D0218935

New Horizons in Multicultural Counseling

Russell Young, 1956–2005
Exemplary multicultural scholar, educator, and loved colleague

New Horizons in Multicultural Counseling

Gerald Monk
San Diego State University

John Winslade
California State University, San Bernardino

Stacey Sinclair
San Diego State University

SAGE Publications
Los Angeles • London • New Delhi • Singapore

Copyright © 2008 by Sage Publications, Inc.

All rights reserved. No part of this book may be reproduced or utilized in any form or by any means, electronic or mechanical, including photocopying, recording, or by any information storage and retrieval system, without permission in writing from the publisher.

For information:

Sage Publications, Inc.
2455 Teller Road
Thousand Oaks, California 91320
E-mail: order@sagepub.com

Sage Publications India Pvt. Ltd.
B 1/I 1 Mohan Cooperative Industrial Area
Mathura Road, New Delhi 110 044
India

Sage Publications Ltd.
1 Oliver's Yard
55 City Road
London EC1Y 1SP
United Kingdom

Sage Publications Asia-Pacific Pte. Ltd.
33 Pekin Street #02-01
Far East Square
Singapore 048763

Printed in the United States of America

Library of Congress Cataloging-in-Publication Data

Monk, Gerald, 1954-
New horizons multicultural counseling/Gerald Monk, John Maxwell Winslade, Stacey L. Sinclair.
    p. cm.
Includes bibliographical references and index.
ISBN 978-1-4129-1676-9 (pbk.: alk. paper)
  1. Cross-cultural counseling. I. Winslade, John. II. Sinclair, Stacey L. III. Title.

BF636.7.C76M66 2008
158′.3—dc22   2007037952

This book is printed on acid-free paper.

07   08   09   10   11   10 9 8 7 6 5 4 3 2 1

Acquisitions Editor:	Kassie Graves
Editorial Assistant:	Veronica Novak
Production Editor:	Kristen Gibson
Copy Editor:	Rachel Keith
Typesetter:	C&M Digitals (P) Ltd.
Proofreader:	Kris Bergstad
Indexer:	Holly Day
Cover Designer:	Candice Harman
Marketing Manager:	Carmel Withers

Contents

Foreword

Kenneth J. Gergen

Life in the helping professions has always been fraught with ambiguity. How are we to understand the strange and often self-defeating behavior in which people engage, what are the origins of untoward and irrational actions, how are we to sort people into tractable categories, what are the best forms of counseling or therapeutic practice, how can we assess the effects of our interventions, and what are the ethical and political implications of our engagement? For over a century, such issues have stimulated lively and sometimes rancorous debate. Only in periods of vast suppression do we seem to approach agreement on answers. For the most part, schools of thought have come and gone, and we seem no closer to the answers today than we were a century ago.

In recent decades this search for clear answers has taken a different turn, at once liberating and perilous. In earlier years the search largely took place within the professional classes, and the grounds for debate were typically those furnished by the then-dominant conception of empirical science. Reason and evidence were the key players in the game. However, as the technologies of communication (e.g., television, mass publishing, talk radio, jet transportation, the Internet) became increasingly available to people, grassroots organization was facilitated. Multiple pockets of consciousness developed; groups of the like-minded sprang to political life. There were sharp differences among such groups in the way they understood the world and the values they placed on various outcomes. Further, for many of these groups the debates within the helping professions not only seemed obfuscating and irrelevant, but also were threatening to the very ways of life they so valued. Thus, the "helping" professions were variously excoriated for race, class, gender, and sexual preference biases. And, too, their assumptions and practices seemed wholly insensitive to the vast ethnic and cultural differences within a society.

This fiercely pluralistic movement has been enormously liberating. It has placed in critical question long-standing traditions, given voice to myriad minorities, and set new agendas for how to think about and foster human well-being. The space of freedom has been substantially expanded. At the same time, these movements have fostered both fragmentation and alienation. There are strong tendencies of the enclaves, just as of the "old-stream," to seek independence; each strives to set its own course for the future. Those outside an enclave are often viewed with suspicion or derision. There is a circulating logic that no group has the right to conceptualize those outside, to study them or offer entrapping practices of help. To extend such logic, we are all invited to live in isolation from each other.

With the publication of the present volume, Gerald Monk, John Winslade, and Stacey Sinclair herald an entirely new era of thought and practice. They write from long experience in the roiling waters of multicultural counseling; they are not afraid to expose their passions and their shortcomings; they have stepped outside the domain of counseling in search of useful insights from other fields of study. And their conclusion is of enormous importance: it is not the clear and compelling answer for which we should be striving, but a continuing and ever-extended participation in dialogue. In effect, they render honor to the full panoply of traditions, values, and visions that now circulate globally, but invite an open and honest sharing. They soften the boundaries of separation and see within dialogue the possibilities for new, more fully informed, more thoroughly sensitive, and more broadly responsible ways of going on. In offering such visions to those entering the field of counseling today, they make a major contribution to a more viable tomorrow.

This spirit of participatory inquiry is secreted into every corner of this work, from the personal openness of the initial prologue to a final chapter in which the reader is invited to join in thinking about the next steps. Traditional understandings are thrust into question at every turn; where clarity on matters of culture, race, ethnicity, identity, community, and competence once reigned, there is now careful and caring reflection. Nor are the authors satisfied by developing highly sophisticated and far-reaching accounts of the subject matter. They also invite readers into experiences that will enable them to add to the deliberation in their own terms. The chapters also bring a wealth of wide-ranging scholarship to bear on the topics they treat, thus adding depth and breadth to the discussions. Yet, and perhaps most salutary, they invite responses to their offerings from authors varying significantly in viewpoint.

I am reminded here of a passage from the poet Rainer Maria Rilke's *Letters to a Young Poet*:

> I would like to beg you . . . to have patience with everything unresolved in your heart and to try to love the questions themselves as if they were locked rooms or books written in a very foreign language. Don't search for the answers, which could not be given to you now, because you would not be able to live them. And the point is to live everything. Live the questions now. Perhaps then, someday far in the future, you will gradually, without even noticing it, live your way into the answer.

To be sure, it is most gratifying to me that the authors have made such excellent use of social constructionist ideas. Deliberations on social construction have absorbed my interests and enthusiasm for over 25 years. In many respects I believe that the same processes that gave rise to the multicultural movement—its liberating potentials as well as its tensions—also contributed to the expanding consciousness of construction. To the extent that any discourse, and its associated way of life, is dominant, there is little questioning of what is real, rational, or valuable. It was thus that in early periods of counseling psychology there was virtually unquestioned respect for observation, systematic evidence, coherent reasoning, and the value of using one's expertise to help others. However, as the many voices of difference found expression, the veil of the obvious began to fall. Behind the veil we began to discern the culturally and historically thrown condition of science, reason, and Western ethics. No longer was there an unquestionable authority. All traditions of interpretation could claim legitimacy.

Yet, as the constructionist dialogues have developed, they have also opened a path to a new level of consciousness. As we have found in the field of counseling, plural legitimacies also lend themselves to plural claims of the real and the good. While social constructionist ideas are used to deconstruct the dominant discourse, they are infrequently turned upon oneself. Thus, we approach a war of all against all, only in this case it is war among traditions as opposed to individuals. Given the potential for any movement to expand globally and the simultaneous democratization of weaponry, we find ourselves approaching a radical condition of crisis. It is at this point that the pragmatic dimension of constructionism plays a prominent role, for we cease to order the world into ultimate goods and evils, locating fault and establishing institutions of censor and control. Rather, we simply ask, "Is this the kind of world *we* wish to create together?" And, if the answer is "No," the invitation is given for a collaborative search into more viable futures. It is precisely here that one can discern the profound significance of this volume. In the case of counseling, the authors answer "No" to an embattled future. Thus, we find within these pages not simply a groundbreaking entry into the domain of multicultural counseling; rather, this volume gives rise to the kind of consciousness on which global well-being will ultimately depend.

Kenneth J. Gergen, Ph.D., is a senior research professor at Swarthmore College and the director of the Taos Institute. He is widely known for his inquiries in social construction and contemporary cultural life. In addition to honorary degrees in the United States and Europe, he has received awards from the National Science Foundation, the Guggenheim Foundation, the Fulbright Foundation, and the Alexander von Humboldt Foundation. Among his major works are *Realities and Relationships, The Saturated Self,* and *An Invitation to Social Construction.*

Prologue

I have had a burning desire to write this book for 20 years. It's taken 20 years because I didn't at first have the courage to write down the conversations, debates, conflicts, and challenges of a field that has been so fraught with accounts of disrespect, injustice, and misunderstanding. What has given me the strength, confidence, and encouragement to undertake this large project has been the major contributions of two of my wonderful friends and colleagues, who bring their ability to write with depth, complexity, and potency to this important subject of multicultural counseling. Together we have grappled with the big issues of advancing the state of multicultural counseling while staying focused on the question driving the movement: how do we all promote justice, respect, equity, and understanding in the counseling process among culturally diverse peoples?

It's a risky business for a group of white authors to write on multiculturalism, inequity, and social justice. So much injustice has been perpetrated throughout the planet by white people and their ancestors, and thus it is easy for many communities across the globe to distrust white people's motives and agendas. Among many communities, there is a suspicion that white people, who appear to have been fused with the most negative aspects of dominant Western culture, have little to contribute to the question of how to address justice, and equity, understanding, and respect across diverse cultures. White people have been described as members of an oppressor group who have access to all kinds of privilege. From many perspectives, they are unqualified to speak about topics such as racism, oppression, and marginalization. Certainly the majority culture in the United States continues to grant privilege to white groups.

Each of us (the authors) can identify aspects of our lives that have been both privileged and oppressive to others. Despite this history, we have a place to contribute to the conversation that relates to respect, understanding, and justice in the counseling encounter across diverse communities. While in terms of ethnicity we identify as white, or, in the case of John Winslade and me, as *Pakeha* (white New Zealanders), we hope that by the end of reading this book you, the reader, will experience our voice as that of a mix of multiple, salient identities that defy a stereotypical, univocal, unidimensional expression and that do not inevitably reproduce oppressive practice.

Like my colleague John Winslade, I have lived for more than half of my life in the land referred to by Maori as Aotearoa ("The Land of the Long White Cloud"), otherwise known as New Zealand. Our third coauthor, Stacey Sinclair, spent her early life in Ypsilanti/Ann Arbor, Michigan, and most of her youth and adult life in Virginia Beach, Virginia.

This book on multicultural counseling had its genesis in New Zealand, in the painful yet deeply insightful interactions I, as a Pakeha New Zealander, experienced with Maori, the indigenous people of New Zealand.

As a brand-new psychologist who had just graduated from New Zealand's esteemed University of Otago, I returned to my small hometown of Gisborne to begin work in my newly chosen field of counseling and psychological practice. I was to begin work in the Department of Education Psychological Services. The year was 1985. I was full of enthusiasm as a newly trained professional, ready to make an impact in my home community. I had been preparing to do this for five years.

Gisborne, a very isolated community, had always struggled to provide an adequate range of medical and psychological services to its citizens. As I prepared for this new job, I felt I must first become acquainted with the services already provided so that I could work alongside my colleagues, who coordinated an appropriate delivery of services. One of my first ports of call was a meeting with Erana, a member of the Ngati Porou *iwi* (tribe) and a senior social worker in a large community agency that provided services to Maori families. I introduced myself and talked to her about how we might work together. In the first two minutes, her response to what I regarded as an appropriate professional interaction was shocking to the point that I am remembering it and writing about it 20 years later.

Erana said, "I have no interest in working with you or the services that you think you could provide to our people."

"I am sorry," I said, reeling with incredulity, "but I don't understand what you mean."

"I place no value on Pakeha institutions and the Pakeha knowledge you want to impose on Maori," she said in a straightforward, unapologetic tone.

Needless to say, it was a very short meeting, and I left feeling confused and upset. I asked myself, how can somebody dismiss and reject me and what I represent, without even knowing anything about me, just because of my ethnicity or my culture and professional background? This was the first time I had experienced such an encounter. I had a lot to learn. I was a 28-year-old man who had been raised in a white New Zealand middle class community and had never suffered rejection on the grounds of my cultural background and the stereotypical assumptions often associated with the people I identified with. In a country where the majority Pakeha culture was dominant in all major public and private institutions, it was rare to be singled out by a minority culture and challenged about anything. This was the first of a number of interactions where my ethnic background and what it represented was rejected and discounted.

Fortunately, I soon realized that I was experiencing, on the smallest of scales, what it feels like to be rejected, devalued, and unappreciated because of one's ethnicity, gender, or class. In another interaction that occurred a few months later, I was told in public to shut up by a young community worker who was "sick of hearing from Pakeha males." These small encounters were enormously impactful and began to require me to confront many issues. I found that I had to reevaluate what I was trained to do as a counselor and a psychologist.

All through my training I had believed I was learning therapeutic and professional skills that would apply to all people. After all, I was trained in a scientist-practitioner model by the latest empirically tested psychological science, which was considered effective with all people independent of ethnicity, class, and gender. Now, on a regular basis I was being told by significant numbers of my community that they were not interested in what I had to offer or the knowledge I was trained in. What did it now mean for me, a Pakeha male professional trained in the Western counseling and psychological traditions, to work in my own community but be rejected by many members of the Maori community? I could have easily written off those Maori community members who said to me, "Thanks, but no thanks." It is very easy to scapegoat members of a minority culture who don't like what is being offered to them from the majority culture. Embedded in this response would have been the arrogant implication that the dominant culture is better and more important than the minority culture. Of course, it was also the easy route to take to make myself feel better.

However, after moving on from feeling sorry for myself, I became very interested in how we as Pakeha and Maori got to be in this place. I had lived in my hometown for most of my life. I had thought that I was particularly good at getting along with Maori and working together for the greater good of all of us. Some of my closest friends throughout my schooling had been Maori. In fact, the teacher I had loved most was Maori; Mr. Callaghan was very proud of his cultural history. I had often been singled out in our class plays to perform in the role of a Maori warrior in ancient tribal legends. Now I was feeling disconnected and estranged from Maori and finding that what I had to offer was not only of no value but also seen as harmful by some of the Maori mental health professionals in my own town. I made a commitment to conduct myself in a manner that would be perceived as respectful to Maori and to get to a better place.

At around this time I was faced with other challenges unrelated to the conflicts between Pakeha and Maori. I attended a Family Therapy Conference in 1986 and was confronted and challenged because of my gender. Halfway through the conference, a woman stood up at the end of a plenary session and challenged all the men in the room to stand up and publicly take responsibility as men for the sexual and physically violent crimes being perpetrated by men against women in the community. Research was presented about the large numbers of men perpetrating crimes against women and children in families and the significant amount of sexual abuse being committed by male therapists toward their female clients. Sarah asked each man at the conference to take a stand against violence and sexual abuse and to pledge to work with men to eradicate violence from our communities. The response was overwhelming silence. Nobody moved or spoke for what seemed like hours, although it was probably a few minutes. Later in the conference, a number of women expressed their indignation over the men's failure to respond to the challenge to address abuses committed by male culture in the community. Interactions like this were to occur again and again in various professional gatherings during the latter part of the 1980s.

At another Family Therapy Conference, a woman who identified as Samoan challenged all of the Pakeha and *Palangi* (Samoan for "whites") to take responsibility for their abuse of indigenous peoples and their imposition of their colonizing therapies on indigenous peoples. These challenges were always painful, and many professionals who worked in the counseling and family therapy arena and were concerned about these serious social issues stopped attending the national and regional conferences because they were afraid of being attacked for their failure to adequately address patriarchal or racially prejudicial behavior. As a result, conference attendance declined, and in some instances national conferences were canceled for a period. A heightened level of concern about issues of racial hatred, colonization, and patriarchy surfaced in the professional community.

In the early 1990s, the national counseling organization in New Zealand was split in two. Many people both within and outside of the counseling and psychotherapy community thought it necessary to separate services for Maori and Pakeha. Pakeha clients were encouraged to see Pakeha therapists and Maori clients were encouraged to see Maori therapists. It was believed that by separating out the ethnic groups, the dominating and colonizing therapies of the Pakeha would not be imposed upon Maori. Thus, Maori could receive services from Maori that would honor their traditions and unique culture and thus avoid being tainted by Pakeha practices.

Men were encouraged to work with male counselors and women were encouraged to work with female counselors. It was believed that male counselors would be in a better position than female counselors to challenge patriarchal behavior and stop violence and abuse in their male clients. It was also believed that if male counselors were discouraged from working with female clients, they would avoid imposing their own patriarchal behavior on women. Thus, during the 1990s in New Zealand, it was common practice to separate groups around particular cultural markers with a view to avoiding prejudicial behaviors by therapists working with culturally different clients. This agenda included the promotion of gay counselors' working with gay clients to avoid the imposition of harmful heterosexual biases and abuses on the client by the counselor.

During the 1990s, I also came to embrace this practice of separating groups around particular cultural markers because I couldn't see any other way to respect the concerns of many Maori and many women about the potential for therapeutic harm. As a result, I worked with men's groups to address sexual and physical violence. I actively discouraged Maori clients from seeing me and encouraged them to take referrals to a Maori counselor. When I became a counselor educator at a university in a neighboring town, I discouraged people who identified as Maori from participating in the training program because it was taught mainly by Pakeha and followed a mainstream counseling curriculum that many Maori deemed harmful. That is, I was concerned that the existing program was not catering to their needs and felt that they would benefit more from training with Maori counselor educators.

For nearly 10 years I promoted the provision of separate services based on shared cultural markers or the shared salient identities of the clients or students. In New Zealand, because the more homogenous patterns in the population are made up of mainly four ethnic groups (Pakeha, Maori, Pacific Islander, and Asian), the majority being Pakeha and a sizable minority group being Maori, it seemed more possible to separate services for discrete groups. Now, more than 10 years later, I can see that we in New Zealand have made some progress in addressing serious social injustices in the delivery of counseling and psychological services in comparison to what was provided before the mid 1980s. However, there are still many difficulties that have not been resolved by separating services along these lines. In fact, I have serious misgivings about providing separate services by counselors and clients who share matching ethnic markers to resolve serious social injustices between different groups, whether the divisions are constructed along ethnic or gender lines or among other cultural groupings whose legitimate concerns need attention.

One of the biggest problems that arise when we start thinking of people primarily as members of specific cultural groups is that we participate in forming unidimensional understandings of who they are as people. We also invite people to conform to a one-dimensional characterization. In fact, we all exhibit a complex array of multiple cultural identities or cultural markers. As we engage with a person's ethnicity, we are simultaneously engaging with him or her as a person who is a man or woman or transgender person, with a particular sexual orientation, social class, religious or nonreligious background, ability, or disability, of a particular age, rural or urban location, and so on. It is difficult to resolve inequity and injustice by believing we can match people on every cultural variable or cultural marker.

The other problem underpinning any unidimensional characterization is that it fails to encompass the dynamic and fluid nature of power relations, and, in doing so, constrains options for change. Placing people in a fixed, one-dimensional characterization is usually predicated on an oppressor/oppressed binary, which conceives of power as a property inherent within categories of people rather than as a relational phenomenon. The deterministic and essentialist quality of these assumptions has the potential to evoke feelings of helplessness and reduce people's abilities to act. However, there is still a profound need to identify and understand systematic social processes at work in a community that become the source of abuse, disrespect, and hatred of people with certain cultural markings.

This book is a genuine effort to expand on an alternative range of theoretical and therapeutic approaches to addressing social injustices without on the one hand resorting to Eurocentric models of practice (the ones that all the authors were trained in) or, on the other hand, creating separate and distinct classes of therapy that somehow match all of the complex, heterogeneous cultural markers experienced by clients. Rather, this book is an effort to provide resources for all of us to use to work respectfully with multiple cultural identities as well as to address systematic social inequities that people live with daily.

While I have been writing about experiences that have taken place far, far away from most readers of this book, there are some very important parallels between what has taken place in New Zealand and what occurs in North America. Experience any multicultural class that is preparing counselors, psychiatrists, psychologists, marriage and family therapists, nurses, and medical doctors to work with diverse populations, and you will hear some version of the statements I have listed below:

"We are all human beings. We all share essentially the same genetic makeup, so surely we can all benefit from the same well-proven methods to assist people."

"You are white and you will never understand the racism I've experienced and can never really understand what it's like to be me."

"You are from a dominant culture and you don't know what it's like to be oppressed. I would never seek counseling from you or people like you."

"I wish I had a culture. Yours is so beautiful and rich, I feel as if I would really benefit from being a person like you."

"I'm color-blind. We're all human beings and that's the shared basis that we need to work from."

"You can't help but be racist and you have to acknowledge that."

"I think we are all one people. We're all American here, aren't we? Don't we all believe in essentially the same things?"

There are many such dividing statements made by participants in North American classrooms and on the street that suggest, "We can be understood only by people of our own kind." These statements are often sincere attempts to manage the difficult challenges we all face in working with, living alongside, and counseling others. Some comments strike me as very naive. Others seem hopeless or pessimistic. But what we believe about one another is not something that we have invented on our own. Each of these statements comes from an elaborate history of thought arising from experiences that often reach back in time well beyond the age of the student who is uttering them. It is through understanding our genealogies and our multiple and diverse histories that we will come to more fully understand what is going on now as we begin our steps into the 21st century.

"History," wrote Arthur Schlesinger, Jr., "haunts even generations who refuse to [acknowledge it]. Rhythms, patterns, continuities, drift out of time long forgotten to mould the present and to color the shape of things to come."

Gerald Monk
May 2007

Preface

Some might say that this is a contentious book—that is, that we, the authors, are seeking to contend. We are conscious that not everyone will always agree with our contentions. We maintain a hope, however, that any field of inquiry will resemble a respectful conversation among a range of contending voices. There are indeed many books currently being published about multicultural counseling. This is a positive development, given that the issues of responding to difference across a range of domains are critical to modern life. But it does raise the question, why yet another book?

To answer this question, we need to be up front about our purposes in writing this text. We have a number of specific goals that we are trying to achieve in this book. We shall outline these here, now, so that they are transparent and so that you can measure your reading of the book against these goals rather than against some other idea of what a book like this should be.

First, we have aimed to write a book that will be of use to students and faculty instructors in a multicultural counseling class. That has been the primary audience we have kept in mind while writing. We hope, too, that others in the field of general helping relations—for example, students of psychology and social work—will find this work of value. We also hope that this book will stimulate interest among practitioners of counseling.

We have been conscious of the requirements of the American Counseling Association's multicultural counseling competencies in the writing of this text. Alongside a discussion of these competencies, our aim has been to introduce some new material into the discourse of multicultural counseling, or at least to gather a number of ideas together from various sources for increased consideration in relation to multicultural practice. This is not because we do not support the multicultural counseling competencies as they exist. Rather, we believe there are a few gaps in them that deserve attention and we want to contribute to the development of this field. We shall go on now to explain the particular intentions we have held to in writing this text.

We have sought to avoid what some multicultural counseling texts offer in the way of a kind of cookbook of suggestions for counselors in working with persons from specific cultural groups. Usually these groups appear to correspond with the

United States census divisions. If you are looking for chapters discussing the traditional ethnic and other identity groups, you will be disappointed. For our purposes, descriptive accounts of group identity have not been helpful to us in conceptualizing multicultural counseling.

What we have done is address what we see as some of the most important domains of cultural influence while seeking to avoid normalizing descriptions within those domains. One book can't do everything. Because our focus has been on the complexity of identity issues and the epistemological underpinnings of the multicultural perspective, we have not been able to adequately address all of the multicultural domains that you might be looking for. For example, you will find very little discussion on the specific counseling needs of ethnic groups, only a modest account (in Chapter 12) of the counseling needs of lesbian/gay/bisexual/transgender persons, and passing allusions to rather than full discussion of the cultural influences of disability, religion, and spirituality or of the cultural experience of the elderly. Fortunately, there are numerous publications that address the discrete needs of identity groups. Recent publications that address some of these issues include the following:

Atkinson, D. R., & Hackett, G. (Eds.). (2004). *Counseling diverse populations* (3rd ed.). New York: McGraw-Hill.

Baruth, L. G., & Manning, M. L. (2007). *Multicultural counseling and psychotherapy: A lifespan perspective* (4th ed.). Columbus, OH: Prentice Hall.

Brammer, R. (2004). *Diversity in counseling.* Belmont, CA: Thomson Brooks/Cole.

Harper, F. D., & McFadden, J. (2003). *Culture and counseling: New approaches.* Boston: Pearson Education.

Rabin, C. L. (2005). *Understanding gender and culture in the helping process: Practitioners' narratives from global perspectives.* Belmont, CA: Thomson Wadsworth.

Robinson, T. L. (2005). *The convergence of race, ethnicity, and gender: Multiple identities in counseling.* Columbus, OH: Prentice Hall.

Sue, D. W., & Sue, D. (2007). *Counseling the culturally diverse: Theory and practice* (5th ed.). New York: Wiley.

We have taken a different aim. Our task has been to articulate some conceptual tools for counselors and students to think with as they make sense of their own experience and the experiences of the clients who seek their help. We consider one of the primary functions of a textbook to be the provocation and stimulation of thought. You may not always agree with our arguments in this book. That is okay. We expect that. But we would invite you to at least consider the ideas we present and to work at articulating your own conceptual framework for working in a multicultural way. We take the multicultural movement seriously enough to believe that it should provoke substantial rethinking of many of the commonly accepted assumptions in the counseling field. Therefore, we invite you to adopt a questioning stance in relation to accepted knowledge and to test it against criteria that place cultural difference at the forefront of your thinking.

Some may argue (we have heard these arguments expressed to us) that we should not focus so much on the "intellectual" issues of culture but should promote the more humanistic concept of "awareness" in this text. We are not persuaded by these arguments. It is not that we are opposed to the idea of awareness. It is just that awareness can only exist within a framework of assumptions about people and about life. There is no such thing as pure awareness, only awareness that is located in culture and discourse and history. We think that students should engage in understanding and sometimes questioning these background assumptions in the process of developing awareness of cultural relations. We prefer not to patronize students by suggesting that they are not capable of such thought.

Our intention, therefore, has been to contribute a problematizing element to the conversation on these issues. To problematize means to take a step back from something that seems familiar and taken for granted and to render it an object worthy of thinking more about (Marshall, 2007). In the process, as we contemplate the difficulties that can be noticed in relation to this concept, the subject matter might become less certain and less familiar. Rather than just asking students or practitioners to, say, be more aware of their own race or culture, we want to ask them to step back and think carefully about some of the problems associated with the conventional concepts of race and culture and to understand these concepts as contestable ideas rather than hard realities, ideas produced through a history riven with power relations. Many texts start with defining the terms of race and culture and so on. We want to encourage a discussion about how these terms get to be so defined, on the grounds that the control of definitions is in itself a basis for power. We trust that the opening up of these terms for searching discussion will also open up new forms of practice.

For these reasons, we have endeavored in this book to bring work on the assumptions and experience of culture and cultural difference from several other fields to bear upon the field of multicultural counseling. For example, we have sought to draw from the recent developments in the field of cultural studies. We have also consciously drawn upon the literature of postcolonial studies and critical race theory. We've used material based in the philosophy of culture and in postmodern social theory. Others in the field of multicultural counseling have dipped into these sources, of course, but not all texts in this field have used them as fully as we have sought to do here. Our aim has been to translate promising ideas into readable and practical form and to suggest ways that they can enhance the practice of counseling so that multicultural counseling becomes not just an add-on to the field but a force that propels it forward into new vistas.

To be more specific, we need to mention some guiding principles we've drawn from these literatures that we believe can benefit the field of multicultural counseling. All texts are written from a philosophical perspective; ours is no different. Sometimes this isn't mentioned because it's assumed that everyone will share the same perspective. Sometimes, too, confusion results when people talk across different assumptions without being transparent about where they're coming from. We want to avoid that. So let's declare our preference for thinking about counseling and multicultural practice from a social constructionist perspective. In Chapter 1, we outline what we mean by that. We have not written this book from a humanistic perspective, or from a structuralist perspective. We certainly have respect for the vast majority of counselors who hold to one or the other of these frameworks of assumption. But, like them, we have our own biases. We would prefer that you know this from the start.

One of our premises as social constructionists is that essentialist ideas about culture should be eschewed. We explain what we mean by this in Chapter 2. Because essentialist thinking about meanings, about personhood, about groups of people, and about culture itself is so familiar in our patterns of thought and in our ways of speaking, essentialism is hard to step out of. Nevertheless, we believe that new possibilities open up when we do so. We have therefore aimed to write about cultural issues using language and concepts that are as nonessentialist as possible.

Some may find this effort Eurocentric. They are, in a sense, right. Essentialist thinking has dominated the modern world from its origins in European culture. Even the word "culture" is itself a European concept, as is the word "race." Indigenous cultures around the world have nurtured very different ways of thinking. Our intention in questioning essentialist assumptions in multicultural counseling is partly to make room for other ways of making sense of life to be granted legitimacy. Even when we're not speaking about different cultural frameworks of thought, we would like you to remember that this is our intention.

Another premise we hold is that cultural relations in the modern world are not just constructed out of contemporary thinking. They have a history and they developed in a social context. We have therefore placed considerable emphasis in this text on locating concepts of culture in context, rather than implying that they exist in the present in some kind of temporal suspension. People do not hold to cultural stereotypes because, for example, they have independently developed faulty thinking in their heads. They do so because they are the products of a history that has produced these stereotypes and passed them down through the generations. We think it's important to make that history explicit without turning this book into a history text. We work with the assumption that locating concepts in history helps deconstruct some of their taken-for-granted authority.

Another way we seek to avoid essentialist thinking lies in how we write about racism, sexism, homophobia, and other ideological issues. We don't believe that these ideologies are essential to any person's existence. Therefore, we have sought to avoid the common practice of assigning their origins to the hearts of persons. We do not believe that people are racist, for example, in the core of their being. Rather, we assume that racism is a social construct that existed long before any individual who now utters its lines. It has been passed on through social discourse and may have achieved a degree of influence over a person's heart and mind. But we shall avoid talking about any individual as a racist person, a sexist person, and so on. Such discipline is based on our philosophical standpoint, and we ask that you consider it. In this discipline, we draw from Michael White's (1989) aphorism: "The person is not the problem; the problem is the problem" (p. 7).

A by-product of this assumption is that we are doubtful about classroom practices that seek to make students more aware of, for example, their own racism or sexism. We would invite students to *step out of* the racist or sexist ideas that may have affected them, rather than to step further into them. We are more interested, therefore, in exercises that help students deconstruct the work done by powerful ideologies, including in their own thinking, to produce life experiences of privilege and disadvantage.

While it may be a risky business for a group of white authors to write on multiculturalism, inequity, and social justice, silence about these issues can be criticized as well. We believe that we have a responsibility to address these issues and not remain silent about them. We prefer to engage with the issues and to join the conversation about them rather than retreat. Our aim in this book and in other contexts is certainly not to upstage people from a range of cultural positions but to work in partnership with those who have not been exposed to privilege.

The book begins in Chapter 1 by raising some questions about the concept of culture. Many texts on multiculturalism simply define culture and move on. We think it is important for a book on multiculturalism to take the concept of culture seriously. We begin, therefore, with a problematizing discussion in which we briefly trace the genealogy of the concept of culture and also note the genealogy of the uses to which this concept has been put in the therapeutic literature. In Chapter 2 we introduce many aspects of added complexity that we believe need to be taken into account in relation to culture. In particular, we argue for a focus on the multiplicity of cultural influences rather than an essentializing of singular cultural belonging. Here we explain the usefulness of considering cultural narratives that run through our lives rather than focusing on simple identities. In Chapter 3 we move to a focus on the major social divisions that were created by the processes of Western colonization of most of the earth's land surface and the psychological effects of this process that are still being worked out. We take a historical perspective here in order to signify that the cultural relations that exist today do so because of a particular history rather than just because of current policies and practices. The historical and genealogical focus continues in Chapter 4, where we pay particular attention to the concept of race. Our focus on these topics before all others signifies the centrality in the modern world of the forms of social organization that have been built on concepts of race through the colonizing practices that assumed these concepts.

Chapters 5 through 8 are more general. They lay out some theoretical and epistemological emphases that we want to make use of through the rest of the book. In Chapter 5 we explore the usefulness to multicultural counseling of the concepts of discourse, deconstruction, and positioning. Drawn from poststructuralism and used extensively in cultural studies, these concepts are, we believe, useful for counselors to master in order to speak in fresh ways about cultural identity influences. Chapters 6, 7, and 8 all address power relations, highlighting and teasing out three different ways of thinking about power. Chapter 6 explains the liberal humanist approach that emphasizes personal power, Chapter 7 explains a structuralist approach to power, and Chapter 8 develops the poststructuralist (largely

Foucauldian) analytic of power. We advocate that the multicultural counseling field take the latter approach much more seriously than it has done so far.

In Chapter 9, we pick up the subject of gender as a domain of cultural experience. This chapter traces some of the different approaches to thinking about gender, again with something of a historical emphasis, and includes a consideration of both women's and men's enculturation into gendered narratives.

Chapters 10 through 12 address the processes of cultural identity formation. We believe this to be a crucial consideration for counselors because it is the material that counselors and clients are dealing with on a daily basis. Our aim in these chapters is to do justice to the complexities of identity formation in the face of the array of swirling forces at work in the modern world. Chapter 10 investigates the effects of globalization on personal lives, Chapter 11 addresses the multiplicity of cultural influences in personal life, and Chapter 12 investigates some models of cultural identity development, such as racial identity development, immigrant acculturation, and LGBT identity development, particularly in relation to the coming out process.

In Chapter 13, we consider the community contexts in which individuals are developing their personal identity. Here we pose the question, just what kind of community can we imagine that multicultural counseling might contribute to? We use Charles Taylor's concept of social imaginaries and explore the shifts away from the melting pot idea to a range of possible alternatives.

The next three chapters pick up particular domains of cultural experience. In Chapter 14, we return to the question of racism. It is such a central and such a damaging ideological formation that we felt this book deserved another chapter devoted to how counselors might think about and respond to expressions of racism. In Chapter 15, we explore social class issues and the positioning of people in places of economic privilege or disadvantage. We investigate how personal stories are formed in relation to socioeconomic cultural formations and the degree of access these formations give people to the "American dream" or its equivalent in other countries. Chapter 16 looks at the cultural context of schooling. It addresses the functions of cultural reproduction that take place in schools as a hidden curriculum alongside the overt aims of education, then invites counselors to consider how they might work with young people to develop their lives and their education in the context of these powerful processes of cultural reproduction.

Chapter 17 brings us to the American Counseling Association's multicultural competencies. In this chapter, we support the intention behind the development of these competencies and also raise some questions about them, especially with regard to the gaps we would like to see addressed, given the perspectives we have already covered in this book.

Finally, in Chapter 18 we bring together the themes we have been pursuing in the previous chapters in a final series of statements about what we see on the horizon for multicultural counseling.

This book has been more than two and a half years in the writing and many more years in gestation. We are grateful to many people who have contributed to it along the way. We have deliberately sought to include a range of voices by taking special care to give space to a richly diverse group of writers. These writers include experts and teachers in the field of multicultural counseling as well as students of these subjects. We have invited them all to contribute their ideas on multicultural counseling in North America (and in other homelands) and to include their reflections on the nature of culture, identity, ethnicity, race, sexual orientation, class, geographic location, disability, religion, and numerous other salient cultural markers. Our goal has been to create a polyphonic range of responses that represents the complexity and multiplicity of perspectives we have been at pains to explain. We trust that the result of this process is that the book has something of the dialogic quality of a conversation rather than of a monologue.

Each chapter ends with a reflection on the content of the chapter by an author who we deem has a perspective to offer on its content. You may recognize some of these authors as established and well-known writers in the multicultural field. Others represent the new generation of teachers of multicultural counseling. When we approached these people to ask them to write their reflections, we specified two things. One was that they need not agree with our perspective but might take issue with it wherever they saw fit. We hope that the differences expressed here will provide readers with stimulation to their own thinking as they work at creating their own perspectives. We also asked the writers to include a story illustrating the impact of the issues in the chapter on their own or others' lives. We are grateful to those who so willingly contributed their reflections to this book, and we acknowledge their thoughtfulness and integrity in doing so.

Our students have also contributed many stories to this book. We acknowledge the richness and poignancy of these stories and the freshness and complexity of lived experience that they exemplify. They serve as valuable illustrations of the ideas we have sought to represent. We acknowledge the contributions of the following people: Sara Ackelson, Lorena Arias, Jason Carney, Abbie Castel, Danielle Castillo, Heather Conley-Higgins, Natasha Crawford, Mark Darby, Joyce K. Everett, Esmelda Gonzalez, Maiko Ikeda, Ryan Jackson, Sarah Johnson, Mikela Jones, Andy Kim, Mayra Lorenzo, Monica Loyce, Homero Magaña, Sarah Mamaril, Jesus Miranda, Courtnay Oatts Mohammed, Fredy Moreno, Mandana Najimi, Rieko Onuma, Elynn Oropilla, Lorena Ortega, Florence Park, Michael Perales, An Pham, Hien Pham, Stephanie Picon, Belen Robles, Deborah Ann Samson, Randy Tone, Deanna Toombs, Jaime Tran, Grace Tsai, Mary Suzette Tuason, Tristan Turk, Lucille Vail, Calix Vu-Bui, Michelle Wiese, and Daphne Zacky.

A number of people read and commented on drafts of many chapters in the book, helping us to revaluate many small and not-so-small issues as we wrote. Some were particularly helpful in asking us to adopt a less strident tone in certain places; we shall leave it to you to judge how well we took their advice. We are grateful to the following people for their comments and suggestions: Fred Bemak, Edward Delgado-Romero, Changming Duan, Brenda Ingram, Richard Lee, Paul Pedersen, Sue Strong, and Allen Wilcoxon.

Collecting background material and locating textual sources is detailed and sometimes tedious work, and we are grateful to the following people for their assistance in bringing the book together: Krystal Colwell, Mia Hardy, Michael Jabbra, Larissa Jefferson-Allen, and Tracy Shelton.

Those at Sage Publications who have stayed with us through the course of producing this book also deserve our acknowledgment and gratitude. We are particularly grateful to Art Pomponio for seeing value in our proposal for this book and for helping us initiate the project. We appreciate Kassie Graves's editorial guidance and her patience and encouragement along the way. We thank Veronica Novak for her hard work in getting the book into production. We would also like to thank Rachel Keith for her meticulous copyediting and helpful additions.

Our universities have provided both general and specific assistance for the completion of this project. In particular, San Diego State University's College of Education and Department of Counseling and School Psychology have given generous research support to Gerald Monk over the last two years. California State University, San Bernardino, through a faculty research leave program, provided John Winslade with one-quarter relief from teaching, which enabled him to concentrate on the latter stages of writing and revision in the spring of 2007.

On a more personal level, Lorraine Hedtke has participated in many discussions about the content and detail of the book and has contributed many specific suggestions for inclusion in the text. She has read draft material with a sharp eye and commented helpfully on it. She has also contributed many aspects of less tangible support, particularly for John Winslade, by way of generous encouragement and her belief that the project was worthwhile. Such encouragement has been necessary at times when the project has felt bogged down. It is fitting that she be acknowledged here for helping to make this book happen.

Gerald Monk, Ph.D., is a professor in the Department of Counseling and School Psychology at San Diego State University and teaches in the Marriage and Family Therapy Program. He teaches multicultural counseling classes at the graduate level. Gerald is a practicing marriage and family therapist in California and a mediator and trainer in collaborative divorce practices and health care. Gerald worked as a psychologist and counselor educator in New Zealand for 15 years before moving to the United States in 2000. He has a long-standing commitment to working with the bicultural issues that have arisen from the abuses of Maori by the colonizing practices of Pakeha in Aotearoa over the last 250 years. He has participated in extensive bicultural programs in New Zealand and introduced many students to working with indigenous healing practices on *marae*, the sacred ground of the Maori.

Gerald has a strong interest in promoting constructionist theories in counseling and family systems work. He is well known for his contributions to developing and expanding the applications of narrative therapy in New Zealand and in North America. Gerald has published numerous articles and coauthored four books on the subject of narrative therapy and narrative mediation. His main professional commitment lies in the development and application of narrative mediation in health care and community-based contexts. Gerald has taught numerous workshops on this subject in the United Kingdom, Ireland, Canada, Austria, Iceland, Cyprus, Mexico, Denmark, Israel, Russia, and across the United States. Recently, he was the recipient of a Fred J. Hansen grant for peace studies to conduct bicommunal workshops in the buffer zone in Nicosia, Cyprus.

John Winslade, Ph.D., is a professor at California State University, San Bernardino, where he is the coordinator of the Educational Counseling Program. He also teaches part time at the University of Waikato in New Zealand, where he was previously the director of counselor education. He is a New Zealander of Pakeha ancestry, and he conceives of Pakeha culture not just as an expression of white, British, or European heritage, but also as being about living in relation to Maori and Pacific cultural narratives in Aotearoa.

His academic work has focused mainly on the application of social constructionist and narrative ideas to the fields of counseling and conflict resolution. His interest in these ideas lies not just in their novel modes of practice but also in their potential for helping people articulate responses to new developments in our conditions of life in the 21st century. He believes that counseling and psychology need to adapt to current cultural shifts, rather than continuing to repeat older solutions. In addition to numerous articles, John has coauthored four books on narrative counseling and mediation and one on narrative grief counseling.

John has a strong interest in conflict resolution and peace building in personal, organizational, and community contexts. He has taught workshops on narrative counseling and mediation in the United States, Canada, Britain, Denmark, Sweden, the Netherlands, Australia, New Zealand, Cyprus, and Israel. In the last two years, through the sponsorship of the Fred J. Hansen Institute for World Peace, he has been involved in bicommunal peace building work in Cyprus.

Stacey L. Sinclair, Ph.D., is director of the University Honors Program at San Diego State University and teaches in the Department of Counseling and School Psychology at San Diego State University. She is a nationally certified counselor and trained mediator. Her research and scholarship concentrate on social constructionist theory, discursive psychology, postmodern feminism, and conflict resolution. She has published numerous journal articles and book chapters on the application of postmodern epistemology in counseling and marriage and family therapy, and she regularly presents her work at the national and international level. Her primary teaching focus lies in the area of cultural studies and grounding culture in political, economic, and social contexts. Stacey has developed an undergraduate curriculum centered around popular culture for the Department of Counseling and School Psychology. This curriculum starts from the premise that popular culture, far from being a frivolous or debased alternative to "high" or "real" culture, is in fact an important site of popular expression, social construction, and cultural conflict and thus deserves critical attention. Stacey's teaching pays special attention to the ways popular culture affects individuals' daily lives, producing a range of physical, social, and emotional consequences.

Stacey also has a strong background in developing and conducting a range of study-abroad programs for undergraduate and graduate students. Recently, she developed and taught study-abroad courses on conflict resolution in Estonia and Cyprus. Her conflict resolution work has included facilitating bicommunal peace building workshops with Turkish and Greek Cypriots in Nicosia, Cyprus, between 2005 and 2007 and in San Diego in 2006.

CHAPTER 1

What Is Culture?

"**W**hat is your culture?" People answer that question in lots of different ways, illustrating the confusion we have about what culture is and what it means to us. Some people answer by referring to a political entity, such as their country or state of origin. Others refer to a geographic location, such as the continent they belong to, or to a region or locale with which they identify, or to their ethnicity or tribal origins. They answer, "I am American," "Cuban," "Indian," "Canadian," "Mexican," "Caucasian," "Asian," "Californian," or "a New Yorker!" Sometimes they mix geography with ethnicity, calling themselves "African American," "Arab American," or "Caribbean American." Or they might say "black" or "white," drawing attention to physical characteristics over geography or ethnicity. In some parts of the world, people more commonly answer in terms of religion, saying, for example, "I am Jewish." Or they might reference a linguistic heritage or mother tongue, calling themselves "Latino" or "Hispanic." You have probably also heard people say they either don't have a culture or wish they had one. Some individuals are referred to (usually by others) as "really cultured."

These differences in response are not trivial. We believe they reflect differences not just in individual thinking but in the general discourse about culture. These differences also frequently have painful and quite real consequences. For instance, when people speak to each other across the gaps created by different points of reference, they make mistakes in hearing what others are saying. For example, in the United States, people have different preferences for whether they wish to be called Mexican, Hispanic, Latino, or Chicano, and the connotations around words like *black*, *Negro*, and *African American* have taken on different resonances in different times. As a result, it is easy for others who have not attuned themselves carefully enough to the nuances of these terms to ascribe identity in ways that create offense. The conversation can easily deteriorate from here into accusations of racism or of failure to be true to one's cultural identity and heated denials of such accusations. We want to explore the possibility that these exchanges illustrate the limits of understanding produced by many prevailing concepts within dominant ideas about

1

culture and the potential frustrations and pain that can result. Indeed, what suffers from our different responses to the question, "What is your culture?" is often the conversation itself. It stumbles and falls. It is left in midair. Fear of the Other grows. People retreat in discontent and resort to bitterness and blame, and possibilities for social change that might promote intercultural justice are shut down. We have been part of and have witnessed many conversations like this. This book represents our effort to find ways forward in such conversations and to stretch the limits of current thinking about multicultural counseling.

In a multicultural counseling class in a North American classroom, one of our students was asked to answer three questions: "What is your culture?" "What is your race?" "What is your ethnicity?" Her answer to all three questions was "Vietnamese!" For others, the answer to each question would be different. One thing seems clear: the answers to these questions often change depending on who asks us, what era we happen to live in, and the context we find ourselves in at the time. Therefore, our understandings of what culture is and of how, as practitioners, we might relate to it, are necessarily multifaceted. As we traverse the territory of culture in this book, we need to remember that the very concept of culture is not stable. It slips out of our grasp just when we think we have a handle on it. It can be complex and confusing. For example, we can develop a neat and tidy theoretical account and immediately run into life circumstances that contradict our carefully constructed categories. We don't need to be intimidated by such complexity, however. Nor should we seek to eliminate complexity by tying the concept down too tightly to singular definitions, for to do so risks discounting someone's real experience.

An Pham describes her culture, race, and ethnicity as "Vietnamese."

In this book, we shall take the attitude that an appreciation of complexity enriches us with more possibilities for making a difference in the world. At the same time, we believe that if we are to explore the horizons of multicultural counseling, it is necessary to take the concept of culture seriously. We therefore invite readers to join us in some careful thinking about many of the complexities that this concept of culture entails. In our view, the function of a text like this should be to provide readers with some intellectual tools with which to think through the issues of culture as they are experienced in life. We can't do the personal exploration part of this exercise for our readers. We can, however, discuss the tools and thus equip you to do the personal exploration.

In this chapter, we shall explore some of the various contemporary definitions of culture and the different meanings of and associations accompanying words like *race* and *ethnicity*. Central to understanding culture, race, and ethnicity is the social context out of which these terms have arisen. To appreciate this, we need to look at the various contexts in which our concepts of culture have developed. We need to look at current debates and also to look back and trace some of the historical meanings associated with ideas of culture. We are always living with the legacies of such history, always to some extent caught by the web of this history, always speaking in ways that echo historical understandings. As we explore these historical influences on our current ideas about culture, we cannot help but do so from a vantage point constructed on the foundations of the overarching influences of European colonization. The modern world has been founded substantially (although not completely) on the basis of colonization. Its social, political, religious, educational, and economic influences continue to this day in contemporary North America and around the world. Like it or not, our current understandings of culture have also arisen in the context of this history. Even as we might seek to escape the bounds of this history, our consciousness is still profoundly shaped by it. To study the influences of culture in our own and in other people's lives, we must wrestle with the effects of history, sometimes grieving over its legacy of pain and injustice, sometimes identifying points of resistance where we might create ruptures within this legacy, and sometimes celebrating the possibilities for cultural development and understanding that grow out of this legacy. Because our history has been profoundly significant in shaping the field of multicultural counseling, we have made it a central theme in this book and have dedicated a chapter to it. A historical exploration of what has shaped our modern world is discussed in Chapter 3 and provides us with a lens to review what is taking place in our communities and in the field of multicultural counseling today.

In this first chapter, we must also use a historical lens to address the confusion around the meaning of culture and the best way to work respectfully with it. We shall seek to ground the discussion of culture in particular historical contexts, rather than constructing it as a timeless, abstract, or universal concept. Even the idea of culture itself is a cultural product. It has a history, and its meaning has developed through a series of changing viewpoints and values.

Box 1.1. An Exercise

1. Take a sheet of paper or a whiteboard and draw a line down the middle of it. Write the heading "Nature" on one side and the heading "Culture" on the other.

2. Brainstorm quickly and without discussion or second thoughts as many words as you can that you would either associate with each of these headings or imagine subsumed under them.

3. Reflect on what you have produced. Where do these ideas come from? What view of the world do they point to?

4. Think further until you notice where the decisions you made to place words under one heading or the other start to break down. Identify complications, contradictions, qualifications, exceptions, gaps, and anomalies.

TO DISCUSS

1. What is the difference among the terms *culture*, *civilization*, *society*, and *community*?

2. What is the difference between *culture and race*?

3. What is the difference between *culture* and *ethnicity*?

4. Who uses these different terms and in what contexts?

5. What are the limits of the use of each of these terms? When would you not use them?

6. For each of the distinctions you make among these terms, reflect further on how these distinctions relate to your own life, your own cultural history, your own national origin, and your own life history.

7. See if you can imagine speaking as someone else who might think differently. What would this person say?

8. Take any particular meaning and ask the question, "Whose experience might be left out by this meaning?"

Another way in which we want to ground this book is by making explicit the particular perspective we're starting from. All books are written from one perspective or another. Even those textbooks that seek to survey a range of perspectives are always written from one of these perspectives or through a particular explanatory framework. We believe it is more honest to declare this from the start than it is to spring it on you later, or to let you guess as you read. This way, you can make sense of what we're saying in relation to a particular view of the world. If you don't share the same worldview, that's okay. We respect that. But at least you know where we're coming from and can make allowances in how you read what we say here.

We call the position we write from *social constructionist*. That means something specific to us, which we shall explain, but it is far from an agreed-upon term. Even many people who share a number of the ideas and concepts that make up what we call social constructionism (see Box 1.2) choose to use other terms to describe what we are referring to. We are not the only writers who have used the ideas of social constructionism in multicultural counseling. Recent examples include the work of Lisa Tsoi Hoshmand (2005) and Garrett McAuliffe (2007).

Box 1.2. Social Constructionism

Social constructionism refers to a philosophical movement in the social sciences that has particular groups of adherents in sociology and psychology. Not everyone who shares at least some of its ideas, however, would choose to call it by this name. Some might call it "postmodernism," referring to the general shift in thinking that has taken place in academic circles in the last 30 years or so. We don't object to this term but find that it sometimes encompasses too many influences, not all of which we share. Some might prefer the term "poststructuralism," referring to the particular academic movement originating in France after the disturbances of 1968 and led by figures such as Michel Foucault, Jacques Lacan, Julia Kristeva, and Jacques Derrida. However, this term is perhaps too localized and means little to those who are not familiar with the academic movement known in linguistics, anthropology, and philosophy as "structuralism." Like the term *postmodernism*, *poststructuralism* describes a concept in terms of something that it is not—in terms of what it follows. It is a reference to something else rather than to itself. It is therefore a somewhat negative description, less precise than it could be, and less helpful in pointing to ways forward. There are others, particularly in Britain, who would argue for the term "discourse psychology" or "critical psychology." They tend to cluster around the discipline of social psychology and are less concerned with the social practice of counseling. They have, however, contributed much to the development of a critical perspective in discourse analysis, and their work shall serve as a useful foundation for many of our explorations of culture.

Social constructionism (some argue that the word *social* is redundant) points to the way our experiences are constructed rather than determined in advance as part of the natural working out of biological processes. Kenneth Gergen (1994, 1999; Gergen & Davis, 1985; McNamee & Gergen, 1992; Shotter & Gergen, 1989) has been a major contributor to the development of social constructionist ideas in psychology. He summarizes the constructionist position in these words:

> In the end all that is meaningful grows from relationships, and it is within this vortex that the future will be forged. (Gergen, 1994, p. ix)

Focusing on relationships as the context in which people form concepts, identities, meanings, and forms of action in the world leads constructionists to pay close attention to the representations in language that we use when we converse. Such representations are not neutral but always charged with sparks of power and therefore able to exert a shaping influence on who we are and what we can say. Examining these representations leads us to rethink many of the taken-for-granted aspects of modern life. For example, the idea that each individual is a self who has unique emotions can be shown to be a truth that is not so simple as we often treat it. Gergen (1999) talks about the usual idea of the self as resting on a "shaky scaffold" (p. 6). The same might be said for the concept of culture and for many other concepts that we shall examine in this book. We find the ideas of social constructionism important enough to use as a platform to stand on in viewing the territory of multicultural counseling. Accordingly, we have made a decision to locate our approach in relation to a particular account of a position that we are currently comfortable with: Vivien Burr's (2003) readable and forthright introduction to "social constructionism". We like the way it includes perspectives taken from postmodern, poststructuralist, and critical psychologists, as well as makes links with the versions of social constructionism that have

(Continued)

(Continued)

developed in North America and with narrative psychologists such as Jerome Bruner. You may come across those who object to the term *social constructionism*, particularly with regard to the loose ways in which people talk about "social constructs" as the opposite of something more real (see Hacking, 1999, for a critique of such loose usages). That is not our meaning of the term. We have chosen Vivien Burr's account of social constructionism, somewhat arbitrarily but also after careful consideration, as a base for what we explore in this book.

Social constructionism refers to the processes by which people use language, or more precisely, discourse, to construct their lives. The term *discourse* refers to the assumptions that develop in a given cultural context to guide people's thinking and acting. Without general agreement on which discourse counts in that context, words and actions remain meaningless. In the process of using discourse, people must wrestle with the ways in which the very language they use presupposes many things and exerts a shaping or structuring influence on what they can think. For example, in contemporary American culture, the term *feminine* typically suggests modesty, gracefulness, nurturance, weakness, passivity, or timidity. The taken-for-granted assumptions that accompany the word in turn influence the behavior of men and women alike. From the constructionist position, the role that language, or discourse, plays to represent or stand in for things is critical to cultural experience. Hence, we aim in this book to develop an understanding of the concept of discourse and to use it often as almost a synonym for culture. It is our belief that the concept of discourse has much to offer, not only to the practice of counseling, but also to the task of sorting out the confusions and finding a way forward in the many stalled conversations around issues of culture. We shall explore it in detail in Chapter 5.

What Is Culture?

Let's embark now on an exploration of the different meanings of the term *culture* and endeavor to sort them carefully. Our investigations suggest that there is not universal agreement on the meaning of the word and that the meanings most people agree on have been through a series of shifts and changes. We shall seek to trace the main threads in the historical development of the concept of culture in order to make sense of where we find ourselves today. One place to start is by trying to separate culture from what it is not. This is a basic move in the method of inquiry known as "deconstruction" (see Box 1.3).

Box 1.3. Deconstruction

Deconstruction, a method of philosophical inquiry into the meanings of words and experiences, was first articulated by the French philosopher Jacques Derrida (1976). Derrida suggests searching for the meaning of a word, not so much in a precise capturing of its essence as in a careful tracing of its relation to other words and concepts used by people in particular social contexts throughout history. Each word carries with it a trace of meaning from its other significant usages. It participates in the general exchange of discourse and develops overtones of usage from those who have deployed the word for particular purposes. Derrida also seeks to uncover the meaning of a concept in its relation to other concepts around it. In particular, he wants to drill a philosophical mine shaft into the relationship of binary conceptual opposites. For example, he argues that the word *light* has meaning only in relation to its opposite *dark* and carries the meaning of the opposite as a hidden referent in its own meaning. In other words, the meaning of a term or concept can be made clearer by searching for the meaning that it negates as much as in what it asserts. In this way, the meanings of binary concepts are always bound to each other in a relationship.

There are a series of binaries pertaining to the subject matter of this book that are bound together in this way. In discourse about race, *white/ black* is an example of a binary pair. Other examples are *male/female*, *rich/poor*, *educated/uneducated*, *normal/abnormal*, and *problem/ solution*. These binary distinctions are important because they become headings under which much of our thinking gets organized in *either/or* terms. Derrida proposes opening up the relation between these binary opposites and then identifying the surpluses of meaning that escape such binaries. The intention of the deconstructive endeavor is not to render everything so relative that it is meaningless. Derrida has been very strong on that point. Rather, it is to open up new possibilities for meaning and fresh openings for living. Therefore, we think that deconstruction has a useful part to play in the process of addressing problems, be they social problems or personal problems, in counseling. Those who have argued explicitly for the value of a deconstructive spirit in counseling include the narrative therapist Michael White (1992) and the psychoanalyst Jacques Lacan (1977). The general spirit of deconstruction, however, is implicit to some degree in many other approaches to counseling.

A deconstructive inquiry would lead us to ask, from what does the word *culture* distinguish itself? To what is it opposed? What is the limit or boundary beyond which we are not talking about culture but about something else? One answer that comes readily to mind is the concept of "nature." What is cultural is whatever is not natural. There are clearly some aspects of every person that are natural characteristics of human beings. They are biological in origin. We are born with them or they develop as a result of biological maturation processes. For example, the development of sexual interest and attraction to others with the onset of puberty is usually considered an aspect of natural maturation resulting from hormonal changes in the body. However, dating and courtship practices are not "natural" human activities. They are always specific to particular cultural contexts and should not be simply attributed to natural causes. The picture is complicated further because there may be huge variations in the biological aspects from one person to another, or from one group of people to another, as a result of biological variation rather than of cultural practice.

Few would disagree with these general assertions. The problems come when we try to sort out just what is natural and what is cultural. The study of psychology and education, in particular, has been for a long time caught in a debate about "nature versus nurture." This has not been just an esoteric academic debate. There are material consequences based on the positions taken in this debate that affect people's daily lives. For example, you're probably familiar with the cultural idea or discourse that "women are naturally more nurturing than men," or the discourse that "men are naturally more rational than women." These pieces of discourse, if accepted by the majority, lead easily to cultural expectations that women will be better suited to stay at home and rear children and men better suited to exercise leadership in business and politics. We know that when such discourses were challenged by feminism, it became a more common cultural practice for women to advance their careers and for men to participate in the nurturing of children. If these behaviors were determined by nature rather than discourse or culture, such shifts would not be possible. These contemporary understandings about men's and women's "natures," about what it means to be born male or born female, have a huge impact on how we conduct ourselves as they shape our educational, professional, and social choices.

In addition, culturally produced mechanisms have been created to calculate the level of one's nature or biological makeup and to evaluate quantified amounts of this nature against social norms. For example, intelligence tests were developed on this basis. Cyril Burt (Butler & Petrulis, 1999) produced falsified accounts of how intelligence was primarily "natural" through his invention of phony identical twins reared apart who scored very similarly on IQ tests. The eugenics movement, now largely discredited, was powerfully influential in the early 20th century and led to the forced sterilization of many people with intellectual disabilities. The worst examples of abuses based on the assumptions of biological primacy were the efforts by the Nazis in Germany to create a "pure" race of "superior" Aryan people through the implementation of the "final solution" for those who were Jewish or Gypsy (racially impure), mentally handicapped or mentally ill (mentally impure), and homosexual (morally impure).

To articulate a full, rich, and nuanced understanding of what culture means, it's worth listening to the academic conversations that have been taking place on this subject. We can access these conversations by reading the articles and books left behind by scholars. One place to start is the academic discipline that has engaged with the dimensions of culture, sought to describe it in detail, and analyzed it from the widest range of perspectives: anthropology. Another starting point is the fields of study pertaining to the interpretation of cultural products such as literature, art, and music. The whole field of cultural studies, an area of recent growth in academia, draws on the academic conversations of these domains. Then there has been in recent years a vigorous movement in the discipline of psychology that calls itself "cultural psychology." This particular domain is worth paying attention to because it is concerned with the personal elements of culture that are so important in the practice of counseling. Finally, still closer to home, there is a multicultural counseling literature in the counseling field itself. We shall conduct a brief survey of the range of meanings that we can identify in these various academic conversations and then ask what they teach us.

From a reading of the history of the concept of culture, we have selected four different meaning clusters that have evolved in the English language. Each of these patterns can be said to be a coagulation of the flow of meaning that takes place in many pieces of writing and many conversations. Each of them can be heard in contemporary conversation with varying degrees of frequency, but there has also been an evolution of meaning as well. We shall represent these meaning clusters in terms of the development of meaning that we believe has taken place.

Culture Signifies a Refined Sensibility to the Subtleties of Artistic and Intellectual Expression

Our current understanding of the concept of culture grew largely out of German philosophical writing in the 19th century (Appiah, 2005; Benhabib, 2002; Kroeber & Kluckhohn, 1952). Since German-speaking people could not identify specifically at that time with one particular country, there was a general concern to articulate and identify with their intellectual and artistic contributions to European consciousness. *Kultur* represented something like the "spirit" or "genius" (in the Romantic sense) of a people as it was expressed in art and literature. Early references to culture, from the 18th to the early 19th century, were usually related to an individual's aspirations to become "cultured" and trained in the sensibility and appreciation of the arts and humanities, which were regarded as the highest expressions of European intellectual life. This meaning grew out of earlier emphases on culture as the product of agricultural processes of "cultivation." The metaphor was then extended to persons. Matthew Arnold (1865), an influential public figure in the Victorian era, drawing upon Neoplatonic traditions, described culture as the pursuit of beauty, truth, and perfection. To be cultured, he said, was to "know the best that has been thought or said" (p. 15). Arnold assumed that the responsibility of the "cultured" was to instill into "barbaric" others the cultural virtues of goodness and truth.

In the 20th century, other voices used the same concept of culture but began to sound not so confident of the grand European vision of cultural progress toward higher forms of civilization. T. S. Eliot (1949), for example, held that it was self-evident that cultures went through periods of advance and decline. He argued that European culture in the mid 20th century was in a period of decline.

Becoming "cultured," nevertheless, was a process of intellectual-spiritual formation. It was sometimes contrasted with a meaning of "civilization" that referred more to the material and technological practices characterizing a particular way of life. This meaning of "culture" persists in some modern usages and is to some extent echoed in recent formulations of the process of "acculturation." According to this idea, a person's relationship to a culture emerges through a process of evolution as she moves toward a higher stage of enlightenment. This idea of an enlightened worldview is different from the 19th century idea of the cultured individual, but the emphasis on a process of growth is similar. We shall discuss the concept of acculturation more fully in Chapter 12.

Mathew Arnold, European aristocrat, poet, and writer, dressed in a style that reflects his role as an arbiter of "high culture."

Culture Signifies the Degree of Civilization of a People

Gradually, the word *culture* began to be applied to the masses rather than just to sophisticated and educated elites. It became more synonymous in some usages with the word *civilization* and delineated stages of evolutionary social development, from lower, "primitive" civilizations to higher, "civilized" ones. By the late 19th century, the newly established science of anthropology worked toward a consensus on the meaning of culture, broadening it to represent the organization of a particular way of life among a particular group of people. Edward Tylor's (1871) publication of *Primitive Culture* eventually proved decisive in establishing the social science meaning of culture, defining it as "that complex whole which includes knowledge, belief, art, morals, law, custom, and any other capabilities and habits acquired by man as a member of society" (p. 1). It was a move toward a concept that included everyone. However, as the book title suggests, the influence of the earlier meaning of civilization remained in the assumption that Europeans had a higher culture and that the culture of "primitive" people, or "savages," was to be an object of curious study, if not pity.

As Clifford Geertz (1995) notes, the concept of culture was used to mark off the colonizing West from the non-West, amid assumptions that all cultures were engaged in a process of evolution to some higher form. Western cultures were, as a matter of course, considered more highly developed along this evolutionary path and assumed to exhibit characteristics of more rational, progressive thought than the more superstitious, magical, and archaic characteristics of non-Western cultures. This view of culture served to provide a justificatory rationale for the imposition of European political authority over other cultural and political systems. It was "for their own good" that such "backward" cultures had been or were being colonized.

We would now call such assumptions racist or Eurocentric, but traces of these assumptions linger in the discourse that is available to frame the way we think and speak. If we want to separate from such assumptions, we sometimes have to work actively to challenge them in our own and in others' words. But we cannot merely by an act of will completely remove such traces of meaning from the repertoire of thinking that is carried not so much in our heads as in the language, or discourse, that we employ. There is a sense in which discourse is all we have as tools to think with. Therefore, the very concept of culture itself, even when we use it to criticize

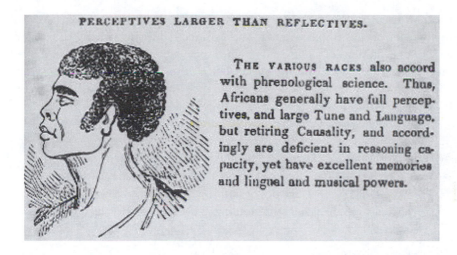

PERCEPTIVES LARGER THAN REFLECTIVES.

THE VARIOUS RACES also accord with phrenological science. Thus, Africans generally have full perceptives, and large Tune and Language, but retiring Causality, and accordingly are deficient in reasoning capacity, yet have excellent memories and lingual and musical powers.

Figure 1.1   The caption underneath this sketch illustrates the racist sentiments explicitly interwoven into 18th century European understandings of the superiority and civilized nature of whites over blacks.

Source: From Jeffries, 1869.

racism or other injustices, carries with it traces of the very assumptions that drove the process of Western cultural domination and colonization. Hence, the confusions we spoke of above are not so surprising, given this historical context. We can understand them better if we take the history into account. We cannot separate the concept of culture from such contexts and still hope to understand it and get past the effects of confusion.

Culture Signifies the Sum of Patterned Behaviors That Make Up a Way of Life

Current dominant understandings of the term *culture* are usually closer to the scientific, anthropological meaning that Tylor's definition began to articulate, namely, a set of attributes of a group of people. This set of attributes is assumed to be stable and knowable. As social scientists developed the study of culture, they treated these attributes as if they had enough coherence to provide the basis for scientific prediction. During the late 19th and early 20th centuries, this meaning became widely accepted and evolved to be less and less associated with judgments about the degree of civilization of any particular culture. Culture became more relativistic (rather than hierarchically ranked) and more inclusive. By the middle of the 20th century, many anthropologists had added their piece to the conversation Tylor had initiated. In 1952, A. L. Kroeber and Clyde Kluckhohn wrote the most thorough examination to date of the history of the concept of culture. They brought together a host of definitions from contemporary anthropologists and explored the various emphases and nuances advanced by many writers. They found a range of definitions of *culture* and grouped them according to their emphasis on matters of history, social norms, psychological features, structural organization, and genetic components. Here is a summary of the range of aspects emphasized in the definitions they found.

Culture can be taken to refer to a social group variously in terms of:

1. Their knowledge, beliefs, points of view, worldview, values, ethics, laws, norms, morals, burial practices, and religion

2. Their customs, behavior patterns, acquired habits, food habits, and rules of etiquette

3. Their art, artifacts, crafts, consumer goods, and products of human industry, and the treasury of their creations (including books, paintings, buildings, and music)

4. Their patterns of organization of social relations, sexual relations, and family relations

5. Their language and means of transmitting information from one person to another through education, instruction, or imitation

6. Their social groupings, institutions, and processes of granting sanction to persons' endeavors

This list appears very comprehensive, and perhaps the meaning of the term starts to break down when it becomes too comprehensive and appears not to exclude very much at all. What became clear, however, was that culture from the anthropological perspective was much more egalitarian than earlier conceptualizations and now included everyone. *Culture* was not just a term used to describe how "primitive" people lived, while the "advanced" societies of the West were civilizations. The objective scientific perspective introduced a sense that all cultures were relative and should not be judged against external criteria. Thus, the idea of general cultural advancement was downplayed and the idea of high and low culture deemphasized.

The classical anthropological studies of culture performed in the old British colonies emerged from this perspective on culture. Clifford Geertz (1995) calls it the "cookie-cutter" version of culture. Many confidently definitive "people studies" (Geertz, 1995, p. 43) were written about the Nuer, the Trobriand Islanders, the Kwakiutl, the Tallensi, and so on. The objective scientific method reigned triumphant and was able to pronounce the truth about tribal peoples in ways that made them seem exotic but known, summarized and packaged into a parcel of established truths.

We shall refer to this viewpoint, by way of shorthand, as the "modernist" view of culture. *Modernist* refers to the particular interlocking network of cultural assumptions that have governed the modern world in the last 300 years. It features assumptions of the triumph of science-led progress based on objective knowledge generated in the academy and promulgated around the world through the mechanisms of modern business, government, law, and media. We shall explain this concept further later in the chapter, but suffice it to say here that the view of culture referred to here is the epitome of modern scientific thinking before the challenges of postmodern thinking arose.

Another important emphasis in the anthropological perspective was that references to culture were references to the sum of all the components mentioned above. An almost metaphysical notion of a culture as an essence, or as a crystallization, of the various components of a system was invoked (Kroeber & Kluckhohn, 1952). The concept of culture referred to a way of living as a singular whole. The result was a tendency to refer to *the* Samoan way of bringing up children, *a* Hindu burial custom, *the* Nuer system of kinship relations, and so on, as though there were little variation, debate, or change within the communities being referred to. Cultures began to look more static and timeless and therefore less in touch with the relentless drives in the direction of social and technological change that were happening in the world around them. This perspective on the concept of culture continues to exert strong pulls on our thinking and can fairly be called the dominant perspective of culture operating in the world today. Some multicultural counseling texts are positioned within the notion of culture as a discrete, somewhat cohesive grouping of people who share certain salient characteristics.

In the past there was a tendency in the multicultural counseling field to characterize culture as a rather static phenomenon. Sometimes sweeping generalizations were made about groupings of people such as Asians, African Americans, and Jewish people that made them sound very similar. The emphasis was often on cultural belonging and similitude over cultural difference and debate. The modernist view of culture has often focused upon coherence and loyalty to rather simplified cultural norms that remain fixed and unchanging. It does not focus very much on cultural relations or tensions. This perspective tends to select exceptions out as culturally inauthentic and consigns them to the margins as the price to be paid for a theory of more rigid convergence.

Not so long ago, questions in counseling licensing and accreditation exams were constructed on the basis of these assumptions. For example, a multiple choice question might ask a candidate to respond to an item about counseling an African American client, presuming a cookie-cutter version of what African American culture is like. While the purpose was to test counselors on their understanding of important cultural differences, this approach deemphasized complexity and difference in favor of a simple reductionist certainty that can be scored as right or wrong.

The test makers might have responded to such an allegation by saying that there is always research evidence for the concepts tested. Even if this were true, the research evidence always depends on the assumptions the researchers built into the research process. Hence, an idea can have research support but still have dubious truth value because of the problematic assumptions on which it is built. Facts never

Figure 1.2   The titles of these books hint at the static and unidimensional descriptions of cultural groups produced by Western researchers in the middle and latter part of the 20th century.

speak for themselves without relying on a framework of philosophical assumptions to make sense. Today, multiculturalism is moving away from cookie-cutter versions of culture. There is a growing recognition that testing candidates in this manner can perpetuate simplistic and unidimensional understandings of their clients because they belong to a particular ethnic grouping.

> ## Box 1.4. Famous Quotations About Culture
>
> What links can you make among the different ways of conceptualizing culture that we have outlined in this chapter and that are expressed in these quotations?
>
> *Culture is properly described as the love of perfection; it is a study of perfection.*
>
> —Matthew Arnold, *Culture and Anarchy*
>
> *The more elevated a culture, the richer its language.*
>
> —Anton Pavlovich Chekhov

Whenever I hear the word culture, I reach for my revolver.

—Attributed to Hermann Goering

No culture can live, if it attempts to be exclusive.

—Mahatma Gandhi

Culture is like the sum of special knowledge that accumulates in any large united family and is the common property of all its members. When we of the great Culture Family meet, we exchange reminiscences about Grandfather Homer, and that awful old Dr. Johnson, and Aunt Sappho, and poor Johnny Keats.

—Aldous Huxley

Culture: the cry of men in face of their destiny.

—Albert Camus, *L'Envers et L'Endroit* [Betwixt and Between]

The concept of culture I espouse . . . is essentially a semiotic one. Believing, with Max Weber, that man is an animal suspended in webs of significance he himself has spun, I take culture to be those webs, and the analysis of it to be therefore not an experimental science in search of law but an interpretative one in search of meaning. It is explication I am after. . . .

—Clifford Geertz, *The Interpretation of Cultures*

We use the word culture in these two senses: to mean a whole way of life—the common meanings; to mean the arts and learning—the special processes of discovery and creative effort. Some writers reserve the word for one or other of these senses; I insist on both, and on the significance of their conjunction. The questions I ask about our culture are questions about deep personal meanings. Culture is ordinary, in every society and in every mind.

—Raymond Williams, *Culture and Society*

An army without culture is a dull-witted army, and a dull-witted army cannot defeat the enemy.

—Mao Tse-Tung, "The United Front in Cultural Work"

Every mingling of Aryan blood with that of lower peoples the result was the end of the cultured people. North America, whose population consists in by far the largest part of Germanic elements who mixed but little with the lower colored peoples, shows a different humanity and culture from Central and South America, where the predominantly Latin immigrants often mixed with the aborigines on a large scale. By this one example, we can clearly and distinctly recognize the effect of racial mixture. The Germanic inhabitant of

(Continued)

(Continued)

> the American continent, who has remained racially pure and unmixed, rose to be master of the continent; he will remain the master as long as he does not fall a victim to defilement of the blood.
>
> —Adolf Hitler, *Mein Kampf* [My Struggle]

Culture Signifies the Diverse and Complex Strands of Discourse Influences on People's Lives

Today there is a shift to new ways of thinking about culture, partly in response to philosophical shifts introduced through postmodern social theorizing and partly through the development of a new academic discipline of cultural studies. This shift has been marked by a series of critiques of the modernist view of culture and by the gradual emergence of some new ways of looking at culture. Stuart Hall (2005) characterizes this shift simply as a shift to an understanding of culture as "shared meanings" (p. 295). This emphasis focuses our attention much more on the work done in language to represent ways of living rather than directly on the ways of living themselves. A culture is a way of interpreting life as much as it is a way of life. As Hall notes, however, meanings and interpretations are slippery, they move about, they are contestable, they are seldom singular or fixed. Moreover, from this perspective, the understanding of culture becomes a matter of understanding how people give meaning to things. Kwame Appiah (2005) also notes a turn to a more linguistic and interpretive understanding of culture as well as an expansion of the kinds and numbers of groups to whom the concept of culture has been applied.

Seyla Benhabib (2002) summarizes some of the major ways in which recent scholars have come to be critical of the conventional concept of culture. She suggests that there are three false premises in modernist conceptions of culture. The first is that cultures are "clearly delineable wholes" (p. 4). It is notoriously difficult in practice to define who is a member of a cultural group and who is not. Arguments develop about whose membership is valid and whose is not. The second false premise is that a "non-controversial description of the culture of a human group is possible" (p. 4). For many assertions of what is a cultural norm, there are conflicting practices by other members of the same group, so much so that many would argue that divisions and differences about cultural patterns are more common than uniformity. The third false premise is that there exists a one-to-one correspondence between groups of people and cultural practices and that political decisions can be made with a degree of certainty about how members of a particular cultural group will respond. Think of how difficult it might be to plan a policy or a counseling program that will meet the needs of women, for example, given that there are vast differences among women with different backgrounds, lifestyles, beliefs, and experiences.

Benhabib calls the modernist version of culture "reductionist" because it reduces groups of people and descriptions of culture to each other without thinking about the problems of doing so. Others have echoed these problems with conventional views of culture. The overemphasizing of the boundedness and distinctness of culture has been criticized by anthropologists such as Terence Turner (1993) and Renato Rosaldo (1994). It is just not as easy as many people think to define who is Latino or what Japanese culture is about. Any definition of cultural membership you come up with will leave some people out, and any description of a cultural belief or norm will encounter immediate contradictions from many who would claim membership in that culture. Being too definite about cultural characteristics has the effect of sidelining those who live on the "borders" of any particular cultural group. In Chapter 2, we shall explore the concept of border and hybrid identities further.

Newer conceptualizations of what culture is make it a much more fluid concept. Culture is not so much a fixed orthodoxy as an open field of meanings. It is always emergent, always in process, and always changing. Therefore, fixed accounts of what a culture means appear inadequate. From this perspective, cultural groups are noticed to be constantly negotiating ambivalences or tensions among themselves as well as in their relation to other cultural groups (Yon, 2000). Claiming that someone is an "authentic" group member becomes less and less possible, because any definition of what is authentic can be disputed.

The search for "indigenous authenticity" is more realistically represented as a "tangled multiplicity" (Geertz, 1995, pp. 52–53). As the concept of culture has itself become more elusive, it has become harder to make straightforward statements of cultural identity. Daniel Yon (2000) researched in a compelling way the cultural identifications of young people in a multicultural high school in Toronto and used the word "elusive" to describe the young people's culture.

Figure 1.3   It is more difficult to identify distinct ethnic groups based on dress in the 21st century, since the majority of people on the planet wear Western style clothing.

From this perspective, a culture needs first to be understood as a construction imposed onto the lives of a group of people by whoever is describing it. The person doing the describing, therefore, comes much more into view, whether this person is describing himself or is an anthropologist, a politician, a journalist, a psychologist, or a counselor. Whatever we might say about another person's culture is now viewed as an interpretation much more than as a simple description. So whose interpretation is it? What assumptions from the worldview of the person doing the interpreting are unwittingly included? The person making the interpretation is always speaking from a cultural position and, in speaking about others, is always revealing something about himself. This is one reason why we want to be transparent about our own theoretical leanings in this book. In other words, "the study of culture is culture" (Wagner, 1981, p. 16). Objectivity is, in principle, one of the cornerstones of modernist social science, but it has started to look a lot more difficult to achieve. How can a description of someone's culture be objective if it is infused with the cultural perspective of the person doing the observing? Thus, studying culture has in recent times become a matter of studying relations between the subject and the object of the speaking, that is, between cultural positions, rather than a simple objective study of the Other.

In recent decades, the academic study of culture has grown a new branch that has opened up different perspectives from those championed within the discipline of anthropology. It is called "cultural studies" (see Box 1.5), and it has developed many new postmodern concepts and perspectives on culture. For a start, it has often been written not so much from the point of view of the colonizing people as from the position of those seeking to shrug off the yoke of colonization. Thus, this field of study has at times become known as *postcolonialism*.

Shifting fields of study reflect shifting experiences of life. Hence, the emergent view of culture is necessarily a less solid and more fluid concept. Cultures are considered less as finished products and more as ongoing processes of production (Yon, 2000). To view culture as discrete and stable now appears always risky because it blinds us to processes by which people are continually remaking cultural identity and belonging in daily life. Rather than homogeneous essential characteristics, cultural identities appear to be much more hybrid. People's cultural identities are in a constant state of revision as they respond to the changing circumstances around them, and this occurs more than is often recognized. At the same time, people also strive for coherence and maintain stable reference points for themselves as much as they can, even while the forms of life around them are shifting and changing. Terms like *race* and *culture* don't mean the same things they did a generation ago. They shift beneath our feet as we walk through life.

This has been only a brief survey of the recent evolution of the concept of culture. The practice of multicultural counseling must be based on some such foundation. Increasingly, multicultural writers and practitioners are embracing postmodern ideas of culture and tracing their significance into the domain of multicultural counseling. Over recent decades there has been growing rejection of what Geertz calls the predominant "cookie-cutter" version of culture.

The four distinct meanings described here are by no means the only ones around—they are merely the ones that have dominated recent conversations about culture. The postmodern conceptualization of culture discussed above may in the future divide into a series of distinctions. It is unlikely to remain stable. It will do so in response to the evolving complexities of people's lives. Cultural worlds themselves are made up of the thousands and millions of interactions between people and between human beings and the physical environment that take place on a daily basis. It is therefore not surprising that among these many events there will be many differences in the patterns of life that people live out.

Box. 1.5. Cultural Studies

The field of cultural studies represents a new way of engaging in the observation and study of culture. While many academic disciplines have applied their particular concerns to the direct study of culture, namely anthropology, history, sociology, psychology, and literary studies, over the past two decades there has been an increased interest in a study of culture that is interdisciplinary and not bound by a singular field of study. This move toward recognizing culture as a distinct field of inquiry reflects the complex history and diverse range of meanings the term *culture* encompasses.

The field of cultural studies does not focus just on cultures as if they could be studied directly without problem. It also focuses on the field of representations through which our knowledge of other cultures must pass. It is a field of study that has rendered problematic conventional understandings of culture. It seeks to represent culture as more complex, more contested, more riven by politics and power relations than traditional cultural anthropology commonly holds it to be. The discipline of cultural studies is multidisciplinary in its focus and its methodologies. It has even been called "antidisciplinary" (Grossberg, Nelson, & Treichler, 1992) in the sense that it actively resists being caught in the conventional disciplines of the traditional academy. It has turned the focus of the study of culture away from exclusive attention to the cultures of exotic Others and onto the cultural trends in all parts of the modern world. It pays serious attention to the products and texts of popular culture as cultural formations worthy of interpretation, rather than treating them as just ephemeral pieces of common life that should be winnowed out in the pursuit of high culture. The cultural studies field has thus granted a new "authenticity" to aspects of culture that were previously not studied.

Edward Said is considered one of the most influential figures in the development of the field of cultural studies, as is Raymond Williams. Other well-known writers who dominate the reading lists in cultural studies include Stuart Hall, Donna Haraway, bell hooks, and Cornel West. Some of these writers are literary critics and some are social scientists, and the cultural studies discipline has tended to offer them a dialogic space within which to talk with each other. The territory has been shaped largely by departures from modernist thinking. Cultural studies scholars usually draw perspectives from critical theory and postmodernism. This field has also contributed to the growth of recognition for studies in postcolonialism and media studies.

In the last section of this chapter, however, we shall turn our attention to the field of psychology and look at how the four meanings of culture outlined above have been represented in selections from major theorists whose work underpins the counseling field.

Representations of Culture in the Psychological Literature

Now we shall trace some of the expressions of the various meanings of culture into the psychological literature that has informed counseling practice. The modern history of therapy and counseling can be said to have begun with the psychoanalytic work of Sigmund Freud, so let's look at some comments Freud wrote that indicate some of his assumptions about culture.

> Primitive man is known to us by the stages of development through which he has passed: that is, through the inanimate monuments and implements which he has left behind for us, through our knowledge of his art, his religion, and his attitude towards life, which we have received either directly or through the medium of legends, myths and fairytales; and through the remnants of his ways that survive in our own manners and customs. Moreover, in a certain sense he is still our contemporary: there are many people whom we still consider more closely related to primitive man than to ourselves, in whom we therefore recognize the direct descendants and representatives of earlier man. We can thus judge the so-called savage and semi-savage races; their psychic life assumes a peculiar interest for us, for we can recognize in their psychic life a well-preserved, early stage of our own development. (Freud, 1938, p. 775)

It is noticeable here that Freud conceived of psychosocial developmental processes in terms borrowed from the dominant European discourses that drove the processes of colonization. It is clear that "savages" will be regarded as objects of "our" study and that "we" who are doing the studying are clearly European. He echoes the assumption that European culture is superior to the culture of "savages." He also echoes the social Darwinism that was very influential in 19th century European academic discourse, whereby "primitive" people were considered to be on an evolutionary pathway toward the kinds of civilization for which "superior" European culture could serve as the model. "We" are already civilized; "they" are stuck in cultures that, while backward, are evolving toward civilization. Echoes of Tylor's definition of culture and of the assumptions of a hierarchy of cultures were present in 19th century conceptions of culture.

Freud also extends the cultural metaphor to describe individuals who might need therapeutic help. They are "more closely related" to "primitive" people than to "us." They are developmentally inferior. They are of scientific interest, but they are most unlikely to have anything to teach "us." Instead, they need to be given the benefit of "our" own superior rationality. He thus creates a distance between the therapist and the patient. The latter is an object of the former's scientific gaze, which is assumed to come from a place of disinterested neutrality rather than from a cultural worldview. Yet, with the benefit of a hundred years of hindsight, we can easily see some of the cultural influences of Freud's day represented in his words. Far from being a culture-free scientist, he is a scientist whose perspective is shaped strongly by his cultural world.

The question that needs to be asked for counseling practice is whether there are traces of these cultural assumptions still present in modern psychoanalytic thera-peutic practices or in the many strands of therapeutic practice that draw to a greater or lesser extent on Freud's foundational work. For example, how do Freud's notions of transference, still taught as simple truths to current generations of counselors, rely on the dubious assumptions of cultural chauvinism represented in these statements? This book is not the place to answer these questions, but we believe they need to be asked in the multicultural counseling field. We can also bring the questions forward to the present. How closely do modern therapists regard their clients as objects of study and assume that their own knowledge is scientific in the sense of being free of cultural influences? How many of the assumptions we hold with little thought today will appear at best quaint in a hundred years? We argue that the study of counseling theory needs to be frequently revisited in response to questions like these and that multicultural counseling texts should lead the way in this reexamination.

Carl Jung was for a time a colleague of Freud's but later developed a rivalry with him. His work has been very influential in the counseling field. By the time he died in 1961, he had written a great deal about therapy and had articulated his own analytic approach to therapeutic interaction. His interest in the study of spirituality led him to many inquiries into the beliefs, practices, and rituals of different cultures around the world. One thing he sought to establish was a series of archetypal symbols that could be found in the waking and dreaming life of all of "mankind." His was a modernist vision of the rational scientific psychologist producing understanding by studying and gaining insight into the more irrational thinking of more primitive people. Like Freud, he was interested in "primitive" culture for what could be extracted out of it by the trained scientific mind; he was looking for what it could teach the civilized European scientist about a universal human nature. As he talks about the force of his "archetypes" in shaping psychological experience, he makes the following comment:

> We carry our past with us, to wit, the primitive and inferior man with his desires and emotions, and it is only with an enormous effort that we can detach ourselves from this burden. (Jung, 1983, p. 88)

The heroic effort, of course, is that of the "advanced" civilizations of Europe, based on rational thought, which stand in contrast to the "primitive" cultures who are left seething in emotions and desires. The rational scientist of enlightenment-based modernism remains the model for everyone else to emulate. While Jung's language reflects some shifts to a more modernist discourse (he was a lot younger than Freud), he still bears the assumptions of the distinction between civilization and culture typical of Tylor's version of culture.

In the next generation of psychological writers, the divide between modernist scientific behavioral psychology on the one hand and the more Romantic vision of humanistic psychology on the other hand became manifest. Our question is not so much about the theories and practices that emerged as about what happened to concepts of culture in the process of these developments.

If we look at the work of the most prominent behavioral psychologist, B. F. Skinner, we find evidence of the shift to a more universal view of culture made into a subject of scientific analysis. Take the following comments from a book on education as an example:

> Men sometimes work towards distant goals. In a very real sense they plant in the spring because of the harvest in the autumn and study for years for the sake of professional career. But they do all this not because they are affected by distant and future events but because their culture has constructed mediating devices in the form of conditioned reinforcers: the student studies because he is admired for doing so, because immediate changes in his behavior make progress towards later reinforcement, because being educated is "a good thing," because he is released from the aversive condition of not-knowing. Cultures are never particularly successful in building reinforcers of this sort; hence the importance of a direct attack on the problem in a technology of teaching. (Skinner, 1968, pp. 155–156)

It is not just "savages" who have culture in this passage. All "men" do. (Women are assumed to be included in a background position, which is one way in which Skinner is representing a cultural perspective and not just a scientific one.) Culture is reinterpreted as a set of "conditioned reinforcers," but they are described as "never particularly successful" in comparison with the superior reinforcers that science can offer. Skinner's remarks assume the position that most modernist social science and professional practice did during the mid to late 20th century: we all have culture, but it is not particularly to be celebrated. Culture was often referred to during this time as "the environment" (before the rise of ecology co-opted this term to refer to the biological context of life) and was viewed as the source of faulty patterns of conditioning that needed the superior perspective of the scientist to correct. The 19th century opposition between culture and civilization shifts here to an opposition between culture and science.

Cognitive-behavioral counseling has achieved enormous influence and popularity in North America as a result of the bringing together of behavioral scientific principles and the therapeutic practice ideas of Albert Ellis. In Ellis's pugnacious writing, we find references to the same commitment that Skinner has to modernist social science standing in opposition to cultural traditions. Consider his comments on religion, for example:

> In the final analysis, then, religion is neurosis. . . . [R]eligion goes hand in hand with the basic irrational beliefs of human beings. These keep them dependent, anxious and hostile, and thereby create and maintain their neuroses and psychoses. . . . Obviously the sane and effective psychotherapist

should not—as many contemporary psychoanalytic Jungian, client-centered, and existentialist therapists have contended he should—go along with the patient's religious orientation and try to help these patients live successfully with their religions. (Ellis, 1985, p. 15)

For Ellis, therapy is about the application of rational, scientific thinking to the problems of individuals' lives. Like Skinner, he believes (you could say he has *faith* in) the possibilities that thinking more rationally can bring, in contrast to the inferior options for making sense of life offered by religious commitment. He is talking here about the relationship between science and religion, but if we consider religious commitment to be an important aspect of a person's cultural identity, then it is reasonable to conclude that Ellis does not place much value on cultural formations other than those produced out of modernist science. He does not even advocate communicating respect for a patient's religious beliefs.

In the cognitive-behavioral literature, it is uncommon to find much in the way of references to the concept of culture at all. Aaron Beck, for example, scarcely gives culture a mention. Like other cognitive-behaviorists, his focus is on the scientific approach that presumably rises above the idiosyncrasies of culture. Donald Meichenbaum is another prominent figure in the history of cognitive-behavioral therapy. He prefers the concept of schemata to that of belief systems, but they mean roughly the same thing. In explaining the importance of a person's cognitive schema, he does make some cultural references by way of analogy:

Harman (1981) has described anthropological examples of people from one tribe having a different "reality" or consensual belief system (set of schemata) by means of which they perceive the world quite differently than do members of another tribe. Each tribe's belief system is validated by experience. . . . The tribe's constellation of implicit beliefs . . . serves as a framework for perceiving and evaluating inputs. Moreover, the members of each tribe have a confirmatory bias to seek and find data that are supportive of their initial beliefs. (Meichenbaum & Gilmore, 1984, p. 284)

The analogy here involves a comparison of the schemata of an individual therapy client with the schemata of a tribe from another culture. The therapy client remains an individual and her schemata are her own. The tribe members, on the other hand, are accorded a common schema that serves a collective function. The word "bias" is used, which typically refers to a faulty perspective on reality that can be corrected by the application of the scientific method of objective observation and measurement. Psychological science has a primary place of authority for the individual who is suffering from a biased schema, as the tribe members are. The question that arises for our purposes is, in just what version of culture is the tribe being portrayed? Since they are now being compared with clients in "our" culture, they are no longer exotic "savages" who live in a primal world of raw emotion. There is a greater level of respect for the tribe members' thoughts, schema, and rational processes than there is in, say, Freud's version of culture. But whereas "we" are individuals, each with our own schema, "they" are spoken of as if they all share an identical schema. This is the cookie-cutter version of culture spread by modernist social science, in which tribal schema are assumed to be uniform, static, and unchanging. There is little room here for postmodern versions of culture in which tribal schemata might be multiple, hybrid, or competing. Meanwhile, members of modern, more civilized societies are treated as individuals who benefit from a science that corrects the "bias" of culture.

A similar scientific universalizing of the relationship between culture and science happens when we look at Carl Rogers's humanistic account of culture, although Rogers positions himself differently in relation to it. Rogers did not often refer to persons as members of cultural groups. His interests were more in the individual's personal experience of life. However, here is a passage in which he refers to the relationships between individuals and their cultural environment. Speaking of what he saw as the clash of values between young people and their elders in the 1970s, Rogers (1973) says,

> Sophisticated individuals in every culture seem unsure and troubled as to the goals they hold in esteem. The reasons are not far to seek. The world culture, in all its aspects, seems increasingly scientific and relativistic, and the rigid, absolute views on values which come to us from the past appear anachronistic. Even more important perhaps, is the fact that the modern individual is assailed from every angle by divergent and contradictory value claims. It is no longer possible as it was in the not too distant historical past, to settle comfortably into the value system of one's forbears or one's community and live one's life without ever examining the nature and assumptions of that system. (p. 13)

In this passage, Rogers refers to a new science-dominated "world culture" that is in contest with the traditional, more local cultures of one's "forbears." This is clearly a reference to the cultural influences of what we would now call the modernist world. But Rogers does not pay great attention to these influences. He is more interested in the existential struggle of the individual to free himself from the restraints of both the unexamined and perhaps primitive cultural world and from the scientific world culture. This is the struggle for self-actualization that Rogers articulates more fully elsewhere. Rogers is also Romantic enough in his orientation to paint an unattractive picture of modernist science as slightly soulless and relativistic. The distinctions between the world of civilization and the world of ethnic cultures that Freud referred to have softened but are still alluded to, albeit less explicitly. The struggle of the individual in Rogers's thinking is primarily a struggle to free oneself from culture, whether it be modern culture or the culture of forebears. He is, therefore, no multiculturalist, because the multicultural movement by its very nature seeks to situate the individual more strongly back in the world of cultural influences, rather than to free him from them. The concept of culture that one might be freed from is more akin to the cookie-cutter version of culture that Geertz alluded to. Everyone has forebears and therefore everyone has culture. Gone is the open allusion to the superiority of European "civilization," although it remains in the background, masked as "world culture."

Similarly, Fritz Perls, in his writings on Gestalt therapy, constitutes the individual as in a process of struggle with the cultural world around her. He seldom speaks of this social world in terms of culture, however, preferring the biological metaphors of "the organism" in "contact" with the "environment." He will speak of "society" at times, presumably a reference to modernism, but it is largely a place of negative reference. It is the source of "shoulds," which are spoken of as toxic for the individual's emergence as a responsible self. Here is one passage where he does make some cultural references, in particular to cultural rituals:

> There seems to be, in all human beings, an inborn tendency towards ritual, which can be defined as an expression of man's sense of social identification, his need for contact with a group. We find this tendency not only among primitives, but among highly civilized groups as well. The play of children is made up largely of ritual acting and repetition. Parades, festivals, religious services, all are expressions of this need. In a perverted way, the need for ritual seems to underlie the obsessional and compulsive neuroses. (Perls, 1973, p. 28)

Perls goes on to contrast neurotic rituals with legitimate rituals that are a healthy expression of human need, if participated in with full awareness. He goes on to tell a story of an individual who is participating in a cultural ritual and in the middle of it becomes aware of a personal biological need (the need to urinate). He argues for the source of neurotic behavior being the unsuccessful resolution of the conflict between participation in cultural ritual and personal needs. For Perls, bodily needs always trump cultural practices. Biology is the stronger authority. Any attempt to deny an individual bodily need in favor of a cultural ritual is considered the source of neurosis. Here we have recognition of cultural influences accompanied by a description of the individual as standing in a place of opposition to culture, governed principally in this place by biological needs. It is a similar Romantic theme to the one found in Rogers's work. Perls clearly does have traces in his thinking of the 19th century assumptions of the difference between civilized people and those who have cultures. His version of Gestalt therapy is not, however, strongly multicultural. In the relationship between the individual and the social environment, Perls does not give much prominence to the role of culture. The needs Perls speaks of are primarily biological, and they are human needs rather than cultural ones. It therefore seems reasonable to align his assumptions with the modernist conceptualization of culture, at least with a version of it that emphasizes the importance of scientific modernism ahead of any investigation of how cultural traditions might shape the experience of counseling clients.

We have seen, therefore, that the place of culture in some of these works by significant contributors to the therapeutic field has evolved through the last hundred years. The version of culture that once was a preserve of savages dripping with raw emotion and standing in contrast to civilization gradually gives way to a more modernist version of exotic culture. In the more modern version, culture is something that we all share, although there are still hints that a civilization based on science can do better for the individual than culture can. This is what we have been calling the cookie-cutter version of culture. The differences between different writers relate more to the role of science than to the role of culture. Science either provides the model method for rising above cultural influences and improving on them, or it is part of the stifling and sterile environment that individuals must free themselves from.

You will look in vain for the newer, postmodern versions of culture in the major figures who continue to dominate the psychology of counseling. These versions of culture have started to be evident in some of the more recent contributions to the counseling field. We shall explore these contributions later in the book. The multicultural counseling movement has itself shifted the ground on which we stand in this regard. It has had a powerful effect in placing culture on the agenda much more strongly than any of the counseling theorists cited above ever envisaged. However, the mainstream practices of counseling have still not strayed far from base with regard to taking the more nuanced versions of culture into account. The cookie-cutter version of culture is still dominant in many counselors' thinking.

The counseling field is now taking cultural influences more seriously. That is a clear implication of the growing interest in multicultural approaches to counseling. The examination we have conducted in this chapter suggests the importance of reexamining major counseling theories. Multiculturalism should be more than just an add-on to existing counseling theory. It should cause us to reexamine our assumptions about the role of culture in the production of our psychology, the relationship between culture and science, and therefore our counseling theories and methods.

TO DISCUSS

1. What links can you make between the concepts of culture used in the multicultural literature on counseling and the four different versions of culture listed above?

2. Which meanings of culture do each of the quotations listed in Box 1.4 rely on?

3. In small groups, construct a role-played conversation between a group of people at a social occasion that embodies each of the four perspectives on culture. Choose from the following list of social occasions: a Hollywood cocktail party; a gathering of anthropologists at a conference; a group of homeless people huddled around a fire; a government cabinet meeting discussing a current foreign policy issue; a political group planning a protest action.

4. Reflect on the usefulness of each of the meanings of culture. What sorts of social practices do they lead to? What social relations do they support or anticipate? What advantages/disadvantages do they produce for colonizers and the colonized? Are these advantages intended or unintended?

5. Name particular groups of people in your community and ask what consequences the use of these concepts would lead to for each of them.

6. Discuss the effects of these concepts of culture on the way people think about the problems they present to their counselors.

Response to Chapter 1

Courtland Lee

Courtland Lee, Ph.D., is a professor and director of the Counselor Education Program at the University of Maryland, College Park. He is the author, editor, or coeditor of four books on multicultural counseling and two books on counseling and social justice. He is also the author of three books on counseling African American males. In addition, he has published numerous book chapters and articles on cross-cultural counseling. Dr. Lee is president of the International Association for Counselling. He is also a fellow of the British Association for Counselling and Psychotherapy, the first and only American to receive this honor. Dr. Lee is a past president of the American Counseling Association. He is also a past president of the Association for Multicultural Counseling and Development. In addition, Dr. Lee is a past President of Chi Sigma Iota, the international counseling honor society. He is a charter member of Chi Sigma Iota's Academy of Leaders for Excellence. Dr. Lee is the former editor of the *Journal of Multicultural Counseling and Development* and the *Journal of African American Men.* He currently serves on the editorial board of the *International Journal for the Advancement of Counselling.* He is also an associate editor of the *Journal of Counseling & Development.* Dr. Lee has held faculty positions as a counselor educator at the University of North Carolina at Chapel Hill and the University of Virginia. A former teacher and school counselor, Dr. Lee has served as an educational consultant in both the United States and abroad.

The authors present a very provocative analysis of the concept of culture in this chapter. They are to be applauded for examining culture through not only a psychological lens, but anthropological, philosophical, historical, and literary ones as well. I believe that this may be one of the very few chapters in a multicultural counseling text that explores culture in such a comprehensive and multidisciplinary fashion.

The two basic assumptions of this chapter, with which I concur, are that culture is dynamic rather than static and that it is multifaceted (i.e., more than just race/ethnicity). The discussion of the four different meanings of culture in this chapter has forced me to once again reflect on my views of the meaning and importance of culture. I have taught multicultural counseling in one form or another for almost 30 years, and my thinking on the nature of culture has evolved over that time. In my early years of teaching, issues of culture in counseling revolved exclusively around concepts of race and ethnicity. Culture was synonymous with a person's racial or ethnic identification and that was the end of the discourse. As my thinking evolved and my experiences grew, I came to see culture as a complex set of identities that described the many facets of individual personality. In addition to race/ethnicity, I now perceived culture to be primarily nationality, gender, sexual orientation, religious affiliation, and ability status. However, upon reading and reflecting on this chapter I must again rethink my ideas on culture. The authors have impacted my thinking about culture in identity boxes (e.g., "race," "sexual orientation," "American") and how this reinforces "cookie-cutter" notions and perpetuates stereotypical, or what I would refer to as "monolithic," views of people as cultural beings.

After reflecting on this chapter, it is now more evident to me that culture must be understood from an individualistic as opposed to a group perspective. Culture must be considered in an existential context. The ideas in this chapter imply that culture as a personality construct is how each individual makes meaning for his or her life. Culture, therefore, is an intensely personal phenomenon made real by how an individual interprets common human experiences as well as those experiences that relate to the degree of his or her group identification or affiliation. Culture as a construct can only really be comprehended by listening to personal narratives and trying to understand how people make meaning for their lives.

This chapter is profound in that it forces us to think far outside the bounds of culture traditionally presented in multicultural counseling texts. It will no doubt stimulate intense dialogue among those who hold differing views on the nature of culture and its place in the helping relationship. I urge the reader to carefully reflect on the ideas presented here and on who he or she really is as a cultural being as the remainder of the chapters are explored.

CHAPTER 2

Complexity and Culture

Culture in North American multicultural literature generally refers first to different ethnic and racial minority groups and then to subcultures based on gender, sexual orientation, and, to a lesser extent, socioeconomic factors and age. There is a debate in the multicultural counseling literature about the nature of these cultural categories as well as about the extent to which group identities should be given prime billing in the world of culture. It is worth exploring some of the debates here to better grapple with current thinking about multiculturalism and counseling. We can then compare and contrast our own position with the debate that has taken place over the last two decades.

Many multicultural researchers and scholars write about multicultural counseling as a practice that deals with the primacy and salience of race. These writers appear to limit the scope of multicultural counseling to that which primarily addresses issues of ethnic oppression and marginalization within the counseling process. They argue that overinclusive definitions dilute the usefulness of the construct of culture because they fail to denote anything beyond individual differences. Clemont Vontress (1988), for example, defines multicultural counseling as "counseling in which the counselor and the client are culturally different because of socialization acquired in distinct cultural, sub-cultural, race-ethnic . . . environments" (p. 74). His use of culture here is synonymous with ethnicity. Other writers have emphasized their concern that broadening the definitions of multiculturalism may dilute the focus on racial and ethnic concerns, particularly the concerns of the four established minority groups that are granted official visibility in America: African, Asian, Latin, and Native American (Locke, 1990). Derald Wing Sue (1993) suggests that when white researchers define culture broadly to include class, affectional orientation, religion, sex, and age, racism is not addressed.

There has, however, been strong resistance to this proposal. A number of writers have criticized those who limit definitions of multicultural counseling to include issues of ethnicity only (Axelson, 1994; Ivey, 1986; Ivey, Ivey, & Simek-Morgan,

1993; Midgett & Meggert, 1991; Pedersen, 1991, 1993; Pope, 1995; Savickas, 1992; Sue, Ivey, & Pedersen, 1996; Wetherell & Potter, 1992). They suggest that all counseling is, to some extent, multicultural, a stance that would be congruent with the social constructionist approach we outlined in the first chapter. The more inclusive definition of culture considers lifestyle, gender, and socioeconomic factors in addition to ethnic and racial differences. It also opens up the concept of culture to include many other aspects of subcultural lifestyle in ways that may be much more radical for psychology and for the counseling profession, such as contemporary urban identities like gang cultures. From this perspective, it becomes quickly apparent that there is a multicultural dimension in every counseling relationship. However, despite this frequent insistence that multiculturalism embodies characteristics other than ethnicity, the literature remains dominated by examples that equate culture with ethnicity and race.

Tracy Robinson (2005) offers an explanation that helps explain this emphasis. She argues for her own primary focus on race, ethnicity, and gender, not so much because they are more important in essence but because in American society they have been more salient as "primary status traits" (p. 2). In other words, the processes of social construction and historical development have been organized more consistently around these cultural dimensions than around others. Of course, this is cold comfort for the person who is experiencing social exclusion as a result of being gay, or disabled, or Muslim and is seeking to make sense of this experience through talking with a counselor. Therefore, we believe the tent needs to be big enough to include wide understandings of culture but also to notice where the major dividing lines have been drawn.

Ajit Das's (1995) definition of multicultural counseling is close to our own. His concept of culture includes all groups who find meaningful ways of coping with the problems that life presents, and he suggests that all counseling is essentially multicultural. Das defines multicultural counseling as that which considers the sociocultural conditions responsible for the problems for which people seek counseling. He describes counseling as a particular form of cultural invention developed in the West to deal with psychological distress, also acknowledging that every culture has some formal or informal way of dealing with human misery.

While our definition includes the points made by Das, the multicultural approach we would like to advance is embedded in a social constructionist analysis. A constructionist approach emphasizes the central role of language in cultural production. From this viewpoint, all cultural expression is produced out of background explanatory systems of human understanding that are in a constant state of flux. Every human interaction is necessarily imbued with cultural meaning and expression. Thus, multicultural counseling from a constructionist perspective refers to the process of addressing peoples' troubles or concerns as products of multiple forms of human interaction and engagement across time and space.

Raymond Williams (1958) argued an important principle that multicultural counseling should take into account. He advocated a recognition that culture is not just something that takes place in communities and in networks of social interaction.

It is also a conceptual schema of the social world that is reproduced in the mind of every individual. The role of language and discourse is crucial to the production of this internalized schema. It is also expressed each time persons speak about any ordinary aspect of their lives. It is through discourse that culture is made manifest, through which it is transmitted, and through which it is repeated and reproduced again and again. This argument provides the basis for thinking of counseling as always a cultural process and never adequately focused on an individual stripped of cultural connections. It is always dealing with the internalized models of the social world as they shape and influence a person's experience of identity and career, or, for that matter, of relationships and traumatic life events.

Over the last 20 years, many multicultural counseling texts have introduced issues of diversity, ethnic difference, and the unique cultural characteristics of different communities by dedicating discrete chapters to ethnic or racial groupings. A number of widely distributed multicultural books introduce readers to chapters on how to counsel African Americans, Native Americans, Asian Americans, Latino Americans, and sometimes other minority ethnic groups in American society. The material presented in these texts is constructed on the assumption that particular ethnic and racial groupings share general characteristics that must be taken into account when counseling services are provided for them. Many multicultural authors have cautioned mental health professionals against exaggerating between-group differences and within-group commonalities (Corey, Corey, Callanan, & Russell, 2003; Sue & Sue, 2007).

There is wide agreement among multicultural researchers that within-group differences of an identifiable group are as great if not greater than between-group differences. For example, even if we focus solely on ethnic or racial groupings, Derald Wing Sue and David Sue (2003) suggest that Latinos, Filipinos, Native Americans, and Native Hawaiians are all multiracial, and 30% to 70% of people who identify as African American have a diverse interracial ancestry. Given this racially diverse pattern, it continues to be surprising that ethnic groups are largely written about in a way that suggests that culture is somewhat fixed, stable, and unyielding to forces of change. Yet there continues to be a strong thrust in the literature to study the discrete history and experience of specific ethnic groups (Falicov, 1998; Hong & Ham, 2001; Mio & Awakuni, 2000; Parham, 2002). Blaine Fowers and Barbara Davidov (2006) propose that it is necessary to develop factual knowledge of distinct ethnic groups in order to counsel others effectively and competently. While we endorse willingness to learn about others' worlds, we also warn counselors to guard against developing understandings of diverse groups as stable and immutable, or of cultural identities as unchanging entities.

Multicultural researchers generally agree that cultures do not exist in isolation but influence one another. There is always diffusion of ideas, values, and technology among cultures, and this cross-cultural contact leads to cultural change. Renato Rosaldo (1993) suggests that culture "can arguably be conceived as a more porous array of intersections where distinct processes criss-cross from within and beyond its borders" (p. 20). Daphne's story illustrates this point.

I have always struggled with my cultural identity because it is customary for people to understand themselves and others by grouping and categorizing them, and my background is so diverse and unique that it is impossible to simplify it into one label. I remember being aware of this at a very young age. I would ask my parents, "What culture do I belong to?" and they would always respond, "Daphne, you are Baskin-Robbins thirty-one flavors." Since then, I have not been able to come up with a better answer. My mother is Spanish, from northern Spain but born and raised in Mexico. My father is Greek-Lebanese, born in Egypt and raised speaking French and Arabic. In addition to this ethnic heritage, there are distinct social classes that have shaped my family's heritage. My mother's ancestors were members of the Asturian culture from northern Spain. My mother describes the women from this community as anything but submissive and traditional. The Asturian women "wore the pants of the house," meaning that they played the traditional male role in the family and were strong and highly intelligent. While my mother is Mexican, as a light-skinned woman she was identified by many as a Spaniard belonging to the ancestors of the arrogant conquistadores. The Asturian heritage, which was matriarchal with a strong female leadership presence, placed my mom in conflict with the patriarchal family life in Mexico, leading her to struggle with "machismo" attitudes.

My father was born in Alexandria, Egypt. His family, members of the minority Christian community in Alexandria at the time, were persecuted by a growing Muslim fundamentalist movement. My father's family took Arab names and spoke Arabic, but their light skin targeted them as people who did not belong. They were driven out of Egypt in 1962. My family provides a good example of living with multiple border identities that are difficult to pigeonhole into discrete categories.

My name is really Daphne Zaki (Arabic), but my dad changed it to Zacky to be more Americanized.

Daphne Zacky describes herself as multiethnic.

Daphne's story illustrates the complex nature of ethnic or racial identity and its intersection with geographic priorities, historical legacies, linguistic practices, complex gender politics, and religious beliefs. Her story is also in harmony with the recognition that the multicultural movement has truly become postmodern in direction (Gonzalez, 1997; Sue et al., 1998). Multicultural writers are now taking these complexities seriously as they try to think through how we should shift our working assumptions and accommodate to the complexity of culture and its application to counseling. Taking into account some of the postmodern notions of culture as we think about multicultural counseling helps position us to respond to people like Daphne without forcing them to fit into our own rigid categories of thought.

Complications With the Concept of Culture

In this chapter, our task is to expand on these postmodern ideas about culture. Processes of globalization over several centuries have rendered simple concepts of belonging to a single cultural home redundant. For example, people often live in one place but refer to somewhere else as their cultural home. Or they trace their cultural belonging through their mother to one tradition and through their father to another one. Or their daily practices are influenced by cultural traditions to which they have no sense of belonging. For example, there are young people of Asian ethnic origins who form identity around their enjoyment of hip-hop music. There are also those who experience abuse or rejection from those close to them and seek to move away from their cultural origins and adopt different cultural practices as a result.

From a postmodern perspective, culture is first of all a social construction, a representation in language or in discourse, rather than an objective truth. As we think about Daphne's story, all commentaries on culture start to appear partial and subjective rather than objective and authoritative. Interpretations of culture from different vantage points should be made subject to constant dialogue and debate rather than finalized through academic consensus. This perspective can appear maddening to those who seek the solidity of the modernist viewpoint. Postmodernists maintain, however, that it is more honest and respectful of the actual complexity of people's lives. We want to argue too that for counseling practice, this perspective opens up much greater possibility for creating conversational spaces where cultural identity can be negotiated and reflected on in a manner that captures its complexity and is not blaming or shaming.

Border Identities

Any definition of a cultural group establishes a boundary beyond which a person is not considered a member of that group. The more elaborate the definition, the more sharply defined the border will be. At the same time, however, the more we define the border between one identity and another, the more likely we are to find individuals who do not fit our definition, or people who either straddle the border or live very close to it. The term "border identities" (Rosaldo, 1993) was developed to describe these experiences. Tightly defining culture may even define the borders in ways that exclude people from cultural belonging. Their experience of life does not count as the "real" experience of being black or Native American, if the experience of those deemed to be at the center is used as the sole reference point for what is true. For example, many African Americans struggle with feeling that they are not being "black enough" or are accused of "acting white" and feel they have to prove to other African Americans that they truly belong. In these circumstances, particular ideas about culture are functioning in ways that create divisions between people who share common cultural histories. Such divisions are often then policed by those who identify closer to the center of the relevant definition. Sometimes people are pitied or treated as almost abnormal if they owe allegiance to more than one cultural group. In identity terms, they are often invited to make a choice and to adopt one cultural position as their true identity.

If these postmodern critiques have disturbed the comfortable assumptions about culture that have become commonplace, then they are gradually giving way to a new view of culture that is more fluid and less essentializing. Rather than stressing the homogeneity of a people, the postmodern concept of culture has become pluralistic or "polyphonic" (Geertz, 1995, p. 48). We have begun to notice that people borrow from different cultural traditions and cannot be defined within one cultural box. We also see that they discard cultural practices when they no longer fit (Narayan, 2000; Yon, 2000).

We would like to emphasize the value of speaking in terms of cultural narratives that run through people's lives rather than thinking of people as identified in a one-to-one correspondence with a particular cultural identity. Renato Rosaldo (1994) suggests thinking of one's life as an intersection through which cultural narratives are always traveling like vehicles. Kwame Appiah (2005) argues for thinking of identity in terms of a "narrative arc" (p. 23). Seyla Benhabib (2002) suggests that the nature of a culture exists much more in the accounts we give of it, that is, in our interpretations, than in a simple observable reality. Lisa Tsoi Hoshmand (2005) notices how in cultural psychology the concept of narrative has taken on the character of a root metaphor. Critical race theorists, such as Derrick Bell (2000), also argue for the use of narratives to uncover the modern workings of racism. And Edward Said (1978/1994) suggests that we are always required to take account of the narratives that other people from other cultural backgrounds tell about our people. As a result, the actual lives that people lead are much more fragmented than simplistic uniform accounts of cultural coherence can admit. Calix's story illustrates the struggles that can arise in people's lives as a result.

At age 8, I learned that I was different from my classmates. I was enrolled in a private Catholic school with primarily white peers, and I learned something about race when one of them pulled the outside corners of his eyes up and down and called me "Ching Chong." Although I didn't understand the terms *Vietnamese* and *Asian*, I understood quite painfully the meaning of difference. Everything outside my home was a different world where I didn't fit, where my parents didn't fit. Too young to embrace my cultural heritage, I was embarrassed by their cultural practices and immigrant accents.

It was hard outside the home, but harder inside the home. As a child in Vietnam, where parents use physical means to teach children respect and obedience, my mother had endured harsh physical reprimanding as a form of discipline. She disciplined me as harshly as if I were born in Vietnam, which sometimes made me think my parents did not love me. My Caucasian friends seemed to have friendships with their parents, while I had authority figure parents who had carried their parenting patterns across the sea and into an American context. Now that I have a language for and an understanding of the dimensions of my various cultural and social backgrounds, I can see that the anger I bore toward my parents was actually a result of the frustration that arises from having multiple identities in a culture that encourages a more singular identification.

Somewhere along the way I abandoned the notion of a singular identity. I blurred the lines between the meaning of American, white, and Vietnamese. Was I white? If I assimilated enough, if I spoke English well enough, if I adopted American ways, could I suppress the Vietnamese in my blood? I used to press into the flesh above my eyelids, thinking that if I held my fingers there long enough, my eyes would look more "American." My face would blend in more.

Family gatherings continue to be alienating, as my siblings and I are the only non-Vietnamese-speaking family members. The decision by my parents to raise their children with only English was made with the intention to give us a better future, a better life in the United States, but it came at the cost of losing the Vietnamese language. Sometime toward the end of my college years, I began the process of coming out as queer-identified. Having been raised in a devout Catholic home, I have not been able to be honest about my sexual orientation with my parents. It is hard enough being a woman of color, but to be a queer woman of color, a minority among minorities, is a constant negotiation process for me. I am not just Vietnamese, just American, just queer, just woman. I am all of these identities, some of which conflict at times. That is part of my multidimensional, multicultural reality.

Calix's story is a good example of how diverse our cultural markers can be. To portray Calix as having only a Vietnamese culture would be to fail to pay tribute to the complexity that exists in her day-to-day life. In this way, she is no different from the rest of us; the cultural meanings we have about ourselves change depending on the cultural contexts we inhabit.

Which cultural definition gets expressed in peoples' lives depends on the context and the discourses available in that context. Different cultural identities emerge from the contextual configurations present at the time. The significance of context in postmodern theory is in stark contrast to its role in modernist theory, which tends to produce context-independent analyses of cultural life. To a large extent, culture emerges within the specific circumstances in which we are placed and through the multiple contexts we find ourselves in. For example, on first appearance, Jason looks like a regular, white, middle class male. A white, middle class cultural group is often portrayed as an identifiable, cohesive cultural grouping. Yet, on closer examination, Jason provides a typical example of within-group differences. These within-group differences

Calix Vu-Bui describes herself as someone possessing multiple identities.

compellingly assign Jason to group identities that are not captured by the cultural descriptions *white* and *middle class*. Jason grew up experiencing the pain of his parents' separation in middle childhood when his father left home. Jason became a member of a cultural community of single-parent households and was jettisoned out of the middle class into a struggling family of lower socioeconomic status while attending an upper middle class school. Wearing out-of-style clothing, he spent time with those termed "misfits" and "detention-frequenting delinquents."

He described the following experience of high school: "I was into independent punk rock while the taunts turned from 'geek' into 'freak' and later into, 'I'll kill you, fag.'" He and his close friend were heterosexual and had steady girlfriends throughout school, although his friend later embraced a bisexual identity. Because of their androgynous and unfamiliar looks, Jason experienced the full-blown prejudice of the heterosexual culture of the high school, which created serious dangers for him and his friend. As the threats of violence increased, Jason carried a three-pound lock on a chain in case he was going to be bullied. As his alienation increased, he turned to music, which became "heavier" at every taunt. It was only after walking into a music club that represented his form of music that he experienced the feeling of community and a shared cultural identity. He had felt like a nerd for not smoking and using drugs, but now a straight edge lifestyle emerged out of the hard-core punk community. His identification with hard-core punk and a straight edge orientation to life was accompanied by a commitment to veganism, which he viewed as a political act to challenge the meat and dairy industries.

Through his diet and lifestyle, Jason is now able to gain power and belonging. His cultural membership has emerged in relation to something other than his being a white, middle class male.

Some multiculturalists would not consider Jason's straight edge lifestyle and its association with the hard-core punk community to be a legitimate culture in its own right. Those who identify as adherents to hard-core punk or embrace a straight edge lifestyle do not compose large communities. No statistics have been gathered on the prevalence of a straight edge lifestyle, nor, perhaps, is there a long history associated with it. You will not likely find articles or books that give advice on counseling straight edge clients. However, for Jason and his community, who share the same cultural meanings, their lived experience is captured by these symbols, which

Jason Carney identifies himself as a member of the straight edge community.

are significant to them within the contexts that they inhabit. Shared lived experience that binds people together around a body of cultural symbols is an example of a culture when viewed from a postmodern perspective.

As a way of considering the fluid and dynamic nature of culture, consider the scenarios in Box 2.1 and immediately identify the cultural grouping that you would identify with.

Box 2.1. A Cultural Identity Exercise

1. What cultural identity were you conscious of when you watched the planes hit the World Trade Center towers?

2. What cultural identity are you conscious of when you visit a gay bar?

3. What cultural identity are you conscious of when you see a Muslim praying?

4. What cultural identity are you conscious of when you walk through a wealthy neighborhood?

5. What cultural identity are you conscious of when you are asked to milk a cow?

6. What cultural identity are you conscious of when you sit next to a man and woman kissing on a bench?

7. What cultural identity are you conscious of while crossing the border to Tijuana?

8. What cultural identity are you conscious of when you try on a bathing suit?

An exercise such as this helps us begin to connect with the multiple overlapping cultural groups we belong to and the identities we can draw from to define ourselves. Changing from one contextual circumstance to another demonstrates in a dramatic way the fluid and unstable nature of cultural belonging. Not only do cultural identities change in relation to context, but they also change in relationship to time. For example, take the instance of entering a gay bar and imagine the difference that a man might experience after coming out as gay compared to before he came out. Or take the example of walking through a wealthy neighborhood and imagine how your experience would change if you had won the lottery the day before. Or take the example of crossing the border into Mexico on attaining residence in the United States. If you reflect on your own development, say, from middle school to high school, or from high school to college, you will very likely see changes in how you identify yourself.

Naming the different conceptual trends in recent thinking about culture is not enough, however. A fuller picture needs to emerge as we consider some of the ways in which cultures, however we think of them, interact with other social institutions or forces. Cultural identity is produced not so much out of singular formations as it is out of a series of layers. Tracy Robinson (2005) refers to this process as one of "convergence," referring to the ways in which the different identity formations converge in an individual person. The individual is without doubt a site of cultural convergence, but we might equally think of the individual as simultaneously a site of divergence, where cultural influences are constantly bifurcating and splitting off into many trajectories. Mikhail Bakhtin (see Morson & Emerson, 1990) has argued something similar, saying that cultural discourse features both centripetal (convergent) tendencies and also centrifugal (divergent) forces at work in the production of lives and identities.

The identities fostered within our families and communities of origin are frequently overlaid with cultural formations drawn from many other sources. One of these overlays will likely be a worldview that is not limited to any one distinguishable cultural group. In the United States, we might call it various names such as democracy, capitalism, America, the economy, the American dream, "our" way of life, and empirical data. We might even refer to multiculturalism, thinking that this ground is covered by our understanding of specific cultural traditions. In separating "culture" from "nature," it is useful to place it in relation to these and other patterns of overlay.

Also overlaid on our concepts of culture are more specific habits of thinking, expressed in particular ways of speaking. For example, it is the habit of many people to speak about culture and race as if they were the same thing. Much confusion can result. One particular habit of thinking that has been so strong in European traditions of thought for so long that it finds its way readily into modernist assumptions is the habit of "essentialism." One of the main purposes of this book is to suggest ways of shedding the assumptions of essentialist thinking in order to advance the practice of multicultural counseling. In the next section, we shall address some of these complications and also define what we mean by "essentialism" and "essentialist" thinking.

Essentialist Thinking About Culture

A social constructionist perspective raises many questions about essentialism and seeks to open up alternatives to essentialist ways of conceptualizing culture and personal identity. This is not easy to achieve on a consistent basis, because essentialism is built into the very fabric of much of our philosophical history and into the academic disciplines, such as psychology, that counseling draws upon. We need to spend a little time here explaining what essentialism is and what the alternatives to it are, because this will equip us to ask questions about many other concepts throughout the rest of the book.

Essentialism is the habit of thinking in which one seeks out the truth value of a concept by searching for its core or central meaning. If we are talking about the meaning of a word, essentialist thinking would have us search for its true underlying meaning. If we are talking about a person, essentialist thinking has us peeling away the layers of the onion to discover the core truth of that person's nature. The assumption of essentialist thinking is that there is a stable, reliable core, or a hidden truth, to be found in the meaning of a word or in a person's life, and that it is indicative of what is true and trustworthy. From an essentialist perspective, if we can come to understand the central "nature" or "essence" of given individuals, that which is born or programmed early into them, we can predict how they might behave (Burr, 1995). Examples of essentialist ideas in counseling include Sigmund Freud's idea of the unconscious, Carl Rogers's self-actualizing tendency, and Carl Jung's extrovert and introvert personality types. The *Diagnostic and Statistical Manual of Mental Disorders* (American Psychiatric Association, 2000) is replete with essentialist thinking. You are all probably used to hearing things like "Homero is ADHD," "Sarah is borderline," and "Hein is narcissistic." Lay examples of essentialist language include "I am shy," "She is depressed," and "He is bulimic." In all these instances, there is no attempt to separate out the complex contradictions of a person's life from the supposed determining essences of ADHD, borderline personality disorder, narcissism, and so on. Neither is there any recognition of the diagnostic labels as culturally produced metaphors that might have effects on a person's life. They are assumed to allow us to see through to an unquestioned natural truth about the person. The characteristics referred to by the metaphors are seen as residing within the individual in an essential or natural way. The assumption of nature underpinning essentialist thinking undermines curiosity. That is, the risk of arrogance accompanies the certainty embedded in essentialist descriptions. Common assumptions that women are good child caregivers because they are women, or that black people are good at sports because they are black, or that Asians are smart, are founded on essentialism. In recent times, political descriptions such as "freedom lovers' or "evildoers" and implications that "you are either with us or against us" are indicative of essentialism. Despite the familiarity of essentialist thinking, you cannot prove the existence of such essences; you can only proceed on the assumption that they exist. The social constructionist perspective asks the question, what if they do not exist? Or, more accurate, what if they are not consistent in their truth value? What if the meaning of a word is less straightforward than that and depends on many things in the context in which it is used? What if the core or heart of a person is not as stable and singular as we often assume, but instead is made up of many fragments that we are always seeking to organize into some picture of coherence or pattern, but that never stay still from one moment to the next, or from one context to the next? In other words, social constructionists challenge essentialism's oversimplification of human beings' attitudes, feelings, and behaviors.

Now let's take this question of essentialism into the realm of culture and the social categories of identity. An essentialist view of culture assumes that our descriptions of social categories (black, disabled, women, etc.) are natural givens. It assumes that we can rely on the language categories we use to describe them to "[stand] in for an essence—a set of intrinsic qualities or characteristics residing within a people" (Gergen, 1999, p. 45). One culture can clearly be distinguished from another culture because each has its own discrete nature. Each is separate from the other. And there is an easy one-to-one correspondence between a culture and a group of people who belong to it. In this view, a culture exists independently of our efforts to study it or come to know it. Our task as learners becomes one of discovery of what is already there. To do this learning from an essentialist perspective, we might seek out the key features of a culture that exist in its center or core and are definitive of the people who belong to it. If we conceive of our own culture from an essentialist perspective, we are invited to identify with known cultural givens and to change ourselves to fit these, rather than to question the cultural norms themselves. Essentialist views of culture promote close identification of individuals with cultural norms and have the function of promoting the stability of cultures. They tend to emphasize cultural preservation and sometimes to hold back cultural change. While individuals may identify with discrete cultures and represent themselves by certain cultural traditions as if they existed in some stable and static form, people outside these groups can constantly stereotype such individuals as people belonging to static and uniform cultural groupings. Native Americans, for example, continue to be stereotyped and caricatured by depictions of them wearing a feathered headdress, a shawl, and moccasins in front of a tepee as if their tribal groups had not evolved over a few hundred years. A glossy magazine advertisement skillfully challenges these essentializing stereotypical descriptions by showing two Native Americans, one dressed in a surgeon's garb and the other dressed as a judge in a professional Western style suit, with the words, "Have you seen a real Indian?" written across their portraits.

What an essentialist view of culture does not do so well is accommodate intra-cultural differences, except as diluted versions of "true" culture. Essentialism plays down the political struggles and conflicts between groups of people who claim the same cultural membership. Kenneth Gergen (1999) goes as far as to say that essentialized identity categories actually "destroy differences" and "suppress enormous variations" (p. 45). For example, essentialism assumes that all African Americans are bonded to one another and share the same preferences, values, and ways of thinking and behaving. It does not help us notice how often so-called cultural norms are products of political debate and reflect current compromises in those debates. A social constructionist perspective, by contrast, is always looking for the

Reprinted by permission of the American Indian College Fund. All rights reserved.

social and political processes by which cultural worlds get established. Social constructionism asks questions about how the boundaries of cultural membership are policed and who gets included and excluded. From this perspective, cultural traditions and norms are not just natural or stable givens, but they have become emblematic of a culture through the decisions made by people in particular times and places. And they are always changing.

Labels given to cultures or cultural norms and assumed to be straightforward descriptions are never really straightforward. They have always been assigned by someone speaking from a position. Take, for example, the terms "Indian" and "Native American." Both terms are assigned to peoples from the outside. They do not correspond to the descriptions that tribal members form identity around, such as Cherokee, Iroquois, and Navajo. The same is true in other parts of the world. "Australian Aboriginals" and "New Zealand Maori" are terms assigned by the colonizer rather than descriptions of the cultural membership that tribal groups traditionally identify with themselves. Many cultures are held together only by terms that arise directly from the experience of colonization. Another example comes from the British colonization of India. India was a political construction of the British Raj and it resulted in the labeling of "Indian culture." But there was no such thing before colonization. Rather, there were many different peoples, some of whom shared similar practices and beliefs and many of whom were very different from each other. Nevertheless, indigenous people's movements have developed to combat the effects of colonization, and they frequently organize cultural resistance around the cultural membership terms assigned by the process of colonization itself. From a social constructionist perspective, this usage should not be criticized as inauthentic. It is just the way that culture always works. All cultures borrow from each other and construct their social practices in relation to the historical conditions of their time.

Social constructionism enables us at times to ask questions about movements for cultural preservation that would be forbidden by an essentialist perspective. From a constructionist view, such movements appear advantageous to certain people in the power relations among groups within a cultural context. Sometimes it is certain persons' positions of power that are being preserved, rather than the cultural advantages for all cultural members. For example, dominant groups within a culture may seek to preserve selected cultural elements to preserve their own cultural power. Indian feminist Uma Narayan (2000) calls this the process of "selective labeling" of "essential" cultural norms. It ignores, she argues, the ways in which cultural groups have frequently discarded cultural practices in response to changing circumstances.

Essentialist thinking invites people to judge each other's cultural worthiness in relation to established essential norms. You may have heard or even been caught up in arguments about who is a real Native American, who has an authentic right to speak for African Americans and who does not, who is more oppressed than someone else on the basis of cultural membership, who is betraying the essential cause of feminism and who is not. Such arguments can never be resolved. The danger is that they fragment people more than create understanding. Polarization is frequently a direct outcome of such essentialist assumptions. From a social constructionist perspective, the problem is the very idea of seeking to establish a "natural" basis for claims of cultural authenticity, which sets up needless competition for the right to speak and works against a more inclusive and complex approach to the diversity of experience. An important danger of essentialist thinking is that it invites a polarizing stance and tempts people to judge the worthiness of others' experiences, including their experiences of discrimination and oppression. What can result from these kinds of essentialist encounters is that particular voices are not recognized as valid, or as having a right to speak. The conversation then quickly deteriorates and groups retreat without any additional understanding.

Equating Culture and Nationality

During the 20th century, many efforts have been made to establish political boundaries on the basis of cultural groups and to whip up nationalistic fervor around cultural membership. The result has often been the exclusion of others who are defined as cultural outsiders. When culture becomes a fetish of national identity, grisly injustices often result that bring discredit to the cultural assumptions on which they were founded. The worst examples are the ghastly results of the assertion of "Aryan" culture in Nazi Germany, but similar patterns of thinking have led to many other examples of ethnic cleansing and xenophobic nationalism in recent history, leading to massacres and genocides. Think of the ugly wars in the 1990s in Yugoslavia, the tribal genocide in Rwanda, the killing fields of Cambodia, or the Baath party's attacks on the Kurds in Iraq. Think, too, of the establishment in some countries of political systems that enforce the practice of one religion (whether Christianity, Islam, or Judaism—or, for that matter, atheism) and encourage persecution or differential treatment of others who have different beliefs. The civil war that has erupted between the Shiites and the Sunnis in Iraq in the last few years illustrates the essentialist and fundamentalist attitudes about culture and identity that these Islamic sects hold. It is often the very assumptions of culture that have been discredited by such events.

Once again, we see essentialist thinking as a problem in these instances. Nationalistic causes often portray certain cultural features or perspectives as essential to a nation that all patriotic people must affirm on pain of sometimes dire consequences. In some instances, national citizenship is accorded only on the basis of an assumed ethnic essence and all others are excluded. Insistence on the coincidence of a person's nature with his political identity is an essentialist premise.

Separating Culture From Modernism

In the last 20 years, postmodern social theorists have developed a new way of thinking about culture that counselors could benefit from taking into account. This evolution of thinking involves one description of a particular stream of cultural development called modernism, which originated in Europe especially around the time of the Enlightenment, about 300 to 400 years ago, and which has gradually been spread around the whole world since. Because it originated in Europe, it is often assumed to be synonymous with "Western" culture and then contrasted with other cultures around the world. However, according to postmodern theory, this story of modernism is inaccurate.

Modernism is a particular cultural stream within and across European cultures that has come to dominate other cultural traditions. It has gone on to dominate other cultures all around the world after being spread by scholars, missionaries, traders, and politicians, all of whom rode in the wake of the military colonizers. There is now nowhere on earth where this modernist culture has not penetrated and overlaid other cultural streams. This dominance has not meant the complete disappearance of other indigenous cultures or even the total eclipse of other cultural streams within Western culture, but it has forced many cultures around the world to accommodate to its authority.

Modernism can be distinguished by a series of common cultural assumptions. These have been summarized by the sociologist Steven Seidman (1994) in the following way: Modernism was founded on the establishment of the scientific method as the chief method of validating truth claims and on the university's displacement of the church as the primary site where truth was sanctioned. It assumes that the ideology of social and economic progress is unquestionable in a way that would have been unthinkable for people in medieval Europe. It established the modern secular nation state and the principles of modern democracy and many of the instruments of government, such as political parties, markets, trade unions, business and legal processes, and modern professional disciplines. It assumes the underlying unity of humanity and believes in the individual as the driving creative force of history and society. And it also assumes the superiority of the West over other cultural traditions.

Postmodern writers have pointed out that there are many places where all of these modernist agendas appear less certain than they did a generation ago. Many of them are in considerable turmoil. But they are still in charge and are far from obsolete. Moreover, you can travel to places on the earth that would seem to be far removed from the reaches of modernist thinking and find its effects very present in the lives of people for whom centuries-old indigenous cultural influences are still very much intact. Educationist Allan Luke (1999), for example, describes visiting the hill tribes in Northern Thailand and encountering children identifying with Bart Simpson, a cartoon figure produced in North America. In addition, the citizens of the ancient kingdom of Bhutan keenly embrace the images and fashions portrayed by the popular Music Television channel produced by American television affiliates.

To the extent that we all live in a world overlaid by modernism, we all share some cultural characteristics. In this sense, we are all bicultural. Our differences lie in the extent to which modernism has penetrated other aspects of our identity and the extent to which we situate ourselves in the other cultural narratives available to us.

Culture and Lifestyle

In recent decades, a new development on the cultural landscape has further undermined the simple essentialisms of previously solid assumptions about culture. This is the development of consciously chosen "lifestyles" (Chouliaraki & Fairclough, 1999). It is not uncommon to hear young people, especially, talk about their practices of living in terms of their identification with a "subculture" that entails the adoption of a definitional set of customary practices and signs. For instance, you can find examples of people who articulate their cultural identification not so much in relation to ethnic ancestry as in relation to musical genres, or surfing culture, or drug culture, or motorcycle bike culture, or a lesbian lifestyle. These identifications clearly mark out cultural reference groups. But they don't fit modernist understandings of culture. They are more ephemeral, more likely to be consciously chosen, and more layered and complex. Nevertheless, such subcultures, or lifestyles, provide their adherents with recognizable language usages, ritual observances, social practices, and affiliations with others.

A decidedly postmodern theme is often associated with the way of envisaging culture implicit in such thinking: the approaching of life from an aesthetic perspective (Chouliaraki & Fairclough, 1999). In the academic discipline of cultural studies, much research has explored such subcultural experience. From this perspective, culture is not so much an encompassing essential birthright within which most practices and assumptions are givens. It is more like something that one designs and crafts as a work of art. Culture becomes an object of play or a field of creative expression. It becomes less about what one is and more about the things one does and how one does them. Ironically, this conception of culture revives the early 19th century ideas of culture as something learned and worked at in the development of an individual's consciousness.

Culture as Heritage

Another subtle variation on the way in which culture is conceived is associated with the links made between culture and the past. In this usage, aspects of culture that refer to what is traditional and unchanging are emphasized. Culture is viewed as a repository from some golden age in the past that is remembered nostalgically but diluted into impure forms in the ways that people live in the present. Margaret Wetherell and Jonathan Potter (1992) have described this perspective as an emphasis on "culture as heritage" (p. 129). From this viewpoint, culture is ancient, constantly under threat, and deserving of preservation. It is frequently associated with indigenous people, or non-Western cultures whose ways of life have been modified and overtaken by modernism.

Wetherell and Potter show how this emphasis has consequences for Maori people in New Zealand, who are portrayed, or may portray themselves, as seeking to "hang on" to their culture in the face of threats to erase it. They must avoid at all costs the danger of "losing" their culture. In this formulation, however, culture is assumed to be like a museum piece rather than an articulation of how people live their lives in the present, and indigenous people are characterized as museum keepers. The cost for Maori and for others who are described in this way, Wetherell and Potter argue, is that culture becomes frozen in an archaic, pure form right out of a Romantic past and separated from the lives of people in the present. Only those who have stronger connections with the past (usually traditional cultural elders) are considered authentic enough to speak as spokespersons for Maori culture. As a result, the issues of power and privilege that might be shaping the lives of minority groups in the present are rendered invisible and less than relevant. Those who contest such issues might be criticized by the dominant cultural majority as out of tune with their own culture or as abandoning their culture. For example, African Americans are accused of "selling out" or being an "Uncle Tom" when they act in ways that contradict traditional customs or expectations.

TO DISCUSS

1. Some people talk about "American culture." What does this mean?

2. What effect does hearing the term used in this way have on you? On others?

3. What is brought to the fore by this meaning and what is pushed into the background?

4. How does the concept of American culture relate to the following concepts: Native American culture, Navajo culture, African American culture, Amish culture, Jewish culture, Inuit culture, Chinese culture?

Moving Away From Unidimensional Notions of Cultural Groups

In the early application of multiculturalism in counseling, culture was treated as an add-on to general theories of the individual rather than as a challenge to the many individualistic assumptions that have been built up in conventional psychology. Today, there is a more comprehensive and rigorous view of multicultural counseling that not only pays attention to the effects of power in the construction of psychological problems, but also raises serious questions about many existing theoretical concepts in the counseling field. In Chapter 1, we began to scrutinize more closely the relationship between psychology and culture.

Like many of our colleagues in the multicultural movement, we are seeking to acknowledge the complex counseling needs and requirements of specific ethnic and other cultural groups and marginalized populations. This is a departure from the stereotypical format employed in multicultural books at an earlier stage in the multicultural field. Cecil Patterson (1996) argues that knowledge of cultures other than one's own can lead to facile stereotyping and that attempting to fit counseling techniques with clients' cultural background is very much a hit-or-miss business.

We have underscored the contemporary complexities of addressing cultural diversity in the practice of counseling and therapy. Our primary purpose here is to outline the ramifications, challenges, and nuances of what it means to work respectfully with the complexity and multiplicity of cultural identification. As we have already suggested, culture is the production of complex social processes through which, for example, race, ethnicity, gender, sexual orientation, class, and religion are constructed. It is also the representation of these processes that we form in our heads. These complex processes make it difficult to identify unambiguous and noncontradictory themes, despite the best efforts of multicultural scholars. Empirical studies of cross sections of populations should always be treated cautiously in this regard. In the first place, such studies always predetermine the "populations" to be studied and therefore to some extent produce what they are looking for. Second, the results of these studies can only ever best be understood as probabilities that can never account for the all of the particularity and variability in human cultural experience. Wise heads in the multicultural field are increasingly cautious about naming certain therapeutic practices that best cater to whites, blacks, Asians, Latinos, and others.

There is an older literature base that suggested that American Indians speak slowly, Asian Americans and Latinos speak softly, whites speak loud and fast, and blacks speak with affect. In this literature, it was asserted that American Indians have an indirect gaze when listening, Asian Americans avoid eye contact when listening to high status individuals, and whites have greater eye contact than blacks. While some practitioners still find this kind of information helpful, researchers are now much more cautious about making such strong claims (Sue & Sue, 2007). Most of us exposed to culturally diverse communities are quickly confronted with the immense diversity in communication styles within identifiable ethnic groups. Stereotypical generalizations can still persist, and these perspectives are granted authoritative status in the multicultural literature. For example, in multiple choice licensing exam questions, examinees might still be asked to identify how you would counsel a newly emigrated Egyptian client or a gay client recently infected with AIDS or choose the best approach for counseling African American clients. The simplistic and naive nature of these questions can be deeply offensive. It is as though candidates were being asked how to treat a particular character disorder or psychological problem rather than a person. Treating another culture as an object of study risks promoting the objectification of individuals who draw from that culture. Additionally, the value of the knowledge produced through such descriptive study may be, as Lisa Tsoi Hoshmand (2005) suggests, severely limited because of cultural trends such as "assimilation and hybridity resulting from migration and globalization" (p. 5). Of course, black clients do not constitute a particular clinical or diagnostic type any more than white clients do. As Edward Jones (1985) suggests, "knowing that a patient is Black fails to inform adequately about his views of psychotherapy, about his personality and psychological conflict, and about his aspirations and goals in therapy, let alone about educational level, social background, or environmental context" (pp. 174–175). To not acknowledge the enormous within-group variability and to treat the person as only a representative of a particular group can be culturally oppressive in itself (Ibrahim, 1991).

While there is value in specific cultural communities gathering together and subjectively asserting some of their shared characteristics and understanding their unique histories, we emphasize caution in how a professional field might represent such a group in an objective (objectifying?) way and then make assertions about their counseling needs. Some categorizations may be experienced as offensive. For example, some people are opposed to being categorized as Asian Americans because they come from a country such as Laos or South Korea. Essentially, the description "Asian American" is a fiction constructed by the official designations of race in American government documents. It does not represent the life experience or the preferred identities of people themselves. Asia is a continent, not a race or ethnic group at all. The racial category *Asian* is seldom one that people from the various countries on the Asian continent use to describe themselves. If we use the term *Asian*, we gloss over the fact that there are at least 29 distinct subgroups represented under that label (Moy, 1992; Ridley, 2005). Each of these subgroups has its own traditions, languages, and customs, which vary tremendously from those of the other subgroups. Recent immigrants from China, Korea, Vietnam, and Taiwan introduce this rich diversity on their entry into the United States. The place where they settle then adds to the complexity and diversity of their identity. American-born Chinese who live in China Town communities will form an ethnic identity very different from that of individuals who live in a rural town in the Midwest (Moy, 1992).

Similarly, Native American populations are extraordinarily diverse in their languages and identities. It is impossible to make general recommendations regarding counseling interventions for those who identify as Native American (Thomason, 1991). Different customs and languages among Native Americans, in addition to the individual differences within tribes, produce huge variation in the lives people live. Perhaps even more significant than these intertribal and within-tribal variations are the differences that most ethnic minorities in the United States experience because of the degree of acculturation to mainstream American culture. As Timothy Thomason (1991) suggests, there is a significant continuum extending from those Native Americans born and reared on a reservation, perhaps even speaking their mother tongue, to persons identifying as Native American who live in a city and have completely lost touch with any tribal ancestry.

In the United States, there is a large and rapidly growing Latino community. At the beginning of the 20th century, half a million Latinos were living in the United States. According to *Newsweek* (Campo-Flores & Fineman, 2005), there are now more than 40 million spread throughout the United States. The diversity among this ethnic community is striking. There is a sizable population of new and first-generation Mexican and Mexican Americans in the United States. Many of this recent wave of immigrants are fluent Spanish speakers in the early stages of acculturating to mainstream American culture. They are learning English as a second language, and many of them struggle tremendously at acquiring English fluency because United States schools do not have the resources to cater to second-language learners. Many recent Mexican American immigrants encourage their children to speak only Spanish at home to maintain their mother tongue and family and Mexican customs. Some parents struggle to speak English and thus require their English-speaking children to communicate in Spanish or "Spanglish." Other families encourage their children to speak only English in their homes to help them acculturate to dominant American culture. Many children from these families grow up as first-generation Mexican Americans not knowing how to speak Spanish.

There is a large Spanish-speaking population in the United States from Central America and South America. Then there are people descended from the Spanish-speaking inhabitants of Texas and California before the United States took over their land. They are not immigrants at all. Thus, the diversity among recent immigrants, first-generation Latinos, and Spanish-speaking nonimmigrants is vast. Because of this enormous cultural diversity, the counseling needs of this population are equally diverse. We must remember that, as Kwame Appiah (2005) points out, both "Latino" and "Hispanic" are germane identifications only in the United States. The people themselves do not come with these labels attached; they are American constructions that people are slotted into and by which their lives are governed in the United States.

Undocumented immigrants have very diverse counseling needs and share many of the common concerns of low socioeconomic status groups. Employment, housing, and health care for the millions of undocumented Latinos are of special concern. The adults in these families are forced to participate in employment that is dangerous, backbreaking work for little pay. They are not allowed to obtain driver's licenses or social security numbers and therefore find it difficult to access services for which these standard forms of identification are required as proof of identity. Individuals may obtain accommodations by sharing small one- and two-bedroom apartments with large numbers of relatives and friends. Without legal status, their access to health care and education is compromised. The counseling needs of this population may be very different from those of documented immigrants who can utilize health care and education resources denied to other members of their ethnic group.

Needless to say, there is significant within-group variation among Latino ethnic immigrants. When second-, third-, and fourth-generation Latinos are included in this same ethnic identity group, the diversity of needs grows exponentially. Latinos who are fully acculturated into mainstream U.S. culture have begun to join the middle classes in large numbers and are becoming a powerful political force. In fact, fully acculturated Latinos are subjected to many middle class challenges, such as dieting and other body shame issues. According to the American Society of Plastic Surgeons, Latinos are reported to receive more cosmetic plastic surgery than any other minority group in the United States. More than 500,000 procedures were done in 2004—a 50% increase from 2000 (Price, Raymond, & Zissu, 2005). It is clear that the counseling needs of middle class Latinos are significantly different from those of new, undocumented immigrants from Mexico and Central America.

According to Joshua Goldstein (1999), one fifth of adult Americans have a close family member of a race different from their own. In the 2000 United States census, the first allowing Americans to register their race in more than one category, nearly 7 million people identified with more than one race.

A Vision of Multicultural Counseling

The vision of multicultural counseling we want to support and reinforce rests on a belief in some form of social justice. In this sense, it is a political vision. It's not enough to just celebrate the rainbow colors of diversity without taking seriously the ways in which cultural divisions lead to differential opportunities in life. It is heartening to witness the multicultural counseling field develop a sophisticated understanding of how power works to shape relations among groups of people and how this plays out in the personal lives of individuals. Lisa Tsoi Hoshmand (2005) refers to this as "the politics of culture" (p. 1). If counseling practice is not based on addressing the effects of power relations, we don't believe it is adequately multicultural. Many of the problems people bring to counselors need to be understood as effects of power relations. The postmodern move in multicultural counseling has more radical consequences for the theory and practice of counseling than has sometimes been acknowledged. Current directions in multiculturalism are critiquing and challenging many of the comfortable assumptions of counseling theory, assessment and diagnostic processes, and practice, because they have been based on largely monocultural traditions of thought.

Because multicultural writers are usually committed to social justice in counseling and therapy, they inevitably are engaged in some kind of political enterprise. To consider the politics of counseling and the politics of culture, we need some overarching theory of democracy within which a vision of social justice can be materialized. Most multicultural theorists and practitioners acknowledge that counseling is not a politically neutral process. It is profoundly democratic in its ideals (see, for example, Rogers, 1970). That is why some people who are not committed to the noblest traditions of democracy, including a vision of fairness of opportunity for all people in life, are either suspicious of counseling or want to make it fit dominant cultural practices. Counseling practice is, in itself, a cultural force that has produced social effects.

Democracy is not just about electoral politics, however. It is about people having a say in the creation of the conditions of their own lives. It is about social inclusion rather than division. And since the necessary conditions for such democracy are frequently not achieved, it is about promoting social change. In the end, multiculturalism is about improving democracy, and multicultural counseling is about envisaging ways in which counseling practices can play a part in improving the experience of democracy in the everyday personal lives of our clients.

Current conceptualizations of multiculturalism in counseling are, we believe, aimed at this kind of vision. But there are places where they encounter conceptual limits that hold back the advance of practice. There is strong support in the multicultural movement for the notion that the cookie-cutter view of culture, so popular in modernist social science, holds back the development of multicultural counseling. Essentialist assumptions of all sorts do not help us notice the sometimes subtle cultural components of our identity narratives or the opportunities for social change that lie around us. It is our aim here to stretch the limits of both theory and practice in multicultural counseling. To do this, we are consciously drawing on social constructionism, because it opens up new questions about both personal and cultural essentialism. As you read this book, we invite you to envisage a counseling practice based on the following assumptions:

- That it is more useful to think in terms of people being shaped and influenced by cultural narratives than it is to simply identify individuals as members of a culture

- That the concept of discourse enables us to think in a more discriminating way about how certain cultural influences become dominant and others remain subjugated
- That cultural identifications always exist in the context of cultural power relations that are constantly shifting and changing
- That counseling knowledge itself needs constant reexamination with regard to its cultural assumptions and its colonizing potential
- That personal identity is not an essential given on the basis of naturalistic versions of either personality or culture but something that is best considered as an achievement of living through the process of engagement with cultural narratives
- That there are always competing axes of cultural membership and that we cannot reduce these to singular dimensions without creating distortions
- That we need to make room in our conceptualizations of culture for the contradictory positions that people take up in response to cultural narratives and not expect that people will fit neatly into cultural boxes

Response to Chapter 2

Allen E. Ivey

Allen E. Ivey, Ed.D., is Distinguished University Professor Emeritus at the University of Massachusetts Amherst, professor of counselor education (a courtesy appointment) at the University of South Florida, and the president of Micro Training Associates, Inc. The originator of the influential microcounseling framework and the integrative theory Development Counseling and Therapy (DCT), Dr. Ivey has won wide recognition and national and international awards, including the American Counseling Association's Professional Development Award. However, he is most pleased and honored by being named a "Distinguished Multicultural Elder" at the National Multicultural Conference and Summit. He is the author or coauthor of over 40 books and 200 articles, and his work has been translated into 20 languages. He did original work on the multicultural implications of the microskills in 1968 through 1974 and has been increasing his work in multicultural studies ever since.

"I do not speak. Rather, I am spoken." French psychoanalyst Jacques Lacan points out that our sociohistorical background (our culture) influences us so deeply that even our thoughts are not our own, but the outcome of our forebears and developmental history. The "feeble ego" is a construction of the past and our present interactions. In effect, we seldom speak for ourselves. Our language and very way of thinking are given to us. As theologian Paul Tillich says, "we are thrown into the world." This "thrownness" determines so much of who were are, perhaps all. Much of who we are and how we think is determined by the immediate family, community, religion, and national world into which we are born.

Let's consider a bit more theory. Consider the multicultural cube presented below. As you examine the figure, are the boxes real or imaginary? Are they as separate as the diagram might suggest? Are all "dimensions" really covered? Can we really divide multiculturalism into a few discrete boxes? I think not, but perhaps this is a beginning to help us all think about ourselves and our clients.

I'm one of those who believes that all counseling and therapy is ultimately multicultural and that failing to be aware of and being unwilling to deal with culture is literally unethical. There is no immaculate construction! We are constructed out of many people—both dead and alive. Our very landscape impacts our conceptions of self and others (e.g., Mississippi vs. New York vs. Colorado).

Thinking multiculturally requires us first to think of ourselves as multicultural beings and to consider how life experience affects our language and our being. The authors of this book present important exercises at the end of this chapter in which they ask you to think about past experiences that help define who you are now. I'd like to follow along and give a brief analysis of myself as a multicultural being.

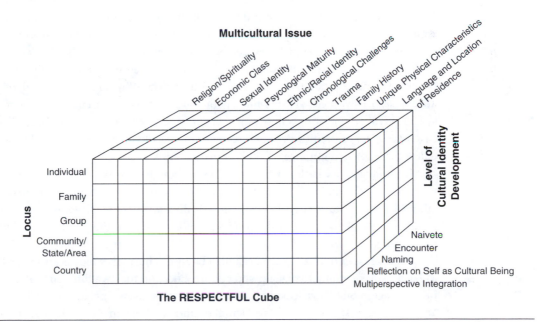

Figure 2.1   The RESPECTFUL cube is used by permission of Allen E. Ivey. The RESPECTFUL concept was developed by Michael D'Andrea and Judy Daniels (2001).

I come from a solid fundamentalist Baptist background, which was first challenged by a wonderful biology course in my university that revealed that all I had been taught was not necessarily true. The university culture interacted with my Baptist foundations, and change quickly occurred. Yet "a boy can leave the Baptists, but the Baptist in the boy will never leave." There is still much in this cultural tradition in my thought and language that I treasure. Interacting with Catholics, Hindus, Latter-Day Saints, and many others constantly changes my thoughts and causes me to think and speak differently.

Born into a working class family and community, as a professor I now find myself in the so-called upper middle class. It is so easy to forget those origins and the redneck racist community in which I grew up. But I have had to work hard to eliminate as much prejudice and racism from myself as I can. Nonetheless, racism (and other "isms") are so deep in our society that I consider any White person (capitalize *White* and *Black*, by the way) who claims to be nonracist both naive and dangerous.

As a heterosexual, the discourse and language of those around me led to homophobia and heterosexist thoughts and actions. My rural background had a deep impact on me, and here we see the intersection of sexual orientation, gender, economic class, and even race. It was a challenging learning experience to remove my many deeply held biases. Can you imagine how my Baptist congregation responded in 1970 when I brought a lesbian couple to speak to the teenage Sunday School class I was teaching!

Psychological maturity speaks cognitive and emotional self-development, always changing and moving. Becoming aware of myself as a privileged White person took a lot of time. For example, I never personally met an African American until I worked with a student in my third year of university teaching. Talk about segregation and a limited cultural experience! I needed a lot of learning and growing.

Seventy-three now, I sometimes feel the oppression of society on the elderly. But, even more, I am aware of the oppression of poor children who don't get the same benefits for medical care that I receive from our nation. Why do I receive good, relatively inexpensive medical care while a poor child has to go to the emergency room?

Trauma survivors also compose distinct cultures. Whether it is cancer, heart disease, war, rape, or even divorce or a serious auto accident, trauma creates distinct cultural groups that impinge on the way people think and speak.

My family history is clearly bicultural, even though I am White. Put together a Celtic father with an English mother and you can sense the confusion I experience ethnically. My history is replete with my dealing with those differences at war inside me. My physical self deals with issues of lookism and the physical ideals of our culture.

Language is central and I can speak only English. This makes me disadvantaged, as I lack skills in another language and culture. Location makes a difference. Raised in Washington State, I've lived in California, Colorado, New England, and Florida. Yet it was time spent learning in Denmark and teaching in Australia that most changed the way I think. I grieve that more U.S. citizens don't spend significant time abroad so that they can learn how narrow this one American culture is. Not that it is necessarily bad, but we take an extremely limited view of the world.

So, I speak from a multicultural base. White and economically privileged, I face the challenges of old age and a society that increasingly wants to ignore me. So far, my physical self is holding together. But all of these intersecting multicultural dimensions remain to define me. *I do not speak. Rather, I am spoken.*

TO DISCUSS

1. Can you think of examples of essentialism in how we think of cultural issues?

2. Consider your own experiences of cultural identity. Then consider others who are close to you and imagine how they might answer this question. In which instances do you find yourself fitting into the center of a cultural identity and in which instances do you find yourself having a border identity?

3. What implications for counseling practice might flow from these ideas about culture? Do you see yourself straddling the borders?

4. How might Allen Ivey's RESPECTFUL cube help you make sense of the complexity of cultural experience?

5. Do an online search and find instances where culture is talked about principally as a repository of the past rather than as a vibrant and living force. Do the same for subcultural lifestyles and culture as equated with nationality.

6. As you read about the questions raised in this chapter, what concerns do you have, or what problems do you see within these ideas?

7. How do other texts that you have read treat these issues of cultural complexity? Where would they agree or disagree with the ideas presented in this chapter?

CHAPTER 3

A Short History of Colonization and Decolonization

I f we assume that a person who seeks out the help of a counselor is living a life caught in a web of cultural patterns, it is useful for us to pause and consider the historical trajectory that has given rise to those patterns, rather than assuming that the patterns began in the psyche of each individual. This is one of the chief contributions that a multicultural approach has to offer the practice of counseling. It helps counselors understand the lives of their clients as produced in a cultural context, rather than as isolated, singular, peculiar events.

The cultural patterns that have a shaping effect on the lives of individual people are not arbitrary, however. They exist as a product of history. They partake in the connections and clashes that have occurred among peoples across the ages and across the oceans and continents. These histories are materialized in the shifting details of everyday, contemporary life. What has happened in the past often places us in a limited range of positions from which we can live. Ulrich Bonnell Phillips (1968) said, "We do not live in the past, but the past lives in us" (p. 269). This statement suggests that history is worth studying not just so we can learn about the past but also so we can obtain rich accounts about our present cultural life. It helps us understand ourselves and each other today—economically, intellectually, and spiritually.

So let's now place the cultural worlds in which we live in some historical context. Why, you might ask, should a counseling text focus on processes of colonization? Our brief answer is that counselors will fail to understand fully enough the problems that people experience in their day-to-day relations with others if they don't take into account the shaping forces that give structure and substance to the backdrops against which individuals speak and act. It is uncommon to focus a multicultural counseling text on history in this way, but to not do so risks promoting a version of culture too abstract and separate from the influences that have shaped it. In this abstract version, cultural influences appear to be free-floating ideas rather than concrete products of the people who formed them in actual places and times. Ahistorical versions of culture also seem fixed and static rather than susceptible to constant debate and social change. Focusing on history is another way of disrupting the essentialized understandings of culture that we raised questions about in Chapter 2.

In order to practice our craft with respect, understanding, and effectiveness, it is necessary to understand the links between the world's recent history and the issues and challenges that face counselors and therapists today. To understand the counseling of diverse populations in contemporary times and to advance the practice of multicultural counseling in the future, we must grapple with our histories and their expression in our current social, educational, and political systems.

This is not a history text, so we shall necessarily offer a cursory sketch rather than a thorough examination. Our scope will be limited to the historical influences that have shaped cultural relations in the modern world, and we shall concentrate on the last 300 years to capture these shaping influences. Our contention in this chapter is that the process of colonization of most of the earth's territory by Europeans between the 16th and 20th centuries has had a significant impact on the lives of all people everywhere. It is not possible to live in the modern world without somehow engaging with or being engaged by these influences. It is not that this is the only colonization that has happened in history. There have been many of those influences, and the European people who perpetrated modern colonizing were no different in their intent from many other colonizers of diverse cultural backgrounds at different times and in different circumstances. What has been different, however, has been the scale of this colonization. By the 20th century, it had achieved a greater scope of political control than any previous colonizing process.

Colonization has been a major shaping influence in the modern world on the entitlements that people claim, the privileges or disadvantages that they enjoy or suffer, the expectations of life that they can "realistically" expect or not expect, the shape of family relations that they might grow up in, the identity stories that they might enact in life, the careers that are possible for them to enter, the ways in which they might make sense of adversity and respond to it, and the feelings that accompany all of these experiences. In other words, it was not just land that was colonized. Part of the experience of colonization was psychological in effect. The psychological effects of colonization that persist to this day cannot be fully understood by counselors and by their clients without taking account of the history of the cultural relations produced by colonization.

On the other hand, the process of colonization has never had things all its own way. From the inception of the modern process of colonization, it has been called into question and often actively opposed. People have found many ways to resist the loss of sovereignty that colonization thrust upon them. Political movements have been spawned, protests have been made, violent and nonviolent resistance has been offered, and gradually, in many instances, political independence has been won. The European political colonization of land and territory has been steadily reversed during the last hundred years in most parts of the world, a movement that has become known as *decolonization.* Just as colonization has produced psychological effects that can be traced into the problems people present to counselors, so too does the process of decolonization require psychological as well as political resistance. Counselors who understand this well are in a much better position to make sense of the cultural positioning of their clients and to help them articulate their lives in relation to the psychological resistance in which they choose to participate. Because decolonization is psychological as well as political, it is associated with the production of good mental health.

With this introduction, let us now turn to a brief account of the modern history of colonization and decolonization.

A Review of the History of Colonization: Domination and Subjugation

In the history of human civilization, many societies have sought to dominate others, and those societies threatened with domination have struggled to resist. Our human history is full of examples where more powerful societies with technological advantages or greater numbers have wrenched physical and economic resources away from less powerful societies. Domination in human history has usually occurred through wars of conquest, which typically lead to the colonization of the defeated peoples by those who are militarily successful. As a result, the colonized may have their entire moral and physical universe destroyed and subsequently reshaped and restructured.

Colonizing societies don't usually stop at dominating and controlling the geography and the available physical resources. They typically impose their own language, their own religion, and their own social and political systems of governance on the colonized. In the process of overpowering and dominating another people, they regularly claim that they are superior to those they have defeated. The victors represent themselves as possessing all that is worthwhile and those that have been vanquished as generally inferior or barbaric.

Christopher Columbus was conscious of this intent from the beginning of his explorations of conquest in the New World. After his first contact with the Arawak people on the island of Hispaniola, he wrote in his log the following comments about the culture of the indigenous people:

> They do not bear arms, and do not know them, for I showed them a sword, they took it by the edge and cut themselves out of ignorance. They have no iron. Their spears are made of cane. . . . They would make fine servants. . . . With fifty men we could subjugate them all and make them do whatever we want. (Zinn, 2003, p. 1)

Important aspects of the history of the next 500 years are prefigured in these words. Europeans and indigenous peoples in many places are still working through the implications of the desire for cultural power that Columbus expressed. Contemporary social configurations around the globe need to be understood as shaped largely by events that have occurred over the last four centuries, featuring generations of dominance, subjugation, and frequently genocide. In particular, wars, famines, disease, technology, and religion over this period have shaped contemporary patterns of relationship across diverse cultural communities. On

Hispaniola (which we now call Haiti), there were an estimated 250,000 Arawak Indians when Columbus arrived. After two years, by a combination of wholesale murders, mass suicides, and disease, half of them were dead. Fifty years later, there were none of the original Arawak people left on the island (Zinn, 2003).

Understanding the Beginnings of British and European Colonization

Today, most discussion about colonization occurs in reference to British or other European countries. An understanding of British colonization helps us understand the cultural forces that have been at work to shape our current Western practices, including the practices of counseling, psychology, and psychotherapy. Since many of the issues that we struggle with in most multicultural counseling contexts are linked back to the impact of British colonization, let's have a closer look at the nature of this powerful colonizing force and the background tensions it contributes to in contemporary Western life.

The beginnings of the European empire were started elsewhere. Jared Diamond (1999), in his book *Guns, Germs and Steel,* provides a persuasive argument to explain European colonization not coincident with the notion of an innate superior European character as implied by the definition of culture as civilization described in Chapter 1. In fact, he states that if a historian had lived at any time between 8500 B.C. and A.D. 1450 and had tried to predict the future trajectories of development, she would have found Europe to be the least likely to develop in comparison to the civilizations of China, India, the Eastern Mediterranean, and the Middle East.

Like other dominating cultural forces in human history, Britain originally emerged from its own history of subjugation. For nearly a fifth of recorded history, Britain was a conquered country. It was made up of thirty tribes who fought fiercely among themselves. To the Romans, Britons were simply "barbarians" (Sowell, 1998). Julius Caesar saw primitive tribal groups decorated with dyed bodies and long hair and living in a society with shared wives (Wolf, 1989). Due to the "backwardness" of pre-Roman Britain, greatly outnumbered Roman soldiers easily defeated these British tribes. In 55 B.C., the Romans returned victorious over the Britons, taking with them British slaves marching behind their procession. The Roman contribution to the development of Britain was profound until around 500 A.D., and then Britain reverted to its former ways and was viewed as a cultural backwater of Western civilization, "an enclave of illiterate pagans" (Sowell, 1998, p. 27). It wasn't until the Norman invasion in 1066 A.D. that Britain slowly began to catch up with its European neighbors. It is valuable to acknowledge the genealogy of powerful empires, because most of them emerged from the ranks of the defeated and disenfranchised at some point in their history. Over relatively short periods of human history, the ranks of the colonized can quickly become the ranks of the colonizing, and vice versa.

In the last 400 years, the most extensive colonizations have been undertaken by the British and, to a slightly lesser extent, the French. The Spanish and Portuguese also maintained substantial colonies in the Americas, and the Dutch, the Italians, the Danes, the Russians, the Austro-Hungarians, and the Germans also participated in the general European colonial expansion. But even during this period, it was not only the Europeans who were engaged in colonization. The Ottoman Empire was an example of an Islamic colonizing movement, and the Chinese gradually accumulated greater and greater territory in countries neighboring China. However, it was the British Empire that became the largest colonizing force in recent times.

The Unique Dimensions of British Colonization

The modern European empires differed from the earlier colonizing powers—such as the Romans, the Spanish, and the Arabs—in that European colonizing practices systematically and continuously reinvested in the colonized world rather than undertaking only a slash-and-burn, loot-and-leave approach. In a period of 200 years, 50 million people from the Old World moved to the New World. British settlers moved to North America, Australasia, and Southern Africa, taking with them their agricultural and horticultural way of life. They turned these landscapes into replicas of what they had left. In fact, by 1878, Western powers had taken control of 67% of the earth's surface, having done so at a rate of 83,000 square miles per year for about 80 years. By 1914, Europe held a grand total of 85% of the earth as colonies, protectorates, dependencies, dominions, and commonwealths (Magdoff, 1978).

European colonization was uniquely constructed on the assumption that the colonizer's *duty* was to civilize the conquered people. It introduced an imperial responsibility to lead people (wherever they resided) away from barbarism and toward truth, goodness, well-being, and modernism. Implicit was the European aristocracy's sense of their right and obligation to rule and civilize others. This eventually became known as the doctrine of "manifest destiny." It was taken up in North America as the mission of Anglo culture with regard to both native peoples and Africans brought over as slaves.

> If we are saved from the ruin of short term conquest, then the idea of redemption takes this one step further. For the imperialist is redeemed by the self-justifying practice of imperialism's idea of mission and reveres this idea, even though it was constructed in the first place in order to achieve dominance over the colonized. (Said, 1993, pp. 81–82)

While Britain had the power and opportunity to take over territory, it accompanied its dominating influence with a self-justification and self-aggrandizement originating in its notion of promising civilized and civilizing values from which the entire world would benefit.

> By the late nineteenth century Europe had erected an edifice of culture so hugely confident, authoritative and self-congratulatory that its imperial assumptions, its centralizing of European life and its complicity in the civilizing mission simply could not be questioned. (Ashcroft & Ahluwalia, 2001, p. 87)

Such a sense of self-appointed mission can still be detected in both American and British foreign policy, leading to a patronizing stance with regard to other "inferior" cultural traditions. Edward Said (1978/1994, 1993) is one writer who has analyzed this mission in great detail. He shows how the British, and to a slightly lesser extent the French, developed a thoroughgoing study of the cultures of "Oriental" peoples in order to enable the "civilizing mission" to be undertaken with great precision.

Box 3.1. The British Civilizing Mission

Modern anthropology grew out of the tradition of studying "the natives," and Said shows how many other academic disciplines joined in the production of knowledge about "other" cultures. He also shows how many of the great books of the established canon of English literature, including works by Jane Austen, Charles Dickens, William Thackeray, Joseph Conrad, and Rudyard Kipling, simply assumed this civilizing mission as a natural truth. He adds to this list historians such as Thomas Carlyle and Lord Macaulay. And he traces the discourses of "Orientalism" into the foreign policy statements of politicians and political theorists as disparate as Napoleon Bonaparte, Karl Marx, T. E. Lawrence, Benjamin Disraeli, and Henry Kissinger. "Orientals," or "natives," goes this argument, can never be expected to understand the principles of democracy or the advantages of civilization the way "we" do, unless we teach them through the process of colonization.

These "civilizing discourses," with the accompanying aesthetic production of "high" culture, proceeded to assert their authority over colonized groups with little regard for the violence and injustices inherent in the political and social institutions they established in these communities. Assumptions about the inherent inferiority of colonized peoples were intimately interwoven into the dominating discourses of colonization and provided the rationale to energize and drive these movements. In the fabric of contemporary life in the West, these forces continue to operate.

However, there is also an implicit irony here. The civilizing mission of European colonization can be argued to contain within it the seeds of its own failure. If it were actually to be successful in its civilizing mission, it would produce leaders among colonized people who would stand up to the forces of colonization on its own terms and challenge its whole rationale. Perhaps it is not surprising, therefore, that many leaders of anticolonial movements, such as Mahatma Gandhi, Martin Luther King, Jr., and Nelson Mandela, or scholars like Edward Said and Frantz Fanon, were professional men, well educated in the discourse of the colonizers, and knew intimately its points of weakness. Because these leaders spoke eloquently in the discourse of the colonizers, what they had to say could not so easily be dismissed.

A parallel can be found in the counseling field. One of the most significant efforts that has occurred in the multicultural counseling movement is the attempt to develop a set of multicultural counseling competencies in order to thwart the extent to which the dominating influences of Anglo culture subjugate the discourses of other cultural communities. Or, to put it another way, to provide a set of standards for the multicultural community so as to give voice to persons and communities otherwise rendered invisible, disenfranchised, and isolated. But it has been written in the discourse of "competencies" to connect with the dominant discourse of counselor education. We focus on these competencies in Chapter 17.

In all the colonizing powers of the modern era, there was a deeply embedded assumption of the superiority of the colonizer in all aspects of life and the inferiority of the colonized. A French advocate of colonialism spelled out all too eloquently the spoken and unspoken assumptions of colonizers of 18th and 19th century Europe:

> It is necessary, then, to accept as a principle and point of departure the fact that there is a hierarchy of races and civilizations, and that we belong to the superior race and civilization, still recognizing that, while superiority confers rights, it imposes strict obligations in return. The basic legitimation of conquest over native peoples is the conviction of our superiority, not merely our mechanical, economic, and military superiority, but our moral superiority. Our dignity rests on that quality, and it underlies our right to direct the rest of humanity. Material power is nothing but a means to that end. (François-Jules Harmand, in Curtin, 1971, pp. 294–295)

It is within this cultural discourse that the early European settlers established their residence in the Americas. These cultural assumptions about their identities and their understandings about their supposedly rightful place in the world were fundamental to the way they engaged the inhabitants of the "New World."

The Expression of British Colonization in North America

In many ways the majority culture of the United States continues to be an expression of British colonial discourse. The settlers who created the colonies along the American Eastern Seaboard had a decisive and lasting impact on the culture and institutions of that society. The United States as we know it now is a society founded by 17th and 18th century settlers from the British Isles. Thus, the dominant cultural ideas and dominant discourses in America arise from the culture of 17th and 18th century English settlers. The Christian religion, Protestant values, moralism, work ethics, the English language, British traditions of law and justice, the limits of government power, and the legacy of European art, literature, philosophy, and music all arise from the imposition of British colonization on the peoples of the land known as North America (Huntington, 2004). Out of this culture, settlers developed the American creed with its principles of liberty, equality, individualism, representative government, and private property.

While subsequent immigrants modified this culture, they did not change it fundamentally. There are rich historical descriptions around the world of how colonizing groups tend to preserve habits of life or speech that are no longer current in their home country. In 1760, Benjamin Franklin declared proudly, "I am a Briton" (Huntington, 2004). Sixteen years later, Franklin signed the Declaration of Independence and thus renounced his British identity. In the intervening years, settlers in North America made efforts to carve out a new cultural identity as relations with Britain deteriorated over trade, taxes, military security, and the extent of parliamentary power over the colonies. In terms of race, ethnicity, and language, white

Americans and the British were nevertheless essentially one people. Hence, American independence required a different rationale—an appeal to political ideas. According to Huntington (2004), Americans argued that the British government was deviating from English concepts of liberty, law, and government by consent. Americans began to invoke universalistic self-evident truths concerning liberty, equality, and individual rights, which ultimately led to the Declaration of Independence. Their enemies were tyranny, monarchy, aristocracy, and the suppression of liberty and individual rights. Paradoxically, while the Anglo Americans stood with great pride alongside these high-minded ideals, the reality for all others was anything but liberty, equality, and any form of basic human rights. Despite the breach with Britain and the establishment of the Declaration, the underlying cultural discourse of British colonization, which perhaps could now be termed American colonization, continued to guide and shape the fundamental identities of Anglo Americans. While America prided itself on "the essential dignity of the individual human being, of the fundamental essential equality of all men, and certain inalienable rights to freedom, justice and fair opportunity," it did not extend these principles even to all of its own people (p. 67). At the same time that the founders of these new political and moral institutions constructed upon British law were articulating their vision of democracy, they were betraying their own principles with peoples who were not members of this Anglo American or white race. Neither did they include women.

Manifest Destiny

The expression "manifest destiny," attributed to the journalist John L. O'Sullivan in 1845, was popularized in American political discourse in the 1840s. It referred to a sense of mission that politicians wanted the American public to take hold of and was used to fuel and justify the westward expansive impulse. Specifically, the mission was to extend the governmental reach of the particular political and social values held dear by the various populations of the Eastern Seaboard of the North American continent into western territories. Eventually, it clashed with the Mexican government's desire to extend its own "destiny" northward. Before that, however, it rode roughshod over the native populations and other nonwhite groups, who were not considered capable of democracy or self-government. The notion of manifest destiny justified the colonizing impulse. At its best, it was a "civilizing" mission. It was an Anglo-Saxon mission. It allowed the colonizers to believe they were doing a civilizing service to those whom they were conquering because they were bringing them into the light of the modernist world, from which they would undoubtedly benefit. At its worst, it led to what would now be called ethnic cleansing and genocide.

Manifest destiny evolved not only as a justification for territorial expansion; it was also closely tied to a Romantic idea of progress. Americans were encouraged to imagine themselves as forging a new power that would carry a torch for freedom to the rest of the world. The United States was constructed in this discourse as having a providential authority to become a world leader in a variety of fields, from industry to commerce, as well as in intellectual achievement. This idea has persisted into the present in American relations with the world. It is sometimes linked with the viewpoint called "American exceptionalism," in which the United States is considered a unique country that serves as a model to other countries, offering the world a special hope that its values of individual freedom will be reproduced elsewhere.

In terms of cultural relations, the doctrine of manifest destiny created a comfortable sense of righteousness among those of Anglo-Saxon descent. Their desire to expand and colonize Indian tribes and Mexican territories was blessed by this concept with something akin to a divine right. It therefore served to justify the subjugation of other cultures and allowed people to do this not only with a clear conscience but also with a conviction of patriotic duty. Critics of the Bush administration view its decision to enter Iraq and impose its version of democracy on the inhabitants as a modern-day version of manifest destiny.

The Role of Slavery in European Colonization

An account of European colonization in the Americas cannot be complete without acknowledgment of the transportation of many millions of Africans from the sub-Sahara on slave ships to many destinations in the Americas. European trade in African slaves had actually begun 50 years before Columbus, when slaves were transported from Africa to Portugal (Zinn, 2003). There is no doubt that much of the accumulated wealth of the European empire, generated from the extensive sugar and cotton plantations of the American Eastern Seaboard and in the southern states, was gained at the expense of the suffering of African slaves. There are no exact statistics covering all the places that African men, women, and children were sent. Howard Zinn (2003) estimates that during the centuries of the modern slave trade, Africa lost some 50 million people to death and slavery. There were an estimated 14 million slaves sent to Islamic nations in the Middle East alone (Sowell, 1998). Hundreds of thousands and possibly millions of people perished in transit, whether it was on the desolate slavery trails in North Africa or on the hundreds of slave ships that crossed the Atlantic. Shockingly, as widespread as slavery was in North America, Brazil alone imported six times as many slaves as did the slave traders in the northern continent (Sowell, 1998). By the end of the 17th century, most African slaves in the American colonies had been born on American soil and were losing many of their customs and traditions. In the slave societies of Brazil, the slaves' African customs and traditions stayed more intact, because the slave trade in this country continued right through until the 1880s.

The brutality that accompanied being captured in one's African homeland and transported to the Americas was matched by the brutality of the foreman in charge of the plantation slaves. Many of the working class whites who traveled from Britain and Ireland in search of employment in North America served the higher class slave owners as foremen who would control, discipline, and punish the slaves. The individuals wielding the whip and lash were often immigrants from the fringes of British civil life. They themselves had come from violent communities dominated by poverty and lawlessness. Many of them were ruthless men used to settling differences with violence, sometimes as graphic as the biting off of ears and noses. Thus, this pattern of ruthless violence was brutally transferred on to the slave societies.

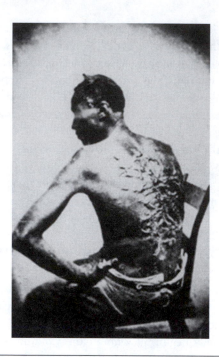

Figure 3.1   This picture, showing a slave's back deeply scarred from whipping, provides an example of how slaves were treated in the 19th century.

Copyright ©2006 by Free the Slaves. All rights reserved.

A significant irony in the history of British colonization is that Britain, the leading slave-trading nation, ultimately became the leading advocate for the end of the slave trade and finally eliminated slavery altogether. This was no mean feat, since England and America had economically benefited so greatly from exploiting slave labors. The significance of this achievement is also hard to understand without appreciating that slavery was a worldwide institution that had been conducted by dominating institutions and nations on every inhabited continent, subjugating people of every color, language, and religion, for thousands of years. Sowell (1998) states, "The dogged persistence of the British in that struggle was a key factor in the ultimate destruction of slavery around the world" (p. 91).

However, the Anglo American culture of the slavery era established laws and systems of education that were in stark contrast to the high-minded ethical principles they had established on that important day in 1776. Through the lens of British-American colonial discourse, Anglo American Protestant values were reinforced in schools, which also served to undermine the capacity of immigrants, indigenous people, and African American slaves to transmit their own cultural histories and cultural fabric to their American-born children. The pressing question from the perspective of the 21st century is, how could the founding fathers appear to stand so proudly by their newly made constitution that espoused life, liberty, and the pursuit of happiness and yet treat so despicably all other groups of people who were not permitted to identify as white? A large part of the answer to that question must surely rest with the construction of race. We shall address the construction of race more fully in Chapter 4.

Figure 3.2   These images of slaves awaiting sale underscore the lived experience of a large number of people in America who had no access to life, liberty, and the pursuit of happiness.

Source: Retrieved July 28, 2007, from http://www.britishempire.co.uk/article/sanders/sanderszanzibarislaves.htm

How the British and the Europeans Were Able to Colonize the World

Europe received all its major technological innovations via the Middle East and China. Even as late as 1450, the flow of science and technology was primarily emerging from Islamic societies stretching from India to North Africa. Jared Diamond's (1999) argument carefully documents how the Europeans were able to conquer other peoples. A combination of serendipitous factors led them to develop European guns, steel tools, and manufactured products, and to carry powerful infectious diseases against which they had themselves developed immunity. Diamond meticulously outlines how the most ancient agricultural and horticultural belt of the Fertile Crescent (now Syria, Israel, Palestine, Lebanon, Jordan, Turkey, and Iraq); the early domestication of animals such as the horse, pig, sheep, goat, and cow; and the centuries-long opportunity for Europeans to develop immunities from diseases carried by domestic animals became of central importance to Europeans in developing powerful armies that could defeat indigenous hunter-gatherers and newly emerging farming cultures. A combination of these outgrowths of thousands of years of Eurasian development led to immunities to influenza, whooping cough, measles, mumps, and chicken pox. These diseases became more effective than military weapons in weakening and ultimately destroying any potential threat to the success of European expansionism in the Americas and the Pacific. For example, in what is currently Mexico, there is wide agreement that these new European diseases were the most significant contributor to the decline of the Mayan, Aztec, and other Indian tribe populations from 22 million to just 2 million (Coe, 1996). The population of the Incas of Peru declined by approximately 90% after the Spanish arrived (Cook, 1981), and the majority of deaths are attributed to European diseases.

In North America, the spread of European diseases decimated the Indians whom the British came into contact with. For example, the Wampanoag on the east coast lost a staggering 90% of their tribe (Steele, 1994). Small Indian populations that were left after the epidemics required less land, so these Indians traded cultivated land to the European settlers. In this manner, the small European settler population began to gain a stronger foothold on accessible fertile land. The Cherokees living in what is now western North Carolina and eastern Tennessee were the largest tribe east of the Mississippi and numbered 20,000 in 1690. Within 50 years there were just 10,000, mostly because of the toll of European diseases (Goodwin, 1977). Indians in the west, such as the Blackfeet, the Comanches, and the Mandans, died of the newly introduced smallpox and cholera in such numbers that their tribes' very survival was threatened; in some instances, they were virtually annihilated (Hagan, 1993). Disturbingly, there is documentation that European settlers traded with and donated blankets—an item sought by the Indians—knowing that the blankets were riddled with the smallpox virus (Sowell, 1998). Human death from the introduction of European diseases occurred at a magnitude that is difficult to grasp. The devastation of indigenous peoples was to be repeated countless times in many lands and continents around the world. In New Zealand, for instance, where two of us authors are from, the arrival of the European settler led to a devastating loss of Maori life after they were exposed to European diseases (influenza and whooping cough). These diseases introduced a vulnerability to this people that they had not experienced since their migration from Eastern Polynesia. By 1896, the Maori population had declined from 110,000 in the early 1800s to slightly more than 40,000. The British sentiment at the turn of the 20th century was to "smooth the pillow of a dying race" (King, 2003, p. 258). How familiar this history sounds when we consider the plight of the American Indian, the Australian Aborigine, and many other indigenous peoples around the planet too numerous to mention!

Perhaps the most dramatic technological advancement in the shaping of human history goes back to the production of iron and steel, from which modern warfare originates. Thousands of years of development, from the making of simple furnaces for pottery to the extraction of copper ores and the production of copper alloys, went into this process. Many more thousands of years of experience in building furnaces capable of generating sufficient heat to produce iron and later steel was necessary for Europe to develop these technologies. Much of this technology was developed far from Europe in China. On the basis of their iron and steel technologies, the Chinese had developed a crude form of musket that was too unreliable to be of use in war. The Europeans were able to refine the Chinese weaponry to such a level that it became lethal to any people who did not possess armor, the sword, and the gun. Perhaps one of the most dramatic illustrations of the superiority of the military technology of iron and steel over less superior technology comes from an encounter between Francisco Pizarro, the Spanish conquistador, and the Incan emperor Atahualpa. Only 260 Spaniards, with their armor, swords, and guns in addition to their horses (unknown to the Incas at that time), were able to capture Atahualpa and overwhelm his followers, despite the emperor's being protected by thousands of warriors. This attack on the emperor ultimately led Pizarro and his followers and allies to conquer the entire Inca Empire with its thousands of soldiers and millions of people (Diamond, 1999).

All of the developments in technology that occurred over a 13,000-year period provided the stability to develop large, coordinated economic and political systems accompanied by a written language. Tracing this particular history of technological development provides us with insights as to how British and European colonization became so spectacularly overpowering to essentially all other peoples in Asia, Africa, the Americas, and the Pacific. This history of technological advantage has constructed the world in which we now live. It has also structured the complex interrelationships around the globe that contribute to contemporary human patterns of domination and marginalization. Every day in the news we are confronted with further examples of how the technologies of war based on European technologies of the last 300 years dictate the current shape of our lives and relationships.

Colonization in Pre-European Societies

Terrible indeed were the consequences of European expansion and empire for indigenous peoples around the globe. It is easy to vilify and hold 16th to 19th century Europe responsible for all of the large-scale human travesties that have occurred in the records of human history. However, what we must remember is that over thousands of years many human societies have exploited technological or organizational advantages to conquer other societies.

Virtually all societies on the planet, small or large, have, at some time in their history, been either conquerors or victims of conquest. Sometimes they have been both at different times. In the continent of Africa, where human ancestry can be traced back approximately 8 million years, there were colonizing empires that arose and declined in the sub-Saharan area of what today would be called Nigeria and Ghana. Evidence suggests that the Oyo empire (founded sometime before 1400 and slightly smaller than Colorado) and the Songhay empire (about the size of France) were huge states in this continent. As in other parts of the world, those with superior strength in organization and well-equipped fighters used their colonizing prowess to subjugate and enslave others, including their fellow Africans. These events occurred completely independent of the Ottoman, European, and North and South American slave trade. According to Martin Klein (1998), most enslaved African peoples remained in Africa in the Sudan and Nigeria despite the enormous numbers of people enslaved beyond African shores.

We know that when the first Europeans arrived in North America, they behaved badly toward the indigenous people they found there. Sadly, as Thomas Sowell (1998) describes it, they behaved

> as conquerors have behaved all over the world for thousands of years—which is to say, brutally, greedily, and with arrogance towards the conquered peoples. Indeed that is very much the way Indian conquerors behaved toward other Indians, long before Columbus' ships first appeared on the horizon. (p. 255)

In southern North America in what is today Mexico, the sophisticated civilizations of the Mayans and Aztecs considered hunters and gatherers to be no more than barbarians. These technologically advanced societies disdained, enslaved, and exterminated or sacrificed hundreds of thousands of peoples who were less equipped to protect themselves. Before European invaders arrived in the Americas, the Incas developed one of the largest empires in the world. It stretched for 2000 miles, crossing what today is Peru, Ecuador, Chile, Bolivia, and parts of Argentina and Venezuela. The Quechua-speaking people who lived in the heart of the Inca Empire spread their hegemony to all those within their reign. Equivalent to the Mayans and Aztecs in their technological superiority over hunters and gatherers, they built stone cities with sophisticated canals, suspension bridges, and irrigated agricultural terraces (Hemming, 1970). Immediately before the Spaniards arrived in what is now Peru, the Incas were entrenched in a bloody and devastating civil war between the forces of Huascar and Atahualpa. Atahualpa instituted a mass slaughtering of Inca nobles accompanied by hideous atrocities against the wider population (Davies, 1995).

Psychological Effects of Colonization

Edward Said was keenly interested in how the colonized were portrayed by colonizing Western powers. Box 3.2 represents, from the viewpoint of European writers, his characterizations of people of the West in comparison with people of the East, who were to become part of subordinated communities dominated by Western imperialism. Such descriptions detail the psychological contours of the landscape of colonization. These comparative descriptions portray Westerners as morally superior, wise, even handed, virtuous, and self-disciplined. An Easterner or Oriental, by contrast, is consistently characterized as undisciplined and unruly, lacking wisdom, rationality, maturity, and morality. Westerners' assumptions of their own superior virtuous qualities fortified them in both their conquering and their civilizing missions and justified their psychological domination of those living in the East. They sealed off the Western mind from caring about the human costs paid by indigenous people for the acts of conquest and colonization. In some measure, the people of the East were assumed to deserve what was happening to them and were, therefore, less to be pitied.

Box 3.2. Some Characteristics of the "East" and the "West" Within Said's (1978/1994) *Orientalism*

East	West
Mysterious	Obvious
Mystical	Sensible
Childlike	Mature
Silent	Articulate
Weak	Strong
Dark	Light
Irrational	Rational
Depraved	Virtuous
Tyrannical	Democratic
Sensual	Self-controlled
Incapable of self-government	Capable of self-government

Source: Adapted from Baldwin, Longhurst, McCracken, Ogborn, & Smith (2000).

As it developed, British colonization became not just about the exploitation of the physical resources of a foreign territory, but also about imposing the colonizing power's political, moral, religious, and economic will on the subjugated societies. When the meaning-making frameworks central to the organization and structure of a community are removed, together with the physical resources that sustain them, people experience a profound sense of dislocation, isolation, and alienation. Their physical, psychological, spiritual, and social fabric is damaged or destroyed. The resulting degradation steadily becomes internalized among its citizens and leads ultimately to their loss of belief in their own worthiness. Ironically, the internalized degradation sometimes mirrors the attitudes ascribed to them by the colonizing power. Even the highly negative assumptions of racism can be psychologically internalized in the thoughts of the very people who are subjected to them.

If we hold this story in mind, it becomes easier to understand how the effects of colonization can show up in the kinds of mental health problems many people present to counselors even today. Native American, African American, and Latino communities in the United States are overrepresented in the statistics of people suffering from mental health problems, drug and alcohol problems, and incarceration. The same disproportionate indicators of personal suffering can be found around the world among other colonized peoples. These figures can be ascribed, in no small part, to the ongoing deleterious effects of colonizing actions of the Western European culture over 400 years. It takes many generations to work through the effects of such damage, especially when the power relations that produce these effects have not disappeared, even though they may have been considerably modified.

Through the potent mechanisms of colonizing culture, subjugated peoples come to abandon the very foundations that give meaning to many of their own cultural practices and identities. As a result, great harm and suffering occurs. The effects of colonization have been eloquently elaborated by Albert Memmi (1967), who describes the bond that creates both the colonizer and the colonized. It is one that destroys both parties, although in different ways. Memmi draws a portrait of the "Other" as described by the colonizer. In dominant colonizing discourse, the colonized emerges as the image of everything the colonizer is not. The colonizer is represented as civilized, hardworking, resourceful, intelligent, moral, and compassionate, while the colonized is positioned as lazy, wicked, backward, immoral, and in some important ways not fully human. Memmi points to several conclusions drawn about the artificially created Other. First, the Other is always lacking in the valued qualities of the society, whatever those qualities may be. Second, the humanity of the Other becomes mysterious and unknown. Third, the Other is not a member of the "civilized" human community, but rather part of a chaotic, disorganized, and anonymous collectivity. Finally, the Other carries the mark of the plural. Whereas "we" are all unique, differentiated individuals, "they" all look alike and can be treated en masse. The colonizing discourse is dehumanizing because the ultimate positioning offered to the recipient is an existence that serves the needs of the colonizer.

What are the psychological effects of this process of "Othering"? We have already spoken about the danger of internalized degradation. It is achieved through the colonizer's imposition of an image of the colonized groups onto those who have been subjugated. They are required to see themselves through the same deprecating lens through which the colonizer views them (Fanon, 1963; Taylor, 1994). In the modern world, this process is frequently replicated by encounters with mental health professionals who fail to take the processes of colonization, still expressed through racism, seriously in their diagnostic assessments. They seek primarily to understand a person's psychological distress in individual, intrapsychic terms. They ascribe problems to personal deficits rather than to cultural positioning in the drama of colonization. And they proceed to work on solutions that address only the limited dimensions identified by their diagnostic procedures. In these ways, counselors and therapists often fail to take into account the historical and cultural trauma suffered by indigenous peoples, African slaves, and indentured workers from Asia and reproduced by racist encounters in the present world. The vile abuses that occurred against these peoples and the subsequent destruction of kinship and community have left serious intergenerational wounds. Drug and alcohol abuse, mental health problems, violence, alienation and economic hardship can be directly related to 400 years of European colonization. Rather than seeing these problems as hangovers of a historical context, traditional counseling focuses on challenging individuals to be responsible for themselves. It ascribes diagnoses of deficiency and pathology to those who cannot maintain this sense of rational responsibility and fails to take into account how the very ability to be self-governing was targeted and undermined by the colonizing process. Neither did these processes all cease centuries ago. Further layers of these hardships are experienced by people from former colonized countries who in recent times have sought to escape harsh living conditions and immigrated into modern European and American cities. Once there, they can often take up positions only on the margins of their new social world. There they experience the same internalized abjection their forebears felt.

Decolonization

The concept of decolonization is a recent one. It refers to the processes by which, throughout the 20th century, people in colonized lands have struggled to overthrow colonial political systems. Such movements did not begin out of the blue in the 20th century, however. They have their seeds in the expressions of resistance to modern colonization as far back as its very beginnings. Indigenous people in many places fought against the invading armies of the colonizers, sometimes winning but more often losing these battles. People captured into slavery made desperate attempts to run away. Organized rebellions took place on the slave plantations. Howard Zinn (2003) counts 18 uprisings aimed at the overthrow of colonial governments, 6 black rebellions, and 40 riots that occurred before 1760 in America. In some cases, poor white people, many of whom came to America as indentured laborers and whose conditions and rights were only marginally better than those of black slaves, joined forces with the slaves in resistance. Bacon's Rebellion was a case in point. Also, some slaves were freed early in the slavery period.

From early in the history of slavery there were also white people who stood against the practice of slavery. The abolitionist movement in Britain developed a large following around the period of the Enlightenment, and this continued through the 19th century. Even that was not the beginning of the antislavery movement in

Britain; slavery and enforced servitude in England had once been abolished way back in 1102. But as the African slave trade began, many slaves entered Britain from the Americas with their masters. They were freed by a decision of the chief justice of the Court of King's Bench in 1772, at which time there estimated to be 10,000 to 14,000 slaves living in Britain. In the rest of Europe, other movements to make slavery illegal sprang from the Enlightenment. One hero of this movement was the French bishop Abbé Grégoire, who had considerable influence in the revolutionary government after the French Revolution. He was immensely popular in France (although hated by the Pope) and led the revolutionary government in a policy of religious toleration for Jews and granting freedom to black slaves in France. In 19th century Britain, the Aboriginal Protection Society campaigned for the rights of colonized people and was responsible for influencing the Home Office to make treaties with indigenous peoples in New Zealand and elsewhere (Orange, 1987).

Throwing off the yoke of colonization is not just a matter of a change of government. In many places around the world, systems of social organization and systems of thinking have continued to maintain privileged opportunity for white people and the racist assumptions of the colonizing era long after the politicians and colonial administrators have left. The process of decolonization has likewise focused not just on regime change but also on the development of ways of thinking that depart from the assumptions and practices of racial and cultural superiority. Decolonization is necessarily in part a psychological struggle, since the colonizing assumptions have penetrated deep into the psyches of people in the modern world. Hence it is important for counselors to understand the psychological process of decolonization and its effects in order to work with people who are affected by it. Counseling can help throw off the internalized images of abjection that have resulted from colonization.

By way of example, Mikela Jones's narrative contains twin stories of colonization and decolonization. As you read it, keep an ear out for the ongoing effects of the atrocities committed by Anglo Americans and settlers in their colonizing quest. And also listen for the decolonizing assertions of resistance and the effort to maintain cultural resilience in spite of the effects of colonization.

Sin ta yabe machi na, ke sheeyay Mikela Jones, ba tenik xabe. Ke nahpo, che ya ta kai casil. My name is Mikela Jones and I am Pomo Hinthil from my mother's side. My people are the indigenous inhabitants of what today is northern California. We are the little river band of Pomo Indians. I am also Paiute Shoshone from my father's side. My people currently reside in northern Nevada. We are from the Duck Valley reservation. I am *che ya*, which in my language means people of the earth and father sky. Today I have grown comfortable calling myself Indian. A lot of people question that, asking, "Are you okay calling yourself Indian, even though Columbus called you that because he thought he landed in India?" Yes, I am okay calling myself Indian, because I know my history. My mother knew what it was like being Indian growing up in a Westernized world; therefore, she felt she had to teach me, to arm me with the tools necessary to defend myself against critics and racist people.

I was told the real story around that term *Indian*, and it is a bit different from what most people believe. During the 1490s, when Columbus arrived, the word "Indian" did not exist. When he landed, his first observation of these indigenous inhabitants was how very religious they were. His exact words were "en Dios," which translated means "of God." He was saying that these people were of God. The term evolved from *En Dios* to *Endian* and continued to evolve to what it is today. I am a child of the creator, which is why I have no problem saying that I am an Indian. But I must also respect my ancestors and give you my ancestry: I am Pomo Hinthil, Paiute Shoshone, che ya. My Indian-ness has not only been instrumental in shaping my life, but it has also been monumental in shaping my family's history and their present and future status as a people.

I would like to share with you how instrumental it has been for my people and me. I am empowered today because of the terrible sacrifices made by many of my people. Everything in my life relates to my culture and the experiences my people have gone through that have led to the creation of my being. Everything follows from my being Indian—my religion, economic class, life choices, and so on. To know where we are going, we have to know where we are, and to know where we are, we have to know where we have been. We must look at the history of our people to find its influence on my family's choices and its effects on me. Indian is not an ethnic group, nor is it a race. It is a political organization. Indians are the only group in the United States that has its own federal agency. That agency is the Bureau of Indian Affairs (BIA). The reason is partly political status, but how did we get that political status? We need only to look at the history of my people. Tribes are sovereign nations to the extent that the government allows them to be. That statement doesn't really make sense, considering the definition of the word *sovereign*, but regardless of its confusion, that is exactly how it is when we consider the relationship my people have with the United States.

It all began in 1492 when Columbus landed on Turtle Island. When European whites left their homes to seek a place where they would not face any religious prosecution, their freedom meant the loss of another's. In the development of the United States, early leaders saw native people as animals, not human beings, which allowed them to treat them the way they did. This perception of "savage" is still around today. Yes, even in the 21st century, I have to prove myself to a lot of people. A lot of my professors wondered what an Indian was doing in their institution. I prove myself by being successful, and the more milestones I complete, the more credible I become in the eyes of Western society.

Countless legal inequities were imposed on my people at the highest levels of government. The brutality and disenfranchisement arising from the United States' treatment of the Indian over these last few hundred years is too enormous to mention here. However, part of this history led to the emergence of the BIA. This institution has played a part in the shaping of native sovereignty and its relation to the state and federal government. Because the Supreme Court gave us the title of a distinct dependent nation, we now have a unique relationship with the United States. By making this precedent, the United States has a responsibility to be that guardian, but there is a disquieting contradiction: tribes wanting self-determination are also being treated as dependent. That is why we have a quasi definition and status of sovereignty. I continue to ask myself this question as I tell you the history of my people: how does this affect my family and me? Sovereignty is a power that has been given to us. It is something that unites us. It seems to me the only light we have in a world of darkness. My tribe and all tribes are working at exercising this power in any way that they can. Casinos are one way, but there is a lot more that tribes can do to be economically sufficient. Sovereignty means self-determination, and for my people self-determination takes us one step closer to the way we used to live and one step away from colonialism. Self-determination allows us to guide each other using traditional philosophies and ceremonies and not live solely by the Westernized ideologies that at one time were forced down our throats. The federal policies that follow are founded on this idea of a domestic dependent nation, in which we are a ward of the government, our guardian.

The year 1887 gave rise to the Dawes Act. The goal of this legislation was to acquire more Indian land by a policy of assimilation. The government enacted policies like "allotment," which introduced the idea of land ownership to the native people, put them on reservations, and gave each family their own piece of land. Prior to this, Indians had been dispersed throughout the land. Allotment put them in distinct areas, limiting their ability to live in their own vast lands. Surplus land went to the government to open up for immigrant homesteading. The settlers' movement west took our indigenous people out of their traditional homelands, removing them from sacred sites where their ceremonies had been practiced. In many instances, my people were separated from their traditional food resources. This made them rely on government-supplied food, which they were not accustomed to eating. Prior to contact with European immigrants, native people had been extremely healthy. What is the situation today? Diabetes is an epidemic for Indian people, and this is due to the diet. Our bodies are not used to the processed foods consumed in our communities today.

From the 1800s to the mid 1950s, the government used boarding schools to assimilate Indians. Children were taken from their families by force and sent away to schools designed to force young people to become assimilated and estranged from their cultural roots. The government had a saying at this time: "Kill the Indian, save the man." The purpose of these boarding schools was essentially to kill the Indian. At these schools, children were abused physically, mentally, emotionally, and spiritually. They were molested sexually and beaten for speaking their language. They were forced to learn positions of servitude, to forget what it was to be an Indian. They were not allowed to go home. They weren't allowed to nurture each other, nor were they nurtured by the staff. They were no longer allowed to practice their traditional ceremonies. Everything was taken, and what replaced that void was the compulsion to be servants to a Western ideology.

Even on the reservations, assimilation tactics were being practiced. A well-known example is the battle of Wounded Knee, which should be called the massacre at Wounded Knee. My ancestor, Wavoka, a Paiute medicine man, had introduced the Ghost Dance—a dance that was supposed to bring back those who had died and make all the white people go back to where they had come from. When practicing this ceremony, the Paiutes were shot down, including women and children. Tribes had no religious protection and were killed for practicing their ceremonies.

Today, when I am asked, "Do you speak your language?" I almost want to cry. I think about what my people went through and why I cannot speak my language fluently. There was a time in my life when I really struggled to figure out what made me Indian. The only thing I could think of was that I had long hair, brown skin, high cheekbones, and a big nose. Oh, and I had Indian blood, but was that it? I didn't know my language, my songs, my dance, and my ceremonies. They were gone because of what had been done to us, the genocide my people had endured. I had to go through a lot of traditional and nontraditional counseling methods. I had to pray to bring those things back into my life. The acts of the past affect me and my family today. We struggle to do research to find our songs, our language, our dance and our ceremonies. It is now our life's work to bring back the Indian within us, for it is the only way we can be whole again.

Even though the acts against Indians were despicable, nothing surely could have been any more horrific than what was done to my people, the Pomo Hinthil, in California. It is a history that doesn't want to be told, nor heard. The late 1840s marked the era of the gold rush. Many history books talk about the development aspect of the gold rush, the building of cities and the histories of the miners. Seldom is there anything written about the original inhabitants of this area, the Pomo, or the many other tribes living in California at the time. California has the most diverse of native populations across the country, and they all have a history that is rarely discussed in the textbooks in our schools. Would it be too violent to talk about in school, or is this a history that people are trying to forget? Federal bounties were placed on the heads of my people: 20 cents for men, 15 cents for women, 10 cents for children. In a period of just 20 years, the United States paid over 2 million dollars in bounties. Tribes in California were decimated. It is estimated that more than 20,000 bounties were claimed. That means that 20,000 of my ancestors were killed by bounty hunters alone. Indians that were not killed were taken into a kind of slavery, known at this time as indentured servitude. My people also have the story of the bloody island massacre, which occurred in the early 1900s. Some of my people who were indentured servants rebelled and killed a white man for molesting their children. All the women, elders, and children fled to an island for safety, while the men, the warriors, stayed behind and fought. The governor of California returned with the United States Cavalry, not to fight the warriors, but to the island. They slaughtered dozens of elders, women, and children, almost annihilating the whole village. There were few survivors. Those that did survive hid in the water breathing through tule vines. The island was red with their blood. These things were happening to my people less than 100 years ago.

Forced assimilation and genocide have left my people in an unhealthy place. Today, many are in a state of poverty, have lost their identity, are in poor health, and have poor living habits. Tribes were given alcohol in their food rations. In many ways, this decision to supply alcohol to my people was designed to take away our focus and our priorities and to further subdue us. Today, many are in a damaging cycle of abuse and have negative self-medicating habits. That is why I feel it is my responsibility to counter the efforts of this abusive policy. Even though these events happened long ago, we are all still being affected by them.

How does this abusive history affect my people and me? Posttraumatic stress syndrome is one way that it is affecting us. Traumatic experiences through history have sent us into a cycle of depression and anger. I had to heal myself in order to see clearly, to forgive and move on. Once I began to see the history, I began to put together the puzzle that shaped my actions and my people's actions. It became evident why my people are in the place they're in, why we are poor, why we drink, and why we have lost our history and cultural fabric.

Understanding this gave rise to my pursuit to find the Indian within. I struggled with substance abuse when I was younger because that was what I was taught—that's what I thought it was to be Indian. I went through a healing process and began to pursue my culture. I also began to think about self-determination and how I could contribute to that. My answer came with the idea that we need more professionals, because the truth is that each day our sovereignty is getting weaker. We are losing it with the court systems. We need people to learn the language of the courts and fight for our people with pen and paper. That is why I pursued a college education. I became the first male from my tribe to graduate from a four-year university and the first from my tribe to go on to graduate school. My history influences my behavior as well as motivates me to be successful, to help my people. My cultural group is not just something I belong to; it's a way of life for me, a way that guides my choices and my ethics. It is something that I live by and protect, something that my people live by and protect. My history makes my people and me who we are.

In my family, we have generations of men being raised by women alone. Could this be related to the acts of oppression and genocide my people endured? I believe so. Of all the things that have been taken away from my people, I think the status of "warrior" is critical. There is also some shame there. Shame that we couldn't defend our people the way we wished we could. Though we are still alive, there is a sense of loss, and the pressure falls on our warriors. When I was with the men of the reservation, I was given a role, a responsibility, though it was hard at times. I was independent. When I was with the women, I was truly respected and didn't have fear; it felt good. I was also taught a lot about what it means to be a good man.

Today, as Indian men, we are in need of new role responsibilities. We are redefining *warrior* and the ownership of that role. Our community is violent because our young men don't know their role. But it's not their fault. There is no one there to teach them about the source of their anger, about their instinct and their warrior-ness. Domestic violence and infidelity are just some of the issues that come because of this loss. Indian men need to learn about their healing issues. They need to not feel guilty. We are still alive, and we are a breathing, beautiful people.

In reflecting on these events, I am able to see how far I have come. I am able to see what my people have done to make it this far. I honor my ancestors and what they endured so that I can live today. Even today, we live in some of the most beautiful areas. Some of us still know our songs, our dance, and our language. It is coming back, and not only is it coming back, but we are taking responsibility for our self-determination. I am not the only one doing this. This renaissance is happening all over. Many Indian leaders are stepping up and becoming professionals. Accepting that responsibility and becoming present-day warriors, fighting for that sovereignty with the pen. We are walking in two worlds, still adapting, but accepting the beauty in both and trying to balance the inequities in one. *Ke sheeyay Mikela Jones, ba tenik xabe.* I am Pomo Paiute Shoshone Hinthil, che ya. *Kadi ho kaline ya nake nake. Yaqui kooto.*

Mikela Jones identifies as Pomo Hinthil and Paiute Shoshone.

TO DISCUSS

1. As you read Mikela's story, how did it touch you?

2. Were there places where you were saddened, enlivened, angered, dismayed, or excited, or felt any other response?

3. What did you find surprising in it?

4. What difference did it make to you?

5. How were the psychological effects of colonization evident in this story?

6. How was the theme of resistance and decolonization present in this story?

7. What are the counseling implications of Mikela's story?

It would be a mistake to think of the forces of colonization as inevitable and inexorable. If we look closely at history, we can trace the development of an alternative story from the beginning of the colonizing process. Colonization was resisted, with varying degrees of success, by many people all around the world. Subjugated groups always sought to maintain the integrity of their cultural perspectives and sometimes organized their sense of cultural belonging around their projects of resistance. They also always made accommodations to the European way of life, adopting practices that they found attractive from the colonizers and discarding some of their own traditional practices.

The political forms of 19th century colonization no longer apply. The general consensus of world politics as expressed in the United Nations is now opposed to colonizing practices, and international law, such as it exists, and has outlawed them. Through the 20th century there has been a steady movement toward the reestablishment of independent status for nation states around the globe. The old British and French empires no longer exist in the form that they did a hundred years ago. German efforts to establish political dominance in Europe were turned back in World War II. The Russian rule over vast territories in Europe and Asia ended with the overthrow of the Soviet system in the 1990s and the breakup of the Soviet Union into many different countries. In more recent times, the invasion of Kuwait by Iraq was turned back by a United Nations–led international coalition. Among nation states, only the United States now seems capable of defying international law and invading other countries to bring about "regime change" (e.g., Iraq, Afghanistan, Grenada, Panama), but even the United States feels the constraint of anticolonial discourse and its own rhetoric of democratic independence and history of the overthrow of colonial rule. The American public would not accept the political intention to colonize as an acceptable goal of American power in the way that the British public would a hundred years ago.

In other words, there has been a worldwide shift in discourse against the practice of colonization. This does not necessarily mean that the colonizing impulse has completely disappeared out of world politics. It can be argued that it now takes on new and more sophisticated forms and that the colonizing process is now not so much about occupying land as about economic control held by multinational corporations and international banking systems. It continues to actively produce both privilege and poverty in systematic ways around the globe with much the same effect as previous practices of colonization. (For accounts of these modern practices of what has been called neocolonialism, look at the work of Noam Chomsky [2003], Arundhati Roy [2004], and John Perkins [2004].)

This shift of general discourse against colonizing practice has, however, produced a strong counter theme of decolonization that has sought expression in numerous ways in different parts of the world. In later chapters we shall explore this discourse of decolonization and some of the expressions it has taken. We shall also relate these to the worlds of counseling and education in order to show that it has had an effect in the lives of ordinary people in many places.

Despite the development of an anticolonization discourse, however, it is important to remember that the effects of the processes of colonization are still being worked out. They are still pervasive in the assumptions of "culture," as we outlined in Chapter 1. And they continue to have material effects in people's lives, constructing their lifestyles and constraining their life chances. We should not expect otherwise as long as we remember that shifts in discourse are not mere acts of personal willpower.

We all must live in a world that is still shaped by the era of colonization in many ways. Its assumptions are woven into our language, our political rhetoric, our academic and social science concepts, and our identity categories. It is shaping our choices each time we fill in a form and write down our cultural identity preferences.

As we conclude this chapter, we hope we have made it clear why a review of colonization is important to the practice of counseling. These practices of colonization can be recapitulated by counselors in the practice of counseling if we are not careful. Specifically, counselors must be acutely aware of how the very counseling theories they adopt may embody certain colonizing legacies constructed upon a Eurocentric vision as discussed in Chapter 1. Counselors must guard against using a solely intrapsychic focus in evaluating and intervening in people's lives when their clients have been victimized by cultural trauma produced by colonizing forces. It is also important to acknowledge that some personal traumas have been caused by the dislocation or destruction of kinship and familial support systems. Some of this fragmentation is relatively recent, given the welfare policies in the United States and Australia where the federal government, even until the 1960s, promoted the policy of removing Indian and Aboriginal children from their parents and placing them in boarding schools to better socialize them to a Eurocentric lifestyle. Many people continue to suffer from the ongoing social and psychological dismemberment of their familial systems.

There are many more psychological effects produced by colonization inequitably affecting those who are the benefactors of colonization and those who have suffered because of it. On the other hand, counselors can exercise the choice to apply counseling theories and practices that explicitly support the resilience and courage exhibited by individuals, families, and communities who have suffered the full negative effects of colonization and who have not only survived but have even restored their communities in the face of the demeaning impact of Western ideologies. When counselors appreciate fully the extent to which their clients' experiences are produced within a particular sociocultural and historical context, they are in a better position to intervene in culturally respectful ways.

Response to Chapter 3

Carol Robinson-Zañartu

Carol Robinson-Zañartu, Ph.D., is professor and chair of the Department of Counseling and School Psychology at San Diego State University and director of the Native American Scholars and Collaborators Projects. An educator and psychologist concerned about social justice, her primary professional affiliation is school psychology. She is Scotch-English by ancestry, has raised two bicultural (Chilean American) children, and has been mentored by numerous indigenous teachers. Her research and scholarly activities focus on issues of social justice, especially Native American issues, systemic approaches to change in education, and dynamic intervention-based assessment.

I have come to believe that to treat or even to claim to educate indigenous peoples and others whose lives have been shaped by the profound implications of colonization and historical trauma without grasping more than a brief history of colonization and its implications is truly unethical. Thus, Monk, Winslade, and Sinclair's chapter provides a much-needed introduction to some of the concepts and consequences of colonization, its historical antecedents, and current attempts to address these issues. This chapter should whet the appetites of mental health and educational professionals for more in-depth treatment of both the theory and practical implications of colonization and decolonization (see, for instance, Battiste, 2000; Cleary & Peacock, 1998; Duran, 2006; Smith, 2001).

The effects of colonization for many indigenous peoples reflect the inseparability in worldview of the physical (land/body), the psychological (mind), the spiritual (spirit), and the emotional (heart). For instance, the land base is central to many creation stories, and when it is defiled or stolen, a profound spiritual hurt is coupled with emotional and psychological consequences. For many indigenous peoples, colonization and attempts at cultural genocide in acts ranging from the forced removal of children to brutal murders of the innocent, the breaking of treaties, seizure and defilement of sacred lands, and degrading government policies designed to remove all vestiges of culture, resulted in traumas that have been passed from generation to generation. Not unlike some of the effects described in the literature on posttraumatic stress disorder, such symptoms as acting out against peers, underperformance, depression, and lack of focus may be displayed by survivors of historical trauma, who can well be the hidden victims of traumas gone unrecognized, untreated, and unresolved. Many are mistakenly identified as incorrigible, unmotivated, or just "bad kids." Too many school and community counselors, psychologists, social workers, family therapists, and teachers are unaware of the complex dynamics of traumatic stress, and thus miss the opportunity to intervene. Therefore, we must take care not to name such behaviors as typical characteristics of people from indigenous or colonized cultures but must instead consider the possibility that we are seeing the effects of colonization.

Eduardo Duran (2006) discusses this intergenerational effect of the attempts to conquer land, heart, mind, and spirit as a "soul wound." Healing that soul wound at the individual and collective levels requires some depth of understanding not only of the antecedent actions but also of the traditions that guide healing within the appropriate culture. Because decolonizing goes beyond voice and reflects the reclaiming of a cultural lens, cultural identity, and worldview, individuals and communities will begin to provide new perspectives, new social structures, new ethics, new actions, and new demands as outcomes of decolonizing work.

I have been privileged to participate in projects with Filipino, African American, Japanese American, Puerto Rican, and Mexican American people engaged in decolonizing work as well as with individuals from the Hopi, Pomo, Tohono O'odham, Zuni, Cree, Yaqui, Creek, Choctaw, Seminole, Caddo, and Diné (Navajo) nations. As the histories vary, so does the work. For instance, Jennifer Gorospe (2007) confronted such issues as high depression rates among Filipino Americans, a passive response of some families linked to their belief in *bahala na* ("come what may"), and "the resignation of a people to a history of repeated colonization." This decolonizing work has been a path marked at times by tears, anger, and argument as well as empowerment, voice, and the emergence of compelling perspectives and ideas. Certain phrases will linger with me for many years: *Why didn't they tell us this? This makes me struggle with everything I believed was the truth! I have such a newfound respect for my grandparents. I want to know my history. I am proud of who I am!* Traversing the annals of an alternative view of history, my students have grappled with information on colonization and the depths of a new reality. Their work will transform future generations, and has also been said to help heal the wounds for former generations.

Those of us typically empowered by the mainstream system must learn this well enough not to recolonize unawarely through such patronizing actions as "giving" to the disenfranchised a place at "our table" with expectations that "they" will now become leaders, thinkers, and writers "like us" with stronger voices than before. Rather, we must be prepared to have our knowledge bases and perspectives augmented as we become learners, collaborators, and followers. We must do our own decolonizing work, letting go of the entitlement that has become a historical legacy of the colonizer mentality.

TO DISCUSS

1. Think about your own family histories. How have they been shaped and affected by the history of colonization and decolonization? Share stories of what you know.

2. How have these histories shaped your own life, your own social location, your own values, your own commitments?

3. As you think about these histories, what difference do they make to the work you are doing, or would like to do, as a counselor, psychologist, social worker, or other professional?

4. Do an online search for statements in the public discourse that support colonization or that support decolonization.

5. What are some examples you can identify of the current ongoing psychological effects of colonization?

6. What are some examples you can find of inspiring stories of resistance and resilience in the face of colonizing practices?

7. Read modern newspapers and find traces of assumptions about the moral inferiority of colonized groups that still persist.

8. What are the most useful roles that counselors, psychologists, and social workers (or other professionals) can play when faced with the effects of colonization?

9. What are some strategies that you know of that would assist in this work?

CHAPTER 4

Race, Ethnicity, and Identity

R ace has played a dominant role in shaping contemporary life throughout the world. The history of race and its role in European colonization has powerfully shaped, and continues to shape, how we perceive ourselves and others in relation to particular defining physical features. Racial categorization has meant for some groups continuous and systematic unearned access to opportunity in important aspects of day-to-day life. These opportunities lead to quality housing, education, health care, political authority, and overall psychological well-being. For less favored racial groups, racial categorization produces systematic denial of opportunity and access to quality essential services.

Access to societal resources, or the denial of access to them, has a profound influence on people's quality of life. It also impacts on what can be accomplished within a counseling and therapeutic process. For example, if a client has privileged access to opportunity and resources, it is easy for a counselor to confront him about taking responsibility for his own choices in life. After all, if systematic advantages are in your favor, it is more plausible to argue that what holds you back in living a satisfying life is what you as an individual make of those circumstances. When those same choices are systematically denied to people along racial lines, such confrontation can have a much more negative impact. In fact, a counselor's insistence on individual personal responsibility may make experiences of frustration and depression in the face of difficult circumstances considerably worse. In a counseling or therapeutic relationship, the issue of race tends to be most salient when the therapist is perceived to be from a more privileged racial background than the client. We will discuss the significance of this issue in counseling in this chapter and again in Chapter 14. Without constant awareness of these themes, they can negatively impact both the counseling relationship and the value of the therapy.

Our dreams, aspirations, long- and short-term goals, passions, attractions, loves, and losses are all experienced through multiple ethnic memberships and racial categorizations. Many of our meaning-making functions are constructed within ethnic history and ethnic membership. Often, our successes and troubles are understood through an ethnic lens. Many counselor and therapeutic exchanges occur within the context of multiple ethnic understandings and misunderstandings.

Race as a Defining Domain

Let us begin with the subject of race. We shall explore the implications of this historical and contemporary cultural formation on the practice and delivery of multicultural counseling in the United States and elsewhere. Like the concept of culture, the concept of race has evolved in particular historical contexts, and it cannot be understood without investigating those contexts. Like the concept of culture, race is not a stable concept. What we mean by it now is not what it has always meant.

British and European colonization is implicated in the ongoing discursive legacy embodied in the concept of "race." The very use of this word carries with it the idea that there are biological differences among groups of people that can be used as markers for organizing our perceptions of and attitudes toward each other. This idea of distinct, biological differences among peoples, usually with a special focus on skin color, is intimately associated with British and European colonizing discourse. A race is generally defined as a human group distinguished by common physical characteristics that are held to be natural and genetic in origin. The modern notion of race, constructed around biological differences, has its origins in pseudoscience, popular culture, and history, rather than in any scientific evidence that is recognized as valid today. There have been many attempts to develop a scientific account that incorporates the concept of race. There is general scientific consensus that these attempts all lack credibility when examined closely. However, the concept of race is so deeply entwined in contemporary consciousness that it is not possible to avoid discussing it. Everyone thinks she knows what *race* means. Yet it remains a problematic concept. We shall investigate the concept a little by asking some questions about it.

What Is the Genealogy of the Term *Race*?

The term *race* first appeared in the English language about 300 years ago (Atkinson, Morten, & Sue, 1993). The notion of race originated from the French language, meaning breed or lineage as defined by physical markers. The markers include skin color, facial and bodily features, and hair type. Categories of persons were invented based on these physical markers. We shall argue here that there is no inherent meaning in these categories. The meanings were simply devised by those in the position to do so.

The genealogy of the term *race* as we know it can be traced back to the period when Europeans began to develop extended contact with non-Europeans. In the late 15th and early 16th century, Europeans started expanding beyond their national horizons in search of wealth and conquest. Noting how others in the far-away lands they visited were different from themselves, they determined that these differences were indicators of some fundamental difference in the nature of human beings. It was a small step for early European explorers to conclude that, since the indigenous peoples of these continents did not have technological developments equal to those of the European, they must be an inferior kind of human being. Usually, they assumed that Europeans were in sole possession of the attributes of "civilization" and frequently referred to other peoples as "savages." Savages, by the logic of the time, did not need to be accorded the same rights and respect as civilized human beings (Huntington, 2004).

As the Enlightenment scientific project developed, one of its major aims in the field of biological study was to document, classify, and categorize all species of plant and animal life on earth. The categorization of types (genus types, species types, subspecies types) through the analysis of characteristics was the dominant scientific emphasis. The analogy of species "type" was readily extended by the European mind, with its assumptions of superiority and manifest destiny, from animal species to human beings who looked different. The concept of the "human race" is actually an older concept than the modern term *race*, which refers to human beings of different physical characteristics. It was the application of the idea that the people the colonizers encountered were not fully human that led to the development of the idea of racial type and therefore the modern concept of race. There were many efforts to categorize racial types according to "phenotypic characteristics," to measure the skulls and brain sizes of people of different "races" in much the same way that the skeletons and skulls of extinct animals were investigated.

Racial discourse of the time assumed that differences among races related to fundamentally different types of blood, a concept that persists in both popular and official discourse through the descriptions of people of color (but not white folks)

Figure 4.1   In the middle of the 19th century, many Western researchers believed it was possible to grade races according to intellectual endowments. John Jeffries's diagram was designed to show how certain skull shapes are illustrative of intellectual capacity.

Source: From Jeffries, 1869.

as "full blooded," "half blooded," and so forth. The science of racial types has long since been discredited, and modern geneticists have replaced the idea of blood type with the idea of populations that share a genetic stock (Lévi-Strauss, 2001). Still, the idea of inherent biological differences of different races has lingered.

As Darwinian ideas about evolution became popular in the 19th century, the assumption of "advanced" and "more highly evolved" races took hold. Although it bore little relation to Darwin's biological project, social Darwinism created an analogue that was readily adopted by Europeans already bent on establishing positions of power over the people who inhabited the lands they wanted to conquer. The concept of superior and inferior races was a welcome intellectual tool that could serve to rationalize and justify the treatment of colonized races as less than fully human. If it had scientific backing, then it had even more authority. It eased the European conscience with regard to moral questions about the treatment of nonwhite people, making it possible to regard them as children to be ruled over for their own good and punished when they were naughty. After all, "they" were not like "us." Their inferior minds meant that they were not really fit to govern themselves.

You can still hear traces of this logic when people talk about the reasons that some countries in Africa and Asia struggle with political turmoil. After all, goes the racial logic, "they" cannot be expected to have the minds that would appreciate democratic and peaceful social systems. It's just not part of their mind-set, meaning their natural mental capacity. The concept of race was deployed to make it seem normal that white people, by their very nature, are superior and deserve to be rulers, and that people of color are naturally inferior and deserve to be ruled. The concept of race thus served as a justification for policies of colonizing conquest and economic exploitation and for practices of enslavement and even genocidal extermination.

The whole idea of the existence of race needs to be understood first and foremost as a construction of European colonizing discourse. It is a modern construct and has not always been around, as some people assume. It is more correct to say that the concept of race has become naturalized in our understandings than it is to call it a description of a natural phenomenon. In the story of European colonization, Europeans created the notion of distinct and identifiable races and by some definitions created categories of subhumans or nonhumans. In the first English settler communities on North American soil, begun in 1607, 1620, and 1630, contact between the English and the indigenous peoples of North America was generally cooperative (Huntington, 2004). However, relations deteriorated in response to settlers' expanding demands for land. Indians developed justified fears that prospects of coexistence were being replaced by the prospect of domination. The result was a long and bloody engagement between settler and Indian.

By the 1660s, European Americans had categorized Native Americans as a race of people who were backward, savage, and uncivilized. In the early 19th century, President Andrew Jackson persuaded Congress to pass the Indian Removal Act, and principal tribes in six southern states were forcibly moved west of the Mississippi in a process that would be described as ethnic or racial cleansing today (Huntington, 2004).

At the same time that Indians were being taken from their homeland and killed in devastating numbers, Africans were being imported and enslaved until the cessation of the slave trade in 1808. According to Samuel Huntington (2004), the founding fathers required high levels of racial, ethnic, and religious homogeneity. At the time of the first naturalization statute in 1790, when citizenship was made available to "free white persons," the first U.S. attorney general, Edmund Randolph, stated that black people were not "constituent members of our society." At this time there was a total U.S. population of 3,929,000, of whom 698,000 were slaves (Huntington, 2004, p. 54).

Thomas Jefferson, along with other political and religious figures of the day, while stating that whites and blacks were "equally free," also stated that they could not "live in the same government." During President Jefferson's term of office, the country of Liberia was created in Africa so that all the blacks brought as slaves to North America could be transported back to the continent from which they had been captured and enslaved. Between 11,000 and 15,000 black people were transported there. Abraham Lincoln wanted all black people to migrate to Africa (Huntington, 2004).

Similar forms of oppression and marginalization were suffered by early Chinese immigrants to the United States. The Chinese were also perceived by the Anglo Americans to be an inferior race. In 1875, after a wave of Chinese workers came into the country to help build the railroads after the Civil War, the first laws restricting Chinese immigrants from entering the country were enacted. In 1882, the Chinese Exclusion Act was implemented, with Justice Stephen J. Field defending this new law on grounds that "Chinese were of a different race, and it seems impossible for them to assimilate." If their migration were not restricted, he said, it would lead to an "oriental invasion [that] would constitute a menace to our civilization." (Huntington, 2004, p. 56). This legal barrier to Chinese immigrants' entering the United States was lifted only in 1952.

Even as the European empires as political entities began to break up during the 20th century, the idea that whites can be deemed innately superior to nonwhites has persisted. In North America, by the early 19th century, the concept of race was playing an increasingly important role in scientific, intellectual, and popular thinking among white Americans. Reginald Horsman (1981) suggested that by the middle of the century the "inherent inequality of races was simply accepted as a scientific fact in America" (p. 134).

From the 19th century to recent times, it was widely believed that humans are divided hierarchically into four major races, with the Caucasian at the apex of the hierarchy followed by, in descending order, the Mongolian, the Indian, and the African. A further differentiation among some Caucasians placed Anglo-Saxon descendants of Germanic tribes at the top (Huntington, 2004). Madison Grant, president of the American Zoological Society and a trustee of the American Museum of Natural History, wrote a best-selling book in the 1920s in which he said,

Neither the black, nor the brown, nor the yellow, nor the red will conquer the white in battle. But if the valuable elements in the Nordic race mix with inferior strains or die out through race suicide, then the citadel of civilization will fall for mere lack of defenders. (Grant, 1921, p. xxxi)

This confident assumption of the superiority of the "Nordic race," referring to those whose ancestry can be traced to northern Europe, along with the assumption of the importance of preserving racial "purity," was later taken up by Adolf Hitler and the Nazi party and pushed to grisly extremes. This same concept of race buttressed white America's comfortable position of assumed superiority. It further legitimated the conquering and ruling of Mexican Indians and numerous other groups. In addition, the hierarchical categorization of people as belonging to particular races based on some innate characteristics served to maintain the racial purity of a white society.

During the 20th century, the concept of race continued to remain important. In the first half of the century, the eugenics movement gained considerable sway. It was popularized in books that sold widely, but it also developed substantial respectability in academic circles and was taught to a generation of students of education and psychology. Eugenics was founded on the assumption of the prime importance of genetic inheritance and concern about the "contamination" of the "race" (meaning the human race) by people with "weak" genes. It was closely linked with the idea that those born of an "inferior" race were to be automatically considered a burden on society. In other words, eugenics was closely intertwined with racist thinking.

What is important for modern students of counseling and psychology to realize is that the people who popularized eugenics in the early part of the 20th century were not extremists or crackpots. They were centrally placed in the psychological sciences and in education (Selden, 1999). They include names that we know today as founders of many branches of study. For example, Francis Galton coined the name *eugenics* and was honored by the Galton Society (which existed to promote eugenics). His work was foundational in starting what we know today as the study of human development. Other eugenicists include G. Stanley Hall (the originator of the child study), Charles Spearman (known still for his method of calculating correlational statistics), Lewis Terman (the early developer of intelligence tests), and Leta Hollingworth (who launched academic interest in the study of gifted children). Theodore Roosevelt was an enthusiastic supporter of eugenics, and it was the basis of several immigration laws passed by Congress.

The point is that the assumption of the primacy of certain hereditary factors, including race, and the ready assumption of a hierarchy of races were commonplace features of American thinking during the first half of the 20th century. Take the words of H. L. Mencken, the popular journalist and social commentator, as typical of the flavor of the times:

> The educated Negro of today is a failure, not because he meets insuperable difficulties in life, but because he is a Negro. His brain is not fitted for the higher forms of mental effort; his ideals, no matter how laboriously he is trained and sheltered, remain those of a clown. He is, in brief, a low-caste man, to the manner born, and he will remain inert and inefficient until fifty generations of him have lived in civilization. And even then, the superior white race will be fifty generations ahead of him. (cited by Rodgers, 2005, p. 119)

Are There Biological Differences Among Different "Races"?

There has, in fact, been little agreement about the nature and number of human races. If there were clear biological differences, we might expect to find greater agreement about what these differences are. Any contemporary scientific study that attempts to tie down the distinguishing biological differences among racial categories of human beings has been doomed to failure. With the completion of the human genome project, in which the genetic makeup of the human being was mapped, there is yet further evidence of the difficulty of drawing genetic or biological distinctions among groups of human beings that could be said to be racial differences. In fact, in genetic terms, the human being shares 92% of his genetic structure with the fruit fly and 99% of the same genetic makeup with the chimpanzee. Genetic differences between any two people in the world amount to no more than 0.2%. So-called racial characteristics account for just 6% of this 0.2% variation. When we calculate this, we find that just 0.012% of the genetic difference is pertinent to racial differences (Green, 2005). In fact, as critical race theorist Ian Haney Lopez (2000) states,

> There are no genetic characteristics possessed by all Blacks but not by non-Blacks; similarly, there is no gene or cluster of genes common to all Whites but not to non-Whites . . . greater genetic variation exists within the populations typically labeled Black and White than between these populations. (p. 166)

Modern genetic science, therefore, does not support the existence of race as a biological category. Scientists and scholars over the last few hundred years have nevertheless attempted to categorize and class groups of people on some kind of biological basis. Agreement among scholars is hard to find, even on the names of different races (Atkinson et al., 1993), let alone on just what the biological differences among them are.

> Linnaeus had found four human races; Blumenbach had five; Cuvier had three; John Hunter had seven; Burke had sixty-three; Pickering had eleven; Virey had two "species," each containing three races; Haeckel had thirty-six; Huxley had four; Topinard had nineteen under three headings; Desmoulins had sixteen "species"; Deniker had seventeen races and thirty types. (Gossett, 1963, p. 82)

Over the last thousand years, there has been even greater variation in human characteristics such as blood type, hair texture, skin color, and body type than there was in previous times. There is dramatic variation in physical characteristics within so-called racial groups. As we have suggested, the genetic variation is so tiny between persons that it can be greater among individuals within a racial group than it is between individuals belonging to different racial groups (Atkinson et al., 1993; Cornell & Hartmann, 1998; Ponterotto & Pedersen, 1993).

Figure 4.2   Five generations of Courtnay Oatts Mohammed's family, which is of African American ancestry (Courtnay is second from left). This photograph illustrates great variation in skin tone. Darker skin color is not always reflective of a black or African American identity. Courtnay identifies herself as a member of a "slave culture."

The problem with racial categorization is that the underlying assumptions on which it was built are not scientific at all. Efforts to distinguish and then categorize differences among human beings based on biological makeup are, in fact, founded on the European colonizing discourse of white superiority rather than on empirical biological data. Scientific efforts to define different races were directed toward legitimating the dominant discourse of the day. Of course, there are a few obvious physiological differences among peoples of different genetic stock, but skin color is only one aspect of genetic difference. Race discourse blows it way out of proportion. The idea of systematic, inherited, distinct biological differences just cannot be made to hold up. Janet Helms (1994) calls it "irrational" (p. 295). Historian Barbara Fields has summed up the current scientific consensus on race in this way:

> Anyone who continues to believe in race as a physical attribute of individuals, despite the now commonplace disclaimers of biologists and geneticists, might as well also believe that Santa Claus, the Easter Bunny and the tooth fairy are real, and that the earth stands still while the sun moves. (cited by Lopez, 2000, p. 167)

And yet the biological concept of race, scientifically flimsy as it is, continues to persist. Not only do notions of race continue to be alive and well in our communities, but the factor of race is intimately involved in shaping the relationship between client and counselor. For instance, some multiculturalists advocate racial matching between client and counselor to maximize cultural empathy between the two. There are significant issues of trust that arise on the foundation of racial difference that need to be worked through for effective counseling to occur. A black client may have significant concerns about trusting a white therapist because of the historical legacy of European colonization that we have described. Therefore, if race is not a biological category, we need to focus more on the social process of categorization.

What Has Been the Social Function of the Term *Race*?

Whether or not the concept of race corresponds with any real biological differences other than at the level of the epidermis, we know that it has real effects through its social consequences. It is in practice a sociopolitical construct rather than a biological one (Helms, 1994; Ponterotto & Pedersen, 1993). Race has served as a major dividing tool among people throughout most of the colonized world, but perhaps more powerfully in the United States than in most other places. Ascriptions of race have been used to mark people out for entry into privileged opportunity or to limit their access to such opportunity. On the basis of racial divisions, the social practices of discrimination have been, and in many instances continue to be, legitimated.

Race is not the only dividing tool, however. There are others based on religion, language, social class, and gender, for example. In some contexts, race is not even the most salient dividing line. Northern Ireland is an example. It is a territory colonized about 400 years ago by the English, and the division between the colonizers and the colonized has been marked on the basis of the Catholic/Protestant religious divide more than on a concept of race. The point is that while race has frequently been marked out as the basis for social division in ways that lead to oppressive practices, it has not been the only basis. Within England itself, although dividing practices built on race are of growing importance, markers of social class, such as accent, have been traditionally more strongly employed in the dividing practices that exclude groups of people from access to opportunity.

Throughout the Americas, Africa, Asia, and the Pacific, however, race has usually served as the prime marker for social division. This is not to say that many of the efforts to blur or remove the race divide have not achieved considerable success. Despite all these efforts, however, it remains in our consciousness. We still frequently notice race and are aware of it, rather than finding that it has slipped back into the background of our thinking. It remains a salient category of thought in our daily lives—for example, in the forms that we fill out for a hundred purposes. Try to fill out the form in Box 4.1 and discuss its implications.

Box 4.1. Please Fill Out This Form

Name:

Gender:
- ☐ Male
- ☐ Female

Age:
- ☐ 0-15 years
- ☐ 15-25 years
- ☐ 25-35 years
- ☐ 35-45 years
- ☐ 45-55 years
- ☐ over 55 years

Race (choose one):
- ☐ Caucasian
- ☐ African American
- ☐ Hispanic
- ☐ Asian or Pacific Islander
- ☐ Native American

Nationality (choose one):
- ☐ American citizen
- ☐ Foreign-born U.S. resident
- ☐ Legal alien

Ethnicity (choose one):
- ☐ European
- ☐ Latino
- ☐ African American
- ☐ Native American
- ☐ Jewish
- ☐ Arab
- ☐ East Indian
- ☐ Chinese
- ☐ Japanese
- ☐ Other (please specify): _____

Income (Estimate your yearly household income. Include your spouse's income):
- ☐ $0-$15,000
- ☐ $15,000-$25,000
- ☐ $25,000-$40,000
- ☐ $40,000-$60,000
- ☐ $60,000-$80,000
- ☐ Over $80,000

TO DISCUSS

1. What was your internal experience while filling out this form? What internal debates did you have to settle in order to choose an answer? What difficulties did you encounter?

2. At which points did you find yourself making a forced choice?

3. What aspects of your experience of life or identity were excluded from visibility through the construction of this form?

4. Who else can you think of whose preferred identities might not fit with the identity categories listed in this form?

5. Speculate on the reasons that the categories used on this form are there. What perspective do they represent?

6. In what sense might data collected from this form be objective or not objective?

7. Where have you been asked to fill out forms like this? What experiences have you had in doing so?

Skin color and other physical characteristics get selected out and tend to obscure an emphasis on cultural distinctions because of race's assumed biological authority. But how are race categories decided upon? The physiological differences that serve as racial markers change according to which cultural constructions are dominant. Defining the boundary between one race and another is more complicated than most people think. In fact, there are no consistent differences among racial groupings. People whose physical characteristics are at the borders or margins of the group are often made into new races.

In the 19th century, the preacher Clare Herbert Woolston wrote the well-known Sunday school song that imprinted one set of racial categories into the general discourse:

> *Jesus loves the little children*
> *All the children of the world*
> *Red and yellow, black and white*
> *All are precious in his sight*
> *Jesus loves the little children of the world*

However, even the words of this song have not remained consistent. Later versions added "brown" to the list.

We might expect the official discourse of government to be more stable, but even here the categories and boundaries are constantly being revised. In 1970, the United States government listed five races in the United States: "White, Colored (Blacks), Colored (Mulattoes), Chinese and Indian. . . . In 1950, the census categories reflected a different social understanding: White, Black, and other" (Spickard, 1992, p. 18). In the 1990s, federal programs, responding to challenges from groups having nothing to do with biological theory, required various community structures to report racial data in five categories again, although by now they had changed the categories to White, Black, Asian, Hispanic, and Indian (Cornell & Hartmann, 1998).

The Hispanic category arose only as a result of political developments and has been used to include people of many different nationalities, ethnicities, and cultural traditions without any consistent physical markers (Birman, 1994). However, it is still primarily focused on immigrants to the United States from Mexico. In the early 1800s, Mexican people were variously categorized as White, Indian, Black, or Asian (Lopez, 2000). When Mexico gained independence in 1821, its citizens were not thought of as a race. As the Anglo-Mexican battles over territory intensified in the 19th century, Mexicans were considered a mixed race (a mixture of white and Indian "blood") and later were explicitly designated as a distinct race (Hispanic) in their own right. Many people who are now classified racially as Hispanic share physical characteristics that are indistinguishable from those classified as white (Cornell & Hartmann, 1998).

The category of Asian is in fact such a catchall that there are no physical features that apply to all people whose ancestry hails from places like Iran, India, China, and Japan. Pacific Islanders are lumped in with Asians despite the vast differences between people from China and people from Polynesia. The determination of which characteristics constitute race is of course a selection of physical characteristics chosen to be salient at a particular point in history. But the determination of salience is not predetermined by biological factors. The categories appear to change not so much in response to the characteristics of the people they categorize as in response to the dominant discourse of the day.

Associated with the concept of race is the concept of "blood," which originated in the completely fallacious idea that racial differences are the product of differences in the blood that courses through the veins of people. This hypothesis has long since been dropped, but the metaphor remains in usages like "full blooded," "half blooded," and so forth. It has even been used in the United States Supreme Court as recently as 1991. In that year, Justice Antonin Scalia rejected a claim in favor of minority broadcasting licenses by charging that the policy "reduced to a matter of blood . . . blood not background and environment" (cited by Lopez, 2000, p. 168).

"Blood" is still used to describe interracial progeny. Seyla Benhabib (2002) points out, however, that it has been used differentially in the United States. The idea of "mixed blood" is little used in reference to people whose ancestors all had the same skin color. Ask yourself if you have ever heard of a person whose parents were, say Anglo and German, being thought of as half blooded. But the minute the black/white skin divide is crossed, the concept seems to come into play. Historically, the "one drop of blood" rule meant that a person was defined as African American or Native American if she had one ancestor among eight who qualified, even if all her other ancestors were white (Helms, 1994). But the reverse did not apply. One drop of white blood did not qualify a person as white.

Here are two examples showing racial categories to be historical social constructions. Virginia Dominguez (1986) describes a well-known case in which a Louisiana woman went to court to dispute the state's conclusion that she was black. She claimed her ancestry was white. The state's argument was that her ancestry was at least 1/32 "Negro," which, according to state law, meant she was black. This woman lost her case because of the one-drop rule (Davis, 1991). These rules have a history. They emerge in particular historical contexts—in this case, the history of slavery in the United States. It is interesting to reflect on the notion that being 1/32 Dutch, Irish, or Japanese does not mean belonging to that grouping, but one drop of black blood has long been considered sufficient for racial categorization. Since the era of the civil rights movement in the United States, many individuals with "1/32 black blood" proudly identify as black (Cornell & Hartmann, 1998). However, such people are often queried about their membership in this category because they are perceived by others who have darker skin pigmentation to benefit from a lighter skin and are thus deemed to not really know or feel the systemic effects of oppression felt by darker-skinned people. Racial categories change over time as they are revised, contested, interpreted, and reinterpreted.

Societies such as the United States pour substantial resources into policing the boundaries of racial groupings, and the outcomes of classification have significant consequences for the individuals involved. An illustration of this occurred in 1922, when Takao Ozawa applied for United States citizenship (Lopez, 2000). In accordance with the Naturalization Act, he asserted that he was white because, born in the northern part of Japan, his skin was as white as most Europeans'. The Supreme Court rejected his claim and in their ruling stated that race could not be defined by "mere color of the skin" (p. 167); otherwise, it would have to exclude from the category of white many Europeans of swarthy complexion. Even the common assumption of skin color as a racial designator can be set aside when it suits the purposes of governing authorities. This paradox (that skin color is sometimes and sometimes not the primary indicator of one's race) gets played out increasingly in our contemporary, globalized world. In our classrooms, we frequently hear conversations and debates about the supposed legitimacy of a person's self-proclaimed race. Consider, for example, the student who is challenged about the amount of "blackness" he possesses, given his biracial genealogy and light skin.

Brazil, because of greater intermarriage among different peoples with different physical characteristics, has officially given up on the notion of distinct races. Overlapping categories have been established that recognize the various mixtures, usually based on a person's appearance but relating to skin color from lightest to darkest. However, the legacy of European colonization continues to play a prominent role in Western society, promoting the definition of the relative merits of a people's status based on how close their skin pigment is to white. Think of all the television shows broadcast from Latino countries in which the majority of citizens have bronze or dark skin, and yet the popular television characters are almost always very light skinned and the maids and servants are typically darker skinned.

Racial categories are always relational (Lopez, 2000). They exist only as points of distinction from other races. The category *black* relies on the assumption of what *white* means in order to make sense, and vice versa. These categories of difference were originally produced in relation to the politics of conquest, colonization, and subjugation. As these politics have shifted and changed and new forms of distinction have become required for the purpose of ongoing subjugation, the racial categories have shifted and changed with them.

Henderikus Stam (1998) states that Brazil's complicated racial categories based on skin pigment do not match other racial typologies. Francis Deng (1997) points out how the South African apartheid system's *black*, *white*, and *colored* categories were different from those of other colonizing classification systems. Koreans and Japanese regard each other as belonging to different races, even though these two peoples are perceived by outsiders to have similar phenotypic characteristics. Within Brazil, the socioeconomic status of an individual frequently affects her racial category.

It is heartening to see that some geneticists consider race to be culturally determined. James King (1981) comments that within the British colonial framework, skin color, hair type, stature, facial structure, and other bodily features became physical markers that identified the limits of group boundaries. Categories were invented according to phenotype but appear to have no inherent meaning. They were endowed with particular cultural meanings that became the basis for how we conduct our relations with others, and in that sense they seemed to become real and true.

What Are the Effects of the Construction of Race?

Race is institutionalized into American culture, and significant levels of human social interaction take place around race. In fact, race is a central organizing principle in most modern nations. The racial category *white* is a highly privileged status in most Western countries, while the racial category *black* generally describes a less privileged status. The great German sociologist Max Weber, when he visited the United States in 1904, was struck by the intensity with which black Americans, more than Native Americans, were objects to be despised (Stone, 2003).

As Stephen Cornell and Douglas Hartmann (1998) outline, "race has been first and foremost a way of describing others, of making clear that they are not us" (p. 27). The purpose is usually to create populations of people who can be governed and managed. Racial designation is always linked to practices of power. Michel Foucault (2000) identifies the designation of people into "populations" as a technological invention in the modern world to make the governing of people's lives easier. Racial categorization serves to distinguish "us" from "them." Mainstream cultural assumptions held by large groups of people do not like to allow movement across racial divides. For example, David Hollinger (1995) points out that "a Cambodian American does not have to remain Cambodian, as far as non-Asian Americans are concerned, but only with great difficulty can this person cease to be an Asian American" (p. 28).

The power that derives from racial categorizing can go both ways. Today, racial categories are used not only for oppressive purposes or to further the cause of a European colonizing agenda. Many state, federal, and private institutions in the United States track people by racial categories. Some of these institutions use racial dividing practices to identify when services are not being provided to specific racial groups and when the government is being successful in catering to a particular group's needs. For example, in education, authorities can track whether the educational needs of African American, Filipino, Latino, and other groups of students are served in the public education system. When a group's needs are not being responded to, advocate groups can use statistics based on racial categorizations to point out to politicians and decision makers the failure of particular practices and campaign for increased resources. Statistics of this kind are used to track many issues in North American society. For example, statistics are gathered on specific racial groups in the domains of mental health, criminal justice, housing, and employment with a view toward resource allocation to promote equity and social justice.

In the last few years in California, many people from majority culture have wanted to change the way that California collects statistics and have promoted doing away with racial categories. The defenders of racial equity and social justice have come out in strong support for keeping racial categorizations intact, recognizing the leverage that can be gained to attract state, federal, and private resources. Advocates for policies of affirmative action in education and the workplace are dependent on the maintenance of racial categorization. These are examples of employing decolonizing moves to systematically undo the injustices perpetrated against groupings of people who have historically suffered the discriminating effects of European colonization.

In Native American communities that have access to casinos, tribal authorities carefully monitor blood ties to determine the level of access tribal members have to the significant financial resources produced by gambling. While these uses of the concept of race are aimed at helping people who are disadvantaged by the very distinctions that historically have been made on this basis, these processes of gathering and keeping statistics also help ensure that the categories of social division remain in place.

The History of White Identity in the United States

During the era of British colonization, colonizing groups created the justifying assumption that human groups are inherently different and that these differences constitute natural physical, moral, and religious hierarchies. Being at the top of the hierarchy legitimated using those at the bottom of the hierarchy as a resource to be exploited. Interwoven with hierarchy is the insidious and widely held belief that some races are inherently more intelligent than others and that those at the bottom of the hierarchy have reached a lower stage of human evolution. All social groups, including those constructed by the identity "race," can make their own hierarchies. However, over the last 400 years, it has been white racial groups who have had the power in the United States to create racial categories that organize the institutions and social relations to which we are obliged to conform.

From a colonizing perspective, whites generally represent what is normal while others are "them" and not "us." Ruth Frankenberg (1993) notes that "the White Western self as a racial being has for the most part remained unexamined and unnamed" (p. 17). That is why it is so common for students who come from an Anglo American heritage to report that they don't identify as belonging to a race or don't have a distinct culture. Whiteness conforms so much to the characteristics of dominant modern culture that it is difficult for whites to distinguish their lives as belonging to a racial group or to have the words to name the way they live their lives as a culture. Failure to register whiteness as a racial category is sometimes assumed to result from an individual lack of awareness, but we would argue that it is more a product of shared discourse than it is of individual consciousness. This point has implications for the multicultural counseling movement and those who advocate self-discovery and self-awareness as the foundation for multicultural competency. That is, there are real, material limits to how much self-understanding can be accomplished (and thus how much multicultural competency can be achieved) within the larger cultural background dominated by a narrow, privileged perspective.

There has been an interesting shift in what we could term the racialization of whites (Cornell & Hartmann, 1998). In the United States, not only were nonwhite categories established, but the category *white* was assigned to certain persons. A distinct set of statuses followed. In the early history of the United States, English, Dutch, and a few others shared the white category. The Irish, Italians, and some Jews were not classified as white. In fact, the Irish, even though they had the same skin pigment as the English, were regarded as a distinctly inferior race. Michael Hechter (1975) quotes a Cambridge University historian's description of the Irish about 200 years ago:

I am haunted by the human chimpanzees I saw. . . . [To] see white chimpanzees is dreadful; if they were black, one would not feel it so much, but their skins except where tanned by exposure, are as white as ours. (p. xvi)

At this time, the Irish were assigned to a nonwhite category. Heather's story of her family's early history clearly illustrates the attitudes of the time.

Growing up, I remember stories of the oppression that my descendants faced on their arrival in America. Dates and generations seem to have been lost; however, the oral tradition of our family's oppression still remains. When my ex-stepfather's Irish descendants stepped off the ship on which they had traveled over, they changed their surname to a slightly less Irish-sounding name—from McNeelis to McNellis. The reason my ancestors had to change their name was the oppression that Irish immigrants received in terms of employment in America. Although my ancestors looked much like the white Americans they encountered, they were singled out and discriminated against if they spoke with too thick an accent, or had a last name which sounded too "foreign." Immigrants were forced to assimilate as fast as possible, sometimes dropping all of their traditional values and customs as well as their last names, in order to make it in America. My ancestors shunned their cultures and assimilated to the American way of life to survive and flourish in America.

The Irish side of Sarah's family faced similar challenges.

My great, great grandfather was black Irish Catholic. This meant that he had an olive skin tone and wavy black hair. He therefore did not fit the mainstream European look. Coming to escape the potato famine, my Irish grandfather was not as welcome as my Scottish ancestors. A large part of this had to do with his being not only Irish, but Irish Catholic. Many Irish immigrants were forced to do jobs that Anglo Americans were not willing to do, like digging canals and working on the railroads. The strong Protestant beliefs in the United States meant that the Irish way of life was not warmly accepted. Having an Irish accent was difficult for immigrants from Ireland, especially since the Anglo population looked down on them.

This was later to change. This example again shows the socially constructed nature of race and how categories can shift. In different periods in American history, whiteness has included some other groups who have, for a short period, been embraced as white and then shortly after been recast as nonwhite. Briefly, some Native Americans and later Latinos were included under a "white" umbrella.

Sarah Johnson identifies with her Irish ancestry.

Is *Ethnicity* a Better Term Than *Race*?

Racial classification assumes that pure phenotypes exist. This premise cannot be proven even if one accepts the conjecture that pure phenotypes existed at some point in history. Ethnicity, as we understand it in the modern world, is a much more recent term. It developed its current meanings around the middle of the 20th century through the work done by anthropologists. Originally a Greek term for Gentiles, it derives from the noun *ethnos*, meaning "foreign people." For many centuries, the term *ethnic* in English meant "heathen." The general consensus now is that ethnicity does not refer to physical characteristics as much as the term *race* does, although there is some overlap. Ethnicity is a group identity based on a common history, a shared set of cultural symbols (which usually means a shared language), and sometimes shared nationality, tribal affiliation, and religious faith. Its historical markers are more identifiable and tangible than those associated with race. Whereas racial groups are considered to be few, there are hundreds or thousands of possible ethnicities.

Max Weber defines ethnic groups as "human groups (other than kinship groups) which cherish a belief in their common origins of such a kind that it provides a basis for the formation of a community" (cited by Stone, 2003, p. 32).

Notice the emphasis here on what we might call discourse in this definition. Weber sidesteps an essentialist definition of ethnicity and privileges the role of *belief* in common origins rather than the role of those origins themselves.

Like race, ethnic identity produces social boundaries that define how people distinguish themselves from others. The boundaries, however, are much more porous and complex. As with race, a particular ethnic membership has meaning only within a social context in which individuals can contrast themselves with others to produce a "them" and an "us." In the United States, many people use the word *ethnic* to describe a minority population that is different from the dominant culture. For instance, "ethnic foods" are non-European cuisine. The expression "That's really ethnic" is used to describe something unique or exotic and not found in European American middle class culture.

However, ethnicity is not really encompassed by these colloquial uses. As a categorizing label, ethnicity is not tied as closely as race is to physical markers. A shared ethnicity is more of a fluid association and is less essentializing than the category of race. It is also not tied to the fallacious analogy of blood. Neither does it make any sense to calculate percentages of ethnicity. When communities generate their own categories on the basis of particular collective histories, they are engaged in the production of an ethnicity (Cornell & Hartmann, 1998).

Another distinction between race and ethnicity is which people have the power to name the categories. A shared ethnicity is not just assigned and defined by an outside group. Belonging is typically named and asserted by group members themselves on the basis of shared experiences. Over the last 300 years in the United States, it has been only Anglo American people who have assigned themselves the role of constructing racial categories for their own purposes. When categorizations that accompany race are invoked, assumptions about biological inferiority or superiority are immediately drawn. All ethnic groups are certainly capable of believing they are superior to others, but the reference point is not biological inferiority or superiority as it is with race. Thus, the moral force of the categories *ethnicity* and *race* operate at different degrees of magnitude. This is why, when a person of color utters a racial slur against another group, it might be racist but does not mean the same thing as it does when a white person utters it, since it does not have the force of the history of racial categorization behind it.

The anthropologist Ashley Montagu (1962) presents an argument for choosing to use the concept of ethnicity instead of the concept of race:

> The term "race" takes for granted what should be a matter for inquiry. And this is precisely the point that is raised when one uses the noncommittal "ethnic group." It encourages the passage from ignorant or confused certainty to thoughtful uncertainty. For the layman, as for others, the term "race" closes the door on understanding. The phrase "ethnic group" opens it, or at the very least, leaves it ajar. (p. 926)

His argument is supported in a recent anthropological review of the concepts of race and ethnicity by Michael Billinger (2007).

While race is the fundamental organizing dimension in most of the colonized world, it is not so in all countries and continents. For example, in Belgium, ethnicity has overshadowed race as a basis for categorizing people. In Canada, French-speaking Quebec places greater weight on a French Canadian linguistically based ethnicity than it does on racial categorization. The concept of the Polynesian race refers to the genetic similarities of many people around the Pacific. But the ethnicity of these peoples is much more diverse and is divided into Hawaiian, Tongan, Samoan, Cook Islander, Tahitian, Maori, and the like (Cornell & Hartmann, 1998).

The terms *race* and *ethnicity* are not mutually exclusive. For example, many American blacks have come to adopt both race and ethnicity to define themselves. They identify themselves as a distinct race by color and bodily features. While using a classification system devised by 16th century Europeans, many blacks have embraced the physical markers as defining characteristics of their group and are redefining race by attempting to remove it from its historical associations with inferiority and superiority. Many blacks who are confronted with historical and day-to-day discrimination based on physical markers embrace these markers as points of shared oppression. Joining together around a history of shared oppression has provided a powerful impetus to build resilience and strength. In addition to identifying themselves as belonging to a race, many blacks embrace a common ethnicity as a self-conscious population who share a homeland, a history dominated by slavery, a religion, and a language.

Categorizations based on physical markers continue to dominate the way our global society operates. Many blacks and people of color continue to be systematically disadvantaged when it comes to jobs, social resources, and political sway. These factors have a huge impact on how problems for which people seek counseling are created. To not acknowledge the significance of race and ethnicity in shaping client problems and in raising important challenges for counselor effectiveness would be to neglect essential counseling dynamics. Most multicultural counseling texts comment on race and ethnicity as central domains to address when they suggest that counselors must be multiculturally competent. The colonizing code that directs many whites to treat blacks and other people of color as inferior continues in covert and overt ways across the globe. Unfortunately, focusing on the construct of race, in our view, maintains essentializing and static categories and keeps our attention on physical markers as the primary site of dividing practices in a multicultural society. The problem with the construct of race for counselors is that it can seduce them into believing in stereotypical, unitary conceptions of who and what a white person is, who a black person is, or who an Asian person is, and thus lead them into simplistic therapeutic directions.

Therefore, we prefer the term *ethnicity*, which, by definition, acknowledges more directly the constructed and fluid nature of human organization while at the same time acknowledging the defining power of physical markers in a person's identity. The term *race* is associated with colonization and is produced out of a colonizing analysis of characteristics of human beings, while the term *ethnicity* does not have such a problematic legacy. Ethnicity more consciously groups human beings by historical events and collective meaning making. Race, while constructed by these same social processes, is understood by many to be natural and inherent. Ethnicity acknowledges more the construction, reproduction, and transformation of social identity, a concept congruent with postmodern thought. As Richard Jenkins (2003) observes, race is more a category to which people are assigned without choice, while ethnicity is a group of people who usually have some degree of choice about their own belonging.

On the other hand, the concept of race cannot just be wished away. It is a highly problematic concept, but it exists in the general discourse and everyone acts daily on the basis of shared assumptions of what it means. Race still has official authority behind it, too. Power relations are constructed on the basis of these assumptions, and these power relations have very real material effects on people's lives. In this sense, the notion of race is by no means illusory. It produces an all-too-real impact on people's lives. Even though it is a social category ascribed from the outside, it becomes internalized into strongly felt identities (Jenkins, 2003). Therefore, we do have to engage with it. But we can best engage with it as a politically charged social construct that can be contested, rather than as a straightforward biological reality. And we can choose to use the term *ethnicity* where it seems to more accurately and respectfully refer to the cultural differences that groups of people themselves regard as salient.

One of the other difficulties with the concept of race is that through evolution and interracial unions, new generations have physical markers different from those of earlier generations. With greater levels of intermarriage and the changing phenotypic shapes of human beings around the globe, it is becoming more and more difficult to police the boundaries where one race begins and another ends. As a result, it is also more difficult for people to embrace race as a criterion for social division. Decolonizing movements in opposition to racist practices have also made it more difficult to sustain as a dividing line.

Some American blacks struggle with determining whether someone deserves to be considered black if his skin color is too light, his hair is not kinky enough, or his eyes are not brown. Conversely, some individuals self-identify as white but have a skin color that is darker than that of many who identify as black. There is also an emerging challenge to the view of race as something fixed, natural, and inherent in the growing numbers of children whose parents form combinations such as Samoan-Chinese, Portuguese-Filipino, and Korean–African American. As growing numbers of people claim multiracial or multiethnic identities, to what extent will federal racial categories hold up? Currently, if a black woman and an Anglo American man bear a child, the child will be considered black. American society still largely employs the one-drop rule, where if you have any black ancestry you are automatically black. It is more difficult to predict what racial classification will be used when Anglo American–Native American or Asian–Anglo American couples bear children (Cornell & Hartmann, 1998).

Ethnicity and Context

Context and situation play a very big part in the ethnicity and identity people present to others. For example, in New Zealand, the indigenous people belong to various tribal identities. When the Ngapuhi and Tainui tribes meet, they engage in ritual greetings that honor the traditions and ancestors of each of those tribal communities. Tribal organization and tribal customs and practices take precedence. However, when these two tribes are threatened by some political or economic action instigated by the dominant Pakeha (white) ethnic group, they invoke their ethnicity as Maori. They will join to identify themselves as the *Tangata Whenua*, or first indigenous people of the land. This contextual organization and situational change of ethnicity doesn't happen at just the community level. It often takes place within extended families. The promotion of one identity and the submergence of another is dependent on a number of factors. For example, when Belen is with her Mexican community, she identifies with that ethnic group and participates in the Cinco de Mayo celebrations. When she travels to Flagstaff to be with her Indian side of the family for Native Heritage Month, she participates fully in Diné drumming and dance activities. Paul Spickard and Rowena Fong (1995) describe a similar scenario with a young woman who lives multiple ethnicities in Hawaii:

> If I am with my grandmother I'm Portuguese. If I'm with some of my aunts on my dad's side I'm Filipino. If I'm hanging around, I'm just local. If I'm on the mainland I'm Hawaiian. (p. 1370)

Due to increased rates of movement, migration, and interethnic marriage, ethnic boundaries can become less obvious, less compelling, and more difficult to maintain. When people are living with multiple ethnicities and multiple heritages, what starts to matter more is not the boundaries that separate one group from another but the sites within these ethnic domains where they will find acceptance. Paul Spickard and Rowena Fong (1995) suggest that when the boundaries around ethnic definition become more permeable, what might matter more will be the potential connections between ethnicities. Boundary policing based on historical orientations to past abuses and violations will then diminish.

Stephen Cornell and Douglas Hartmann (1998) envisage one possible future scenario as a result of patterns of global migration in which there will be fewer identifiable ethnicities but more multiethnic individuals. They suggest that brothers and sisters will share combinations, but "each combination will last only a generation before some other set of ancestries joins in to produce offspring whose ethnic lineages are more complicated still" (p. 245).

The fluid and complex quality of ethnicity reminds counselors that they cannot always assume that a person has one particular ethnicity. Counselors and therapists need to be respectful of and curious about the meaning making systems with which *every* client is engaged. Ethnic understanding is vital to successful and effective counseling, but it is impossible to know by looking at people, or by hearing or viewing a label that describes an ethnicity, what these important defining characteristics might be. Only through conversation can these characteristics be understood. Because of the fluid and dynamic quality of ethnic membership, one cannot even assume that all the members of the same family will share the same identities or ethnic categories. In all counseling interactions, open curiosity and naive inquiry are essential to understanding the complexity of a client's multiple identities and ethnic histories and the client's construction of her various problems. What's more, multiple ethnic sources of identity can provide clients with a richer resource bank for use in overcoming problems.

Just as it may be possible for ethnic boundaries to become more permeable and dynamic, it is also possible for ethnic boundaries to harden. There is every prospect that racial categories will continue and thus permit the alienation, separation, and conflict that are founded on these socially constructed barriers. These dynamics play out in very different ways in popular culture and in the media.

Ishmael Reed (1989) talks about the well-publicized book and movie *Roots*, in which Alex Haley (1996) traces his genealogy for many generations on his mother's side through the period of slavery and finally back to Gambia in Africa. Reed comments that if Alex Haley had followed his father's ancestry, he would have traveled back 12 generations and ended up not in Gambia but in Ireland. The historian David Hollinger (1995) points out that Haley never had any real option to place any weight on his father's bloodline. American social conventions classify him as black, and his white, Irish ethnic heritage is perceived as unimportant. Haley could hardly choose his Irish heritage, as he would be crossing a racial divide and would be perceived to be siding with those historically responsible for the oppression of his mother's bloodline.

Constructing Ethnic Identities

There is good evidence to suggest that the more one possesses physical features of the majority white cultures, the more choice one has to inhabit, experiment with, and claim a variety of ethnicities and identities. The farther removed one's physical characteristics are from white, Anglo American facial features, such as a white complexion, straight or wavy hair, almond-shaped eyes, a pointed nose, and certain chiseled features, the less one can claim an ethnicity unaffected by racial classification.

To illustrate, we shall use an example from New Zealand, which has been just as influenced by European colonizing values as has North America. A Pakeha, or white, mother adopted Karen, who had physical features that were Maori, including the classic Polynesian brown skin, brown eyes, and black wavy hair. The child was not exposed to any Maori or Polynesian people, nor did she have any knowledge of Polynesian history or ethnic ancestry. Karen did not eat the traditional foods, know the popular Polynesian music forms, or learn the linguistic subtleties of Maori communication styles. Karen was very confident in a middle class English register. When she was nine, Karen's white peer group began to communicate to her that she no longer belonged with them because she was Maori. The child had no conception of what it was to be Maori. By the time she was 14, her peer group was Maori. To gain membership as Maori, she had to learn all of the significant cultural meanings of this peer group. Since she looked like them, the assumption was that she belonged to the Maori group.

Karen clearly had limits imposed on her as far as the ethnic reference group she was allowed to belong to. Most often, middle class whites have genuine ethnic identity choices. They can choose to be Irish or Italian, French or Polish. They can choose cultural identities pertaining to religion, urban versus rural orientation, and even class. A gay or lesbian person can decide to come out or not. A person with an accent that distinguishes him as, say, lower class can sometimes change his accent to show that he belongs to a higher class. However, bodily markers and the dominant meanings that accompany them cannot be so easily changed.

Many Asian, Latino, and Native American communities, but much more obviously black communities, have fewer ethnic options because of dominant cultural assumptions formed around physical markers. These markers make it difficult for people with nonwhite physical features to embrace their forebears' Italian or Irish ethnic heritage. Of course, the same can occur for those that look white but wish to claim a heritage that includes slavery and an African ancestry. Yet the consequences for white-skinned individuals wishing to identify as black are very different from those of black-skinned individuals wishing to identify as white (Cornell & Hartmann, 1998).

Natasha reminds us of the contemporary versions of racism in the United States.

Throughout my life I've heard many blacks say, "I'd rather live in the South than in the North. At least you know where you stand." The South has a history of overt, in-your-face racism. If people are going to discriminate against me because of skin color, I know it. It's apparent in their attitudes, actions, and words. There is no question about it when you encounter it. In the North, however, there is a history of subtle racism. It will come out in racial proofing, hiring practices, being passed up for promotions, and unfair housing practices. You'll just be told, "There are no more apartments available," not, "We don't allow_____ [fill in the blank] to live here." I have to constantly question whether someone's actions against me are racist, or whether the person is just being rude. I become hypersensitive, dare I say paranoid. When it's overt, you know how to avoid it, what neighborhood not to go in. When it is subtle, I am forced to live a life of wonder: Was that a racist act? Did I just get discriminated against? It would be nice if the options were (a) overt racism, (b) subtle racism, or (c) no racism. I know which one I would choose.

Veronica talks about some painful recollections in her own family.

In my family we African Americans favored narrower noses, big lips, neutral eyes, and being tall and skinny. Having lighter skin was also favored. The darker the skin that people had, the more unfavored they were. Darker-skinned people did not get paid as much as the lighter-skinned people. In the 1960s, it was known that the lighter, the better.

My father (Don) had darker skin than his sisters and he was not shown favor. Jacqueline, among other relatives, did not favor Don because of his skin color, and he was aware of it. Jacqueline would take Bruce and Frank out to different places and leave Don at home. My mom told me that Don knew he could not go out with his mom, because he had picked up the fact that he had darker skin and his mom told him that he was too dark. My father tried to commit suicide because of the way everyone was treating him on account of his skin color. I had never known Don had tried to do such a thing. I knew he had a hard life growing up, especially with racism being so well known to him. I hate that skin color is such a big deal to people.

> Some of the stereotypes that Don believes others have of African Americans are that they have big noses, are lazy, and are not smart. Some stereotypes that Don said he had of African Americans, which is an example of turning racism on ourselves, are that they eat fried chicken and that the women are overweight.

According to American colonization, the physical features (such as eye shape, stature, and hair) of whites are deemed superior to those of Asians. Since skin color has been enlisted as a powerful dividing practice for 400 years, it is not surprising that ethnicities form around the privileges associated with being white and the oppressive experiences associated with being black or yellow. We are slowly working out the consequences of this history, but it will probably take much longer for it to be consigned to distant history.

Some ethnic groups strategically use the essentializing of ethnic bonds as a basis for organization and purposeful action. Originally, the markers of race and ethnicity were used by the colonizers to identify, separate, organize, and subordinate groups. In the last few decades, some ethnic groups have essentialized and reproduced the rigid boundaries of the colonizing cultures to build a base for struggle and empowerment. The Maori in New Zealand are a good example of this. The move by disadvantaged groups to wholeheartedly endorse race as a meaningful construction has been largely fueled by ongoing disparities of status, wealth, and well-being.

As Stephen Cornell and Douglas Hartmann (1998) suggest,

> there is little inherently good or bad about ethnicity and race. . . . What makes them significant is what human beings do to them. . . . The critical issue for the 21st century is not whether ethnicity and race will continue to serve as categories of collective identity but what kinds of ethnic and racial stories groups tell and how these stories are put to use. (p. 252)

Counseling Implications of Race and Ethnicity

"Why can't we just treat everyone as a human being? Why not just treat everyone equally, and surely the problems of race will disappear!" This cry is not infrequently heard from many counselors (usually white). Nor is it very surprising. Many counselors want to believe that all human beings start on an equal footing and have the same life chances. They are supported in this assumption by the dominant ideology in all modern Western economies, which endorses and supports the practices of universalism and individualism. This ideology is built into the legal system, the organization of capitalism, and into political systems.

One corollary of this ideology is that if people are not thriving, it is assumed that there is something wrong with them as individuals. Such a person must possess some dysfunctional personality trait, such as laziness, idleness, or lack of motivation. On the basis of these assumptions, widespread attitudes are built that either deny or completely underestimate the impact of powerful sociohistorical factors at work. Denial of the power of present-day colonizing practices protects those who are beneficiaries of the dominant discourse from confronting it in their counseling practice.

Counseling diagnostic practices that alert counselors to look first at the intrapsychic processes of the client to the exclusion of cultural and contextual factors will always risk blaming clients for their difficulties and problems. Some clients who are suffering from problems in gaining access to quality housing, adequate education, and basic health care, not to mention sustainable employment, may be struggling because of systemic inequities in the community in which they live. Clients subjected to these inequities may easily be invited to internalize their suffering and blame themselves for their plight. They may feel ashamed of the way they are living and direct their energies into self-loathing, depression, and despair. They may be convinced that their problems result from personal lack of assertiveness, irrational thinking, or negative feelings about themselves as individuals.

On the other hand, other clients in this same situation may direct their frustration, outrage, and anger outside of themselves onto members of their family, or onto community representatives such as teachers, police, health care workers, and the like. A counselor or therapist can be an easy target for the client's outrage, particularly if the client is a person of color and the therapist is white. White therapists must be particularly careful to locate the causes of depression, self-hatred, anger, and violence in a wider sociohistorical context, rather than simply attributing these troubles to personal deficits inside people. The white therapist can come to represent for some people of color a modern-day version of a colonizing master by using practices that build on assumptions of individual deficit.

Contextualizing and situating clients' problems in a social and historical context can help defuse any inclination of the therapist to blame clients for their own plight. Some understanding of the complexity of social relations can be generated, and this by itself can help shift the dynamics onto a positive footing.

Whites can also have their identities totalized and stereotyped when people of color accuse them of embodying practices of superiority and uncritically assume them to be benefactors of racism. Where such accusations are true, there might be massive constraints on the counselor's helpfulness. But it is not a given that white counselors are practicing in ways that perpetuate their own privilege. The white counselor or therapist is wiser to pay close attention to any legacy of privilege and to be acutely aware of how this can play out in counseling sessions.

Issues of trust pertaining to the legacies of race and ethnicity can become critical in the counseling relationship. These issues are sometimes best addressed by making them explicit. Potential concerns can be raised as legitimate topics of conversation early in the counseling relationship. For example, the white therapist might begin the session by asking a person of color whether he has any misgivings about working with her. The counselor should be ready to acknowledge that ethnicity and race might be a factor in their work together. Not raising the possibility that sociocultural undercurrents might be present limits the prospect of effective therapeutic work. It makes it much harder for counselors to help clients situate the challenges that confront them within the history of cultural practices built on the assumptions about race discussed above.

A culturally aware white counselor can also help a client of color tease out the difference between the dominant cultural practices of race, which cause oppression, and the practices of this particular white therapist. Identifying contradictory experiences does not have to undermine the validity of experiences of racism. Instead, it can become the basis for hope that things can be different. For a client of color, seeing a white therapist committed to standing against racism could be enormously helpful in engendering trust and hope.

We have been discussing the counseling challenges that may arise between a white therapist and a client who is a person of color. Yet the legacy of colonization might make it even more difficult for a black or Asian therapist to work with a white client. Racist discourse can influence white clients to dismiss or minimize the expertise of the black or Asian therapist, which significantly disrupts the therapeutic process. We don't believe therapists who are persons of color should have to educate clients or to sustain their therapeutic efforts in these circumstances. It is preferable that the client be referred to somebody of his own ethnicity who can challenge unjust and prejudicial behavior as part of the therapeutic contract.

Sometimes it might be difficult for counselors of color to see past the white privilege certain clients have. They may underestimate the suffering white middle class clients experience even while benefiting from particular racist traditions. It is not uncommon for people who have been subjected to oppression, when given the opportunity, to engage in subtle oppressive practices themselves, either intentionally or inadvertently.

Just because the counselor and client are of the same race or ethnicity does not mean that the sociohistorical factors are not playing out in their therapeutic relationship. Within ethnic groups, established hierarchies can be built around physical markers but based on the underlying dividing lines of race. For example, many light-skinned blacks may have access to privileges that are less available to darker-skinned blacks. They may be perceived as more attractive and benefit from being able to pass for white.

Natasha has lived her whole life being subjected to what she terms intraracial prejudice.

> When I was growing up I was made to think that lighter is better. During the time of slavery, many of the light-skinned slaves, most often the illegitimate children of the slave owners, became house slaves and were spared from working in the fields. Even though they were treated badly, they were perceived to get better treatment than plantation and field slaves. Many light-skinned blacks

found it necessary to pass for white in order to succeed, which meant leaving their family. It was a better life. I recall when I was a kid being called "tar baby" by another kid who was the same shade as me. Many times I have felt "less than" because of my color. Those with lighter skin and "good hair" (meaning straight or wavy) always got all the attention in my community. I have experienced the desire to marry a light-skinned black; it would help increase the chances that my own children will be lighter than me and won't be subject to feelings of self-loathing due to something they can't change about themselves. When I was younger I probably did have some negative feelings toward my lighter brothers and sisters. Now, sometimes it's envy.

Natasha Crawford identifies as black American.

Sometimes, light-skinned blacks can feel marginalized by members of the black community because they don't possess the physical markers that truly define them as black. LaShanda, a lighter-skinned black with other racial heritage, describes such an experience.

My grandmother on my father's side has told me and my siblings that we don't love her as much as our cousins do because we aren't fully black. My older sister has told me that I deny my African American heritage, based on her own opinions. I believe that I am who I am; I know and accept myself. I can't make myself more African American than I am.

How do we make sense of the practices that Natasha and LaShanda experienced? Are they evidence that blacks can be just as racist as whites? We would argue that this meaning relies too heavily on the essentializing of racism in those who express it. A better way to think of such experiences starts with the concept of discourse. Racist discourse has been internalized in nonwhite people's consciousness just as it has in white people's consciousness for over 400 years via European colonization. Racist discourse is expressed in a variety of ways, and sometimes the practices of racism are used by people against themselves as well as against others.

Significant distinctions also occur among people of the same ethnicity as a result of social class differences, relative wealth or poverty, and level of education. These distinctions can strongly alter a person's experience of the effects of racial discourse. This discourse often exceptionalizes certain individuals as models of the "good black person" and grants them special status within otherwise white worlds. An upper middle class black therapist with a college education may sometimes really struggle to build trust and empathy with a client from a poor inner-city community. While they are similarly positioned in terms of race, the effects of poverty may feel much more foreign to the counselor. A white therapist who was brought up in a lower class community may have more understanding of the problems that a person of color who is poor may face. Differences in sexual orientation or problems with homophobia may also present barriers for a counselor and client from the same racial group.

There are many racist practices that take place among nonwhite ethnic groups. Some who are committed to a structuralist analysis of power (see Chapter 7) argue that this is not possible and that racism is solely a white phenomenon. But this argument does not reflect the many day-to-day, painful experiences suffered by members of diverse ethnic and racial groups. We believe it is more accurate to say that racist practices are expressions of power and that they can be employed by anyone who chooses to use them to gain some advantage for herself by hurting someone else. Whatever the background of the person using racist discourse, the background of the discourse itself comes from the history of colonization. It is still true that the origins of the ideas of racism lie in the stereotypical, prejudicial assumptions woven into the arbitrary European nomenclature of race. Individuals of diverse races can plug into this systemic discourse of race at the moment that they choose to deploy racist discourse for their own reasons. They can join in the game of innate superiority and inferiority.

The point we are arguing here is a subtle one, but we believe it is important. *Racism is a term that should be reserved for practices, rather than persons*. The assumptions on which these practices are built, however, are not invented by any one individual. They are products of the history of colonization and the justifications that underlie it. The practice of making racist remarks is, therefore, available for any individual of any race to utter. At the same time, racist remarks are products of a systematic discourse that is white and European in its genealogy.

Natasha explains it this way.

Unfortunately, throughout the course of American history, those in power and in the media have perpetuated stereotypes of each group. Since many of us were segregated and may have had little interaction with those in other ethnic groups, the stereotypes were believed and passed down. Growing up, I was surrounded almost exclusively by blacks and Puerto Ricans. I am sure that I had stereotypes of members of other ethnic groups. Even though we know better, we still assume all Asian Americans are smart, all blacks are lazy, and all Latinos are dirty. We are afraid of one another. This hinders us from working together to educate the nation and the world about the wonderful contributions we have made to making this country what it is today.

Sometimes therapists assume that because they belong to the same ethnicity, they will be able to empathize with their clients and grapple with concerns that only persons of that ethnicity could understand. Assumptions may be made about the client's experience on this basis when, in reality, the client's experience is very different from what the counselor imagines. Such assumptions undermine trust and empathy and diminish the effectiveness of an exploration of major client concerns. In practice, the degree of shared outlook between a counselor and a client of the same ethnicity may be minimal. We have outlined above many ways in which the concepts of ethnicity and race are much more complex than they are often presented as. Their meanings are multiple, and thus it would be surprising to find empathic understanding to be a straightforward process of ethnic matching. Creating shared understandings of issues of race and ethnicity between counselors and clients always needs to be worked at, and we believe it needs to be founded on a clear analysis of the genealogy of these concepts and of the present-day cultural formations in which they are being lived out.

While we have laid out an argument explaining the genealogy of racism in the history of European colonization, the world is a complex place and many contradictory patterns are also occurring. Within popular culture, there are frequent contradictions of the assumptions of racial privilege. Often they occur as a result of the inroads of decolonization into modern culture. More than ever before, we have successful and powerful black, Asian, and Latino political leaders, artists, and sportspeople featured on prime-time mainstream television. These people of color have a huge following among Anglo Americans. They clearly are accorded positions of authority and privilege that contradict the history of race. A phenomenon occurring among middle class white youths and young people from around the globe has been the idolization of black music artists. These artists may embody in their art forms experiences from their own recent history of significant oppression that can clearly be attributed, at least in part, to race discourse. Many successful black artists come from the poorest and most downtrodden communities and display the cultural symbols of those neighborhoods with their dress, dialect, and cultural accoutrements. They even use these symbols as badges of resistance and decolonization. Ironically, however, after becoming cultural icons, these artists assume the trappings of privilege, and white youths now mimic their dress and style of communication. They are now in positions of power and influence that apparently belie what they are saying in their music. The point here is that it is not easy to make generalizations about the patterns of relationship that form around some ethnic territories.

These people are not being inauthentic in the process. They are merely illustrating the complexity of cultural positioning in the world that we live in.

Figure 4.3   Mottie and Dewey Haugabook, the great, great, great, great grandparents of Courtnay Oatts Mohammed. Dewey (right) was a bridge builder, janitor, and slave owner. Mottie was a mother and housekeeper and originally Dewey's slave. In order to be a family, Dewey and Mottie moved from Georgia to West Philadelphia, Pennsylvania.

Response to Chapter 4

Angus Hikairo Macfarlane

Angus Hikairo Macfarlane, Ph.D., is of the Te Arawa tribe of central North Island, New Zealand. He is an experienced educator and practitioner and has been an advisor for Special Education Services of the Ministry of Education. The thrust of his research is concerned with the exploration of cultural concepts and theories that affect classroom practice. He is the author of numerous articles and four books. In 2003, he was awarded the inaugural Research Fellowship by the New Zealand Council for Educational Research, at which time he took up residency in Wellington to carry out further research in his area of interest. In 2004, he was a recipient of the Tohu Kairangi award, a citation for academic excellence in Maori education. Dr Macfarlane is an associate professor at the University of Waikato.

In New Zealand, year after year, Maori students are suspended from school at a much higher rate than their non-Maori counterparts. While any number of reasons are cited for this anomaly, it seems to be the education system's version of the conflicts in New Zealand associated with prejudice, exclusion, and discrimination that have persisted over the generations. Out of these struggles, however, has evolved an awareness of the need for people to get along with persons of diverse backgrounds and to better understand each other's expectations and worldviews. The realization that this requires commitment and effort on the part of all of us is not insignificant.

An underlying theme of this chapter is the important role that race and ethnicity play in the lives of people and the implications of that role for counseling processes and approaches. In New Zealand, a number of programs have been developed in the education and health sectors to help professionals be more culturally responsive as they work with Maori clients and their families. One such approach is the *hui whakatika*, which literally means "restorative conferencing."

People from one ethnic background are likely to enter a conferencing situation with very different views and expectations from those of people who come from another background. Conferencing is not new to Maori people. Traditional Maori societies had this down to a fine art, and many examples are magnificently manifested in mythology, legends, and history. Contemporary Maori society has retained an abundance of what their *tipuna* (ancestors) had to offer, despite the infiltration of Western processes into their conferencing techniques. For Maori, oneness of *tinana* (body), *hinengaro* (mind), and *wairua* (spirit) is often perceived to be distinct from the rationality and logic that influence Western thinking. If the conferencing process is going to be of value to Maori students who find themselves in trouble at school—and at risk of being excluded from it—then it needs to embrace Maori philosophy and logic.

Four quintessential features illustrate pre-European Maori counseling. They are:

1. An emphasis on reaching *consensus* and involving the whole community

2. A desired outcome of *reconciliation* and a settlement acceptable to all parties, rather than the isolation and punishment of the offender

3. Not the apportionment of blame, but *examination* of the wider reason for the wrong, with an implicit assumption that there is often wrong on both sides

4. Less concern with whether or not there has been a breach of law and more concern with the *restoration* of harmony

Let me recite a case where I facilitated a hui whakatika. The hui whakatika was convened to consider the plight of Piripi, a 14-year-old Maori student. The head of the junior school had referred Piripi to me because of his rudeness, absenteeism, nonadherence to rules, and bullying of other boys by intimidation, including the use of stand-over tactics. He was not willing to share his problems, and attempts by the school counselor to reason with him through conventional approaches had led to a dead end. Piripi had recently stolen a car belonging to a retired couple and had damaged it while showing off to his mates. Consequently, the police had become involved. He was in dire straits.

A number of phases had to be worked through in this hui whakitika, including:

- Setup. Determining who needs to be involved, preparing those involved for what will happen, and establishing Piripi's willingness to make amends.
- The conference proper. Opening, conducting, and closing the conference, adhering to (Maori) rituals along the way. This involved clarifying the desired outcomes and declaring that the problem, not Piripi, was the problem.
- Seeking out new possibilities. This involved the consideration of alternative stories, planning, monitoring, and reviewing. Where to now for Piripi?

The hui whakatika process is intricate and demanding of people's time. Many people attend, including school personnel, family members, and those who have been affected or offended by the individual concerned. Maori protocols apply, such as *karakia* (prayer), *waiata* (song), *kai* (food), and copious *korero* (discussion). People of all ages and backgrounds attend the hui whakatika and are encouraged to actively participate. This approach is not about stipulating who is to be in the room or what checklists should be attended to. It is about preparing to speak with one another about difficult things in a way that avoids regression into the dynamics that gave rise to the problems in the first place.

In daily life, it is commonplace to encounter the use of punitive and judgmental forms of speech, particularly where there is a desire to rein someone in. These habits of judgment are hard to break. In this sense, conferencing is about developing new ways of speaking. All instances of conferencing are, by definition, intended to promote discussion. Speaking respectfully does not cost a great deal, and it can be extremely effective in achieving desirable outcomes. The hui whakatika approach is particularly interested in the types of conversations that are able to turn people and events around, not frighteningly, but assertively. The outcome sought is the restoration of a person from a state of disorientation to a state of optimism. The conversations are constantly searching for ways of going forward and developing new directions.

For students in situations similar to Piripi's, new opportunities and directions are sought and the punitive measures of expulsion are, where possible, avoided. The counselor and all others present at a hui whakatika are required to consider all the relevant matters and then draw up a plan to address the concerns. A good plan obviously includes aspects that would benefit the school (e.g., nonviolence pacts, attendance undertakings) as well as aspects that would benefit the student (e.g., having him or her join a sports club or receive counseling). It may also need to include aspects that benefit the community (e.g., the removal of graffiti) or the family (e.g., active parental interest in the school community). These options were applicable in Piripi's case, and satisfactory outcomes, while not guaranteed, did ensue in this instance.

The hui whakatika places culture at the center. It opens and closes in a manner compatible with Maori processes; there is an order to who should speak and when. There is a place for talk and debate, laughter and tears, food and song. There is also a wairua, a spirituality, that exudes *mana* (authority)—and mana can move people!

Many voices are heard as the English and Maori languages blend. The dignified presences of *kaumatua* (older Maori people) provide a net of safety to younger members of the conference. Throughout the conference, the feelings of *whanaungatanga* (relationships) and the intensity of the *kaupapa* (discussion) are the *taonga tuku iho*, the treasures of history and mythology that have been handed down from the past. The hui whakatika has traditionally been the focal point of Maori counseling—and for many, it still is.

TO DISCUSS

1. The topics of race and ethnicity are sensitive topics. What sensitivities were stimulated in you as you read this chapter?

2. When would you prefer to use the term *race* and when would you prefer to use the term *ethnicity*?

3. Can you think of instances in which the ways that people use the terms *race* and *ethnicity* have affected you personally? How?

4. Do an online search for articles on the validity of the concept of race. What did you find?

5. Search online for examples of official government documents that use the concept of race. How is it used? Which races are given official status?

CHAPTER 5

Discourse, Positioning, and Deconstruction

In this chapter, we want to introduce some new concepts into the literature on multicultural counseling. We shall introduce and explain the concept of discourse and the idea of being positioned in relation to discourse. We shall also explain the approach to understanding discourse usage called deconstruction. These are not-so-new concepts in social theory (they have been used in the fields of philosophy, cultural studies, sociology, literary studies, and anthropology for a couple of decades, even though not universally by all academics in these domains), but they have only to a modest extent been picked up by psychologists and are still not widely understood in the field of counseling.

We have reasons for introducing these concepts here. This isn't just a matter of keeping up with academic fashions, and we certainly don't want to add jargon for its own sake to the field of multicultural counseling. But we think these concepts help us get around some recurrent problems in our field. We think that using these concepts gives us a fresh perspective in the field of culture and on the work that counselors do within it. Fresh concepts can allow for new ways of speaking, and we ourselves have experienced these concepts as opening up productive ways to think about culture and about counseling. We shall introduce these concepts in this chapter so that we can use them in the rest of the book, in the hope that readers will be assisted in their practice. We should warn you that it might take a bit of work to master these concepts. That is because they are not always familiar. We would encourage you to persist, however, because we think that the ability to make clearer decisions about a range of issues can be gained from such persistence.

One of the main reasons that we want to use the concept of discourse is because it often serves as a sharper instrument with which to discuss things that are more problematic to talk about when we use the word *culture*. *Culture* is often a blunt instrument because of the history of essentialist thinking attached to it. Discourse, on the other hand, allows us to capture more of the complexity of the situations in which people often live as they are pulled in contradictory directions that can never be adequately described by the idea that each individual belongs to a single culture. The word *race* is an even blunter instrument than *culture* in this regard, as we have made clear in earlier chapters. We think that identity construction is always a complex process of being positioned by a swathe of competing discourses, established through large-scale historical movements but having a unique impact on each person at every moment of their lives. We are seeking to talk about these impacts and the struggles people go through to position themselves in relation to dominant discourse in ways that fit their own hopes and ambitions in life. This is the stuff that people see counselors about. To us, the concept of discourse seems uniquely suited as an explanatory framework for making sense of the diversity and complexity of human engagement that multicultural counseling is all about.

Another argument that we want to mount for our use of the concept of discourse is that discourse is always a product of the social world in which we live. Therefore, thinking in terms of discourse always makes the social and cultural aspects of the problems that people bring to counselors more visible. This visibility is in contrast to the use of, for example, biological metaphors, which can render the social and cultural world invisible or irrelevant. We believe it is in the interest of the multicultural counseling field specifically, and of the counseling profession generally, to reexamine many of the ways in which people are thought of, problems are diagnosed, and counseling interventions are conceived. From our perspective, the concept of discourse provides a new language to name the social processes operating in clients' worlds that is in stark contrast to the essentialist understandings expressed in many models of counseling. It also provides a way forward in a manner that isn't blameworthy.

Deploying the concept of discourse also includes a focus on the language used in the counseling profession itself and invites us to pay closer attention to it. It may often be part of the problem that the multicultural counseling movement is seeking to address. This is where the other concept mentioned above, deconstruction, comes in. Deconstruction lays bare the work done by discourse, makes it visible, and leads to openings for change.

Let's now discuss each of these concepts in turn and explain them in more detail before outlining some examples of how they might be used to constructive effect.

Discourse

In a general sense, discourse is both the process of talk and interaction between people and the products of that interaction. The things that people say or write are examples of discourse. In the more precise meaning that has developed in academic writing, the term *discourse* refers to a set of meanings, concepts, images, and/or statements that produce a particular representation of an event, object, person, or other entity to the world (Burr, 2003). Such meanings tend to become patterned and well known through constant repetition in hundreds and thousands of conversations. This concept of discourse, influenced chiefly by social constructionist and poststructuralist theory, is based on the work of Michel Foucault (1972), who described discourse as a "social practice" disseminated through cultural space that exerts a dominating effect on what can be thought or spoken. That is, we speak from discourse, feel from discourse, and behave from discourse. In simplest terms, you can think of discourse as a cultural idea.

You can get a sense of a discourse by listening to any statement that someone makes and asking yourself, what are the background assumptions on which that statement rests? For example, consider this woman's statement: "When I am going through a crisis, I find that the first thing I do is take control of my weight and eating habits—one time I even came close to the edge of a devastating eating disorder." There are a number of assumptions that lie in the background of this statement. They are not things that are often said out loud, but at the same time everybody within the cultural world that the speaker comes from knows these assumptions and thinks of them as just normal, everyday truths. We can render these assumptions understandable by spelling them out as simple assertions of what is obvious and taken for granted just below the surface of the words. For example, some of these assumptions may be:

- "Thin is beautiful."
- "Women should take care of their appearance and make themselves desirable for men."
- "A successful woman measures her weight and brings it under control, mainly by dieting."
- "Eating disorders happen to women who are too controlling."

These are examples of discursive statements that we may find by analyzing a given utterance in a discourse.

At any given moment, a variety of discourses will be in circulation in a particular social or cultural world. Notice that the last of these assumptions may have points of reference in standard professional discourse and may influence writers of academic articles and books as well as laypeople. Discourses can also compete with one another. For example, with regard to the above discourses, there are competing ideas around them, such as:

- "Fat is just as beautiful as thin."
- "It is wrong for anyone to be subjected to judgment of her personal worth on the basis of her body's appearance."
- "Eating disorders are produced by cultural pressure on women, not by individual controlling personalities."

Discourses are not simply abstract ideas, ideologies, or theories (although theories and ideologies must be talked about in language and, therefore, in discourse). They are not as formally constituted as theories. They are, however, implicit in social practices and often lie just beneath the surface of our understanding as assumptions that are necessary to make what we say or do make sense. In this way, discourses construct meaning and shape individuals' behavior, their perceptions of the world, and the sense they make of lived experience. Discourse is the realm in which what is "normal," what is "acceptable," what is "right," what is "real," and what is "possible" are constructed.

Box 5.1. Defining Discourse

Here are some well-known conceptualizations of discourse:

[Discourses are] practices that systematically form the objects of which they speak.

—Michel Foucault, *The Archaeology of Knowledge*

A discourse is a system of statements which constructs an object.

—Ian Parker, *Discourse Dynamics*

Instead of gradually reducing the rather fluctuating meaning of the word "discourse," I believe I have in fact added to its meanings; treating it sometimes as the general domain of all statements, sometimes as an individualizeable group of statements, and sometimes as a regulated practice that accounts for a number of statements.

—Michel Foucault, *The Archaeology of Knowledge*

A discourse is any regulated system of statements.

—Julian Henriques, Wendy Hollway, Cathy Urwin, Couze Venn, and Valerie Walkerdine, *Changing the Subject*

Discourse is a mode of action, one form in which people may act upon the world and especially upon each other, as well as a mode of representation.

—Norman Fairclough, *Discourse and Social Change*

Discourses should be understood as statements with a material existence.

—Michel Foucault, *The Hermeneutics of the Subject*

TO DISCUSS

1. What different perspective does each of these definitions make clear about the concept of discourse?

2. How do these definitions compare with your previous understanding(s) of discourse?

Dominant Discourse

One of the advantages that the concept of discourse affords is a view of the relationship among competing discourses. The concept of culture is more static and is usually assumed to be more universal, less driven by conflict. Different discourses, however, are often quite contradictory. They can be thought of as being like political parties, clamoring for your vote at election time. While there are always a range of discourses, however, they are seldom competing on a level playing field. Some discourses always come to dominate others. We can thus talk about dominant discourses and subjugated, or alternative, discourses. Dominant discourse refers to those cultural ideas that have a privileged and dominant influence on our behavior in the world. That is, dominant discourses reflect prevailing ideology, including popular norms, values, and beliefs. Sometimes they are embodied as law or have official authority behind them, or are bestowed by the most prominent academic commentators of the day. As a result, they are often so persuasive in a community that their implications for how life should be lived are completely taken for granted (Hare-Mustin, 1994).

All these discourses reflect what is often considered common sense about how people should behave and exert a powerful influence in day-to-day interactions. In fact, it is the familiarity and taken-for-granted nature of dominant discourses that seduce us to adopt these popular cultural views. That is, "their influence can most easily remain hidden and difficult to identify and, therefore, to resist" (Gavey & McPhillips, 1999, p. 352).

Consider how the dominant discourse of one woman's family shaped her own understandings and experiences.

My grandparents and parents have raised me to have a certain ideal for the family. The perfect family starts with a man and a woman who are married before they have children. Then they have two children, a boy and then a girl: a boy to pass on the family name and to please the father, and a girl to please the mother. The parents are not too old, so that they can still enjoy their kids. They are financially secure before they have children. They do not divorce, ideally. The perfect family keeps their problems private. Since my aunt married my late Uncle Steve in Vegas and my sister had a child out of wedlock, there is a lot of pressure on me to make my grandmother proud in the way that I choose to live that part of my life. I have really thought a lot about marriage and its importance, so my Nanny's ideals have had a huge impact on my life.

What this woman is describing is a pretty ordinary picture of how family is imagined in the modern world. She speaks of this "ideal" in terms of how it has been passed down from her grandparents and parents, but there are surely many other people who have had the same messages. They were not invented specially for this woman by her parents or grandparents. They are actually drawn from discourse. Discourse theorists would argue that this picture is not just an image of an ideal family, but an image of what has been instilled into us by dominant discourse as a "normal" family, that is, one that we should all measure our own family against to decide whether it is normal or not. The speaker in this extract actually starts to register this pressure to be normal in the last few sentences. She mentions a couple of marriages in her family that did not fit the normal picture, and she is now personally feeling increased pressure to construct her own life to fit the designated norm.

These dominating discourses shape every aspect of human functioning, embracing thought, behavior, and affective responses. It is not as if our feelings are somehow part of an authentic world that is untouched by culture, as is often suggested by liberal humanism (see Chapter 6). Some counseling theories have suggested this idea and have argued that we should concentrate on helping people get in touch with their inner feeling worlds and that there they will encounter a sense of self that is free of cultural influence. This is of course an essentialist idea. From a social constructionist perspective, this quest does not work. Our feelings are also produced out of a world of discourse and culture, such that we do not have some responses that are "pure" or culture free. Even our dreams have discourse symbols in them, which is not surprising if they include language.

Discourse and Knowledge

One of the aims of modern science has been to establish a body of knowledge that can be relied on for its truth value. In the last 200 years, we have witnessed the growth of the role of the university in modern society as the principal institution where such knowledge is produced, taught, and disseminated. The foundation of the system of knowledge creation that the academic production of knowledge is built on is a set of rules that constitute recognized research methods. These are, first of all, the rules of systematic observation by observers who are separate from what they observe. These observers are neutral and unbiased. The rules are also the rules of scientific categorization, experimentation, and logical proof, embodied in the end in mathematical calculations.

The goal of research production within this modern framework is to produce knowledge of the world of nature. By definition, the world of nature is that which is free of cultural influence. Hence it is not too far a stretch to say that modern science has tried to eliminate as far as possible cultural material from the knowledge that it produces. All this makes a lot of sense in the fields of physics and chemistry and other "natural" sciences. You don't want the culture of the scientist to interfere with knowledge of how the atoms of the universe interact, although even then scientists have to use linguistic metaphors to describe what they are discussing, and language is a cultural product. When we are studying human sciences, the issues become more complex. Human beings studying cultural worlds are studying themselves. Hence the human sciences have developed methods to create distance between the observer and the observed (experimental methods, control groups, calculation of statistical probabilities, etc.).

This is where the concept of discourse becomes important. Early in his career, Michel Foucault (1972) wrote a book called *The Order of Things: An Archaeology of the Human Sciences*, which received extraordinary attention in France and eventually in other parts of the world. He used the concept of discourse to show that the human sciences like psychology, constructed as they were in language, were full of cultural presuppositions. Foucault argued that social scientists were much less able than everyone believed to separate themselves from their own cultural perspectives and pursue objective knowledge. This is not just a matter of removing "bias," either. The whole academic exercise is located deeply in a set of philosophical, and, therefore, cultural, assumptions and is used for purposes that are profoundly political.

The meaning of Foucault's work for our purposes here is that we cannot separate knowledge from the world where discourse operates. Knowledge is constructed out of discourse and for discursive purposes. Knowledge, then, is a cultural product. Indeed, to know anything is to know it in terms of discourse (Davies & Harré, 1990). If we look back through the history of knowledge about culture, this is not hard to see. Nineteenth century anthropology is replete with assumptions about race and ethnicity that we would regard as at best quaint and at worst racist. If we extrapolate this experience of reading 19th century human sciences, we have to be concerned about how the simple "truths" of today will look to people living in the culture of future societies.

This viewpoint is a challenge to the assumptions of simple empiricism. Facts no longer speak just for themselves. From their conception to the explanation of their significance, they are always interpretations of the world. Interpretations are made by human beings imbued with cultural worldviews, and they are spoken in discourse that embodies the dominant perspectives of an age, a locale, and a people. Therefore, not only do we need to ask about a given topic, "What are the facts?" We also need to ask questions such as, "Whose facts are they?" "Who benefits from this version of the facts?" "Under what cultural 'regime of truth' have these facts been produced?"

Counseling knowledge is of course no exception. It is always built on the discourse of the day. Thus, Michel Foucault posited that social practices, including therapeutic engagements, are informed by discourse. If we look at the various theories of counseling and read them as pieces of discourse, they reveal a lot about the cultural worlds inhabited by the persons who developed them. A social constructionist perspective encourages us to do this. Sigmund Freud's theories do not, therefore, just speak about the human mind. They speak about the discourses that dominated the thinking of medical professionals in late 19th and early 20th century Vienna. Carl Rogers's work can be read as a product of the discourse of the Anglo-Protestant, midwestern United States from the middle of the 20th century. Such readings do not necessarily mean that these counseling theories are wrong or are any less valuable, but it does change our relationship with them. We know that discourse changes over time, and in response to events in history, and through encounters with different cultural perspectives. Hence, treating knowledge as discourse enables it to come down off the pedestal of grand narrative (Lyotard, 1984) and be more reachable for all of us. We can also expect ideas about counseling to change in response to the discourse of our day and to not remain frozen in the grand narratives of the past.

For the cause of multiculturalism in counseling, the concept of discourse has great importance. It enables us to ask questions about the relationships between counseling ideas and the particular cultural worlds occupied by those who speak them. It enables us to examine patterns of cultural dominance in the literature of counseling itself. It enables us, too, to open up the field of counseling to cultural perspectives that otherwise are kept silent by the dominant discourse of the day.

It is not only the theory of counseling that can be investigated in terms of discourse. Counseling conversations in practice contexts are, of course, also conducted in discourse because they involve language. The ways that clients present problems to counselors are imbued with discourse, as are the counselor's responses. For example, the following discourses commonly circulate and capture many clients in counseling: "I expect my partner to take care of me forever." "My partner is my true soul mate." "A good family consists of a nuclear family." "Divorce is not good for the sake of the children." "Families should not discuss private matters with strangers."

Discourse and Identity

Discourse provides the material out of which we form identity. Who we are depends on the circumstances we are placed in and the discourses available in the setting we find ourselves in. Identity is made up of both personal preferences and cultural specifications for the range within which we are allowed to form preferences. For example, gender specifications are one domain in which identity patterns are laid out by gender discourse. Both men and women learn to perceive the world, and their experiences in it, through such gender discourse. Categories such as *feminine* and *masculine* are organizing headings within gender discourse, as men and women define themselves with reference to this division. For instance, to be considered "masculine" or "feminine," men and women must conform to certain cultural standards endorsed and enacted through discourse. For example, masculine men do not wear makeup and are active and competitive and make jokes and emphasize strength and taking initiative. Feminine women shave their legs, wear makeup, spend hours talking with their friends about personal troubles, and are caring and nurturing.

In discourse theory, identity is thought of in terms of subject positions. However, "while all discourses offer subject positions that suggest particular ways of being in and experiencing the world, they vary in their accessibility and power" (Gavey & McPhillips, 1999, p. 352). The idea is that discourse sets up patterns of relationships among people, but rarely on an equal basis. Particular discourses are always being contested and debated, and groups of people typically seek to shift the discourse so that it tilts in their favor. As a result, the discourse that dominates always gives some people more entitlement to speak, to do things, and to be recognized in their social world. Other people, meanwhile, are always up against it to have their voices heard, to be recognized by others who matter, and even to feel justified in having an opinion in the first place. They have to find places to live on the margins of the dominant discourse. Hence, we may talk about their being marginalized by this discourse.

Here is an example of one such struggle between discourses that produce differential subject positions. Hong, a Korean woman, speaks about traditional Korean discourse as it specifies gender roles and family configurations. She also comments on how this discourse has impacted her own life.

> Confucianism defines family members as descendants along the male line. The family headship system decrees that a baby boy becomes the family head if his father, the family's only son, dies. Even though sons are no longer entitled to inherit the bulk of their late parents' wealth, most fathers still hand over their fortunes to the eldest son before they die. There has been a lot of change in Korea, but these ideas still remain in Korean society. As an educated Christian woman, I refuse to comply with the gender roles of my family. However, sometimes I realize that I am affected by these gender roles unconsciously. For example, I take care of my parents-in-law more than my own parents because I feel more responsibility as a wife of the only son of the family.

In this statement, Hong references a series of competing discourses—Confucian and Christian, traditional and modern, educated and uneducated—each of which alters the mix of subject positions she can choose from. She mentions efforts to change by legal decree the traditional dominant discourse that is tilted in favor of men, but indicates that there have also been widespread efforts to mitigate the effect of these reforms that have been designed to benefit women. The dominant patriarchal discourse thus remains dominant because it dominates the practice that actually takes place on the ground.

Notice, too, the subject positions Hong takes up and builds identity around. She claims for herself positions as educated, Christian, woman, and wife. She "refuses to comply" with some gender roles in her family. On the other hand, she finds herself unconsciously acting out practices specified by dominant discourse with her parents-in-law. Her final statement is an interesting one. It suggests how discourse works inside the minds of people, shaping what they do almost without their knowing. Discourse practices are so ordinary and everyday that they often slip by unnoticed, because they are just what everyone expects.

These workings of discourse are the very material that makes up culture. They are also the material that makes up people's identities. Identity is formed partly out of personal intention and preference on the one hand, but, on the other hand, it is chosen and constructed in social exchange and dialogue that is beyond any individual's express control. For counseling, the work that discourse does in the construction of a person's problems in life is very important. The places where a person might experience painful problems are very often the places where he is refusing to comply with dominant discourse and experiencing consequences as a result, or they might be the very places where he is unconsciously complying with dominant discourse and feeling discontented as a result. Therefore, there is a sense in which counselors who are working with their clients about personal struggles are always working with the cultural dimensions of life. Our argument is that the concept of discourse enables us to see the swirling and changing forces at work and not to pigeonhole Hong as a stereotypical Korean woman who thinks the way textbooks say Korean women think.

Positioning

The concept of positioning (Davies & Harré, 1990) is built on the concept of discourse. It can serve as a bridge between the personal and the social aspects of discourse. It is a metaphor used to describe the fluid and dynamic relationship between people and discourse. Positioning refers to the way in which every utterance in a conversation establishes, even for a moment, a relation that is made up of discourse and discursive assumptions. In this moment, a speaker establishes a position for herself in relation to a set of meanings, including identity meanings. She also positions other people in a place of meaning from which they are invited to respond. A conversation is made up of a series of position-taking utterances that install moments of "moral oughtness" (Linehan & McCarthy, 2001) based on particular discourses. Each utterance also issues a position call to listeners. It calls them into positions from which to respond. In this way, positioning enables us to examine the influence of discourse on individuals' lives, or how we come to take up certain identities and not others (Drewery, 2005).

Let's examine an example. In a conflict situation, someone says, "Look, I'm only trying to be reasonable here." At face value, this is a straightforward piece of communication. When we think of it in terms of positioning, it becomes rich and dynamic. The speaker is seeking to establish a position in a relation from which he will be taken seriously. The basis for the claim to be taken seriously is one of "being reasonable." If we ask what being reasonable means, we start to enter a world of discourse where certain behaviors will be regarded as reasonable and others will not. The dominant discourse of the modern world privileges a certain display of self as a rational person who can exhibit a degree of control, unless tested beyond reasonable limits. There is a small element of threat in the original utterance that suggests that if the listener does not respond with the same degree of rational behavior, then the speaker will not continue to be "reasonable." Along with the establishment of the position of being reasonable, there is also an implied opposite that is being ascribed to the listener. "You" are clearly being "unreasonable," or "overly emotional," or "crazy," and this is testing "my" long-suffering patience. In other words, the speaker establishes a position for himself, the rational and reasonable one, and calls the other person into a position from which to respond, that of the unreasonable and irrational one. In the background of both these positions lies a discourse and a history and a literature that specifies what will be taken to be rational and reasonable. Thus, even this simple sentence has a cultural world that it relies on to make any sense. It may also be a gendered world, in which men are assumed to be more rational and women more emotional by "nature."

The discursive concept of positioning has only recently begun to be described within the counseling literature (Drewery, 2005; Drewery, Winslade, & Monk, 2000; Sinclair, 2007; Sinclair & Monk, 2004; Winslade, 2005) despite the potential it holds for culturally and socially responsible work. In fact, we would argue that the concept of discourse is inadequate without incorporating the concept of positioning. Positioning points to the manner in which individuals are located in conversations as active participants in producing what they experience. That is, individuals always speak and act from particular contexts and in response to other conversational moves that have gone before. Therefore, discourses are manifest in how we go forward in our therapeutic engagements. There is a dynamic back-and-forth quality to how we are positioned by discourse and how these discursive moves influence the changing assumptions and expectations we have about one another and ourselves. As Carla Willig (2001) explains, "discourses make available particular subject positions (certain ways-of-seeing the world and certain ways-of-being in the world) that when taken up, have particular implications for subjectivity and experience" (p. 107). For example, sexist language provides exclusionary positioning for women to the extent that unequal conditions of possibility are created (Winslade, 2005). In the family counseling arena, this can look like a husband asking his wife (without any prior negotiation), "I'm going to the gym; when are you picking up the kids from soccer practice?" In this instance, the woman is excluded from any possibility other than engaging in the caregiving of the children.

In emphasizing the subjectivity that is produced through the positions we take up (or are positioned in by others), the concept of positioning helps direct attention to the dynamic aspects of interactions (Davies & Harré, 1990) and prevents a static and fixed understanding of discourse. Moreover, the discursive fields within which people live inevitably provide some degree of subjectivity and thus an agentic position. The emphasis on the subjective (as opposed to subjected) quality of positioning permits individuals to exercise choice in relation to the discourses available. As Bronwyn Davies and Rom Harré point out, "choice is inevitably involved because there are many and contradictory discursive practices that each person could engage in" (p. 3). From this perspective, then, the power of dominant discourses is not absolute and invitations to take up certain positions in discourses can be accepted or rejected. For example, sometimes an initial move by the therapist as the dominant identity in the therapeutic conversation will influence the other speaker, the client, into positions she may not have ordinarily taken up. However, this framework recognizes that positioning in discourses creates space for resistance and renders our interactions in therapy visible, contestable, and amenable to change. Moreover, the agency conceptualized here is distinct from the agency within liberal humanism (see Chapter 6 for more about this concept), since it exists between people rather than within the individual (Drewery, 2005). As Vivien Burr (2003) describes, "agency is only possible in relation to others" (p. 190).

This understanding of our participation in the creation of new discursive possibilities allows us to consider how invitations for incorporating dominant discourse (in a nonreflexive manner) can be challenged or adapted. In other words, positioning allows room to actively engage with discourses in a way that is liberating. To be exact, disrupting dominant discourses opens up spaces for competing discourses in which alternative ways of being can be constructed. Indeed, there are discourses that do not typically bear such a dominant and oppressive influence in people's interactions. These *alternative* discourses challenge the more dominant discourses and are often representative of marginalized cultural ideas circulating within a context or community. Examples of alternative discourses around families include the following:

- "Husband and wives are equally suited for economic and domestic activities."

- "Single parent families raise successful and well-adapted children."

- "Children's voices are an integral part of family life."

- "Same-sex couples are legitimate and deserving parents."

Examples of Positioning

In order to make the concept of positioning more explicit, let's look at some examples. Here is an exchange in which a young girl is positioned in gender discourse. The speaker is Rieko, whose ancestry is Japanese.

> When I was about 10 years old, I became aware of the fact that I was a girl. My mother used to say, "Help me with the cooking and cleaning the rooms. You are a girl." My brother did not have to do any work at home. We were not treated equally. When I was at home with my brother, I was given instructions to do dishes and prepare dinner for my father and my siblings. I would complain, and my mother would reprimand me and say, "You are a girl. This is your training to take care of your husband and children in the future."

Rieko is issued an explicit instruction that positions her in the place of either refusal or compliance. She makes an effort to complain, using the word *equal* to indicate her awareness of the existence of an alternative discourse. In the end, however, the force of the identity position, "You are a girl," is too much and she has to comply. This is an example of a statement that has behind it a matrix of assumptions that are not spoken but that everyone knows. What is also of interest is that Rieko remembers this exchange as an adult and maintains within herself a sense of the injustice in this differential positioning of boys and girls. In other words, the dominant discourse still works on her, but she is not completely subjugated into acquiescing to this discourse inside herself. Counseling should help someone like Rieko to articulate more fully the objections she has to the dominant discourse and to grow places of resistance in her own mind and in her interactions with others.

Now let's look at an example of positioning, from a counseling session, that is focused on both abuse and social class issues (Winslade, 2005).

Janine: When I was seven, I just had to do one little thing wrong and my mother would beat me. She wouldn't hold back. It was awful. I used to hate her. We used to live in a trailer park and the neighbours used to hear me scream and then look at me funny for a few days. Then when I got to be a teenager she would tell me sometimes you're never going to be worth anything, you're not going to do anything.

Counsellor: What effect did that have for you?

Janine: It has stayed with me and when I am feeling down it comes back and haunts me.

Counsellor: So it has wormed its way inside you and it affects you. What does it affect in your relationships with others?

Janine: It makes me feel like I am different all the time and that I don't really belong with people who are smart or have a nice house or a good job.

Counsellor: So it undermines your sense of being OK in yourself.

Janine: Yes, I think it's half the reason why my identity always seems to be lacking something, because of all the self-doubt that I have accumulated. (pp. 358–359)

Like the previous example, this extract from a counseling conversation shows how positioning works to create both social and personal effects. Janine's mother made comments that positioned her in a place of self-doubt and of inferior social worth. Such comments were supported by the conditions of her life. Hence they are difficult not to internalize. Janine works hard to challenge these positions in her own mind and in how she is raising her daughter. Again, the counselor's job is to help her to counteract the pieces of cultural positioning that are still negatively impacting her and to reposition herself in an alternative discourse, one in which she is accorded a place of worth.

The importance and practical value of the dynamic concepts of discourse and positioning cannot be overestimated. The advantage of taking up these conceptual tools is that it provides counselors with a way to keep the cultural backdrop of contemporary life visible and invites clients to think and be otherwise, which can be extremely freeing (Drewery & Monk, 1994). In other words, an examination of the discourses and positions available to therapists and clients helps work toward taking up positions in discourses that are less personally damaging (Burr, 2003). In this way, the concept of discourse takes change for granted.

Deconstruction

A feature of discourse is that it often does its work right under our noses without our noticing. There does not have to be anything deeply buried that must be found by tunneling deep down in the psyche. It is more that the surface evidence is often being overlooked because it is so obvious. We have become so used to it that we have taken its truth value for granted. Still, it sometimes takes some effort to uncover the work being done by discourse behind our backs, as it were. This is where the concept of deconstruction becomes useful.

The process by which discourses and positions are unpacked is called "deconstruction." Deconstruction refers to the practice of exploring and uncovering the taken-for-granted assumptions and influential discourses that underpin our conversation, behavior, and emotional expression. The term *deconstruction* derives from the work of the French philosopher Jacques Derrida (1978). It was introduced into the therapeutic literature by Michael White (1992). Derrida developed the concept of deconstruction in the context of literary theory. He was interested in the problem of how to understand the meaning of a word in a piece of text. The conventional answer is to consult a standard authority (e.g., a dictionary) on the meaning of the word, or to inquire into the intentions of the author who is using it. Derrida argues, however, that neither of these approaches will do. The reason is that there is no trustworthy authority that is not itself part of the discourse context that the word refers to. And the intentions of the author are not free of the influence of other texts produced out of that same discourse context. Derrida says that the use of a word is always bound within a social and linguistic context and carries with it the many other uses of that concept in the thousands of other conversations that have taken place in the history of a language. Mikhail Bakhtin (1986) argues a similar point and refers to the way in which a word or a meaning echoes down a "long corridor of voices" (p. 121). This corridor of voices is another term for what we have been calling discourse. It is also another metaphor that refers to the world of culture.

Derrida's concern in proposing deconstruction as a method of inquiry is not to make everything relative and meaningless, as some critics contend. It is not a destructive or nihilistic aim. Derrida has even asserted that there are some things that cannot be deconstructed. He cites a moral concern for justice as an example.

If anything is undeconstructable, it is justice. The law is deconstructible, for-tunately: it is infinitely perfectible. I am tempted to regard justice as the best word, today, for what refuses to yield to deconstruction, that is to say for what sets deconstruction in motion, what justifies it. It is an affirmative experience of the coming of the other as other. (Derrida, 1994, p. 36)

Deconstruction aims to break up rigidities of thought, particularly where they are having oppressive consequences, and to open up a field of inquiry to previously unnoticed possibilities. It achieves this by disassembling pieces of discourse that are actually "constructions" that pose as "natural" truths. In the modern world, natural truths are regularly accorded the highest form of truth status.

Giovanna Borradori (2003) has offered a summary of Derrida's deconstructive method that can be summarized as follows.

1. Identify the conceptual construction of a particular discourse. Find the key words on which decisions turn or identities are assigned.

2. Identify the conceptual pairs that make up the polarized options for thought around which a discourse is organized. This move is based on the idea that every concept exists not just as a positive identity but also as a negation of something else. Male is not female. Light is not dark. Educated is not illiter-ate. Normal is not abnormal. Healthy is not sick. Ideal is not material. White is not black. Culture is not nature. Derrida contends that meanings rely on their polarized opposite and that the meaning of the positive meaning depends on the negation of its opposite. Hence, they are tied together in a binary relation. Moreover, the pairing is organized in a hierarchy that privi-leges one meaning over the other. The construction of race is a case in point. It consistently privileges white over black.

3. Derrida invites us to play with this binary pairing and invert it so that the normally subordinated meaning is privileged. For example, we might ask, "What would it be like if black were the privileged meaning?"

4. Derrida invokes a search for surplus meaning, for third and fourth possible meanings that escape our attention if we focus only on the binary pairing. The aim is to break down the structure of the binary pair by overloading it with new meanings. The result is that new choices about how to respond to a text or a situation might emerge.

The concept of deconstruction is relevant for counseling because counselors, like literary critics, are vitally interested in carefully making meaning of the things that their clients tell them. Clients are frequently caught in binary oppositions. They experience them as internal dilemmas or problems and they bring them to counselors. They are also living in circumstances prescribed within discourses that divide their worlds in binary ways. For example, our lives are constructed in ways that require a choice between two binary genders, male and female, out of perhaps four possible biological sexes that people are born into. Of the multiple ancestries and cultural influences that we grow up among, the binary pairing of white and nonwhite is selected out, not by nature but by social construction, as the major dividing line around which people are allocated opportunity and privilege or denied these things. Of the wide range of human sexual responses, two major identities are selected out as a binary pair: heterosexual and homosexual. Other binaries include Christian and non-Christian, able-bodied and disabled, intelligent and learning-disabled, law-abiding and criminal, sane and insane.

Michael White (1992) was the first to introduce the concept of deconstruction into the practice of therapy. His use of the term is, he admits (p. 121), a little looser than Derrida's. It is, however, directed toward the same objective: that of helping people overwhelmed by the effects of rigid discourses in their lives to identify how things might be otherwise. White uses the term *deconstruction* to refer to processes of therapeutic inquiry in which the counseling aims to "subvert taken-for-granted realities and practices" (p. 121) by "rendering them strange" (p. 122). He directs the deconstructive focus specifically on ways in which dominant cultural narratives work to produce aspects of a person's self-narrative or identity.

The use of deconstruction in counseling involves a tentative, curious, deliberately naive posture. It differs from a more oppositional social critique in this way. For example, it leads a counselor to ask of any problem story, "What was left out? What was covered over? What was paid attention to and what was not?" (Monk, Winslade, Crocket, & Epston, 1997). Counseling from a discursive perspective focuses on the contextual staging of problems rather than on essentialist aims such as personality change or symptom removal. It is also less preoccupied with seeking definitive and objective answers for individuals. Deconstruction is also not something that counselors do to clients. During counseling, clients are themselves invited to engage in the deconstruction process that challenges the ways in which cultural systems maintain the status quo. This is achieved especially through developing curiosity about the meanings that dominate clients' understanding. Deconstructive questioning asks where these meanings come from, whom they benefit, what discourse grants them authority, and what other preferences or competencies they mask. When deconstruction is applied successfully, the client questions his preoccupations and preferred points of reference, familiar habits, social practices, beliefs, and judgments, which are often regarded as common sense.

The practice of deconstruction is differentiated from other forms of counseling, including what can be considered "best practice," in that it appreciates fully the extent to which people are seduced by culture and its imperatives to behave in certain ways. It therefore avoids the assumption that a person's cultural background provides her with authoritative identity prescriptions that must only be respected and followed. Deconstruction rather suggests that the world of culture is always riven with contested meanings and that the dominant meanings are not necessarily optimal. Deconstruction practices are especially helpful in addressing some of the more subtle effects of dominant discourse on the client; "because dominant discourses are so familiar, they are taken for granted and even recede from view" (Hare-Mustin, 1994, p. 20). Furthermore, when individuals are unaware of the particular discursive influences impacting them, they have a much more limited range of discursive responses available to them. In other words, deconstructive analysis of very particular discourse usages opens up choice and frees up the position taking that is possible.

Deconstructing Identity Stories

Having outlined the three concepts of discourse, positioning, and deconstruction, we are now ready to put them to use. To understand these concepts better and to see how they can be useful, let's look at a series of identity statements and consider them as pieces of discourse that can be deconstructed. They are also position statements that can be analyzed so that the work that they do to form social relations can be made more explicit.

Here is LaShanda's story. Her mother is Japanese and her father is African American.

> The union of my father, coming from the lower middle-class, and my mother, coming from the middle class, did not make my Grandma Rochelle happy. Grandpa Graham said he did not want his children marrying anyone of color. Grandma Rochelle felt that my mother shamed the family, so she was disowned. Marrying out of the race was not acceptable. All of my uncles and aunts had married Chinese people or another type of Asian. Rochelle herself was not treated nicely by her mother-in-law, yet she treated my father wrongly. Grandma Tracy and her family were extremely happy to see Ron getting married, but my Grandma Tracy has said some really hurtful things to me and my siblings. She told us that, because we are not "full" African American, we do not love her as much as her sisters and their grandchildren do. My mother is dead to her extended side of the family; therefore, I do not know much about them. If my mother's relatives found out about me and my family, they would be shamed again, and it could lead to my Grandma Rochelle's being disowned from the family. The division of my extended family is due to the union between my father and mother.

In La Shanda's story, many questions are raised about the meaning of race and also about social class. There is a background discourse in place that specifies that marriage with a person of another race breaks a rule in a social world where the dividing lines are sharply drawn around race. A similar discourse about marrying another of one's own "station" is also in place. If we were to take an essentialist approach, we might locate the source of the disowning, the hurtful comments, and the family schisms in the prejudiced thinking of individuals. If we deconstruct the motivations behind these actions, we might be more inclined to locate their origins in the discourse about race and class that circulates in the wider cultural background and that has exerted a powerful influence on the thinking of these people.

For example, the idea that there can be such a thing as "full" African American presupposes the opposite possibility of a person being "half blooded." We have seen already that the whole idea of full and half bloodedness is based on 19th century biological discourse that has long since been discredited as unscientific, and yet it persists in popular discourse. It assumes the existence of racial "purity," a notion that has continued to operate as a piece of discourse that builds on efforts to divide people into discrete racial groups. If we were to invoke Derrida's principle of turning a dominant discourse on its head and consider for a while the possibility that being born to parents or mixed ancestry might be more the norm than is imagined and that, if we dig a little, no one is actually purely anything, then perhaps the meaning of this family conflict might look different.

None of the people who are playing out this family drama invented these divisions or these concepts of racial purity. Therefore, it makes no deconstructive sense to talk with them about their prejudices or their personally faulty logic. The discourse that has influenced their actions has enveloped them and shaped their working assumptions. As a result, LaShanda's parents and LaShanda herself have been offered positions from which to respond in conversations that are not those of fully legitimate members of a family. Such positioning is hurtful and engenders shame and anger. And yet, each of these people has choices about whether he or she will choose to join with the background discourses of race and class or not. LaShanda seems to indicate that she is aware of at least the possibility of a very different approach. Even though she does not spell this out explicitly, LaShanda's comments give a hint of an opening to some ways in which things could be otherwise in her family. Counseling that focuses on deconstruction can potentially open up these implicit surplus meanings for exploration and future decision making.

Bridgette, who has Irish and Finnish ancestry and describes herself as heterosexual, tells the next story.

Gender roles and sexual orientation are very important issues in my family. Many of the men and some of the women would be considered homophobic. My Grandpa Brian is disgusted by gay men and complains whenever my Nanny wants to watch *Will & Grace*. My Aunt Rosemary's son Dennis is also homophobic and just does not understand gay people. My dad, on the other hand, is pretty liberal and laid back. My family's beliefs about homosexuality stem from their beliefs about gender roles. I believe that the males in our family were raised to be men's men—very tough and strong and manly. The idea of homosexuality is so foreign to them that they don't accept it.

Personally, I don't mind homosexuals being the way that they are. It does gross me out a little to see two men kiss, but I have worked on this over the years and have gotten a lot more used to it after living in Toronto. We have a lesbian in the family—my Grandpa Brian's sister's daughter. She is accepted but referred to as the "gay cousin," and she is somewhat distant from the family.

In this instance, the cultural world that Bridgette lives in has a sharp dividing line running through it based on gender and sexual orientation. Again, this dividing line is built around discourse. There is nothing about being male that, in itself, requires a person to adopt an identity of "very tough and strong and manly." However, such an identity is sanctioned in many social worlds. In this discourse, being heterosexual and macho is considered normal. Presumably, being gay or effeminate is abnormal, something to be disgusted or "grossed out" about. There is, on the other hand, a counter discourse that is about acceptance, being liberal, and "working on" one's less tolerant responses. In this counter discourse, it is presumably okay to watch *Will & Grace*.

Esmelda identifies herself as a Chicana.

There are strong views in my family about women and their roles in marriage and having children. My brothers have had children out of wedlock, and, although my mother was disappointed about it, it was accepted and the family moved on. However, when my sister was pregnant before getting married, she was kicked out of the house and spoken of really badly by my father, and we all let her know how upset and disappointed we were with her.

It is important for the daughters to be married to be considered somebody. The stress on marriage is not as apparent for the males. In nuclear and extended family, the question of marriage pops up at almost all family gatherings. "So, when are you getting married? Your sister is already on her second and you haven't even had your first."

My question to them would be, "How many marriages are you supposed to have?"

Although getting a divorce is looked down on, being married equals success.

To some of our more traditional family members from Mexico, having an education is not as important as marriage.

As my sister kindly put it the other day, "it doesn't matter that we graduated from college and are both doing our master's; we are nothing because we aren't married."

One of my father's sayings about my sister and me is, "Ya estan dejadas" ("They have already been left behind").

This saying is often used in my culture to refer to women; no guy is going to want to marry them because of whatever reason. To my father and to his family, my sister and I, at the ages of 26 and 27, are already considered old for marriage.

Now I am all grown up, and unfortunately things haven't changed much. My family's beliefs are still the same. Because I am a Chicana, I am still expected to become married and have children. It has been hard for my father to say that he is proud that my sister and I have bachelor's degrees and are both currently in graduate school. For him and other members in the extended family, our educational accomplishments are mere awards. We will be considered successful the day we are married and the day we have children.

> This struggle has had an impact on me for the longest time. I think about how I will raise my children and how I will attempt to keep some, if not all, of those beliefs out of my immediate family. It is a struggle to try to balance my family's beliefs with my own, and I can see how this has affected me and will continue.
>
> In certain situations, such as at extended family gatherings or at events with my ex-boyfriend, I have felt the need to act differently. For instance, instead of being together with everyone, I feel I have to stay separated with the women. I have to serve my father and brothers, or ask my partner if he would like to be served. If I don't, my family or significant other will look bad, and that would be the last thing I'd want. At these times I feel as if I'm being a hypocrite because I believe these kinds of roles shouldn't exist.
>
> Therefore, my biggest struggle is trying to keep the idea that women and men are equal without embarrassing my family or a significant other. How do I maintain my own beliefs while still keeping my values and respecting the family? It is as if I have to go along with the idea that women are less than men in order to not put the family to shame. I need to keep up with the cultural idea of the female gender role and still maintain what I consider to be right.

Esmelda is struggling to establish a position that she feels comfortable with in relation to gender discourse. Her own preferences are compromised by the strength of patriarchal discourse in her family. Within this discourse she has been positioned as "left behind" and therefore not normal or legitimate. This positioning gives her a narrow range of options from which to respond, and she experiences being squeezed. We can distill the dominant discourse from Esmelda's comments and represent it in statements such as the following:

- "Marriage, more than education, defines a woman as a success."
- "The right age for a woman to marry is in her early 20s."
- "A man should be the primary breadwinner and more educated than his female partner."
- "A woman can attain true happiness only after marriage."
- "A good mother devotes her entire life to her children and family."

Deconstructive counseling with Esmelda might examine the cultural and gendered discourses at work and their effects on her. It might notice the places where she is willing to make compromises with the dominant discourse (we all have to do that on occasion) and also the places where she wants to exercise her own preferences and position herself in places of resistance. In those places, good counseling might encourage her to articulate more fully the alternative discourses she would like to draw on and examine with her the conscious positions she might want to take up.

In this chapter, we have introduced some concepts that we think of as tools to think with when discussing cultural issues. We believe that they can be used more extensively in the multicultural counseling field than they have been to date. These tools have potential for opening up the tensions and contradictions within cultural worlds, as well as the consistencies and commonalities. To us, they seem to make cultural worlds come alive as sites of difference, movement, and contest, rather than rendering them narrow and static. They enable us to understand processes of change, and since counseling is about the facilitation of change, we believe this is an important advantage.

However, the process of change in relation to dominant discourses will necessarily encounter obstacles. Dominant discourses, by their nature, seek to remain in positions of dominance. Many people who are committed to aspects of them in their daily experience will act to keep them in place, so there will often be struggles that take place in families, in communities, and in cultural worlds. To make sense of these power struggles, multicultural counselors need to develop an analysis of how power works, and that is the subject we shall turn to next. In the next three chapters, we will explore some alternative readings of power.

Box. 5.2. An Exercise in Deconstructing Dominant Discourse

Read the following examples, and then discuss and identify the discourses at work in these examples as you respond to the questions that follow.

Rieko (Japanese)

It is true that some Japanese people have undergone plastic surgery to make their eyes appear round. Recently, a number of women have undergone cosmetic surgery in Korea, where cosmetic surgeries are more popular and cheaper. I understand their feelings and their reasons.

I believe that attractive people have more social power. They are able to exercise power on a daily basis and negotiate their lives more efficiently. Physically attrac-

Rieko Onuma describes herself as Japanese.

tive women are more likely to get privilege than unattractive ones. In many situations, they seem to be treated better and get more opportunities. I had hoped to be an attractive woman. I wanted bigger eyes, long eyelashes, a higher and narrower nose, bigger breasts, and longer and thinner legs. If I had these things, I would have lived a different life.

Michelle (white and Latina)

The American media shows Hispanic women that are exotic looking but not too dark. This idea that being light skinned represents wealth is playing out in Hollywood, and it stems from the views held about skin color in Latin America. The

(Continued)

(Continued)

ideal of light skin goes back to the perception that the Spanish are the wealthier class in El Salvador; the lighter you are, the less "local" blood you have in you. When one does not fit this ideal, oppression is often played out.

My Aba did not fit the mold of a wealthy Hispanic woman. She was very dark skinned and at a young age was given the nickname "Negro," which means black in Spanish. She was constantly reminded that she was a Ladina (a name given in El Salvador to those who are a mixture of Spanish and indigenous), and when

my mother was born she was very relieved that my mom was light skinned. In the United States, my sisters and I have had our own oppression because of our skin color. While living in Texas, we were never seen as children from the same father because our skin tones were so different. In fact, my oldest sister is darker than either of my parents, taking more of the color of my grandmother. People's assumption that we were of different fathers caused oppression within our own community. We as children were also not allowed to play in people's homes because we were half brown. This oppression is the reason why we left Lubbock.

Michelle Wiese identifies herself biracially as white and Latina.

Sarah (heterosexual)

My family is accepting of heterosexual and homosexual choices. My aunt is bisexual and for many years dated only women. Although this took time for my grandparents to accept, they had sensed it before she told them, so it was not a complete shock. Being exposed to gay culture at an early age has positively affected me. I am comfortable interacting with individuals who are gay and strongly support gay rights.

Mandy (Iranian)

The woman's role is primarily based on maintaining innocence and purity. Virginity is imperative for a woman before she is married. Otherwise, she is considered worthless. Once married, women take on the roles of submissive wife, domestic keeper, and loving mother. Although education and a career are attainable prospects, women are more respected for their domestic skills than they are for their individual achievement. On the contrary, Iranian men are honored and tenacious. Sexism in the culture is ubiquitous, as men are not judged for engaging in premarital sex. Furthermore, Iranian law supports the claim that one man is equivalent to two women. This chauvinistic mentality tolerates no deviance.

1. What are the major concepts around which identity can be built in each of these pieces of text?

2. Where are the dividing lines around which differences are marked?

3. What background assumptions do these stories rely on?

4. What discursive statements can you construct that represent the taken-for-granted assumptions of this discourse?

5. What examples can you find of persons being positioned in relation to a dominant discourse?

6. What examples can you find of people drawing on a counter discourse or of resisting the position calls they are offered?

Response to Chapter 5

David Paré

David Paré, Ph.D., is a psychologist and counselor educator at the University of Ottawa. He is the director of the Glebe Institute, which provides therapeutic services, supervision, and training in postmodern therapies. David writes widely and presents internationally on the subject of narrative and postmodern therapies and has coedited two books on the subject, *Collaborative Practice in Psychology and Therapy* and *Furthering Talk: Advances in the Discursive Therapies*.

There was a time when there were no words for the complex interplay of ideas and beliefs, symbols and social rituals that constitute the ways of being in the world that we call "culture" today. Culture was just people living their lives and expressing their humanness in familiar patterns. But as homogeneous local communities expanded outward, they encountered others whose histories and values were unfamiliar, whose ways were strange. *Difference* became manifest, and the language of "culture" emerged to create distinctions never made before. This made it possible to talk about, to think about, and even to act in relation to each other in novel ways.

As John Austin (1962) reminded us, words help us *get things done*, not the least "thing" of which is what Nelson Goodman (1978) called "worldmaking." Language introduces distinctions to make sense of the "great blooming, buzzing confusion" that William James (1890/1981) described infants as perceiving until language helps them organize their experience (p. 462). This is all useful stuff when it comes to counseling and therapy. The dizzying complexity of persons' lives is organized in critically helpful ways through the language we bring to our work. Of that language, "culture" (along with many other words, meanings, and constructs that reverberate around it) has been eminently serviceable for alerting us that therapeutic conversations always take place across a divide. The introduction of culture as a key term awakened the field to its own traditional ethnocentricity. It reminded us that difference characterizes the social world and that homogeneity is an unattainable myth.

These reflections on words as tools for getting things done bubbled up in me as I read through Chapter 5. I see the chapter, indeed this book, as a generous offering of additional tools for practitioners to share with the persons who consult them as they construct new paths forward in complex lives. The chapter takes on theory of distinguished vintage but with a reputation for opaqueness and distills it to the point of transparent clarity. And it does so for some eminently practical purposes. Monk, Winslade, and Sinclair suggest that the trusty tool that is the word *culture* may not always be enough to take on the increasingly complex task of counseling in the 21st century. They offer *discourse* as a valuable addition to counselors' repertoire of worldmaking implements. In what remains of my response, I would like to reflect briefly on three of the many aspects of culturally rooted lives that discourse helps us to engage, and to share an example to illustrate the ideas.

Discursive Multiplicity

Where "culture" reminds us that the persons who consult us come from distinct backgrounds, it's been less helpful in illuminating the many strands of often contradictory ideas and practices that converge simultaneously, like threads of alternate histories, in persons' lives. This may be because the word *culture* has echoes of past meanings that located persons in one *or* another culture, usually separated geographically. In recent years, globalization has brought a massive intermingling of cultures, and contemporary uses of *culture* in counseling transcend the notion of a fixed geographic location. Not only that, but the word now encompasses categories like gender, class, and sexual orientation in addition to race and ethnicity, opening things up further. But *culture* falters in trying to capture how the myriad influences that surround us (someone once said, "We are the fish; discourse is the water") are present *at the same time,* and recede in and out of the foreground as contexts shift. In "cultural" terms, this would be like saying we are both members and nonmembers of particular cultures concurrently: a confusing idea. Understanding persons as at the crossroads of multiple discourses helps to clarify things and opens conversational options not available when we view them as rooted in particular cultures.

Power and Dominant Meanings

I have leafed though the indexes of dozens of contemporary counseling texts in search of the word *power* and found to my dismay that it is rarely included. There is a rich thread of social analysis that comes with the introduction of the word *discourse* to the counseling lexicon. It makes it more possible to join with people in identifying how certain meanings (and the thoughts, feelings, and actions accompanying them) have taken hold because they are attached to powerful stories circulating in the broader culture. It trains the eyes and ears for alternative meanings obscured by dominant versions of "the way things are." And, equally useful, the attention to discourse leads counselors to turn a mirror on their practices and to consider the way that their theories and models, and the institutions in which they are embedded, can be at the service of maintaining normative standards versus opening the door to new possibilities.

The Co-Construction of Meaning

As this chapter reminds us, discourse refers to "both the process of talk and interaction between people and the products of that interaction." Here's another way to put it: discourse is both a verb and a noun (Strong & Paré, 2004). We don't just "draw on" existing meanings generated elsewhere when we talk with each other—talking itself brings new meanings into the world. The importance of this distinction may be easier to understand if we revert to the language of culture. The implication is that our work doesn't just happen *in* culture and isn't just talk *about* culture. Counseling conversations are in effect sites for joining with others in "culture making."

Alain is a working class, 18-year-old French Canadian (known as a Francophone in Canada), self-identified as gay, enrolled in an English-speaking high school mostly attended by wealthy Anglophones. His slight French accent just adds to his energetic, extroverted charm, and he is popular among his circle of mainly gay friends at the school. Alain wants to speak to a counselor not because of problems associated with familiar "cultural" categories like sexual orientation, class, or language group. Rather, he has found he derives more joy in impersonating celebrities and making people laugh than he does in sitting still for hours reading, writing, and working out equations. Alain's gifts are invisible to his father, an electrician, who expects his son to take up the trade that he himself learned from his father. And they are frowned on in a school system that assigns merit according to its own scorecard. Increasingly, Alain feels like a failure.

The construct of "culture" in the broadest sense helps to locate Alain in society. But it is less useful for identifying the meanings that position him as not measuring up and thus unworthy. Those meanings are threaded through the wider culture he inhabits and can be traced intergenerationally through his family. They are a "dominant discourse" that exists alongside *other* versions of events that become more available to Alain as we explore his gifts, connecting them to his Uncle Jacques, who made a career as an actor. There is a multiplicity of stories in Alain's life, and our conversations help to foreground useful ones overshadowed by dominant meanings.

At the same time, it is important that we pay attention to the language of "attention-deficit disorder," which could be taken up in ways that position me as the expert assessor of pathology and Alain as the holder of the deficit. This is where the tool of discourse helps alert me to the risks of merely reinforcing normative prescriptions that Alain is already finding problematic. This is not to say we ignore the possibility that his learning style presents challenges in the school context. But it allows us to grab on to alternative threads and to construct new meanings. In asking Alain, "How have you been able to hang on to your creativity in the face of these messages that surround you?" I am not merely seeking information. This is discourse as verb: Alain and I are co-constructing culture as we speak, and over time it becomes a home for his abundant gifts.

CHAPTER 6

Power and Privilege: Part One

A Liberal Humanist Perspective

This chapter and the two chapters that follow address the issue of power. This is a thorny issue in the helping professions, which are mainly oriented to working with one person at a time. When you are engrossed in the process of counseling one person with regard to his or her struggles in life, it is often hard to conceptualize how the problems he or she is talking about are part of a larger picture of cultural relations. But that's what's required in a multicultural approach to helping relationships. An emphasis on culture invites us to see persons not just as individuals with their own thoughts and feelings about their lives, but as participants in discourse exchanges that shape what they think and feel and as members of social groups that define and legitimate in important ways what they might feel and think about. Even seeing people as members of social groups, though, is not enough, because social groups, like individuals, never exist in isolation. They are always in some form of relation with each other. Hence, we do not really learn enough about a person by knowing about his group membership without considering how the social groups that he identifies with are drawn into relation with other social groups.

It would be nice if all the social groups to which people belonged were equally valued in our communities and if members of all these groups had equal rights and opportunities in life. Then all we would have to do from a multicultural perspective would be to appreciate and celebrate difference. In fact, this simple notion of appreciating and celebrating difference commonly appears in much professional talk about multiculturalism. From this perspective, counselors would only need to learn about and honor the experiences of each social group that they worked with in order for the counseling process to be socially just. A moment's reflection on life in the United States at the moment, however, is enough to see that this situation does not exist.

There are clearly inequities and differential opportunities in life in many dimensions. Another moment's reflection would lead most people to the idea that the ideal situation in which members of all identifiable social groups are equally regarded and have equal opportunities in their community has never really existed anywhere else either. Ideal social justice, while a noble idea, cannot be found on the ground in relations between social groups in any totally satisfactory form. You can find those who claim, usually from a position of privilege, that there is such a situation, but there are always others who object and protest that their chances in life are limited in some material way. Such protests may come from the African American community, which bore a disproportionate share of the effects of Hurricane Katrina. Women still do not command the same salaries as men. Organ transplants are given more frequently to white individuals. Large numbers of the poor do not receive adequate health care. Obese people are commonly overlooked for employment. Unjust power relations can be found in many domains of life. Gay men are sometimes targets for taunting and violent hate crimes. Prostitutes are arrested but their clients are not. These are just a random selection of injustices that can be traced back to power relations.

In order to account for this state of affairs, we need to develop an account of power relations. Such an account needs to explain how inequalities between people and between groups of people are produced and reproduced and how they shape and affect people's lives. It needs to tell how persons influence and shape the lives of other persons. It needs to specify the ways in which institutional authority impacts the lives of individuals. It needs to be an account of both privilege and disadvantage and of the relations between them, and of the ways in which these are not produced randomly or by chance but systematically. It also needs to consider the complexities of people's identity stories that often do not produce uniform and simple distinctions between positions of privilege and disadvantage. An account of power relations needs to give us conceptual tools with which to make sense of the things that people say to counselors about their lives and about the social limits they encounter. How we as professionals conceptualize these things will make a difference in how we respond to our clients, in how we conceive of their problems, and in which remedial strategies we choose to engage with them. The task of the next several chapters, then, is to outline some possible ideas about how we might conceptualize power.

As is the case with many other domains of thought and practice, simple consensus or agreement on these terms and concepts does not exist. We shall need to deal with some contests and debates about the very terms in which power is talked about. To this end, we shall seek to outline the main ideas about power that we perceive to have dominated the counseling literature in recent decades. We shall also address some recent postmodern developments in how power is conceptualized that we believe offer fresh promise for new forms of practice. Contemporary approaches to multiculturalism bring to our attention that counseling is not neutral or objective. We do not believe it ever could be. Especially in relation to questions of power, neutrality and objectivity can render us like the news reporter who takes photographs of a drowning person instead of trying to save her. Therefore, our goal is not to be objective but to represent our beliefs about the most useful ideas we have encountered and to discuss them in relation to other possible conceptualizations and say why we prefer them, in the hope that readers will be stimulated to develop their own thinking about these matters.

Three Approaches to Power

We want to describe three main approaches to the analysis of power relations. They arise out of three different views of the world and lead to markedly different orientations to social practice. The first is the *liberal humanist* view of power that has given rise to most of the world's democratic systems of government, the American Constitution among them. This view is based on a privileging of the individual as the prime mover in the social world. Advocates of this perspective therefore concentrate on how power is attached to individuals. In psychological parlance, this analysis translates into an understanding of "personal" power. This will be the main focus of this chapter.

The second view of power is based on structural thinking. It analyzes power in terms of positions in an underlying social structure rather than as the personal property of the individual. Hence, it is typical of what is sometimes called a *structuralist* analysis. A structuralist approach can be seen to inform the social analysis of Karl Marx and the psychoanalytic theorizing of Sigmund Freud. This view of power has had an enormous influence on social thinking in many fields of academic study, such as politics, economics, history, and sociology. A structuralist analysis has spurred a series of social movements that seek to address structural inequities and hence has been influential in the development of multiculturalism in social practice. This analysis of power will be the focus of Chapter 7.

A third approach to the analysis of power is much newer. It is based on the still emerging *poststructuralist* philosophical perspective, which has brought challenges to both the liberal humanist and the structuralist view of life. In relation to the analysis of power, the work of Michel Foucault (1980, 2000) has made a major contribution to the development of this way of thinking. We believe he offers us some revolutionary tools with which to think about power relations and how they affect the lives of counseling clients. Therefore, we want to explain his conceptualizations of power relations and explore their implications for counseling practice. We shall address this approach to power in Chapter 8.

A Liberal Humanist View of Power

The liberal perspective focuses on the individual and postulates a notional equality of citizens who are, in theory at least, born equal. The emergence of differences among people is accounted for by the choices they make, the extent to which they make use of their genius or potential, and the accidents of genetic endowment. The idea of political equality, or the theory of democratic equality in power relations, had its modern origins in the 17th century and was embodied in the work of John Locke. It was Locke, in his "Treatise on Government," who first articulated the theory of individuals having "natural rights," which he elaborated as the economic right to own property and the intellectual right to freedom of conscience. These natural rights, forerunners of the modern idea of "human rights," were God given and superseded the rights of kings. As such, they constituted a challenge to the premodern idea that people are certainly not equal but instead slotted into a hierarchically organized Chain of Being, and that communities will function best if everything is in order in this hierarchy (Taylor, 2004). The idea of these individual rights drove the English revolutions of 1642 and 1688 and eventually gave impetus to the French Revolution a century later. The American Revolution picked up on the same notions of individual freedom and political rights, and they were written into the American Constitution.

From this perspective, free and equal citizens participate in the marketplace of life and set about influencing each other to varying degrees. They are the authors of their own decisions and act in their own interests. The idea of individual rights requires the notion that persons are independent, rational, unitary beings who are freely responsible for their own decisions and fundamentally separate from the social and historical world around them. Personal change is thus initiated by the individual and is dependent on an individual's choice. Change processes occurring within the individual are initiated by the individual's drawing on personal power. This focus is favored over any assumption that external sociocultural and historical influences might determine human volition and action.

The emphasis on individualism as opposed to collectivity led to the modern tendency for liberal humanist thought to universalize human experience. Mainstream psychology has consistently maintained that its primary focus of study is on a human nature that represents the core functions of the universal human psyche. This perspective assumes an underlying commonality among people. However, this is an unusual emphasis in the history of culture. In a widely quoted summary, anthropologist Clifford Geertz (1983) commented on the narrow, culturally prescribed nature of the person described by liberal humanistic discourse.

> The Western conception of the person as a bounded, unique, more or less integrated motivational and cognitive universe, a dynamic centre of awareness, emotion, judgment, and action, organized into a distinctive whole and set contrastively against other such wholes and against a social and natural background is, however incorrigible it may seem to us, a rather peculiar idea within the context of the world's cultures. (p. 59)

In other words, the perspective from which we might analyze the phenomena of power in cultural relations is itself rooted in a cultural worldview.

In recent decades, liberal humanism has dominated the counseling field. Gaining momentum through Rogerian psychotherapy in the 1960s, this perspective has consistently identified the individual as the agent of all social phenomena. In 1998, Stephen Weinrach and Kenneth Thomas stated that counseling theories (all of them) are rooted in humanism, the individual being the center of any focus. They suggested that abandonment of humanistic counseling theories would leave the counseling movement bereft of any viable theories. We would not agree. We can see a number of burgeoning counseling theories that are steadily abandoning the liberal humanist agenda.

Nevertheless, as personality theory has evolved in psychotherapy, healthy identity has been consistently associated with the dominant white Western cultural norms of achievement, individualism, self-determination, mastery, and material success (Ivey, 1993; Maslow, 1956; Olssen, 1991; Ridley, Mendoza & Kanitz, 1994;

Sampson, 1989; Spence, 1995). Therapeutic goals such as self-actualization, independence, creativity, competence, and autonomy are all based on an individualistic ethic and an individualistic orientation to therapy.

If power is about the ways in which people get other people to do their bidding, then a liberal view of power seeks to explain how this is achieved with reference to internal qualities and attributes of the individual. Some individuals are strong and powerful and others are weak and powerless. Power is thought of as something that individual people "hold" and then exercise. Power is like an object that can be accrued and amassed over time in greater and greater amounts. And if it can be held and accrued, there is at least a notional sense in which it can be measured and calculated. One individual can be talked about as "more powerful" than another. Indeed, whenever you hear someone say that one person is more powerful than another, there likely is a liberal humanist idea of power lurking somewhere in the background.

According to this view, there are certain specific ways in which you can accrue power. You can advance yourself to a position of greater personal authority and become a manager, a judge, a politician, a chief executive; or, for that matter, a gang leader or a terrorist mastermind. Through the authority of the position, you can make and execute decisions that impact other people's lives and in this way exercise power. You can accrue wealth and buy more influence over others. You can threaten others with physical force and get them to do what you want. You can become more educated and develop the kind of authority that comes with being able to speak with greater knowledge than others. You can develop a charismatic presence and eloquence that attracts others to you and allows you to influence them. Power in this sense is emblematic of a position in a social hierarchy of one kind or another. You get more of it by advancing up the ladder of the hierarchy. Where the specific hierarchy is more diffuse, we might substitute the idea of social "status," which is conferred on individuals by various means: titles, leadership roles, ownership, recognition of achievements, academic degrees, election to office, and so forth.

The flip side of this coin is the idea that other individuals are not so lucky, or that they have not had the strength of character or foresight to accrue much of the various currencies in which power is measured. They have not worked hard enough or made good financial decisions and are not wealthy. They have not put time into study and acquired the kind of knowledge that makes others defer to their judgments and opinions. They lack enough personal confidence or strength of character to assert themselves very strongly in conflict situations or in relations with other people. They are physically weaker and less able therefore to back up their influence with force or the threat of it. In the discourse that developed during the 1980s, such individuals are sometimes described as "disempowered," in sharp contrast to those who are powerful.

But simple accounts of power in the liberal humanist tradition have also developed greater sophistication and complexity. Sometimes, those who apparently do not have access to the main currencies of power are described (consciously or unconsciously) as resorting to subterfuges in order to have more power, such as using covert means of "manipulating" others. Psychology has been particularly interested in this idea. Such moves were interpreted as deceptive games in Eric Berne's (1973) runaway best seller *Games People Play*. An example of Berne's analysis is the "Yes, but . . ." game in which someone with few opportunities to address a problem apparent to him or her responds to each effort by another person to make a helpful suggestion with the words, "Yes, but . . ." and then proceeds to say why it will not work. Berne's suggestion is that the person saying "Yes, but . . ." is not sincere but merely seeking to increase personal power by frustrating the other person. The trouble with this analysis is that it can potentially blind the helper to the understandable frustrations of those who live on the margins and actually have restricted opportunities to move. In the therapeutic literature, Fritz Perls's (1972) comments on the competition between top dog and underdog are also built on the assumption that people "pretend" to be underdogs in order to exert subtle manipulative influence over others. Again, the individualistic therapeutic interpretation preempts any kind of appreciation of social circumstances that make for top dog and underdog conditions of life. Stephen Karpman's (1968) drama triangle that analyzes interpersonal interactions in terms of victim, persecutor, and rescuer is another example of thinking in such terms. The three roles are assumed to be interchangeable and more or less equal in their ability to influence people in the other two roles. Playing the "victim" role is thus understood as exercising power in a more manipulative way, rather than as having no power. In each of these accounts of personal power, what is left out is any possibility that those engaged in this relation might not start from a place of equality or that social advantage might not be conferred on them equally.

Personal power has also been talked about in the counseling literature with reference to the concept of "assertiveness" (e.g., Twenge, 2001). This is a description of a personal quality or skill set to be used in influencing others. It is assumed to be possessed by an individual or to be lacking in those who need more of it. It is also distinguished from outright "aggression," which might be conceptualized as the excessive use of assertiveness in ways that do not leave room for others to be assertive as well.

A related idea that developed from the notion of assertiveness is the idea of "empowerment." It can be thought of in various ways, but in the liberal humanist tradition empowerment is often spoken of as the action of a professional to teach skills to an individual who is assumed to be personally lacking in the ability to exercise power. They may be skills in "saying no," focusing on strengths, building individual resilience, or taking risks to stand up to powerful people. What is often noticeable is the equation of power with individual strength, rather than with more relational ideas of, for example, group solidarity.

When racism is explained from the perspective of personal power, it is assumed to be a product of individual thought processes. Racism exists because some persons are racists. These individuals have thought patterns that are irrational in some way, perhaps because of damaging early childhood experiences, or of being trained into authoritarian personality structures (Adorno, Aron, Levinson, & Morrow, 1950). The origins of racist practice are thus assumed to lie in the individual psychology of the person who exhibits it. There have been many research studies into racism that start from this problematic assumption. Even when their findings are methodologically "valid," we believe that empirical data produced by such studies are still faulty because they are grounded in inadequate starting assumptions.

There is a strong tendency toward essentialist thinking in this theory of personal power. It is there in the links postulated between power and personal qualities such as charisma, intelligence, and personality. Freedom and autonomy of action are considered essential givens for the individual "man." (At the time of the origins of the liberal humanist account of individual rights, women, along with slaves, were not included in the equation.) "We hold these truths to be self-evident" said the framers of the American Declaration of Independence, "that all men are created equal." While all persons are theoretically born with equal opportunity, some have talents or develop abilities that make them more powerful than others.

What is the place of culture in this account of power? In the first place, a liberal humanist account of power does not emphasize cultural belonging very strongly. Its emphasis is on the individual's creation of his own life. Culture still has a place in this schema. It is the collective result of the exercise of many individual acts of initiative. Social groups are thought of as "collectives" made up principally of individual actors. Social privilege is often assumed to be earned largely by hard work, strength of character, or extraordinary genius rather than conferred by one's social origins or group membership. Social structures and institutions are assumed to be the products of the autonomous decisions of the individuals who construct them.

Social change happens first on the individual level too. A common catchphrase that has emerged from this worldview and been picked up by some advertising campaigns is, "We are changing the world, one person at a time." Many counselors buy into this idea as they think about their own work. The success of such change is measured by counting the number of individual changes that happen. So, changes in the social relations of privilege and disadvantage would be measured by counting, say, the number of African Americans or women entering positions of leadership, or the number of Latinos gaining graduate degrees, or the number of persons with disabilities earning a particular annual salary, or the number of openly gay and lesbian people being appointed as CEOs.

All this emphasis on the individual as the source of power is not, in itself, culturally neutral. This idea, like most ideas, comes from a cultural background, has a history, and fits into a matrix of other cultural assumptions. It has its origins in a Western view of the world and works best among people who hold other ideas originating in the dominant discourse of the European cultural tradition. For those who are not so culturally attuned to the Western worldview and who are more influenced by collectivist cultural narratives, this way of thinking about the relation between the individual and the social group makes less sense. For them, the liberal humanist version of power often does not fit. The history of the last few hundred years that we discussed in Chapter 3 means that the Western assumptions of the individual are everywhere, are accorded most airspace, and are often assumed to coincide with universal truths. Such is the modern world.

But there are problems with this liberal humanist idea of power other than those that relate to fit. The emphasis on individuals as the source of power does not account well for the role of institutions in the construction of powerful effects on individual lives. It tends to portray persons as autonomous beings who are primarily responsible for their plight in life. It easily turns into personal blame, even in the hands of counselors who profess to be nonjudgmental. What gets left out are the ways in which, for example, racism, sexism, and homophobia get built into the structure and practices of institutions like schools and courtrooms beyond what any one individual ever intends. Liberal humanism does not take into account the ways in which people act or respond to others' actions, not always on a unique individual basis but in patterns that are typical of, for example, their social class position or their gender, or the culture of an institution. Culture is not just a matter of individual difference but of group allegiance, and cultural patterns act on the consciousness of individuals in powerful ways. It is therefore not uncommon for people to feel that they are helpless to exercise their own choices in the face of systemic forces that constrain them.

The dominance of liberal humanistic values has nevertheless been so taken for granted in contemporary counseling practice that practitioners regard it as the natural prescription for addressing human misery. Yet this stance has, albeit inadvertently, blamed people who are marginalized for their very marginalization. It is a small step from taking a personal view of power to criticizing those who are victims for their irresponsibility or their lack of individual effort in addressing their problems.

In contrast to the liberal humanist position, structural approaches, which we discuss in the next chapter, reject outright the mainstream humanist assumption that the individual is both the source of all human action and the most important unit of social analysis. Despite these criticisms, a liberal humanist focus maintains momentum. Stephen Weinrach and Kenneth Thomas (1998) argue,

> Although it is clear that in the twenty-first century fewer and fewer clients (and counselors) will be White, there may be some reason to believe that widespread assimilation may reduce the urgency for radical modification of existing counseling theories. (p. 117)

Even in the face of their own recognition of the inevitability of a multicultural perspective, these writers maintain their defense of the liberal humanist discourse. We believe, however, that the liberal humanist account of power relations is seriously limited in the extent to which it can acknowledge systemic influences, hence the appeal for a more structural analysis of how power relations are formed. We shall look at this contrasting model of power in Chapter 7.

Counseling Example Influenced by a Liberal Humanist Perspective on Power

Now let's look at this perspective on power in action and discuss how it might look in the middle of counseling. Our intention here is to make clearer the argument outlined in this chapter by giving an example of some practices that embody the ideas we have talked about. This is necessarily an interpretive act on our part, and, of course, it is difficult to provide straightforward examples of what we are discussing. This difficulty arises because counseling conversations are messy things that are not easy to pin down in relation to a philosophical issue in a brief section of a chapter.

We also want to avoid asking readers to wade through lengthy counseling transcripts in order to understand the points we're making, and therefore we have constructed a brief example, adapted from some reconstructed actual counseling sessions, of a story that illustrates the perspective on power that this chapter has explicated.

Daneesha came to her counseling appointment with Rebeka appearing visibly distraught. They had been meeting for counseling weekly for the past six weeks and had been working on some issues of self-esteem that Daneesha was concerned about. On this occasion, Daneesha was tearful and shaken about what she described as an upsetting conversation at a recent committee meeting at her church.

Rebeka inquired about what had happened.

"Well, I'm on this committee with a group of women. I've known them all for about a year and some of them for several years. There are only a few African Americans at my church and I'm the only African American on the committee. The other women are mostly Mexican American."

"Okay," said Rebeka. "So did something happen at the committee meeting?"

Daneesha recounted an uncomfortable exchange at the meeting earlier that day.

"We were discussing a social event that we're supposed to be planning as a fund-raiser. One of the women told a story to the group about how her husband referred to her as a 'nigger.' She said it was like a joke, and she was just laughing as she said it."

"Sounds like you didn't feel very amused," said Rebeka.

"Actually, I was shocked to hear her use the *N* word," said Daneesha. "And I was even more uncomfortable because the other women chuckled at the incident."

Daneesha stated that nothing was said about its being wrong or that it might create discomfort for her.

"I don't know which is worse—that they used the *N* word or that they laughed about it," she said.

"It upset you that they laughed and that they were using the *N* word. Which do you think is worse?" her counselor asked.

Daneesha thought about this as she wiped away tears.

"Actually, what is the worst is not the use of the word or their laughter, but that I didn't say anything about it!"

"I don't understand," said Rebeka. "How is that worse? Can you explain it to me?"

"I should have told them how offensive this was and left the room. Instead, I just kind of looked at the woman who said it."

As she told what she should have done, Daneesha became more animated and upset. Rebeka moved forward in her chair and began to respond in a calming voice.

"You sound angry," she commented. "She must have hurt you."

"I am angry. Now that I'm talking about it, I realize what was wrong with it. And it does make me boil. I tried to talk to my neighbor about it before coming here, but she wasn't home. I have been thinking about it over and over since it happened."

After a full exploration of the problematic experience, the counselor attempted to locate the client's reaction in the historical context of her life.

"Have there been other times when you've noticed feeling upset by people talking about race or using disrespectful language?"

Daneesha thought back to a time when she was much younger, perhaps only 12 or 13 years old, and shared the recollection with Rebeka. She had been with her mother at a grocery store in Tennessee, where she grew up. Her mom had asked for assistance from a young clerk.

"I don't even recall what my mom wanted," she said, "but the clerk sneered and rudely said, 'I don't do anything for niggers.'"

As Daneesha recounted this event, her tears returned.

"It must have been really hard for you to hear someone express racial hatred in front of you and your mother," the counselor commented.

"It was. My mom told me to be quiet about it, and she said the godly thing to do was to pray for the young man, and we simply walked out of the store."

"So, in both of these situations you felt angry and powerless, right?" said Rebeka.

"Yes," Daneesha answered with resignation, and was silent.

"So what could you have done this morning to claim more power for yourself?"

"I could have told her that I was offended and to knock it off."

"What would that have felt like?"

Daneesha said that it would have felt good.

"Would it be helpful for us to rehearse what you might say on other occasions when you experience this kind of silencing and lose your voice?" asked Rebeka. "'Cause it sounds like in situations like this you want someone to know what's in your heart and to be assertive about it."

Daneesha smiled, and they continued to discuss strategies for empowering her in this situation and others like it.

How is the liberal humanist analysis of power present in this counseling scenario? We need to examine a series of assumptions that underlie the counseling practices used here. First, both of the interactions are talked about as incidents between two individuals. The counselor makes no attempt to help the client locate the incidents in a wider cultural context. Instead, they are referenced as personal experiences. The origins of the racism are connected to feelings of "racial hatred" on the part of the clerk in the store and to enjoyment of humor on the part of Daneesha's fellow committee members, rather than to any systemic structures or discourses. The responses the counselor makes reinforce these assumptions by centering on the feeling content of the experience in the client and offering empathetic support. Daneesha is assumed to have a primarily personal response to both exchanges. Her responses are not apparently considered to be produced out of her structural social position. Rebeka does provide acknowledgment of Daneesha's sense of powerlessness. To be powerful is to have the ability to be assertive and express anger on one's own behalf. In this way, one might get other people to take notice of one's feelings and modify their hurtful behavior.

Another assumption in this work is that powerlessness is a personal deficit that Daneesha has developed within her. The question about Daneesha's past suggests that personal deficits usually arise out of formative childhood experiences in one's family of origin that have been internalized. The therapeutic strategy that Rebeka uses is one of helping Daneesha to get more in touch with her feelings of anger and strength, to learn how to express these in powerful ways, and to strategize to find ways to apply this knowledge in future situations she might come across.

TO DISCUSS

1. In the counseling conversation with Daneesha, what specific things did the counselor do that fit with a liberal humanist perspective on power?

2. Search counseling texts or videotapes for examples of the expression of a liberal humanist perspective.

3. Role-play a counseling interview similar to the one between Daneesha and Rebeka and discuss how it is experienced from the client's point of view.

4. What value can be obtained from a focus on individual rights? What does a focus on individual rights not address?

5. From your experience or from your reading, identify some cultural traditions that do not give the individual the prime place of honor.

Response to Chapter 6

Judy Daniels

Judy Daniels, Ed.D., is a professor in the Department of Counselor Education at the University of Hawaii. She received her doctorate from Vanderbilt University, her master's degree from the University of Tennessee, and her bachelor's degree from Washington University. Dr. Daniels is well known for her work as a social justice advocate and scholar. She has published over 40 refereed book chapters and articles and several books, and she has conducted over 85 national and international presentations. She has received a number of awards from the American Counseling Association, including the prestigious Wrenn Award and the Fellow Award. She has also received two teaching awards from the University of Hawaii.

This chapter is about how counselors and clients conceptualize power from a liberal humanist perspective. More specifically, as the authors of this chapter note, counselors need to explain "how inequalities between people and between groups of people are produced and reproduced and how they shape and affect people's lives" (p. 142). In the case presented in this chapter, Daneesha explains to her counselor the ways in which inequalities were manifested when the Hispanic members of her church group expressed comments reflecting unintentional forms of racism and relates how this dynamic has adversely impacted her psychological well-being.

The authors effectively demonstrate how the culturally competent counselor can help clients like Daneesha overcome their sense of powerlessness in such encounters "by centering on the feeling content of the experience in the client and offering empathic support" (p. 150). Centering on the feeling context of the experience and offering empathic support are important considerations in dealing with the client's sense of powerlessness so that the client may acquire personal affirmation and confidence as well as obtain a sense of personal power. However, the next step of the helping process is essential and cannot be ignored. This next step focuses on power issues involved in helping clients like Daneesha develop new behavioral strategies that can be used to effect change in both themselves and their environment.

Consequently, my approach to working with Daneesha would extend beyond what is discussed in this chapter. I would build on the positive effect of communicating empathic support and encourage Daneesha to process her feelings so that she might now explore specific behavioral strategies that she can implement to effectively express her concerns with the other members of the church group and start to effect change in her environment. In doing so, Daneesha is likely to benefit from a mild confrontation presented by the counselor. This sort of confrontation might be manifested simply by the counselor's presentation of the following statements: "Now that we've talked about the feelings you had when the women in your church group made the racial comments they did, I wonder if we can take some time to brainstorm what you might do in your next meeting with these woman that will assist them in understanding how you felt about the last meeting. Let's think of how you might help these women better understand how we're all prone to manifesting unintentional forms of racism that adversely impact friends and potential alleys in our daily lives."

When I have implemented this type of strategy in my own work with individuals, I have waited to see the client's response to this challenge. Sometimes, allowing the client to express her feelings and engage in empathic communication about experiences such as the one Daneesha had is sufficient to encourage the client to express her newly found sense of personal power by directing her situation. On the other hand, I have noted that some clients benefit from having me initiate a collaborative process, characteristic of feminist counseling, by offering a suggestion that I think might be useful for them to implement in the future. Of course, the emphasis here is not to provide all the answers, but rather to assist in mutual problem solving with clients who, like Daneesha, are likely to benefit from developing new behavioral strategies that complement the affective and cognitive gains acquired by exploration of their feelings.

It is important to note that the primary purpose of adding a behavioral component to counseling sessions is to foster the personal power of clients to effect change in their situation and to begin to effect structural change in their environment. If I were working with a client like Daneesha, I would find it useful to encourage her to extend her impact even further by considering the benefits of developing a consciousness-raising group at her church. This type of group could intentionally focus on issues of racism, internalized oppression, and the need to build allies to promote a greater sense of justice in the church members' interactions with each other and with the community the church serves.

In summary, I have found a five-step approach useful in helping women like Daneesha utilize their growing sense of personal power to explore and implement positive personal and environmental changes.

- Step 1. Build a positive and trusting relationship based on the communication of empathic understanding that facilitates the client's exploration of vulnerable feelings that arise within her when she is subjected to racism.
- Step 2. Assist the client in understanding how the expression of such feelings and the validation of their experience is an important component in discovering new dimensions of personal power.
- Step 3. Extend the client's sense of personal power by exploring new ways that she can effect positive changes in her environment and then exploring the strengths and weaknesses of each strategy.
- Step 4. Encourage the client to make a commitment to take action steps aimed at creating change in herself and in her environment.
- Step 5. Begin the next counseling session with an evaluation of the positive and/or negative outcomes of implementing these new strategies in the client's world.

Clearly, there are many ways that counselors can utilize a liberal humanistic perspective in counseling settings to help clients realize new and untapped dimensions of their personal power. I hope that my own counseling approach expands this perspective of building on personal power by exploring new behavioral strategies that extend our thinking beyond just creating changes in individual clients and create a greater impact through systemic and environmental changes.

CHAPTER 7

Power and Privilege: Part Two

A Structural View of Power

Whereas a personal account of power relations focuses on the individual, as we saw in the last chapter, a structural analysis constructs the individual as a product of her position in a social structure. Individuals are less than completely free because their choices are, to some extent at least, determined for them by social structures, or by "the system." It therefore becomes more important to analyze the structures that shape and determine us and to set about working out how to change them. A structural analysis helps explain how some people seem to have unearned privilege and enjoy the right to have others do their bidding, not on any personal account of talent or hard work but on the happenstance of their position in a set of social relations. Indeed, people are often born into these positions, and the power that they exercise precedes the entry of any one individual into such systems. From this perspective, power is a product of deep-seated social forces that produce structural sets of relations among groups of people. Individual power is the downstream effect rather than the cause of these intergroup relations. It is produced in individuals by virtue of their membership in a group or by their position in a social structure that is not entirely of their own making.

Indeed, a structural analysis suggests that the conscious thoughts and intentions of individuals are not to be trusted as the primary sources of their actions. They are rather the surface effects of much deeper structural systems. People's thoughts, desires, motivations, and intentions are not just their own. They are determined by systematic forces outside the individual. Individuals are to a certain extent puppets of the system. When they open their mouths, they speak the lines of their position in an organized system of social relations more than they speak of their personal experience.

A structural analysis is founded on the idea that below the surface of any social phenomenon lies a deep structure that gives shape to what is visible. This structure is hidden from view but is nonetheless real and determining. It can be deduced from its effects rather than immediately sensed. The metaphor "structure" suggests an edifice as solid and permanent as a building. Those who build models of social structures often argue that they are foundational for human experience and that many of the things that people talk about, or get upset about, are less important. These things are the superficial epiphenomena that shift and change, not through processes of conscious persuasion but through fundamental shifts in the underlying social structure. For example, a structuralist argument about the reasons for a war would not concentrate on the explanations politicians articulate but on the underlying economic forces that produce the conflict, such as access to oil, competition for markets, or contradictory national interests.

A structural analysis is often compelling because it appears to see through immediate and confusing detail to more solid and enduring forces at work. It enables us to make sense of a large number of different events by reducing them to a single unifying explanation. The individual experiences of discrimination against women are explained better by a structural analysis of patriarchy than by an analysis of the negative oppressive intentions of the individual men in their lives.

For example, male violence has been viewed in the mental health and counseling field as arising from patriarchal patterns of male power and control. Ellen Pence (1993) and her colleagues reported how male violence is promoted by an attitude of entitlement by men within their relationships with women. She stated that men who are violent believe they have a right to be the sole authority in the home. With this authority comes control over family financial resources, decisions over whom their partners can associate with, and a belief that they are entitled to access to their partners' bodies. Around this same time, the counseling profession was criticized for its failure to address issues of patriarchy and male violence in particular (e.g., Drewery, 1986; Goldner, 1985; McKinnon & Miller, 1987; Treadgold, 1983; Waldegrave, 1985).

The structuralist perspective on patriarchy and Eurocentric practices divides people into opposing camps of oppressors and the oppressed. Belonging to a defined group rather than individual intention is the main criterion for such division. The actions of professionals, however, may be analyzed for whether they collude with oppression or not. Many feminist researchers and practitioners have confronted mental health professionals for colluding with culturally oppressive practices and failing to attend to the structural inequalities that support racism and sexism (Calvert, 1994; Hindmarsh, 1987; Lawson–Te Aho, 1993; McKinnon & Miller, 1987; Ohlson, 1993; Smith, 1992; Tamesese & Waldegrave, 1993).

Karl Marx's analyses remain the most extensive theoretical accounts of social structure. Marx sought to explain the shaping of human consciousness by the relentless structuring power of economic forces. In Marx's analysis, within a given social system of organization, the structural economic base, that is, the means of economic production (including the social relations of production), determines social class relations (Tucker, 1978). On this economic base is built a superstructure of ideas and beliefs, but these are not independent of economic forces. They are determined and structured by the economic base. Thus, from a Marxist perspective, ideology, rhetoric, art, religion, fashion, and politics are all assumed to be products of social structure rather than producers of it. In order to understand the ideological and political world, it is necessary to refer back to the economic or material base to understand the major organizing forces (Tucker, 1978). Political, religious, and philosophical ideas are thus relegated to the position of social effects and stripped of the possibility of originary force. As Vivien Burr (1995) points out, in Marxist analysis, ideology per se is always to be suspected as "false consciousness" and human beings are considered almost to be irrational and unwitting puppets of social and material forces beyond their control.

A feminist analysis of systemic patriarchy is often also structuralist in its orientation. It does not credit individual men with the oppression of women through the exercise of their personal power as much as it stresses a systematic structural organization of life chances for men and women that grants considerable privilege to men and oppresses women. Hence, the feminist movement of the 1970s and 1980s worked by organizing consciousness-raising experiences for women. It was most often consciousness about the structural organization of gender relations that was being raised. Paulo Freire's education work with the poor was based on a similar practice of raising people's consciousness of structural conditions. Freire's "conscientization" was based on an educative and liberatory process that empowered subjugated peoples to recognize and ultimately challenge structural oppression (Freire, 1976).

In its strongest form, a structural analysis thus takes the view that most people's difficulties are caused by social conditions over which they have little or no control (Poster, 1989). Indeed, from this perspective, counseling sometimes seems to have little point at all. At best, it might provide temporary relief from the ravages of systematic oppression, or place a Band-Aid over deep wounds, but it cannot alter a social structure by meeting with individuals one to one.

According to Jennie Harré Hindmarsh (1993), structural theorists have concentrated on dealing with the outcomes of struggles around issues such as capitalism, patriarchy, and racism. The goals of a structural analysis are always structural change. Some kind of revolution, some universal law change, some mass transfer of wealth or power is always envisaged. The danger of this kind of analysis is that it always runs the risk of thinking in terms of the macro struggle and ignoring the particular complexities of personal experience in the individuals whose interests it purports to represent. In always focusing on the masses, it can sometimes be disrespectful to individual members of these masses. Individuals tend to be viewed primarily as members of groups, and their interests are considered to be the interests of the group rather than their own concerns.

A structural analysis shares with a liberal humanist analysis the understanding of power as a commodity. The difference lies in how the commodity of power is obtained. Rather than being a product of individuals' talents, power is vested in individuals on the basis of their structural positioning or group membership. However, it is still viewed as a finite quantity that is distributed unevenly among groups of people. Since power is assumed to be a commodity accrued by those in structural positions of advantage, it follows that those who are the objects of the operation of this power must be powerless. From this position, there seems little that the powerless can do to change things.

The Concept of Hegemony

A problem for a structural analysis of power is how to account for the times when people appear to be acting or speaking against the interests of their class or race or gender. It was in response to this problem that the concept of hegemony was developed. This idea originated from the Italian Marxist, Antonio Gramsci (1971), in his writings from prison. Hegemony is the process whereby the consciousness of the powerless is locked into an interpretation of experiences within the fixed categories and perspectives of the dominant (Lears, 1985). Jackson Lears defined Gramsci's hegemony as the

> spontaneous consent given by the great masses of the population to the general direction imposed on social life by the dominant fundamental group; this consent is historically caused by the prestige which the dominant group enjoys because of its position and function in the world of production. (p. 568)

The concept of hegemony is a move toward an understanding of how power operates inside the heads of those whom it oppresses. From inside their heads, power can get people to "voluntarily" give consent to the conditions of their own oppression. Such practices are evident in the phrase, "Even when they say no, that might not be what they mean." Thus, unsuspecting oppressed groups consent to the definitions of their experience by social elites and speak about their lives in these terms. Since they are participants in the operation of power, they are less likely to later object to it, even when it produces adverse effects in their lives. A marginalized person who has not been enlightened about hegemonic processes may not even be in a position to identify the source of his oppression and thus take any action. From a structuralist analysis, the liberal humanist analysis of power itself serves a hegemonic function.

There is, however, a trap in this structuralist analysis. It tends to end up with a self-appointed enlightened person knowing better about what someone else is saying and reinterpreting it for her. This in itself might be thought of as an act of power. Thus, when counselors practice from within a structuralist discourse, they run the risk of communicating profound disrespect to their clients. When an "oppressed person" gives an answer to a question, the counselor might recognize this opinion as a reflection of a colonized mind-set and might proceed to reinterpret events to the client. This has the effect of suggesting that colonized people cannot "know their own minds." Thus, a structuralist analysis ironically risks adopting a position of superiority and thereby disrespecting even those whom it aims to support.

Gender, Race, and Class

Structural analysis often shares with a liberal humanist analysis the assumption that power is owned by those in structural positions of privilege. From the perspective of most structuralists, power is a commodity or property possessed by those at the top of the social hierarchy. Hence, social justice requires us to identify who owns the power when we respond to social injustice. Power is viewed as a finite quantity, distributed unevenly between groups, particularly on the basis of gender, ethnicity, class, and sexuality (Jones & Guy, 1992). This analysis of power views oppression as being structured hierarchically, with those experiencing the worst oppression on the bottom and their oppressors on the top. Typically, white middle and upper class men are identified as accumulators of more power than anyone else on the basis of their structural membership in these identity groups. You can add to these oppressor identity categories heterosexuals, the able-bodied, and Christians. The oppressed groups, meanwhile, are made up of those categorized as women, people of color, gays and lesbians, the disabled, and non-Christians. Discussions about empowerment tend to view power as a property that can be appropriated and redistributed among these groups (Gore, 1992).

Julian Henriques, Wendy Hollway, Cathy Urwin, Couze Venn, and Valerie Walkerdine (1984) argue that the orthodox Marxist's position in relation to the theory of patriarchal power is that power is the property of men as the dominant sex class and that women are victims, the objects of power. Within this analysis, the group with the power is oppressive and the group without the power is oppressed. Since the oppressed don't have any power, it appears that there is very little they can do to change things. The oppressor group is seen to benefit uniformly from the status quo, and the oppressed group must pay the price. Indeed, a structural analysis tends to make social change seem very difficult. It is suspicious of, and sometimes even cynical about, any changes that do not amount to a significant overturning of structural arrangements. Anything less than a decisive transformation or revolution may be dismissed as cosmetic or token. Until such a moment, the role of helping professionals should be one of educating the oppressed about the nature of their oppression and producing an anger that might motivate change. Brian Fay (1987) suggests that "critical oppressive moments" are opportunities to educate those suffering from unjust hierarchical structures to help them develop the necessary volition to produce a transformative experience.

The difference between a structural discourse of power and a liberal humanist discourse is the ability to critique the simplistic assumption that individuals are free agents with equal ability to extricate themselves from unjust circumstances. Unlike liberal humanists, who emphasize individual will and motivation, structuralists focus on the centrality of repressive social practices that contribute to oppression, marginalization, and powerlessness.

During the 1970s in the United States, the major structural emphasis in therapy was the recognition of the structural politics of gender relations and the idea that the therapist-client relationship should be structurally egalitarian (Gilbert, 1980). As a result of feminists' work on sex bias and sex role stereotyping, psychologists became more aware of the importance of informing clients about procedures, goals, and potential side effects of counseling and psychotherapy. During this period, some feminist therapists believed that limiting one's practice to counseling individuals was a form of treating the symptoms and avoiding the cause. They highlighted the need to work with the social disease represented by society. Edna Rawlings and Dianne Carter (1977) suggested that social action is an essential professional responsibility of therapists.

Much of the structuralist literature in the 1980s and 1990s, typified by a radical feminist analysis of patriarchy and male violence, focused on the variety of abuses perpetrated by men against women. Women were portrayed as being trapped by patriarchy and were thought to believe their role was to be subservient to men, and thus they were considered to collude with patriarchy.

Imelda Whelehan (1995) gives an example of the kinds of statements that were made by radical feminists in the United States around this time:

> All men are our policemen, and no organized police force is necessary at this time to keep us in our places. All men enjoy male supremacy and take advantage of it to a greater or lesser degree depending on their position in the masculine hierarchy of power. (p. 536)

From this analysis, male counselors were challenged regarding their ignorance of historical and contemporary institutional patriarchy and its effects on their practice (Calvert, 1994; Chesler, 1972; Ehrenreich & English, 1979; Hindmarsh, 1987; Lawson–Te Aho, 1993; Plath, 1963).

Karen Offen (1988) stated that in order to counsel women in a respectful way, the counselor needs to first assess a woman's status in society relative to men and then encourage her to claim her own values rather than be trapped by the ideal of what a woman should be according to patriarchal specifications. Offen also suggested that counselors should encourage women to challenge the coercive authority of male privilege. Structuralists have criticized the individualistic focus promoted by liberal humanism, which directed the counseling practitioners' gaze away from the domination of patriarchy in the counseling profession. Mental health researchers adopting a liberal humanist position can be tempted to pathologize the experiences of female clients.

Those advocating a structuralist approach to addressing gender issues in counseling note that women enter therapy more frequently and more often present with affective distress and anxiety-related disorders and relationship-related problems (Moore & Leafgren, 1990). Royda Crose, David Nicholas, David Gobble, and Beth Frank (1992) commented that women suffer from more debilitating chronic disease, whereas men suffer from more life-threatening illnesses, such as heart disease. They cited numerous examples of the psychological costs of patriarchal and androcentric culture to women. These authors suggested that women are more likely than men to receive a diagnosis of mental disorder by their physicians. Women are more often prescribed psychotropic medication and take more prescription and over-the-counter drugs. Crose and her colleagues suggested that women are also more likely to be informally labeled with a hypochondriacal, psychosomatic, hysterical, or dependent personality.

In studies that address differential diagnoses by gender, men are found to have four or five times higher rates of alcohol abuse and antisocial personality. Judith Daniluk, Monika Stein, and Diana Bockus (1995) suggested that men who seek assistance frequently present with problems related to career, impulse control, and alcohol or other drug abuse, while women are twice as likely to exhibit depression, anxiety, or phobic disorders. Maye Taylor (1994) reported on recent surveys revealing that a high percentage of individuals with signs of depression, anxiety, panic, anorexia, and phobia are women, and that they constitute a very large percentage of the client population.

Structuralists make a link between patriarchal practices and an overdeveloped male gender role, which sometimes gets expressed by increased risk taking, self-destructive activities, high stress, emotional inexpressiveness, an emphasis on control, and the drive to accumulate money (Kimmel & Levine, 1989; Meth, 1990; Pleck, 1981; Stewart & Lykes, 1985). James O'Neill (1990) stated that men can display "rigid, sexist, or restrictive gender roles" because of the structural influences of patriarchal practice (p. 25). For both men and women, differences are attributed to group membership in structural relations.

To avoid further exacerbation of the structural inequalities between men and women, some counseling researchers have proposed that male therapists should avoid working with female clients. The commodity metaphor of power would make it impossible to attain equity, understanding, respect, or indeed justice between counselor and client when a client is positioned in an oppressed group and the counselor in an oppressor group. Not only is it unlikely that a counselor from an oppressor group could empathize with a client who is a member of an oppressed group, except on the basis of an unequal relationship, but he might also have some unconscious investment in maintaining the oppressive status quo. To do anything else might undermine his privileged position. From this standpoint, it would be congruent to match counselor and client on the basis of a shared experience of oppression. Separatist developments in counseling, promoted by structuralists, use this form of commodity analysis of power in relation to understanding oppression and achieving their goal of equalizing power relations. In fact, radical feminists employing a structural analysis view gender matching for clients as a legitimate method of seeking justice for women in the counseling relationship. Maye Taylor (1991) suggested that female clients can achieve independence in the counseling process by being unencumbered by "male transference." Edna Rawlings and Dianne Carter (1977) suggested that in most instances, men should not counsel women. And, based on their clinical experience, "two feminist therapists" (Fisher & Maloney, 1994) concluded that women should work with a female therapist, stating, "In our experience we have not met a woman who has benefited as much from a male as from a female therapist" (p. 18).

Structuralism views relationships between different groups as a hierarchy of oppressions where the power relations are understood to be both monolithic and fixed. Wendy Larner (1995) identified how structuralist interpretations produce binary frameworks not only on the basis of gender but also by ethnicity, class, and sexual orientation. Binary distinctions are either/or distinctions that limit possible interpretations to two options only. You are either oppressed or an oppressor, for example. Such formulations do not allow gray areas, contradictory positions, or complexities in experience to be noticed.

The barriers to educational achievement experienced by those living in poor working class communities are better understood in terms of systemically produced economic disadvantage than by an explanation that focuses on the personal motivation to succeed of the individuals in those communities. Charles Waldegrave (1992) believed that many therapists address problems without reference to the real cause (which he suggests is often poverty and oppression). After therapy is concluded, people are sent straight back to the condition that created the problem in the first place. From this perspective, counselors are not benign helpers but rather functionaries of a system, there to help people adjust and adapt to the dominant group's values and conditions. Numerous authors have presented similar arguments (Hindmarsh, 1993; Katz, 1985; Szasz, 1974). Jessie Bernard (1969) suggests that counseling practice is often concerned with reconciling and adjusting people to the failure and defeat that are products of a capitalist and classist system. He criticizes counselors for colluding with this system to help people who have genuine grievances become pacified in unjust situations. Bernard maintains that a competitive and capitalistic society requires that there be failures despite all that might be done to minimize them. Saul Alinsky (1969) graphically illustrated a structuralist analysis in describing how appointed helpers adjust people to poverty:

> They come to the people of the slums under the guise of benevolence and goodness, not to help people fight their way out of the muck but to be adjusted so that they will live in hell and like it too. It is difficult to conceive of a higher form of treason. (p. 18)

For some, a structural analysis renders counseling virtually redundant. As a practice, so this argument runs, counseling is much too focused on the superficial aspects of individuals' lives to ever get at the important underlying forces at work in the production of their oppressive experiences.

Derald Wing Sue and David Sue (1990), referring to counseling in North America, summed up the argument as follows:

> While counseling enshrines the concept of freedom, rational thought, tolerance for new ideas, and equality and justice for all, it can be used as an oppressive instrument by those in power to maintain the status quo. In this respect counseling becomes a form of oppression in which there is an unjust and cruel exercise of power to subjugate or mistreat large groups of people. (p. 6)

In this analysis, the difficulty people of color experience in reaching positions of seniority is better explained with reference to structural institutional racism than it is with reference to each specific instance of personal discrimination.

The examples above illustrate the three major axes that have occupied the academic attention of those who have pursued a structural social analysis: race, gender, and class. This analysis has produced an account of patriarchy, an account of racism, and an account of economic privilege that are founded on a systematic organization of relations between binary social groups of oppressors and the oppressed, rather than on the conscious decisions of individuals.

While race, gender, and class have been the most intensely analyzed features of systems of social relations, there are other forms of social structure as well. For instance, organizations and corporations have a systemic structure and can be analyzed for their institutional determination of personal experience. Institutions such as the family, the peer group, and the school can be analyzed for their structural features. Governments, courts, banking systems, markets, and the media all have structures that have shaping effects. You have no doubt heard talk of a community's "infrastructure." Anthropologists have applied structural analysis to the study of kinship systems and myths (Lévi-Strauss, 1967, 1969). Linguists have studied the "deep structure" of language (Chomsky, 1966; Saussure, 1986). Psychologists have pursued the method of structural analysis into the domain of the psyche (Freud, 1938) and have sought to explain the dynamics of personal experience with reference to the enduring structures of personality. Family therapists have analyzed families in terms of their structural organization (Minuchin, 1974).

This kind of analysis has implications for how change happens. It suggests that the most important kinds of change happen not on the surface but in the deep structure of a system. It is therefore not so important to understand the surface phenomena as it is to get at what at first remains hidden, to get at the underlying structure. Only through a thorough analysis of this underlying structure can "real" change be brought about. Real and lasting change can only be structural change. From this perspective, it makes little sense to change the world "one person at a time." Some kind of major restructuring is needed.

The idea of pursuing major structural change has been a common theme in many fields. It has driven major restructuring projects in businesses, organizations, and government agencies. It has provided the rationale for many political revolutions. It has shaped the goal setting agendas of civil rights movements for many groups of people in many places. And without a doubt, a structural analysis has driven many social changes as diverse as the civil rights movements in the South of the United States in the 1960s and the economic restructuring undertaken by the Reagan administration and the Thatcher government (among others around the world) in the 1980s.

Problems With a Structural Analysis

The major critiques of a structuralist analysis of power have come from the school of thought that has become known as poststructuralism. These criticisms have been directed against the grand narratives of structuralist social analysis. It is, in fact, difficult to make sense of the complexity of relations among people if we rigidly divide them into categories of the oppressed and the oppressors. Even when such divisions are compelling, there are many exceptional circumstances in which oppression appears to happen in reverse.

As a result, many arguments have developed among "oppressed" groups. During the early 1980s, when white middle class women argued that the category *woman* joined all women together in solidarity and hope for emancipation, they made the assumption that black women shared the experiences of white women. However, many women of color made it clear that this argument was too simplistic. They argued that the experience of black women was not always analogous with that of white women and that their allegiance was shared across a spectrum of identities (Poindexter-Cameron & Robinson, 1997). *Woman* was only one of these. The radical feminist notion of "sisterhood," rather than becoming a universal rallying cry, was fractured into competing discourses. The problem was, as Jennifer Gore (1992) suggested, that some structural theorists failed to explore how the concept of liberation was bound to particular contexts, rather than being of universal appeal to women, just as Marxist concepts of revolution were not welcomed universally by the working class.

Structuralist analyses of power began to appear too monolithic. Julian Henriques and his colleagues (1984) argued that power is not singularly the property of one side in a power relation, nor is it inherent in the apparatus of the state. To describe a group of people as powerless is in the end to insult them. What was needed was an analysis that accounted more adequately for the many sites of resistance and social conflict that could be identified.

The other main problem with a structuralist analysis is the limited place of agency it gives to individual intentions and actions. While not quite ruling out personal initiatives, this analysis accords them less value than it could. The system, by contrast, is granted too much authority. Where a liberal humanist perspective inappropriately aggrandizes the possibilities of the individual counseling client in the construction of a life, the structuralist perspective appears often to minimize and constrain such possibilities. What is needed is some kind of bridge between the individual and the structural. It is at this point that we need to move to our third approach to power, an approach that we believe creates a much more effective bridge between the personal and the political. We shall outline this perspective in Chapter 8.

Counseling From a Structuralist Perspective on Power

At the end of Chapter 6, we illustrated the liberal humanist analysis of power with a scenario constructed for this purpose. For the sake of comparison, let's use the same scenario in this chapter to illustrate the structuralist analysis of power. There are a range of different structuralist approaches we could use for the purpose of illustration, but we can't use all of them. Therefore, we have decided to use an approach that is based on a feminist orientation to therapy.

The first concern that a structuralist approach to issues of power in counseling needs to address is the structural setup of the counseling. Many things, according to a structuralist perspective, are determined before the client and the counselor meet. A structuralist approach cannot maintain a strict here-and-now emphasis, which doesn't mean that a structurally oriented counselor is not vitally concerned about what is happening in the here and now. It just means that she considers the here and now of events to be structured by things outside the two people present in the room.

The counseling therefore begins when Daneesha makes an appointment to see a counselor. The agency's policy in this case is to ask the person making an appointment to fill in a form nominating her or his gender, ethnicity, and sexual orientation. Daneesha writes down that she is an African American, heterosexual woman. She is therefore assigned to a counselor who is an African American, heterosexual woman. Unfortunately, Rebeka, the counselor who fits this bill, is away on the day that Daneesha is first due to come for her appointment. The agency receptionist telephones and says that Daneesha will have to reschedule. Daneesha asks if she can see another counselor, but the receptionist responds that it's agency policy to match people with counselors of the same gender, ethnicity, and sexual orientation, because it produces more useful counseling. She will have to wait until Rebeka comes back to work.

What has already happened? Daneesha has been understood to occupy a position in the hierarchical structural relations of gender, ethnicity, and sexual orientation. These are the positions from which she will be viewed. Even if she'd once had a lengthy lesbian relationship, her grandfather on her mother's side were a Navajo medicine man, and her job were as the CEO of a company that employed mainly men (who worked under her), her positioning in the structure of power would be defined according to the hegemonic structures of patriarchy, race, and homophobic heterosexuality.

Early on in their first counseling session, Rebeka introduces her approach to counseling: "The way I see counseling, it's the two of us working together to find out what's best for you. I think of you as the expert in your own life, not me. But I am the expert in counseling. I work from a multicultural, feminist perspective. I think this means two important things. The first one is that I'll work hard to understand your concerns as you experience them. I want to respect your knowledge about yourself and your life and even about your problems. The second thing is, I bring a social and political perspective to how I make sense of what you tell me. A lot of counselors don't do this. I believe that many of the problems women bring to counseling are produced by the politics of gender and that many of the problems African Americans bring to counseling are produced by the politics of race. So I won't be scared to talk about those things. In general, black women are not valued by our society, and this creates psychological distress."

This is an example of the feminist therapist's effort to establish a structural position as a companion alongside the client rather than to take up an expert position over her. It is expressed overtly and transparently and includes the counselor's beliefs about the sources of problems that women experience and that African Americans experience. These sources will be interpreted in terms of the dominance of white male racism and the patriarchal dominance of men over women.

Daneesha expresses some concern that Rebeka will expect her to take up a feminist perspective, which she is not sure will fit comfortably with her religious beliefs.

Rebeka assures Daneesha that she will respect her viewpoints but says that she wants to be up front about her politics so that she is not hiding anything. Daneesha feels relieved about this, and they move on to discuss the problem that is clearly weighing on Daneesha.

> "Well, I'm on this committee with a group of women," Daneesha explained. "I've known them all for about a year and some of them for several years. There are only a few African Americans at my church and I'm the only African American on the committee. The other women are mostly Mexican American."
>
> "Okay," said Rebeka. "So did something happen at the committee meeting?"
>
> Daneesha recounted an uncomfortable exchange at the meeting earlier that day.
>
> "We were discussing a social event that we are supposed to be planning as a fund-raiser. One of the women told a story to the group about how her husband referred to her as a 'nigger.' She said it was like a joke, and she was just laughing as she said it."

"So she used a term of racist abuse of African Americans in your presence. How did you feel about that?"

"Actually I was shocked to hear her use the *N* word," said Daneesha. "And I was even more uncomfortable because the other women chuckled at the incident."

Daneesha stated that nothing was said about its being wrong or that it might create discomfort for her.

"I don't know which is worse—that they used the *N* word or that they laughed about it," she said, looking a little sheepish and trailing off.

"Did you feel kind of bad about yourself a little bit?" asked Rebeka.

"I should have made a statement telling them how offensive this was and left the room. Instead, I just kind of looked at the woman who said it."

"Okay, so you froze up in this situation and later felt a bit responsible for what you didn't say. Let me ask you something, though. Were you responsible for the racist slur being spoken?"

"No," said Daneesha, smiling through a few tears.

"Are you responsible for the ways in which the *N* word has been used for centuries to keep African Americans oppressed?"

"No," said Daneesha again.

"Are you responsible for the ways in which Mexicans sometimes get tricked by racism into currying favor with whites by putting down blacks?"

"Do you think that's what was happening? I never thought of it like *that*," said Daneesha.

"Well, it's possible. What do you think?"

"I suppose it makes sense," said Daneesha. "And no, I'm not responsible for that either. But I still feel upset about it."

"I guess I would too. In fact, I've experienced something similar myself," said Rebeka. She went on to share with Daneesha her own experience a couple of years back. She had been in a situation where she was forced to overhear the *N* word, even though it wasn't directed at her. When she objected, she was told to lighten up and not take things so seriously.

"Thanks," said Daneesha, after listening to Rebeka's story. "I don't feel so stupid when I hear you had a similar experience."

"I'm glad," smiled Rebeka. "We need to stand together against racism. It's too hard to handle on your own. So what would you have liked to do to stand up to it in this situation?"

"I could have told her that I was offended and to knock it off."

"What would that have felt like?"

Daneesha said that it would have felt good, but she was frowning as she said it.

"What is the frown about?" asked Rebeka. "Has something else bothered you?"

"Yes," said Daneesha. "It's odd, really. I just remembered something I haven't thought about in a long time."

She then told Rebeka the story of what had happened when she was 12 or 13 years old. She had been with her mother at a grocery store in Tennessee, where she grew up. Her mom had asked for assistance from a young clerk.

"I don't even recall what my mom wanted," she said. "But the clerk sneered and rudely said, 'I don't do anything for niggers.'"

As Daneesha recounted this event, her tears returned. "My mom told me to be quiet about it, and she said the godly thing to do was to pray for the young man, and we simply walked out of the store."

Rebeka listened patiently to the story. Then she asked Daneesha if it would be all right for her to comment on this experience from her perspective. Daneesha was curious and said yes.

"Well, some of the legacies of slavery and colonization are psychological. Just because we got freedom from slavery and made major advances in civil rights in the sixties doesn't mean that those psychological effects don't keep on happening. I don't blame your mother for doing what she could to protect you at that age. My mother likely would have done the same. But what it seems is still happening for you is that you have internalized some of the effects of racism and they get under your skin and make you feel that sense of inferiority in yourself, so that you can't stand up and object like you want to. I think that's how racism works. It's also how sexism works on women; have you noticed that?"

Daneesha and Rebeka then spend some time exploring the internalized effects of racism that have affected Daneesha. Then they begin to work on strategies of strengthening her to be able to stand up more for her right not to be abused, intentionally or otherwise. They talk about empowerment and solidarity with others engaged in similar structural struggles. Rebeka suggests some reading for Daneesha to do to sharpen her consciousness of the structural issues.

The counselor is taking up the role of educator here. She is doing some consciousness-raising work with Daneesha about the structural inequities at work in the race issue as they are experienced on a daily basis. As another African American woman, she places herself structurally in a position similar to Daneesha's in relation to the forces of racism. She indicates to Daneesha that she is in this struggle with her. They are not just personalizing the problem but conceiving of it as part of a structural problem that needs to be addressed structurally. The daily details of personal interactions become material through which to understand better the ways that personal experience is determined by structural conditions. In the end, the goal of therapy from this perspective is social change.

This, then, is an example of how counseling might look different if we operated from a structuralist perspective on power. There are some points of similarity between this perspective and the liberal humanist analysis of power, which is far more widespread in the counseling domain. And there are some definite points of departure. The counselor is much more inclined to represent his or her own structuralist analysis and to interpret the client's experience in terms of this analysis. He or she adopts a position of solidarity alongside the client. And he or she is more committed to an educational and consciousness-raising role than the counselor in Chapter 6. But these are not the only options either. In Chapter 8, we shall introduce you to a new perspective, one that as yet only a small number of people in the counseling field have taken up. We introduce it because we think it helps address some of the limitations of both liberal humanist and structuralist versions of power relations and because it therefore opens up new possibilities in counseling.

TO DISCUSS

1. In the counseling conversation with Daneesha, what specific things did the counselor do that fit with a structuralist perspective on power?

2. Search counseling texts or videotapes for examples of the expression of a structuralist perspective.

3. Role-play a counseling interview similar to the one between Daneesha and Rebeka and discuss how it is experienced from the client's point of view.

4. What is the value of focusing on structural issues with clients? What are some problematic issues that might arise for clients exposed to a structuralist approach?

5. What do you find to be the central distinctions between the liberal humanist and the structuralist approach?

Response to Chapter 7

Michael D'Andrea

Michael D'Andrea, Ed.D., is a professor in the Department of Counselor Education at the University of Hawaii. He has been a professional counselor for the past 31 years and a faculty member at the University of Hawaii for the past 18 years. He has also served as the executive director of the National Institute for Multicultural Competence for the past 14 years. Dr. D'Andrea has coauthored six books and more than 200 publications, most of which address issues related to multicultural and social justice counseling. He is also known for his social justice activism in the mental health and education professions.

It is agreed that it is important to build a bridge between the individual and structural issues when using a structural approach to counseling. In the case presented in this chapter, the client (Daneesha) is assigned to an African American, heterosexual, female therapist because she self-identified with these characteristics in a form she completed during her intake.

This is sound reasoning, not only from the structural approach to counseling that is described in this chapter, but also because researchers have noted that matching clients and counselors/therapists in these ways often facilitates the establishment of a positive therapeutic relationship and contributes to positive counseling outcomes (Atkinson, Morton, & Sue, 1998). However, it is important to keep a couple of other important issues in mind when doing so. These issues are briefly discussed below.

First, it is suggested that many clients will predictably identify themselves by using certain race, gender, and sexual orientation terms (e.g., as African American, female, and heterosexual) when presented with an intake form before receiving mental health services. However, the sort of self-identification that Daneesha asserted on the form she completed is not necessarily helpful in understanding her psychological readiness to explore structural issues relevant to the problem she presents in counseling. Given the tremendous psychological differences manifested by persons of the same racial or ethnic background, gender, and affectional group, structural counselors and psychologists would do well to assess their clients' level of racial/cultural, gender, and sexual identity development before addressing structural issues in the helping process. This can be done by utilizing any of the racial/cultural (Helms & Cook, 1999; Sue & Sue, 2003), womanistic/feminist (Daniels, 2007), and sexual orientation (Browning, Reynolds, & Dworkin, 1998) identity development models that have proliferated in the fields of counseling and psychology over the past 30 years.

Second, although clients like Daneesha may readily use racial, gender, and sexual orientation terms (e.g., African American, female, heterosexual) to describe themselves in the situation presented in this chapter, there may be other aspects of their cultural being that are more salient for their psychological functioning, worldview, and receptivity to exploring structural issues in counseling and psychotherapy. Dr. Judy Daniels and I have developed the RESPECTFUL counseling framework, which we use when gathering such information in intake situations with the clients we work with.

This theoretical model provides guidelines for exploring, in both individual and structural terms, clients' religious/spiritual identity (R), economic class identity and experiences (E), sexual identity (S), psychological maturity (P), ethnic/racial/cultural identity development (E), chronological challenges (C), trauma and threats to one's well-being (T), family identify and history (F), unique physical characteristics (U), and language preference and location of residence (L). Using this multidimensional model to learn about the salient aspects of our clients' personal, cultural, and gender development provides a means to understand which structural factors are likely to be more relevant to the challenges they face in their lives and thus more appropriate to address in individual counseling and therapy situations that operate from a structural perspective.

We have found the use of the identity development models and the RESPECTFUL counseling framework described above to be very useful in different counseling situations that are designed to promote clients' psychological well-being and personal development. Counselors and psychologists who use a structural approach to counseling and therapy are likely to find these theoretical models particularly helpful when addressing one of the central challenges discussed in this chapter, which is to build "some kind of bridge between the individual and the structural."

TO DISCUSS

1. How does the RESPECTFUL model outlined by Michael D'Andrea connect or not connect with a structuralist understanding of power?

2. What are your experiences of being thought of as a member of a group? Have these experiences been helpful or not so helpful?

3. What are the advantages of thinking in terms of oppressor/oppressed binaries? What are the disadvantages?

4. Think of examples of social changes that have taken place. Discuss how these examples would be talked about from a structuralist perspective.

CHAPTER 8

Power and Privilege: Part Three

A Poststructuralist View of Power

In recent decades, there has emerged an analysis of power that offers some new insights into how power works. It is markedly different from the commonly understood analyses of power that we featured in Chapters 6 and 7. It has been loosely associated with a postmodern worldview and has been strongly influenced by the account of power relations developed by the French philosopher Michel Foucault. This account is often called poststructuralist. As the name suggests, it grew out of a structuralist analysis but in the end moves beyond what can be accounted for in structural terms. We believe that there is much value to be gained from an understanding of Foucault's analysis of power and, in particular, that there is potential within it for a very different approach to counseling. It opens the door for many shifts in thinking that are not possible from a liberal humanist or a structuralist analysis and gives cultural influences a much greater place of importance in psychology than they have previously been given. We want to advocate that the multicultural counseling movement take careful account of the possibilities that Foucault's analysis might reveal. Therefore, we shall explain Foucault's analysis of power carefully and discuss some of his concepts that we believe are useful tools for making sense of power.

Positive Power

Foucault starts from the assumption that power is everywhere. It is certainly centralized or concentrated in some places, but never exclusively. Everyone participates in relations of power at every moment of their lives. People are constantly seeking to exert influence on each other, and this is not a bad thing. Foucault therefore seeks to make the exercise of power a routine aspect of life rather than an exceptional and automatically objectionable dimension. This is not to say that the exercise of power is not at times objectionable, but it does suggest that the effort to influence others is not essentially bad. It is impossible, from this perspective, to conceive of relations between people that are not in some sense power relations. Therefore, the question of which practices of power are acceptable and which are not is an ethical one. If power relations are inevitable and are not always bad, then we need to think about which processes of power are acceptable and just and which ones are damaging and unjust.

Foucault (2000) also argues that it is not enough to follow the common path of assuming that power is basically about stopping people from doing things. He regards it as curious that most analyses of power focus on its negative functions. The word *negative* does not refer to a value judgment as much as to how power *prevents* people from pursuing opportunities in life, *blocks* them from participating in decisions that affect them, *silences* them, and *excludes* them from social benefits. In other words, the usual focus has been on how power is used to actively oppress people. Power is usually identified as "a law that says no" (Foucault, 2000, p. 120). In psychological language, this has led to an analysis of what gets repressed in personal consciousness. Hence, we have a range of counseling processes aimed at helping people get rid of internalized taboos, the influence even into adulthood of parents who said no, and the blocking of the expression of traumatic experiences. Foucault (2000) describes this negative emphasis on power not so much as wrong but as insufficient and "skeletal" (p. 120). It represents the bones of power without muscles and nervous system.

Foucault also challenges the common metaphor whereby power is assumed to be a commodity. As a commodity, power is reified as an object that can be held. The power as commodity assumption is present in both liberal humanist and structuralist versions of power. Individuals are frequently thought of as holders of power. Membership of a structurally organized group is often described in terms of a person's amassing a certain quantity of the commodity of power. Foucault suggests that this metaphor produces distortions. He prefers to speak of power as something inherent in a relation and associated with a set of discourse practices, rather than something held by an individual or amassed as a quantity. This is a less essentialist way of thinking and has potential for noticing and describing greater complexity and nuance in how power works.

It is not that Foucault wanted to argue against the existence of oppression or repression. Far from it. However, he did not believe that this is the only, or indeed the main, way in which power works. Instead, he believed that power is primarily productive rather than just repressive. In other words, he pointed to the ways in which power works to get people to do things rather than just stops them from doing them. "It makes people act and speak" (Foucault, 2000, p. 172). His oft-quoted maxim describes power as "the conduct of conduct" (Foucault, 2000). It refers to the effort to shape and influence the ways in which other people conduct themselves. His argument is that the largest effort in all power relations goes into producing people in particular molds, rather than on repressing in them actions that do not fit the mold. Repression exists around the outside of the processes of producing people in particular ways. It is the backup system that kicks into play to deal with the failures of the productive processes of power. It is important, but secondary to the primary function of power that works in productive ways.

This is a whole new domain of interest in social science. How do we produce people to be the way they are, feel the way they feel, think the way they do, act the way they act? You can't even ask such questions if you think in an essentialist way and assume that people do things because they're "natural" and that power operates mainly to keep people from expressing their natural essences. The exercise of power that must be understood in Foucault's terms becomes much more of a technical question about how people's consciousness is constructed. It is about the design of social processes that have effects on individuals' lives, their bodies, and their psyches. Once Foucault began to think in this way, he found and began to investigate all sorts of technologies of power that operate in the modern world. He also began to trace their emergence and development from premodern European traditions and practices.

It has also been customary in analyses of power to focus on the role of the "state" in the functioning of power. This is the domain that we normally think of as political and is where we might look to notice the workings of power. Foucault does not overlook the role of the state, but he is also clear that power exists well beyond the places where we have traditionally looked for its functions. In other words, it is not just in the institutions of government that we might find the processes by which people's lives are governed. The governing of people's lives, or the processes of power that exert influence on people, are much more widely diffused than that. Feminist analysis of gender power was one of the first places where this was made this clear. There is clearly no central cabinet or politburo where male dominance of women originates. Nor is it uniform. There are many places where women exercise power to govern their own lives and at times the lives of men and children. And yet there is still plenty of evidence of pattern and structure in the relations between men and women. In many contexts, women do not enjoy all the same opportunities in life that men routinely expect. How do we account for this? A simple structural analysis of women's rights does not explain enough. It is not nuanced enough to account for ways in which women sometimes act that are against their own interests or even downright oppressive toward men. Nor are all the techniques by which gender power operates embodied in legal rights.

The poststructuralist analysis helps us make sense of things here. It suggests that power relations are based on the use of discourse. Foucault (1978) argues that "discourse transmits and produces power, reinforces it, but also undermines and exposes it, renders it fragile and makes it possible to thwart it" (p. 100). From this perspective, power cannot be a commodity to be owned but instead is a property of a relation. If it is constituted in discourse, it is vulnerable to shifts in discourse. Hence, it is dependent on the context in which discourse is used, rather than essentially tied to a person or to a group of persons. It is likely to cut across individual lives in ways that can entail privilege and oppression for the same person in different respects. Such fluidity, however, does not preclude the possibility of systematic and patterned applications of discursive power so that some individuals are more consistently disadvantaged than others.

There are discourses of family relations and of gender relations that underlie many of the decisions and actions of men and women on a daily basis. These discourses equip us with a matrix of assumptions that we repeat and reproduce each time we open our mouths. Where this discourse favors and privileges life opportunities for men and diminishes the extent to which these same opportunities are available for women, the repetition of this discourse in our speech patterns and in the media is likely to blind us to ways in which things could be otherwise. Hence, feminists in the 1970s and 1980s paid a lot of attention to the ways in which sexist discourse produced relations between men and women in lopsided ways. For example, the use of the word *chairman* carried with it the assumption that the position of leadership on a committee would be taken up by a man rather than a woman. The struggle for the substitution of the word *chairperson* ensued. Some people who don't understand how power works through discourse get impatient about these differences and dismiss them as mere semantics or complain about undue "political correctness." Often this accusation is a substitute for thinking and understanding quite substantive issues. Calling something "politically correct" and calling something "sexist" are themselves both efforts to exercise power. The task is always to figure out how a piece of discourse usage serves to govern the lives of others, what is at stake, who might benefit if one of these meanings gains ascendancy and who might lose out. From a poststructuralist perspective, the decision between one version of events and another is, in the end, an ethical decision. It is a matter of deciding what is fair and just.

Power, then, is everywhere and pervades the social body. Foucault uses the metaphor "capillary" to describe it, referring to the tiny blood vessels that carry life to the extremities of the body. It does not simply accrue to some groups and not at all to others. We all exercise it to some degree, and therefore it makes no sense to describe anyone as powerless. Power is not centralized as much as structuralists would believe. However, it is still true that there are some places where power concentrates. There are those who more easily access the authority to shape the lives of others and those for whom the path to that access is overgrown with obstacles. There are authorities in many places who exercise the right to govern the lives of other people, and their positions are not just organized around race, gender, and class, as a structuralist analysis has often emphasized. We often assume that the exercise of authority refers to the government, or the state. But there are many other places where authority is exercised over the lives of people. For example, bankers and credit agencies govern people's financial lives. Teachers govern children's lives in school. The fashion industry governs people's clothing tastes. Marketing and advertising govern people's consumption patterns. Public health authorities govern people's bodies, including the housing of them. Captains govern the crew of a ship. Employers govern the lives of their employees. Foucault uses the word *govern* in the sense of producing or eliciting the desired forms of behavior in a population of people.

However, in this formulation, the world is not neatly divided between the dominant and the oppressed, or even between dominating and subjugated discourses. Things are not so strongly determined as that. There is always a degree of indeterminacy in the midst of power relations, and people also make efforts at many points to govern themselves, individually and in groups. Hence, we need to pay careful attention to the microdynamics of power and to the effects of these in order to make the most of opportunities for change. This is as true for the kinds of changes for which people seek counseling as it is for social changes in a community of people.

A brief word is necessary here about the difference between power relations and domination in Foucault's analysis. People often don't make a distinction between the two. According to Foucault's analysis of power, power relations are in a constant fluid exchange of relational expression. Whenever someone attempts to govern the conduct of others, he must engage in a strategy of struggle and contest in which there is always the possibility that the others may refuse to submit. There is always a reciprocal relation. Domination occurs from time to time when the usual flow of exchanges between people in contests of power are frozen into patterns that are very hard to even talk about, let alone contest (Foucault, 2000). Domination occurs when the reciprocal process of struggle and the ebb and flow of give and take and compromise is no longer possible.

Sovereign Power and Disciplinary Power

Foucault adds to this picture by making some distinctions between power as it is frequently exercised in the modern world and power as it was in premodern times. He refers to these two forms of power as sovereign power and disciplinary power. His contention is that it is necessary to study the technologies by which people's lives are governed in order to understand how power operates and that the modern world can be distinguished from earlier times by the development of some sophisticated new technologies of power.

According to Foucault, sovereign power was based on instilling in the general populace a fear of the authority of the sovereign. This was achieved through punishing wrongdoers or political enemies by enacting all manner of physical torture on their bodies or putting them to death. It was maintained by making a show of the power of the person of the king. Hangings and beheadings, for example, were often public events done as much to warn the general public against rebellion as to punish the offender. The final scenes of the movie *Braveheart* (Gibson et al., 1995) demonstrate one of the techniques through which sovereign power works. The ancient Roman practice of crucifixion is another example. Similarly, the long history of lynchings in the South of the United States served the function of keeping black people afraid and docile. And those men who beat their wives in order to maintain power and control can be understood to be seeking to use sovereign power to produce submissive behavior in women.

Disciplinary power, says Foucault, developed from about the 17th century on and has become the chief means by which modern states get their citizens to be loyal, law-abiding citizens. This does not mean that sovereign power has been completely outmoded. It still exists wherever the use of force is deployed. People are still tortured and put to death. However, we have developed modern distaste for such technologies of power and like to think of ourselves as more "civilized" than societies of previous eras. Foucault would say that it is not that we are actually more civilized, but that we have developed new technologies of power that often work far more effectively, and there is less need for the exercise of sovereign power to the degree that it was exercised formerly. How is this achieved?

Foucault argues that from the 17th century on, there has been a general movement (which is still accelerating today) to place the mechanisms by which power operates inside people's heads so that they have to monitor themselves and keep themselves in line rather than be afraid of the power of the king to kill and maim. This shift began with the move to create modern prisons. Before this time, prisons were mainly places where people were held temporarily until they were put to death or were places where torture took place. It was in the 17th century that the idea of holding people in prison to teach them to correct their ways and become law abiding again came into being. For this purpose, Jeremy Bentham developed the panopticon design for the modern prison. The panopticon design allowed the prison guards to be able to look into the individual cells of every prisoner at will. The prisoner never knew when she was going to be watched and so had to take care to monitor her own behavior and obey the rules of the prison all the time, just in case at any moment she might be observed. The prisoner became a new object of study. Her behavior was now a matter to be documented, and files were developed about it. Interviews of various kinds were developed to gather information for these files. Forms to fill out standardized the questions that uncovered the information by which people were to be governed.

Foucault has suggested that Jeremy Bentham deserves to be recognized as the most influential thinker in the modern era because of how this idea has contributed to the shape of people's lives everywhere. Said Foucault (2000), "Today we live in a society programmed basically by Bentham, a panoptic society, a society where panopticism reigns" (p. 70). Bentham's idea of the panopticon has been taken from the prison and applied in every domain of modern life as the principal technology by which power operates. The same process of organization that began in the prison, designed to make governing people's lives easier, was copied in every other institution of modern life that developed in the same era: the factory, the military barracks, the modern school, the government department, the immigration system, and the hospital. "Panopticism is one of the characteristic traits of our society" (Foucault, 2000, p. 70). It focuses on producing the individual in an acceptable mold through three main processes: "supervision, control and correction" (Foucault, 2000, p. 70).

Let's take schools as an example. Schools are organized on the basis of individualizing each student, and the main method by which young people are kept docile and well behaved is not the threat of punishment. It is through the prescription of a curriculum that each child must learn and through the process of tests and exams by which children's progress through this curriculum is measured and calculated. Such progress is planned out, supervised, and measured from the earliest days of kindergarten to the completion of Ph.D.s. Examinations serve the same function as the guard tower in the prison. They subject children to the gaze of the education authorities. Each child knows that sooner or later the truth about his learning will be accounted for and that he must work to produce himself as a successful student in order to be granted access to the privileges of the adult world. In other words, children's learning is turned into an object of calculation and study. This enables norms to be established that specify rates of learning progress and enables distinctions to be made between different groups of students: those who are above average or normal and those who are below average and abnormal. And it requires children to produce their sense of self in terms of the identity categories laid down within the dominant system of schooling. Those who are deemed abnormal must be corrected.

Another feature of the modern operation of power is the role of norms. In the last 150 years, we have seen the rise of the normal curve. This statistical invention

(Foucault points out that *statistics* are so called because they were developed as the science of the state, or the science of governing) has made it possible to map out a normal distribution of the population along a predictable bell-shaped curve. Those within two standard deviations of the norm are called normal. Those outside this range are to be treated as abnormal, or as if they require some corrective or remedial treatment. In the education system, children are routinely established in such positions by a large variety of tests. Most of these tests have been developed over the last hundred years and are usually assumed to be objective, neutral measures of people's personal qualities or abilities. Foucault would argue that such objectivity is a ruse designed to obscure the function of these tests, which is not objective at all. Their purpose is to create social divisions and to assign responsibility for those divisions to the persons who are being so divided. You can't object to being assigned the category *abnormal* if it is established by a scientifically designed, impersonal testing procedure. Instead, you must internalize the results of the test and adopt it as an aspect of your identity. This is the process of normalization. I *am* an average student. I *am* learning disabled. I *am* a nerd. The use of the verb *to be* indicates a powerful essentializing force at work. As a result of this normalizing judgment, a whole array of totalizing identities are developed and assigned to young people in ways that define who they can expect to be. These identities are then kept in place by the processes of surveillance and internalized monitoring (such as ongoing testing) that were first developed in the prison built on the panopticon design.

Foucault also studied sexuality as a site of power relations. He describes the process by which people's sexuality became a concern of the government of people, especially in the 19th century (Foucault, 1978). He argues that this concern arose as a product of the conceptualization of "populations" in response to the population growth in the 18th century. Foucault maintains that the dramatic population increase during this time led to numerous health and housing problems. As a result, the government became much more interested in birth rates, age of marriages, illegitimate births, frequency of sexual relations, and the like. Those in authority became inquisitors into people's formerly private affairs. As Vivien Burr (2003) writes, "the practice of scrutinizing the population's sexual behaviour and of encouraging people to confess their sexual 'sins' developed into a powerful form of social control as people began to internalise this process" (p. 70). It was during this time that scientific concepts of what is normal and what is abnormal developed and accounts of "perversion" became the focus of intense public scrutiny. The problematization of sexuality remains important today, especially for those who don't conform to heterosexist standards.

Through the development of modern discourse about sexuality, the body became a site for the operation of power. Western culture's current obsession with thinness can thus be analyzed as a manifestation of disciplinary power. Women especially, but increasingly men too, are placed under constant surveillance by such disciplinary power to look a certain way and encouraged to engage in whatever means necessary to fit the thin ideal.

Power can thus be understood to be at work inside us every time we look in the mirror or stand on the scales. We are incited to look at ourselves and measure ourselves against a "normal" ideal by advertising and the fashion industry, which work tirelessly to inscribe on women's bodies their expectations for attractiveness, including certain clothing and hair styles. At this time, the most prominent standard for attractiveness for women is the cultural ideal of thinness, or the "tyranny of slenderness" (Chernin, 1981, p. 3). To prepare themselves for the evaluation of others, women must watch themselves with a critical eye and sometimes submit themselves to self-torture (diet and exercise regimens) to ensure that they conform to cultural body standards and to avoid being judged negatively. Internalized bodily self-surveillance invites women to be preoccupied with their physical appearance, to be concerned about ascribed deficiencies, and to see themselves as objects and to respond to other women as competing objects. In learning to prepare for the inspection of others, a woman becomes skilled at seeing herself as others see her. "Through no small amount of labor, women within dominant culture are given the task of watching themselves from a position that is both inside and outside the body" (Spitzack, 1990, p. 34). John Berger (1972) suggests that, given the primacy of women's personal appearance within dominant culture, it actually behooves them to anticipate the repercussions of their appearance, "to be their own first surveyors" (p. 46).

This monitoring and controlling of behavior begins with a governmental concern about sexuality and population but is eventually inscribed onto the individual body through a process of self-discipline. Thus, the ultimate testament to the success of the governing body's use of disciplinary power is when individuals take up the practice of self-discipline. These technologies of power are conceived by individuals and function through institutions, but it is important to notice that they are not owned by anyone, or any group, and that their effects are diffused through the actions of thousands and millions of people who all participate in policing themselves and each other. Anything that is so diffused through the many actions of many people must therefore be understood as a cultural phenomenon and should be of interest to counselors who are working with individuals struggling with how to discipline themselves.

Power/Knowledge

The argument in the previous section illustrates another of Foucault's concerns: the close relationship between scientific knowledge in the human, or social, sciences and processes of social and political control. Foucault views the human sciences as far from maintaining a neutral or objective stance in relation to political and social issues. Rather, he charges medicine, psychiatry, psychology, and education in particular (he was trained as a psychologist himself) with enthusiastic complicity in the operation of power in people's lives. Psychologists have actively contributed to the design and elaboration of processes of normalizing judgment for the purposes of measuring people's personal qualities and assigning them identity categories from which they are required to make sense of their lives. The human sciences, he says, have provided the tools for the production of modern practices of governing people's lives. They have developed the social categories, or populations, to which people have been assigned, and to which we willingly assign ourselves membership. Race and gender are examples. Social scientists have developed vast knowledge about these populations, which make people more easily governed. They have elaborated the technologies of this government too, in the form of the psychological gaze and the ways in which it is applied by professional practitioners to produce citizenship along specified lines.

What is more, Foucault argues that knowledge in the human sciences consistently represents the interests of the dominant discourse of its day. Social scientists are, after all, members of a social world. They are influenced, as much as anyone else, by the ebbs and flows of discourse and sociohistorical trends, and these influences shape the knowledge that is produced in academic writing. Erica Burman (1994) elaborates on this point by suggesting that we cannot adequately understand psychological research without noticing "the circumstances in which the research was carried out, the social and political influences that made the topic seem relevant, and the role and impact of that research" (p. 5). Here are some examples: The development of psychological practices and knowledge has been influenced heavily by the wars of the last hundred years. World War I gave us new psychological accounts of trauma as a result of what was called in those days "shell shock." This was updated after the Vietnam War, which left scars in the American political discourse in many ways. One of them was the development of the individualized and depoliticized account of posttraumatic stress disorder to describe the suffering of soldiers who returned from that war deeply troubled by what they had witnessed. Posttraumatic stress renders the problem an individual abnormality rather than an understandably normal outcome of a political process. It blames the inadequacy of the individual soldier for his suffering, rather than the government that put him in harm's way. In this sense, no diagnosis of posttraumatic stress can ever be politically neutral, even though it claims to be objective. World War II left behind in Britain a large number of orphaned children who were cared for in orphanages amid political concern that they not grow up to become juvenile delinquents. It was the study of these children that led John Bowlby to develop his theory of attachment, which was connected with an associated discourse of motherhood (Burman, 1994). This was, initially at least, a response to a political issue of the day, and it served to create new worries for women about their responsibilities as mothers and encouraged them to stay at home rather than work.

Jeffrey Masson (1984) also argues that Freud's oedipal theory of early childhood fantasies of desire for the parent of opposite gender was influenced by the current discourse of his day. Masson shows how Freud probably founded his theory of the oedipal complex on stories of sexual abuse told to him by patients, stories that at first he believed were true. Later, however, he was cold shouldered by his own professional community of doctors when he delivered a paper on the subject of the effects of traumatic experiences of sexual abuse. Disturbed by this rejection, or as we might say, by the dominant discourse of his day, he eventually shifted his thinking and began to explain the tales he was told by his women clients as sexual fantasies (to be understood as deep-seated oedipal urges) rather than as accounts of actual abuse.

The result of Foucault's analysis of the relationship between power and knowledge in the modern world is that it leads us to a different reading of much of the knowledge produced within the modern academy. Scientific studies, by Foucault's account, are not to be read as simple truths, in which empirical data can be trusted to speak for themselves. Instead, they are to be read as products of particular "regimes of truth" (Foucault, 2000). This does not mean that they are devoid of all truth value, merely that our reading of the truth that they offer needs to be understood more modestly than as universal truth about the essential human experience. Nor is Foucault suggesting that truth is completely relative. Scientific truth is rather grounded in the power relations of its cultural location, and we should gain more benefit from understanding it this way.

The Confessional Society

One of the effects of the role of modern power/knowledge in the lives of ordinary people has been the development of what Foucault calls the "confessional society." In the process of the government of people's lives in ways that produce them to fit the dominant norms, a strong incitement for people to bring their inner worlds into the light of public scrutiny has developed. We all know that in modern life it is considered a good thing to speak openly and honestly to designated others about deeply personal experience, to express feelings, to give personal testimony to one's failures and achievements, and to assign oneself identity categories. In short, we are incited constantly to produce ourselves to fit the dominant norms by confessing our inner deviations from these norms and then to set about aligning ourselves more fully with those norms.

This is not a new idea. It was developed originally in Western culture by the Catholic Church. The institution of the confessional, whereby people confessed their sins to a priest and were granted absolution and given the admonition to sin no more, was a major practice for the governing of people's lives in medieval times. It is aligned in Foucault's (2000) analysis with the development of what he calls "pastoral power" (p. 352). It is about governing people on an individual basis through coming to know what is happening in their innermost thoughts and inciting them to tell this to a person in authority. Foucault's argument is that this technique was taken over by the modern state and secularized. It comes into play every time in the modern world that we have to fill in a form (a daily practice) and routinely and repetitively "confess" our identity characteristics in response to guided choices about who we can be. We are regularly interviewed by various professionals who maintain files on our private worlds. We must confess our earnings and spending to the tax authorities once a year. We now expect our politicians and our movie star and sports heroes to make their personal lives available for scrutiny so that we can compare ourselves with them and learn how to live. We watch endless talk shows and reality shows on television in which people reveal their inner lives before the camera and are taught moral lessons about how they should live while the rest of us vicariously watch and learn. We are incited by advertising to internalize personal lessons and then to perform the daily practices of living in line with dominant social norms (and of course to consume the products that will help us to do so). Foucault's insight helps us see all this as the (somewhat hidden) operation of power. It is power because it is shaping and producing people's lives. It constitutes personhood in particular patterns, including gender roles, ethnic identities, social class norms, and sexual orientations. Viewed from this perspective, the social structures emphasized within a structuralist view of power are produced and reproduced out of these technologies of power and the discourses on which they rely.

Counseling has had a special role to play in this endeavor. The general acceptance of counseling as a social practice has been built on its role as a place where people can go to confess their private worries and explore their souls. It is also intended, however, to bring these private worlds under the governance of a particular kind of rationality (Guilfoyle, 2005; Rose, 1990). It follows from this analysis that counseling has become part of the culture of modern Western democracies as a result of the growth of the confessional society. There is a strong trend to "send" people to counseling to fix a variety of social ills. Counselors have not often thought of themselves as participants in the governing of people's lives, but a poststructuralist analysis of power invites them to consider this carefully. It has brought about a renewed interest in the operation of power in the counseling relationship, because it means that counselors should consider whether or not they are being used to adjust people to fit the social norms of the day.

Dividing Practices

Another concept that is necessary to Foucault's analysis of power is the idea of "dividing practices" (Foucault, 2000, p. 326). Dividing practices are those that mark out and define the social categories in a social sphere that will be used to allocate status to individuals as legitimate or not, as having a voice that can be heard or that will be ignored. Dividing practices separate the mad and the sane, the sick and the healthy, the criminal and the law abiding, the good student and the poor student, the normal and the abnormal. This concept recognizes that while all people's lives are being governed and produced to fit within the specifications of dominant discourse, the process does not happen in the same way for everyone. This is because dominant discourse also produces dividing lines along with identity categories. Some identities are produced to be recipients of social privilege and others to have limited access to privilege. Some are given ample opportunity to step into positions that govern the lives of others and some are expected to submit to being governed by others.

What are these dividing lines? Every society has them, although their particular expression varies substantially as well as in subtle ways from one context to another. In ancient Rome, for example, there were dividing lines between patricians, plebeians, and slaves. In traditional Indian society, the divisions were constructed along caste lines. In Britain, there have been social divisions along social class lines that are marked out, in part, by the accents people use when they open their mouths. In Northern Ireland, particular histories of colonization have led to fault lines of division on the basis of Catholic or Protestant religious allegiance. As we have shown in Chapter 3, the massive exercise of European colonization of many other parts of the world created the very concept of race and the institution of it by sharp dividing lines. The practices of slavery, for example, were organized around sharp dividing lines between slave owner and slave. In other places, the dividing lines were organized around racial distinctions between farmer and indentured laborer, or between factory owner and waged worker. These dividing lines are not essential structures as they are conceived of from a structuralist analysis, but they are products of culture and discourse.

These dividing lines have persisted as underlying organizing ideas for the social world, for personal identity categories, and for inequitable relations between those identity categories. This persistence continues to happen despite the trends toward decolonization that have been expressed in, for example, the American Revolution, the American Civil War, and the civil rights movement. None of these events have succeeded in completely dislodging the concept of race to keep it from operating as a dividing practice that marks out lines of privilege and disadvantage for many people.

The concept of rights captures only a small part of how this happens. Therefore, the modernist campaigns for civil rights have succeeded in democratizing some parts of the operation of power in the modern world but have also been restricted in their achievements by the limited scope of their analysis. In other words, campaigns for human rights have not always produced the desired experience of freedom when practices of governmentality have leapfrogged over legal rights and manipulated discourse by operating inside people's heads to limit that experience of freedom.

Dividing practices along gender lines is a case in point. Campaigns for women's rights have succeeded in many places in giving women the vote, in granting property rights that used to be denied, in securing greater access for women to positions of leadership in workplaces and in the public sphere, in equalizing, to some degree, financial independence for women in situations of divorce, and so on. In other words, they have had effects in terms of the versions of power that are recognized within liberal humanist discourse. What has been left underanalyzed, however, has been the ways in which dividing lines on the basis of gender continue to be produced through the more subtle operation of discourse on men and women. It starts with the assignment of pink and blue to babies to mark off their gender position. It develops through the assignment of different kinds of toys and games for girls and boys. It trains girls to measure their worthiness in terms of their looks and their body image and their ability to constantly attend to relational processes in ways that are not expected of men. Most of this is not set down in laws that can be changed through human rights campaigns. Therefore, the feminist movement has needed to analyze it in terms captured by the slogan, "The personal is political" (see Chapter 9). It has been necessary to develop understandings of how differences between men and women have been produced inside our heads and then assumed to be natural.

The role of education has to be taken into account for its role in dividing practices. It is noticeable that in recent decades, in a number of countries around the world, education has become an increasingly sensitive political issue. This reflects the increasing role that education plays in the creation of social divisions more complex and sophisticated than simple exclusionary regulations along the lines of race, class, or gender. Nevertheless, parents and students implicitly know that their life chances to access all manner of material privileges hinge on success in school. In the United States today, going to college has become, to a large extent, although not uniformly, a marker of entry to privileged lifestyles. Going to Ivy League colleges marks a person as eligible for higher positions that have even more authority to govern the lives of others.

As a result of this trend, school counselors need to think of their every conversation with young people in schools as focused on issues of power, because they are working in the domain of the production of people's lives and of the identity categories that will dramatically affect their life expectations. They need to make a close study of the particular microtechnologies of power in which children's lives are situated and to help children negotiate their own paths through this.

Resistance

It is easy to reach a mistaken conclusion when we start to understand power from a poststructuralist perspective, however. We can gain the impression that because modern power has developed these new capabilities and efficiencies by getting inside people's heads to produce docile citizens, it is therefore impossible to resist. We can reach conclusions of despair about the possibilities of social justice and change, simply because these modern technologies of power are so pervasive, and we can start to notice them happening everywhere all around us and even in our own practices. We can develop a picture in our minds of power operating as an all-encompassing net that catches us all and determines the shape of our lives. It may be true that, in a certain sense, we are becoming less and less free as discourse is deliberately shaped and molded by those who govern our lives to affect our very thinking about ourselves.

It can even be tempting to give way to a very cynical and deterministic view of the world. There is a danger here. Cynicism needs always to be examined for its contribution to the operation of power. It can easily be co-opted into the role of constantly viewing change as impossible and therefore undermining the efforts of those who seek to bring about social change by telling them that whatever they attempt will not really make a difference. In this way, a cynical analysis can lead to what Michael White (2002) calls a "paralysis of will" (p. 37). An alternative is to adopt a position of optimism, not on the basis of available evidence so much as on the basis of an ethical stance.

There is a flip side to the coin of modern power. Its very strength is also its weakness. Foucault was at pains to point this out. In fact, he even went so far as to say that he was concerned that his earlier work had overemphasized a dark and implacable story of modern power. In his later work, he sought to correct this impression and to spell out the various ways in which people have considerable freedom to resist the operation of power in their lives.

The key difference between the operation of sovereign power and modern disciplinary power in Foucault's analysis is that the sites from which power is exercised are multiplied and diffused everywhere. Power is not so centralized in the modern world. It is dispersed into every crevice of life, into every relation, into myriad dividing practices that are produced and reproduced on a daily basis. It works because it gets people everywhere to participate in its functions as the instruments of their own and other people's oppression. The corollary is that so are the opportunities for change dispersed everywhere. It is no longer as necessary to mount a centralized structural revolution in order to effect change that makes a difference at the local level. Instead, opportunities for resistance are multiplied exponentially. They exist all around us at the local level where disciplinary power operates. In this sense, modern power has a fragile core. It is susceptible to challenge from within the very sites where it operates. If people are active in producing themselves to fit a system of normalized judgment, they can potentially understand this and refuse to participate. If modern power operates principally at the local level in prisons, schools, businesses, social service agencies, health clinics, and personal and family life, then opportunities for social change exist all the time in these same places at the local level too.

Moreover, modern systems of power are never total in their effects. They are never completely dominant. There are always gaps in their ability to reach into every situation. Indeed, if a system of power ever succeeded in complete domination, we could simply not imagine change. Therefore, there are always places where we can find people expressing their opposition to practices of power. Even when such opposition is not organized, it might exist in the tendency to refuse to allow oneself to be defined by a power relation. For example, a 13-year-old boy who has been diagnosed by a psychiatrist with attention-deficit hyperactivity disorder announces to his school counselor, "I'm ADHD but I don't believe it!" (Winslade & Monk, 2007, p. 84). This is a moment of refusal of the operation of modern power, even though in the same breath this boy acknowledges the authority of the practices of power as he identifies himself with the diagnosis.

The close relationship in Foucault's analysis between practices of power and modern academic knowledge is also always open to challenge. There are always alternative knowledges that exist or that can be developed. People learn about and act on these "counter knowledges" (White, 2002) and make changes in their daily lives. Feminism is an example of a counter knowledge that raises questions about the operation of power along the dividing lines of gender. Many women have called on this counter knowledge to initiate myriad changes in the gender relations in which they participate. Antiracism movements that develop counter knowledges about practices of race (e.g., Wise, 2005) offer bases for challenging the dominant practices in race relations. The literature on decolonization (Fanon, 1963; Said, 1993) serves to unravel many of the taken-for-granted "truths" of Western European superiority in ways that allow many people around the world to develop an account of their own lives that is less defined by this set of assumptions.

It is not always the case, however, that people's resistance to practices of power is coherent or well strategized. Foucault (2000) talks about some expressions of resistance as "muddled" (p. 155). Such resistance might serve as an expression of rebellion without having a clear focus on bringing about change in the practices of power to which it is an objection. This may be because the person who is expressing resistance instinctively recognizes herself as an object of power but can't quite determine how. In this case, there is always the possibility that the actions of resistance are in the end more damaging for the person herself than for the relations of power objected to. For example, young people who instinctively realize that schooling practices are shaped in ways that will lead them to eventual exclusion from social privilege may develop a culture of resistance to what is being done to them through subtle breaches of dress code, through skipping class and smoking cigarettes, or through extreme actions like taking automatic weapons to school and shooting at other students. But these actions may succeed only in placing them in further trouble and in bringing down further operations of power on them that limit their opportunities for freedom. Good counseling, in such cases, may actually help these students articulate more clearly the particular operations of power that they object to and develop more targeted strategies of resistance that produce changes in their relations with others in their school community.

The key difference here between a structuralist and a poststructuralist analysis of power lies in the position of the individual person and his options for the exercise of personal freedom. Daniel Yon (2000) expresses this aptly when he argues that understanding the work of discourses of racism and multiculturalism from a post-structuralist perspective means noticing how they are being reworked on a daily basis in everyday experiences. This means that the individuals are seen "not merely as objects of structures but as subjects who are producing and acting upon structures even as they are being constrained by them" (p. 126).

What Are the Advantages for Counselors of a Poststructuralist Analysis of Power?

In the counseling field, Michael White has done more than anyone else to translate Foucault's analysis into a form that is relevant for the practice of counseling. He describes his experience of first reading Foucault's writings in these terms:

> Upon first reading Foucault on modern power, I experienced a special joy. This joy was in part due to his ability to unsettle what is taken-for-granted and routinely accepted, and to render the familiar strange and exotic. Apart from other things, I found that this opened up new avenues of inquiry into the context of many of the problems and predicaments for which people routinely seek therapy. (White, 2002, p. 36)

White's response is important. It envisages possibilities for professional practice rather than dwelling primarily on the role of such professional practices in the reproduction of power relations. It gestures toward a vision of professional practice that serves as a "counter-practice" (White, 2002, p. 37). Such a practice would be based on an adequate recognition of how modern power works to produce people's lives in certain molds and on an appreciation of people's efforts to resist such power.

A poststructuralist analysis of power also directs attention to the detail of the counseling relationship itself on the assumption that it will always be a power relation. The exercise of power in this relationship will be constantly fluctuating and changing in response to the deployment of discourse in the counseling conversation. At the same time, there are many discursive practices around the setup of the counseling relationship that structure privilege for the voice of the counselor (Guilfoyle, 2005). The ethical question for counseling is how counselors approach the exercise of power in their practice. Does a counselor stand on her own expert knowledge or make room for the client's knowledge? Does the counselor decide the topics of conversation or grant the client some decision making authority in the counseling process? Does the counselor name the problem (diagnosis) and decide on the "treatment" with reference to published psychological discourse, or does she share this authority with the client? An ethical counselor cannot remove the operation of power from the relationship and create some kind of ideal power-free zone by practicing in ways that are nonjudgmental, client centered, and dialogic. But the counselor can conceive of the counseling conversation as an exchange in a power relation and seek to ensure that the flow of power is mutual rather than unidirectional.

Less consistent with a poststructuralist analysis of power would be the argument that a counselor cannot possibly understand the experience of his client if she is from a different social group. It has been argued, for example, that men should not counsel women and that white counselors can never appreciate the experiences of disadvantage from which a black client suffers. Such arguments are more structuralist in origin because they fix identity in a structurally determined place.

Now that we have outlined a poststructuralist analysis of power, it is necessary to address its value. How does such an analysis of power help advance the conversation in multicultural counseling? Let's list a series of arguments for taking this analysis seriously.

In the first place, it helps us see that power does not always operate in terms of structures. Therefore, changing the structures is not the only way to bring about change. Most people who emphasize a structural view of power claim a position exterior to the operation of power (White, 2002). They are helpless in the face of "the system." The poststructuralist account of modern power places us all in the place where power relations are produced and reproduced—that is, in daily conversation. Therefore we are much closer than we think to the site where social change can take place. Potentially, this position gives counseling a more critical role in social change than it has ever assumed before. Sociologist Norman Fairclough (1992) has commented that counseling is an "ambiguous practice," not essentially either oppressive or emancipatory, but potentially either, according to how and in which contexts it is practiced. Foucault's analysis allows counselors the opportunity to understand the processes of modern power, which, if they are not careful, they can easily reproduce in their conversations with their clients. It also enables them to base their practice on counter knowledges when they detect the operation of power in the production of oppressive circumstances in their clients' lives.

Second, the poststructuralist analysis of power allows a more extensive vision of the operation of power. It is not as if the liberal humanist and the structural versions of power are not still relevant. There are places where they can still be useful. But there is a much wider range of practices that can be included under the heading of power when it is viewed from a poststructuralist perspective. The potential for counseling to produce personal and social change that makes a substantive difference is increased if the analysis of power is more extensive in this way. What is more, there are many ways in which new elaborations of the principles of modern power are being invented every day, particularly through the ever-widening deployment of computer technology to place people under surveillance. This analysis positions us in a place where we can immediately understand some of the implications for people's lives.

The emphasis in a poststructuralist analysis of modern power is on *practices* that produce relations of power. Foucault talks about a "regime of practices" as being more foundational than the structure of an institution. Power is assumed to begin in social practices, not in individuals, nor in membership of social groups. We believe that a focus on practices is inherently practical. This is not to deny that people operate as individuals or that they are members of social groups. It is rather to argue that they are produced as individuals out of social relations and that the social groups to which they belong are produced out of social relations too. Practices produce structures. This difference requires us to focus on a person's participation in social practices rather than on his or her essential nature. Hence, the literature on cultural identity development that focuses primarily on either individual identity or on belonging to social groups is, to some extent, misguided. From a poststructuralist stance, it is addressing the wrong question with regard to how power operates. For example, from our perspective, racism does not continue to happen because there are too many white people who are unaware of their cultural identity or because there are too few people of color who are prepared to stand up for their cultural identity. It happens because we all participate in a range of daily social practices, or discourse practices, that set up relations among people along the dividing lines of color and that privilege those who are white and disadvantage those who are not white. Racism is the ideology produced by this discourse and the justification for it. It reproduces itself over and over again through the repetition of its assumptions. A poststructuralist analysis directs us to pay attention first of all to the language practices rather than to what lies in the hearts of people. The latter is assumed to be a by-product of the former rather than its source.

Another advantage of the poststructuralist analysis of power is that it spotlights the practices of power in counseling itself. It cautions counselors about becoming unwitting operatives of the confessional technologies of power that Nikolas Rose (1985) calls the function of the psy-complex. If these functions are illuminated, rather than remaining in the shadows, their power can be used to different ends. An example is the trend within the modern management of persons for individuals to become thought of as "cases" (Foucault, 2000, p. 172). The language of counseling has often adopted this piece of discourse from the medical disciplines. If we recognize that such discourse usages are cultural pieces of the operation of power, then we can refuse to talk in this way. We can refuse to participate in one of the key steps in the operation of power, that of turning persons into objects first so that they can be governed (treated) second. This can be difficult to achieve when counselors are required by their employers to fill out "treatment" plans couched in the language of objectification. However, creative counselors everywhere are finding ways to meet such requirements and still respect their clients by, for example, giving clients a say in what gets filled out on the form.

An acute sensitivity to the work done by power relations to construct people's lives also helps counselors hear what is of critical importance in the experience of persons and to separate this from other material. Foucault (2000) has argued that "the most intense point of a life, the point where its energy is concentrated, is where it comes against power, struggles with it, attempts to use its forces, and to evade its traps" (p. 162). If this is true to even a small degree, then counselors should consciously direct their work to this place, where they can potentially have the most critical impact. They can help their clients discover different ways of governing themselves, not just of being governed by others. Foucault (2000) called this domain of practice "political spirituality" (p. 233). If counseling can be situated at this place, clients will seldom find counseling irrelevant or lack motivation to participate in it.

The poststructuralist analysis of power focuses our attention on its cultural nature. Power conceived of as a network of social practices that get stamped into our psyches emphasizes the technical role of culture in the production of psychological experience. This emphasis elevates the position of culture in the human sciences. It requires us to take more seriously the daily operations of power in cultural relations and gives us some tools with which to make sense of them. Moreover, it enables us to see that power and privilege are seldom monolithic and that cultural relations are often complex and nuanced fields of negotiation. We can thus avoid the mistake of thinking people are powerless or completely lacking in freedom. We believe that the multicultural counseling field would do well to embrace this perspective more than it currently does.

Counseling From a Poststructuralist Perspective on Power

At the end of Chapter 6, we illustrated the liberal humanist analysis of power with a scenario constructed for this purpose. In Chapter 7, we used the same story to illustrate the structuralist analysis of power. For purposes of comparison, let's use the same scenario, for a third time, in this chapter. We invite readers to notice the differences in the conversation as the counselor proceeds from a poststructuralist analysis of power.

There are only a small number of different poststructuralist approaches we could choose from to use for illustration purposes. We've decided to use the approach that we're most familiar with: a narrative orientation to therapy.

A narrative therapist shares with a structuralist the understanding that the setup of the counseling is structured before it starts. The difference is that for the poststructuralist, the structuring is not just done by the system, whose nerve center exists elsewhere. Rather, it exists in the practices that surround the counseling. These include the ways in which the workers at the counseling agency talk about their clients. Rebeka has actually led a staff discussion among the counselors at the agency where she works about how to make agency practices respectful of clients as agents in their own lives. As a result, the use of the word *case* in reference to people is banned from the agency. Clients are not even spoken of as clients. They are spoken to and referred to by the names that they prefer. Secret files are not kept on them, and they are made aware that ownership of their file is shared between them and the counselor. They have a say about what goes in the file and what does not. Neither are they asked to fill in a form as soon as they arrive at the counseling center. When a form does have to be filled out, it is done as a joint exercise with the counselor. The form does not invite clients to assign themselves categories of identity along the lines specified by the government. The counseling center still has to submit statistics to insurance companies, but the identity categories on the agency's forms are sensitive to the multiple identity categories that clients might prefer to nominate. Rebeka is careful to ask about these issues in ways that leave the questions open rather than force rapid closure.

Early on in their first counseling session, Rebeka asks Daneesha if it's okay for her to ask some questions about what brought her to counseling and what she wants from it. Daneesha agrees, and they begin to talk about an issue that has just arisen and is at the front of Daneesha's mind, even though it's not the reason she initially asked for counseling.

"Well, I'm on this committee with a group of women," Daneesha explained. "I've known them all for about a year and some of them for several years. There are only a few African Americans at my church and I am the only African American on the committee. The other women are mostly Mexican American."

"Okay," said Rebeka. "So did something happen at the committee meeting?"

Daneesha recounted an uncomfortable exchange at the meeting earlier that day.

"We were discussing a social event that we are supposed to be planning as a fund-raiser. One of the women told a story to the group about how her husband referred to her as a 'nigger.' She said it was like a joke, and she was just laughing as she said it."

"So what effect did that incident have for you?" asked Rebeka.

"Actually, I was shocked to hear her use the *N* word," said Daneesha. "And I was even more uncomfortable because the other women chuckled at the incident."

Daneesha stated that no one said anything about its being wrong or was concerned that it might create discomfort for her.

"I don't know which is worse—that they used the *N* word or that they laughed about it," she said, looking a little sheepish and trailing off.

"Were there some other effects of this incident as well?" asked Rebeka.

"I should have made a statement telling them how offensive this was and left the room. Instead, I just kind of looked at the woman who said it."

"Are you saying that one of the effects of what happened was that it produced some negative self-talk in you about what you should have done? In fact, it almost tried to convince you that you were more responsible than the person who uttered the racist slur. Is that right?"

"Yes," said Daneesha. "I guess that's what happened."

"How did it do that? How did it get under your skin so easily and persuade you that there was something wrong with you?"

"I guess that's what I always do," Daneesha smiled. "I always take the responsibility myself."

"Does that mean that when you encounter a racist remark, you are likely to take responsibility for the effects of that remark on yourself?"

"It sounds dumb, doesn't it? But yes."

"Well, I wouldn't call it dumb, but I am interested in whether you think that's what you would prefer to do in such situations."

Daneesha thought for a few seconds.

"No, I would like not to have to do that. I'd like to feel okay about standing up against racism and objecting to it when I come across it without getting all knotted up inside."

"Okay," said Rebeka. "So can we explore a bit how you learned to respond in a way that you don't want to keep repeating. Would that be of interest to you?"

Daneesha was happy to engage in this conversation, and they talked about several experiences that had been similar for her. Eventually, during this conversation, she remembered something that had happened at a grocery store in Tennessee when she was 12 or 13. Her mom had asked for assistance from a young clerk.

"I don't even recall what my mom wanted," she said, "but the clerk sneered and rudely said, 'I don't do anything for niggers.'"

As Daneesha recounted this event, her eyes filled with tears. She told Rebeka that her mom had told her to be quiet about the incident. Her mom had said that the godly thing to do was to pray for the young man, and they walked out of the store.

"Did your mom's comment help the voice of responsibility taking or help your other voice of wanting to stand up against it?"

"Well, it made me ashamed . . . and I didn't pray for that man. So I think I ended up feeling guilty myself, too."

"As you think about it now, do you think you were guilty of doing anything wrong?" asked Rebeka.

"No," said Daneesha.

"So is it kind of like racism can trick you into feeling guilty even when you're not the one who's done something wrong?"

Daneesha smiled at this. It sounded absurd and yet also strangely accurate.

"Tell me," said Rebeka. "Are there times you can remember when you didn't allow this to happen? Are there any occasions when you've chosen not to feel guilty and to stand in a different place?"

After some thought, Daneesha came up with a couple of instances. They related to more recent events in her life, particularly the discussion group on race and Christianity that she had attended at her church.

"So what was it that you took from that discussion group and how was it helpful for you?" asked Rebeka.

"I guess I just saw how the whole racism thing works and is so powerful and I got mad about that," said Daneesha, "and that was just before Hurricane Katrina hit and made it all in the news, too."

"So if you had been able to hold the spirit of that discussion group with you this afternoon, what would you have done differently?"

The conversation went on to explore the identity that Daneesha would like to have enacted that afternoon and in other situations of her life.

We would like you to notice several things that are different about this piece of counseling. First, it treats identity neither as something given by the usual categories to which people are assigned by cultural dividing practices nor as a product of personality. The counselor does not assume that Daneesha's childhood memory is determining her personality in any way. Nor does she assume that there is some deficit condition in her because she feels guilty instead of angry.

Notice, too, the way that racism is talked about. It is not spoken of as if it originates in the hearts of persons. Instead, the counselor uses the narrative technique of externalizing language and speaks of racism as an effect of discourse. It is something that can be challenged and contested rather than something determined by a structural essence. On the same basis, the experience of guilt is not assumed to be an identity characteristic of Daneesha. Instead, it is understood to be produced in her as an effect of the operation of power along racial dividing lines. She is governed by the practices that embody racist discourse to the extent that it has psychological effects on her.

However, there are also counter stories, and they exist in Daneesha's experience and in the world around her. As she takes steps to govern her own responses in accordance with her preferred identity, she is able to ameliorate the effects of the governing power of racist discourse. This is admittedly a small moment of resistance to this particular operation of power, but it happens at the local and immediate level of a person's psychological experience. Such moments are always available. They do not take cataclysmic social changes to become manifest. They do not require structural revolutions to be underway before counseling can enable them to be effective. They are as ordinary as people's everyday problems. In fact, from this perspective, it is inevitable that people's everyday problems will always be shot through with the effects of power relations of the kind that Foucault analyzed. We believe that the multicultural cause in counseling has much to gain from taking these ideas seriously.

TO DISCUSS

1. In the counseling conversation with Daneesha, what specific things did the counselor do that fit with a poststructuralist perspective on power?

2. Search counseling texts or videotapes for examples of the expression of a poststructuralist perspective.

3. Role-play a counseling interview similar to the one between Daneesha and Rebeka and discuss how it is experienced from the client's point of view.

4. What difference does it make to counseling to think of power in a positive or productive way rather than as just oppressive?

Response to Chapter 8

Susan Brotherton, with Felix Esquivel

Susan Brotherton, Ph.D., is a professor of educational psychology and counseling at California State University, San Bernardino. She coordinated the program for five years and teaches Multicultural Counseling, Introduction to Counseling, Ethics and Law, Consultation, Advanced Child and Adolescent Development, Field Experience Supervision, and Clinical Practicum. At CSUSB, Sue served six years as the cochair of the University Diversity Committee, served on the president's Strategic Plan Diversity Action Committee, and chaired an annual diversity conference for four years.

Sue is a well-known motivational speaker, trainer, and consultant in the realm of diversity. She is a regular trainer for the National Multicultural Institute in Washington, DC, trains new social workers in a five-county region, and provides workshops and keynote addresses for public schools, universities, private business, and nonprofit groups. She has authored numerous articles and a book titled *Counselor Education for the Twenty-First Century*.

In addition, Sue is a foster parent caring for infants. She participates in team decision making as a community member. Sue has assisted San Bernardino County in designing Family to Family training curriculum regarding mentoring between foster parents and birth parents.

Tears have a language of their own; a counselor's tears may have the ability to defrost the frozen patterns of cultural power relations. Here is a "story."

We understand that a school counselor usually represents and "speaks" for the educational institution, whose main goal is student retention and behavioral control, that is, the production of student lives in certain cultural patterns. This ethical stance is most prevalent in alternative and continuation high schools where the students are well aware of the operation of educational power in their lives. Often an alternative school setting may be the last resort for students who have had poor attendance, pregnancy, truancy, problems with the law, or resistant behaviors at school. The counselor speaks the voice of privilege: "I am well educated, successful, and far above you in the hierarchy," and the voice of power: "I have the ability to kick you out of the system if you do not meet the criteria" (behavior, attitude, attendance, and achievement.) One might see this as a "dividing practice," whereby counselors select students who stay in school and those who do not.

On the other hand, the school counselor can also speak in ways that resist this operation of power. When the school counselor advocates for the client, he is often standing alongside practices of resistance. Or when the school counselor helps a student articulate her experience of failure and at the same time her determination not to be determined by that failure, he is engaged in a different kind of ethical practice. Let me illustrate this by telling a remarkable story.

As a counselor educator, I often speak to my graduate students about the issues of power in the counseling relationship. Yet it was not until I read about a post-structuralist analysis of power, and then personally observed a counseling conversation as an exchange in power relation, that this concept came alive for me.

Felix is a graduate student in the educational counseling program at California State University, San Bernardino. He is middle aged, changing careers (from barber to school counselor), and, in the last year of a three-year graduate program, was diagnosed with advanced cancer. His field experience placement was in an alternative high school setting. As a university fieldwork supervisor, I visited the site to observe and evaluate Felix's counseling skills.

Felix was seeing a male student, "Juan," who had the potential to be an achieving student and wanted to return to his original high school. Yet he lacked self-confidence, school credits, and support, perhaps as a result of the cultural dividing practices that were impacting on him. His narrative contained a combination of the effects of a discouraging, failing discourse and, on the other hand, a glimmer of hope. Felix brought out the contrasting story elements in his counseling.

During the counseling conversation, Juan mentioned that he wanted to be a dialysis nurse and maybe help save lives, or at least be a part of that endeavor. At this moment, Felix made the choice to share that he had just had his last chemotherapy treatment, and he spoke about the wonderful, caring nurses he had met and how they had affected his life. As he spoke about what he had received from these nurses, tears overcame him. Juan asked if they should stop at this point, and Felix mumbled, "And I'm supposed to be the counselor." At this moment, he stepped out of the position of power that the role of counselor granted him and spoke to Juan as an imagined recipient of his services. In doing so he positioned Juan in the position of honor as the future expert carer with much to offer.

As a cancer survivor myself, I knew what Felix's tears were saying. I very rarely become involved in a counseling session during observation and student evaluation. Yet this time, I spoke to Juan. I explained to him that the tears were about deep gratitude and that he would see many of them with his future patients. The student then had tears in his eyes. I continued, "This is the moment, right now! You can decide to go to college and become a nurse."

There was a strikingly positive energy shift, partially unseen and unspoken. All of us moved to a position of optimism. Juan responded by acknowledging that he understood the importance of how Felix and I felt and how he as a nurse could have an impact on people. He knew that his life could have meaning and he said that now was the time, that at his age and in this moment he could make that decision and act on it. The counseling session had become a transfer of power, yet counselor and student both knew their place and respected it. Felix skillfully brought the session to closure.

I used to teach that if you "stay in the role of counselor," then you will not, should not, cry with or in front of your clients. Of course, this is about holding a stance of power in the relationship. Felix and Juan changed my thinking. The flow of power was mutual, not unidirectional, which is not to say that the position of counselor does not continue to be located in a power relation. But the expression of it was fluid in that moment and Juan was invited to step into a subject position that was potentially powerful in terms of his life. I cannot say what the long-term results of this counseling conversation will be, but what I intuitively know is that we were all changed in that moment. My hope is that Juan will always remember Felix as a counselor who possessed the strength, wisdom, confidence, and skill to allow a mutual exchange of power between the two of them. Through this mutual exchange, a counter story emerged.

CHAPTER 9

Gender and Identity

Gender discourse is one of the most powerful shaping influences on people's lives. Multicultural counselors generally acknowledge that gender is key to the cultural context of living (Brooks & Good, 2001; McGoldrick, 1998). This recognition has largely arisen from the efforts of feminist therapists who argued that female clients' experiences should be considered in the context of a pervasive sociocultural patriarchal system (e.g., Avis, 1987; Hare-Mustin, 1987; Lerner, 1987). From our perspective, gender narratives provide us with many of the most important identity templates that we live by. Together with race, ethnicity, and class, gender is institutionalized through the organization of complex cultural and social locations that shape every person's life from birth. They impact men's and women's thought patterns, emotions, nonverbal expressions, life expectations, career aspirations, moral reasoning, value systems, and relationship moves. While some societies are comparatively homogenous in terms of race or class, no society can ignore gender. Every society is founded on assumptions of gender difference (Kimmel & Yi, 2004; Lorber & Farrell, 1991).

There is no problem with the acknowledgment of gender difference when it involves an appreciation of and a valuing of the different biological functions in, for example, childbirth. What is problematic is how biological sex differences have been layered over with differential entitlements in the social world. Gender differences have often solidified into dividing lines, according to which opportunity to act in the world is distributed unevenly. More often than not, it has been men who have been privileged by an emphasis on their generally greater physical strength and the development of unified accounts of "superiority" in other domains (intellectual, moral, etc.). And it has been women who have been assigned second-class social positions on account of their supposed physical, intellectual, and moral "inferiority." Sexism, like racism, has depended on assumptions of superiority and inferiority. And, like racism, gender differences have been developed as elaborate narratives about what is natural about these differences. In this way, power relations that have their origins in discourse and narrative have been accorded an authority that is harder to question. To question this authority, one has to question the raft of essentialist assumptions that underlie the process of "naturalizing" what is really work done by discourse.

To ignore gender as a cultural variable that shapes our interactions, experiences, problems, and attempts at counseling would therefore be problematic. To do so would also reinforce a simplistic analysis of culture and identity that would center race or ethnicity as the sole focus of multicultural practice. This oversimplification would not be surprising, though, considering that gender and race have historically represented different fields of study. But if the contours of gender difference and gender entitlement are based more on discourse and narrative than on male and female nature, then we are necessarily talking about cultural differences.

We should be careful here, however, not to present an oversimplified, monolithic account of gender relations. Consistent with the account of greater complexity that we outlined in Chapter 2, gender-based power relations do not fit easily into a story of long-standing pervasive oppression and then simple feminist-inspired liberation. The history of gender and power has been long and contested. It takes different forms in different cultural contexts and is constantly shifting, never static. We should also be careful about reading Eurocentric analyses of gender politics onto the cultural positions of women from outside the Western tradition. Even in the West, the position of women in relation to men has been through periods of greater and lesser power. Stephanie Coontz (2005), for example, in writing a history of marriage, shows how many of the particular concerns that have occupied feminists in the last 30 years developed out of the industrial revolution, the modern evolution of the love marriage, and the 20th century breadwinner/homemaker norm for family arrangement. Women in earlier centuries might have identified with some but by no means all of the concerns of modern feminists. At the same time, incidentally, Coontz disputes the conservative narrative of the family as a stable institution from time immemorial that is only now being threatened by such cultural developments as sole-parent families and gay marriage. Coontz shows that the institution of marriage has never been singular or stable and has in fact been through many shifts and changes.

Feminist therapists and feminist writers have nevertheless for several decades voiced serious criticism of the counseling and therapy field for its failure to adequately address issues of patriarchy (Drewery, 1986; Goldner, 1985; McKinnon & Miller, 1987; Treadgold, 1983; Waldegrave, 1985). The expressions of gendered power relations that are evidenced in male violence and its effects on the psychological experience of women have been a particular focus of this criticism. However, the distinctive problems that women present to counselors are not only those of domestic violence, rape, and sexual abuse. They reach far into the identity stories that encompass women's lives and through which they envision what is possible for them to aspire to. The deeper we look into these issues, the more questions that can be raised about psychological theories of human functioning that sometimes appear to ignore gender.

The dominance of the liberal humanist perspective in therapy in the latter part of the 20th century, which we described in Chapter 6, alarmed many feminists. Liberal humanism was identified as emerging from patriarchal and Eurocentric belief systems and was criticized for lacking the teeth to address social justice concerns for women in therapy. From a feminist perspective, patriarchal and Eurocentric practices systematically silence women who do not conform to dominant cultural norms. In this way, they require the majority of women to fit their identities into gendered norms and to police those who stray from such norms. These insights inspired many feminist researchers and practitioners to confront mental health professionals for colluding with culturally oppressive practices and failing to attend to the structured inequalities that support sexism (Calvert, 1994; Hindmarsh, 1987; Lawson-Te Aho, 1993; McKinnon & Miller, 1987; Ohlson, 1993; Smith, 1992; Tamesese & Waldegrave, 1993).

Jean Marecek (1995) shows that the history of psychology is full of examples in which esteemed "scientific knowledge" justifies gender inequality. For instance, Marecek cites research that claims that the female brain was thought to be less highly evolved than the male brain. While research no longer supports the idea that the female brain is less evolved, Marecek's purpose in citing this research assumption is to demonstrate the androcentric bias of science. The effort to establish an essential difference between men and women that might be used to justify the structuring of social dividing lines has been long-standing. More subtle has been the development of a psychology of human beings that ignores gendered cultural experience and conflates men's psychological experience with women's. Thus, it is not surprising that the exploration of social justice issues in therapy has been a central focus for feminists.

Box 9.1. Women in Statistics

A United Nations global survey conducted in 1980 showed that women do 2/3 of the work in the world but own only 1/100 of the property, earn 1/10 of the income, and comprise 2/3 of the illiterate population (Kahn & Kahn, 2003). Female infanticide and female circumcision, or what often amounts to female genital mutilation, are still carried out in many countries. Females are still victims of forced marriages or are exposed to divorce systems that are directly biased against women. In some communities, honor killings continue to occur. In communities all over the world, women are victims of sexual crimes and suffer serious psychological scars, sometimes described in psychiatric terms as posttraumatic stress syndrome. It is clear that physical and sexual abuse, partner violence, and rape or sexual assault are also strongly related to the prevalence of suicidal thoughts, depression, and anxiety in women.

Many research studies show that women are systematically disadvantaged in the workplace. In 2001, in the United States, the median hourly wage of women workers was 78 percent of the median hourly wage of male workers, whereas in 1979 it had been only 63 percent. While the gender wage gap between men and women has narrowed, women earn 25% less than men on average. Sexual harassment is another impediment that women suffer in the workplace. Unwelcome sexual advances interfere

(Continued)

(Continued)

> with a woman's ability to perform her job and enjoy its benefits. As many as one quarter to one third of all working women report having been sexually harassed in the workplace (McNamee & Miller, 2004). There are many successful businesswomen who report numerous barriers to advancement to senior management (Lyness & Thompson, 2000). For example, when women behave in the workplace in a manner not considered feminine, disadvantages result. When women display a task-oriented style that goes against the dominant discourse of women as, "by nature," relational and demure, they might be rated competent but will receive low likability ratings. When men display the same task-oriented leadership style, they tend to be perceived more favorably (Rudman, 1998, cited by Sue & Sue, 2007). Talented women leaders are often excluded from business domains where male camaraderie exists (e.g., on the golf course), which also excludes them from access to good mentoring and to information that might assist them with on-the-job performance.

The Influence of Feminist Therapy Over Three Decades

The 1970s in the United States are often called the first decade of feminist therapy. A major feminist emphasis that developed out of feminist consciousness-raising groups into the therapy field in this decade was the recognition that "the personal is political." This phrase became a catch cry of the feminist movement in general, and it had particular significance for counseling. Through participation in consciousness-raising groups, women in this time set about deconstructing their situations in relation to marriage, child rearing, sex, work, and the wider culture. Even the personal use of language was analyzed and deconstructed (see Deborah Tannen's [1991] account of gender differences in conversational language use).

One result of this deconstruction was that women began to see that what they had thought of as their personal suffering was related to the wider systemic politics of gender relations. Experiences that they might bring to counseling were not just shaped by their personal preferences and choices, or even by their unconscious "penis envy," but were downstream effects of sexism or patriarchy. "The personal is political," therefore, described how women's personal lives were in considerable part politically shaped and delimited. Several implications followed. One was that addressing personal suffering meant collectively addressing the structuring of political relationships. Another was that every personal choice had political implications for all gender relations. Yet another was that the front where struggle for significant social change might take place was to be found not just in the public domain of politics but also in the private and personal domain of the family. This last point fits well with Foucault's analytics of power, as described in Chapter 8. Foucault also saw the sites of power and of resistance to be dispersed in millions of places in the social world.

If the personal was political, then there were clear political implications for therapy practices focused on the personal world of clients. One implication was that therapy needed to focus more explicitly on political consciousness raising. Another was that the personal relationship between the counselor and the client needed to come under scrutiny. Feminist therapy began to advocate a more egalitarian therapist-client relationship (Gilbert, 1980). As a result of feminist work on sex bias and sex role stereotyping, gender-aware psychologists became more conscious of the importance of informing clients about procedures, goals, and potential side effects of counseling and psychotherapy. The power of the therapist to intervene in the lives of clients began to be treated as worthy of suspicion. During this period, some feminist therapists believed that limiting one's practice to counseling individuals was a form of treating the symptoms and ignoring the cause. They highlighted the need to work alongside clients against the social disease represented by patriarchal society. Edna Rawlings and Dianne Carter (1977) suggested that social action was an essential professional responsibility of therapists.

During the 1970s and 1980s, many feminist counselors emphasized the different natures of men and women. There was a need to establish differences between the psychological experiences of men and women, which were often obscured by an emphasis on human nature. Some felt that they could map out possible problem trajectories determined by gender. In addition, many feminists suggested that there was a moral obligation for counselors to teach and attempt to change their clients to embrace nonpatriarchal practices.

For example, Sari Dworkin (1984) stated that the therapist has a responsibility to intervene directly or indirectly in the client's value system if it reflects a patriarchal bias. She argued that women are systematically taught to accept and conform to social roles and therefore have learned that they are less capable and need the approval of others to feel good about themselves. Because women's sense of worth is externally defined, said Dworkin, a healthy self-concept is difficult to attain. She suggested that therapy should provide the opportunity for women to explore and reflect on the origin and meaning of their feelings and behavior outside prescribed roles. Like Dworkin, Maye Taylor (1991) thought that both women clients and counselors need to examine what they have been taught about being female in the light of their actual competencies, interests, and needs. Likewise, male clients and counselors needed to examine what they have been taught to take for granted about women.

Karen Offen (1988) believed that in order to counsel women in a respectful way, a counselor needs to first assess a woman's status in society relative to men and then encourage women to claim their own values rather than be limited by a patriarchal specification of what a woman should be. Offen also wanted counselors to step away from neutrality and a nonjudgmental stance and actively encourage women to challenge the coercive authority of male privilege.

During the 1980s, feminist therapy was becoming recognized in its own right (Ballou & Gabalac, 1985; Chaplin, 1988; Russell, 1984). Writers in the early and mid 1980s pointed out ways in which exaggeration of women's gender role stereotypes were codified and reinforced through diagnostic categories (Enns, 1993). Despite the powerful and articulate challenging of patriarchal practices by many women, the revised third edition of the *Diagnostic and Statistical Manual of Mental Disorders* (DSM-III-R), published by the American Psychiatric Association (1987), introduced a "Self-Defeating Personality Disorder." Carolyn Zerbe Enns contended that this category described 85% of women based on normative socialization.

Neither did this diagnostic label acknowledge the survival value of learned submissive behavior in reducing emotional or physical violence in abusive relationships. Wendy Drewery (1986), using a structuralist analysis, emphasized the value of showing how patriarchy and socially unjust practices contribute to unacceptable conditions in people's lives. She suggested that the immense burden of individual guilt and self-deprecation from which many women suffer is likely to be relieved when their experiences are located within the sociocultural practices from which their private experiences have developed.

During the early and mid 1980s, feminist therapists in the United States increasingly directed their focus toward helping female clients understand the personal, cultural, and social aspects of their distress (Greenspan, 1983). Some feminists promoted separate counseling services for men and women as a method of protecting women from male therapists' sexist or androcentric bias. Some feminist therapists (e.g., Rawlings & Carter, 1977) asked male therapists to abandon working with female clients. David Orlinsky and Kenneth Howard (1980) reported that women with depressive reactions, anxiety reactions, or schizophrenia had more positive experiences with female therapists. They also found that single women, particularly young single women, benefited more from female counselors. Mary Nomme Russell (1984) concluded from a summary of various studies that young women in the process of defining their identities would be best served by female therapists who have an awareness of gender role issues. Maye Taylor (1991) claimed that feminist psychotherapists are at an advantage in assisting women clients because they have firsthand experience of male oppression and patriarchy. Clearly, many feminists saw gender matching of clients and counselors as a legitimate method of seeking justice for women in the counseling relationship. Being unencumbered by "male transference" (Taylor, 1991, p. 102) was a further benefit claimed for such gender matching.

By the late 1980s, the reemergence of liberal humanism was contributing to a growth in conservative and individualistic versions of feminist therapeutic practice less explicitly connected with the sociocultural and historical context (Kahn & Yoder, 1989). A dilution of passion for the social action issues that had been fundamental to the work of many feminist counselors at an earlier time took place. A parallel return of some client-centered therapies to romantic individualism was reflected in the encouragement of individuals to look within for solutions. Less emphasis was given to the impact of social contexts and to dominant and oppressive discourses. Carolyn Zerbe Enns (1993) claimed that romantic individualism returned the burden of responsibility and transformation to clients, rather than enabling a repositioning in social contexts through the educative process as advocated by feminist therapists.

Yet, in the 1990s, feminist concerns were not completely marginalized. What's more, they began to be taken up in therapy with men. In *Invitations to Responsibility*, Alan Jenkins (1990) outlined many of the traditional gender patterns that position male clients in a very limited and constrained role repertoire in their relationships with women. Working with men who had used violence or abused women or children, he used the language of male entitlement to explain many men's expectations of women to attend to their physical and social needs. When these men's female partners failed to conform to stereotypical relationship patterns, they would feel entitled to resort to abusive behavior. Jenkins also discussed how patriarchal cultural patterns invite men to leave the primary responsibility of parenting to women, even when both partners are working outside the home. Many women are frequently positioned in families as primarily responsible for the socioemotional development of both their husbands and their children (Jenkins, 1990). The challenge for counselors is to help men recognize how gender discourse has often placed them in an unearned position of social privilege, which becomes so familiar that an exaggerated sense of entitlement in their relationships with women remains unquestioned.

Raquel's story is one woman's account of gendered relationship norms within the family. Notice how she experiences personally the effects of the politics of gender, even though neither she nor her husband is responsible for creating them.

I am an American wife. I wish that meant that I am in an equal partnership where responsibility for income, romance, parenting, entertaining, and so forth are shared. But for me, the word *wife* frequently means sacrifice, inequality, oppression, powerlessness. This is not just the fault of society, or of my husband, or of myself. Each plays a role in its continuance.

Of course I learned most "rules" from my parents. Popular culture and entertainment also greatly supported what I was learning. The husband is the breadwinner. The wife is the homemaker, cook, maid, hostess, relationship counselor, single parent, "arm candy," and entertainment manager. All these titles, but no power. Lesson: husbands are superior and are expected only to make money. Wives are expected to do everything else.

The husband is the boss of the home and the decision maker. The wife may speak her opinions, but they do not carry as much weight as the man's in the final decision. By watching my mother, I learned that sometimes it is easier to hold your tongue in the moment and just do what you want later. Lesson: it's easier to say, "Oops!" or "Sorry" than "May I . . . ?" and risk hearing "No." But that is not power.

While I know he loves and cares for me, my father was not a hands-on parent. In addition to his lack of interest in equal parenting, his career in the military meant he was away from the family a lot, sometimes for months at a time. The emotions he most frequently showed ranged from anger to worry or annoyance. Because I was a girl, I enjoyed a relationship with my father that was not available to my brothers. Earning his love and approval was very important to me, and I learned which behaviors made him happy and which did not and I adapted. Lesson: if you show your true, imperfect self, you will not be loved. As with many military families, the ability to adapt to situations and people was necessary and greatly valued. For a long time, it never occurred to me that adapting so much for my father's love might be potentially damaging to my personality. But, through years of playing a role, suppressing my opinions, and learning to ignore my gut and natural tendencies, I lost touch with the real me. In doing so, my own power atrophied from disuse.

I also watched my mother change and suppress her true self in hope of winning my father's love. When my father was away, I observed that my mother was almost a different person. We had fun, certain rules of the house were temporarily lifted, and her dynamic, joyful personality shone more brightly. This shift occurred over and over again each time my father deployed. I learned that it was only safe or appropriate for a wife to be her true self outside the company of her spouse. Lesson: power and freedom are available only when your husband is away. I struggle greatly with this in my own marriage.

Because I was taught to be this way, believing it was "normal," I have made major choices in my life based on that oppressive rule book. I chose a college close to home because I was sure as a girl that I couldn't make it completely on my own. When I chose my major I was free to choose whatever I wanted because I would never really use it anyway. It was assumed or expected that I would become a wife and mother. When I did leave home, I moved directly from my father's house to my husband's house. It never occurred to me, nor was it suggested to me, that my life, my marriage, and my personal worth might benefit from time on my own, from earning things and truly deserving them. In following my husband's career, we moved across country and I had difficulty finding a job relating to my field of study. I was told that any job would do, even part time at the mall, because he made enough already. He believed he was saying the right thing to relieve my stress and make me feel better. Additionally, he received much fulfillment from his ability to provide for me. But his telling me this did not bring relief. I felt stupid, incapable, held down, and powerless. I equated a job to my own personality, independence, and power, so what I heard was that it didn't matter anyway because my place in this marriage was subordinate to him.

Only within the last three or four years have these old lessons come angrily rushing to the surface. My oppression is apparent in different ways, now that I am fighting to change it. When I chose to work a second job in order to feel more personally challenged and financially independent, I was scolded by my husband for being ungrateful for his provision and for being selfish with my time. But it is okay that he work 12-hour days and deploy for months at a time! When we discussed power issues in counseling sessions, he seemed oblivious and yet defensive about my complaints. He finds traditional gender roles safe and appealing. I'm sure he is quite conscious of the power he holds in our marriage. One reason I think he is scared to give up some of that power is that he fears it will mean losing my love. I find it sad that he views my love as an obligatory response to his power or conditional on his bank account. Who taught him that? It does not escape me that, with every oppressive "rule" I follow, there is a corresponding oppression that bears on him.

Immediately following every word I write about my oppression, there is a little voice inside my head saying that I am responsible for my situation; on a logical level I know I am not without power. I know I am a strong, independent, capable person. Yet I remain a victim of this deep-seated belief that as a woman and a wife I cannot make it in this world on my own power, intelligence, and ability. At the end of the day, I am still carrying around with me that same old rule book—and my husband and my culture carry it as well.

A number of researchers in the United States have continued to express concern that gender awareness in therapy has not been adequately addressed (Rigazio-DiGilio, Anderson, & Kunkler, 1995; Twohey & Volker, 1993). Regarding the supervision of therapists, it has been suggested that supervisors need to be more aware of themselves as gendered beings. Mary Lee Nelson and Elizabeth Holloway's (1990) study illustrated this point when they found that supervisors often failed to encourage female trainees to assume power in supervision. Females tend to defer to more powerful authority figures more quickly than males do. Sandra Rigazio-DiGilio, Stephen Anderson, and Kara Kunkler (1995) suggested that counselor educators must accept the effect that gender differences have on male and female counselors' work. These authors claimed that the socialization of men and women produces different "voices" in clinical practice.

The Effect of Postmodern Feminism on Contemporary Counseling Practice

There was a growing consensus in the 1990s among postmodern writers and postmodern feminists in particular that while the ascriptions "male" and "female" have deep social meanings, women and men are not simple, unproblematic, self-evident gender categories (Butler, 1992; Connell, 1995; Davies, 1993; de Lauretis, 1986; Enns, 1993; Flax, 1990, 1992; Gavey, 1996; Grimshaw, 1986; Gunew, 1993; Haraway, 1990; Hare-Mustin & Marecek, 1994; Jones & Guy, 1992; Larner, 1993, 1995; Marecek, 1995; Mouffe, 1992; Real, 1995; Yeatman, 1993). There has been insufficient evidence to suggest that either women or men can be categorized into meaningful social groups on the basis of biology alone. During this time, gender was increasingly being reconceived as a highly variable and historically contingent set of human practices that pervade many aspects of human experience.

Recently, considerable attention has been paid to the oversimplified, dualistic, and essentialist explanation of gender generally, and men's oppression over women specifically, within radical feminist theory (Bordo, 1993; Diamond & Quinby, 1988; McNay, 1992). The traditional feminist analysis presented women as passive recipients of cultural practices and was argued by postmodern feminists to ignore the reality of women's collusion with and resistance to these practices (Bordo, 1993). In fact, this essentialist perspective actually "confirms the naturalness of their [women's] passivity and the rightness of their objectification" (Waterhouse, 1993, p. 108). In addition, essentialist understandings of the mind/body dichotomy and resulting cultural practices reflect a pessimistic, if not harmful, view of men (Scott & Morgan, 1993). Susan Bordo (1993) summarizes the limitations of this traditional feminist account:

> Subsuming patriarchal institutions and practices under an oppressor/oppressed model which theorizes men as possessing and wielding power over women—who are viewed correspondingly as themselves utterly powerless—proved inadequate to the social and historical complexities of the situations of men and women. (p. 23)

Nita McKinley (2000) acknowledged the limitations of essentialist accounts of men's and women's behavior in general and of women's body experience specifically. Thus, she included a nonessentialist feminist perspective in her efforts to understand women's body experience in American culture.

Gender and its Intersection With Other Identities

When we explore the meaning of gender, we are immediately confronted with the difficulty of understanding gender independent of ethnicity, class, religion, sexual orientation, and a whole host of other identities. Maria Julia (2000) quite rightly identifies how ethnicity and gender, for example, are "simultaneous, interconnected, inter-determining processes, rather than separate systems" (p. 3). Discussing gender separately from other identities creates an artificial construction.

The diverse experiences contained within the categories *men* and *women* make it hard to squeeze women and men into relatively stable or unified subjects as defined by consciousness of gender oppressiveness and oppression. Jean Grimshaw (1986) illustrated this by suggesting that

> the experience of gender, of being a man or woman inflects on much if not all of people's lives. . . . But even if one is always a man or a woman, one is never just a man or a woman. One is young or old, sick or healthy, married or unmarried, a parent or not a parent, employed or unemployed, middle-class or working-class, rich or poor, Black or White, and so forth. Gender of course inflects one's experience of these things, so that experience of any one of them may well be radically different according to whether one is a man or a woman. But it may also be radically different according to whether one is, say, Black or White, or working-class or middle-class. (pp. 84–85)

Cultural practices and political activity may reinforce gender identities, but so do class and ethnic factors (Curthoys, 1988). Judith Butler (1990) emphasized this point by suggesting that it is impossible to separate gender from its political and cultural intersections, including class, ethnic, sexual, and regional modalities of discursively constituted identities. Many gender studies have white women as the universal female subject, and this leaves the experiences of women of color marginalized. Doman Lum (2000) described women of color as a "double minority" because they are subjected to both racist and patriarchal discourse. Claire Rabin (2005) described the powerful prejudicial imagery and stereotypical forms that impact minority women today. For example, a black woman can be perceived as the mammy and a submissive, obedient servant, or the aggressive boss of an unruly family and the breeder of countless children, or the dependent welfare mother, or the jezebel, whore, or sexually aggressive woman. Latina women are often portrayed as Madonnas–virtuous, self-effacing, self-sacrificing mothers—or as spitfires, hot blooded and smolderingly erotic. Asian women are depicted as demure china dolls, or as dominating dragons. This discursive imagery is demeaning and implicitly victim blaming.

White women have been largely exempt from ethnic labeling and stereotyping and have often benefited from white privilege, thus making their day-to-day experiences qualitatively different from those of ethnic minority women. In some cases, white women have acted as oppressors of women of color, who have been child care workers for them while having to abandon the needs of their own children.

Critiques of a Postmodern Analysis of Gender

Some feminist theorists have been concerned about these recent developments in postmodern theorizing, which critique any group's sense of a common core or cohesive unity. This concern is strongly expressed in relation to the deconstruction of the category *women*. Judith Butler (1992) argued that while there can be no universal content to a gender category, that is not to say that the term *woman*, for example, should not be used. On the contrary, she suggested that the term *woman* "designates an undesignatory field of differences, one that can not be totalized or summarized by a descriptive identity category" (p. 16). Chantal Mouffe (1992) proposed that because the category *woman* can no longer correspond to any unified or unifying essence, there is no need to develop a set of questions to unearth the essential meaning. Far more pertinent are the questions, "How does *woman* become constructed as a category within different discourses?" "How is sexual difference made a pertinent distinction in social relations?" and "How are relations of subordination constructed through such a distinction?" (Mouffe, 1992, p. 373).

Postmodern feminist and social constructionist writers have challenged not only essentialist feminist assumptions. Applying the same critique, they have challenged the masculinity politics advocated by those espousing an innate or essentialist perspective of the kind proposed by Robert Bly (1990). A constructionist lens views masculinity as a sociocultural phenomenon, in contrast to the liberal humanist politics emphasized by "new age" writers who privilege an innate masculinity. Social constructionism's primary emphasis on the cultural production of gender has not been without its critics.

While postmodernists have challenged essentialist and unitary categories of persons, particularly in relation to gender and ethnic groups, there has been an objection to this analysis by what Imelda Whelehan (1995) calls cultural "outgroups." She has observed that some groups feel unprepared to dispense with their own totalizing and unitary categories, such as those described as *black* or *gay* or *lesbian*. She suggests that many nonwhite, nonmale, nonheterosexuals feel that they are excluded by what she calls the postmodern mainstream. On top of these feelings of exclusion, these groups have been urged to dispense with their old-fashioned ways of thinking. bell hooks (1991) points out that when ethnicity is discussed in a postmodern context, black women are seldom acknowledged. She states,

> It is sadly ironic that the contemporary discourse which talks the most about heterogeneity, the decentered subject, declaring breakthroughs that allow recognition of otherness, still directs its critical voice primarily to a specialized audience that shares a common language rooted in the very master narratives it claims to challenge. (p. 25)

This challenge from hooks that postmodern thought has been directed at the most privileged in Western society coincides with concerns from a number of feminists about postmodern explorations into the axes of gender, ethnicity, and sexual identity in particular (Hare-Mustin & Marecek, 1994). Michèle Barrett and Anne Phillips (1992) noted how many feminist groups consider postmodern concepts such as discourse theory to be ideologically suspect and believe they undermine the work of feminists in addressing patriarchy. Many feminists are at odds with the fragmentation of identity, a strong feature of postmodern theorizing. Barrett and Phillips argue that while gender relations could potentially take an infinite number of forms, there are in actuality some widely repeated features and considerable historical continuity. They suggest that there is sufficient historical and cross-cultural continuity, despite some variation, to warrant such signifiers as *women* and *men*. Imelda Whelehan (1995) stated that the luxury of female antiessentialism is still accorded to only the privileged. She says, "Non-white, non-heterosexual, non-bourgeois women are still finding political impetus in summoning up womanhood as identity, and femininity as a construct which excludes and punishes them most painfully of all" (p. 211).

Diana Fuss (1989) agreed that there are problems with implying that there is an essence within identity that is fixed and can be unearthed through the discussion of an oppressed group's experience of subjectivity. However, she also asserts that we cannot challenge the notion that groups of people who are systematically marginalized by the dominating cultural norms of patriarchy or Eurocentrism are strengthened by standing together and thus allowing previously silenced individuals to be heard. These political acts have been transformative in history and have advanced many communities in dealing with prejudices relating to sexual orientation, ethnicity, and gender, to name just a few.

However, we argue that when these groups begin to essentialize and totalize their identity based on one dimension, a new set of problems is generated. When exploring the intimate issues that a client wishes to address in counseling, it is a gross mistake for the counselor to see the client in unidimensional terms. It remains our view that experiences are never universal but that they reflect differing relationships to class, ethnicity, and sexual orientation, not to mention more localized variables. Bronwyn Davies (1990) suggested that postmodernism gives access to a range of new discourses that enable many women and men to present the multiplicity of their experiencing selves. Homero Magaña's story is an example of the dramatic discursive shifts that can occur in men's and women's lives in a very short time. The changes in Homero's life occurred largely through his migrating from one country to another and moving from a rural setting to an urban one.

As I was growing up in El Rincon de Don Pedro, Michoacán, Mexico, I experienced the division of roles between men and women. As early as when I was three or four years old, I remember seeing the men, including my father, grandfathers, great grandfathers, and uncles, as the breadwinners and the women, including my mother, grandmothers, great grandmothers, and aunts, as the housewives. As the seasonal farming began in El Rincon, I remember all the boys, including me, going with our fathers or uncles to cultivate the land, produce crops, and raise livestock to support and feed the family, as well as to trade, sell, and buy crops and livestock to monetarily support the family. Since I was the oldest and only man of five siblings, my father began teaching me the different duties a breadwinner "man" did to financially support his family. For example, I remember his always telling me how to do every single task he did in relation to cultivating and raising livestock and the different methods of selling them. Often, though, I would not learn as fast as he wanted me to learn, and he would yell at me because I didn't do what he wanted. He would tell me that I had to learn fast because he was going to immigrate to "El Norte," or the north, by which he meant immigrating to California to work in the fields. He used to tell me that, when he was gone, I was supposed to be "the man of the house," to take care of my mother and sisters, and to help my mother with everything that needed to be done on the farm. By the time I was nine years old, I had already learned how to cultivate the land, produce crops such as corn, wheat, squash, garbanzo beans, and lima beans, and raise livestock (cattle, goats, horses, chickens, pigs). My father had realized that cultivating the land, producing crops, and raising livestock for sale was a good way to make ends meet. He would also tell me that when I was 14 or 15 years old, I would also go to El Norte and be a breadwinner for our family. In El Rincon and among the many villages and cities in Mexico, all boys at the age of 13 or 14 still immigrate every year to California legally or illegally to work in the fields and be the breadwinners of their families along with their father. They are supposed to help their fathers this way for an average of six to eight years until they get married. Even though the men get married in their early or late 20s, they are still supposed to help their father financially until he dies.

In contrast to the men, women in El Rincon, and in other small villages and cities in Mexico, are mostly expected to be housewives. Just as the men develop an awareness of their place as breadwinners early on, the women begin to develop, as early as three or four years old, awareness of the housewife role they will take on later in life. As I grew up, I rarely saw women working in the fields or raising livestock. I saw them mainly in the home, rearing the children and managing the household while their husbands and sons worked in the fields or in El Norte. The only exceptions were when a household was composed mainly of women. At home, the teachings I received from my mother dealt with learning how to make my bed, behaving well, and doing well in school. While my father taught me how to work with my hands, my mother reinforced in me the idea that my future wife was supposed to cook for me, wash my clothes, do the bed, and take care of me, and that she should stay home running the household just as my mother had done. Women were expected to be in the house and not go out of the house unless they were accompanied by an older sister or mother. They learned to fully dedicate themselves to doing the chores of the house from early morning until late in the afternoon.

The above description of my early life might seem very specific to a particular community. However, these breadwinner and housewife roles are very much set throughout Mexico. If families stay in Mexico and never migrate to the United States, the roles stay pretty much the same. However, when families migrate to the United States, the roles change, sometimes drastically. My mother is working part time and is a full-time student. My father is encouraging her to get an education so that one day she can get a better job than working in the fields. My father is still the main provider at home, always picking oranges or lemons or building homes. However, the expectations of my parents regarding my sister's upbringing have changed drastically. They want her to attend the university and never depend on a man economically. I have made big changes in my attitudes toward women and their roles since being in the United States. This has to do with the education I have attained and the different gender roles that exist here in the United States as opposed to Mexico. Now I do not want my sisters to depend on a man economically; they have to learn to provide for themselves and learn how to use their intelligence.

Recently, I proposed to Paola, who was raised in Mexico but also immigrated to the United States. We had been dating for a year and a half. After analyzing our situation, I realized that after she graduated from the University of California, Riverside, her parents would want her to return home and live with them until she got married. She and I did not agree with this idea, because we knew that if she went back to live with her family, she would have to take care of her parents and nephews, as she is the youngest of two. She is 24 years old but has always been deprived of extracurricular activities that might require her to be out of the house regularly. Her father specifically would never allow her to live anywhere but in his house. We believe that if we live together, we both will be able to work; both of us will be the breadwinners and the "housewives." We are already breaking the traditional roles that we were raised in.

Homero Magaña identifies himself as Mexican American and as a farm worker.

Gender-Related Presenting Problems

Men seek out therapy only half as often as women do (see Box 9.2). There are also differences in how women and men present themselves to counselors. The counseling literature suggests that men are less aware of their feelings and present more work-related issues (Daniluk, Stein, & Bockus, 1995). Martin Heesacker and his colleagues (1999) found that counselors tend to view men as hypoemotional or emotionally unexpressive. In a series of six studies, these authors demonstrated that counselors are more likely to blame men for marital difficulties because of their emotional demeanor. In terms of diagnosis, men are overrepresented in the antisocial personality disorder category, a negative male stereotype.

> ## Box 9.2. Utilization of Counseling Services by Women and Men
>
> Historically, women have used the mental health system more often than men. About two thirds of all clients seeking psychological services are women (McCarthy & Holliday, 2004; Vessey & Howard, 1993). This difference occurs even when men experience rates of distress similar to if not higher than those experienced by women (Robertson, 2001). There are suggestions, however, that this trend might be changing. More men are seeking psychological help than before (Betcher & Pollack, 1993; Freiberg & Sleek, 1999), and the necessity to address the counseling needs of male clients has become more salient (Brooks & Good, 2001; McCarthy & Holliday, 2004).
>
> In the higher echelons of the mental health system, men continue to be the largest majority of health care professionals. According to John Archer and Barbara Lloyd (2002), approximately three quarters of psychiatrists and over half of psychologists are male, while only a quarter of those in the social work field are men. Among counselors, women are by far the majority.

Women, on the other hand, are more likely to attract diagnoses such as histrionic personality disorder, borderline personality disorder, and dependent personality disorder. Susan Nolen-Hoeksema (1998) suggests that this is because many women have a heightened concern for their appearance, are stereotypically perceived to be more dependent than men, and often fit a negative feminine stereotype. Women have been found to present with greater affective distress and more anxiety-related disorders, and they more often present relationship-related problems (Moore & Leafgren, 1990). These circumstances provide the very conditions that lead mental health researchers to construct pathologizing descriptions of the experiences of female clients.

These gender differences in how and for what reasons women and men seek counseling might be explained in various ways. We might ask, for example, whether women's experience of life is more difficult and more likely to produce the experiences of pain that lead people to seek out counseling help. We might posit a greater habit of dependence on others and therefore on counselors as a result of women's economic positioning as more dependent on men. We might more positively argue that women are more alert to the need for counseling or more at ease with talking about their feelings. Our preference, however, is an explanation that refers to the discourses that shape the socialization of women and men. These discourses shape the positions that women and men occupy in relation to counselors and counseling as well as to each other. The same discourses also shape how professionals respond to what they are presented with.

Royda Crose, Donald Nicholas, David Gobble, and Beth Frank (1992) commented that women suffer from more debilitating chronic disease, whereas men suffer from more life-threatening illnesses, such as heart disease. They cited numerous examples of the psychological costs of patriarchal and androcentric culture to women. They also suggested that women are more likely than men to receive a diagnosis of mental disorder by their physicians. Women are more often prescribed psychotropic medication and take more prescription and over-the-counter drugs. These authors suggested that women are also more likely to be informally labeled with a hypochondriacal, psychosomatic, hysterical, or dependent personality. Women are also reported to be twice as likely to exhibit depression, anxiety, or phobic disorders. Maye Taylor (1994) reported on surveys revealing that a high percentage of individuals with signs of depression, anxiety, panic, anorexia, and phobia are women, and that they constitute a very large percentage of the client population.

The positions assigned to men by dominant gender discourse are not without their liabilities. In studies that address differential diagnoses by gender, men are found to have four or five times higher rates of alcohol abuse and antisocial personality diagnoses. Judith Daniluk, Monika Stein, and Diane Bockus (1995) suggested that when men seek assistance, they frequently present with problems related to career, impulse control, and alcohol or other drug abuse. Keith Hawton (2005) notes that suicide rates vary according to age and ethnicity but that men kill themselves in much larger numbers than women. Women, on the other hand, have a higher rate of self-mutilation and self-injurious behavior than men.

A number of researchers have suggested that an overdeveloped male gender role sometimes gets expressed by increased risk taking, self-destructive activities, high stress, emotional inexpressiveness, an emphasis on control, and the drive to accumulate money (Kimmel & Levine, 1989; Meth, 1990; Pleck, 1981; Stewart & Lykes, 1985). James O'Neill (1990) stated that men can display "rigid, sexist, or restrictive gender roles learned during socialization, which result in personal restriction, devaluation, or violation of others or the self" (p. 25). While much of this research on presenting problems has focused on the differences between men and women, there appears to be compelling evidence that gender histories shape and influence many of the problems that clients bring to counseling. In addressing these concerns, it is important to note how the relationship between counseling problems and gender-influenced lives is an ongoing sociocultural issue.

Men and Therapy

Increasingly, gender studies are reflecting on the experiences of men through a lens other than that of the oppressor/oppressed binary. Susan Faludi (1999), Michael Gurian (1999), and William Pollack (1998) have provoked considerable debate regarding their assertion that boys, as well as girls, are harmed by a culture that poorly recognizes their needs and stresses (Brooks & Good, 2001). Yet much of the therapeutic literature continues to overlook men as occupants of a unique cultural position that needs to be understood (Brooks & Good, 2001; Dienhart, 2001). Anna Dienhart (2001) points out that "there is limited literature in the family therapy field specifically exploring therapeutic techniques aimed at engaging men in the process of therapy" (p. 24). Others agree that there is a particular need to investigate the relationship between emotions and men's problems and to design therapeutic interventions to address the restriction of men's emotions (Good & Sherrod, 2001).

Cultural changes have resulted in a rethinking of what were once taken-for-granted certainties about who men are and how they should behave, and many men have resented these changes (Rowan, 1997). It is perhaps not surprising, then, that there is a growing body of literature that demonstrates that traditional masculine attitudes and adherence to traditional male gender roles are associated with negative outcomes for men (Wester, Vogel, & Archer, 2004), including anxiety (Cournoyer & Mahalik, 1995), depression (Good & Wood, 1995), relationship difficulties (Fischer & Good, 1997), and anger (Blazina & Watkins, 1996). Moreover, the relationship between traditional masculine attitudes and willingness to seek help has been explored, and the results support a connection between male socialization and reluctance to seek psychological help (Blazina & Watkins, 1996; Good, Dell, & Mintz, 1989; Robertson, 2001).

David Jolliff and Arthur Horne (1996) point out that an interesting paradox exists regarding explanations for the low utilization of mental health services among certain groups of people, including men. The low usage of mental health services among individuals of non-European ancestry raises questions about the cultural awareness of counselors. When similar low levels of mental health service utilization are observed for men, there is a tendency to view men negatively as not open to counseling services. The assumption of a gender deficit precludes any examination of how the mental health system can become more relevant to men (McCarthy & Holliday, 2004). Some therapists may often view male clients as impenetrable and "difficult" to work with, or as "resistant," unwilling participants (Dienhart, 2001). Other therapists may unintentionally view men who seek therapy in more negative terms based on traditional notions of masculinity (Dienhart, 2001; Robertson & Fitzgerald, 1990).

As a result, many scholars have noted that rather than trying to change the individual to fit the environment, and in doing so blaming men for their deficits, it might be more helpful to alter the environment to fit the person (Robertson, 2001; McCarthy & Holliday, 2004). Therapy involving men "should be considered as a form of cross-cultural counseling, calling for special considerations" (Brooks & Good, 2001, p. 8). A variety of efforts have been aimed at improving men's access to psychological information and the use of mental health services (Good & Sherrod, 2001). One trend has been reframing or changing the name of mental health services from *counseling* or *psychotherapy* to *seminar, classes,* or *coaching* in order to attract those men who may hold traditional views of masculinity (Good & Sherrod, 2001; McCarthy & Holliday, 2004; Robertson & Fitzgerald, 1992). Some researchers have argued that therapy is too reliant on "feminine" modes of intervention that require verbal expressivity, vulnerability, and emotional awareness, all skills that are difficult for men to acquire in our society (Meth & Pasick, 1990), and that new therapies should be developed that are more congruent with "masculine" styles (Brooks & Good, 2001; Heesacker & Prichard, 1992; Shay, 1996; Wilcox & Forrest, 1992). While these modifications may prove useful, we suggest that family therapists pay closer attention to the culture of masculinity as a means of working more effectively with men in families.

We would argue that masculinity is an identifiable cultural identity that demands special attention from therapists. In saying this, it is not our intention to suggest that all men adopt traditional ideologies of masculinity. Masculinity has been conceptualized in a number of ways.

A number of theories have attempted to explain the etiologic roots of men's behavior, or why men are the way they are. There are two dominant explanations in the gender literature. Some scholars maintain an essentialist perspective for male behavior, suggesting either a biological (e.g., Bancroft, 2002; Guay, 2001; Leiblum, 2002) or psychoevolutionary basis (e.g., Archer, 1996; Buss, 1995, 2000). Those advancing a biological perspective propose that essential (genetic and hormonal) differences exist between men and women and that these biological qualities are the source of men's attitudes and behaviors. Others promote a psychoevolutionary account of masculinity, speculating that men have a completely different evolutionary heritage and face different adaptive challenges compared to women.

Essentialist views of masculinity remain popular and influential within the psychological literature as well as within popular culture. In fact, John Gray's bestselling book *Men Are From Mars, Women Are From Venus* (1992) explicitly advances an essentialist perspective, arguing that physiological differences between the sexes account for psychological differences, which then create relationship difficulties. Essentialist explanations for masculinity are often expressed most plainly in the area of sexuality. For example, it is commonly taken for granted that men's sexual urges are natural and compelling (Hare-Mustin, 1994), while women's sexual urges are assumed to naturally have much less intensity (Crawford, Kippax, & Waldby, 1994). Many men and women subscribe to the belief that a man always wants and is always ready for sex, while women need only to be loved, held, and cherished (Braun, Gavey, & McPhillips, 2003; Potts, 1998).

While essentialist explanations of masculinity offer a certain level of understanding and remind therapists not to ignore biological factors, they fail to capture the nuanced complexities of men's attitudes and behaviors, including their particular professional ambitions, personal aspirations, relational needs, and patterns of relating. Essentialist theories also fail to explain those men who act in ways contrary to their "biological makeup." Moreover, "because of their high regard for the relative immutability of the inherent differences between women and men, essentialist theorists tend to be relatively conservative in their view of possibilities for change" (Brooks & Good, 2001, p. 8).

The primary implication of essentialist explanations for therapy is that they invite a universal and totalizing description of the client's problem(s). What follows is often a blaming interaction in which partners are pitted against one another's "truth-based" assumptions about desirable human behavior. For example, suppose a family therapist is working with a couple struggling to find mutually satisfying ways of communicating with each another. The wife complains that her husband is withdrawn and won't "open up," while the husband complains that his wife has unrealistic expectations of him and constantly nags him to talk about "touchy-feely stuff." From an essentialist framework, the family therapist would likely urge the couple to develop greater appreciation and acceptance of each other's inherent differences and learn to create respectful communication (Brooks & Good, 2001). We see this focus on "acceptance" as potentially very limiting, inasmuch as it emphasizes simplistic, totalizing notions of male and female nature. Such totalizing limits the change options available to both the couple and the therapist. Many family therapists remain captured by essentialist accounts of men's and women's behavior, and thus it is not surprising that the above intervention appears quite familiar and common.

In response to the limitations of essentialist approaches, many theorists have shifted their focus away from biology and instead have emphasized the influence of the social context in explaining men's experiences. In particular, *social role theory*, or *gender role theory*, has garnered much attention and is the predominant account of masculinity within the literature (e.g., Archer & Lloyd, 2002; Brooks & Good, 2001; Eagly & Wood, 1999; Messner, 1998; Pleck, 1995). Within this framework, theorists have observed that traditional gender roles hinder men in asserting their emotions and vulnerabilities. Generally, men are expected to take on assertive, independent, dominant, and other instrumental and agentic roles, whereas women are expected to take up expressive and communal roles and to be relationship oriented, selfless, emotional, and submissive (Alexander & Fisher, 2003; Cejka & Eagly, 1999).

While role theory offers certain insights into men's experiences, it fails to encompass the dynamic, complex aspects of masculinity. In particular, role theory, and the closely related script theory (e.g., Mahalik, Good, & Englar-Carlson, 2003; Mosher, 1991) and socialization theory (e.g., Rabinowitz & Cochran, 2002; Rowan, 1997) largely ignore men's subjectivity and instead highlight static, formal, and prescribed aspects within men's and women's behavior (Burr, 1995; Davies & Harré, 1990). That is, the concept of role thinks of people "as occupying pre-ordained societal 'slots' that come with a pre-written script or set of expected behaviors, which people somehow 'slip on,' like an overcoat, over their real selves" (Burr, 1995, p. 140). Through this emphasis on a self-contained and presocial individual, role theory is not particularly responsive to the nuanced contextual, relational circumstances that people find themselves in.

While the role perspective identifies salient cultural practices, it does not respond to the ways that men resist these practices. From this perspective, therapists can easily ignore the enormous variation in men's attitudes and behaviors and unwittingly reinforce notions of men as passive participants in their lives. Popular gender aware (Good, Gilbert, & Scher, 1990), gender sensitive (Philpot, 2001), and gender fair (Nutt, 1991) therapies all reflect the role framework in their attempts to engage men more fully in the context of family therapy. Carol Philpot (2001), describing gender sensitive family therapy, recommends that the therapist act as a "gender broker" who explains the "male code" to female family members and the "female code" to male family members (p. 628). Philpot cites the case of a couple in conflict over the sharing of child care and domestic responsibilities to illustrate this approach:

> In this common situation, the therapist can help the wife understand that the husband is doing exactly what he believes is expected of him—providing for his family through hard work and dedication to the good provider role. When she understands that his intent is good, she can then approach him from a more compassionate stance. She can correct any misconceptions he may have about her expectations of him and clarify exactly what she wants most. If she chooses, she can ask him to show his love and support in a different way. By reframing the husband's behavior in a positive way, the therapist opens the door for negotiation and change. (p. 629)

While this approach is potentially useful, we think it reflects the limitations associated with the role perspective in that it does not fully appreciate the cultural constraints placed on men, nor does it adequately engage men to challenge and resist those constraints. Rather, in privileging universalizing and static "codes" of behavior, this approach appears one dimensional and does not capture the nuanced complexity within men's subjectivity.

Like other identities we have discussed in this book, masculinity is of course embedded in competing discourses. For example, a "real man" is conceptualized as "strong, omnicompetent and rational-logical in [his] expression" (Dienhart, 2001, p. 22). With a focus on self-reliance, control, and invulnerability, dominant discourses invite men to put on a tough guise, or a masculine shield, which can constrain emotional expressions and relational intimacy. Most of us are familiar with the following discourses that commonly circulate and capture many boys and men:

- "Boys don't cry."
- "Crying is for sissies."
- "Keep a stiff upper lip."
- "Keep your cool."
- "Be tough."
- "A man doesn't show weakness or emotion."
- "A man doesn't need others for emotional support."
- "A man should be preoccupied with work, achievement, and success."
- "It's a man's duty to take care of his family financially."
- "A man's sexual desire is natural and compelling."

These discourses reflect what is often considered "common sense" about how men should behave, and because they are "left largely unchallenged and unexamined, they take on an unchangeable and natural nature" (Larsson, 1997, p. 7). Moreover, these discourses exert a powerful influence on the day-to-day interactions of men and women in intimate relationships. In fact, it is the familiar and taken-for-granted nature of dominant discourses that often constrains men's choices. That is, "their influence can most easily remain hidden and difficult to identify and, therefore, to resist" (Gavey & McPhillips, 1999, p. 352).

Given the insidious and seductive nature of dominant discourse, it makes sense that men are invited into discourses of emotional containment. Furthermore, men's reluctance to enter therapy and men's perceived "resistance" in therapy makes sense within the context of the above discourses. In particular, the discourse of the strong and self-contained rugged individual (which is celebrated over and over again through images of heroes on television and in the movies) is predominant in North America, Britain, and Europe. This discourse presents a significant obstacle to men considering entering therapy. It is important to note, however, that people are capable of exercising choice in relation to discourses. In other words, individuals are not enveloped by discourses in passive ways. The central metaphor used to describe the fluid and dynamic relationship between people and discourse is positioning (Davies & Harré, 1990).

This understanding of our participation in the creation of new discursive possibilities allows us to consider how invitations into traditional masculine identities and emotional containment for men can be challenged or adapted. Because there are multiple and competing discourses circulating at any given time, there are also discourses that offer the potential to separate from the tough guise. Indeed, there are discourses that do not typically bear such a dominant and oppressive influence in people's interactions generally and in men's subjectivity specifically. These *alternative* discourses challenge the more dominant discourses and are often representative of marginalized cultural ideas circulating within a context or community, such as those of gay, rural, or lower class men (Courtenay, 2000). Examples of alternative discourses around masculinity include the following:

- "Men express vulnerability and emotions."
- "Men are concerned about the relational needs of partnership."
- "Men value interdependency in relationships in the home and in the workplace."
- "Men are not controlled by their sexual desire."
- "Men sustain responsible and loving relationships with children."

Ryan Jackson's story illustrates, in a compelling fashion, the contradictions and complexities of dominant and alternative discourse in the shaping of his life as a man and what that means to him in a marriage.

By traditional American standards, the man is considered the "head" of the house. It is expected that the man in traditional male-female relationships will not only be the provider or breadwinner but also handle all major life decisions, specifically those decisions surrounding money. During the process of two becoming one, traditionally the woman leaves her family and symbolically mirrors that leaving by taking the man's last name, thus becoming one in whatever the man's last name happens to be. I have even heard of girls, longing for some relationship, practicing their new name by writing it and even verbalizing it aloud. It is often said that young girls dream about their wedding day—what their dress will look like, where the ceremony will take place, how their father will walk them down the aisle to the expectant groom, the huge celebration to follow the beautiful ceremony with all their friends and family in attendance, and finally the announcement of the new couple: "I now present to you Mr. and Mrs. Fill-in-the-blank."

In the case of my own wedding, much of this "dream" was in fact a reality, right up to the point where my wife and I were announced to all those in attendance. To the average reader, this may not seem to be a big deal, but believe me, in our case this was perhaps the most discussed part of our wedding ceremony. We chose not to be announced as Mr. and Mrs. Ryan Jackson, because Jackson is and was my wife's last name, and we feared a long and awkward silence or even a collective groan following an otherwise fantastic ceremony. For a number of reasons we made the decision that I would be the one to change my last name instead of my wife. In the United States in the year 2005, the woman's taking the man's last name is more than an expectation; it's almost a fact (in the event that there is a name change taking place). If discourse truly is ". . . a set of meanings, metaphors, representations, images, stories, statements and so on that in some way together produce a particular version of events" (Burr, 1995, p. 48), then I definitely both subscribe to and also struggle against the dominant discourse that says men should be the head of the household and women should be accountable to their husbands. In some instances, I find myself buying into it and wanting to be just as the discourse says I should, but in the very next instance, I recognize I/we are not living that way. Men are expected to be the head of the house and women are expected to be submissive in the marriage relationship in almost all aspects. Generally, roles that are in disagreement with these expectations are both questioned and scrutinized. This discourse is so powerful and prevalent in our culture that I sometimes find myself questioning my own manhood. My very identity as a man sometimes feels threatened by the fact that I have chosen to take my wife's name, and that currently I am able to not work and concentrate solely on school because my wife is the breadwinner. Even as I sit here and type these very words, I feel a sense of weakness and frailty. I feel as if I'm not doing my job as a man and husband.

Challenging this discourse personally inevitably leads others to the mocking question, "Who wears the pants in your family?" I will reiterate that it has been somewhat difficult to not feel that I am somehow failing in my duties as a man. Right now, my wife works, I go to school. My wife handles and organizes our finances and many of our financial decisions. When I was working, I turned over all of my paychecks to her. In actuality, we had direct deposit into our joint back account. On one occasion as I was filling out some survey, I had to ask my wife what my monthly income was because I actually didn't know, since she is the one who takes care of our finances. I have been somewhat ridiculed by my male friends a number of times for the roles that my wife and I take on in our relationship. Honestly, there are often times when that ridicule leads me to believe that I really am "less of a man." I, too, buy into the belief that the man is to lead the marriage, be the primary provider, and perform as the so-called head of the body.

This account of Ryan's relationship and his willingness to take his wife's last name is illustrative of significant resistance to the positioning of men in dominant gender discourse. Such resistance can be found taking place in surprisingly many places if we are prepared to look for it and seek it out. We believe that counselors should be very much on the lookout for opportunities to celebrate such possibilities.

Body Image, Physical Attractiveness, and Physical Well-Being

In a discussion of the impact of gender discourse on people's life experiences and on their presenting concerns in counseling, we would be remiss not to address the issues associated with the body, physical attractiveness, and physical well-being. There is abundant research examining the negative experiences women encounter that relate to their physical bodies. There is a much smaller base of research addressing men's concerns with body image and physical attractiveness.

Body Shame in Women

For women, the counseling and psychology literature has the most to say about dieting, eating disorders, body image, body satisfaction, and body esteem. Many findings indicate that a large proportion of women are dissatisfied with their bodies and are constantly monitoring their weight and dieting. Most perceive themselves as overweight, regardless of the accuracy of this assessment (e.g., Rodin, Silberstein, & Striegel-Moore, 1985; Wooley & Wooley, 1984). For example, in a 1993 national survey, 48% of American women reported experiencing dissatisfaction with their overall appearance as well as a fear of being or becoming overweight (Cash & Henry, 1995). In addition, a recent meta-analysis of 222 body image studies from the past 50 years revealed continual increases in women's body dissatisfaction (Feingold & Mazzella, 1998). Furthermore, females are becoming more concerned about their weight at younger ages (Cavanaugh & Lemberg, 1999). Survey estimates of restrained eating range as high as 45% in third-grade children and as high as 80% among fourth- and fifth-graders (Mellin, Irwin, & Scully, 1992). Finally, studies have demonstrated that females constitute 90% of the eating-disordered population (Striegel-Moore, Silberstein, & Rodin, 1986).

Given the "normative discontent" (Rodin et al., 1985, p. 267), or the widespread nature of women's dissatisfaction with their body and appearance, it is not surprising that a body of literature has been assembled that targets a number of sociocultural factors for their potentially harmful effects on women's status and on their physical and emotional health (Bordo, 1993; Foucault, 1980; Gremillion, 2003; Heinberg, 1996; Maisel, Epston, & Borden, 2004; Thompson, Heinberg, Altabe, & Tantleff-Dunn, 1999). For example, women's bodies are inscribed with expectations for attractiveness, including certain clothing and hair styles, and at this time the most prominent standard for attractiveness for women is thinness (Rodin et al., 1985). The increasingly thin representation of the feminine body has frequently been referred to as the cultural ideal of thinness or the "tyranny of slenderness" (Chernin, 1981). This representation, or more accurately normative expectation, remains the most frequently implicated sociocultural factor contributing to women's negative body experiences.

Sociocultural constructions of the female body and expectations of physical and sexual appeal lead to myriad negative experiences for women, including constant monitoring of one's appearance, body shame, negative body esteem, restricted eating, and eating problems (McKinley, 1998, 1999; McKinley & Hyde, 1996). Mariette Brouwers (1990) has made a link between negative emotional responses arising from body shame and the eating disorders of anorexia nervosa and bulimia.

Therefore, a woman's preoccupation with appearance appears "natural," masking the extent to which external pressures influence women's daily practices, such as makeup application, dieting, and exercise. Because cultural standards for the feminine body are virtually impossible to attain, women often feel shame about their bodies when they internalize these standards (Bartky, 1988; McKinley, 2000). Negative experiences associated with body shame are widespread and have greater consequences for women and their psychological well-being than they do for men (Hesse-Biber, Clayton-Matthews, & Downey, 1987; Mintz & Betz, 1986; Silberstein, Striegel-Moore, Timko, & Rodin, 1988). Ellie gives a personal account of this experience.

I internalized the message that a woman's value is proportional to her looks at a very young age, as many girls nowadays probably do, especially those who grow up in places like Southern California. Once, when I was about 13, boarding a chairlift in Vail with my mother, one of the two male attendants gazed at me in a way that made my skin crawl and then commented loudly to the other, "That's a nice shirt. If it was bigger, I'd wear it." I was disgusted and ashamed, as was my horrified mother, but somehow felt that it was my fault. I had attracted his attention, so there must be something wrong with me. Things like that just don't happen to nice girls. In a sick way, I was secretly glad that at some level, I must be desirable. It was horrible to hear comments like that, but in my mind, it would have been infinitely worse to be ugly, or fat. What would people say then? If I continued to be pleasing, I would be safe from criticism that could be devastating to my fragile self-image. The way I looked on the outside became my most salient survival tool, because I was terrified of not being good enough.

I was 18, a freshman in college, the first time I threw up my food. I had gone to dinner with one of the guys I'd met. He and most of his teammates at school were from the Midwest. I went to the bathroom at one point, and when I returned to the table I approached him from behind. He was on his cell phone, several drinks deep and talking too loudly, telling his buddy on the other end, "You're going to owe me that eighty bucks because I'm totally going to fuck her tonight." Too angry and humiliated to call him out, I waited several seconds, then sat down as if nothing was wrong. I was too uncomfortable to address what he had said, and I pretended at the end of the meal that I felt sick. He drunkenly drove me home to my dorm, where I sat and cried.

I had been at school for only a month and I had never gotten too drunk at a party, danced on a table, taken my clothes off, or done anything that would have somehow justified his (and his teammate's) evaluation of what I apparently was. I cried for a while, then walked to the bathroom and stuck my fingers down my throat. Everything came up so easily and it was like a switch flipped inside of me. That was easy. For the next month I ate nothing, just drank coffee all day and had small salads at night when I ate with my friends. When I got too hungry and ate something "unacceptable" or felt too full, I would throw up. I'd had a perfect body before this, although I didn't think so at the time, but my weight began to fluctuate wildly. I wouldn't eat for months. Then I would get so hungry I would eat everything and throw up. I felt awful all the time. My period stopped and I became extremely depressed. I cut myself with razors and had intrusive thoughts of suicide literally every few moments for several months.

I found out that acquaintances of mine at school, my sorority sisters actually, many of whom did cocaine and got blackout drunk every weekend and many weeknights, all talked about how they thought I was a drug addict. Eventually, I dropped out of the house. I had never felt so completely alone. I could not understand what was wrong with me, why this was happening to me, why I was inherently so horrible and couldn't have a normal functional life like the proverbial "everyone else." My boyfriend became exhausted with me and our relationship deteriorated. I was hurt and newly ashamed of myself and wondered what he must be telling his fraternity friends, who had all probably heard the rumors about me from my sorority "friends." I have never felt so utterly alone.

Somehow I managed to make it through school and overcome the eating problem. It is still a major part of my life, something that will never be completely eradicated, but it is no longer what controls me. I can't say for sure why this happened to me, since there are women who are raped or molested or have encounters far more devastating than my own.

The constant pressure our culture and media bombard women with about how their inherent worth is derived from physical beauty doesn't help. I couldn't help internalizing this and doing the very thing I shouldn't: place all importance on appearance. So how can I blame all the men that hurt me by treating me like an object for doing the same thing? I am working on myself, trying to realize who the person inside is, what she wants and likes. It is still well-nigh impossible for me to approach relationships with the mentality that I have a lot to offer and should do so. I am still terrified of failure of any kind, and I am still learning to accept the simple lesson that mistakes are all right. I hope someday that I will finally be able to do all these things and be happy in my own skin, as a woman.

A few researchers have compared Asian and Hispanic women with white and African American women on measures of body image, body satisfaction, and disordered eating (Akan & Grilo, 1995; Ahmad, Waller, & Verduyn, 1994; Altabe, 1998), and one study has compared American Indian women with white and African American women on measures of weight satisfaction (Story, French, Resnick, & Blum, 1995). These findings suggest that body-related concerns are not confined to white females, but that body-related concerns appear less significant among ethnically diverse women *relative to* white women as a whole (Cash & Henry, 1995). The experiences of individual women within each ethnic group, of course, may differ from the normative experience for the group as a whole. What appears to be clearer is that women who identify as lesbians tend to report less concern for physical appearance and less drive to be thin than heterosexual women (Beren, Hayden, Wilfley, & Striegel-Moore, 1997; Bergeron & Senn, 1998; Herzog, Newman, Yeh, & Warshaw, 1992; Strong, Williamson, Netemeyer, & Geer, 2000). One explanation for this is that support within the lesbian community buffers lesbians and helps them keep from internalizing the increasingly thin ideal (Heffernan, 1996). This is another example of how alternative discourse positions can provide resources that enable resistance to the norms specified by dominant discourse.

Issues pertaining to body dissatisfaction have led to an enormous increase in plastic surgeries for women. According to Gloria Steinem (1992), 87% of people undergoing plastic surgery are women. In growing numbers, women undergo rhinoplasty to obtain a nose that is small and narrow, liposuction to reduce the size of their thighs and stomach, and breast augmentation. Women of color use bleaching agents to lighten their skin, Some Asian women have surgery on their eyes so they will appear round and Western. As Tracy Robinson (2005) reported, women will suffer from bunions, corns, and all manner of foot problems to conform to restrictive but socially desirable shoe fashions.

Body Shame in Men

Many men are also increasingly affected by negative body images because of societal notions of attractiveness. A sculpted, triangular body with washboard abdominal muscles is portrayed in popular culture as an attractive male body. Lillian Emmons (1992) noted that adolescent boys in particular are very prone to a negative self-assessment of their bodies and often engage in unhealthy dieting. Men, like many women, have resorted to fasting, the use of laxatives, and purging. Males are often less concerned with overall weight and much more consumed with muscle definition and the avoidance of fat and flab (Robinson, 2005). Because men are socialized to believe that manliness is associated with being a protector and provider, being athletic or having superior body strength becomes intimately wrapped up with this identity. Elvynn's story illustrates how this discourse gets internalized.

What is difficult about being a male in today's American society is that men are supposed to be the protectors of their friends and family. This means that men need to appear larger than life to create an intimidating persona that others will respect and back down from without any major confrontation. The problem with becoming bigger, faster, and stronger is that men still need to have the defined body that resembles the classical images of ancient Greece, meaning that men need to have the cut washboard abs, tapered V-shaped body, broad shoulders, and well-defined calves. This double standard of "manliness" is an issue that I continually face every day.

Being of Asian descent, I am already faced with the fact that most Asians are short. Being short is a genetic shortcoming that cannot be overcome no matter how much weight training or dieting I do. This puts me at a disadvantage on the "manliness" scale because, when compared to the European American male, whose average height is 5 inches taller than mine, I cannot appear to be a better protector or a better man. To appear appealing and to be an attractive prospect as a man, I would need to compensate for the height disadvantage by focusing on what I can control: my weight and body definition.

I grew up as a slim, fit child who was constantly playing sports. I was never too concerned about my body size or image, but I was constantly hearing the mantra "Bigger, faster, stronger!" To do better and dominate the competition, I felt that I had to be those three words. Not knowing much about muscle resistance weight training, I thought that to be bigger I should just eat more. So that's what I did. Unfortunately, that made me everything that was unattractive and unwanted. While I was not incessantly obese, I was large enough to warrant such comments as "Oh my gosh, you're getting so big," and, "Wow, you need to lose weight!" All that for a kid who was only 13 years old. That was the first time I became overly concerned with my body image, and that insecurity has constantly affected me to this day.

Hearing those comments from family members made me wear bigger clothes and eat next to nothing just to keep them from saying these things. I also started attending a gym, where I did weight resistance to bulk up and convert the fat into muscle. While I was seeing improvements in my body, I never got big enough to feel confident or "cut" enough to show off the washboard abs that are so desirable. Wanting to reach these standards, I started developing a disorder known as exercise bulimia. I would constantly work out at the gym. Before meals and after meals, I would go to the gym, because each meal felt like a detriment to my "diet" of achieving a large yet cut body image. I would not have time for any fun or recreation because the only thought in my head was that I was still fat and needed to bulk up. This mentality actually made problems worse, because it's almost impossible to do both bulking up and cutting fat.

Today I still struggle to feel confident as a man in American society. I don't feel that my body is attractive enough to be perceived as manly, powerful, and respected. I still hear the negative comments of people calling me fat and over-weight and still find myself comparing myself to every other male out there, never feeling confident because they have the look I am still striving for. As I see women comment on and fawn over the triangular, defined body shape, I know that that is what is desired and attractive and that that is what a man should be.

Men with physical disabilities often struggle to a great degree with a negative body image because they are not able to command the same physical strength as able-bodied males. Men sometimes address their negative body image by using and abusing steroids to create a hypermasculine body image (Ham, 1993). Anabolic/androgenic steroid hormones, for example, are used to enhance body size for those seeking to achieve a chiseled body. Steroids are well known to produce adverse effects on the liver, the cardiovascular and reproductive systems, and the psychological health of the steroid user.

Tensions Between Ethnicity and Gender in Cultural Discourse

The underlying premise of the multicultural movement in counseling and therapy is the promotion of social justice and cultural democracy among diverse peoples. But therapists can be criticized for promoting and supporting certain ethnic cultural practices on the grounds that they are aligned with cultural traditions that can be harmful to women. Susan Moller Okin (1999), for example, has raised questions about the ethical implications of some forms of multicultural practice for women. She suggests that the defense of certain cultural practices and traditions has the potential to subjugate the rights and the quality of life for women. In many communities, there is very real discrimination against and at times hatred for females, and their freedom and even their right to live are sometimes seriously compromised. The very worst illustrations of these practices, including the ongoing abuse of women through genital circumcision and genital mutilation, female child trafficking, bride burning, infanticide, and the aborting of female fetuses, still occur in many countries of the world.

In North America, there may in some instances be tension between the promotion of multicultural sensitivity and gender equity. For example, the promotion of gender equity may heighten the possibility of punitive oppressive practices against women. Some cultural traditions urge negative consequences for women who seek outside help. For example, the support by counselors and therapists of women who wish to take a stand against rigid and harmful machismo behavior may not be welcomed in some Latino families. In such instances, therapists who defend traditional ethnic cultural practices ahead of gender equity can produce more negative impacts on women than on men. Susan Moller Okin (1999) suggested that

> because attention to the rights of minority cultural groups must ultimately be aimed at furthering the wellbeing of these groups, there can be no justification for assuming that the group's self-proclaimed leaders (invariably composed of their older male members) represent the interest of all the family members. (p. 24)

Therapists who unquestioningly support particular ethnic traditions without consideration of gender inequalities can become complicit in the ongoing subjugation of women among immigrant cultures. It is also likely that, in some instances, counselors' promotion of women's rights within a counseling relationship may inadvertently subject female clients to more risk. This retribution effect arises in many situations when women are in abusive relationships and are at risk of being killed, physically hurt, or socially and economically isolated. Therapists must not violate the ethical principle of doing no harm and must be careful and wise in helping women and children to be removed from potentially lethal situations. Sometimes counselors have to manage the complex tensions between what is best for the family and what is best for the individual.

Gender Effects on Therapists

According to research conducted by the American Psychological Association's Task Force on Sex Bias and Sex-Role Stereotyping in therapy (Sue & Sue, 2007), the perpetuation of patriarchal practices by therapists and psychologists throughout the helping process continues. While this research was conducted some time ago, Judith Myers Avis (1996) found that the concerns that were brought to light continue to be pertinent and relevant in therapeutic practice. Here are some examples that display gendered assumptions held by therapists about family life: There was evidence that some practitioners had a bias toward assuming that women would benefit from remaining in a marriage. In some instances, there was a bias toward showing more interest in a man's career than a woman's. Often, therapists would hold women more accountable than men for a child's problems and for child rearing. There was also evidence to suggest that men's needs were often deferred to over women's needs. Derald Wing Sue and David Sue (2007) cite research that suggests that therapists interrupt female clients more often than they interrupt male clients. In addition, there is clear evidence to show consistent biases for certain diagnostic categories that reflect dominant discursive ideas about gender attributes. Women are often identified as having exaggerated emotional expressions, including intense fluctuations in mood. Women appear in much larger numbers than men on Axis II of the DSM-IV diagnoses, such as histrionic personality disorder, borderline personality disorder, or dependent personality disorder.

Counseling Implications

When mental health professionals name some of the gendered patterns of identity construction for female and male clients, they are taking the first step toward ensuring that negative patriarchal attitudes do not dominate in the counseling room. Here are some guidelines that male and female therapists can consider when they addressing gender issues in counseling:

1. There needs to be acknowledgment that in many communities the devaluing of women is a common occurrence. For example, Darcy Haag Granello and Patricia Beamish (1998) identified how women can be pathologized for being codependent when their behavior could be reconceptualized as a nurturing and self-sacrificing demeanor toward family members. At the same time, counselors, especially male counselors, need to guard against chauvinist behaviors that suggest that women need to be protected and adored.

2. Therapists need to continue to update their knowledge of the biological, psychological, and sociological factors that uniquely impact men and women. For women, counselors can acquire recent knowledge on issues related to menstruation, pregnancy, birth, infertility, and miscarriage. For men, therapists can become knowledgeable about prostate issues, vasectomies, steroid use and abuse, the negative effects of patriarchal behaviors, and the like.

3. When cultural traditions emphasize strongly patriarchal assumptions, men and women are ascribed distinct roles in the family and in the community. Communities often place considerable investment in maintaining these elaborate gender narratives, and counselors must, therefore, proceed slowly and respectfully with clients who identify with such cultural traditions so as not to alienate them. Rhea Almeida, Rosemary Woods, Theresa Messineo, and Roberto Font (1998) have proposed models that include consultants from the very cultural communities that clients draw from. Clients are invited to participate in culture circles to grapple with relevant gender, class, and race issues.

4. Whenever gender issues arise in counseling, other identity factors are also likely to be in play. It will be important to take into account other environmental issues that need addressing, such as poverty, racism, sexism, ageism, and other sociocultural and socioeconomic factors. For example, women are subject to pressures to be pretty, feminine, and the loving caregiver, while men are pressured to be the protector, the primary income earner, and the head of the household. When it comes to ageism, older women are often viewed more negatively than older men. Counselors need to be aware of the psychological pressures that accrue for clients as a result of these wider cultural practices.

5. Therapists can use a deconstructive approach toward the impact of gender discourse on clients. Here are some examples of questions that therapists can ask their male and female clients that might open up conversations about the cultural aspects of gender experience:

- "Antonio, when you were growing up, what was the significance of work outside the family?" "Where did you get the idea that it was a good idea to work so hard?" "Where do ideas about a man's being financially successful and taking care of the family come from?"
- "Xiomara and Andre, to what extent are these ideas about men being the primary breadwinners currently working for you?" "How helpful have ideas about a man's being better suited for money-making activities been to your relationship?"
- "Christina, how did you expect that Jaime would show and share his grief after his friend died?" "Jaime, what did you expect to happen when you lost someone close to you?" "Where did you get these expectations about expressing your feelings from?" "Jaime, what does it mean for a man in this society to realize that being strong can be stressful and take a toll on interpersonal relationships?" "What would it mean to you if you didn't have to be strong and feel responsible all the time?"
- "Ian, are there any areas of your life where expressing emotion is appropriate?" "Could it be that the constraints on men to be invulnerable and stoic are not as solid as we sometimes think?" "Ian, is it possible that you don't have to be so subject to culture's demands?"

Through deconstruction, an astute therapist can support the discovery of alternative discourses, which allow for both personal transformation and also reconstruction of new understandings of how to be in the world.

TO DISCUSS

1. Make lists of what standard gender discourse specifies for women and men.

2. Choose one of the stories in this chapter and compare your own experience with that of the student's.

3. Construct a simple questionnaire exploring the effects of gender discourse in couple or family relationships. Answer this questionnaire among the class. Discuss the results.

4. What has the impact of feminism on your own family been?

5. What has the impact of feminism on your career choices been?

6. Collect and share stories of people who defy normal gender specifications in some area of life.

7. Collect a selection of magazines aimed at women and aimed at men. Deconstruct the images presented and speculate on the effects on men and women.

8. Share stories of the impact of gendered norms for body image on your own experience.

9. Watch a counseling videotape and focus specifically on the gender aspects portrayed. How would the counselor responses be different if the client were of a different gender or if the counselor were of a different gender?

Response to Chapter 9

Brent A. Taylor

Brent A. Taylor, Ph.D., identifies himself as European American, heterosexual, middle class, and able-bodied. He grew up in Wisconsin and attended Brigham Young University for his undergraduate studies in psychology. He received master's degrees from Northwestern University and the University of Southern California in counseling psychology, marriage and family therapy, and sociology. He completed his doctoral studies at USC in sociology with a clinical emphasis on marriage and family therapy. He is an associate professor at San Diego State University in the Department of Counseling and School Psychology and is the program director for the master's degree in marriage and family therapy. His research interests related to this chapter response include fatherhood, Latino men and their families, and men's issues in training. He is married and has three children.

You have been exposed to a plethora of theories in this chapter, and yet I want to introduce you to one more: black feminist thought. If you are reading this book, it is likely that you are in a counselor training program; I would like to tell you briefly about my graduate training. I recall discussing with fellow graduate students who identified as female and as people of color that they felt as if their experiences weren't being adequately expressed in the theories and research they were studying in the program. Interestingly, as a white male, I also felt that there was a void in terms of scholarly understanding regarding my experiences as a man. It felt as though we were all being marginalized, and we were left wondering who was at the center, since everyone perceived themselves to be at the margins. Although I embody all the privileges society has to offer, I felt that none of the theories written by scholars of my own gender or ethnicity accurately described my lived experience. While decades of research and countless volumes of scholarly work have been documented by men, it is the work of women that I felt resonated with my belief system and experiences.

In particular, postmodern feminism and black feminist thought (developed by the sociologist Patricia Hill Collins) had the most powerful impact on my theoretical development. My being trained in a strict psychoanalytic style during my master's program left me feeling isolated and that my own belief system was unacknowledged. There was no room for important parts of me, such as my spirituality. I will never forget the impactful moment that came when I read an article about postmodern feminism in the *Family Therapy Networker* magazine and felt a sense of validation. For the first time in my graduate training, I felt that my experience mattered. The power of postmodernism came to fruition for me when I realized that there was room for my own beliefs in the scholarly world. There has always been room for white men in this world, or at least they have made room for themselves by oppressing or annihilating others. Yet my spiritual beliefs, which are the most powerful force in my life, set me apart from most other white men. My spirituality has led me to feel both attuned and responsible to the oppressed and their experiences. Since I view us all as interconnected, the traumas of colonization and oppression affect me and all white men; the white man becomes the oppressor of himself.

I pursued my doctorate in sociology and the theory that spoke most potently to my experiences and beliefs was black feminist thought. This theory articulates the notion that black women have created knowledge that is not known or respected. In her book *Black Feminist Thought: Knowledge, Consciousness, and the Politics of Empowerment*, Patricia Hill Collins (1990) develops an Afrocentric feminist epistemology that puts concrete experience at the core, along with an ethic of caring, an ethic of personal accountability, and the use of dialogue in assessing knowledge claims. The book has three central tenets: (1) the oppressions in society according to race, class, gender, sexuality, and nation are inextricably interconnected; (2) external definitions of what it means to be a black woman through controlling images created by dominant society have been constricting and restricting to black women; and (3) this has created the need for black women to create self-definitions that reflect their worldviews and to work on behalf of social justice. At the outset, it may seem quite odd that this speaks to me so powerfully, since I am an able-bodied European American male raised in an upper middle class Mormon family in the Midwest. How is it that a theory that views race, class, and gender as interlocking systems of oppression makes so much sense to me, since I am a product of interlocking systems of privilege? In short, the paradigm of postmodern feminism provides room for such possibilities.

My work often revolves around people of color, both in training and as my clientele. I frequently work with the Latino community and have found that while immigrant Latino males often experience much privilege in their country of origin due to machismo, when they immigrate to the United States, they experience multiple oppressions. My extensive research on Latino fathers suggests that the concepts of black feminist thought fit well with the experiences of Latino immigrant fathers, since they are often up against negative dominant discourses that do not reflect their self-definitions or worldviews. By working with Latino fathers through the lens of postmodernism, I find that empowerment can be a powerful antidote to the disenfranchised experiences of these men.

Traditional feminist approaches have cast men as culprits and left little hope for change unless men completely transform themselves. Under radical feminist thought, it can feel as though being a man is the "original sin" and that this identity must be shed before effective relationships can emerge. This stridency damages hope and can leave clients stuck in patterns of anger and resentment. Alternatively, I find postmodern approaches more useful in that they create the necessary space for all to be understood and in that they normalize instead of pathologize client lives.

Gender does not act alone; it is part of a matrix of our social identity and constantly interacts with our race, ethnicity, spirituality, ability, and class. Gender in context is a powerful impetus to how we think and act. Conversations in therapy will create new avenues of change as we incorporate postmodern ideas into the therapeutic work. For example, toward the conclusion of the chapter, discursive questions are given that can help open up new possibilities and aid clients in shedding their cultural constraints and creating new ways of relating.

In conclusion, postmodern feminism opens the doors for endless explorations about how gender colors our world. I am grateful to postmodern feminist theorists who have created a space for my experiences as a white, heterosexual, well-educated, able-bodied, Mormon man to be heard and understood. A space where black feminist thought articulates my views on the world better than someone of my same identity does. Perhaps no one needs to be at the center, but we should all have a shared space where men and women of various social locations can care for each other and live and learn together.

CHAPTER 10

The Globalization of Identity

The era of globalization has arrived, and with it come new directions in cultural politics (Eko, 2003). It is now impossible to talk about how identities are formed in the modern world without taking account of the ways in which globalization slices through the middle of traditional cultural identifications. Like it or not, globalization produces common habits, shared cultural norms, and common knowledge systems across diverse cultural populations. These emerging global cultural trends are promulgated by transnational media, mass travel and migration, and technological change. In order to better understand the intimate and personal issues going on in our clients' lives and to be better equipped as counselors, therapists, and psychologists to address clients' concerns, it is helpful to grapple with the wider sociocultural dynamics that are currently taking place around the globe.

The Pros and Cons of Globalization

Globalization is a controversial phenomenon. For many, globalization is a contemporary process identified with the accumulation of power in the hands of a limited number of powerful corporations that are now larger than many national economies. In their hands, the globalization of cultural influences can be understood as a subtle new vehicle for political, economic, and cultural domination, a colonizing movement of the 21st century that recapitulates the colonization of previous centuries. There is plenty of evidence of the link between globalization and cultural hegemony. The new global culture certainly seems to privilege Western consumerism, the spread of uncontrolled capitalism and the free market, and deregulated commercialism and to most benefit those in the most privileged positions in American and European societies.

Nobel Prize–winning economist Joseph Stiglitz (2003) has shown how policies instituted by the International Monetary Fund (IMF) have served the agendas of the richer industrialized countries at the expense of the developing countries of the world to the extent that globalization (especially the globalization of economic markets) has acquired a bad name around the world and become the target of considerable anger. It is often associated with the continuation of neocolonial policies that ensure that America and Europe maintain exploitative economic advantage while developing countries are coerced into implementing stringent economic regimens whose negative impact is borne in the end by the poorest people on earth. Stiglitz nevertheless argues that the problem is not globalization itself as much as unfair and ill-conceived economic policies that need to be and can be corrected.

Koichiro Matsuura, director general of the United Nations Educational, Scientific and Cultural Organization (UNESCO) in the late 1990s, warned that globalization is dangerous because it floods the third world with cultural artifacts from industrialized countries, leading to homogenization and subsequent "global impoverishment" (Caramel & Laronche, 2000). Historian Arnold Toynbee (1987) argued that the world goes through a series of evolutionary stages and predicted that the one we are currently in would be shaped by the rapid speed in which knowledge is disseminated throughout all human societies. Michael Peters and Tina Besley (2006) argue that the "global interconnected space of communication" (p. 1) is producing new forms of knowledge and new knowledge cultures in which knowledge is exchanged with increasing rapidity. One product of this process is that human societies are tending to become less and less differentiated from one another. When people in many places form identities around the same musical genres, television shows, and hit movies, there is a strong theme of cultural homogenization at work.

On the other hand, while the West appears to dominate the cultural flow across borders and across space and time, globalizing social processes are not rigid, one-way flows of cultural production. There are numerous examples of reverse flows. For example, film festivals celebrate movies from increasingly diverse local cultural traditions. Musical cultures from Brazil, the Caribbean, and sub-Saharan Africa find audiences in the mainstream of global popular culture. Japanese style management systems are have been introduced into Western companies. It might be possible to argue now that what is Western and what is Eastern is more fluid than it once was. Cultural products emanating from both the West and the East mingle with each other, resulting in hybrid forms of cultural expression. Some writers describe this process as "glocalization," referring to a complex interaction of globalizing and localizing tendencies (Scott, 1997). Globalization seems to be accompanied by a resurgence in and assertion of indigenous and minority cultural practice of various kinds. As a result, the cultural homogenization that globalization threatens has not been and may not ever be fully actualized because of the multiplicity of new cultural identities that are forming. There is a phenomenon taking place that Joseph Chan and Eric Ma (2002) refer to as transculturation, a creative and exotic mixing where human encounters between established modern societies and developing ones produce reciprocal patterns of relating. In these exchanges, dominant global motifs are constantly impacted by local preferences. This dynamic is shaped by the interchanges between the dualisms of universalism versus particularism and homogenization versus differentiation.

Lisa Tsoi Hoshmand (2005) suggests that impactful social processes occurring right now all over the planet are leading to profound changes in human experience and identity. As a result, cultural knowledges are being subjected to processes of assimilation and hybridity. She suggests that we can no longer straightforwardly categorize particular groups of people when the pace of identity formation and identity choices are greater than ever before in the history of the world.

Horizontal and Vertical Culture

French historian Marc Bloch (1886–1944) once said, "Men are more the sons of their time than of their fathers" (Maalouf, 2000, p. 101). This statement is perhaps more relevant today than it was when Bloch wrote it, as it underscores the point that a citizen today often has greater connection and more shared understandings, values, and meanings with his contemporaries than he does with his own ancestors. This phenomenon is increasingly the case as social change occurs at faster and faster rates. Reflect on the fact that our oldest citizens have to make an effort to recall what their outlook was like in their childhood. In order to understand the self that lived 40 or 50 years ago, we must shed a frame of reference and a lifestyle of habits shaped profoundly by products and tools that a person today cannot do without. Most young people don't have the slightest idea what their grandparents' way of life was like, let alone that of earlier generations. We share some affinities with our contemporaries more than we do with our ancestors. Random passersby on a street in San Diego or Beijing probably have many cultural reference points that are more in common with each other than with their great-grandparents.

Amin Maalouf (2000) suggests that we have two heritages: a vertical one that comes from our ancestors and a horizontal one transmitted by our peers. For example, "I am Mexican American" is a reference to a vertical cultural heritage, whereas "I am into reggae music," "I am a Red Sox fan," and "I am a vegetarian" are more horizontal cultural allegiances. All may be held by the same person. Nevertheless, the cultural inheritance that most people habitually invoke is the vertical one. Subcultural groups like street gangs demand allegiance to horizontal heritages that construct for their adherents the currency in which identity claims are traded. In the age of globalization, vertical cultural groups often attempt to assert their differences more fiercely in order to ensure that their cultural identities stay distinct. Meanwhile, in other respects, as each day goes by, many of our differences are reduced and our likenesses are increased. Joseph Straubhaar and Antonio La Pastina (2003) describe contemporary citizens of Brazil as acquirers of multiple layers of identity that respond to the world media as well as to regional and local media.

Even 50 years ago it was likely that most people lived and went to school and worked and worshiped in a community that contained largely the same overlapping group of people. This is no longer true. Through modern means of communication, we are daily and routinely in touch with multiple communities of people in many parts of the world. Our relationships have, as Kenneth Gergen (1999) observes, "gone electronic" (p. 1). We exercise choices about which groups we do which parts of our lives with. Our points of cultural reference are multiple. This condition of life is more true for those who are more affluent, but it is rapidly becoming true for many of modest economic means as well.

Three Major Global Processes

Within the last century, perhaps more than at any other time, life has brimmed with diversity, complexity, discontinuity, and the transitory, chaotic nature of human expression. This is one reason why it is increasingly difficult for us to sustain elaborate descriptions about the specific counseling needs of discrete cultural groups. More than ever before, human beings are simultaneously engaged in both producing new forms of cultural life and carrying forward cultural traditions from their ancestors. As Lisa Tsoi Hoshmand (2005) suggests, we are both culture bearing and culture creating. Cultural life is profoundly shaped and constrained by contemporary social forces.

In this chapter, we have chosen to survey three major social forces at work in the process of globalization that play a profound role in shaping contemporary cultural identity. These are: migration, the proliferation and influence of mass media, and the growth of technology. Each of these social phenomena can explain the complexity of the cultural challenges that our clients face us with as we learn about the diverse struggles that they encounter in the process of constructing a life. Since this is not a book about globalization, we have necessarily been selective in our choices, but we would argue that these three themes are usually relevant to the psychological challenges that clients present to counselors.

Migration

Migration across the globe is occurring at levels never before witnessed in human history (Dovidio & Esses, 2001). Such movement of people contrasts starkly with how most human beings lived their lives for many thousands of years prior to the last couple of centuries. While over the centuries there have always been enormous human upheavals caused by war, famine, and widespread disease, numerous communities have lived in relative stability for hundreds of generations. Stability is characterized by generations of individuals and families living in the same place, practicing the same religion, eating the same foods, speaking the same dialect, pursuing the same livelihood, and following the same child rearing practices. Cultural practices in many communities around the world have changed very slowly and almost imperceptibly over hundreds of years.

Today, people all over the planet are on the move. In the last few decades, over 150 million people have moved to live outside the country in which they were born. This number is increasing by approximately 4 million each year (United Nations, Population Division, 1999). Today, the largest migration flows are from Latin America and Asia into North America, and from Eastern Europe, the countries of the former Soviet Union, and North Africa into northern and western Europe. The Middle East receives immigrants from Africa and Asia. The United Nations expects that between 2005 and 2050, at least 98 million people will migrate internationally (United Nations, Population Division, 2004). While there are significant numbers of people on the move between countries, there are an even greater number of people relocating their place of residence within their own country's borders. This trend has been occurring for over 200 years since the industrial revolution, but the acceleration of rural to urban migration in the 20th century was unprecedented and is continuing unabated in the 21st century. For example, in 1800, 3% of the world's population lived in towns and cities. By 1900, the number was 14%. From 1900 to 2000, the urban population increased from 14% to 47% within just 100 years. In 2005, more people around the globe live in an urban setting than a rural one. In China, the 1980s and 1990s witnessed the largest single migration in human history when approximately 90 million people migrated from rural areas dominated by peasant economies to the new cities of southern China. The Population Reference Bureau, which provides data to the United Nations, has predicted that 60% of the world's population will live in a city by 2030 (United Nations, Population Division, 1999). Today, the cities in countries in Africa and South America and in India and China are growing at such an unbelievable rate that in most instances they are stretched beyond capacity to accommodate this human avalanche.

Movement around the globe is not just about changing residence, however. People from all parts of the globe are traveling for business and vacations in numbers not dreamed of just 20 years ago. Currently, 1.6 billion people per year engage in air travel. China leads the world in rates of new travelers, with a projected annual increase of 12.5% per year. Poland, Hungary, and the Czech Republic are not far behind (Gilden, 2005). It is evident that the world no longer operates as if cultures and communities are isolated from each other, unchanged by contact with other cultures. This volume of people moving around the planet constantly provides opportunities for people to meet face to face with others who follow different cultural practices and lifestyles. As a result, people are continually examining and in some cases modifying their own lifestyles and cultural ideals as they are attracted to and embrace new ways of thinking and new modes of life. In the words of James Clifford (1986), people in different countries now "influence, dominate, parody, translate, and subvert each other . . . enmeshed in global movements of difference and power" (p. 22).

These dramatic changes in physical location simultaneously produce profound social, psychological, and cultural changes. Today, there is virtually no place on the planet that is insulated from the powerful cultural forces of urbanization. Life in a city demands dramatic shifts in the way family life is conducted. In the United States, many Anglo American families who have lived here for five or six generations have had many years to adjust to the huge social upheavals brought about by international migration and urbanization. However, for more recent immigrants, these upheavals are still having dramatic effects on their family relationships and personal identities. In many of the indigenous and black communities, individuals continue to suffer from the circumstances leading to their imposed physical relocation, either within the United States, in the case of Native Americans, or, in the case of African Americans, from the enslavement forced on their ancestors from the continent of Africa.

Huge numbers of citizens have come to the United States in the last few decades to escape atrocious circumstances in their homeland. Large Ethiopian, Somali, Sudanese, Laotian, Cambodian, and Vietnamese communities, among many others, have formed throughout the United States. Many of these people share horrific stories of arriving in North America as refugees fleeing from civil war, violent dictatorships, poverty, and persecution. On their arrival in the United States, they are subjected to new hardships as they attempt to adjust to the cultural life and structural inequalities prominent in the United States. These communities experience profound ruptures of their traditional ethnic identities as younger family members attempt to acculturate to majority norms in a country dominated by European American middle class cultural ideals.

Changes in Family Organization

In addition to the growing Asian and African communities in the United States, a sizable proportion of the American population consists of immigrants from Mexico, Central and South America, and the Pacific. Because of dramatic changes in physical location, many extended family systems become stretched, if not ruptured and fragmented. Migration and urbanization push the organization of families toward a nuclear model rather than extended family structures. The days when grandparents and uncles and aunties lived in the same house or were close by are being left behind. Marlene Brant Castellano (2002) notes that in Native American communities, two-generation households consisting of parents and children are increasingly becoming the units of family organization in both rural and urban contexts.

In the United States in 1970, 11% of children under the age of 18 were living with a single parent. In 2000, the number was close to 30%. Among those who identify as African American, the number is around 85% (Sue & Sue, 2003). This demographic trend has implications for the standard of living in which children grow up. By 2003, over 20% of children under the age of six in the United States were living in poverty (Payne, 2005). This trend also has implications for the life opportunities of women, who head up most one-parent families.

These changes to family organization create increased demands for counseling services. Because of the powerful social and economic forces operating around the globe, peoples' cultural identities are increasingly being shaped by their access to or exclusion from economic resources. For example, living together in extended families and large groups now often has less to do with ethnic preference for extended family living and much more to do with economic survival.

Social Impacts on Migrating Families

City life is fast paced and demands that recently arrived urban dwellers quickly develop new cultural strategies just in order to survive. Until a few decades ago, extended families were necessary to plow the fields, plant the crops, harvest the mature produce, and deliver it to the local market for sale. They were also depended on for social security. The struggle for material well-being in cities compels people to compete in ways that rural settings do not. As a result, city life places constraints on how large a family can be. In China, state regulations have for decades dictated how many children a family can have. But in many other developed countries, the same restrictions have been achieved without state regulation. In most cities in the world, families have had to become smaller in order to successfully compete for material resources and manage the high material costs of feeding, housing, and educating children. In response, the cultural fabric of kinship systems has necessarily been reconstructed. Many new immigrant mothers and fathers in the United States need to work long hours away from home, leaving their children alone in their homes for long periods. The absence of adults in the family home leaves many children and adolescents to fend for themselves without supervision. These circumstances have a huge influence on family systems and their organization and therefore on the problems that are presented to counselors. Read Mayra's account of the effects of immigration on one family.

I immigrated to the United States from Guatemala with my parents in May 1983. We were the first to come here from both my father's and mother's family. Our immigration was both forced and voluntary. The immigration was forced because my father was trying to escape execution by the Guatemalan government. It was voluntary because my mother decided that she wanted the family to move to the United States.

A new political party had taken over the police force in Guatemala. My father was in the police force and worked as a detective. The new political party wanted to clear the force of corruption, so they fired and executed those whom they believed had corrupted the police force. My father was among those on the list to be executed. Fearing for his life, he fled to the United States in 1981. He left behind his new family: my mother, who was 25, my sister, who was six, and me, three years old at the time.

My father's departure was hard on our family. It was difficult for my mother to take care of two children and work at the same time. My *abuelitos* (grandparents) were able to provide little support to my mother. My mother struggled for a year on her own to keep my sister and me from going hungry. She rarely heard from my father. On a few occasions he mailed her some American dollars that he had slaved for.

When my father first arrived in the United States, he came to California. He lived in a small city in Los Angeles County named Hawaiian Gardens. He lived there for a few months, then moved to a part of Fresno called Madera. There were many job opportunities for unskilled immigrants in Madera. Jobs were abundant in the fruit fields. My father lived on a ranch. The rancher rented out little shacks to newly arrived immigrants. My father lived in one of those shacks with many other immigrant men. In those days, there were a lot of deportations in Fresno. *La Migra* (the immigration authorities) would raid the fruit fields and deport people by the hundreds. My father was deported within a year.

When he returned to Guatemala, he arrived with absolutely no money. There was a lot of tension that came with my father's arrival. The fact that he was back from "the land of opportunity" with absolutely no money was viewed by the family as very bad. My mother knew that our family would live in poverty if we stayed in Guatemala. So one day in May 1983, she took our family's meager savings out of San Martin de Porres. The money would be used to get my mother, my father, and me to California. Both my parents would leave their families behind in search of a better future in the United States. My sister, who was seven years old at the time, would also be left behind. We had so little money that my mother knew that it would be impossible to bring my sister along with us, so she decided to leave her with my grandmother and come back for her as soon as we had saved enough money. Being left behind devastated my sister.

In May 1983, my mother stuffed a duffle bag with a pair of clothes for each of us, and we set off on our journey to the United States with a duffle bag, 100 dollars, and a heart full of hope. Hope that we would find a better life in the land of liberty and justice for all. Our immigration was very difficult because we had to cross both the Mexican and United States borders. I don't remember much about crossing the Mexican border, but I do remember crossing the United States border. I remember running in the dark over a dirt field surrounded by bushes with about 20 other people. My little heart was pounding, yet I didn't know why I was so scared. I was on my father's shoulders holding on tight to his head, hoping that he would not drop me. I asked him where we were going. He responded, "To Disneyland." We attempted to cross the United States border several times. During our last attempt, my mother and I were separated from my father, who was caught by la Migra. My mother and I were left alone with a Mexican coyote (a person who smuggles undocumented people into the United States), no money, and an address scribbled on a piece of paper. My mother was scared, knowing that this man could harm us if he wanted to. We had no power to stop him, because she was a woman and I a child, and because we were immigrants with no rights in Mexico.

Things got worse for my mother and me as the journey to the United States progressed. After we successfully crossed the border, we waited with the coyote at the San Ysidro train station for a train that would take us to Santa Ana. The coyote would deliver us to the address we had and in return receive money for guiding us across the border and delivering us to our final destination. While we were waiting for the train, the coyote went to the restroom. In the restroom he was caught by la Migra and taken back to Mexico.

Once again, my mother and I were left all alone. Neither of us spoke English, and we had no idea where we were going. When the train arrived, my mother decided that we would not turn back. We would move forward and somehow arrive at the address scribbled on the paper. We boarded the train, hoping that we would not be caught by la Migra. My mother is very light skinned and can pass for a white person. I, on the other hand, am dark skinned. In this situation, my brown skin could get us deported, so my mother wrapped me in her arms to cover my brown skin so that we would not be found out.

During the ride, my mother spotted a Latina, so she moved next to her. My mom began talking to her and told her our story. The lady offered to help us as best she could. She said she would ask her boyfriend, who would be waiting for her at the train stop, to take us to the address we had. The lady knew we had no money, so she offered to buy us some food. My mother thanked her and took up her offer, but only to buy food for me. My mother was too embarrassed and didn't want to take advantage of the lady's kindness by accepting food for both of us. I still remember sitting in that train, eating a sandwich made with wheat bread and drinking milk from a small carton. I was a young child who did not understand the pain and suffering my mom was enduring to get me to this "land of opportunity."

When we got off the train, a tall white man, standing next to a brand new shiny car, was awaiting the arrival of that kind Latina. I remember seeing her walk to him, watching them look at a large paper (which I now know was a map), and then seeing her walk toward us with a sad look on her face. She told my mother that her boyfriend did not know where Hawaiian Gardens was. Even though I was just a little girl, I knew that this was not the truth. In my heart I felt that the Latina's boyfriend wanted nothing to do with us. She handed my mom 20 dollars and wished us luck. So there we were again, alone with nowhere to go.

It was getting dark and my mom began to panic. Where would we sleep, where would we go? We were standing by a liquor store, and my mom saw a Latino man coming out of the liquor store. Desperately she approached him and told him our story. She showed him the address we were trying to get to, and luckily he knew exactly where it was. He told my mother that it was too late to take us to our destination, but that we were welcome to stay the night at his house and that his brother would take us in the morning. He told my mom that he was divorced and lived with his three sons. My mom was scared and hesitant to believe the man. What if he tried to rape her or hurt us? She did not have much choice, so she accepted the man's offer. The man took us to his house and luckily was very respectful and kind to us. He stayed in a room with his sons and offered his room to us. He provided us showers and food from his kitchen.

The next morning, the man was gone. His brother came in the morning, as promised, to drive us to Hawaiian Gardens. We arrived at our final destination and were welcomed with open arms. This was the same house my father had come to when he first came to the United States. Two weeks later, my father arrived. I was in the front of the house, buying an ice cream from the driver of an ice cream truck, when a car pulled up and my dad jumped out of it. I remember feeling so happy that my mother and I were no longer alone.

So far, this is a story of the hardships and stresses of migration. Leave aside the question of immigration legality that may arise in some counselors' minds. Counselors should maintain a position of nonjudgmental responsiveness to the personal and cultural experience that Mayra relates. It is not a counselor's job to engage in the enforcement of legality anyway, but to care for the experiences of their clients no matter what their status with authorities. Read this way, Mayra's story draws on our cultural empathy. Her account of migration does not end, however, with the journey to the new country. It continues through a series of ongoing demands and struggles. Let's take a look at more of Mayra's story from the years that followed.

My parents began to work in the grape fields. I was not old enough to be enrolled in school yet, so my parents would take me to the grape fields with them. One of my first childhood memories is of those grape fields. I was walking up and down the dirt-packed aisles, surrounded by green vines packed with red, plump grapes. I strutted behind my parents, helping them pick the grapes from the vines. My little feet were tired and my hands couldn't reach to pick another grape. I remember looking up at my mom and telling her, "Let's go home now. I think we have enough grapes. Why do you want so many grapes?"

My mother looked at me with a warm, sad look. Now I realize how much meaning that look had behind it. It was an apologetic look that screamed out, "I'm sorry for putting you through this, I'm sorry that you have to work as I did when I was a child. I'm sorry for mistaking this for the land of opportunity." My mother told me that the grapes were not for us and that the reason we picked them was to earn some money.

I was eventually enrolled in school, and that was an experience in itself. I remember walking into the classroom and seeing all the little white, blue-eyed, blond children turning to look at me. I was so different from them. Their language was foreign to me, and my Spanish tongue was foreign to them. I hated being in that classroom. The teacher was a white lady, who was not able to communicate with me. In her frustration to figure out what to do with me and at the same time continue to teach her English-speaking students, she would instruct me to go to the back of the classroom, where I would play all day. I remember yearning to engage in all the activities the other children engaged in. I wanted to read and write as they did. I wanted to learn and was tired of sitting in the back playing by myself. I remember that my first words in English were "Can I go to the restroom, please?" Often I would raise my hand and ask the teacher, "Can I go to the restroom, please?" Once she excused me, I would sit on the toilet seat, dangle my little feet, and listen to the class speak. I wondered what they said and wished that I could understand. I remember feeling so safe in that little restroom; the four walls protected me from a teacher who did not seem to care and from children who did not accept me.

Working has kept my parents in poverty, from being engaged with their children, and in poor health. They come home so tired from work that they have no energy left to be present with the family, thus creating dysfunction within the family. One of the biggest things my siblings and I have struggled with is the fact that our parents have not been very involved in our lives. We all grew up with little parental supervision and all got into mischief with our freedom. Work shifts have varied for my parents; sometimes they worked regular hours from 8 a.m. to 5 p.m., but at other times they have worked from 4 p.m. to 1 a.m. and sometimes on weekends, making them unavailable for us. Many people can't choose working hours that will allow them to be with their families; they just take what is available so they can support their families.

Most jobs available to people who, like my parents, are undocumented and don't speak English pay a minimum wage or less. The income of two parents working full time at minimum wage is barely enough to pay for rent or mortgage and food. Sometimes there is only one parent in the home, leaving the family to struggle to make ends meet. In both cases, people live in poverty, and sadly stay in poverty because there is little or no room for advancement in jobs open to people like my parents.

I was the first person in my family and one of the few in Hawaiian Gardens to graduate from high school and receive a degree from a university. In my family, I was expected only to graduate from high school, and then to work to help support the family. My family, the community, and my teachers expected this of me. Many youths in Hawaiian Gardens don't graduate from high school for many reasons, the main ones being gangs, drugs and alcohol, poverty, and family dysfunction. Many come from families where there hasn't been a high level of educational achievement, so parents don't know how to encourage and support their children in school. Many times, education is not a value in the home. Many parents are struggling to make ends meet for their family, so when their children reach working age they are expected to help support the family and not pursue education. Other parents are addicted to drugs or alcohol, and their children struggle to simply survive the pain present in their homes. Many of these homes are very dysfunctional and not the best environment for children to grow up in.

I was kicked out of high school during my freshman year and was not expected to return. At that time I was involved in the gang, doing drugs, and acting out violently in the name of the gang. When I returned to high school, all my teachers and counselors were surprised. I was angry that they expected me to just drop out of high school, angry that at the time when I was expelled they had expected me to never finish my high school education. There are many factors that contribute to a youth's dropping out of high school. Unfortunately, many of those factors are present in low-income neighborhoods.

After I graduated from college, I was able to develop my awareness of all the social injustice around me. I have started to talk to my family about the social injustice present in the community we live in. It amazes me how my desire to help the community has been fostered by my parents and their selflessness in helping the community. My parents are like the social workers of the community. When people first arrive in Hawaiian Gardens from Mexico, or sometimes from Guatemala, they help establish them in the community. They help them find a place to live, and sometimes these immigrants stay with us until my parents find them a place of their own. My dad will teach the men how to work in construction so that they can pick up a job as day laborers. My mom will find jobs for the women in factories. Because my father is one of the older men in Hawaiian Gardens, people look to him for help in getting free of alcohol and drugs. My dad helps out many of the street junkies in the neighborhood. He takes them to rehab homes, or church, and helps them get back on their feet. My mother is like the community counselor for the women. Many of the ladies in the community look to my mom for support when they are having difficulties in their lives. I feel that my parents contribute to the community and try to help the people in it when no one else will. We have a system set up that closes its doors to immigrants. My parents are helping people overcome homelessness, unemployment, drug and alcohol addiction, and poor mental health.

Mayra Lorenzo and her family endured great suffering and danger when they entered the United States.

Migration can take a terrible toll on families fleeing from one oppressive culture to another. In Mayra's story, the cycle of oppression continues to keep migrant communities oppressed. In the United States, many poor migrant families are highly vulnerable and are exposed to the ugliest underbelly of life in North America. Many become addicted to street drugs and alcohol. With family cohesion stretched to the breaking point, there is much teenage pregnancy, school truancy, and family violence. Despite the grim struggles Mayra describes, she reports that the family life of U.S. immigrants, even undocumented workers, is possibly easier than the life these people escaped from. Here there is also a story of courage and resilience and of drawing from cultural narratives to create new cultural formations in a new context.

Changes in Religious Belief

The spiritual and religious practices of some people have undergone rapid changes as a result of migration. In an urban environment, people can choose from the wider selection of religious and spiritual practices and not be limited to the faith of their parents and grandparents. With the focus on material survival and material success that so characterizes city life, many young people are replacing deeply held and long-standing family religious values with secular ones or becoming invested in religious or spiritual expressions very different from those that their parents were brought up with. In August 2005, *Newsweek* and Beliefnet asked 1,004 Americans how they worshipped and what they believed. Twenty-four percent reported that they had different religious beliefs from those of their parents, and 30% had made some changes in their religious orientation in comparison to their parents (Adler, 2005). Monica McGoldrick, Joseph Giordano, and Nydia Garcia-Preto (2005) reported that 50% of Americans are marrying out of their ethnic groups and that 33 million American adults live in households where at least one adult has a different religious identity from that of other family members.

Often younger family members acculturated to the many social requirements of success in the urban school and workplace resent the efforts of their parents and grandparents to maintain the social, religious, and linguistic cultural practices brought with them from their rural communities. On the other hand, grandparents and parents become alarmed by the speed with which their children abandon age-old customs, rituals, and ways of life. Family counselors working with immigrant families will encounter the playing out of these themes in people's lives with great frequency.

Indigenous Renaissance

Nowhere is this pattern more starkly illustrated than with the demands on families to change their dialect or their language as they enter a new urban environment. Indigenous languages and dialects spoken in small rural communities are often quickly lost in the shift to the large urban environment. In their efforts to help younger family members adjust to the changing demands of life in a new and strange city, parents insist that their children quickly acculturate to the dominant patterns of communication and mode of life in their new place of residence. They encourage their children not to speak their native tongue in order to quickly learn to speak as if they belong with the majority group. José Joachín Brunner (1998) suggests that by the year 2100, based on current projections, fewer than 600 of the world's current 6,200 languages will still be spoken. This trend supports the homogenization argument about globalization. Losing one's mother tongue is a powerful force in disrupting traditional cultural identities and producing dramatic shifts in cultural expression.

There are, however, counter trends that support the localization argument. While families encourage children to move away from their indigenous roots to join mainstream cultural communities, a counter movement often occurs in which families attempt to hold on to or become reacquainted with the language and cultural histories of their ancestors. There are numerous cultural communities on the brink of losing their indigenous languages who take action to reclaim their linguistic traditions. For example, where aboriginal community membership becomes more heterogeneous, a vigorous movement arises to conserve and revitalize traditional languages, teachings, and ceremonial practices (Castellano, 2002). Formal associations and informal networks emerge to support traditional cultural themes, deliberately embracing norms of "sharing and caring" and extending spiritual and practical support to those made vulnerable by family breakdown.

While the dominance of Western cultural ideas is far reaching, the world is not merely divided between indigenous recipients of cultural messages from the West and cultural transmitters from the West to the developing world. There are societies in every continent that are holding on to their traditions, cultural practices, and, most important, their language. In New Zealand, the indigenous Maori people have revitalized their cultural traditions sufficiently to profoundly shape the national landscape. Through a dedicated campaign, Maori have reintroduced their language and cultural practices into the institutions of education, law, commerce, and entertainment. While engaging with wider globalizing processes, Maori have negotiated a strong and vibrant presence in the nation. For example, in the last few years they have operated a Maori television channel. There are other examples of such indigenous renaissance. Australian aboriginal art has been successfully traded in the global art markets. The Icelandic culture has strengthened its indigenous language in the face of anglicizing trends. Israeli society has prospered to a large extent following the embracing of Modern Hebrew as a linguistic force that helps keep the country together.

Changing Identities

Amin Maalouf (2000) argues that globalization is owned by only some people. He comments that it is like a huge arena in which there are thousands of jousting matches and complex interactions taking place all at the same time, producing an indescribable and shattering din. The world he suggests has become like "an amphitheatre that anyone is free to enter with his own motto or theme song" (p. 126).

Box 10.1. Migrating indigenous ethnic communities typically face traumatic shifts in their social order and cultural identity upon entering Western style, consumer-driven societies. The Hmong are a good example of people who have had to survive enormous threats to their social fabric and daily family life.

Many Hmong people who arrived in the United States as reluctant immigrants in the 1970s and 1980s explicitly did not want to immerse themselves in the culture and values of middle class America with its nuclear family patterns. Even so, they have gone through profound changes in their family organization and social structure as a result of living in American cities. The Hmong have been historically regarded by many researchers and scholars as one of the most robust and ethnically cohesive social groups in the world. They have deflected many powerful acculturating forces from within Asia over the centuries and within Southeast Asia specifically more recently. Now they often find their youth suffering from serious identity crises. Like many American adolescents, some Hmong youths rebel against their parents and elders and reject the cultural practices so carefully protected by their forebears. Instead, they embrace cultural ideals modeled by their adolescent peers (Yang, 1991).

In circumstances of rapid urban migration, elderly members of the family, who were looked to for guidance in addressing life problems in rural settings, find themselves isolated and redundant because they are not able to provide guidance to younger family members and assist them in dealing with the trials and tribulations of city life. As a result, it is often the young people who become resources for their families as they acquire the necessary dialects and languages spoken in the cities, in the schools, and in the workplace. Older family members come to rely on younger family members to help them adjust to the changes required to survive in the cities. Customary social roles are thus reversed. Children are cast in the role of primary educators or translators for their families in negotiating with the education system and understanding the economic, health care, legal, and political systems. Conflict can result between the older and younger generations.

Anne Fadiman (1998), in *The Spirit Catches You and You Fall Down*, writes about the collision of Hmong culture with middle class American culture. She describes the phenomenon of role loss that many older migrating family members experience when settling in North America. She describes observing an exercise led by psychologist Evelyn Lee, who asked a group of people at a Southeast Asian mental health conference to role-play a family and line up according to status within Asian culture. She cast each of the individuals in a family, including a grandfather, a father, a mother, an 18-year-old son, and a 12-year-old daughter. They ranked themselves by traditional notions of age and gender, with the grandfather placing himself at the head of the family and the 12-year-old daughter at the bottom of the hierarchy. Lee now told the role players that they had moved to America, where the grandfather has no job, the father is employed performing menial kitchen duties, the son has dropped out of high school because he can't learn English, the mother

and older daughter work in a factory, and the youngest child has successfully gained entrance to and graduated from the University of California,
Berkeley. In the new lineup, there is a reshuffle in the hierarchy such that
it is completely altered. The youngest daughter now earns the most status in the community. This change for the male heads of the household
from positions of power and influence to positions of low influence produces "role loss" and all the symptoms of anxiety and depression that
accompany this state.

The Mass Media

Perhaps the most powerful cultural force shaping cultural identity today is the
mass media. Its influence is much less abrupt and dramatic than migration but nevertheless drives deep into the psyche of the consumer. North American and
European popular culture, including music, texts, magazines, movies, television, and
the Internet, all convey Western political, social, religious, and moral content that
provides interpretive commentary about all aspects of human life and produces in
us guiding strategies for how to live. Contemporary media images dictate what food
should be consumed, what clothing should be worn, how families should be organized, which relationship values should be privileged, and what moral values should
be performed. By far the preponderance of mass media content comes from the
wealthy developed world and is exported worldwide. By contrast, people living in the
United States are exposed to very little of the mass media content produced elsewhere in the world. The impact of the transmission of this cultural content around
the globe can easily be characterized as a modern-day form of European and
American colonization. It is surely a powerful expression of cultural dominance.

Consumerism and Culture

There is a growing consensus among sociologists and researchers that cultural
perspectives conveyed by the mass media supplant among young people many cultural practices previously primarily modeled by families of origin. The increasing
availability of mass media outlets threatens the authority of traditional sources of
influence, such as the family, school, community, and religion. As a result, many
young people brought up in communal and collective cultures are being attracted
to individual values rather than collective or societal values. Lyombe Eko (2003)
describes how multinational mass media conglomerates like Disney plunder
African cultural motifs, music, landscape, and culture, then de-Africanize them,
reduce them to clichés and stereotypes, and repackage them for mass audiences.
Robbin Crabtree and Sheena Malhotra (2003) analyzed television programming in
India and highlighted an increasing trend toward the promotion of middle class
values, where money is equated with power, authority, and economic advancement.
Indian television programmers are now emulating Western television shows by
staging soap operas in lavish settings where the main characters are wealthy and the

poor are peripheral. Earlier Indian soaps showed the protagonist as the common person whose goodness was derived from virtue. Indian television portrays prominent characters as breaking away from traditional cultural practices and using Western consumerism as a conduit to do so. Subir Sengupta (1996) compared Indian advertisements with American ones and found that while the United States still had more materialistic values, Indian public media were clearly moving in the American direction. Crabtree and Malhotra (2003) give a powerful example of how advertising and consumerism, so intimately interwoven with globalizing trends, are changing family dynamics and cultural values in India:

> What is a kid in a village going to do? Let's take a bar of chocolate. It costs 10 rupees. He is never going to be able to buy a bar of chocolate his whole life. But the commercial is telling him that if his parents love him, they'll buy him that bar of chocolate. (p. 222)

The advertising industry's ability to conflate consumption with love and desire is what consumer culture is built on. These powerful commercial forces have huge shaping influences on identity and family relationships. There is every reason for young people who are not able to attain the monetary goals and wealth promised by the commercial media to be dissatisfied with cultural traditions that have eschewed individualistic agendas. Consumerism is a powerful disruptive force in societies that construct cultural identities on discourses of collectivism and communality.

Corporate Culture

One of the globalizing forces that has brought serious disruption and sometimes devastation to collective and communal societies is the expansion of international multinational corporations, usually based in Europe or the United States, into many other countries around the world. While sometimes their contributions to their host countries have been helpful through the provision of investment capital and the introduction of goods and services to communities desperately in need, they have also imported corporate culture based on materialistic values, fast-paced competition, and the promise of happiness to be delivered by the quick acquisition of products. American life has been inundated with corporate culture for decades.

In the United States, corporations compete with elected politicians to govern people's lives, and it can be argued that they have achieved the upper hand over the democratic electoral system. Although they often claim to be politically neutral, they also clearly promote particular middle class norms and practices. Their influence is spreading rapidly as other nations all over the world join the corporate way of life. In Moscow in 2006, we saw an enormous billboard displayed over Red Square, advertising an icon of corporate culture: the Rolex watch. Corporate culture sanctions greed by expecting people to devote most of their time and energy to getting richer. Wal-Mart entices thousands of young Chinese to work long hours in its factories six or seven days a week for 3 dollars a day in the hope that they can join in the benefits of the corporate economy.

The expansionist behavior of corporations and the adoption of Western consumerism all around the world are widely admired by those seduced by corporate culture. It compels the wealthy to keep acquiring wealth, even though this behavior could be viewed as compulsive and unhealthy. Ultimately, the corporate promise is usually unsatisfying. When people view themselves through the lens of corporate culture, they become defined culturally through their roles as workers and consumers. The corporate discourse provides them with a personal model of a successful life. It demands that corporate objectives and needs be given the central place of honor in employees' lives. The culture wants all of them. Employees often face demands to work longer hours and struggle to cater to the socioemotional needs of their family. Arlie Russell Hochschild (1997, cited by Kasser & Kanner, 2004) did research on a Fortune 500 company and investigated how parents were able to cater to their children's needs when they were sick.

> In one case, the son of a single mother needed surgery, but because she had already used up her sick days and her vacation days, she chose to wait six months to schedule the surgery so she could arrange a day off. In response to her delay, her son's doctor threatened to press charges of child abuse. On another occasion, a supervisor threatened to fire a mother who left work to care for a daughter with a dangerously high fever. (Kasser & Kanner, 2004, pp. 169–170)

Such claims on people's lives need to be understood as penetrating not just into work ethics but into the shape of family life. We can see the modern technologies of power (described in Chapter 8) at work through the operation of corporate culture. Corporate culture creates powerful norms that have a structuring effect on the lives of people, who are described as economic units and are required to internalize these descriptions into their cultural perspective on their own lives. The merit of peoples' lives in corporations is measured by their contribution to a level of production and economic output. Materialistic cultural norms invite people to trivialize any areas of their lives that do not relate to economic substance. As a result of this normalizing judgment, consumer identities are developed and assigned that have intimate effects on all areas of peoples' lives.

On these grounds, we would argue that we cannot talk about the cultural dimension of life or construct a multicultural perspective in counseling without considering the impact of corporations on people's lives. Corporate culture is a horizontal force that impacts the vertical aspects of cultural identity formation. Its demands are insistent and its control is pervasive. But no one is in control of it. The heads of large corporations may have more decision making power, but they are just as caught up in the discourse rolling out around them as the consumers at the end of the chain are. And there are examples everywhere of resistance to the power of corporate culture. For instance, local communities in many parts of the United States have joined together to prevent the entry of Wal-Mart into their local cultural context.

Identities Produced in Hollywood

Hollywood movie and television production companies play a significant role in producing contemporary cultural identities. Despite many efforts to develop exceptions, mass media continue to endorse dominant cultural stereotypes. While the world is made up of diverse ethnicities, heterosexual, white, middle class males still tend to be the main characters in movies and on television. They are especially likely to be portrayed in heroic roles, while other cultural groups are either assigned supporting or villain roles or remain in the margins. Despite the influence of feminism, the mass media frequently continues to encode authoritative gender patterns and reinforce stereotypical gender relations by portraying men as strong and active and women as passive, or as confined to domestic nurturing roles. The way many movies are edited compels the audience to identify with the male character, with the female character often appearing as the "love interest" and frequently being objectified from a male point of view. According to Harry Benshoff and Sean Griffin (2004), there are twice as many men on the movie screen as women, and Hollywood director and producer roles continue to be dominated by men. Historically, Hollywood films have been about men, while women have been portrayed in secondary roles drawn from the virgin/whore dichotomy. For example, in Westerns, the guys had the guns and women's roles were reduced to those of either the saloon girl (a euphemism for prostitute) or the virtuous daughter of the mayor of the town or honorable rancher, or perhaps a faithful school teacher. This type of positioning is frequently repeated in music videos.

These gender images are taken up by viewers as powerful cultural prescriptions for the development of their own identities. People mimic the dominant images of the media. As people watch movies, they internalize values and relationship ethics. These images (and the cultural values implicit within them) reach far beyond the borders of America, where the movie narratives are usually constructed. Since young people seek role models from the mass media, the impact of these images on how cultural identities are formed cannot be underestimated.

Early Hollywood films drew from the Victorian era, where women were portrayed as innocent and childlike and in need of protection. Devotion to fathers was transferred to husbands upon marriage. Women were sexually virtuous, cute, and defenseless and in need of protection by their male suitors from the advances of other men. Many female actors in early Hollywood films were portrayed as childlike. The actor Mary Pickford, featured in films in the 1920s, embodied this innocent character on screen. The set would be constructed with oversize props and chairs to emphasize her innocent, vulnerable, and childlike demeanor (Benshoff & Griffin, 2004). For a short period in the 1920s, some strong female characters, like Greta Garbo, Mae West, and Marlene Dietrich, made it to the movie screen, challenging the dominant images of women at the time. However, when the movie industry in Hollywood became more regulated, these strong female images were eclipsed once more, and challenges to the patriarchal status quo were fleeting. It took World War II to change the popular images of women. Women began to appear as powerful, assertive figures in their own right when women in the United States served in industry and helped run the economy during that period. However, these images never dominated the Hollywood film industry.

After World War II, women continued to be identified as wholesome girls next door aspiring to be stay-at-home mothers and housewives. In the 1950s and 1970s, actors such as Doris Day, Debbie Reynolds, and Sandra Dee epitomized these cultural identities. If it wasn't an innocent, passive female identity being portrayed on television and in the movies, it was an image of women as sexual objects to be lusted for. Movie stars such as Marilyn Monroe, Jayne Mansfield, Mamie Van Doren, Elizabeth Taylor, and Sophia Loren embodied these stereotypical sexualized images.

Today, the media portrayals of the cultural identities of men and women are more diverse and more complex. However, young women continue to be bombarded with heterosexual images that convey a dichotomous view of women as either virtuous and innocent or whorelike and wayward. Men, on the other hand, are subjected to powerful images of rugged individualistic heroes—physically powerful, decisive, independent, and psychologically hardened. The Marlboro Man portrayed in advertising beginning in the mid 1950s is prototypical. Heterosexual images of men as strong protectors and providers dominate, while women are still the nurturers and supporters of their man. It is increasingly common to see gay or lesbian relational images on television and in the movies, but overall they remain in the margins. In the most watched blockbuster movies, black, Asian, and Latino characters continue to be in secondary roles while their white counterparts continue to have prominence. These dominant mass media images are mapped onto the lives of audiences. They are never the sole cultural influence, but people who come to counseling will be influenced by the messages contained in them. Multicultural counseling should not ignore the influence of these images in the construction of clients' lives.

Media and Bodies

All forms of media are defining and redefining in astonishingly regular detail the norms for male and female beauty. David Garner, Paul Garfinkel, and Donald Schwartz (1980) examined the changing body shape of *Playboy* centerfolds over a 20-year period (1959–1978), choosing *Playboy* models because they may be said to personify the current ideal of the female body shape. Examinations revealed that the mean weight for the centerfolds was significantly lower than that of the average female for the same time period. In addition, models' weights and bust and hip measurements decreased significantly over the 20-year period, even though the centerfolds were becoming taller. Replicating and extending this research project by 10 years (1959–1988), Claire Wiseman, James Gray, James Mosimann, and Anthony Ahrens (1992) found that models' bust and hip measurements continued to decrease. These researchers found that the average weight reported for the centerfolds was 13% to 19% lower than that reported for average or normal females' weight. Similarly, Brett Silverstein, Lauren Purdue, Barbara Peterson, and Eileen Kelly (1986) surveyed major magazines and television programs from the 1930s to the 1980s and found that women in the 1970s and 1980s were portrayed as thinner and less curvaceous than they had been in earlier years. The Barbie doll, undeniably revered for her purported beauty, keenly reflects the idealized body shape and illustrates the unrealistic nature of this ideal. For example, in 1997, the average woman measured 37–29–40, a department store mannequin measured 34–23–34, and Barbie measured 38–18–28. It was calculated that the probability of a woman's having Barbie's measurements was less than 1 in 100,000 (Rogers, 1999).

The Pervasiveness of Western Media

There are no citizens or communities frozen in time and isolated from the influences of the mass media. Many have been irrevocably changed by this encroachment. Nigerians in Lagos regularly witness in their homes American public confession television, such as the *The Jerry Springer Show. Who Wants to Be a Millionaire* comes in multiple versions, with over 70 countries broadcasting the show. World Wrestling Federation shows are seen on television in Kenya, as are martial art films from Hong Kong, and Hindi melodramas add to the variety (Eko, 2003).

Box 10.2. Mangaia

What immediately becomes apparent when one travels from country to country is the extraordinary reach of the mass media and mass communication. During one trip, two of us authors, Gerald Monk and Stacey Sinclair, traveled to a remote Pacific island (Mangaia) where Monk had lived and worked as a secondary school teacher 25 years earlier. Twenty-five years ago, the 1,600 people who lived on this island were virtually cut off from what was going on in the rest of the world. The majority of the population received no newspapers or magazines. There was no electricity other than that produced by seven or eight private generators, no television, and no radio signal strong enough for residents to pick up on an inexpensive radio receiver. Returning to this island 25 years later, we found that most residents had electricity. However, more surprising to us was the view of a large satellite dish dominating the typography, channeling cell phone and television signals to island residents. Today, most Mangaian homes have a television set. At any one time, island citizens are in a position to view a selection of hundreds of television channels broadcast from around the globe. This change in the level of mass media exposure that has occurred on the island of Mangaia over the last quarter of a century is occurring in virtually every corner of the globe.

Countries as remote and culturally protected from outside influences as the kingdom of Bhutan, where citizens up until recently were required by the king to wear the traditional Bhutanese dress, are undergoing significant cultural changes. Fifty years ago, Bhutan had no public hospitals or schools, no paper currency, no roads, and no electricity. The first invited Western visitors were allowed into the kingdom in 1974. According to Cathy Scott-Clark and Adrian Levy (2003), Bhutan became the last nation in the world to turn on television in June 1999. The king of Bhutan, in an effort to modernize, introduced a cable service that provided 46 channels of round-the-clock entertainment, a move that abruptly changed a cultural context that had barely changed in centuries. Lyonpo Sangay Ngedup, Bhutan's minister of health and education, has commented that that there is a gulf opening up between the old Bhutan and the new: "Until recently, we shied away from killing insects, and yet now we Bhutanese are asked to watch people on TV blowing heads off with shotguns. Will we now be blowing each other's heads off?" (Scott-Clark & Levy, 2003).

Young Bhutanese people report their attraction to and fascination with MTV (Music Television) and television series from America. The most-watched television stations in Bhutan include ESPN, STAR Sports, and HBO.

Reality television in its various forms is found in many communities all over the world. Countries such as Thailand, Egypt, Japan, and China have experimented with their own reality shows that mimic what has taken place in the West. When traveling around the globe, it is not uncommon to see a variety of versions of the same popular reality shows. For example, Egyptian television has its own home-grown version of *Who Wants to Be a Millionaire*. It has grown in popularity as the media have played a prominent role in shaping a new generation of consumers captured by the materialistic and individualistic goals of many societies in the West (Hammond, 2005). Many themes of these shows illustrate cultural practices that hinge on competition, individualism, and materialism, powerful cultural forces that are shaping cultural identities in all communities throughout the world.

Performing New Identities

In a global society increasingly shaped by the role of media and telecommunications, young people are performing identities that arise from multiple cultural sources. Many and varied cultural sources are appropriated by young people in their production of their identity. There are countless examples of people who draw from horizontal as well as vertical cultural influences. For example, Maiko, a Japanese woman in her early 20s, brought up by relatively traditional Japanese parents, traveled to the United States to dedicate her career to hip-hop music. Having been introduced to hip-hop in Japan, she immerses herself in the black community in central Los Angeles. Many hip-hop lyrics (like other forms of Western music) embody the rhetoric of individualism and the Western cultural formations of the "me" generation. These are not the symbols that one typically associates with a collective Asian culture. And yet they are being invoked by Japanese young people.

The Media and Poverty

Repeatedly, around the globe, the media portray the growing gap between the "haves" and the "have nots," even as the cultivation of consumerism escalates. Consumer behavior must surely be counted as much a part of cultural practice as expressions of family kinship ties. James Petras (1993) graphically describes the effects of consumer culture on the masses everywhere:

> The TV "table of plenty" contrasts with the experience of the empty kitchen; the amorous escapades of media personalities crash against a houseful of crawling, crying, hungry children. . . . The promise of affluence becomes an affront to those who are perpetually denied. (p. 147)

These are the social forces shaping cultural identity today. As a result, the identity struggles of counseling clients everywhere are made more complex. The influences from traditional vertical cultural traditions are constantly moderated by the immediacy of these horizontal, globalized, cultural influences. How we think about multiculturalism needs to take these complexities into account. Counselors are always working with clients in their struggles to define an identity. If cultural influences provide the building blocks for such struggles, then counselors need to listen for the echoes of globalized cultural influences as well as the traditional vertical messages from ancestral traditions.

Technology

Access to Technology and Consumer Goods

Consider these events and their potential impact on culture and identity: In Moyabi, Gabon, in the heart of the equatorial rain forest, Africa's most popular commercial FM station broadcasts American and European commercials to societies that are now being bombarded by consumer culture. Timbuktu in Mali was one of the first places in Africa to be wired for the Internet. African television has been overtaken by the regular transmission of American, European, and Asian programming on stations across the continent. From Morocco to Zimbabwe, American popular music, most prominently rap music, blares from radios.

Large sections of humanity are locked into ongoing relationships across the world, because that is how they produce their livelihood. For example, China is producing statuettes of Mexican's patron saint, the Virgin of Guadalupe. The Chinese are also producing traditional Ramadan lanterns to be held by Egyptian children during the fast of Ramadan (Friedman, 2005). These Muslim lanterns play traditional Ramadan tunes and the theme to a television cartoon series in Egypt called *Bakkar*. Who would have guessed the intimate involvement Chinese entrepreneurs have in the religious celebrations of Muslim people thousands of miles away?

Large multinational retail chains like Wal-Mart perpetuate this trend. Wal-Mart has over 8,000 suppliers of goods in China alone and outlets in 44 countries. It now has 2,276 stores outside the United States. We can travel to the remote reaches of Mexico and find ourselves shopping for groceries alongside the local indigenous Mexican citizens at a Wal-Mart store. There are emerging trends in technology that will continue the march toward an interactive global society.

Technology and the Poor

In most countries around the world, cellular telephone technology has been rapidly introduced. Cell phone access is getting closer and closer to the poorest of families in the poorest countries. Phones are getting cheaper and cheaper and soon may be purchased for a few dollars. It is estimated, based on current projections, that by 2010 there will be 3.5 billion cell phone subscribers (Kendall, 2006). That's nearly half the world's population. In 2006, Somalia was one of the cheapest places to make an international cell phone call. In Afghanistan, there were 20,000 telephone lines in 2003, and in 2006 the number of Afghans communicating by cell phone had grown to 1.3 million ("Dial M for Mujahideen," 2006).

Within five years, poor families who can afford a television set will also be able to afford laptop computers, which will be available for less than 100 U.S. dollars. This technological explosion could connect the entire world with a networked international media in a way that has never been witnessed before. Very different cultural communities are having greater and greater contact because of these profound changes.

Thomas Friedman (2005) argues that we have moved into an era in which human activity around the globe is becoming completely interconnected. He cites examples of how component parts of computers are built in seven or eight countries and constructed and delivered to consumers by companies located in at least three or four other countries. Friedman also describes how Boeing builds its airplanes. Russian engineers based in Moscow help design the planes; contractors at Hindustan Aeronautics in Bangalore, India, digitize the plane designs; and Japanese subcontractors build the wings on some of the aircraft. With computer-designed assembly, they will build the next generation of planes each in three days because the "global supply chain will enable [them] to move parts from one facility to another just in time" (Friedman, 2005, p. 196).

There are vast numbers of citizens around the globe benefiting from this "flattening of the world." The sharing of technology and multinational activity has raised the standard of living for millions of people in numerous countries. Increases in income influence and shape the cultural practices of life in many families. With lowering of the costs of owning satellite-connected television sets, cellular phones, and networked laptop computers, a world has opened to many of those previously excluded from it. These technological shifts create a context in which it is possible for complex cultural identities to form within very short time frames around the globe. On the other hand, while it is clear that cultural landscapes and languages are being transformed, millions experience new forms of alienation and disenfranchisement as it becomes clear that they are not the recipients of the promises of consumerism.

Technology puts culturally different communities into contact with one another faster than they can be prepared for it. This new form of global intimacy leaves vulnerable communities threatened, intimidated, frustrated, and in many cases humiliated by close contact. Thanks to the reach of technology, people see in a graphic way where they stand in relation to everybody else. While this new knowledge may be culturally enhancing, it is equally likely to allow the marginalized and disenfranchised to immediately evaluate their life circumstances and find themselves more disadvantaged and unsatisfied, leading to even stronger experiences of unease and discontentment.

Disruptions to Discrete Patterns of Communication Among Ethnic Groups as a Result of Migration, Media, and Technology

In the past, multicultural scholars were able to identify distinct communication styles that specific ethnic groups possessed. Some multicultural texts identify how specific ethnic groups exhibit communication patterns that are unique to these groups. For example, Derald Wing Sue and David Sue (2007) suggest that American

Indians have a cooperative and noncompetitive communication style, while Asian Americans show silence to be respectful and blacks emphasize nonverbal behavior. Because of the powerful cultural forces that we have described above, it is increasingly difficult to identify discrete ethnic communication styles. Differing levels of acculturation to Western middle class culture and the dissimilar socioeconomic statuses held within ethnic groups complicate the picture. The ability to identify uniform verbal and nonverbal styles among large ethnic communities in modern cities is becoming more difficult. The verbal and nonverbal images portrayed on, for example, the television channel MTV compete with parents' behaviors and traditional cultural influences in shaping young people's communication styles. A complex array of social forces at work around the planet and particularly in the large urban centers produces countless disruptions to the formation of stable and neatly described ethnic identities with ethnically distinct forms of communication in modern-day families.

Historically, there have been variations among ethnic groups in their approach to goal setting. Derald Wing Sue and David Sue (2007) suggest that Asian Americans, African Americans, Latinos, and Native Americans have immediate, short-range goals while whites tend to have long-range goals. Our experience is that goal setting is more a product of class differences and economic advantage. People from a variety of ethnicities and backgrounds who are struggling to survive materially are more focused on finding a job, paying for the monthly rent, and getting food on the table than they are on the needs of themselves and their families in two years' time. Survival goals in many poor families are certainly short term. Those who are materially secure can afford to project into the longer term to make decisions about where their children will be educated, how they can acquire new skills to gain a higher income, and how they can borrow sufficient funds to buy themselves and their family a home. Long-range goal setting may also be a product of the modernist grand narrative of technological and social progress rather than a specific feature of European cultural tradition.

Counseling Implications of Globalization

In this chapter we have underscored the contemporary complexities of seeing cultural groups as neat, stable, and discrete categories. Our primary purpose here is to point to the ramifications, challenges, and nuances of working with cultural diversity in a global context in the 21st century. Human identities are produced through complex social processes, through which the vertical dimensions of race, ethnicity, gender, class, and religion all exert influence. As we have argued in this chapter, the picture is complicated even further by horizontal global forces like migration, the mass media, and technological change. These complex processes make it difficult to identify unambiguous and noncontradictory themes, despite the best efforts of multicultural scholars. As many have commented, within-group differences of an identifiable group often outweigh between-group differences, even when groups of people identify themselves as separate and distinct. Thus, we are very cautious about specifying certain therapeutic practices that might best cater to whites, blacks, Asians, Latinos, or others.

While we are concerned about the tendency to overstate the unique needs of one ethnic group in comparison to others (and then extrapolate from there about their specific therapeutic needs), we do not want to lose sight of the real effects of systematic patterns of oppression that have targeted particular ethnic groups. In earlier chapters, we have addressed the disparities that have occurred between many white communities and African Americans, Latinos, and Native Americans as a result of 400 years of European colonization. Such effects are not easily washed away and continue to be reproduced. Significant disparities continue to interact with the horizontal cultural influences outlined in this chapter.

We have described above some of the challenging dynamics confronting individuals and families in the era of globalization. These developments raise serious questions about whether it is adequate for counselors to base their practice on advice about how to counsel an African American, an Asian American, a Latino, or the like. Within a single family, the counseling needs may be very different from one member of the family to another. For example, a Latino family that migrates to the United States will bring with them their traditions, language, and cultural symbols, which are very likely to be different from some of the dominant American cultural practices. The parents have models of child care, discipline, family rituals, religious practices, and established gender roles that they will likely continue with. Their children, however, are growing up in American communities very different from their parents' place of origin. They are subjected to very different gender role models and religious practices. They learn that their American friends have very different levels of freedom and rights in the family.

As we have suggested in this chapter, young people today are increasingly exposed to a horizontal heritage from which they take many of their social cues and much of their cultural guidance. This dynamic produces the occurrence of very different cultural practices within the same household at the same time. Different cultural practices are forever competing and colliding with one another. The result is sometimes serious conflict between parents and children and between siblings, who are all at different places with regard to Western acculturation. This situation is being played out in hundreds of thousands of homes across the United States. Not only are these cultural tensions occurring within families who have recently immigrated from another country, but they are also to be found in families migrating from rural to urban areas and from city to city. Competing cultural practices affect not only migrating families. In fact, in every family whose children are being subjected to significant volumes of horizontal cultural influence, where parents hold to cultural practices that are different from those their children are exposed to, there is great potential for a family culture war. It would not be an exaggeration to suggest that, given the speed of cultural change, many children are brought up in a very different culture from that of their parents. This is the impact of a horizontal heritage at work.

In these circumstances, counselors need to be equipped with more than singular ideas about cultural belonging in order to make sense of what their clients are experiencing. They need a conceptual framework that enables them to identify the complexity of competing background cultural discourses that shape family interactions and produce family conflicts. A counselor's helping the family to name the competing and conflicting discourses at work can begin a process in which she assists the family in negotiating, in a more productive and stress-free way, how these cultural forces can be managed. This is very delicate work. It is a big challenge to establish effective and acceptable connections with parents and grandparents as well as to have the skills to connect with and understand children's and young people's perspectives. Democratic problem solving methods that might be successful with the children may present problems to parents who embrace a more autocratic parenting style. Since every family's needs are different, a way forward can be worked out only on a case-by-case basis.

In addition, rapid social change has led to the fragmentation of extended families especially. Two or three generations ago, it was much more likely that the children, parents, and grandparents, and even the cousins and aunts and uncles, would live in the same community. This has changed for most families today. Family members are spread throughout the country and in some cases throughout the world. Previously, parents could sometimes rely on grandparents to care for the children. Now, in many cases, families have two parents working, which sometimes leaves young children alone in their homes for long periods. The level of stress increases as parents juggle jobs and child care. There are many sole-parent homes and blended families. New family configurations, produced to some extent by rapid social change, present unique challenges to the health care professional. Many families have no models for how to be a blended family or a sole parent. There are few cultural resources these new families can draw from to give them guidance about how to organize their lives. This is another example of where cultural knowledge gained from a horizontal heritage becomes more influential. Therapists need to help families gain access to peer resources for information and guidance that fit with the unique family constellations being created in our communities today.

The reliance on horizontal heritage for cultural resources often has a serious negative impact on the role of the elderly. Older people, who once played such a central role in guiding the affairs of a community and family, now have a diminishing presence. In addition, older people who in communal or collective societies could have relied on their children to take care of them through their old age are increasingly having to fend for themselves. The disjuncture between being honored as an integral and guiding cultural resource to the family and taken care of until death and being isolated and alone leaves many older people feeling depressed, disoriented, and lonely. Therapists have an important role in supporting the elderly in their quest to make sense of and find positions of integrity in relation to a changed cultural environment. Older people who are not able to keep up with rapid technological change occurring with computers can also be further isolated from what is going on around them. Therapists need to develop specific expertise in working with the elderly, particularly because the numbers of older people are rapidly increasing as the baby boomers age.

With rapid social and cultural change comes rapid change in the cultural practices associated with gender relationships. Historically, men were the primary income earners and family providers. With the growing economic pulling power of many women in families, women's voices have grown in the areas of family life that were traditionally the men's domain. Increasingly, women are less willing to hold down three jobs—one as an income earner for the family; one as a domestic servant who cooks, cleans, and maintains the house; and the third as an emotional and social care giver for the children and the husband. In many homes, there has been a serious deterioration in couple relationships because of the changing cultural factors that influence gender roles.

When men and women fail to adjust to these changing cultural trends or women try to sustain all of their previous roles in addition to being a central income earner, the consequence is debilitating stress, conflict, violence, and depression. Therapists have an important role in helping couples and individuals understand the changing gender discourses influencing men's and women's lives. They can help couples renegotiate gender arrangements to fit the new cultural imperatives of gender equity in order to prevent the negative mental health consequences that can otherwise result.

Because of changing cultural trends around income earning, domestic activity, and child care in families, there are also significant challenges around dating practices and sex. Increasingly, there is confusion about what is the correct cultural behavior. Serious conflicts can occur within families around what is deemed appropriate dating or sexual conduct. Again, the counselor therapist has an important role as a cultural broker to help families negotiate a way forward around what were once intractable cultural positions on these matters.

In many ways, rapidly changing cultural processes taking place around the globe have created serious confusion about how to live in relationships. While there is a sense that particular persons are in charge of these emerging cultural trends, the evidence suggests that nobody is really in control. Religious leaders, politicians, business executives, and educators, while appearing to be leaders in the community, are just as captured and caught up in the cultural changes as everybody else. Nobody is at the helm who can single-handedly influence the discourse. In many ways, we are all participants in creating the direction that our world is heading.

Additional consequences of these changes include the many emerging subcultures, which are developing their own cultural identity narratives. The Chicano movement is an example of an emergent cultural identity constructed by a disoriented generation among the children of Latino immigrants who felt they belonged to neither a Mexican identity nor an American one. Thousands of young people were simultaneously alienated from white middle class America and from their immigrant families. Many Chicanos developed an identity that was not dependent on their speaking Spanish or on their ability to acculturate to the practices of mainstream middle class America. But in the face of oppression and prejudice, they did develop a strong political consciousness and a desire for civil rights, together with a deep pride in their Mexican American heritage.

Some of these cultural identities are highly evolved, and the cultural norms underpinning them give clear directives for engaging in day-to-day life. Other subcultural groups are less politically conscious. The most destructive of the new subcultures are the armed gangs in urban and now in rural communities that commit acts of violence against others and against each other. Counselors and therapists who wish to work with the new cultural communities, including gang communities, need to develop a working knowledge of the cultural norms and dominant discourses that prevail in these systems. To build trust and create therapeutic effectiveness, counselors must acquaint themselves with the nuances of these subcultures and their emergent cultural practices.

The increasing focus on material values and the associated Western obsession with body appearance and body shape are powerful cultural themes that many counselors and therapists also need to contend with. Wherever modernist cultural discourses have taken root, there has been serious cultural disciplining of the body. This disciplining produces problems with dieting, starvation, steroid abuse, and overeating. These health problems are lifestyle problems directly related to the dominant cultural messages reinforced every day in the media.

To conclude this chapter, let us reiterate our main theme: counselors and mental health professionals who take seriously the cultural influences on their clients' lives should develop an appreciation of the complexity of cultural narratives that impact the identity development of people's lives. As well as studying the conventional categories of social division formed around ethnicity, sexuality, religion, language, and socioeconomic class, they would do well to attend to the newly emergent elements on the cultural landscape. Cultural influences are not just vertical; they are horizontal as well. Among the horizontal influences, globalization deserves considerable attention. Counselors need to understand especially the profound influence of the media, technology, and mass migration on the shaping of contemporary identities. These cultural strands are becoming pivotal in the task of formulating counseling responses to the bewildering array of complexities that cultural diversity is now composed of.

TO DISCUSS

1. Make a map of the world and locate on it where everyone in the class was born. How many experiences of migration are in the room? Do the same exercise for your parents' generation. And for your grandparents'.

2. Share stories of the effects (positive and negative) of migration on (a) family relationships and organization, (b) schooling, (c) work and career opportunities, and (d) personal identity.

3. Investigate the positive and negative economic effects of globalization for (a) people in Asia and Africa and (b) people in Europe and the United States.

4. Interview someone over 70 about how his life was different when he was young. Bring back stories to class to share and discuss.

5. Make a list of horizontal subcultural influences that have shaped your life in some way. Share these with others.

6. Identify one new technological development. Investigate the new cultural forms of life that have developed as a result of this technology. Use online searches and library searches to explore this topic and bring your findings back to class to share.

Response to Chapter 10

Soh-Leong Lim

Soh-Leong Lim, Ph.D., is a licensed marriage and family therapist and assistant professor in the Marriage and Family Therapy Program at San Diego State University. She is a third-generation Malaysian Chinese and a first-generation immigrant to the United States. She teaches multicultural family therapy, among other courses. She has a passion for bringing global and international awareness to her students in U.S. classrooms. Her research interest is immigrant and transnational families with a focus on acculturation and intergenerational relationships. She lives with her husband in San Diego. They teach internationally and maintain close transnational ties with their family and kin in Asia.

This chapter makes a good case for how vertical and horizontal cultural processes help shape a person's cultural identity. However, I think there needs to be more emphasis on the significance of our vertical cultural processes in addition to the horizontal influences that are going on in our day-to-day lives. My cultural history has been hugely significant in shaping who my family and I have become.

Like weavings of a tapestry, horizontal processes seem more apparent to the observer. The splashes of color catch the eye. Vertical processes, however, are the influences at work that go on silently in one's multigenerational family tapestry. They are passed down from one generation to the next, whether or not the person consciously acknowledges or embraces them at any particular point in his or her life. Though the vertical processes can be masked by globalized forms, they are what constitute the solid framework of one's ethnic identity.

To illustrate this, I would like to share my story. I am a third-generation Malaysian Chinese and a first-generation immigrant to the United States. In my family of five, we have three nuanced identities: my husband and I are OBC (overseas-born Chinese), my first two daughters are ARC (American-raised Chinese), and my youngest daughter is ABC (American-born Chinese). These identities we connect to are a product of horizontal influences, specifically the geographic location of our birth and growing up. However, the common denominator of our identities is that we are Chinese. This is our shared heritage. The vertical influences are very strong for us, although it may appear as if we are losing our Chinese heritage and adopting more American or globalized ways of being through succeeding generations. However, we each tap into these vertical veins and express our Chinese heritage and pride at different junctures of our lives, often in diverse and unexpected ways.

My grandmother migrated to the Malay Peninsula from southern China during the Qing dynasty in the late 19th Century. Following her example, my mother carried on the family tradition of ancestor worship blended with elements of Daoist and Buddhist beliefs. We were also deeply influenced by Confucian philosophy, especially the values of education and filial piety. My nine siblings and I grew up in a traditional Chinese home, no different from most Chinese immigrant homes in Malaysia. My father was a magistrate's court interpreter of English, Malay, Mandarin, and seven Chinese dialects; however, with his 10 children, he emphasized mastery of the English language. This was the period after British colonial rule in Malaysia when English, used in all official business, was also the medium of instruction in school. My father was a pragmatic man. He saw good education and mastery of the English language as our passport to secure jobs, reflecting the determination of an immigrant set on seeing his young family succeed in the host country. My father did not stress continuity in the Chinese culture, nor did he emphasize mastery of the Chinese language as such. Consequently, while my ethnic heritage is Chinese, I grew up cosmopolitan, imbibing blends of both Eastern (Malay, Chinese, Indian) and Western cultural influences (I had an English education, grew up with BBC News, and enjoyed listening to Johnny Cash). I spoke English, Malay, and the Chinese Fukien dialect. I also became a Christian at 13 years of age through a deep spiritual experience.

Last year I visited China for the first time in my life. I went to China because I had a teaching assignment. I did not go there with conscious intent to find my roots or to reconnect with my Chinese heritage. Up to that point, I had aligned myself more with my Malaysian Chinese cosmopolitan cultural identity. I was surprised that my time in China stirred in me a pride in being Chinese—a Han Chinese. This was the first time I embraced and celebrated my Chinese identity in such a deep and conscious way. The Chinese in China identified me by the term *hua-chiao*, which means "overseas Chinese." Prior to my trip, I was worried that I could not converse well enough in Mandarin Chinese, and that the fluent Mandarin–speaking Chinese people would look down on me, as those in Malaysia and Singapore often had. This did not happen. Instead, I experienced a sense of homecoming, even though I am not a citizen of China, nor do I have any plans to be one. It had to do with a profound sense of ethnic pride. I am telling this story to illustrate how strong the vertical processes of a Chinese heritage are for me. It seems as if it has been there all the time in the background. It really is the backdrop of my life.

I have three lovely daughters. In all their childhood years, I did not consciously make it a point to instill Chinese culture in my children, but I see these vertical processes at work. For example, three years ago, my American-born daughter, then 16 years old, was at her grandfather's funeral in Malaysia. While surrounded by a throng of relatives, many of whom she had not met before, she took an interest in documenting the family tree of the large extended family network and became known as the Lim family historian. She also took copious pictures of the funeral service, which was a traditional Chinese one, complete with a brass band and Buddhist chants over the five days. She wanted to document this part of her Chinese heritage; all this was of her own accord. She came back to the United States and shared her stories with her two older sisters, who had not been able to leave the country to attend the funeral because of visa restrictions. At that time, my second daughter, a student in visual arts, was struggling with a lack of artistic inspiration. She asked for all the photos, found inspiration from the Chinese rituals and symbols, and incorporated the themes in her metals artwork. Her vertical connections are quietly reflected in her metalsmithing pieces. They are not as loud as the techno music that she dances to with her fun-loving American friends, but they are surely there, treasured as her finely crafted art pieces are. At her senior art show in Texas, I saw her artwork reflecting our heritage, and I was filled with a deep and awesome pride.

To me, this phenomenon is not static. Multigenerationally, I see ebbs and flows. We have our Chinese culture to return to when we so desire or when she stirs in us an awakening. She is like our old faithful friend. We know her strengths and her weaknesses, her prides and her shames. This is what I hope the readers of this volume will understand—that our friend is here to stay; she is strong and she endures the horizontal currents of change. We need to acknowledge her adequately. Counselors should still pay close attention to vertical cultural traditions, as much as they are aware of horizontal forces, in order to be culturally effective.

My therapist friend from China, who grew up under the Cultural Revolution, observed how deeply Confucian and Daoist thought have influenced her and the Chinese people in spite of decades of Maoist rule. "It is in our blood," she reflected. I, as a *hua-chiao*, agree with her. It is indeed in our blood.

CHAPTER 11

Identity Construction

Previous chapters have dealt with macro-level social processes and power relations that emerge in the multicultural counseling field, and we have explored how they play a part in the creation of culture, ethnicity, race, and gender. Considerable emphasis has been placed on the impact of the historical forces of European colonization that have shaped the modern world. This chapter shifts our attention to the micro-level processes of identity construction but attempts not to lose a sense of the impact of the social dimensions of culture, history, race, ethnicity, and power relations.

The global sociohistorical processes at work around the planet—in particular, the impact of the mass media, technology, and migration, as well as the sustained efforts of many people to generate decolonizing social movements—disrupt the possibility of a stable identity and also the possibility of cultural constancy. The self is saturated (Gergen, 1991) with multiple influences that shape our identities. We have already detailed the complexity of cultural membership in previous chapters and would argue that this complexity is not honored by an approach to multicultural counseling that reduces identity to singular dimensions. We shall now consider the counseling implications of catering to the needs of individuals living with a multiplicity of identities.

In this chapter, we use the notion of identity as a conceptual tool to understand how people make meaning in their personal lives and in their relationships with others. Understanding the process of identity construction as a set of narratives rather than as emerging from a singular core, or personality, can help us understand how psychological problems are produced, and this is at the same time a resource for exploring creative ways to address those problems. We find the construct of identity more useful to us than the notion of personality and would argue that a multicultural perspective in counseling should exercise a preference for identity over personality. In our view, personality is an essentialized, stabilizing construct that does not adequately account for dynamic changes that people make in their lives as they respond to the influences of powerful sociohistorical processes. The notion of ongoing identity construction better represents the dynamic, shifting, and evolving patterns of life that are always responding to the changing cultural contexts that people inhabit.

First, let us specify what we mean by identity construction. The term is used in different ways in accordance with different philosophical traditions.

The Notion of the Singular Self and Personality

Many of us were raised within the influence of a Western cultural tradition to assume without question that we are born with a unique self that expresses itself via a particular personality. From much of the mainstream psychological literature and popular culture, we come to know that we each have different personalities based on certain biological predispositions that we develop when we are young. Most of us accept the fact that these characteristics or dispositions will provide us with a unified, stable sense of who we are throughout our lives. We embrace a pre-fixed psychological structure that shapes and determines the way we behave. Most of us accept that that personality structure stays with us until the physical break-down of our bodies. As Vivien Burr (2003) suggests, personality is so taken for granted in Western culture that we could almost imagine that surgeons could open us up to show us our personality. In both academic discourse and in everyday talk, we accept global descriptions of people and their personalities. For example, people are known by their personalities to be extraverted or introverted, generous or mean spirited.

It would be logical, given our understandings about the self, to expect all cultures to embrace the notion that we have a prefixed personality, but this is clearly not the case. Some cultures don't define certain characteristics as belonging inside people. The Ifaluk, for example, describe people in relationship to community events, rather than as separately locked within their own individual sphere. They talk of justifiable anger not as a privately owned domain but as a moral and public account of some transgression of accepted social practices (Lutz, 1982, 1990). Yet we habitually see qualities such as competitiveness, greed, caring, and love as descriptive of a person rather than of a type of action.

In many ways, the Western or modernist construction of personality could be viewed as pessimistic about possibilities for change. This is due to the widespread notion that deep inside everyone there is just one kind of fundamental truth or essence that really matters and is difficult to change. One could almost say that, in terms of personality, the rest of a person's life journey doesn't really count for much. Mainstream trait-personality theorists suggest that we are born into a particular set of characterological configurations that remain stable over our lives. Other personality theorists suggest that we are shaped by both traits (the biological inclinations we are born with) and states (the situational and environment influences), from which our personalities are created. This means that heredity and environment play a part in shaping a core identity. People talk about babies having their own personalities and how these personalities will define them as they grow. Certainly we don't dispute the notion that children express certain temperaments and habitual patterns of relating very early in their lives. However, these characterological patterns of relating are a far cry from a fixed set of personality attributes that inherently drive a person's life. The question is whether we think of these patterns as fixed or as constantly changing. Some developmental theorists have proposed that once a person has reached a certain age, her personality is set and not subject to change. Sigmund Freud's (1938) theories of personality remain a foundation from which many developmental theorists think about personality. The Freudian view of personality is deterministic to the extent that it believes personality is defined by the interplay of irrational forces, unconscious motivations, and instinctual drives.

Today, counseling and psychotherapy approaches wrestle with the extent to which people are capable of fundamental and lasting change. In North America, insurance companies will pay counselors and psychologists to work with clients troubled by psychological problems that are perceived as treatable. They will not pay for counseling and therapy for people whose problems appear to emanate from a personality disorder, since it is believed that a personality disorder is a fixed, stable entity and thus that people with such disorders are not capable of changing their lives. The latest version of the *Diagnostic and Statistical Manual of Mental Disorders* (DSM-IV–TR; American Psychiatric Association, 2003), one of the most significant cultural artifacts shaping the fields of psychiatry and psychology, guides mental health professionals in understanding and assessing client problems. It is designed on the basis that we all have a core stable personality and that when that personality is not operating correctly it is disordered in some particular way.

Psychology's Preoccupation With the Self

Psychology and mental health professionals have historically been preoccupied with the notion of the individual and the personality. As we have shown in Chapter 6, liberal humanism has dominated mainstream counseling, psychology, and psychotherapy over the last three decades. Gaining momentum in the 1960s, the liberal humanist tradition, pioneered by psychologists such as Gordon Allport, Abraham Maslow, and Carl Rogers, has traditionally identified the individual as the central agent of all social phenomena and has celebrated the self as independent, stable, and knowable, emphasizing an individual's capacity for choice, freedom, and self-development. The field of counseling and psychotherapy has been dominated by the notion of the unitary self. The central premises of individualism in the helping professions are based on the injunction to "be your own person" and "stand on your own two feet." Clients are supported to be functional human beings who are independent, rational, moral agents responsible for their own welfare and individualistic lifestyle.

Sarah's story clearly illustrates the tensions she experiences with her peer group, who perceive her to be weak and dependent because she is not following the dominant Anglo American pattern of living in a separate dwelling from her parents in her mid 20s.

I graduated from UCLA a short while ago. I had a full undergraduate experience, including living in a dormitory and in an apartment separate from my family. Many family members and friends beamed with excitement at the news of my graduation. Then they would ask me, "So what's next in your life?" I'd happily reply that I would be moving back home with my mother and attending graduate school. The mere mention of graduate school brought a sense of pride and joy to their faces, but adding the fact that I would be living at home seemed to make them sneer. I wondered about that, because at first I had no idea what the negativity was all about. In dominant middle class Western society, there is the notion that a person over the age of 18 is supposed to be out in the world living on her own. Certainly she should not be living with her mother.

In traditional Filipino culture, it is customary that when the children grow up, they take care of their parents. This means that they could all be living under the same roof for as long as they all live. According to my mother, the concept is that they (the parents) took care of you (their child) when you were young, and you should return the favor. The origin of this cultural concept is not known, but it could have to do with the Filipino value of respecting one's elders. Friends and family members who have embraced the Western idea that children 18 years of age and older have to move out affects me when I am at family gatherings (usually family parties) or social events with my friends. I mostly feel hurt when they think that it is negative for me to be living at home with my mother, because I truly believe that living at home is a very positive affair. Sometimes I have to stop and self-evaluate for a moment my reasons and objectives for being at home.

My mother and I have a very close relationship, and she has told me time and time again that she loves my being at home. I show, in many ways, that I value the Filipino belief of respecting one's elders through my interactions with my mother. Growing up, I saw how my mother treated my grandmother with utmost respect and kindness, and I have internalized that Filipino value. I plan to take care of her more and more as I get older and have a good career. I use this self-evaluation whenever I feel that people try to impose the stigma of living at home with parents after the age of 18. In other words, I always try to think of my close relationship with my mother and the positive aspects of living at home. At times, however, this dominant cultural attitude of individualism is difficult to weaken.

Interwoven with the liberal humanist perspective of the individual as an independent, autonomous, and unitary being has been the notion that people are fundamentally separate from the social and historical world. With its celebration of individualism, liberal humanism has tended to locate human problems within individuals as distinct and separate from the social, cultural, and political contexts in which they live (Neimeyer, 1998; Winslade, Monk, & Drewery, 1997). This dislocation of individuals and their problems from the larger cultural context reflects the humanistic focus on intrapsychic processes. From this viewpoint, the essence of individuality is the feeling self. Feelings are seen as products of nature and bearers of truth about the individual rather than as products of culture. People's feelings have been revered in counseling as representing a higher level of truth about their nature than their thoughts or words. The dated but nonetheless popular notion of self-actualization, for instance, epitomizes the liberal humanist position that individuals are capable of being in charge of their own lives and grants individuals the freedom to be self-guided, self-governed, and effective in their pursuits of personal growth and development.

Sarah Mamaril identifies herself as Filipino.

The excessive individualism promoted in the liberal humanist movement has tended to ignore the larger sociocultural issues impacting therapists and clients alike. Foreshadowing a contemporary criticism, Allan Buss (1979) observed, "A theory that predisposes one to focus more upon individual freedom and development rather than the larger social reality, works in favor of maintaining that social reality" (p. 47). As a result, the effects of various oppressive practices have frequently been overlooked. For example, the relevance of the humanistic position to the situation of people of color has been challenged (Carter, 1995; Durie, 1989; Jenkins, 2001). Skeptics maintain that because liberal humanist doctrine has portrayed persons as autonomous beings who are primarily responsible for their plight, practitioners within this framework may easily dismiss how racist, sexist, and homophobic discourse impacts them and their clients.

The monolithic conception of the self continues to play a dominant role in modernist schools of thought and continues to be accepted as a fundamental truth on which psychology is founded. This continues despite psychology's best efforts to construct itself as a discipline founded on objective, independent, scientific criteria. The mechanisms by which a society produces fundamental truths were explained by the philosopher Michel Foucault (1969, 1972). In his early writings, he shows how over long periods societies produce certain widely held assumptions about human beings and how these assumptions come to be accepted as true. Foucault explains how a society then constructs certain protocols and practices based on these "truths." In Chapter 5 and Chapter 8, we saw how, in the modern world, processes of normalization and surveillance have been constructed to keep these established truths in place. Human behavior is judged in accordance with established norms and found to be appropriate or aberrant. Foucault's argument is that if we examine the work done by the social processes of production of personhood, many of the features of personal identity do not turn out to be straightforward, natural expressions of innate personality. Rather, they are produced into a person's identity as an outcome of the systematic interplay of power relations. We believe that this perspective offers much richer veins to be mined in the development of the multicultural counseling field than those offered by conventional individualistic notions of personality.

dern Psychology and Its Implications

A growing number of social science researchers have rejected the monolithic categories of personality and the notion of the stable self on which the traditions of modern-day psychology are based. They reject the assumption that the individual is both the prime source of all human interaction and the most important unit of social analysis. It is clear from previous chapters that using the individual as the central point of social analysis obstructs our understanding of the profound role that sociocultural processes play in the construction of human expression. The postmodern movement is keenly interested in the link between wider cultural processes and individual identity construction. Postmodernism has emerged as a powerful challenge to the traditional Euro-American science of psychology (Fukuyama & Sevig, 1999; Hare-Mustin & Marecek, 1994; Harvey, 1989; Lax, 1989; Lyotard, 1984). The term *postmodernism*, however, can be used in a number of ways, and we need to specify the sense in which we are using it here.

Postmodernism is a term applied to a loose collection of intellectual movements in a variety of social fields stretching well beyond the social sciences. Some suggest that its center of gravity lies more in the arts and architecture than in social science (e.g., Burr, 1995, p. 12), but it needs to be considered part of the background against which we can understand the general principles of social constructionist psychology.

As the term suggests, postmodernism as an intellectual movement is a reaction to the dominance of modernism, a term referring to the approach to knowledge and truth that grew out of the Enlightenment in Europe in the mid 18th century (Seidman, 1994). Postmodernism casts doubt on the idea that the world can best be understood in terms of the grand narratives or meta-narratives (Lyotard, 1984) of modernist science (based on rationality and objective observation) with their promise of ongoing social progress. Steven Seidman (1994) has summarized modernist culture as built on the following set of organizing assumptions or grand narratives: "assumptions regarding the unity of humanity, the individual as the creative force of society and history, the superiority of the west, the idea of science as Truth, and the belief in social progress" (p. 1).

On the basis of these assumptions, Seidman (1994) details a series of institutional edifices that have entrenched the modernist cultural perspective:

> an industrial-based economy; a politics organized around unions, political parties and interest groups; . . . the market and state regulation . . . ; role specialization and professionalism . . . ; knowledges divided into disciplines and organized around an ideology of scientific enlightenment and progress; the public celebration of a culture of self-redemption and emancipatory hope. (p. 1)

Charles Taylor (2004) would add to this picture of emancipatory hope a more pessimistic note. He suggests that the modern world has also been characterized by a profound personal sense of alienation.

From a postmodern perspective, modernism is characterized as "in crisis" but far from "abruptly coming to an end" (Seidman, 1994, p. 1). Postmodernism asks uncomfortable questions regarding the adequacy of modernist assumptions about truth, knowledge, the relations between the individual and the social, and the possibility of progress, and argues that many historically and culturally specific assumptions have been masquerading as timeless, universal truths. As Derald Wing Sue and David Sue (2007) have stated, postmodern psychology has fueled interest in understanding alternative realities, spirituality, and indigenous methods of healing. This movement has also raised serious questions about the commonly held assumptions about the nature of the self.

Much of the postmodern literature holds that cultural assumptions of a single definable reality are impositions that dismiss or distort the diversity and indeterminacy of human life. Postmodern writers suggest that understanding anything is a consequence of the coming together of a unique set of circumstances at a particular place and time. Descriptions of human behavior emerging from postmodern literature are generally concerned with local and specific occurrences rather than global descriptions based on context-free laws (Hoshmand & Polkinghorne, 1992).

Many counseling models tend to emphasize the primacy of the rational mind over body and emotion and its capacity to take up one noncontradictory position. Postmodern theorizing, on the other hand, emphasizes the significance of the person as a multipositioned subject, a view quite contrary to unitary notions of the self.

Postmodernism has tended to challenge all boundary fixing and the hidden ways in which people subordinate, exclude, and marginalize others (Bernstein, 1983). Advocates of a postmodernist approach, such as Charles Jencks (1992), have suggested that this means an end to a single worldview, a resistance to single explanations, a respect for difference, and a celebration of the regional, local, and particular. David Harvey (1989) suggested that the postmodernist position has been characterized as the total acceptance of ephemerality, fragmentation, discontinuity, and the chaotic while contemporary psychology views chaos and fragmentation as problems to be overcome. The self from this perspective is considered to be in a constant state of change and disequilibrium. The postmodern conception of the self is in stark contrast to the humanist notion of a single, stable, unitary identity.

The nature of the world in the 21st century is characterized by chaos and fragmentation, disorientation and complexity. From a postmodern perspective, the question, "Who are we?" becomes increasingly difficult to answer in the lives that we lead and in the way we describe ourselves in this new century.

Multiple Identities and Multiple Selves

To assert that a person has a single identity means to believe that he has a fundamental allegiance, often religious, national, racial, or ethnic, and that having found it he may flaunt it proudly in the face of others. In fact, every person is a meeting ground for many different allegiances. Sometimes these allegiances conflict with one another, and this confronts the person with difficult choices.

The reality is that people's identities change over time. Amin Maalouf (2000) writes of a man who proudly stands up as a Yugoslavian in 1980. Twelve years later, this person denies his identity as a Yugoslavian as the war in Bosnia is waged. Now this same man stands proudly as a Muslim. Today, he may be Bosnian first and Muslim second. What identity will he be in 20 more years?

In the following identity statement, Rosa reflects on the shifts she has made in her religious identity over time.

My great grandparents prayed the rosary every morning and evening and attended Mass every day, and on Sunday they went twice a day. As a child, my mother was told that if she did not attend Mass and pray, she would be committing a mortal sin. These beliefs were taught and believed by many Catholics. In fact, my mom describes my great grandparents as "Catolicos de más" (too Catholic). Today, many among the working class will say, "Si Dios quierre" ("If God wants") or "Si Dios nos da licensia" ("If God permits us"); these sayings are said out loud whenever one is planning on doing something. For example, if a child says that he or she is going to work hard to get better grades in school, the mother will finish off the sentence by saying, "Si Dios te da licensia." Working class Mexicans believe that if they don't say these phrases, then they are jinxing themselves and will make God mad at them.

Turning to their faith is the only way many working class Mexicans are able to keep hope despite their unjust living conditions. If one stands outside La Villa, a temple the Virgin Mary asked to be built, one will witness many indigenous and working class people walking on their knees down the center aisle toward the image of the Virgin Mary. This is done as an act of faith to the patron saint of Mexico.

Because of this heritage, I came to believe that religion was imperative for survival. I remember attending Mass every Sunday and praying the rosary every night. This routine carried on until my siblings and I got older and began to work and have other responsibilities. Now that I am older and have had many different experiences in my life and have been exposed to new ways of thinking, I have found myself confused about my own religious and spiritual beliefs. This dissonance originated for me in my first year as an undergraduate. For the first time, I had the opportunity to be exposed to different people, different cultures, and a different environment and did not have my parents deciding what I was to believe. Having these new experiences changed my thought processes. I found out that the religion I practiced does not accept homosexuality; in fact, it is considered a sin to be gay or lesbian. Since many Mexican Americans are Catholics, they are influenced by these teachings and look down on homosexuality. Among the working class, homosexuality is also perceived as a shameful way of living. I imagine that these ideas are not influenced just by religious beliefs but also simply by people's being uneducated. My confusion has led me to feel guilty and to feel as if I am a bad Catholic. I am still struggling with this confusion. I know I have faith in God, but I'm not certain I follow all Catholic beliefs. It's a little scary for me to discuss this openly.

My great grandfather told my grandmother that to get married in the Catholic Church meant that *"el matrimonio no es para un dia ni dos, es para toda la vida. Si tú cruz es libiana o pesada, Dios decidará si va haber una seperación. Si te sale mal el marrido, si te golpea, maltrata o lo que sea, tú vas a morir fiel a tú cruz."* Meaning, "Marriage is not for a day or two, it's for life. If the weight of your cross is heavy or light, God will be the one to determine if there will be a separation. If your husband turns out bad, if he hits you, mistreats you, or whatever, you will remain loyal to your cross." The advice my great grandfather gave my grandmother exemplifies how marriage was viewed as an extension of Catholic beliefs. During those times, divorce was unheard of, especially among the working class group. First, there was no money to spend on the process; second, you went down the social class ladder; and third, it was forbidden by the Catholic religion. Witnessing my parents' interactions with each other, I was taught that in a marriage there will be difficult times but that divorce is never an option. Yet, in my American present, I am being taught that divorce is an option. I deal with these two contrasting beliefs by believing that marriage is a sacred union and should not be taken lightly, but not disregarding divorce entirely. I am not saying that I believe in divorce and do not find anything wrong with it; on the contrary, I just don't want to feel trapped, as I think my grandmother once felt.

It is clear that Rosa, like thousands of people, is actively engaged in identity construction. The models of identity laid down for her in her family system about how to be a Christian and a woman do not provide her with all of the cultural knowledge that she needs to negotiate her way into a postmodern world. Migration, the media, and education become powerful contextual elements for Rosa that require her to revise some of her important salient identities.

Mikela is another person in the midst of identity reconstruction, reconciling his Indian-ness with his college education. This is how he describes his identity right now:

I was the first male from my tribe to graduate from college, and I am the first person from my tribe to go on to graduate school. I am doing things that my people haven't done before, and I fear that this will make me an outsider. Although I do get a lot of praise for what I'm doing, I also get a lot of criticism. My own people think that I'm not Indian anymore because I have a college education. They think that I have "turned white." The process that I have undergone to make it to being a professional has large implications for my culture and me. The more educated I become, the less Indian I am. I fear that when I get everything done, I won't be accepted back into my community. So for those that tell me otherwise, usually the ones that solely live on the "rez" but are not connected with their Indian-ness, I sing my songs, and I know in my heart I'm Indian. Another question is, will I not be accepted into the counseling profession because of my Indianness? Much racism against my people is still evident, and I fear that being an Indian will create a lot of barriers in my profession. My worldview is different, my philosophy is different, and my way of working with kids will be different.

Every individual without exception possesses multiple identities. One only needs to ask a few questions to uncover a person's forgotten divergences and unsuspected allegiances. Sadly, on a large scale, many of us lump the most different people together under the same cultural identity and ascribe to them collective crimes, collective acts, and collective opinions. For example, it is common for people to say, "The Sunnis have massacred . . ." "The English have gone on the offensive . . ." or "The Saudis refuse . . ." We unthinkingly express sweeping judgments about a whole people in a single breath.

To be born black is a different matter according to where in the world you come from, whether it be New York, São Paulo, or Addis Ababa. In Nigeria, people are not labeled black or white but recognized as Yoruba or Hausa (Maalouf, 2000).

At the local level of identity construction, identity can take a number of forms, and the context is enormously influential in shaping one's way of understanding oneself and way of relating to the world. Rosa's identity as a Mexican American woman is significantly affected by the contexts produced by national borders. She discusses the day-to-day conflicts and feelings of identity dislocation that she experiences because of the arbitrary divisions produced between Mexican Americans born in Mexico and those born in the United States.

I remember witnessing this division in high school—those born in the United States were perceived as higher class. Often some of the United States–born Mexican Americans did not know the Spanish language as proficiently as the Mexicans, which created a wider division between the two. I was born in the United States, but I had friends from both groups. I remember that one time I wanted to join an organization on campus called MEChA (Movimiento Estudiantil Chicano de Aztlán). I thought that by joining I would learn more about my Mexican roots. At the first meeting I attended, I felt like an outsider. Most of the students were born in Mexico, they were all speaking fluent Spanish, and they had negative images of the "American" lifestyle. I wanted to be a part of them, but at the same time I felt as if I was perceived as the enemy. Needless to say, that was the first and last meeting I attended. Another division among these two groups relies not just on language differences but also on social standing. Those born in Mexico perceive those born in the United States as "fake Mexicans." It's unfortunate that these divisions are a part of growing up as a Mexican American, because they are what make me feel as if I don't belong in the United States or in Mexico. I remember being in Mexico on vacation when I was about 10 and overhearing some ladies refer to me as "the one from the other side." I know that I was born in the United States, but I also know that my roots lie in Mexico. Knowing that my own *raza*, my own people, do not want me in Mexico or America makes it difficult for me to feel accepted and wanted.

Mexican Americans consider members of their own group sellouts if they speak English better than Spanish. They believe that those who are not in touch with their Mexican heritage and do not identify with the struggles they may have experienced are not legitimate. I know I have experienced this prejudice.

Rosa clearly demonstrates the powerful complexities that individuals have to negotiate inside an ethnic category such as Mexican American to feel that they belong. Her identity shifts repeatedly in response to her social context. Rather than seeing her as unfortunately abnormal, we would contend that her experience of multiple reference points is far more normal than dominant discourse usually recognizes. The sad thing is that, rather than feeling valued for her flexible multiplicity, she feels she is required by this discourse to establish singular "roots."

Tristan's story provides some very interesting insights into the nature of identity construction within changing contextual boundaries.

Tristan's first public identity was declared in her mostly white elementary school: she was surfer girl. She took after her mother, who wiped "Browns rule" (meaning Latinos) off the blackboard and replaced it with "Surfers rule." She described her parents as a cute beach couple who embraced the surfing lifestyle. When she entered high school, her identity took on a dramatic revision. She transitioned from a predominantly white part of town to a high school that had a large Mexican American population. This was the early 1990s, when rap and hip-hop were becoming popular. This was also a time when gangs and cliques were the thing to be part of. To identify as a gangster was perceived as trendy. Tristan remembers wanting to be part of a gang so badly, but she knew that Mexican students would not allow white people to identify as gangsters. She says her Mexican peers looked down on white people who tried to act like members of another race. However, as time went by, she spent more time with her Mexican peers. She changed her style of clothing and her makeup and started hanging around with students who identified as gangsters. This led to her long-standing white friends' turning against her and terminating their friendship. Her mom took notice of her changes and disapproved of this new direction. Tristan began to live an identity that her mother completely despised. Now Tristan was projecting a gangster image that her Mexican friends were beginning to accept. Tristan also became successful in developing an understanding of and adaptation to the expressions of Mexican American culture in her community. She would spend endless amounts of time at her best friend's house, where they would participate in quinciñeras, baptisms, and other important rituals shared by the Mexican American communities. Because of her brown hair and eyes and the people she spent time with more and more, people assumed she was half Mexican and half white. She began to confirm to others that she did have this ethnic heritage. She now began to hide her association with her family. She began to identify so strongly as Mexican American that she no longer felt white. Her dialect, accent, and tone mimicked the tonality of Mexican Americans who speak English as a second language. Her behavioral mannerisms, style of dress, and musical interests were a perfect fit for an Anglo-Mexican American.

Tristan says that since starting college, she has "grown out of that gangster stage." Yet today, as she is in her early 20s, the majority of her friends are still Mexican, as are the men she dates. She keeps her Mexican identity intact. In her workplace, people still consistently speak to her in Spanish or ask, "Aren't you Mexican?" When she replies that she doesn't speak Spanish, Mexican Americans seem to get very upset and ask her why her parents didn't teach her. On the other hand, when white people meet her for the first time and notice her Mexican English accent, they scathingly reject her white identity through their looks and comments.

For our purposes, rather than privileging or emphasizing the understanding of people as singular personalities or particular characters, we find it preferable to view the person in terms of complex relational processes manifesting themselves at the site of the individual body. It requires work, however, to shake off some of the individualistic assumptions. We find the term *relational selves* useful in describing the complexity of human identity. We can view the "I" not as a single entity, although it can be portrayed as a singular point from which to view the world, but rather as a product of history that has evolved from institutions and traditions. From this standpoint, the self as a speaking voice is not an individual voice at all but a collective voice, carrying the collective stories that people tell one another. These voices carry cultural traditions over hundreds of years. Thus, it becomes critically important to trace cultural histories to understand how contemporary identities are formed.

Numerous writers have spoken about multiple selves. For instance, Jeffrey Escoffier (1991) referred to overlapping identities. He stressed that the self is often simultaneously connected to a number of different identity discourses and resides within overlapping identities. Kenneth Gergen (1991) described the self as "saturated" with multiple identities. Similarly, John Shotter (1990) stated that "although the postmodern self may be something of a mosaic, no self is completely an island. In postmodern everyday life, as well as in postmodern science, one occupies a multiplicity of standpoints" (p. 19). Maria Root (2003; cited by McGoldrick, Giordano, & Garcia-Preto, 2005, p. 8) proposed a creative challenge to the tendency of people to categorize others in simplistic unitary forms. She was concerned about how many people have a need to categorize others and themselves in uniform boxes, such as one specific ethnicity, religion, or sexual orientation. Root proposed a bill of rights for people who identify themselves as belonging to multiple categories. Her bill of rights seeks to give people permission to not identify as strangers expect them to. She invites people to identify themselves differently in different situations, rather than having to subscribe to a particular category. People can identify themselves differently from family members, if this better describes their lived identity. She encourages us to recognize loyalties to more than one group and to develop new vocabularies to help communicate about multiple identities.

A therapeutic process must accommodate to people's multifaceted ways of being in complex, changing, and often contradictory patterns of power relations. As we have suggested, our identities are not fixed or essential, although they are grounded in our lived experience and so are not free floating. Our identities are produced by our physical location, generation, gender, religion, class, status, and numerous other factors. They are products of culturally mediated interpretations arising within dominant, systemic, and continuous social orders woven together in a series of historical, contextual, and dialogic maneuvers within a community (McNamee & Gergen, 1999). We have laid out in earlier chapters the importance of understanding the contextual and historical influences from which specific cultural identities are formed. Granting significance to the social contexts we inhabit and their impact on the shaping of identity contrasts starkly with individualistic theories and context-independent analyses of the self.

Language and Identity

Since our ways of understanding the world do not come directly from an objective reality, the role of language becomes pivotal in the production of our concepts and categories. Language is significantly more important in shaping human life and identity than traditional psychology has believed. From a social constructionist perspective, language is more than simply a medium in which we express ourselves. Traditional psychology looks for explanations and understandings inside persons and labels them attitudes, motivations, cognitions, and affective states. When people talk about their personality, they tend to assume that the dimensions of the self exist prior to and separately from the words used to describe them. Language is assumed to serve a representational function to give expression to things that already exist in themselves (Burr, 2003; Davies, 1993; Lather, 1992). Language is regarded as a bundle of labels from which we can choose to describe our internal states. From a constructionist perspective, however, language structures our experience of ourselves in the world and produces the meanings and concepts that make us up. Rieko, a Japanese school counselor, illustrates this point well as she reflects on her experiences of living in Japan and in the United States.

> When I am speaking in Japanese, I need to speak in a very polite way. I feel very constrained. When I speak English, I feel independent. It reminds me that I have a voice and am allowed to express my opinion and assert myself. In the United States, I feel very confident. I can say what I want to say. I express my ideas and

beliefs. I feel that people listen to me and they don't judge me. They seem to appreciate my contributions. It feels to me that English provides a level playing field. The Japanese language is more hierarchical, and as a young woman, in order for me to be respectful in Japan, I must present myself as submissive and quiet. I cannot be as direct, as straight talking. This is particularly the case when I am working in my school and am addressing the principal or senior managers in the school. The language itself directs me into a submissive way of relating. I want to speak in English with my students so I that I can feel independent and self-assured.

Built into the structure of some language forms are social hierarchies that give clear directives to language users about what is allowed to be expressed within the culture. In Japanese cultural communities, it is typical of younger people to convey deference to older people. The language register gives explicit instructions in how to converse across the generations. Rieko was reconfronted with the power of these language hierarchies on returning to Japan. Her experience demonstrates how the Japanese language permits one kind of identity to be lived and expressed. In different social and linguistic contexts, she is permitted different kinds of identity.

Significant shifts of identity occur for most people when they migrate from one country to another and from one language world to another. Members of the family who are not taught the native language of their migrating parents experience profound changes in their identity and in how they make sense of who they are and where they belong. In the following identity statement, Abbie captures the complexity of identity construction played out by millions of people who, as a result of migration, speak a different language from their parents.

I do not speak Tagalog, and language is a vital part of Filipino identity. Since I was born, I have been taught to speak English. My father had to endure an American boot camp with no grasp of the English language. He could curse you in English before he could ask where the restrooms were, and once he did learn English, there was nothing he could do to erase the accent he spoke it with. He wanted to spare his children the inferiority he felt when he spoke English. Among my cousins, my sisters and I sound perfectly American, look purely Filipino, and we are the outsiders. I do not speak the language and hence I always feel alienated from other Filipinos.

I do not speak Tagalog, the language of my family, and I have no desire to live outside the United States. I'm slowly gaining independence and learning that, while my family is important, I must also take care of my own needs and wants. In these respects, I am very American. I tried variations of naming what I am to include my American citizenship: *Filipino-American* with the hyphen, without the hyphen, *American citizen who is Filipino*. I feel that I am quite simply Filipino American. When I'm with my Tagalog-speaking aunts and uncles, I feel as if I'm an outsider even more keenly than I do in a room full of white people. I become subdued and try to melt into the walls, cloaking myself in invisibility. I wonder why I feel such a profound change in how I feel about myself when I am with my Filipino extended family. Despite incredible feelings of discomfort at times like this, I still embrace a Filipino identity. In fact, in many ways, how I perceive the world is filtered through that identity. However, things are still not that straightforward. Being in a relationship with an Anglo American has been an interesting experience and impacts how I express myself when I am with him and when I am with my family. That's not to say I change who I am. I just become more overt in certain respects when I am with different people. When I am with my family, we are very vocal, loud, and energetic. I also become much more sensitive to family obligation when I am around them. Some of the main stereotypes that people have about Filipinos are that they are loud and codependent on their families. My friends and my Anglo American husband believe that I am simply an American who happens to have a Filipino background. However, there are certain values and perceptions that I hold that are a result of my being Filipino. A primary example is that I will always be family oriented and I will always emphasize the importance of education.

Because of the changing face of our cultural communities and the elasticity or reconstruction of ethnic membership in the 21st century, there are fewer and fewer familial models and mentors that can help individuals negotiate the kind of person they will be and how they will identify. Historical familial models and ancestral cultural practices are increasingly merging into the background. Abbie comments on the reality of this social process.

Being an American woman is a valued identity for me, which has been problematic for my parents in that I have lived my life according to ideals that are not acceptable in a Filipino Catholic culture. I value the independence that is the cornerstone of American culture and which is denounced in Filipino culture. I value the roles of a female insofar as there should be no traditional roles of a female and that the value of a female is more than just in the preservation of her virginity and in her utility as a housewife and mother. To this day, the fact that I have lived my life a certain way has been a source of conflict between my parents and me. It took a long time before I was able to learn that their approval will not be enough to make me happy if I have to compromise my own self-will, and I would have no one to blame but myself if I did not exert any independence.

My sisters are able to see me and understand that the way my parents live their lives does not necessarily mean that their lives have to be lived in that same

> manner in order for them to obtain happiness and success. They are slowly becoming able to exert their independence and learning to make moral choices for themselves without having to accept what my parents tell them. I think that they value me as a role model of someone who is able to be independent and still value my family as a Filipino. I think that my independence as a woman is of value to my husband, because I am able to take care of myself and to take care of my needs without being dependent on him for complete support. With the multiplicity of ways that people view themselves and how that changes over time, I feel that it is important to take how they see themselves at the present moment into context. I think that it is difficult for people to really think about how they identify themselves, ethnically, racially, gender wise, and so forth, and to think about what that identity means to them is also a challenge.

As ethnic categories change, individuals look increasingly to the mentors and models from their peer group or from cultural sources portrayed in the mass media for guidance to help them negotiate how to define themselves. Reality TV shows, soap operas, self-help programs, daytime talks shows, magazine stories, sports stars, music artists, television and movie stars, and Internet chat lines all provide cultural material that young people (sometimes unknowingly) model themselves after. At no other time in recorded history have there been so many choices of identities for people to engage with and perform in their day-to-day lives.

Counseling Implications of Expressions of Multiple Identity

Personality theory suggests that human beings are born with a central observable core and hold a set of character traits that are set early in life. Therapists influenced by this fixed account of human personality may be constrained in their efforts to support clients because they believe that nothing can be done to change the core. Common notions of a singular and immutable personality can keep counselors from understanding the complexity of human identity and its multiple facets. Axis II disorders in the DSM are examples of problems assumed to be characterological and thus unresponsive to therapeutic efforts.

Curiosity in therapeutic practice can become a casualty of the notion that people have only single-dimension personality traits. Once a personality is discovered or tested for, the therapist can believe that this is who a person is. Personality diagnosis draws attention away from the complexity, ambiguity, and dynamic nature of human functioning. For example, when presented with a behavior that is regarded as symptomatic of a popular personality description, a counselor can quickly assume, "Oh, that's Johnny's ADHD," rather than spending time exploring the meaning of the behavior in its own right. Many of us engage in contradictory behaviors because we are so heavily influenced by contextual factors that influence the identities we perform. Remaining curious about the complexity of individual lives presents counselors with many more therapeutic possibilities with which to respond.

Clients diagnosed on Axis II of DSM-IV seldom receive resources from health insurance providers, because it is believed that a dysfunctional personality pattern is not susceptible to change. These assumptions are widely held in the field of psychiatry. Yet many of us know of individuals, perhaps including ourselves, who have made profound changes in the way they live their lives. People who were formally perceived as paranoid may have become more trusting in their relationships. People who were written off as having an antisocial personality can become more respectful and considerate of others. Individuals perceived as avoidant or dependent may in some situations exhibit more confidence and social skill. Descriptions of personality type are usually located within individualistic traditions of psychiatry and psychology, and they are argued to be independent of culture and context. But there are counseling models that are more responsive to complex and multiple identities.

Much of psychology, psychiatry, and counseling is focused on the individual as the unit of analysis. This orientation is in alignment with many other modernist practices in the West and follows our attraction to the exploration of human phenomena from deductive and reductionist protocols. What it doesn't allow for is the profound influence that human systems have in shaping human behavior. The DSM invites us to look primarily at what is taking place within the individual rather than between people. While there have been efforts in DSM-IV-TR to include more context data, the DSM is still essentially an instrument that privileges individualistic constructions of life. As therapists use the DSM, they can be drawn away from an appreciation of the relational, systemic, and societal factors in human functioning. In other words, the DSM frequently makes multicultural counseling more difficult. Our thrust, by contrast, is to take the cultural world more seriously and to place greater emphasis on the wider systemic and societal influences that shape identity construction. We are conscious that this emphasis renders problematic many counseling theories that center the individual and treats contextual factors as relevant but peripheral. We don't believe that form of multiculturalism is good enough. Our theoretical orientation to identity construction could therefore be characterized as "outside in" rather than "inside out."

From the stories of people who have described their lives in this chapter, it is clear to us that a person's identity remains always in constant revision. There is no point one can reach in life where one can say, "My identity is set." New contextual factors in the culture at large will always emerge and invite us to reconfigure ourselves. Our response may be to fall back on old habits or to find the wider contextual factors so compelling that we don't have a choice but to make a new response.

At the same time, we are bombarded with many cultural prescriptions that invite us to figure out who we "really" are. People call for therapy to help them be made whole. Some therapeutic models suggest that it is healthy for people to integrate their lives and eradicate ambiguity. We would suggest that our lives are so complex that integration and wholeness need to be abandoned as therapeutic goals. It is surely impossible to not respond to compelling stimuli in contradictory ways. A more helpful therapeutic response would be to embrace multiplicity and to normalize the experience for those who are troubled by their multiple identities.

From our perspective, it is pivotal to recognize that the boundaries surrounding ethnic membership are in a state of flux. There are no static cultural practices that straightforwardly guide people's life paths. All cultural patterns of life are constantly in a state of revision, reconstruction, or even upheaval because of the globalizing trends circulating the planet. Cultural groups cannot be treated as if they were museum pieces frozen in time. People everywhere have to respond to the complex and contradictory cultural forces that run through their lives, whether they want to or not. Everyone has to choose how to proceed. Awareness of these processes of flux and change, fluidity and complexity, will better equip counselors to work in our multicultural world.

TO DISCUSS

1. In what contexts have you experienced challenges to cultural messages you received from your family?

2. In what ways are your own practices different from your parents'? Can you identify the cultural influences that you drew from to make these changes?

3. Can you identify contradictions within your thinking, your experience, your story of who you are?

4. Share stories of situations in which you have been pulled in two (or more) different directions by competing ideas or messages from others. What was that like? Analyze the cultural forces at work in producing these competing ideas.

5. Find examples in the counseling literature of statements that assume the existence of a singular self.

6. Watch a videotape of a counseling session and look for evidence of the counselor's belief in a singular self or in a multiple identity.

7. What are the advantages of thinking about identity as being produced by multiple stories? Are there disadvantages?

Response to Chapter 11

Leah Brew

Leah Brew, Ph.D., is a licensed professional counselor, a nationally certified counselor, and a biofeedback therapist. She works as an assistant professor in the Department of Counseling at California State University, Fullerton. Her areas of research, writing, and teaching primarily regard (a) issues of diversity and (b) basic counseling skills, with a strong emphasis on empathy. She has presented on these areas both nationally and internationally.

My identity has most definitely been transformed. I remember being without any sense of self or definition; I just was, without self-consciousness. Then, I defined myself according to various cultural affiliations that changed based on my growing knowledge. And I am now returning to an identity-less way of existing but in a transcended way.

In the third grade, my family moved me to a small town in the South, and other children began to make fun of me because I looked different. They taunted me for being Chinese. I didn't know what this meant, but I was sure it must be bad. I went home and asked my mother if I was Chinese, and to my great relief, she informed me that I was not; I was Japanese. And so I went to school prepared to defend myself. I still didn't know at all what this meant, but I assumed it must be better than Chinese. The kids continued to taunt me. I tirelessly worked to understand what was wrong with being Japanese. Eventually, I recognized through their teasing that my eyes were my downfall; they were small, not large and open like the other kids'. I despised my eyes and would practice making them larger, but to no avail. Thus was the birth of my identity. I defined myself according to this ethnic heritage. That is, until I went to Japan. I quickly recognized that I wasn't Japanese at all. I was much larger, since my father is American. I couldn't use chopsticks. I didn't eat fish for breakfast. And, most prominent, I couldn't speak the language. I made many cultural mistakes. I felt lost, without an identity.

In high school, I remember asking my friends if they ever questioned who they were. They looked at me confusedly and had no idea what I was talking about. I felt crazy and weird. I felt certain that something was wrong with me. What I didn't realize then is that they were all part of the dominant culture (white and Christian); I was not. They were fine with their identity.

In college, I met other nonwhites and defined myself as nonwhite. I also met my ex-husband, who was Thai, and then we defined ourselves as Asian American. I still felt lost, though, because his Thai family was certainly different from the way I was raised. We may both be Asian, but we were no more similar to each other than we were to our white friends. It was only in my culture class as I worked toward my master's degree in counseling that I began to understand race, ethnicity, and their differences, and began moving through my own identity development.

After completing my degree, I moved to California. I met people from all walks of life: people from various ethnic and religious backgrounds, people with varying gender and sexual identities, even other biracial Japanese Americans. I was so excited! I was in paradise. However, after talking with other Japanese Americans, I realized that we'd had such different experiences that I didn't necessarily belong with them either. I was back to square one. Then something quite fortuitous happened to me. On a trip to Thailand, I attended a presentation on Buddhist psychology. The speaker said something profound. He said that Westerners have a need to create boundaries, boxes, or lines around everything; we are pragmatists. He said that in Thailand, those boundaries don't really exist. I was blown away! Suddenly, I had a solution to my identity problem. I didn't need an identity. That isn't to say that I don't enjoy studying cultural constructs; I do. Instead, I believe that we can transcend our boundaries of self. As a result, I now attempt to respond creatively and consciously (rather than habitually) to each moment in my life, to each person, and to each environment. I recognize how cultural constructions are created, are modified, and affect each of us personally and interpersonally. I am dynamic. I'm a composite of my biology, my interactions with others, my environment, and myriad other things that are constantly changing and impossible to pinpoint. I am like a drop of water in the ocean. How can you define where I begin and end?

CHAPTER 12

Cultural Identity Development

In this chapter, we shall address the topic of cultural identity in relation to particular models that focus on a developmental approach. In earlier chapters, we have attended to aspects of identity in relation to various forms of culture, race, ethnicity, and gender. We have also explored the effects of globalization on these identity patterns. A developmental approach, however, widens our perspective by suggesting that any particular identity position is not fixed. The simple fact of cultural belonging does not say all that can be said about an individual person's identity as it moves through time. It is especially this dimension of time that a developmental approach takes more into account. Through time, identities change. They grow and mature, develop new practices, and extend themselves into new nodes of cognitive functioning. Such development is far from random, however. It can readily be seen as patterned and similarly structured among groups of people. It has its sociological aspects, but for each individual it also has psychological dimensions.

It is these patterns of development that models of development seek to map out. There are many such models, and we cannot possibly cover them all in this chapter. Therefore, we have had to make some choices based on our assessment of the significance of these models to the current discourse on multicultural counseling. We shall present here three models of cultural identity development. The first is the model of racial identity development that has received a lot of attention in multicultural counseling literature. It deals specifically with the construct of race, particularly in the context of black-white relations in the United States. The second model deals with the experience of immigration and the developmental challenges that the process of acculturation throws up for new immigrants. Traditionally, this process of development has been assumed to be aimed at assimilation, but a more recent approach affirms both the immigrant's host culture and his culture of origin. The third model we shall present in this chapter features identity development in gay, lesbian, bisexual, and transgender persons. We include this model as a specific example of identity development in relation to a frequently excluded minority group that has its own particular challenges. The similarities and differences among these models are, we hope, instructive. We shall attempt to present each model faithfully and then to list some apparent strengths and problematic aspects of each model. We shall not attempt to draw any final conclusions in relation to any of these models but shall leave that to you, the reader.

Racial Identity Theory

Racial identity theories are based on the attempt to describe and analyze the effects of the social construct of race in psychological terms. As theories of identity, they address the internal experience of the social world, specifically in relation to the construct of race. They introduce the idea that the psychological experience of race is not the same for all people of a given race, but that it varies from person to person. The variation, according to these theories, is not random, however. It involves processes of development, of movement from lesser to greater maturity. These theories account for the personal journey that individuals go through in the process of living and of coming to terms with the current effects of the history of race and of racism in the world in which they live. Tracy Robinson (2005) states the focus of racial identity development nicely. She suggests that it is about the work people do to establish identity positions based on the shared belief that "I am because we are and since we are, therefore I am" (p. 130).

Like many other psychological theories of development and of individual growth, these theories often introduce models of predictable stages that people go through in a process. In this way, they aim to help us make sense of the different kinds of responses we might find ourselves and others making in the midst of relations between people on either side of the black/white race divide. The importance of this work for counseling is that if we can identify a predictable racial identity development process, then as counselors, we can work with people to help them advance their development toward greater maturity. After all, much counseling work is about identity development in response to the problems that life throws up for people. Racial identity development is a domain in which this might take place.

We shall not attempt to cover in depth all of the various theories that abound in this field. We shall instead mention several of them and choose one as an example for greater attention and evaluation.

Jean Phinney (1989, 1990) proposed a model of racial identity development that focuses mainly on adolescent identity development. She called it "ethnic identity development," but we shall set that distinction aside for the moment. It was built on earlier general work of identity development by James Marcia (1966), which outlined four categories of identity status that described the degree and depth of a person's commitment to a particular identity. The four categories of identity status are organized in ascending order of maturity from diffused identity to foreclosed identity to a moratorium identity and finally to an achieved identity. The first status of diffused identity represents the lack of any identity commitment or the absence of any experience of identity crisis. The foreclosed identity status describes the adolescent who has adopted identity commitments based on childhood influences without going through much in the way of identity crisis or exploration. When adolescents enter the moratorium status, they can be said to be in the midst of an identity crisis or identity search marked by intense exploration and experimentation. Out of this search emerges the more settled status of achieved identity, which signals an arrival at a committed personal identity. Questions have been raised about whether this model applies as well to females as it does to males (Ponterotto & Pedersen, 1993), but there is nevertheless modest empirical support for the identity development process that Marcia's model postulates.

Phinney started from the assumption that developing a clear, singular, ethnic identity is a major indicator of positive mental health and used Marcia's model to describe the status of racial or ethnic identity. Phinney collapses Marcia's diffused and foreclosed identities into a single initial stage of "ethnic identity diffusion/ foreclosure." Adolescents at this stage may lack interest in racial identity or see it as a nonissue. The second stage of moratorium status is marked by increased awareness and exploration of racial identity, often spurred by some kind of encounter with racism. It may involve anger and outrage as well as a search to learn more about one's own identity. The third stage of achieved identity involves acceptance of oneself as a member of a minority group, less anger toward the dominant group, and the development of a healthy, bicultural identity.

There are other models that postulate a similar process of movement from naive conformity, through some process of encounter, exploration, resistance, or dissonance, toward a more mature and secure acceptance of one's racial identity and a respectful attitude toward other groups. For example, Donald Atkinson, George Morten, and Derald Wing Sue (1989; see also Sue & Sue, 2007) have proposed a minority identity development model, and Joseph Ponterotto and Paul Pedersen (1993) distill the commonalities of a number of models into their own four-stage model. There are identity development models that focus on specific ethnicities, such as Filipino (Nadal, 2004) and Hispanic (Ferdman & Gallegos, 2001). There is also a "biracial" identity development model (Poston, 1990).

For reasons of space, we shall not go into these and other models in depth but shall concentrate on a typical and also highly elaborated example of a racial identity development model. The work of Janet Helms (1990a, 1990b, 1994) is widely cited in the recent multicultural counseling literature on the subject of racial identity theory. Her work was built on foundations laid by William Cross (1971, 1978, 1991), who began in the 1960s to study "nigrescence," the process of becoming black. Rather than covering each model in a cursory way, we shall examine Helms's approach to the theory of racial identity in greater depth. Her model incorporates much of Cross's earlier work and has been examined in empirical studies.

A starting place for this examination is to ask, what exactly is racial identity, according to Helms? The following comment, while not quite a definition, is instructive:

Many people erroneously use a person's racial categorization (e.g., Black versus White) to mean racial identity. However, the term "racial identity" actually refers to a sense of group or collective identity based on one's *perception* that he or she shares a common racial heritage with a particular racial group. (Helms, 1990a, p. 3)

The care Helms is taking here to avoid a simple essentialist argument is important. Racial identity is being separated from simple correspondence with the categories to which one is assigned by governing authorities. To be born black or white does not automatically confer a black identity or a white identity. Nor is racial identity equated with the "reality" of one's race. In fact, Helms (1990a) refers to racial designation in the United States as "confusing" (p. 3) and instead links racial identity to the more phenomenological process of "perception." We might say, slightly differently, that racial identity refers to a process of social construction or discourse stemming from the interactions between official social designations and the internalized consciousness of these designations. Helms's statement is noticeably describing an outside-in process. People are not born with racial identity. The group or collective identity of the reference group preexists the individual perception and internalization of membership of the group.

Helms goes on to assert that "racial identity theory concerns the psychological implications of racial-group membership; that is belief systems that evolve in reaction to perceived differential racial-group membership." (1990, p. 4).

The term "belief systems" is presumably borrowed from cognitive behavioral theory. It was first popularized by Albert Ellis (1961). These belief systems are said to "evolve." (Developmental theories often have in the background echoes of 19th century ideas of social evolution.) And *perceived* group membership (rather than, say, *actual* categories) is argued to form the basis for such membership's psychological implications. Helms explains further that these psychological implications are borne out in intrapersonal and interpersonal functioning. The assumption is that more evolved belief systems will lead to more optimal psychological functioning. There is, therefore, an implicit assessment of the quality of a person's racial identity in its current state of development. Some identity formations are assumed to be of superior quality (i.e., more highly developed) compared to others.

So what constitutes a high-quality (or, for that matter, low-quality) racial identity? The first criterion for a high-quality identity is the degree of "awareness" that a person achieves with regard to her own racial identity (Helms, 1990a, p. 7). Conscious awareness of identity is preferable to subliminal or repressed identity. Counseling might therefore be helpful if it assists a person to increase her level of awareness of her own racial identity and decreases the degree of unconscious identity formations within her psychological functioning.

A second criterion for high-quality identity is that the individual identifies "with the racial group with which he or she is generally assumed to share racial heritage" (Helms, 1990a, p. 5), rather than with a group from which she or he is generally assumed to be excluded. Thus, a black person identifies more strongly with a black racial identity and a white person identifies more strongly with a white racial identity. Two problems can occur at this point. In a social system where white identity holds dominant sway and guards the entry gates to social privilege, those who are "generally assumed" to be black can seek to overcome less favored or negatively indexed black racial identity and to overidentify with white racial identity (i.e., seek to assimilate into white culture) at the risk of personal or relational confusion. The second problem is that those "generally assumed" to be white can fail to see any need to identify as white (or black) because their lives do not frequently encounter social barriers established on the basis of racial designation. Therefore, they can easily make the erroneous assumption that such barriers do not exist for black people either. Blindness by whites to the whole function of race as a category of identity can make it doubly hard for black people to overcome the challenges of developing an optimal racial identity.

A primary assumption of racial identity theory is that identification of oneself as either black or white (monoracial identity) is preferable and psychologically healthier than either identifying as a member of neither race (marginal identity) or identifying as both white and black (biracial identity). As you might guess from your reading of earlier chapters in this book, we might want to raise some questions about this assumption, because it appears to exclude the possibility of multiple identities. Helms also argues that racial identity is best thought of as relatively stable. This is another assumption that might be questioned by the arguments of social constructionism, in which all identities, or personalities, are regarded as more unstable than psychology usually considers them.

Stages of Black Racial Identity

While the constructs of racial identity are argued theoretically to be relevant for both black and white people, black racial identity was established first (originally referred to by William Cross [1978, 1991] as "nigrescence"), and white racial identity was developed later by extrapolation. Nigrescence refers not to a black identity gained simply on account of skin color but to the process by which a person "becomes Black" (Helms, 1990a, p. 17) in the sense that he develops thinking that positively evaluates him and his reference group belonging. It is about the development of a self-concept with regard to race. Humanistic assumptions of the development of a healthy self-concept through the process of self-actualization underpin the nigrescence model, which later developed into racial identity theory.

Building on the earlier work of William Cross (1971, 1978), Janet Helms's (1990a) model of black racial identity presents a four-stage model of development. Each stage represents a "worldview" or a "cognitive template" (p. 19) out of which a person adopts a sense of self and organizes meanings about other people and social institutions. The four stages are *preencounter, encounter, immersion/emersion,* and *internalization.* Each stage may also be broken down into two forms of expression and is therefore thought of as "bimodal" (p. 19). We shall explain each stage in turn.

Preencounter

A person in the preencounter stage claims to be "just a person" rather than a member of a designated racial category. Race is deemphasized in order for the black person to assimilate into white society and to compete on "equal" terms with whites. White society is idealized as the model that black people should use as the basis for envisaging a future. Preencounter racial identity involves assuming a radically meritocratic view of socioeconomic positioning. A meritocratic view in this context means arguing that people achieve success in the world largely on the basis of their own individual effort and talent and that race does not play a very significant role in whether the doors are open or closed for them. The price paid for maintaining this worldview is dissociation from other black people as a personal reference group. Belief in the existence of a meritocratic world implies blaming the disproportionate numbers of black people who live in poverty for their own laziness or lack of effort. Evidence of racism and its effects on the lives of black people has to be screened out or denied in order for this identity to be maintained.

Preencounter racial identity may be expressed in passive or active forms. Active expression features greater denigration of other black people, while the passive form just accepts negative stereotypes of black people and positive stereotypes of white people.

Encounter

This stage is characterized by an event in the life of a black person in which she is faced with racism or exclusion from white society or firmly assigned an inferior status. Such an event is so powerful that it can no longer be denied, and it touches the core of her racial identity. It is a disturbing event that overwhelms the preencounter racial identity and brings about a conscious awareness that it must change. The person sets off on a quest to discover a new black identity. But the struggle that ensues between the previous worldview and the emergent new identity produces an experience of oscillation, often accompanied by feelings of confusion, anxiety, and anger. Sometimes, says Helms, the experience of this shift is like that of a religious rebirth and is accompanied by feelings of euphoria. But it also can be experienced as a loss of identity, producing profound discomfort. Some may throw caution to the wind and begin a frantic, almost obsessive, search for a new identity. But this stage is marked by the search rather than by any profound discovery. That must wait until the next stage of black racial identity. Consequently, this stage may be like a window that opens for a short time, rather than a place where people dwell for a considerable part of their lives.

Immersion/Emersion

As the name implies, this stage has two modes of expression. Immersion refers to the mode in which the person withdraws into a black world and judges others on the basis of whether they conform to so-called authentic racial standards. He may adopt white stereotypes of black people and act them out in the belief that these are features of true black identity. Adoption of such exaggerated black identity forms is often accompanied by intense anger at white people and at other black people whose eyes have not yet been opened. The person may also direct anger against himself for his past blindness. Whereas in the encounter stage he denigrated blackness and idealized white cultural practices, now he idealizes black cultural practices and denigrates whites. However, black identity seems to be put on like a piece of clothing rather than deeply internalized at this stage.

In the Emersion mode of this stage, the individual joins black or African groups or engages in political activities, and gradually his anger at whites begins to level off or become less intense as he begins to develop a greater sense of control over his own feelings.

Internalization

In this stage, the person develops a positive, more internalized black identity. This identity is also more nuanced and less stereotyped. It may include unique aspects drawn not so much from stereotypes of black culture as from the particular life experiences of the person. People in this stage recognize other blacks as their primary reference group. Rather than embracing a blanket rejection of white culture, the individual begins to develop greater discernment in her relationships with white people while still holding on to a clear rejection of racism. Relationships with white people that were terminated in the anger of the previous stage of development may be reestablished at this point.

Strengths of the Black Racial Identity Model

The first thing that the black racial identity model achieves is the rendering of the general historical process through which black people have traveled in a version that is localized to the individual. It provides a psychological map of a sociocultural relation that is bigger than any one person. By doing this, the model enables counselors to work with issues of race with individual clients and to help them process a complex array of responses to everyday situations within a framework that renders such experiences understandable.

Black racial identity theory has the potential to be inclusive of a range of experiences and therefore forestalls some arguments about whose experience is more valid than others. Different positions along the developmental path can be included in a vision of the same path, rather than being seen in opposition to one another. The model equips counselors with a cognitive map that they can use to address issues of race and its effects on clients without judging them for their choices. These choices can be understood as steps in a larger process, rather than being allowed to totalize the individual in one particular step along a path of development. A model that focuses on the choices individuals make in response to racism also has value in that it leaves theoretical room for blacks to have agency. It is an improvement on theoretical models that cast blacks just in the role of victims of racism. To be only a victim is to remain objectified. A model of racial identity development at least positions people in a place of subjectivity.

In terms of face validity, it seems clear that people do go through processes of development as they form identity around issues of race. We can all think of people who have made identity shifts in this regard. So the idea of identity development in itself makes sense.

Another aspect of the black racial identity model that has explanatory value is the place it gives to the actions of people who are described by the model as in the separatist stage of immersion/emersion. Pronouncements of separatist intent (i.e., when black people want to interact only with other black people) can be unsettling for some people, especially whites, who feel excluded and can resort to accusations of reverse racism at this point. The racial identity model renders this separatist response understandable and contextualizes it, not as reverse racism, but as an understandable, or even necessary, stage of racial identity development. Its value lies in the consciousness-raising development that can take place at this stage as a person engages with and learns from others who have experienced similar forms of oppressive experience. The model therefore has the potential to form the basis for mutual understanding at points where friction can otherwise result.

As an assessment tool, the black racial identity model holds out the potential at least for counselors to make informed decisions on where to concentrate their efforts in identity development work. When clients present in response to an encounter experience, the counselor might concentrate on helping them move into the immersion/emersion stage. When they are in the immersion/emersion stage, the counselor might help them balance out emotional content so that they can enter the internalization stage.

From our social constructionist perspective, this model to a certain extent opens up the recognition of multiple identity positions. It avoids the postulation of a singular black identity that might be taught to counselors and then imposed on their clients. Rather, it validates a range of identity positions without making any one of them permanent. It thus allows for a sophisticated and nuanced account of black identity that is both flexible and complex enough to be inclusive of more people than accounts based on identity type are.

The black racial identity model has been adapted into a measurement tool in the form of a pencil-and-paper questionnaire (the Racial Identity Attitude Scale–Black, or RIAS-B scale [Parham & Helms, 1981]) and has been used to gather empirical support for the model itself. There appears to be some modest empirical support for the model, although Helms acknowledges that the empirical support lags behind the theoretical development.

Robert Carter (1990) states that the racial identity model was developed as an alternative to "what might be called the race perspective" (p. 145). Here he refers to the perspective from which it is assumed that knowing the client's and the counselor's race is enough to be able to develop understandings about how they might influence each other. The racial identity model enables us to develop a more complex picture of what happens in counseling based on the client's and the counselor's stage of racial identity development rather than on the basis of race per se. Carter conducted a study of counseling relationships that appears to provide modest support for this contention. In his study, racial identity attitudes were more predictive of significant counseling relationships than race alone.

Problematic Aspects of the Black Racial Identity Model

Questions can be raised about the black racial identity scale, as they can be asked of any stage theory, on the basis of whether it describes an inevitable process that everyone goes through or whether it models only some people's experience. The clear implication is that it is a universal scale. It is therefore subject to the general postmodern epistemological questions about the worth of "grand narratives" (Lyotard, 1984) and the anthropological preference for "local narratives" (Geertz, 1983). Helms, in fact, acknowledges these possibilities. She cites work by Thomas Parham that speculates that "every person may not enter the developmental cycle at the same place" (Helms, 1990a, p. 32) and that people often recycle through the stages. These possibilities break down the rigidity of the model as a lockstep process of stage progression.

A further limitation of the black racial identity model, as Helms presents it, is that it appears to be centered solely on experiences of race within the United States. Dina Birman (1994) comments that this racial identity model is so contextually specific to African Americans that it has limited generalizability value for other groups. By definition, then, it has to be a limited local narrative rather than a naturally occurring grand narrative that applies to all experiences of race. This does not make it less valid. It only suggests caution in interpreting its validity outside the particular context of its development. If the national context in which we live can alter the experience of racial identity, then logically it would seem likely that other aspects of social context might also produce different developmental paths. Perhaps regional differences within the United States, or rural/urban differences, for example, might produce differential racial identity pathways too.

There is a question mark that hangs over the reification of the construct of race in this model too. The implication that the process of racial identity development follows a natural pattern through a series of stable stages seems to leave unchallenged the idea of race itself as a natural category. We have seen already in Chapter 4, however, that race is not so much a natural category as it is a constructed category. The implicit danger is that the very construct of race, which many who are anxious to undo racism are eager to undermine, is unintentionally solidified by this model.

While there is promising survey research that appears to give some empirical support to the black racial identity model through the RIAS-B instrument, caution has to be used in interpreting this data. Any pencil-and-paper survey must have limited relevance to the situated processes of lived identity development. The model would perhaps better be tested by the analysis of what people actually say about their identity in counseling sessions. Like many psychological studies, the RIAS-B instrument was developed and tested on college students. Since college students cannot represent the full spectrum of experience across all social classes and in all age groups, what can be interpreted from this instrument is limited. Moreover, research that allocates responses to categories along a scale does not in itself prove that over time people move along the same scale. Helms herself allows that the RIAS-B survey is only as good as the theoretical assumptions that are built into it (Helms, 1990a, p. 36) and admits that some built-in assumptions are not tested in the empirical data. For example, two such assumptions are that racial identity is relatively stable and that people move in only one direction along the scale.

Helms (1990a) notes that the reliability measures for racial identity are moderate, rather than outstandingly strong, and suggests that they are comparable with other personality measures (p. 44). This leaves us in a position of choice. Do we accept these measurements of racial identity theory as reliable and trustworthy measures of a naturally occurring phenomenon? Or do we continue to hold doubts about racial identity theory along with all the other measures of personality as well? Such questions cannot always be resolved on empirical grounds. Convention suggests that we should just accept what is so commonly accepted in psychological literature with regard to personality. But the social constructionist argument is that such acceptance is not automatically warranted. The question of essentialism that we raised earlier in this book needs to be addressed here. Essentialist accounts of personality are by their nature reductionist. They reduce the complexity out of life and represent it in a one-size-fits-all approach. One size will certainly fit some people. But the danger is that others will be squeezed uncomfortably into it.

Therefore, we need to ask whether the black racial identity model accounts for all the complexities in people's experience or whether it channels all these complexities into too narrow a channel. We do not doubt that for many people it speaks to their experience. But what about those whose experience of race is more multiply faceted? What about those whose identity is hybrid? What about those referred to as biracial? Is it always necessary for them to adopt one racial identity as their psychological home? What about encounters between blacks and Latinos? Or between Latinos and whites? What effect do they have? We acknowledge that the social world and the requirements of governing bodies of various kinds require such forced choices. But should psychological models not be more open to multiple dimensions of experience than this model at present is, rather than just reproducing the choices required by the authorities? We shall not attempt to answer these questions in any final way. That is for you, the reader, to decide for yourself. Our task here has been to present the model in good faith and also to raise some possible questions about it.

White Racial Identity Development

The idea of white racial identity development (Helms, 1990a is founded on the back of black racial identity development. It asks the question, "What is the converse experience of white persons to the black experience of personality development in relation to race?" The description of a white racial identity development model highlights the idea that the construction of race does not serve just an organizing function for the psychological experience of people of color. It impacts white people as well, shaping their assumptions, governing their interactions with each other and with blacks, and setting up often unconscious experiences of privilege (Robinson, 2005). The goal of white racial identity development is to bring much of what remains as unconscious privilege to the light of day. A healthy white identity is defined as a nonracist identity. It entails a view of self that is not founded on a belief in the superiority of whiteness over blackness. Helms suggest that there are two parallel processes involved in the development of such an identity: the abandonment of racism and the positive development of a nonracist white identity.

An assumption that is built into this theory is that racism expressed by white people on the personal level is first of all injurious to those black people who are on the receiving end of it but second that it is also harmful to the perpetrators of racism. Those who express racism may benefit from its privileges, but they also suffer from a twisted and distorted experience of life. They may perform psychological contortions within themselves to deny the existence of race or racism; they may develop overly rigid personality styles; or they may suffer from underlying guilt and shame, even self-hate, as the price to be paid for maintaining a racist identity (Helms, 1990a).

White racial identity development begins with the acknowledgment and understanding of the sense of entitlement that whites have internalized as a result of living in an America in which they are the numerical majority and are in positions of socioeconomic and political dominance. This sense of entitlement is founded on an assumption of racial superiority, whether this is consciously articulated by an individual or not. This assumption is a function of the history of colonization and slavery and is built into many institutional and cultural practices. Helms (1990a) argues that in America the primary "outgroup" whites can look to in relationship to a belief in their innate superiority over blacks is African American (p. 50). This may be true in many contexts, but it may also be questioned in communities like California, where the Latino population may serve as an equivalent outgroup, or in Hawaii, where Native Hawaiians may serve this function. White racial identity development involves arriving at an understanding that goes beyond not even seeing oneself as white. Racism, as Helms argues, is not just a preserve of hard-core racial supremacists. It exists in the privileged position, not available to blacks, of being able to choose whether or not to "attend to or ignore one's own Whiteness" (p. 50). Helms also acknowledges that there do exist some white people who have not developed an identity based on racist assumptions. Such people do exhibit consciousness of being white in a society that privileges white people and they actively disavow racist assumptions. White racial identity development theory details a model for movement toward this state of psychological consciousness.

Stages of White Racial Identity Development

Helms (1990a) proposes a two-phase model of white racial identity development in which the first phase concentrates on "the abandonment of racism" (p. 55) and the second phase concentrates on "defining a positive White identity" (p. 55). Each phase is then broken down into three stages. Phase 1 involves movement in a linear direction from *contact* to *disintegration* to *reintegration*. Phase 2 involves movement from *pseudo-independence* to *immersion/emersion* to *autonomy*. We shall examine each stage in turn.

Contact

The contact stage is said to begin when a white person first encounters the existence of black people. This stage is characterized by naïveté about issues of race born of limited interaction. A person in this stage may be curious about black experience but largely unaware of his own position of privilege and of differences in the ways in which whites and blacks are treated in the United States. Unconscious racism may be present on a personal level, and blacks may be evaluated according to white criteria. Black people may be judged against stereotypical criteria absorbed from white culture, such that a person might be heard to say something like, "You don't act like a black person" (Helms, 1990a, p. 57). Persons in the contact stage may also assert that they don't even see people in terms of race and feel quite confident in their own viewpoint, although perhaps a little cautious and fearful of black people in general. The contact stage ends when the person is exposed to enough instances of racism, or stories of it from black acquaintances, or criticism from other whites about his interactions with blacks, that his comfortable assumptions are disturbed. This disturbance signals entry into the disintegration stage.

Disintegration

The disintegration stage entails the conscious recognition of a moral dilemma with regard to racism. The person may hold to ideal beliefs about democracy and freedom and compassion and justice and the dignity of all people and be confronted at the same time with information that these ideals do not exist in the world as she had supposed. The person is thrust into a period of questioning what she has been brought up to believe. Her view of race no longer fits what she is encountering. Helms (1990a) connects this experience with Carl Rogers's description of the experience of "incongruence" and with Leon Festinger's account of "cognitive dissonance" (p. 59). Various strategies may be used to reduce the cognitive dissonance, with the most likely outcome being a conscious assertion of one's white identity and a tendency to explicitly speak aloud the assumption of white cultural superiority. But this expression is also accompanied by a deep sense of guilt. It heralds the move to the next stage: reintegration.

Reintegration

The reintegration stage involves a reintegration into dominant white culture and an assertion of white superiority. Black people's negative life circumstances are justified in terms of their inferior moral or intellectual qualities, and negative stereotypes are reasserted. Persons in this stage may remove themselves from contact with black people and speak honestly and frankly only with other whites. Helms suggests that it is fairly easy for white people to become fixed at this stage and to stay there. This is a position of racism that receives enough support from the surrounding world to be sustained and not challenged. However, individuals may also from time to time receive challenges, insightful encounters with black people, or jarring events that push them out of the essentially racist position of the reintegration stage.

Pseudo-Independence

The pseudo-independence stage is the first stage in which redefinition of a positive white identity begins to take place. It is marked by a questioning of the previously assumed superiority of whites and inferiority of blacks. This questioning is largely intellectual, and the person may still unwittingly perpetuate a belief in white superiority in his behavior. A person in this stage may seek out the company of black people and may try to help black people behave more like whites. But he may encounter suspicion from both blacks and whites as a result: from whites for violating a norm and from blacks for making such an effort to help black people change rather than to help bring about change among whites. This stage is marked by a feeling of discomfort and of being on the margins with regard to race issues. This discomfort eventually gives way to a quest for more positive aspects of a white identity that are free from racism. This quest marks the emergence into the next stage.

Immersion/Emersion

In this stage, people often really begin to search for identity in relation to race. They will likely ask questions such as, "Who am I racially?" "Who do I want to be?" and "Who are you really?" (Helms, 1990a, p. 62). This is the stage where people join consciousness-raising groups, read books, and seek out information. Rather than seeking to change black people, they start to focus on changing white people. Inside themselves, they go through a cognitive restructuring process, experiencing perhaps some kind of catharsis or rebirth. This is often accompanied by a feeling of euphoria.

Autonomy

The final stage in the process of the development of a white identity involves nurturing the understanding of whiteness within and applying it to life situations without. The person no longer feels a sense of threat with regard to issues of race. Neither does she hold on to stereotypical assumptions of people of other races. She actively opposes forms of personal and institutional oppression and avoids thinking idealistically about either blacks or whites. A person in this stage is always open to new information and responds to it without passing it through the lens of racist assumptions.

Strengths of the White Racial Identity Model

Once again, the value of such a model is that it does recognize that people go through processes of development. It avoids typecasting people on the basis of a singular expression of thinking or behavior. We can hold out for the best possibility in white people as a result of seeing them as in a process of development, rather than writing them off as inevitably racist on the basis of what they say or do. This model therefore contains an implicit respect for whites as worthy of perhaps more than they are currently able to demonstrate. They can be regarded from the perspective that one day they may reach the stage of autonomy, reject racism, and achieve a healthy and realistic view of racial issues. There is, therefore, an implicit sense of hopefulness in this model. It suggests that engaging with people, if they will allow it, is always worth it in the hope that some form of educational interaction may be possible and that development can ensue. In this sense, this model counter-acts to some extent the totalizing or essentializing of individuals.

The white racial identity model also has the value of recognizing multiple positions from which white people might respond to issues of race. It posits a process of linear development toward a more mature position and argues for a range of stopping points along the way. From a social constructionist perspective, we always welcome the recognition of multiplicity in various forms, although we would not be so committed to such a linear account of developmental progression. What's more, the model is also a relational model of development. Development does not just unfold from within the individual. It is produced through interaction. At significant points in the development of a healthy white identity, the individual is propelled forward by significant interactions with blacks or other whites that are salient enough that they cannot be ignored and therefore force a process of cognitive restructuring.

Another positive value of this model lies in its mirroring of the black identity model. Taken together, these two models postulate a vision of healthy relationships between blacks and whites who are willing to work through these stages of development. There is something of an implicit view of community involved—a community of people who are aware of the salience of race in their own experience, who are committed to working against racism, who are sensitive to expressions of racism both in personal interactions and in cultural and institutional formations, who are realistic in their assessments of the effects of racism, who are able to listen to each other without the interference of stereotypical responses, and who are not defensive with each other. In short, a vision of healthy racial identity holds out a promise of healthy race relations in a community.

Problematic Aspects of the White Racial Identity Model

The concentration on race in the development of racial identity models is both a strength and a limitation. This model's strength lies in its intense focus on the psychological correlates of power relations, such that the roles of oppressor and oppressed around the issue of the black/white divide are thrown into sharp relief. One has to wonder, though, whether growth in an identity that eschews racist stereotypes is also accompanied by, or aided in its development by, other aspects of diversity consciousness. Not all oppression is constructed around race. Whenever we consider oppressor and oppressed binaries occurring around identity, our attention can be drawn to gender, sexual orientation, class, disability, and religious oppression as well as racial oppression. Anti-Semitic prejudice, for example, does not cross the black/white color line. In the black racial identity model, Helms (1994) rejects ethnicity as a euphemism, but in many instances those who assume Anglo superiority deem it a sufficient basis for actions of exclusion and prejudice.

In Chapter 4, we discussed the racist notion of a hierarchy of races that places people of African ancestry on the bottom rung. But oppression is still oppression, and no matter what rung a person of color is placed on by the discourse of race or ethnicity, the experience is still painful.

Another concern we have about this model is that it is still a little too monolithic and static in its interpretation of oppression. It does move a little away from a view of oppression in which the roles of oppressor and oppressed are conferred automatically on the basis of group membership. But it is still structurally based. As we argued in Chapter 8, we believe that oppression and power relations are matters of practice rather than simply manifestations of structural arrangements. We therefore believe that racism is sustained because it is reproduced in practice on a daily basis. And it is also contradicted and resisted in practice on a daily basis. The model does provide recognition of the way that people move toward attitudes and cognitive structures that assist in the contradiction of racism. But we are doubtful of whether individuals stay in stable positions in relation to these practices. We would expect that contextual demands play a larger part than the model allows in the reproduction of racism and that the model exaggerates the influence of a linear internal identity development. We believe that in many aspects of life, people are more fluid, more inconsistent, more contradictory, even more hypocritical, than psychology has often assumed (D'Augelli, 1994; Gergen, 1991). Moreover, we believe that racism, ethnocentrism, and oppressive practices are not just the preserve of white people. They can be acquired by people of all races and ethnicities. To say this is not to deny the enormous cultural and structural privileges that have been systematically created on the back of white expressions of racism. In fact, we believe this perspective strengthens that understanding, because it sets it in a more realistic and nuanced view of the world and accounts more powerfully for apparent contradictions.

Any stage theory is always a reason for concern, too. While it appears attractive in the abstract, and may have modest empirical support, as Helms outlines (empirical data to support the white racial identity model are more flimsy than for the black racial identity model; see also Ponterotto & Pedersen, 1993), questions have to be raised on philosophical grounds. There is an essentialist assumption built in, and the progression of persons from one stage to the next is always hard to trace. Demonstration of this progression always involves a large degree of interpretation, and such interpretation is always open to contest. Other models of development that include stage theories (think of Jean Piaget's model of cognitive development, Lawrence Kohlberg's theory of moral development, and Elisabeth Kübler-Ross's theory of progress through grief) have all been subject to critique and dispute. They are still around, but there are many holes in them. The racial identity development model is much newer, but there is no reason to believe that it too will not attract its share of criticism.

It is not actually necessary, in our view, to propose a series of lockstep stages in order to sustain an idea of development and change. The model is a little too clean and tidy, while life as it is lived is often much more messy. Stage models always risk excluding some people's experience while they affirm others'. An alternative approach is to regard processes of change as multiply dimensioned and to map the variations with regard to the contextual features of relations and interactions that produce them. A focus on interactions might in the end be more productive for counselors than a focus on the diagnosis of individual personality features. After all, relationships are the domain that counselors know best.

Acculturation

We saw in Chapter 10 how one of the features of globalization is a dramatic increase in the numbers of people migrating from one country to another. Here we want to explore the developmental processes that people who migrate go through. Because migration from one cultural context to another requires some degree of adjustment to the new cultural context, we can speak of this move in terms of cultural identity development. Since identity, particularly from a social constructionist perspective, is rooted in relations with others who share similar cultural knowledges and practices, the experience of migration must bring with it demands for some kind of identity transition. New identities form as a person lives in relation to a new group of others who have cultural knowledges and practices different from those of the migrant's culture of origin.

The word used to refer to the process of transition is *acculturation*. This concept grew out of anthropology and was first used to refer to the shifts that groups or populations of immigrants negotiate in a new context. But it has also been developed in a psychological discourse to refer to the internal identity changes that individual members of such populations negotiate in their own personal journey of migration. The term *acculturation* needs to be distinguished from the concept of *enculturation*, which is reserved for children who are born into a culture and are growing into an internalized identity produced by that cultural context. Acculturation presumes that one has already been enculturated elsewhere and now needs to adjust to a new cultural context. So acculturation is about adjustment to something new. It is a process of change brought about by contact with a different group.

Under the influence of colonialist discourse, and later of the melting pot ideology, the overriding assumption was always that immigrants "naturally" had to do all of the adjustment work. They had to accommodate to their new context and work to produce their identities in ways governed by the idea of "assimilation." This governing idea created a pressure on immigrants to give up their unique cultural characteristics and to adopt new cultural practices drawn from the majority culture. Until the 1970s, this idea remained largely unchallenged in the discourse of psychology.

As the multicultural discourse has developed, the emphasis has shifted away from a unidirectional process of assimilation. Some recent work has suggested that immigration requires mutual processes of accommodation for the immigrant and for the host culture, rather than requiring all of the adjustments to be made by the immigrants (Birman, 1994). For immigrants, the idea has developed that it is psychologically preferable to maintain allegiance to one's culture of origin while at the same time developing participation in the new host culture. Cultural identity is no longer required to remain singular, and forced choices between the old and the new are avoided. Dina Birman (1994) argues that cultural identity development for immigrants involves two parallel processes of adjustment, one in relation to the old culture and one in relation to the new cultural context. She suggests that it is theoretically possible to be highly acculturated to either, both, or neither culture. She also assembles four possible styles of handling the relations between these cultural influences: *assimilation, separation, marginalization,* and *biculturalism-integration.* She prefers these descriptions of acculturative styles rather than notions of stages and notes that people can vacillate from one to another of these styles. Some people will choose different styles in different contexts. Others will blend them together in unique forms. Still others will try on each style at different times in a process of exploration.

Acculturation always involves a relation of power. The influence of the dominant culture cannot be resisted by immigrants and is to some degree forced onto them. This domination often produces psychological effects within immigrants, such that the achievement of identity change may be "difficult, reactive and conflictual" (Berry, 1980, p. 10). John Berry argues for a straightforward three-phase course to acculturation. The three phases are *contact, conflict,* and *adaptation.* The first and third phases are inevitable, while the shape and intensity of the second phase depends on the degree of resistance shown by immigrants. The adaptation phase can take different forms. It may feature adjustments that decrease the level of conflict experienced, reactions of retaliation against the dominant culture, or withdrawal into protected contexts that reduce exposure to the conflict.

Berry (1980) also brings together some of the psychological effects of the process of acculturation under the heading of "acculturative stress" (p. 21). This term refers to identity developments that are "mildly pathological and disruptive to the individual and his group" (p. 21), such as deviant behavior and psychosomatic symptoms. Although Berry suggests that these psychological effects are not inevitable, they do reflect a negative assumption of individual pathology that can beset immigrants. It is almost as if immigration produces acculturation as a disease to be suffered through rather than as a learning process to be embraced. Counselors who adopt such a perspective might be tempted to look out for pathological symptoms rather than to be more respectful of the acculturative learning struggles that an immigrant is engaging with. The weight of the problem is also laid on the immigrant, to whom a pathology is imputed, rather than on the cultural conditions in which he is engaging.

Subsequent writing about acculturation has moved away from the deficit orientation and adopted a more positive and respectful representation of the process of education and development that individuals go through (Pedersen, 1995). Paul Pedersen, for example, adopts the racier term "culture shock" to replace the term "acculturative stress." Drawing on previous work by others, Pedersen outlines a five-stage model of psychological progress through culture shock. In this model, the negatively contoured deficit orientation is replaced by a U-curve in which the individual first goes through a process of disintegration and then moves toward a more constructive growth.

The Honeymoon Stage

The first stage is that of initial contact, or the "honeymoon stage" where the newly arrived immigrant is captured by the curiosity and excitement of her new cultural context. The person's identity is still rooted in the home culture, but she is experiencing the new culture like a tourist.

The Disintegration Stage

This second stage involves the disintegration of what is familiar. Cultural cues that were once strong are not as available in the new cultural context. Meanwhile, the individual is to some degree overwhelmed in the face of requirements of the new environment. Difficulties encountered in the new cultural context often produce an undermining effect on personal identity. Individuals feel personally inadequate with regard to what they don't know and are likely to reach conclusions that feature self-blame in situations where they don't know how to conduct themselves.

The Reintegration Stage

In this third stage, the individual has begun to integrate aspects of the new culture and to get used to them. However, rather than a sense of personal inadequacy, this reintegration is often accompanied by anger and resentment toward the host culture for having caused so many difficulties. Pedersen comments that "persons in this stage of culture shock are often difficult to help" (p. 3). If counselors bear this in mind, they are less likely to become defensive in the face of the person's resentment.

The Autonomy Stage

The fourth stage is marked by an increased ability to make discerning distinctions. The immigrant can now see the good and the bad in both the old culture and the new one. The anger is replaced by a more balanced view and an ability to interpret both cultural contexts in their own terms.

The Interdependence Stage

The fifth stage involves the development of a fuller bicultural identity. It is assumed to be the ideal target stage for immigrants. Those who reach this stage are able to be relatively fluent and comfortable in both the old and the new culture.

Strengths and Limitations of the Acculturation Model

For counselors, there are definite advantages to understanding people as working through a progression of cultural identity development in the context of acculturation. From such models, counselors are afforded the possibility of helping people to envisage where they are heading and to take steps in a positive direction. Models such as this one allow counselors to support their clients in the daily negotiations of intercultural life. Such support can become more than general support for what is being experienced and can become more intentional and purposeful support as a result of the counselor's having in mind a concept of developmental trajectory.

This model also allows and encourages counselors to avoid assuming that any one response that an immigrant client makes is definitional of his individual personality or is emblematic of the experience of all immigrants. The model encourages counselors to recognize multiple positions with regard to the acculturation process and validates differences in position. When we meet in counseling individuals whose responses seem confused and contradictory, we may be encouraged by such a model to view them as being in a process of development rather than as pathological by way of their personality.

There are some drawbacks to this model of acculturation, too, especially if it is treated as a universal model to be applied to all immigrants. Experiences are quite possibly widely variable among different immigrant groups. International politics play a role here. Muslim immigrants may be very conscious of how they are perceived in the United States in ways that are not an issue for immigrants from Christian Europe. Experiences also vary according to the educational and social class background of the immigrant and according to the occupational slot she is offered in the host country. Certain occupations offer the kinds of legitimacy and status that are not available to an undocumented farm laborer. And age also makes a difference. The grandmother who comes to the United States from Mexico in her 70s and does not get much chance to learn or practice speaking English may well go through a very different acculturation experience from that of her grandchildren, who are attending school. Immigrants from English-speaking countries who come to the United States may fare very differently from those whose first language is not English. One-size-fits-all models of acculturation may not be adequate for describing the range of different experiences immigrants go through. To be fair, though, Pederson's (1995) model is applied in his book primarily to American college students living temporarily in other cultural contexts. But the point still stands with regard to acculturation models in general.

Acculturation models, like all pieces of knowledge, should also be read as cultural products themselves. Dina Birman (1994) makes an important and pertinent comment: "Acculturation theories are themselves a function of the cultural context in which they were created" (p. 267). Therefore, we should ask about this model, as we should any other model, out of which cultural context does it emerge? Whose perspective does it represent and whose interest does it serve? For example, the representation of "autonomy" as a staging post on the road to "interdependence" is an interesting choice. These might be rendered the other way around in some people's preferences or within some cultural traditions.

Like many models of acculturation, this one appears to be neutral with regard to the host culture. No distinction is made with regard to whether the host culture is welcoming or hostile, for example. We would postulate that the relational context into which immigrants are either invited or thrust plays a significant role in producing the particularities of the psychological experience of acculturation. This relational context can be expected to produce a power relation in which immigrants are differentially legitimated for their cultural expressions. But such power relations are absent from most models. Instead, immigrants are usually treated as individuals without regard for the politics of the context, which serves as the backdrop against which options are possible for the individual. This individualistic assumption may itself be assumed to emerge out of the dominance of a Western tradition of thought. The question that needs to be asked of any model of acculturation is, "Out of whose world of psychological experience does the model itself emerge?"

For these reasons, we think it is best to be cautious about reading such models onto the psychological experience of immigrants. They may sometime be helpful. But they also may have limits that don't extend far enough to include the daily experience of many immigrants.

Development of a Lesbian, Gay, Bisexual, or Transgender Identity

In the final section of this chapter, we want to represent another model of identity development that comes from the field of lesbian, gay, bisexual, and transgender (LGBT) studies. There are many such models of identity development in the literature on homosexuality, not all of which we have the space to represent here (e.g., Coleman, 1982; Falco, 1991; Fox, 1995; Morales, 1989; Sophie, 1985–1986; Van Wormer, Wells, & Boes, 2000).

Frequently cited early examples are the stage theories for the development of a homosexual identity, such as those proposed by Vivienne Cass (1979) and Richard Troiden (1988, 1989). Cass postulated a six-stage model that was principally about the move from a heterosexual identity to a homosexual one. His model moves from an initial stage of *identity confusion* (where the person first perceives thoughts and feelings of same-sex attraction) to *identity comparison* (where the individual becomes aware of and starts to deal with social stigma) to *identity tolerance* (where the individual first seeks out other homosexuals) to *identity acceptance* (where the individual develops the recognition of positive connotations of homosexuality) to *identity pride* (where the individual minimizes contact with heterosexual peers and focuses strongly on being homosexual) and finally to *identity synthesis* (where the individual balances the role of sexual orientation with other aspects of identity and also becomes more balanced in relationships with others so that relationships with both homosexual and heterosexual people are included).

Other approaches to gay and lesbian identity development have built on this same kind of stage theory, with all the advantages and drawbacks that models of stages bring with them. There have been some differences in where the stages are delineated and how they are described, but the patterns have been similar. An attractive model in terms of its simplicity is Ruth Fassinger's (1998) model, which moves from *awareness* to *exploration* to *deepening commitment* and finally to *internalization/ synthesis.* But all of these stage theory models have the drawback of being essentialist in character and of characterizing some people's experience as universal. They also tend to focus on the abstract individual while taking little account of the processes of social construction going on around the individual. By contrast, we want to select out a model that makes an effort to avoid simple essentialism and to work within a social constructionist framework that fits with the themes we are endeavoring to promote in this book. We shall explain this model in more detail.

Anthony D'Augelli (1994) has articulated a model of sexual orientation development that takes cognizance of social constructionist misgivings about "notions of personal consistency" (p. 312) and focuses on the construction of identity in a context of discursive power relations. It draws on approaches to identity development that regard identity not as something essential or naturally unfolding but as something achieved in the context of social relations. He also suggests that being gay, lesbian, or bisexual requires "living a life of multiple psychological identities" (p. 313). Therefore, we need to develop identity constructs that feature "plasticity" more than stability.

Identity development as an LGBT person requires two processes. The first is about developing a response to the dominant culture in which LGBT persons live, which is largely heterosexual. The dominant discourse of this cultural world lays down a set of personal, relational, and social norms to which adherence is demanded. To establish a position of difference as an LGBT person, therefore, means performing a conscious distancing from some of the assumptions of the mainstream heterosexual culture. The second process is about developing a positive identity with regard to sexual orientation as an LGBT person.

From the 19th century until recent times, LGBT identity stories have been officially regarded as abnormal. It was as late as 1987 that the *Diagnostic and Statistical Manual of Mental Disorders* (American Psychiatric Association) removed "ego dystonic homosexuality" from its list of categories of mental disorder. There are still many who criticize LGBT identity as unnatural or disordered. Even within the models of human development that are still current in the psychological academy, development of an LGBT sexual orientation does not fit. Because of the sociopolitical contests that are still taking place over the legitimacy of LGBT identities, it is impossible for a person to develop such an identity without engaging with the politics of identity. One must actively resist and reject some aspects of what is considered "normal," including well-known assumptions of sexual identity development, to develop a positive view of oneself. Until recently (and this is still true in many jurisdictions around the world), an LGBT person had to risk legal or social penalties in this process. As a result, public identity statements have often been guarded. Identity development has therefore often taken place in private contexts. This is an option that has not been available to blacks, for example. Their identity development in the face of the definition of white as normal has always been publicly visible.

The achievement of identity as an LGBT person has necessarily involved the overcoming of barriers put in place by the dominant sociopolitical authorities. It is, therefore, achieved in a spirit of resistance and is frequently embodied in specific acts of resistance. Psychologically, such resistance often involves an internal struggle against internalized myths about LGBT people that often run wild in the dominant heterosexual culture. This process is akin to the struggles that are referenced in the racial identity models with regard to black people's having to deal with a form of internalized self-hate as a result of the general cultural negative images of blacks. Some of these myths about LGBT people are overt and easily challenged. Others are subtle and more covert and are harder to resist, because they lie hidden as cultural assumptions that we are scarcely aware of because they are swallowed along with other assumptions about sexuality and relationships. Examples of myths that have internalized components include the assumption that people become gay as a result of dysfunctional family upbringing, the notion that LGBT people are not capable of forming long-lasting partnerships, the prejudiced view that LGBT people should not be engaged in child raising, and the assumption that being publicly LGBT rules out the taking up of positions of power and authority in the community.

D'Augelli sets his model of identity development within a general theoretical context of life span developmental theory. Life span approaches to development avoid an exclusive focus on childhood and adolescence in a way that assumes that culturally dominant patterns of adulthood are to be regarded as normative. Therefore, life span approaches to development avoid setting up mature adult identities as endpoints for development. These approaches also emphasize that development is a lifelong process and that models of identity development should be open ended. Within this context, D'Augelli outlines some "steps" toward a model of LGBT identity development. His model eschews the idea of simple linear stages and instead talks of processes that individuals might be expected to negotiate. There is, nevertheless, a sense of progression along a continuum inherent in the relation between these processes, but there is no suggestion that one never goes back once one has moved forward along the continuum, or that each of the processes are exclusive of others. All of these processes are accommodated within cultural and sociopolitical contexts that take on specific local forms, which are defining in important ways. D'Augelli demonstrates, for example, how being LGBT in North America is currently very different from how it was in the 1980s or 1960s.

Exiting Heterosexual Identity

The first process D'Augelli describes involves developing an understanding of one's own attractions. It has to be achieved in the face of prevalent assumptions of the "normal" heterosexual development of attractions. It proceeds through the move from keeping such attractions private to acknowledging them to others. "Coming out," says D'Augelli, begins with the first person one tells that one's attractions are different from the heterosexual norm. But coming out is not just a one-time event. It is repeated many times and has the internal effect of developing identity strength as it is repeated. D'Augelli (1994) calls it a "lifelong process" (p. 326) of self-assertion.

Developing a LGBT Identity Status

The second process is the development of a socioaffectional stability. It involves the claiming of an LGBT identity within oneself and coming to terms with it. To do so means confronting the messages about LGBT persons that have been internalized from the surrounding culture. These are encapsulated in the myths referred to above. They will often be accompanied by a negative story of self with regard to one's LGBT affectional orientation that must be consciously challenged or deconstructed in order for the individual to develop a positive self-evaluation. D'Augelli characterizes this process as learning how to be, for example, gay, and to feel positive about it.

Developing a LGBT Social Identity

A third identity development process involves the creation of a set of relationships in which one's personal orientation is known and accepted. D'Augelli carefully distinguishes between the kind of acceptance that amounts to a limited, resigned tolerance and the kind of acceptance that is positively affirmative and provides social support for identity development. It is the latter that needs to be sought out and built by the person who is developing a LGBT social identity. The social constructionist aspect of D'Augelli's model is very evident in his description of this process. From a constructionist perspective, an identity is never solely owned by the individual but is constructed through its performance in a social context. Nor does an identity just unfold naturally from within. It is to some degree at least an outside-in process of development. (We can argue endlessly and probably pointlessly about the proportions of outside-in vs. inside-out influences.) The social interactions in which an identity is affirmed serve a constitutive function in relation to internalized psychological development. In the process, a person develops an internalized counter story to the previously internalized negative story of identity constituted by the dominant discourse. The interactions that are required involve the members of a person's social network, who, through their acknowledgments to others, participate in and indeed widen the coming out process. D'Augelli also stresses that this process takes time. It is not like a momentary cognitive shift in which a person suddenly "gets it." Time needs to be taken to build a network of relations, to learn about other people's reactions to one's affectional orientation, and to learn to distinguish more supportive from less supportive responses.

Becoming a LGBT Offspring

The fourth developmental process involves family relations. One's family of origin must play a significant role in any identity development, and therefore it makes sense to give special attention to what happens to an LGBT identity in the context of family relationships. There is a wide degree of variation in family responses to an individual's coming out as an LGBT person. Responses range from angry rejection and the cutting off of all contact to warm acceptance. There is therefore likely to be wide variation in how early this process begins and in the degree to which it can be fully achieved. Some dare not risk coming out to family members until their own sense of LGBT identity has moved to a position of sufficient positive strength. Others have a greater degree of trust in family members and greater reason to expect to experience such trust in return. D'Augelli describes this process as one of initial disclosure, followed by the reestablishment of the state of relationships with family members along the lines that they were before the disclosure. The difference is that the LGBT person's affectional orientation is now acknowledged and affirmed as part of the relationship. Therefore, this is often a process of sudden disruption followed by gradual reintegration. The reintegration phase may take widely varying amounts of time. For some families, this means years. During the worst times of the AIDS epidemic among gay men in North America, the reintegration phase had often not been worked through before the death of the gay man, leaving the gay community to take on surrogate family status for the dying man. D'Augelli indicates that families often seek to "contain" the "deviance from the norm" as much as possible, perhaps not coming out themselves to other friends and relatives as parents of, say, a gay son. He therefore notes that the initiation of the family's own coming out process often falls to the LGBT person.

Developing a LBGT Intimacy Status

The fifth identity development process involves the development of intimate relationships that are sustaining and fulfilling on the basis of one's LGBT identity. Often LGBT persons form long-lasting partnerships, and in some parts of the world there have been recent legislative moves to provide acknowledgment of these partnerships as either legitimate marriages or civil unions. In the United States, there has been widespread contention over this issue in recent years, and there will no doubt be further developments in this debate between the time of our writing and when this book is printed. At the moment, some states allow civil unions, some allow marriages, and the majority allow neither. LGBT persons, understandably, are not sitting and waiting for the law to legitimate their relationships before getting on with the identity development process D'Augelli refers to. But the legal argument points to the difficulty they encounter, because all the social norms for relationship are based on heterosexual couples. Most of us internalize such norms from fairy tales, literature, and Hollywood movies as the basis for what used to be called courting. There are widespread sociocultural apparatuses for heterosexual bonding that are readily available for heterosexual persons to perform. These apparatuses are largely closed off to LGBT persons. Think, for example, of school dances and prom events and consider what would happen if an LGBT person wanted to bring along a same-sex partner as a date. According to D'Augelli, the result of the lack of cultural scripts for the development of intimacy in LGBT relationships has two effects. On the one hand, it can lead to painful experiences of uncertainty and experimentation that have negative identity effects. On the other hand, the lack of fixed norms leads to a degree of freedom that almost forces people in the LGBT culture to create new forms of normality. Such new norms are often personal, couple specific, or community specific. D'Augelli regards this freedom as a potentially positive context for the development of an intimacy status as an aspect of identity.

Entering a LBGT Community

The final process that D'Augelli outlines is more related to the public world of social and political action. He postulates an identity development that takes place in individuals when they make a commitment to involvement in such action. This kind of commitment by no means appeals to all LGBT people. Many are interested only in getting on peacefully with their own lives. Their affectional orientation remains largely in the private domain. D'Augelli does not criticize those who choose this path. He does, however, note that for those who do make the commitment to take a public stand, the inequities of heterosexual domination come more sharply into focus. He suggests that those who don't make this move may not benefit from the sharper focus that results. Political engagement, he suggests, has several effects on the individual that prompt identity development. One is the fuller awareness of the structuring influences of heterosexism and homophobia. Fuller awareness of these structuring effects leads to the noticing of opportunities to counter them. Another effect is more internal. People have more opportunity through political engagement to revisit the history of their own experiences of oppression and pain. Each of these opportunities provides another occasion for the deconstruction of what was internalized and the concomitant development of a more positive narrative of personal identity.

Strengths and Limitations of D'Augelli's Model of LGBT Identity Development

A strength of D'Augelli's model is its avoidance of essentialist assumptions about the development of an LGBT identity as a naturally occurring phenomenon. Instead, he presents a model of development as a social construction against a backdrop of particular historical and cultural developments. More precisely, he details the process of construction in a series of particular sets of interactions. He acknowledges the role played by dominant discourse and allows for a shifting context of development as this dominant discourse shifts as a result of sociopolitical action. This model is therefore admirably responsive to discourse and social context.

Like the racial identity model, D'Augelli's model is inclusive of individual differences in response to oppressive features of the social context. Individuals are constructed as always in a process of development in one sphere of interaction or another, and those engaged in each of the processes of development are recognized as in a process of development. There is still an implicit continuum of development in this model, but it is less tied to particular stages. Neither are the processes described made too rigid or postulated to be exclusive of other processes. One can engage in any of these processes at any time. The model nevertheless allows for movement toward a place of greater psychological strength in oneself and in one's consciousness of the features of the dominant discourse in the surrounding culture. The model posits a strong element of political consciousness as a conscious goal of development and argues that this consciousness aids in the individual's psychological development.

There are also some limitations of this model. Like most other theories of LGBT identity development, the development of this theory has been largely based on the life of college students in the 18 to 25 age range. Apart from the fact that this is a narrow age band, a question mark hangs over the extent to which college students represent the identity experiences of others who never attend college. Typical of many of the models built around the identity development of this age group, this model is built on the centrality of the coming out process. One might ask questions about what it omits for those who came out long ago and for whom the issues attended to in this model are well past. And yet such individuals are still engaged in ongoing identity development.

Another gap in this model is that it has not developed the equivalent of the white identity model that Helms outlined for racial identity. Presumably, friends and family members of LGBT persons also go through a process of development in response to the process of coming out. This process also has the potential of being mapped. D'Augelli suggests that this is so, but his model does not develop far in this direction. There is literature on this topic, however. For example, James Croteau, Julianne Lark, Melissa Lidderdale, and Barry Chung (2005), in a book specially aimed at counselors, include examples of the development of "allies" of LGBT persons.

Another limitation of the model is the extent to which the experience of particular groups of gay men have been generalized to refer to others. There is perhaps an elision of differences in the experiences of gay men and lesbian women. D'Augelli certainly acknowledges such differences in the process of identity construction. For example, he notes the role played by the women's movement in providing support for lesbian women. But the developmental model still brings these experiences together. There is therefore a concern, as there is with many of the available models, that the focus is too strongly directed toward the experience of gay men and less toward the experience of lesbian women, or bisexual or transgender persons. It is arguable that the politics of gender will impact the identity development of, for example, lesbian women and gay men, in different ways. Indeed, there is evidence that the coming out process is qualitatively different for lesbian women relative to gay men: it is described as less abrupt, less likely to be associated with psychiatric symptoms, more fluid, and more ambiguous (Gonsiorek & Rudolph, 1991).

There are also questions that may be raised concerning the intersection of sexual orientation with race, ethnicity, and social class. Models of gay identity development have tended to approach the topic from the perspective of white, middle class persons. It is hard to see this model as different.

Finally, there are newer developments in queer theory that raise many questions about these models, including D'Augelli's. These perspectives draw on constructionist and poststructuralist thinking to question the very idea that a stable identity can emerge, even in the way that D'Augelli suggests. Drawing on concepts of multiple identity, they question the simple binary distinctions between gay and straight, for example, and argue that the equation of sexual attraction with a social identity is itself a questionable social construction.

The Coming Out Process: Matt's story

In the following story of identity development, featuring Matt, a young man who is now studying to be a counselor, it is possible to trace the developmental processes that D'Augelli maps. Notice how Matt tells of the important relationship events that catalyze identity shifts. Listen, too, for the effects of background discourses that have been absorbed into his identity and sometimes have to be actively deconstructed. Notice also the significance that Matt attributes to the coming out experience as a developmental milestone.

The entire first 18 years of my life I lived the life I thought all boys lived. I went to school, had a select few friends, was loved by my parents, and had hobbies and goals for my life. It seemed that what would happen in my life was pretty set, because I had never hit any major road bumps. I couldn't see anything going wrong now.

It wasn't until I looked back on my life later that I saw my life was not as ideal as I thought. There was always something a little different in me that I didn't know how to explain. I can trace those feelings all the way back to elementary school.

It wasn't until I got into my first year of college at the age of 18 that I found out what homosexuality was and that there were many people who identified as such. When this new revelation came about, I had to examine my own life, because I knew that deep down my feelings for other people were not the typical ones that most guys would feel toward girls. I recall having some sort of inner feeling for the other boys in class when I was in elementary school, but not knowing that this could be normal, I just kept pushing myself to like girls.

After getting out of high school and starting fresh at college, I thought it was time for me to explore my emotions and where my life should take me. I found out that the college I was attending had a Lesbian, Gay, Bisexual, and Transgender (LGBT) Center. I knew that if I wanted to learn more about my feelings and emotions, that would be the place to go. I fought internally for several weeks before I would even step foot in the building that housed the LGBT Center. The first time I went into the building, my heart and mind were going a mile a minute, so I walked past the room and just peeked in. I was so scared of the unknown that I started second-guessing whether or not my feelings were right and whether or not I should try to figure things out on my own.

It took several attempts before I was approached by someone who worked in the LGBT Center. He asked me if he could help me with anything. I shyly told him no and walked away. I walked around the corner and took some deep breaths, then went back to the room and went in. The people in the room were very friendly and inviting. The individuals in the LGBT Center made me feel at home and knew that I was not "out," as they called it. They answered any questions I had and directed me to their extensive library of books. It was great to finally feel some sort of weight being lifted off my shoulders for the first time and to feel some sort of belonging.

I attended the LGBT Center on a daily basis and made it a second home where I could explore my life and find out who I really was. It was great to meet people who struggled with the same issues in life that I did and could tell me of their experiences. Of course, living what became a double life took its toll on my emotional well-being. I would stay at school all day and not come home until late in the evening, at which time my parents began to question me on a regular basis. They wondered how I was doing in my classes because I never studied or did homework at home. I became more reserved around them and went directly to my room as soon as I got home from school.

I tested the waters of coming out, which means telling someone you're gay, with one of my close friends. I was pleased to find out that she was very accepting, and it actually brought us closer together. It was a great experience. For once, someone close to me knew who I was and was okay with it. I would bring up the thought of coming out to my parents and the fear I had that they would kick me out of the house and that I would have nowhere to live. Of course, my parents never gave me any reason to believe that they would ever do such a thing. Being kicked out of the house and losing my family because of my sexuality was not something that I wanted to happen. I kept my secret inside for as long as I could, but one day the line was crossed.

It was sometime in mid-December that I came home late from school and both my parents were sitting on the couch watching television. My mom told me to sit down because she wanted to talk to me. I reluctantly sat, and she asked me where I had been so late and why I hadn't called. I told her I was at school. She told me that she never saw me studying or doing homework and asked me how my classes were going. I told her that I studied at school and didn't have anything to do when I got home. My mother and I got into an argument about the possibility of my coming home more often at an earlier time so I could spend time with the family. That was when I told her that I had a secret that would crush the family. She immediately went quiet and then began trying to guess what it was that I was talking about. She asked me if I had gotten a girl pregnant. I laughed and told her no. Her second guess was that I was gay. I responded with a rather quick "Yes." The room became extremely quiet. My mom asked me if I was serious and then asked me many other questions, which I tried to answer to the best of my knowledge. My dad, meanwhile, sat quietly on the couch. Right before he went to bed, he said he couldn't believe this and left the room.

The rest of the night my mom and I exchanged words so she could try to understand. It was an extremely emotional evening, and both of us shed more tears than we needed to. I wanted nothing more than to leave the house that evening just to get away for a short while. Because I was crying and emotional, my mom told me that I was not in my right mind and should not be driving. I begged her to just let me go. She made me promise her that I would not leave and would try to get some sleep. I told her I would.

The next morning, my mom told me that my father wanted to talk to me when he got home from work, so I couldn't make any plans. I was scared because my father and I don't really have a very close bond with each other, and expressing feelings is not something my dad and I have ever done with each other. I knew that it would be a very interesting conversation. When my dad got home from work, my mother left the house so that we could talk by ourselves. I did not like that at all. My dad started out by saying that I had hurt my mother really badly the previous night. He didn't understand why I would do something like that to her. I was speechless. This conversation was the one and only time I ever saw my father cry. It hit me harder than anything I can recall. I felt like the lowest person at that moment because I had made my father cry and my mother was crushed. Knowing that I had everything to do with why they were feeling this way, I felt like a horrible son and person. I felt so ungrateful for everything my parents had ever done for me.

The entire experience of coming out to my family made me a stronger person. I am better able to handle touchy subjects now. I have a sense of understanding because I have been there. It was very tough because my family always lived the "normal" life that most think of when they think of a family. They had no experience with dealing with someone they knew who was gay, and for it to be someone in their immediate family didn't make it any easier. My parents raised my siblings with the ideals provided by the rest of society as to how one should live life. That is what made it more difficult when it came time for me to accept my life. Luckily, I had a lot of support along the way.

The experience of coming out to my family was by far the toughest thing I have ever done in my life. Five years later, I would not take back that night for anything, because I was finally free. It may not have been the best coming out experience, but it was not the worst either. My family has come a long way after my coming out experience and I think for the most part have accepted my life. My ability to accept being gay was made possible by the unconditional support I received from friends, other people who identify as gay, and my family's effort to accept the change. The experience of coming out and accepting my life has had a great influence on why I chose the field of counseling.

I wish that during my time of need I could have had a counselor to talk to who could have helped me through one of the toughest times in my life. I know that our society is becoming more accepting of homosexuality, but there are still those individuals who do not accept it. I want to be there for those kids who are struggling with coming out and need someone to talk to about their feelings and emotions. It may help some to realize that it is not a bad thing to be part of the LGBT community and that there are plenty of positive role models out there to look up to.

Many counselors may find themselves working with people who are going through identity development processes such as the one that Matt outlines. In fact, it is not uncommon for LGBT people to seek out the help of counselors in the process of charting an identity course when the dominant culture around them does not provide them with a readable chart. In fact, Laura Brown (1995) cites research suggesting that 78% of lesbian women who responded to a survey had sought help from a therapist. While this figure may not be beyond dispute, it still underlines the importance of developing a model of LGBT development, such as the one that D'Augelli proposes, as a guide for practice.

Concluding Questions

We shall end this chapter by raising some general questions about these identity models from a social constructionist perspective. These questions are not intended to criticize and undermine the models in a destructive way. Rather, they are intended to help us think of how we might use them in a way that opens up more possible readings. The questions we want to pose come from constructionist accounts of the status of knowledge and truth claims.

The first set of questions has to do with the social context out of which these models emerge. How representative can they be? How specific are they to the United States and to the specific configurations of race, ethnicity, and sexual orientation or to the specific immigration procedures in this country? If such specificity exists, how often is it acknowledged or investigated? And what value do these models have both within the United States and outside it? Do the truth claims of these models rest on the assumption that they describe something universal in human psychology? Or can they be appreciated for their local value without losing credibility?

A second set of questions has to do with the age applicability of these models. How extensively can they be applied to different age groups? There appears to be a noticeable emphasis on the identity struggles of youths, particularly college age students, in all of these models. Does this suggest that identity development ceases or diminishes in early adulthood? Or does this have more to do with the ready availability of college students as subjects for psychological studies? Do these models imply an underlying reliance on assumptions about the centrality of identity development for adolescents and young adults, as theorized by Erik Erikson (1950, 1968)? If Erikson's ideas do constitute the general foundation for these models, are they necessary? Are there alternative models of adolescence around? Do Erikson's assumptions of adolescent identity growth through crisis stand up in different cultural circumstances? Or are there implicit cultural assumptions, somewhat hidden from view, that have been imported into these models?

Another set of questions has to do with the historical context out of which these models have developed. Are they specific to a particular set of historical influences? Does their emergence reflect a particular time in history? Do psychological theories of acculturation, for example, rely on a particular set of social conditions and governmental immigration policies? Are they specific to particular waves of immigrants and to the general social attitudes of hospitality or its absence that these immigrants meet? Would the models change if the immigrants came from other countries?

Do the models of racial identity development apply primarily to race relations in the United States in the decades after the civil rights movement? Would they have had any relevance before that? Are there any current historical influences that presage the need for different models?

Have the particular historical conditions in which sexuality is talked about and governed shaped available models of LGBT identity development? Have these conditions changed since the 1980s or 1990s? How are they shaped by the current debate about gay marriage?

The final set of questions has to do with language. We know that over time, the language or discourse with which things are described shifts. Note, for example, the shift from the description "nigrescence" to "black racial identity." Or the shift from "homosexual" to "gay" to "LGBT" (some would add "queer"). How do we account for these shifts? We need to ask questions about the general discourse that serves as the background context in which such models make sense. How relevant is this discourse to the lives that people lead? Are there those for whom these models are less relevant because their lives are shaped by different discourses? Do the particular assumptions of identity in the life of the individual represent universal truth values? Or are there different ways of thinking about identity altogether? What about multiple, hybrid, or contradictory identities? How do they fit within each of these models? What happens to these models in the context of alternative notions of identity?

We might also ask questions about how models begin to act as norms against which people are required to compare themselves. Once they do so, what effects do the models have? What happens to the comparisons when the model does not fit? For example, if coming out experiences for LGBT persons become the norm, are there situations where the norm becomes coercive? This question has recently been raised by Sekneh Hammoud-Beckett (2007) in an article about LGBT persons who are also Muslim. She suggests the alternative metaphor of an LGBT person inviting selected trusted others to "come in" to a person's membership club of life.

We are not posing these questions for the purpose of destruction. Our intent is more to widen the conversation about these identity development models. We suspect that there are places of relevance for each of these models but that their relevance needs to be investigated in order for us to better understand their specific value. The usual reflex in social science research is to investigate models through empirical measures that produce statistically differentiated categories of data, leading to claims for generalization. Each of these models, to varying degrees, has some such empirical support. We are not disputing the value of these empirical studies by any means. But we don't think they resolve all of the questions that need to be addressed. Nor can they. Seeking statistics-based empirical data is only one method of inquiry. Careful thinking is also required. So perhaps the questions about the value of these models need to remain open for now.

TO DISCUSS

1. Consider the questions raised in the concluding section of this chapter. Discuss your provisional answers to these questions.

2. What experiences of racial encounters have challenged you to go through developmental shifts?

3. How does reading about white racial identity impact you? What experiences does it bring to mind? What challenges does it raise?

4. From books or articles, or from the Internet, find examples of stories of racial encounters that have led to significant cultural identity development. What form does it take and how well does it match models of cultural identity development?

5. What stories of acculturation have you experienced, heard from family members, or learned about from others?

6. Share stories of people you have known who have developed LGBT identities. (These stories can be about yourself, but please be careful not to create pressure for others to come out in public without their having a choice about it.)

7. As you read Matt's story of coming out, what developmental experiences do you imagine others in his life were going through? What about his parents? Siblings? Friends?

Response to Chapter 12

Todd Jennings

Todd Jennings, Ph.D., is a faculty member in the College of Education at California State University, San Bernardino. He teaches courses in development psychology, educational psychology, and gender issues. His research and writing focus on two areas: human rights education and gay and lesbian issues in the field of education, particularly in the preparation of education professionals.

I am a white gay man born in 1960. The date matters because "back in the day" the world was less accepting, less knowledgeable, and less affirming of gay and lesbian folk than it is today. I knew I was gay as a young boy and have lived all my life with the knowledge of this immutable fact. Like many gay men of my generation, I thought at times in my youth that it would have been much easier to be heterosexual. There were certainly times when I struggled to reject the toxic messages about homosexuality and gay men that are embedded in my society. Fortunately, my own identity formation process led me to embrace being gay with a deep sense of gratitude. I came to realize that being gay contributed greatly to my life, providing me opportunities for joy and celebration, and offered perspectives on myself, others, and the larger world that I might have otherwise overlooked. In short, being gay would become one of the most important characteristics of my identity and would ultimately shape all other identities I assume (social, emotional, physical, professional, and political).

In reflecting on the chapter at hand, I am struck by how the process of constructing identity is, as the authors propose, so tied to the time in which one lives. Admittedly, my experience was redolent of many of the models referenced in the chapter. These models are predicated on social contexts that openly endorse and promote homophobia and heterosexism. In such contexts, it is difficult to not define oneself in opposition to a privileged heterosexuality. However, the chapter discussion, with its emphasis on the D'Augelli model, also reminds me that society is changing and that professionals must embrace models of development that reflect evolving, contemporary realities for new generations of gay and lesbian youth. While many of the traditional models clearly speak to my experience as a gay man in an oppressive society, I wonder if they will have the same descriptive power for future generations of gay male youth. In fact, I wonder if the explanatory power of past models may already be diminishing as *normative* models for gay and lesbian folk. This is particularly true for any model that makes normative seeing oneself in a marginalized status vis-à-vis heterosexuality. In a more affirming society, youth may not have to journey through self-hatred, comparison to heterosexual norms, and forced marginalization. Social progress (if that is not a normative idea in itself) may be working to help gay and lesbian youth avoid altogether, and not just later reject, the errant beliefs that would position them as "less than" their heterosexual peers.

The larger literature in counseling and education typically frames gay and lesbian youth as victims. As such, the models, and the professionals who use them, risk reinforcing heteronormativity (the notion that heterosexuality is both "normal" and desirable) by default. As a researcher in gay and lesbian issues in education, I, along with many of my colleagues, am questioning the damaging messages inherent within the victim narratives so common among descriptions (explicit or implicit) of gay and lesbian youth. While admittedly these models speak to the experience of many, we worry that these victim narratives have themselves worked to reinforce victimization by continually positioning lesbian and gay youth as "at risk." The models rarely highlight that the majority of gay and lesbian youth demonstrate assets that outweigh and subvert negative concepts of them *as* gay and lesbian. While I would not argue that current society guarantees the affirmation of gay and lesbian folk (quite the opposite), the larger public discourse has begun a movement from universal condemnation to more frequent instances of ambivalence and even affirmation. I have no doubt that this social progress will continue. Despite dominant messages within the society, empowered gay and lesbian people are challenging their characterization as victims. As an alternative, more gay and lesbian folks are beginning from positions of power, whereby sexual diversity is not interpreted as problematic but as strength. There is a subtle but important difference between recognizing that one lives in an unjust society and participating in the hegemonic act of defining oneself as a victim.

Admittedly, describing the risks associated with being gay and lesbian in an oppressive environment has had its political purposes. For example, it has been a useful way to get both politicians and educators to respond with policies that promote safety for all. However, one is also left to ask, at what cost do we perpetuate any victim narrative in the interest of political advancement? Do models that promote a victim narrative reinforce the notion that gay and lesbian youth should consider themselves at risk, when in fact the majority of these youth may not be working under such beliefs? Does our allegiance to victim-based models keep us from developing alternative models that retain the importance of sexual orientation in the lives of gays or lesbians but don't position homosexuality so close to risk, victimization, and self-destruction? With social progress may come more youth who see that being gay or lesbian is a natural, *normal variation* of human sexuality rather than a deviance *from* heterosexuality. The continued use of any models that imply comparison to heterosexuality reinforces heteronormativity.

Counselors and educators must be careful to not hold on to victim narratives that promote clients' embracing these negative notions. It is a heterosexist counselor who assumes that self-loathing or comparisons to heterosexual "ideals" are a *necessary* or *inherent* part of gay and lesbian identity formation. We may find that future youth simply bypass the victim narratives and comparisons that some expect or would impose. Make no mistake, being gay or lesbian matters significantly in identity formation, but not because it defines one as a victim or just on the margins. For increasing numbers of gay and lesbian folk, the story of identity may be a positive and empowered one that altogether avoids or dismisses self-loathing and victim narratives, even while they work to transform a society that they see as unjust. This would represent a fine world indeed. In short, are gays and lesbians still at risk for victimization in a heterosexist society? Undeniably, *yes*. Are these risks the only narratives we can use to frame our contemporary understandings of all it means to be gay or lesbian? Increasingly, *no*.

CHAPTER 13

Models of Community

Communities, cities, nations, and international bodies must all find a way to respond to cultural diversity. To do so, they must fashion some model of a community in which relations between cultural groups are structured. They must have some image in mind of how cultural relations might look; some sense of ideal community, within which social groups are subsumed. Such an ideal community may not even exist in the present as much as it represents a project to work toward. At the very least, communities will develop a social formula as a basis for including immigrant newcomers, recognizing indigenous populations, and providing social inclusion for former slave populations. In this chapter, we shall map out some possible models of community and seek to make sense of them. These are all models that have been recognized, articulated, and sometimes argued over in the last hundred years.

In many counseling texts, even though they focus primarily on working with individuals, we can detect a background imagined community to which a person might aspire to belong. It may be a community that is equitable and just, for example, or warm and sensitive, or respectful of responsible assertiveness. The word *multicultural* in the discourse of multicultural counseling refers more to a community than to an individual, more to social relations than to intrapersonal struggles. Yet counseling practice is enormously influenced by the theoretical, philosophical, and day-to-day "in-use" ethics, values, and beliefs that guide counselors and therapists in how they work with clients on a one-on-one basis. Counselors might not explain what they do by referencing a model of community, but they will nevertheless be implicitly influenced by larger ideas about what kind of outcome they want to achieve with their clients. Reflecting on and naming the background social processes already at work in our day-to-day lives will give us a language with which to name, challenge, or embrace the models of community advocated in our contemporary modernist society. In addition, by exploring discrete models of community, we can more clearly articulate the political, economic, and social forces bearing down on the fields of counseling, psychology, and psychiatry and shaping of the multicultural field of counseling.

In this chapter, we will explore the genealogy of the melting pot model of community and consider the role it plays in counseling and therapy to support the cultural practices accompanying individualism. We will also give an account of the social forces of segregation in North America and elsewhere as we consider the role of models of segregated service delivery in the helping fields. Dominant multicultural counseling models advocated today have to some extent arisen out of the tensions between culturally specific models of counseling and culturally universal models. Culture-specific models align at least partially with a segregationist model of community. They include, for example, the cultural matching models where client and counselor are matched by racial membership, by gender, or by religion or sexual orientation. Universal models of counseling align more with integrative models of community. The background histories and contemporary expressions of those segregation and integration models will be examined later in this chapter. In addition, counseling implications of the social movements spurring civil rights, affirmative action, biculturalism, and cultural pluralism will be investigated.

Charles Taylor (2004) refers to this kind of image of a community as a "social imaginary." By this he means something like an implicit sense of how cultural relations might be organized in practice, even if such a sense has not been articulated as a grand idea. He distinguishes carefully between a social imaginary and a theory. The latter is more formal and sometimes may embody a social imaginary. A social imaginary, as Taylor uses the term, is a construction that can be deduced from social practices. His focus is not on academic theorizing so much as on "the way ordinary people 'imagine' their social surroundings" (p. 23). Such images are shared by large groups of people, are often expressed in stories or legends, and give legitimacy to a range of common practices. Taylor's main concern was to articulate some of the major social imaginaries that have evolved in and can serve to characterize the modern era. These are constructs like "the economy," the democratic notion of "popular sovereignty," the "rights" of the individual, and the secular state. Taylor does not extend the concept of the social imaginary to relations between cultures, but we want to use it here for our own purposes to describe implicit models of community that set up cultural relations in particular forms.

There are many different models that can serve this purpose. Which version will apply is usually decided by the group that has political dominance, frequently in the shadow of a history of colonization. Each policy model in effect communicates a message to minority groups, such as, "Come and make sure that you become like us," or "You will never be like us, but we'll tolerate your presence as long as you don't demand too much," or "You can stay for a while, but expect to return home rather than outstay your welcome." Many of the problems that people struggle with on a personal level and sometimes bring to counselors are the downstream effects of these messages, and their shaping effects on people's lives can be traced back.

In the modern world, we have developed the concept of populations who can be governed (see Dean, 1999; Foucault, 2000; Rose, 1999). These populations represent categories of belonging for groups of people. In order to be governed, they are first defined in language, often in law. Individuals are assigned membership of these categories through some process of decision making. Policies are then determined about how populations of people will be counted, treated, legitimated or excluded, manipulated, and, in the worst cases, expelled or eliminated. Counseling is just one of the practices that becomes part of this matrix.

A series of models have been developed for the purpose of developing public policies for the managing and governing of populations of people. Each of these models has been drawn from the discourse of the day and from the available social imaginaries. Each has also been elaborated to some degree in academic knowledge and discussed in public fora of various kinds. The necessity of governing populations of people has led to decisions about how and on what terms people with allegiances to varied cultural traditions will be included in, or excluded from, the mainstream society. Much of this governing function has been administered by the state, by Government with a capital G, through its policing functions, its immigration policies, and its executive spending priorities. Less commonly noticed, however, is the degree to which governing functions have been dispersed throughout a range of bodies. Corporations, health systems, education systems, and the media all exercise part of the function of governing populations of people and of managing how cultural groups will be invited to relate to each other. Each governing body may operate on a slightly different variation of the dominant model of the day for cultural relations. Nevertheless, there is often a rough consensus about the model that everyone knows and tries to operate from. From time to time, however, there may be contests over which model should dominate.

Following Foucault, Nikolas Rose (1990) has proposed that counselors and other mental health practitioners also play a part in the governing of people's lives through their participation in what he calls the "psy complex." The term is an analogical reference to the military-industrial complex that governs people's lives in other ways. The question that arises is how various counseling practices attempt to govern people's lives. To what sorts of ends do they aspire? What assumptions of cultural relations are, perhaps inadvertently, built in? Our aim is to invite counselors to think carefully about the choices they make. As counselors work with their clients, what kind of world are they seeking to contribute to? What sorts of structural arrangement of cultural relations do particular counseling practices support and reproduce? For that matter, what sorts of structural arrangements do particular practices resist and disrupt? The multicultural agenda requires counselors to distinguish among possible visions of the world and to make informed choices about how they will commit themselves in practice.

It is commonplace to suggest that the need to manage life in the midst of diversity is a new demand and that we have never been so diverse. People talk glibly about how "we are becoming more diverse." How accurate is this assumption? It refers, perhaps, to shifts in the demographic trends that shape proportions of identified ethnic groups in the United States, especially the proportion of the population who are identified as white in census data: from 83.5% in 1970 to 69.1% in 2000 (Iceland, 2004). The assumption that we are becoming more diverse, however, deserves further questioning. In the first place, it relies on the existing categories of census data, particularly on the categories of race that are specified by the discourse of the day. These are not fixed categories and have gone through a series of changes historically. The assumption also deserves to be examined in terms of who is saying it and from what background they are drawing in order to say it. It is possible to argue, from the point of view of a minority group, that diversity has always been there and that not much has changed, or perhaps that, as the group's own numbers grow, diversity is actually decreasing. Perhaps, too, there have been shifts in public policy that have made the issue of diversity more visible to those who belong to groups whose traditional privileges have become more visible. The assumption of greater diversity nevertheless persists and often serves to inject a sense of urgency into the conversations about difference, diversity, and cultural relations.

As we study the various models of community that follow, we can notice that none of these models arose out of a social vacuum. Each was a response to particular historical events and trends. Each also gestures toward a future horizon. Each has particular communities of people in mind and rarely encompasses all possible contexts. Some are constructed to address situations of mass immigration. Others address ongoing relations between settlers and colonizers on the one hand and indigenous populations on the other. Still others are rationalizations of social relations around which the labor market, another social imaginary, is organized. In different countries around the world, the models have emerged differently, although parallels can often be drawn.

The Melting Pot

In 1908, a play opened for the first time in Washington, DC. It was written by a Jewish playwright named Israel Zangwill, who had immigrated to the United States from England. The play has long since been forgotten, but its title has entered the public lexicon. The play was called *The Melting Pot* (Udelson, 1990). The image was that of a crucible in which various metals are liquefied and then mixed into a new alloy. It was a reference to the vast wave of immigration from Europe that was taking place at the time. Some 18 million people entered the United States as new citizens between 1890 and 1920, first from Ireland and Germany and later from Italy and eastern Europe. A significant proportion of them were Jewish people escaping from various forms of anti-Semitic discrimination, while others were escaping grinding poverty in search of new economic opportunity. The immigrants spoke a variety of languages and brought with them a range of religious and cultural practices.

It is commonly agreed that the melting pot metaphor captured the spirit of what was expected of people by the dominant discourse of the day as the immigrants entered their adopted country. Their cultural identity and traditions would be melted down and they would blend with the dominant Anglo Protestant majority and develop an identity around their newfound position as American citizens. The new alloy that was to be formed was "American." They would feed off the American dream and contribute to the American democratic tradition. The assumption was that immigrants should let go of their cultural past and enthusiastically embrace their new national identity as their preferred cultural identity. The immigrants were expected to assimilate the cultural customs of the new world, rather than the new world being expected to accommodate itself to include the cultural practices that the immigrants brought with them. It was a one-way accommodation. Theodore

Roosevelt made this clear: "There can be no fifty-fifty Americanism in this country. . . . There is room only for 100 per cent Americanism, only for those who are American and nothing else" (cited by Rumbaut, 2003, p. 237).

For example, immigrants were expected to learn English and let go of their native languages. Advocates for this model frequently pointed to the immigrants who began in waged jobs and rapidly took up entrepreneurial opportunities and started their own businesses.

The image of a society formed in the melting pot was one in which all the contributing "metals" are melted down to form a new American identity. It was a vision of equality in a sense, since in theory all cultural backgrounds were to be melted down in order to contribute to the new alloy. However, it was also clear that it never quite worked that way. In the first place, there was never any expectation that the existing white, Anglo, Protestant majority should be required to go through the melting process and surrender their culture to help form the new one. It was only the immigrants who were required to assimilate. Second, the metaphor was only ever extended to those from Europe who did not disturb the color bar. You could assimilate as long as you were white. Africans and Asians, for example, were not included in this model of community (Birman, 1994). In 1882, for example, the United States Congress passed the Chinese Exclusion Act specifically to ensure that immigrants from China would have minimal impact on the emergent American culture (Atkinson, Morten, & Sue, 1993). Third, the melting pot metaphor was primarily located in and limited to the experience of New York. It therefore was of less significance for areas of the United States as different from New York as the South. Even in New York, it was invoked principally in relation to European migrants and was not so readily applied to African American migrants from the South or to the later waves of Puerto Rican, Dominican, Jamaican, and Asian immigrants. Entrepreneurship has not been as possible a pathway to full admission to the American dream for the later waves of immigrants.

Moreover, by the 1960s it was clear that the melting pot ideal was not even working. Nathan Glazer and Daniel Patrick Moynihan (later Senator Moynihan) published their classic analysis of this social imaginary entitled *Beyond the Melting Pot* in 1963 (Glazer & Moynihan, 1970). It argued that while immigrant populations did abandon their native languages and work hard to learn English, they did not on the whole melt their cultural practices down and adopt "American" lifestyles. Rather, their own cultural expressions evolved in a new context in a wide variety of patterns.

It is interesting to note that the melting pot metaphor was also taken up as an officially sanctioned social imaginary in the new state of Israel. It has since been abandoned, but it was used for a time to organize Israeli thinking about the bringing together of Jewish people from a wide range of countries of origin who brought with them widely divergent cultural practices.

What is now to be made of the melting pot idea? One criticism of it is its tendency to produce cultural blandness, to remove much of the colorful richness of cultural difference from view. If we all melt into one culture, we lose some of leavening influences that different perspectives can bring. We merge into some kind of drab homogeneity. We might also lose a sense of the difference between modernist cultural expressions and the other streams of Western cultural tradition that have been subsumed under it.

More worrying is the possibility that the melting pot might serve as a ruse to mask something more unpalatable. Behind the scenes of the melting pot crucible, it can be argued, lies a process of cultural domination. As John Berry (2001) comments, when strongly enforced, the melting pot easily "becomes a pressure cooker" (p. 620). The melting pot idea refers really to a process of cultural absorption (Entwhistle, 2000) of all comers into the dominant white, Anglo culture. Those who do not trace themselves back to this tradition should take care to mimic it if they want to get ahead in the "real" world. The process of assimilation it requires means abandoning one's cultural origins and traditions. From the modern point of view, this seems like a tragic loss, but it has to be remembered, as Dina Birman, (1994) points out, that in the early 20th century common discourse considered this a better option than the alternative, which was to remain on the margins of the new society.

There are those who argue that the melting pot metaphor still has worth (see Entwhistle, 2000). They claim that some kind of inclusive political vision is needed because the alternative multicultural vision does not clearly enough specify how to settle intercultural disputes in situations where differences rub against each other. Some worry that multiculturalism wanders off into the marshes of relativism and eventually gets bogged down there. They yearn for a return to the days before postmodern critiques disturbed the settled certainties of modernism.

Our belief is that such a return is not possible. Multiculturalism and postmodernism are not just academic ideas. They are responses to the material experiences of people who demand more inclusion and more opportunity in life. They are attempts to articulate people's yearnings for something more and their protests against the limits of what is. As attempts to map out a new vision of a social imaginary, they need to be taken seriously, even though there might be flaws in them.

In the counseling field, we might recognize expressions of the melting pot ideal by the tendency to de-emphasize cultural difference and to emphasize the commonalities of culture. The expectation would be that new immigrants should accommodate themselves to the dominant culture, learn English as soon as possible, and seek to get ahead as individuals in the modern world. Hence, this social imaginary would not expect counselors to go out of their way to affirm the cultural knowledges of an immigrant's home country. Bilingual counselors would not be a major priority in schools and mental health settings. This imaginary would have counseling focus on the future and consign the past to history. Each client would be treated first and foremost as an individual human being, rather than as a member of a cultural community, and the focus of counseling would be primarily on individual intrapsychic phenomena. There are, in fact, many approaches to counseling that work in just this way. Their theories are about individuals primarily and not so much about how cultural patterns get inscribed into individual lives. Such theories fit well with a melting pot social imaginary. However, if we are not endeavoring to implement the melting pot agenda, then perhaps we need to look beyond counseling approaches that are focused in this direction.

Segregation

An alternative to the melting pot model of community is the social policy of segregation. It is founded on the assumption that relations between social groups are less troubled when these groups are kept apart. Its ideal community is one in which racial or other groups maintain *separate but equal* communities. Groups of people live parallel lives with minimal interaction. However, in its idealist forms, the segregation or separatism model has usually operated as a smoke screen for practices of domination in which one group maintains control of the separate conditions of the other group and ensures ongoing second-rate levels of opportunity. Such was the case in the long-standing policy of apartheid in South Africa, which finally broke down in the 1990s. It was also the case in the Warsaw ghetto during World War II. There, Jewish people were herded into a separate community as a precursor to being shipped off to the Nazi death camps. These are two of the most well-known examples of segregation used to mask power relations of extreme inequality.

In the United States, the Jim Crow laws in the South also formalized relations between whites and blacks in a pattern of segregation. Separate housing, restaurants, shopping facilities, water fountains, bathhouses, schools, and churches were established. Seating on public transport was separate. Intermarriage was prohibited and white children could not be adopted by black families. White motorists even had right of way over black motorists at intersections. In order to maintain these separatist laws, voting rights for nonwhites were severely restricted. As in South Africa under apartheid, separate clearly did not mean equal. These laws were challenged and abolished during the civil rights movement of the 1960s.

Around the world, there exist other examples of communities where groups of people are kept separate by legislative or administrative policies of segregation. Sometimes this is the result of intercommunal conflict and segregation is used as a policy to reduce opportunity for contact to produce outbreaks of violence. In Ireland, for example, the "partition" was introduced between the north and the south for this reason. Catholic and Protestant peoples have continued to live alongside each other in Northern Ireland but in segregated communities. In response to ongoing troubles over many decades, the civil rights of the Catholic community especially have been restricted. In Cyprus, since the civil war in 1974, Greek Cypriots and Turkish Cypriots have lived in a totally segregated situation with a border between them policed by United Nations troops.

In Israel and Palestine, a similar situation exists where Jews and Palestinians are strictly segregated by law and by military force. The Israeli government is currently building a wall around the Palestinian community. It is being built for political reasons, but one of its effects is to further entrench segregation. There are other segregations in Israel, too, which are less entrenched by operations of administrative power and are more voluntary, such as the segregation of the old city of Jerusalem into its Moslem, Jewish, Christian, and Armenian quarters. Israeli Arabs live in their own segregated communities, as do orthodox religious Jews. And the Druze people live in their own segregated community.

Segregation is not always achieved by legislative fiat. This is especially true of residential segregation, which is defined as "the unequal distribution of groups across space" (Iceland, 2004, p, 250). Often such segregation is achieved by individuals' "mobility decisions" (Iceland, 2004), which are in turn influenced by a range of socioeconomic factors and personal preferences. Housing discrimination can play a role, too, for example, in the steering of African American home buyers and renters into certain neighborhoods. There are also a range of social policies that can effectively produce segregated communities even when they are not required by law. The establishment of expensive gated communities achieves the effect of segregation when there is economic disparity between communities. Social policy decisions to deliberately build high-rise housing projects right alongside existing African American neighborhoods are also a case in point (Iceland, 2004). Indeed, the most common form of segregation is that established along socioeconomic lines (Iceland, 2004). Wealthier and poorer people do not tend to live beside each other but withdraw into their own communities (although it is only the wealthy who have the full range of choice). Land values and house prices serve to govern such forms of segregation (the poor cannot afford a wide range of choice about where to live), and in many instances de facto segregation along racial and ethnic lines tends to piggyback on economic segregation. The growth of ghettos or barrios in the middle of cities or on their outskirts houses the poor and the working class in ethnic enclaves. There is also segregated housing on the basis of age (Iceland 2004), often fully supported by legislation and public administration. It occurs in the establishment of retirement communities that welcome people only over a certain age.

The development of ethnic homogeneity in what are often referred to as ethnic enclaves is enhanced by the common inner-city phenomenon of "white flight" to the suburbs (Iceland, 2004). No one legislates for white flight. It happens as a result of the personal choices of thousands of individuals and has the effect of producing a pattern of segregation. Research has suggested that whites have the strongest preferences for living with their own people (Iceland, 2004). As a social trend, segregation is never completely uniform, of course. There are always exceptions, but the exceptions allow those who refuse to see patterns of differential opportunity in life to make the claim that people choose their own lifestyles and that therefore there is no issue of injustice involved. As we have shown in Chapter 4, this is a naive view of how power works. In this way, nevertheless, the existence of exceptions works to support the ongoing effects of segregation.

Jonathan Kozol (1992) presented a graphic picture of the results of residential segregation in major American cities. His focus was on educational opportunities in poor and predominantly black neighborhoods. He showed how a policy of unofficial segregation works just as effectively as any official policy to keep people divided along racial lines with regard to housing, employment, and educational opportunity. Schools in poor neighborhoods in parts of New York and Chicago that are more than 90% African American may not have segregation enforced by law, as schools in the South did before the civil rights movement, but they are effectively segregated all the same. Across town, there are usually suburban schools that are predominantly white. In parts of Los Angeles, there are schools that are predominantly Mexican. Nor is the segregation a case of "separate but equal," as Kozol also shows. Funding for education is sharply differential, and the white kids in the wealthier neighborhoods get usually twice as much spent on their education as the children in the poorer neighborhoods. Kozol presents a series of examples of schools in poorer neighborhoods that do not offer students the same counseling services that children in middle class neighborhoods are offered. The same is true of quality teachers, because teachers are often paid substantially less in poorer neighborhoods than they would be in wealthier communities. The kind of education offered differs markedly as a result. Often the effects of segregation and differential educational opportunities are then blamed on the poor and minority families themselves. "They are not motivated to learn" and "The parents don't care about their kids' education" are typical comments that circulate in the discourse that justifies the persisting inequalities. Despite the gains made by the civil rights movement in removing official segregation, unofficial de facto segregation is still firmly in place in the cities of the North as much as in the South, and it has the same effects in people's lives as if it were officially sanctioned.

What is happening to residential segregation? Is it diminishing in response to civil rights changes? Or is it increasing in response to recent immigration patterns? John Iceland (2004) has reviewed United States census data on this subject and concludes that the pattern is mixed. Segregation of blacks in relation to whites has decreased modestly in recent decades, but segregation is increasing with regard to Hispanics and Asians. He suggests that it is white people who are most sensitive to desegregation and most averse to multiethnic areas. On the other hand, the development of more multiethnic living areas has allowed Hispanics and Asians to serve as "buffers" in the relation between whites and blacks, which has assisted the desegregation of blacks in the United States to a modest extent.

Not all segregation, however, is imposed. Voluntary segregation appears in many forms among many social groups. It arises from the desire of people with shared interests and backgrounds to meet together and support each other. Therefore, there have been forms of separatism that are justified by their supporters in terms of their ability to build strategic power and strengthen the voice of a community. The Black Power movement of the 1970s was an example of this. Many people also choose to live in the ghettos out of preference for being close to family and their own people. Voluntary segregation extends well beyond racial and ethnic groups as well. Members of the deaf community, for example, have asserted their preference to be together with others who share their language and perspective on life and to have their own schools and their own university (Gallaudet University in Washington, DC). Feminists have argued for social spaces that can be occupied only by women so that they can share voices that might be silenced by men if brought into the larger community. Gay bars are an example of segregated entertainment venues.

In the field of counseling, segregation is largely a question of access to counseling. Where there is residential segregation, then social services will often experience de facto segregation as a downstream effect. More deliberate policies of separatism have been advocated in the counseling field on the basis of social justice agendas. A frequent expression of this principle is the desire to match clients and counselors along the dividing lines by which social groups are defined. Hence, some argue, only women should counsel women; only African Americans should counsel African Americans; only gays and lesbians should counsel gays and lesbians; only deaf people should counsel deaf people, and so forth. Often such decisions are made on the basis of client preferences. When they are made on the basis of agency policy, they are more likely expressions of segregation.

Integration

The first response to the inequalities of forced segregation has often been to call for the opposite social imaginary of integration. Rather than keeping people in separate social institutions, integration throws them together again. Integration stresses the common humanity of people of different cultural backgrounds and invites equality of opportunity through inclusion of difference. It needs to be understood as a response to segregation, and usually to enforced segregation rather than voluntary segregation. Without a previous history of segregation, the social imaginary of integration makes no sense.

Particularly after the overthrow of the Jim Crow laws in the South of the United States in the 1960s, integration was a common catch cry. Rosa Parks's protest about segregated seating on buses led eventually to integrated seating. The *Brown v. Board of Education* decision (1954) led to integrated schooling in the sense that public schools accepted black and white students into the same schools and classrooms. Integrated housing was harder to achieve, because it was a socioeconomic as well as a racial issue. But some local authorities, particularly in smaller towns, have pursued deliberate policies of granting housing permits and building public housing according to a pepper pot formula that prevents poor areas from developing into large ghettos. Such policies are built on the basis of a social imaginary of integration.

In the United States during the 1970s and 1980s, the cause of integration in education was pursued by means of "busing" students across town to schools outside their immediate neighborhoods in order to ensure racial balance in schools (Pride & Woodard, 1985). The racial composition of each school in a school district was required to reflect the composition of the district as a whole. This was generally achieved by transporting children to a school in a different area of the district. Busing was usually a court-supervised program aimed at combating the lingering effects of segregation in schooling. Without the existence of segregation, it would have made no sense. But it was in the end an unpopular policy that inconvenienced parents and students, and during the early 1990s, in response to a series of court rulings, the policy was tapered off.

One of the aims of the Americans With Disabilities Act (1990) and the Individuals With Disabilities Education Act (1975) was to counter the frequent segregation of persons with disabilities in schools. It gave rise to the mainstreaming movement in special education, which is, in principle, based on the social imaginary of integration in schooling. It envisages equality of educational provision for persons with disabilities through placing them alongside their nondisabled peers, rather than segregating them into special education facilities where they are not expected to achieve educationally to the level of their able-bodied peers.

Integration as a social imaginary has made possible some significant changes in the direction of equality. This has been particularly so with regard to rights of access, whether they be rights of access to education, voting rights, equal employment prospects, or housing. But access is not the full story. Take education, for example. Giving African American children access to the same schools as white persons does not in itself ensure that they will all receive a better education. They may well encounter substantial backlash to integration, a greater likelihood of being tracked into lower classes or special education programs, and a greater likelihood of being expelled or of not graduating from high school (Blanchett, Brantlinger, & Shealey, 2005). De facto segregation of housing based on socioeconomic stratification has for many proved just as limiting as blatant segregationist housing laws (Blanchett et al., 2005), which further affects educational achievement, given that living in poverty strongly affects educational achievement (Berliner & Biddle, 1995).

Integration is always a policy formed in response to situations of segregation. Once the rigid structures of segregation have been abolished and have receded further into historical memory, then the need for ongoing assertion of integration also recedes. Integration is in the end a policy that is difference blind. It works in contrast to discrimination by working for everyone to be treated the same. Where it is limited is in the contexts where equality does not mean equity. Equity sometimes can be obtained only by treating people differently on the basis of their differences. Clients often present to counselors with problems that result from outright discrimination. Good counseling can help a person decide how to respond in such situations. But discrimination is, by definition, intentional and overt, and many of the actions of power, as we saw in Chapter 10, are not personal or intentional but nevertheless have powerful effects. For these effects, the social imaginary of integration does not necessarily help, and therefore counselors need to equip themselves with a more sophisticated vision. Being difference blind is not enough. We need to be sensitive to the particulars of difference in some way that goes beyond integrating them into the melting pot again.

Civil Rights

A strong social imaginary that galvanized social movements of various kinds in the 20th century is that of civil rights. As we suggested in Chapter 6, the concept of civil rights has developed as a product of the modern era. It grew out of the 18th century idea of "natural rights," as argued by John Locke. Natural rights were those that you were born with just by virtue of being human, rather than some privilege that you earned. Premodern societies would not have been likely to think in this way at all. Gradually the idea of natural rights evolved into what we now call "human rights." They have since been embodied in a variety of landmark legal documents in many countries around the world (the American Constitution was one of the earliest examples of this trend) and into international documents like the United Nations' Universal Declaration of Human Rights, the Geneva Conventions, and so forth. Once the idea of human or civil rights was written into constitutional documents and into laws, it became a lever to be used by social movements seeking to lay legal claims to personal rights in the face of the systematic workings of power to deny these rights to groups of people on the basis of race, gender, class, or disability.

In other words, the concept of civil rights has become not just a philosophical idea; it has become a legal term. Claims for civil rights, as we know them, are in the end legal claims. This means that they are the kinds of claims that can be established through legal means, and the limits of the civil rights social imaginary is likely to be marked by the limits of what can be achieved by the application of law. Laws are by their nature built on universal principles applied across a range of social relations in a way that is supposed to ensure orderly resolution of conflicts. Not all experiences of injustice are illegal. Nor can every expression of power relations be legislated against. Laws cannot reach into the hearts of people and remove hatred or prejudice. Laws cannot exert complete control over discourse either, although they can play a role in determining which discourses will be granted authority and sanction. So there will always be limits to what can be achieved in the way of social change by the application of universal principles through the law.

The social imaginary of civil rights has nevertheless been utilized to powerful effect. The latter half of the 20th century has been notable for a series of assertions of power by cultural groups on the basis of claims of civil rights. The black civil rights movement of the 1950s and 1960s was the earliest example of this approach. It succeeded in changing the laws in the South of the United States that had institutionalized segregation. It secured legal access for African Americans to voting rights, better educational and employment opportunities, and civic participation. But it also did more than this. It drew attention to the depth of the expressions of racism in American society. In the words of Martin Luther King, Jr., it inspired people to "dream" of a more just society. Around the world, it inspired other racial and cultural groups to mount their own campaigns of civil rights and indigenous people's rights.

Did it eliminate racism? No, because legal rights and legal processes cannot change people's hearts. Did it shift the dominance of racist discourse in America or elsewhere? To a limited degree, it did, perhaps, but not completely, because laws cannot completely control discourse. If unjust, racist practices are founded on the discourse of race, then civil rights will only ever go so far to challenge them. Other methods, based on other social imaginaries, will need to take over once the limits of the rights discourse are reached.

The civil rights discourse, based in liberal humanist philosophy, was nevertheless copied by other social groups who saw what it could achieve. The women's movement of the 1970s and 1980s adopted the rhetoric of civil rights in order to advance the cause of women's rights. It challenged a range of laws and practices that rendered women less than full citizens and mounted many successful challenges to male-only exclusionary systems. After the women's movement, the gay rights movement took up the same rhetoric, as did the disability rights movement.

All of these social movements have achieved various degrees of legitimacy for their members by claiming legal rights for individual women, gays, persons with disabilities, and so forth. Civil rights, however, focuses on changes to laws and regulations and on how these are policed. It is a legal focus and does not respond so clearly to situations where there is no law that needs changing, merely practices that serve the purposes of power. Sexual harassment is a case in point. There have been laws passed to outlaw sexual harassment in certain workplaces, but in public and in private it often escapes the radar of the law. Often, counseling clients are experiencing problems in their relations with others that do not cross the threshold into legal rights issues, and in these circumstances the rights discourse does not have so much effectiveness.

Affirmative Action

One method of addressing inequality of opportunity for members of disadvantaged social groups is the introduction of affirmative action policies. In the United States, this has been a topic of huge controversy, because it is seen by many to run counter to the assumption of equal opportunity for individuals by giving "undeserved" preferential treatment to some. Affirmative action policies, however, are not uncommon and have often been accepted as fair without being contested. Official affirmative action policies were first instituted in all United States federal agencies (they applied also to private contractors with federal agencies) by President Johnson's administration in 1965 (Crosby, Iyer, Clayton, & Downing, 2003; Middleton, Flowers, & Zawaiza, 1996), although the term *affirmative action* has a history in public policy going back to the 1930s (Woodhouse, 2002). The result of Johnson's executive order was that 20% of the American labor force has since been covered to some degree by affirmative action programs.

Affirmative action can be formally defined as "voluntary and mandatory efforts undertaken by federal, state and local governments; private employers; and schools to combat discrimination and to promote equal opportunity in education and employment for all" (American Psychological Association, 2007). The initial aim of affirmative action policies was to end racial discrimination in employment. Sexual discrimination was added to this agenda by means of the Education Amendments Act of 1972 (Woodhouse, 2002). The goal of affirmative action is not to create unfairness or preferential treatment but to "address the systemic exclusion of individuals of talent, based on their gender or race, from opportunities to develop, perform, achieve and contribute" (Bill Clinton, cited by Middleton, et al., 1996, p. 4). It takes aim at the effects of past injustice and seeks to eliminate existing discriminatory policies. The most frequent targets of affirmative action have been women, who are often prevented from gaining access to gender-exclusive careers and to positions of leadership through the existence of the "glass ceiling," and ethnic minorities who have been traditionally excluded from employment or educational opportunity by the existence of systematic prejudicial discourse.

A distinction can be made between active efforts to promote equality of opportunity and more passive assumptions that such equality already exists. Advocates of "equal opportunity" rather than affirmative action argue that the absence of evidence of overt discrimination can be taken to mean that equality of opportunity actually exists. There is a tendency in the United States to assume that constitutional guarantees of individual equality are sufficient to militate against prejudicial stereotyping and the effects of racist or sexist discourse. The intention of affirmative action policies, however, is to redress situations where the existence of systematic discriminatory discourse currently prevents equality of opportunity based on merit in employment or education. At their best, affirmative action policies do not recruit or promote individuals who do not merit the opportunity. They prevent the exclusion of those who do merit it.

Critics of affirmative action primarily object to the institution of quotas for members of minority groups, thus granting some individuals unfair, preferential treatment. For example, an affirmative action policy at the medical school at the University of California, Davis, was successfully challenged in court for listing applicants in two lists—one white and one for racial minorities—and reserving 16% of admissions for minority applicants (Crosby et al., 2003). The United States Supreme Court upheld the complaint that setting aside quotas can lead to the granting of access to some on the basis of racial identity rather than on merit. On the other hand, Faye Crosby and her colleagues (2003) contend that affirmative action is primarily an effort to strengthen the meritocratic distribution of opportunity. They argue that the primary effort of affirmative action is to set in place systems for monitoring the proportions of underrepresented groups in workforce statistics. When such monitoring reveals unmerited preferential treatment, affirmative action policies should affirm the right of minority groups to equal treatment based on merit, and corrective action should be taken. In fact, in the realm of government employment, the institution of quotas and consequent preferential treatment for minorities has never been part of public policy in the United States. And yet the perception persists for many opponents that this is exactly what affirmative action is about.

Let's now consider the model of community envisaged in the affirmative action idea. It is clearly a policy intended for the governing of relations between social groups. It embodies the hope of creating greater social justice by ensuring a more equitable distribution of opportunity to individuals. It is based, however, on the assumption that individual merit exists and that it can be measured and estimated accurately. It relies to a large extent on a liberal humanist analysis of power relations. In this model, power is conceived of as being in the possession of individuals, and it is fairly shared if individuals from various cultural backgrounds are given proportionate opportunity. It leaves the categories of distinction along ethnic, racial, and gender lines in place and even strengthens them through turning them into facts that can be counted and measured in the workplace. On the other hand, it involves a small shift away from the exclusively individual model of community relations. Crosby and her colleagues (2003) argue that affirmative action policies place the primary responsibility for creating social justice on the institution or company rather than on the individual. The company or the government department has to take responsibility for actively monitoring its own practices. The onus is taken off the individual, who must otherwise register a complaint against unjust treatment and risk being accused of being a troublemaker. Crosby and her colleagues summarize evidence from psychological studies to support the existence of stereotyping and of (usually unconscious) systematic injustice in testing processes and selection criteria. They also cite evidence that opponents of affirmative action are more likely to support racist or sexist discourse. Such evidence suggests that the need for affirmative action is based on the power of racist and sexist discourse to have effects on the life chances of persons and that passive assumptions of equal opportunity do not undermine these effects.

What are the implications of this discussion about affirmative action policies for counseling? Counselors, especially career counselors, are likely to meet individuals who are in the midst of constructing educational or employment directions in their lives. As they do so, they will be experiencing the effects of employment or education practices of one kind or another, whether or not such practices are shaped by affirmative action policies. One of our counseling tasks needs to be to help individuals to make sense of the employment or education environments they live in. We believe that counselors are better equipped for this task if they have developed a strong understanding of discursive and systematic forces at work in the construction of such social contexts. This can position them to respond to clients in ways that do not encourage them to take personal responsibility for unjust situations and that also do not encourage an unrealistic sense of entitlement when they are the recipients of privilege. Another possibility is that individual clients may overestimate the influence of discriminatory discourse in situations where affirmative action polices do exist. Crosby and her colleagues refer to the phenomenon of perceived "stereotype threat" and its inhibitory effects on performance in, for example, job interviews or tests.

Counselors need to have their eyes open to the workings of injustice. They may at times need to be advocates on behalf of those on the receiving end of racist or sexist discourse. This may mean advocating the introduction of affirmative action policies where they do not exist. But counselors also need to help their clients make assessments of the world in which they live and to chart their own pathways in life. Sometimes this will mean helping them find expression for resistance to injustice. Sometimes it will mean helping them develop greater consciousness of how injustice works. Sometimes it will mean helping them name injustices that they were scarcely aware of, and sometimes it will mean helping them reconsider internalized conclusions of self-blame when they are rejected as a result of unjust practices.

Multiculturalism

A social imaginary of a new form of community that has developed in recent decades as an alternative to earlier proposals for a melting pot or for either segregation or integration is the vision of a multicultural society. The multicultural society has its historical roots in the concept of a society that grants religious toleration to people of different faiths. The ideal of religious toleration (which is by no means universal) grew out of the stalemates that emerged in Europe after centuries of religious wars. It was expressed in the American Constitution as the separation of church and state. Charles Taylor (2004) traces the shift from the premodern to the modern world as being founded on the social imaginary of a more secular state. In the last few decades, the model of religious toleration has been extended beyond religious differences to cultural differences. However, as Jacques Derrida (Borradori, 2003) points out, the idea of "toleration" is a flawed one. It is in the end based on the position of the dominant group, who are entitled to exercise their magnanimity and grant a place of toleration to those who are "different." Thus, it leaves the dominant group's dominance in place, it relies on the continuance of generosity by this group, and it positions minority groups in the expectation that they should be vigilant for opportunities to show gratitude and accept without complaint what they have been offered. Toleration is extended like charity.

Nevertheless, despite a history of many setbacks, there have been a series of significant openings created for people who are different as a result of policies of religious toleration. For example, despite his ruthless colonization of the Irish in the 17th century, Oliver Cromwell introduced religious toleration for the Jews into England during his reign. In France, Abbé Grégoire persuaded the revolutionary council in the aftermath of the French Revolution to grant religious toleration to Jews. And it is well known that Queen Elizabeth I told Parliament as it established the Church of England that she would not "make windows into men's souls."

In the multicultural social imaginary, people are not required to relinquish their cultural distinctiveness. They are instead urged to retain it and value it and to wear it proudly for all to appreciate. Cultural difference should be given greater visibility rather than remain hidden in the background (Entwhistle, 2000). From this perspective, those who have been cut off from their cultural history have been encouraged to find their cultural "roots" (Haley, 1976) and develop their cultural identity. Multiculturalism is about embracing cultural particularity rather than merging into the generality of the dominant culture. Searching for roots, immersing oneself in one's cultural history and traditions, centering oneself in the heart of a cultural identity—all this has been encouraged, usually at the expense of acknowledging the complexity of competing pulls.

Nowhere has the vision of a multicultural society been articulated more fully and given more formal public substance than in Canada. Multiculturalism was granted official status as Canadian government policy in 1971 and has since been written into a series of laws (Mock, 1997). The 1982 Charter of Rights and Freedoms entrenched multiculturalism in Canada as a constitutional principle, and in 1988 the Canadian Multiculturalism Act specified further the responsibilities of government departments to implement multicultural policies. This act clearly states that it "recognizes the diversity of Canadians as regards to race, national or ethnic origin, colour and religion as a fundamental characteristic of Canadian society" (Mock, 1997, p. 127).

It is instructive to look at how the meaning of multiculturalism has evolved in Canada over the last three decades. It began with the recognition of English and French as two official languages and was expanded to include the perspectives of "other" communities. In contrast to the melting pot impulse, multiculturalism was at first declared to be about programs to encourage "cultural retention and cultural sharing" (Mock, 1997, p. 123). Rather than allowing their cultural background to be melted down, new immigrants were encouraged to retain their cultural practices in a society that would celebrate differences among groups. Laws against hate crimes were introduced or strengthened. Immigration policy was liberalized.

Later, in response to ongoing dissatisfaction among cultural groups (especially aboriginal Canadians) and in the face of some racial incidents, it was realized that celebrating difference was not enough. Attention began to turn to more active policies of promoting equality. Systemic inequality required more than freedom from discrimination if it was to change significantly. It also could not be addressed by policies that focused mainly on individual freedoms. The emphasis in Canada has therefore shifted to programs that actively promote equality across a range of social institutions.

A variety of metaphors have been suggested as shorthand references to the social imaginary of a multicultural society. Rather than the melting pot, multiculturalism has envisaged the "cultural mosaic" (Benhabib, 2002; Entwhistle, 2000; Sue et al., 1998). In this image, each cultural group contributes a distinctive color to the overall picture of a society. Others have imagined a multicultural society as a "salad bowl," in which each cultural group contributes a flavor to the meal (Anderson, 2000). Another frequently used metaphor is the "tapestry," in which each different colored thread is woven into the overall effect (Entwhistle, 2000). More critically, some have questioned the shallowness of multiculturalism, conceiving of it as merely celebrating differences without performing any analysis of power in cultural relations, and likening it to putting "parsley on the plate" (Wise, 2005). It adds color but little nutritional value.

The social imaginary of multiculturalism has often been invoked in the field of education. The vision of multicultural schooling is not just about access to public schools for people of all cultures. It is also about what happens at school. For example, it is about curriculum designed to be inclusive of the experiences of all students. Multiculturalism, as a social imaginary, works well for this purpose. It supports moves toward the study of a history that does not portray just white men as heroes and leave out the experience of other people (Lawrence, 1997). It urges a study of art and literature that goes outside the established canon of European art and includes artists and writers who speak to the life experience of many cultural groups. Inclusion of the stories of many peoples provides students with role models, validates their cultural identities, and gives people the experience of recognition. Charles Taylor (1994) argues that "recognition" is one of the chief goals of multiculturalism. If policies that promote integration are difference blind, then multiculturalism is the opposite. It pays attention when people demand to be treated differently on the basis of their cultural identity. Multiculturalism is not about equal treatment for individuals as much as it is about equal recognition of different cultural groups and equal respect for cultural practices (Taylor, 1994). One problem that critics of multiculturalism have brought up is the question of how to decide on the merits of pieces of art, music, and literature once you have disestablished the traditional canon. Multiculturalism itself does not establish grounds for decisions on this issue. Taylor (1994) suggests that such decisions will become possible only if we work toward a future horizon where diverse cultural values meet and fuse in a way that allows for cultural respect that goes beyond condescension.

However, other problems have been emerging with the multicultural vision in recent years. For example, an issue has arisen in France during the last decade over Muslim girls wearing the *hajib* headscarf to public schools (Benhabib, 2002). This was taken as a symbol of religious expression, which contradicted the modernist tradition of secularism in school. So the French government in 2004 banned the wearing of the hajib, arguing that it contradicted school dress codes. At the same time, the wearing of Christian crosses, Jewish yarmulkes, and other religious symbols was also banned. An uproar arose among the large Muslim community in France as a result. The issue is not an easy one to resolve. On the one hand, the hajib is a piece of clothing closely associated with personal modesty as it is understood from a Moslem cultural perspective. On the other hand, it is read as a religious statement and criticized from a Western feminist perspective as restrictive for women. Moreover, as Seyla Benhabib points out, some of the students claiming the right to wear the *hijab* did so explicitly as a political statement, not just as a religious expression. From the perspective of government, some kind of decision that promotes equality for all is needed. One of the aims of democratic secularism in education is just such difference blind equality. From the perspective of a minority community, however, this decision is interpreted as an instance of the cultural hegemony of the majority. They claim the right to differential recognition as a minority, and special protection of their cultural practices, not just same-as-everyone equality. Official policies of multiculturalism here ran afoul of administrative decision making. A decision was made that could not please everyone and attracted accusations of cultural hegemony.

Similar issues are raised in courts of law. Seyla Benhabib (2002) cites several examples of criminal court cases in which a defendant has successfully mounted a defense on the grounds that "my culture made me do it." Here is one example:

> In California, a young Laotian American woman is abducted from her work at Fresno State University and is forced to have intercourse against her will. Her assailant, a Hmong immigrant (one of the boat people who fled Cambodia and Laos in the final stages of the Vietnam War) explains that among his tribe this behavior is accepted as the customary way to choose a bride. He is sentenced to 120 days in jail, and his victim receives $900 in reparations. (p. 87)

Benhabib shows how, in this instance and in other instances, the law courts are helpless when it comes to establishing principles to accept cultural differences and at the same time provide equality of protection for individuals, especially women and children.

A question often asked regarding a multiculturalist vision that seeks inclusion for all is, inclusion in what? Clearly, inclusion in a singular nationalistic vision dominated by the majority culture is just a path back to assimilation. Opponents of multiculturalism therefore frequently fall back on the melting pot at this point (e.g., Entwhistle, 2000; Schlesinger, 1991). Proponents of multiculturalism have to work hard at constructing an alternative vision of a social world that might contain different rights within it and resolve disputes between cultural groups over competing demands.

Counseling Implications of Multiculturalism

Counseling that takes a multicultural vision into account has evolved through a series of cycles. At first, it focused on the white counselor and invited her to break out of the place of being "culturally encapsulated" (Wrenn, 1962). The development of cultural sensitivity through the gathering of knowledge about other main cultural groups was advanced as a goal of multiculturalism (Patterson, 1996; Sue & Sue, 1981). Training a more diverse generation of counselors was another goal of the multicultural counseling movement (Patterson, 1996). Culture-specific counseling methods have been advocated and advanced (Pedersen, 1976; Waldegrave, Tamasese, Tuhaka, & Campbell, 2003) and also critiqued (Patterson, 1996). More recently, multiculturalism in counseling in the United States has settled on an agenda of competencies that counselors should master (see Chapter 17). These involve a strong emphasis on developing awareness of one's own and others' cultural assumptions and processes of cultural identity development.

The multicultural social imaginary is strong on inviting counselors to become aware of diversity and valuing it. What has been less evident in most of the mainstream approaches to multicultural counseling is what is generally missing from multiculturalism in general. The mosaic metaphor does not specify an analysis of power relations among the various races and cultures. How the pieces of the mosaic should relate to each other is always a little vague. The conception of a social world in which differences among cultures might not just be appreciated and valued in our awareness but actually debated and negotiated with some give and some take is seldom articulated. Such a conversation is probably limited by the available social imaginaries of a multicultural world. These social imaginaries rarely embody any elaboration of the assumption that culture is dynamic and always evolving, rather than static and fixed. We believe that this is the challenge for the future of multiculturalism.

Biculturalism

The social imaginary of biculturalism differs in its history from multiculturalism. It has been developed in circumstances where the community has been founded on the basis of an indigenous culture and a colonizing culture. This idea has had the greatest currency in New Zealand, but it is known in other parts of the world as well. The ideal community imagined from a bicultural perspective is founded on a partnership between the indigenous people and the former colonists.

In New Zealand, this partnership was founded on an actual treaty, known as the Treaty of Waitangi, which was signed in 1840 by representatives of the British Crown and about 150 Maori leaders (Orange, 1987). Similar treaties were signed in other parts of the world—for example, in Canada and the United States—between European colonizing powers and indigenous cultures. However, the New Zealand treaty happened some decades after the colonization of North and South America and Australia, at a time when the British Home Office was influenced by a liberal group in London called the Aboriginal Protection Society (Orange, 1987). This group's influence led the British government to send an emissary to sign a treaty that would afford the Maori people some protection from the worst ravages of colonial rule that had taken place in other parts of the world, such as wholesale theft of land and genocidal slaughter. Maori leaders, for their part, were fully cognizant of what could happen to them and were eager to negotiate a partnership that would advantage their people in the future. The result was the founding document of New Zealand as a nation. However, because the British settlers who came to New Zealand in the wake of the treaty did not always have the high ideals of the Aboriginal Protection Society at heart, they hated its provisions and sought to set it aside at every opportunity. It was not until over a hundred years later that the treaty was actually honored by the New Zealand government and gradually written into constitutional law as a founding document. (Maori had campaigned in a series of mostly nonviolent movements for this to happen for over one hundred years.) The result has been the rise of a movement arguing for New Zealand to embrace biculturalism as a national social imaginary.

Biculturalism entails the official recognition that two cultures have equal roles to play in a social world. It is echoed in countries that have officially instituted bilingualism. Canada comes to mind in its embrace of English and French as official languages. The imaginary of biculturalism has evolved into a call for the recognition of the roles and obligations of two different peoples to each other in a relationship. These roles are not necessarily exactly the same. Hosts and guests have different roles in a situation of hospitality. Biculturalism does not require each group to melt down and form a new alloy. It rests on the remembering of a partnership agreement that represents the best moments of a shared history, rather than looking at the history and shuddering at the sight of the ugliness of the colonizing process. This is not to imply that there were not ugly aspects of the colonizing process in New Zealand. There certainly were many abuses of power by the colonists, but the Treaty of Waitangi rendered many of these illegal, and since the latter part of the 20th century many Maori have been pursuing legal means of exacting compensation for the worst excesses of illegality (especially illegal land confiscation).

It is worth taking note here that there is another usage of the term *bicultural* that we are not referring to here. Sometimes in the literature on race and culture, the term *bicultural* is used to refer to an individual born of parents from two different racial or cultural groups. This usage is not uncommon in the United States. The parents may be referred to as a bicultural couple and the child as a bicultural child. However, the focus in this usage is on the individual and not on the social imaginary. Therefore, the two meanings are quite different. In this chapter, we are focusing on the social imaginary rather than the individual. It is the meaning that is common in New Zealand that we are employing.

The advantage of a bicultural social imaginary is that it specifies, in a way that multiculturalism often does not, the official recognition of the places of two different cultural groups in legitimate partnership. It has strength because of its location in history, rather than seeking to be the expression of an abstract ideal. It recognizes the colonial past out of which current debates and conflicts have arisen. It even acknowledges the power relations that have shaped that history and specifies a model for shared power. Even when that model is not honored by one of the partners, it creates a ground from which critique can be mounted. It assumes that there will be an ongoing dialogue between the bicultural partners and that neither partner's position will be completely negated in that dialogue. It avoids the call for a singular base for a social world, such as that expected in a social imaginary of integration or a melting pot. In so doing, biculturalism recognizes a dual perspective on reality and rejects the singular definition of truth that science has often sought.

However, there are some downsides to the social imaginary of biculturalism. One question that quickly arises is, what about other cultures that come to settle in the arrangement set up by two initial partners? The bicultural partnership can appear to them like a comfortable binary that leaves them out. An answer sometimes given in New Zealand is that there needs to be a special place of privilege for the indigenous people in a partnership, since there is nowhere else that their culture will be protected. But this answer does not always satisfy people of Asian or Pacific Island descent who have immigrated to New Zealand in the wake of the British colonists. Neither does it address the situation of succeeding generations of the settlers' descendants, who have nowhere else to call home.

A better argument perhaps is that the two partners who signed the original treaty have set up the form of a relation. Other immigrants have been slotted into this relation in different ways. It is a power relation in which a contest of different interests is worked out. Subsequent immigrants are typically slotted into this power relation in the position of either of the two original partners. The bicultural social imaginary allows for an analysis of the privileges and disadvantages of both of these positions.

Still, in the long run, this social imaginary has limits. It may have historical value and serve particular purposes in particular contexts, but it should not be regarded as applicable to every aspect of relationships between all cultures. It leaves out too many people. What it does offer to other countries is the vision of a different ideal, that of deliberate partnership. This is a vision of a power relation that has been set up not to favor one side over the other. Even if this ideal is not lived out, it can serve as a model for what might be. There is no such equivalent in multiculturalism, which does not usually have a highly developed analysis of power relations or such a potent vision of an ideal.

Cultural Pluralism

Another social imaginary that is sometimes invoked is that of cultural pluralism. It is often used interchangeably with multiculturalism, and many writers make no distinction between the two. We think there are possibly some subtle differences and shall try to articulate them here. Nowhere that we know of does there exist any kind of formalized consensus on the kind of cultural pluralism we imagine. Rather, we see signs of an emergent perspective that is arriving in the discourse and that may eventually lead us a step beyond multiculturalism and biculturalism. Some writers, such as Iris Marion Young, Seyla Benhabib, and Jürgen Habermas, have been endeavoring to articulate this vision in theoretical terms. And there are some emergent social trends and social practices that we can point to that suggest that in many places people are extending feelers toward an as yet unknown social imaginary. Cultural pluralism is simply the best name we can think of for this chimerical image.

Cultural pluralism refers to an image of a social world in which there is pluralism of cultural difference not just in a positive sense, but also in a normative one. In other words, it is not just that different groups of people exist, but that they are granted differential rights to exist. They are recognized as members of a group as well as individuals, and perhaps there are rights granted to groups of people as well as to individual human beings.

Given that the Enlightenment-sponsored democratic vision has extended rights only to individuals, such an idea amounts to new forms of democracy that recognize cultural forces more directly than democracy does at present. It is a vision of a democratic system that gives overt legitimate status to differences. It is more than just tolerant of differences; it welcomes them. Imagining such a world is difficult, because there is as yet no consensus on this emergent social imaginary, just a sense of movement toward some new cultural forms that have not yet been born.

One of the problems that cultural pluralism needs to solve is how to address the needs of minority cultural groups and protect them from the tyranny of the majority. In other words, it needs to address the problems that limit the melting pot and integrationist visions. Another problem is how to settle differences when cultural groups come into conflict without falling back into segregationist solutions. Currently, these issues are dealt with in most democratic traditions on the level of individual rights. But there may be other alternatives. Let's list some examples that come to mind.

In New Zealand and in Canada at the moment, some experiments are being undertaken with regard to the handling of criminal offenses. In New Zealand, the Maori people have lobbied for, and in some cases been granted, the right to try their own people using protocols drawn from pre-European traditions. "Marae justice" experiments have been cautiously explored and have achieved some success—so much so that "family group conferences," as they have become known in the youth justice arena, have been made normative for all youth offenders, regardless of cultural background. What is distinctive here is that a cultural minority group succeeded in establishing a differential practice for its own people, and then had this extended to the whole community. In Canada, "sentencing circles" for dealing with crimes in native communities have been introduced by a similar process (Stuart, 1997). These practices are linked together under the banner of restorative justice.

New Zealand is also an example of a nation that has moved politically (during the 1990s) toward a proportional representation model of parliamentary elections. Seyla Benhabib acknowledges that this political model allows a greater opportunity for minority interests to be represented in government decision making. Two-party, first-past-the-post electoral systems such as those that prevail in Britain and the United States do not include the range of political and cultural voices that proportional representation does, and minority cultural interests are forced to remain represented by lobby groups on the outside of the official decision making process. Exceptions to this include the granting of limited sovereignty to cultural minorities, such as that given on Indian reservations. In the cultural pluralism social imaginary, this kind of sovereignty would increase but would also be matched by greater opportunity for the negotiation of differences among cultural groups along the lines envisaged under bicultural partnership models.

In Boston, the Public Conversations Project (Chasin et al., 1996) has developed a method of facilitating conversations between groups of people who are polarized on cultural issues. Their approach draws from the experience in family therapy of most of the key members of the project. It is not a method of mediation aimed at producing an agreement as much as it is a method of building within each group an understanding of and greater familiarization with the other group's experience and commitment to a different viewpoint. Public conversations began with the abortion debate, bringing "pro-choice" and "pro-life" people together to talk. Other topics that the public conversations model has been used with have included environmental land use, gay priests in churches, and the terrorist attacks of September 11, 2001. The authors of this book also used the public conversations model to generate conversations between Greek Cypriots and Turkish Cypriots, who are divided by the Cyprus problem. This is an example of how it is possible for conversations across differences to occur without there being a need to reach a synthesis that produces unity.

These examples suggest some principles that the cultural pluralism of the future might embody. First of all, they are not just about equality before the law in the sense of everyone's being treated the same. A pluralistic social imaginary has room for people to be treated differentially according to their cultural preferences. But it also does so within an overall system that does not end up in separatism or segregation, but engages people in dialogue. It is a dialogic vision, in the sense that Mikhail Bakhtin (1981) envisioned, of a never-ending exchange in which mutual learning continues to take place. This does not have to be dialogue in which a unified outcome is produced. This is its key difference from an integration model. Neither does it conclude that "never the twain shall meet" and surrender to a spirit of segregation. Instead, it regards cultural groups as capable of a degree of sovereignty within their own jurisdiction, on the condition that they will also play a part in the creation of an overall society. It deliberately creates situations of mutual accountability among the different cultural groups within a polity, rather than a winner-takes-all form of democracy. It is built on a trust born of mutual accountability rather than on treating everyone exactly the same.

Those who try to articulate a vision of what a culturally pluralist social world might look like speak of the need for a unifying vision as well as a recognition of difference. This vision is sometimes referred to as one of "deliberative democracy" (Benhabib, 2002). Along with the vision of pluralistic cultural values that a person can borrow from, as from a lending library, comes a vision of serious efforts to communicate across differences rather than regard them as incommensurable. It involves the formation of a basis for commitment from places of difference to create a sense of belonging without insisting on a comprehensive national culture or uniform values or ways of doing things. This needs to be a more robust vision of citizenship than the current American liberal emphasis on tolerating difference (in culture and religion) in the private sphere while requiring uniformity in the public sphere. Its precise forms are still to be elaborated and the social imaginary is nowhere near as clearly captured in metaphor as the melting pot or the cultural mosaic. Perhaps such metaphors will emerge in the future. We believe, however, that there is a need for a new social imaginary that takes into account the more pluralistic, less essentialist versions of culture that we have been tracing through this book. Counselors are already working with this pluralism, whether they recognize it or not, as they listen to the complexity of the stories that their clients tell them.

TO DISCUSS

1. What is your understanding of the concept of the "psy complex"? How are counselors involved in the governing of people's lives?

2. What are the arguments for and against affirmative action?

3. Debate the pros and cons of each of the social imaginaries with regard to relations among cultures.

4. Investigate the word *rhizome*, suggested by Gilles Deleuze and Felix Guattari (1983) and below by Jung Min Choi. What might be its implications for multicultural counseling?

Response to Chapter 13

Jung Min Choi

Jung Min Choi, Ph.D., is an associate professor of sociology at San Diego State University. His areas of interest are race relations, globalization, democracy, and postmodern theory. He has published numerous articles and book chapters and has coauthored several books on issues related to social justice and democracy. His recent work revolves around the issue of democratic education. He is writing a book titled *Pedagogy of Imagination: When Students Have Hope.*

In this chapter, the authors do an excellent job of providing a historical sketch of the various perspectives on communities and communal identities that have emerged in sociopolitical writings throughout the 20th century. Beginning with the melting pot theory and progressing to integration, multiculturalism, and pluralism, the authors point out how each has attempted to explain, and at times justify, the existing social order. Of all the perspectives mentioned throughout this chapter, multiculturalism and "cultural pluralism" seem to be most viable within the tenets of democracy. Indeed, both perspectives seem to be grounded on the notion of "inclusion" as a basis for maintaining society. The problem, however, is that neither perspective (along with all the other perspectives mentioned in the chapter) truly embraces the ontology of difference that is necessary to sustain an egalitarian society. Albeit in different degrees, all the perspectives mentioned in this chapter maintain a form of essentialism that restricts interaction among individuals as equals.

Beyond the various perspectives of society described in this chapter, what other imageries are viable in maintaining society? Martin Buber (1978) believes that in a democratic society, all social relationships should reside in the "in-between," or *dazwischen* (pp. 202–205). For Michel Foucault (1983), communities are "discursive formations" where communal boundaries are (re)interpreted and (re)understood continually without a particular telos. A "patchwork" of locally determined frameworks is the most appropriate way to describe society (Lyotard, 1984). This understanding of linguistic communities defies predetermination, essentialism, genetic superiority, and structured hierarchies based on fallacious concepts of integration, a melting pot, assimilation, and pluralism. Having said this, there is no question that in our society, the impact of assimilation and pluralism has been enormous.

For example, as a nine-year-old Asian American boy growing up in the outskirts of East Los Angeles in the 1970s, I wanted to be integrated into the "norm" that I was surrounded by. Even at an early age, it was evident that fitting in was important. There were no other Koreans in my neighborhood and I was constantly looked at by the other kids as weird in many ways; the language I spoke, the food I ate, and the culture that I practiced were all ridiculed. I got picked on just about every day in school. At times, I got into physical altercations, which usually ended in my being jumped by two or three other students. Rather than having fun and playing games during recess, I either stayed inside the classroom or just sat in a corner out in the quad. Going to school became a recurring nightmare.

So I did everything I could to assimilate as fast as possible. I learned to speak English, ordered my mom to cook burgers and fries, and shunned many of my cultural practices and beliefs. Slowly but surely, this worked! I had friends who would stand up for me and protect me from bullies, and I was able to play tag during recess and lunch. Unwittingly, I was pursuing assimilation and integration at the expense of my cultural identity.

This pursuit of assimilation continued throughout my adolescence into the early part of my college years. In fact, as a high school kid living in Riverside, California, in the early 1980s, I was ashamed to be an Asian American. I didn't want to be associated with the newly arriving "boat people" (as they called many of the Vietnamese refugees), nor did I want to be associated with the "model minority" status given to many Asians. It seemed to me that being an Asian American meant that I had a truncated existence. I was either a war refugee who had no rights or privileges or a bookworm who lacked any other human desires—such as dating, playing sports, being mischievous, or simply being lazy. The model minority status really bothered me. It seemed as though they were saying that I was the "best of the worst." How flattering! I so desperately wanted to have blue eyes and blond hair so that people could see me as a person and not an abstraction.

Once in college, the pursuit of assimilation turned into an obsession with pluralism. This idea seemed really liberating. I heard someone say that rather than a melting pot, we should have a society that resembles a salad bowl. This, I thought, was so progressive. I could hold on to my cultural and ethnic identity and still be an integral part of the larger society. However, many argued that the problem with pluralism is that there is too much difference and diversity, which will eventually destroy the basic fabric of American life.

Nevertheless, as I write this piece 20 some years later—having neither been melted in a pot nor chopped up like a salad—I muse about the power of certain social imaginaries, like assimilation and pluralism, that place individuals into discrete categories.

If we are to have a truly open society where diversity is protected and celebrated rather than feared and repressed, we need an ethical social order where all views reside on a single horizontal plane. A rhizome, according to Gilles Deleuze and Felix Guattari (1983), provides an excellent social imaginary of this kind. Rhizomes have no apparent beginning or end, and these plants do not have centralized roots to sustain their growth. At the same time, rhizomes do not sprout haphazardly. In fact, the dispersion of these plants is orderly, yet decentered. By adopting the image of the rhizome, Deleuze and Guattari attempt to illustrate the applicability of difference in constructing social order.

Without a firm anchor to sustain society, isn't chaos inevitable? Absolutely not, claims Alfred Schutz (1976). Chaos can be averted with people's "growing old" together, where each person is tuned in to the experiential realm of the Other. A "multiplicity of worlds of names, the insurmountable diversity of cultures" does not require a grand narrative to provide a fixed formula for sustaining social order (Lyotard, 1993, p. 31). The point is that social order can emerge from individuals' asserting and accepting each other's opinions in the absence of an imposing structure. According to Deleuze and Guattari (1983), so called-universal structures that are uncompromising may only serve to alienate citizens. Instead of relying on static constructs for guidance, persons are able to use interpretations to lead them down the "path of the dancer's soul" (p. 71). By employing the image of a dancer, Deleuze and Guattari emphasize creativity. Unlike a programmed robot, a dancer's next step can change without a moment's notice and yet not disrupt the harmonious movement. This is why Deleuze and Guattari view social order as a process of "becoming" (p. 49). Clearly stated, order is not the product of a preestablished reality, but rather order and reality "become," or emerge, out of direct interaction between persons. Living at the boundary of one's interpretive reality allows the Other to approach and be approached. Instead of the traditional asymmetrical version of social reality, society can be based on "a series of exclusively lateral relations" (Foucault, 1983). According to Michel Foucault, an ethical social order is one where all views reside on a single horizontal plane. In a society modeled after the rhizome, persons living in different interpretive communities are able to construct reality in the absence of a metaphysical presence such as the "melting pot," or "integration," or even "multiculturalism."

CHAPTER 14

The Question of Racism

Failing to address racism is a form of racism itself. It is like having the ability to rescue a drowning child but failing to do so.

—Charles Ridley, *Overcoming Unintentional Racism in Counseling and Therapy*

This chapter addresses the destructive influences of racism—the ideological legacy of European colonization that has material impact on the lives of people across diverse cultures. Applications of counseling and psychology must not only deal with people from diverse backgrounds; they must deal with the effects of racist ideology on their lives. Combating racism, however, is not just a matter of agreeing that it is a bad thing and starting from there. It involves thinking through some issues in order to ensure that the work of combating racism is effective. Because there are some different approaches around, it also involves considering just how we will talk about the subject of racism. We suspect that some of these approaches are more helpful and less counterproductive than others. This chapter considers a variety of approaches to addressing and combating the effects of racism in and through counseling practice. As we have been doing throughout this book, we shall highlight and explain some specific strategies that utilize the social constructionist metaphor and the application of discourse, deconstruction, and positioning concepts to more productively undermine the discourses of racism and their effects.

Definitions of Racism

Among complex societies in an era of globalization, there is no single kind of racism or single definition of it. As David Theo Goldberg (1993) suggests, "there is no unified phenomenon of racism, only a range of racisms" (p. 213). Racism is fluid in nature and takes on both covert and overt forms. In part, this is why it is so harmful and dangerous to the well-being of all. Various racisms are tied up in all social conditions covering the gamut of economic, political, legal, and cultural realms. For a behavioral description, we could define racism as what occurs when individuals of one racial or ethnic group are denied access, on the basis of their race, to resources and opportunities that are available to and enjoyed by another group (Ridley, 2005). Charmaine Wijeyesinghe, Pat Griffin, and Barbara Love (1997) invoke a commodity metaphor of power to describe racism as "the systematic subordination of members of targeted racial groups who have relatively little social power . . . by members of the agent racial group who have relatively more social power" (p. 88). In both of these definitions, there is an underlying assumption (conscious or unconscious) of superiority of one racial group over another that is used to justify and support oppressive or paternalistic practices. Here is another definition of racism from the anthropologist Ruth Benedict (1945): "Racism is the dogma that one ethnic group is condemned by nature to congenital inferiority and another group is destined for congenital superiority" (p. 87).

This ideological component is central. Any word that ends in *ism* refers to an ideology or a matrix of ideas. There can be little doubt that for different reasons one cultural group can develop specific aspects of superiority in certain dimensions of life. Inuits have superior ability to survive in cold climates. Japanese culture is superior in producing sumo wrestlers. Brazilian soccer teams are consistently superior to those of other countries. The racist assumption, however, is that such superiority is global and applies to all aspects of all people who belong to a racial group. A second assumption is that it is tied to biological inheritance in general and marked by skin color in particular.

Each of these definitions is founded on the assumption that racism is a cultural phenomenon. It is a product of cultural history and is shared among groups of people and aimed at other groups. It is not primarily an aspect of individual psychology, even though it takes on individual psychological formations and is expressed in individual behavior. If racism did not exist as a cultural phenomenon, any individual expression of it would not make sense and would be dismissed as irrational behavior. Its lethality lies partly in the way that individual expressions of racism line up with and reproduce cultural assumptions that many participate in.

Racism and the Body

A significant theme in this book has been an emphasis on the complexity of identity, and we have noted repeatedly that the modern world makes us up as people with multiple identities. A constructionist analysis takes this into consideration in relation to racism. Yet, at the same time, we are sometimes confronted with circumstances that force us to act on the exact opposite assumption. Take, for example, a young man who commits a crime and is incarcerated in a California state prison. He is white in appearance and has a Spanish last name and a Latino heritage. On entry to the prison, he is told by inmates, "You have to choose—are you going to be white or Mexican? You can't be both. Your life depends on your joining one group or the other. If you don't choose, you will die in here."

When people are asked to quickly identify how they perceive themselves, white Anglo American students typically talk about their personal qualities while people in underrepresented groups and people of color typically identify themselves by their outer exterior. Very rarely do we hear a white student in the United States say he is white as the first marker of his identity, but a person of color might claim Asian, African American, black, Latino, or Native American status as her first salient identity. Because so many settings are dominated by whites, color becomes marked as a feature of difference. People of color notice how they are marked as different, and thus color and phenotypic characteristics become internalized as their most salient marker of identity. As Jerry Diller (2007) suggests, many whites see themselves as ordinary members of the human race but not in the first instance as a racial or ethnic group. It continues to surprise many white students when people of color relate to them as a distinct racial group. The experience of surprise, or even shock, does not necessarily identify these individuals as harboring racist intent. It is more likely an effect of the existence of racist assumptions built into the wider social world.

This situation may change in future in response to demographic changes. The tide is turning against what was once an unquestioned assumption (among the white majority in the United States) that white European culture was superior in every way. In settings where white people are a minority, which according to population growth projections will become increasingly more common, it is likely that whiteness will gradually become a more salient phenomenon. Whiteness is already perceived as salient by people of color, and identity is always partially constituted in relation to how one imagines one is seen by others.

The Role of Colonization and Racism

The act of choosing one's salient identity features to present to the world sounds benign enough. In actuality, however, people of color are often denied this choice. Their options are always constrained by the way their skin color and physical features line up with a painful history of racial denigration and abjection produced out of the European colonizing discourses of the last few hundred years. (We discussed this history in Chapter 4.) It is still reproduced in the consciousness of a black child as an experience of inferiority. For example, a black child is exposed to many beliefs and values of a dominant white culture while black culture is represented to the same child in terms of lower academic achievement, association with crime, and lower-paying employment.

At ten years old, Monica was already sharply aware of the negative stigma associated with being seen as dark. She says her own aunt was stigmatized by the family and called Blackie. Children at Monica's predominantly white school would say,

"Why is your hair like that? Why do you say 'acts' instead of 'asks'? You're not say-ing it right." She says she felt so much like an outcast at school.

For people in North America and in many other parts of the world, people with black skin, kinky hair, or stereotypical Asian features and other nonwhite physical features have been historically assigned inferior status and diminished life oppor-tunity. These markers continue today to be associated with systematic, oppressive experiences of social exclusion, if not outright hatred and loathing. Physical char-acteristics and linguistic patterns immediately identify people who have been victimized by these colonizing patterns, while Anglo or white populations are asso-ciated historically (and sometimes currently) with oppressive and hateful acts. Huge pressures are applied to people of color to avoid the covert and overt acts of racism. Take Sarah, for example.

> I would be scolded for playing outside for fear that my skin complexion would darken. Light skin was emphasized as a symbol of beauty. Time and time again, I was informed that I was very blessed to have such a light complexion. My com-plexion has been considered a strong trait of beauty and is a sign of status within the Filipino community. My mother and my grandmother ensured that my complexion would remain light by utilizing whitening and bleaching creams on a regular basis. Nose shape was also an important physical characteristic in our ethnic group. Each night when I went to bed, my grandmother or mother would pinch the bridge of my nose because they believed that I would have a narrower nose rather than the stereotypical Filipino "pug" nose. At times, they would pinch my nose so hard that I would go to school the following day with a bruise.

Colonizing discourses force people in the margins to try to conform to domi-nant cultural ideas about beauty and to escape from the effects of racism and racial hatred. Let us pause to note that the origins of racism do not all begin with hatred. While there are gross examples of racial hate, an overemphasis on reducing racism to hatred can lead to the distorted assumption that racism has its origins in hate. It is probably more closely associated with a smug sense of superiority, while anger and hatred are only triggered when this sense of superiority is challenged. The same mistake can be made if we assume that domestic violence always has its origins in the experience of anger. The analysis of violence as an expression of the desire for power and control (often quite coldly expressed) has yielded a more powerful explanation of domestic violence than an explanation based on an excess of anger, and the same might be said for racism. Racial hate often arises when the victims of racism rise up and defy erroneous or arrogant notions of superiority. People cap-tured by racist attitudes of superiority often resent being challenged by those they perceive to be inferior and undeserving. It is this resentment that is the basis of racial hatred. It is fueled by the same resentment harbored by people who commit acts of domestic violence when they perceive the person in a subjugated position making an effort to resist controlling and oppressive behavior.

While most overt forms of active racism, such as the practices of the Ku Klux Klan and white supremacists, have gone largely underground, the legacy of the story of colonization persists. The European colonizing discourse today supports softer versions of what Beverly Tatum (1997) calls passive racism, where people laugh at racist jokes and support or leave unchallenged many forms of exclusionary practice against people of color in education, housing, health, and the workplace. As Tim Wise (2005) argues, racism is also expressed in the easy acceptance of social privilege as earned and deserved, along with the assumption that people of other races earn and deserve their exclusion from the same privileges and opportunities.

Noticing Ethnic Differences

Racism is founded on the division of people into groups along racial lines, but consciousness of such divisions is not natural. It is learned in the process of being enculturated. As children progress through school, they learn to notice racial markers and to accumulate assumptions on the foundation of such noticing. Their own race or ethnicity is also increasingly noticed by others. Ethnic or racial differences are not noticed as much at elementary school, where there is much more mixing in self-contained classrooms. By middle school, recognizable racial groupings are emerging. For example, many white students are tracked into honors programs while many blacks find themselves in lower tracks. This kind of sorting sends a powerful message to young people. As adolescence continues, the mixing between white and black is lessened. Interracial dating has always been uncommon in the United States (more so than in some other countries) and continues that way today, though there are also many exceptions. Black students are confronted by powerful dominant cultural discourses that suggest that to be black means you are not smart or will become a mugger, drug dealer, gang member, or some other kind of criminal. The dominant cultural discourses reinforce notions that whiteness is superior and blackness inferior. White is the norm and black or colored is the exception, or the excluded other. Signithia Fordham and John Ogbu (1986) have observed that there is a growing awareness by adolescence that black youth are excluded from many aspects of mainstream American society. These authors suggest that as black youth become more conscious of inequities, they sometimes develop an oppositional identity. This identity could be characterized as self-protective but outwardly defiant. It serves to provide some self-protection from the suffering caused by racist practices and also serves to keep the white majority population at a distance.

Barack Obama (2006) speaks about the ongoing effects racism on nonwhite populations:

> None of us—black, white, Latino, or Asian—is immune to the stereotypes that our culture continues to feed us, especially stereotypes about black criminality, black intelligence, or the black work ethic. In general, members of every minority group continue to be measured largely by the degree of our assimilation—how closely our speech patterns, dress, or demeanor conform to the dominant white culture—and the more that a minority strays from these external markers, the more he or she is subject to negative assumptions. (p. 235)

According to the stereotypes that Obama refers to, if a white person fails to show normal intelligence at school or engages in borderline criminal activity, it is more likely to be considered an instance of individual difference. A person of color in the same situation is more likely to be assumed to be typical of his race.

For seven years, I (Gerald) have walked around our ethnically diverse university campus and noticed many black students congregating in one area on campus. In middle and high schools across the United States, black students tend to congregate together, as do Asians and people of other groups. Beverly Tatum's (1997) popular book, titled *Why Are All the Black Kids Sitting Together in the Cafeteria?"* speaks to this phenomenon. While there are great within-group differences in all identity groups, the self-selection of social groups formed along ethnic and racial lines continues to dominate many social institutions in North America. It is most notable in schools, prisons, and the residential communities where people live. Part of this gravitation relates to feelings of shared oppression that people of color experience on a day-to-day basis. Sometimes feelings of oppression shared with others who look similar provide a sense of safety, support, and even protection. Sometimes they also relate to a fear of difference and a desire to keep other groups out. Other factors such as economic resources impact where and how people group together. Read the following stories for examples of how racism is made manifest in individual people's lives.

As I grew older, I was undoubtedly exposed to racism and discrimination. I realized I was a black woman in a white world, and often that was not a good place to be. I repeatedly heard the *N* word not only being used but being accepted in the workplace. Coworkers would make racist comments to my face and then try to convince me they were not racist. When I was bold enough to tell them I did not appreciate the *N* word or challenged them to explain what they meant by their "innocent" or "I didn't mean you" racist comments, I was often labeled hostile and confrontational. This is a stereotype that many African American women are subject to.

At the beginning of an interview for a job, the interviewer said, "Oh, you are black. That is not at all what I was expecting. Your name is not typical for a black girl."

—Heather Conley-Higgins

"Nigger." Six little letters that when put together in that order have such power over my life. It is more than an insult. It is more than a racial slur. In that one word is a reminder of all that my ancestors went through at the hands of Europeans and whites in America. In that one word is a reminder of the villages in West Africa that were destroyed and the people who were captured, held in slave castles, and shipped to the "New World." In that one word is the reminder of all who died in the middle passage. In that one word is the reminder of the centuries of backbreaking work from sunup to sundown for no pay. In that one word is the reminder of the women raped, the men beaten, the children separated from their families. In that one word is the reminder of being counted as three fifths of a person. In that one word is the reminder of the law forbidding blacks to learn to read. In that one word is the reminder of the years of apartheid in America—also known as Jim Crow. In that one word is a reminder of the water hoses, the dogs, the burning crosses, the lynchings. In that one word is a reminder of the four little girls bombed in a church in Birmingham. In that one word is a reminder of racial profiling, being followed in a store, ladies clutching their purses.

So you see, there is a long history behind those six little letters. When I hear it out of the mouth of a white American, it cuts deep down in my soul. I feel it for all my brothers and sisters in the struggle. I feel it for all that came before me. I feel it for my brothers, my sister, my parents, and my grandmother. I feel all of the unsaid that goes with it. *You're nothing. You're worthless. You're nothing more than a chattel. Your opinion doesn't matter. Your thoughts are irrelevant. Your life is unimportant.* The hatred behind "nigger" runs too deep.

There is life and death in the power of words. I choose not to let them define me or destroy my spirit. However, I cannot ignore the historical, social, and racial implications of those six little letters.

James Baldwin once said, "You can only be destroyed by believing that you really are what the white world calls a nigger."

I know that I am worth more than gold. I know that my opinion matters. I know that my life is important. I will not be destroyed. But it still hurts. It still cuts deep. Real deep.

—Natasha Crawford

I shouldn't have to work 20 times harder in this world. I shouldn't have to accept your view and ways of life just because you feel you own this land. On the outside I look like I have had an easy life, but on the inside my heart is aching and I long to cry so that I could shed a tear for all the pain my people and I have endured. The anger that I feel inside is boiling from what you have done, so that sometimes I want revenge. But I am better than that. Two wrongs don't make a right. Do you see me now? I don't think you do, because you've heard my story before but you have chosen to ignore it. You have oppressed my race, my family and friends. You are my oppressor. So the hate gets stronger, but so do I, and no matter what you have done or will do to me and my people I will fight for what is rightly ours . . . Life!

—Deliah

I am writing hoping that maybe, just maybe you'll listen with more than your ears. What you see before you is a typical Asian girl. I've got straight black hair, dark brown eyes, flat nose, and a short physical stature. That's Asian, right? But sometimes people call me Chinese, Japanese, Vietnamese, or even Oriental! Correction, "Oriental" is for rugs. I am Filipino. And I'd like to tell you that it hurts. It hurts to be described like a rug. But, you know what, most of the time I keep quiet.

What you see before you is an Asian American. I am a citizen of the United States. But sometimes people ask me, "Why don't you just say you are American?" or "Why don't you just be an American?" And I think, why should I have to choose between being Asian and being American? I already feel the pressures to assimilate at the cost of my Filipino culture. And if I don't assimilate, I am going to be labeled as a foreigner in America. Sometimes people see me as a foreigner, a foreign exotic Asian female; like some captive creature you point to in the zoo, or like a mail-order bride who is docile, sexual, and mysterious. I feel dirty, degraded, and dehumanized when treated like a commodity.

Some people tell me that I can achieve the "American dream." From my experience, the American dream is not an equal opportunity for all Americans. There have been institutional barriers, such as laws, that have served as obstacles for those who desire the American dream. Historically Asian immigrants were prevented from owning land and other property, from attaining citizenship, and from being allowed to immigrate to be with their loved ones. While these laws no longer apply, their legacy and negative effect has influenced the present social, political, and economic struggles of Asian Americans.

—Mary Suzette Tuason

Mary Suzette Tuason identifies herself as Filipino.

When I started school I could not speak English. When learning English, I could not speak it to my Mandarin-speaking parents. My teachers interpreted my inability to complete work and my lack of participation as a reflection of incompetence. They wrote unsatisfactory comments on my report cards. Because of these reactions, I associated my Chinese heritage with shameful ignorance. I focused on creating an "American identity." I learned to hide my Chinese identity. However, I had limited success. Classmates mocked my Chinese foods, such as rice porridge with dried eel. When I was able to eat hamburgers and fantasize about American pop stars, I began to be accepted by some Anglo American schoolmates.

Despite my very Chinese heritage, Euro-American colonial images were very impactful on my family. As a swimmer, I spent time in the sun and began to develop a strong athletic frame. My mother threatened to pull me out of the swim team because my skin was getting too dark. In my family, dark women were associated with servants or field workers and pale, thin Chinese women were seen as attractive and of high social status. My mother used to pinch my nose, which was a little flatter than she wanted it to be. She tried to mold it to look like an Anglo American nose. My eyes were not large enough; my lips were too thin.

—Grace Tsai

TO DISCUSS

1. Persons of color might be reminded of their own stories of similar experiences and be willing to share them with the class.

2. White students should listen to these stories respectfully and afterward discuss how they are affected by hearing them.

3. What difference does it make to bring these stories into conversation, where they can be heard?

4. How does holding a conversation about racism in class affect relationships in the class?

5. How might holding a conversation about racism in class affect the work you will do as a counselor, social worker, or psychologist?

6. What are some useful strategies that both white counselors and counselors of color can pursue to combat the effects of racism?

Many members of the white majority are quite oblivious to the ongoing effects of racist behavior toward people of color. Some are even convinced that racism is a thing of the past. They focus on the legal changes that have outlawed many of the more egregious overt expressions of racism and ignore the fact that the cultural assumptions and values that live in people's conversation and in their thinking are not instantly removed by changes in law. The past continues to cast shadows over the present.

Meanwhile, the media continue to bombard us with stereotypical images of ethnic and racial groupings. Blacks in the United States and other people of color continue to bear the brunt of the harshest forms of racism as they are continually reinforced by media images. These racist discourses are like a fog that penetrates every aspect of people's day-to-day lives.

Elizabeth Martinez (2007) points out that much of the multicultural literature on racism focuses on white-black relations and minimizes the Latino/Latina community's experience of racism. Martinez argues that Latino/Latina experiences with racism are ignored because they are invisible. When racism against Latinas and Latinos is recognized, it is often in the form of an insinuation that these people endanger the positions of other ethnic groups.

White Privilege

One cannot understand racism in North America without considering the prominent role that white privilege plays in contemporary society. White privilege is the unearned power that most whites accrue in American society simply because they are white. It has grown out of the last few hundred years of European colonization. The genealogy of many of our struggles today can be traced to the history of racial interactions that we described in Chapter 3. The identities that we experience in the present are shaped by complex historical patterns of ethnic, racial, gender, religious, sexual orientation, and class relations. For example, dominant American cultural discourse honors the founding fathers' efforts at building the American institutions that continue to this day. It is easy to join with this discourse of admiration if you are white. If you are Indian, black, or Asian, identifying with these historical political figures and honoring their achievements is more complicated. Joining with this discourse may produce conflicting feelings about how your ancestors were treated by these same founding fathers. This is one tiny example of the different positions that history creates for people. And yet white privilege largely rests on the story that racism is solely historical. In this story, slavery ended after the Civil War and civil rights were won in the 1960s, and these structural changes ended the matter.

For many whites, race and racism are invisible. Joyce King (1991) constructed the term "dysconsciousness" to describe how whites take for granted their privileged position in society. Many hold to comfortable and unquestioned assumptions of equal individual opportunity. In these assumptions, racism is conceived of only as a set of individual beliefs that get expressed in forms of discrimination and prejudice. Sometimes the word *discrimination* is part of the problem. This word transports the issue of racism into the discourse of individual motivation and intent. For discrimination to be proven in court, such intent needs to be established. The problem is that often the origins of racism and the origins of privilege have little to do with individuals' intended actions. They are instead built into the dominant discourse, into institutional processes, and into taken-for-granted assumptions about how life is. There are, of course, many examples of deliberate discrimination that still take place. But the problem of racism is much larger than anything a word like *discrimination* can encompass. It fails to elucidate situations where there is no personal intent to discriminate and yet inferior status is still ascribed to people of color and privileged status is given to white persons who have not earned it.

Conceiving of racism in terms of individual attitudes blinds people to the more systemic aspects of privilege and disadvantage on racial grounds. As Charles Ridley (2005) says, "Few whites attribute racial inequality to the structural framework of American society—a social order where racial victimization is normative" (p. 163). (Notice the structuralist emphasis in this rendering.) White privilege also comes with the option of deciding whether or not to take the initiative in discussing racism.

Another aspect of white privilege is seldom having to think of yourself in terms of race. Not having to identify as a particular race implies choice about the acknowledging or declining of a racial identity. This is a choice black people do not have. Having the choice, therefore, is itself a privilege. This privilege exists regardless of personal attitude and is therefore not the same as active prejudice. Hence it is often denied on the grounds of lack of personal culpability. Such denials miss the point, and thus the responsibility of whites to address racism is dismissed. The same lack of primary consciousness exists around other social dividing lines as well. Gender can similarly be less of a defining identity for men than it is for women. Socioeconomic class can be less salient as an identity for the middle class than for those in the lower classes.

Danica Hays and Catherine Chang (2003) define white privilege as the straightforward belief that one's own standards and opinions can be taken for granted as true and accurate (to the exclusion of others'). This taken-for-granted acceptance of one's viewpoint obscures many white persons' perceptions of themselves as located in racial and ethnic relations. A common attitude among the white community is expressed as "If you work hard, you can succeed in the United States" or "Everybody has the potential to become the president." These ideas illustrate naive assumptions about equality and access to resources. Ronald Jackson (1999) refers to white privilege as a phenomenon that enrolls certain people at birth, without their consent, and brings them up in a favored status. Jerry Diller (2007) suggests that it is easy to deny the existence of white privilege and see oneself as "colorless" so as to avoid noticing ongoing inequalities for people of color.

> If I am White and truly understand what white privilege means socially, economically, and politically, then I cannot help but bear some of the guilt for what has happened historically and what continues to occur. If I were to truly "get it," then I would have no choice but to give up my complacency. (Diller, 2007, p. 49)

Many multicultural counseling texts refer to the well-known article "White Privilege: Unpacking the Invisible knapsack" (McIntosh, 1989), which explains the contemporary systemic advantages of being white in American society. Peggy McIntosh, a white feminist scholar, identifies a long list of societal privileges that she received simply because she was white. It includes major advantages for middle class Anglo Americans, such as access to a wider range of jobs and housing. She describes the luxury of being confident that the teacher would be unlikely to discriminate against her child on the basis of whiteness. She lists being able to walk around a department store with little likelihood of being followed by suspicious salespersons. She could be late for meetings and be fairly confident that her lateness wouldn't be attributed to the fact that she was white. She could also express an opinion in a meeting that would not be labeled a white opinion. Many people of color relate easily to McIntosh's list. However, the article is now 15 years old and some people think times have changed.

How much they have not changed may be indicated by a study recently released by the University of California, Los Angeles, which found that 22.7% of freshmen said racial discrimination was no longer a major problem in the United States (Silverstein, 2005). Opinions differed, however, between whites and minorities on race-related questions. For instance, 23.5% of white freshmen believed that helping to promote racial understanding was essential or very important, while 54.8% of black freshman and 43.6% of Latino freshmen deemed this essential or very important.

From a social constructionist perspective, privilege is not a static or constant, structurally determined state of being, even though it is recognized as patterned systematically. Rather, it might be considered a property of a relation that is reproduced each time we engage in social practices that assume privileged entitlement. It also shifts in response to contextual events. If a white person enters a black or Native American context, she may temporarily experience the inverse of white privilege. Neither is privileged entitlement guaranteed for all whites. Some white people may be excluded from privilege on account of their gay, lesbian, or transsexual identity, or through being seriously disabled, or elderly, or homeless, or from a white underclass.

These exceptions mean that whites have to work at maintaining positions of privilege. The need to work at constantly reproducing privilege has two corollaries. It means that privilege is actively reproduced over and over again. And it also means that there are many places where it can be noticed and contested. Many whites have regular experiences of preferential status. In most business and professional work contexts in North America, white males dominate senior management positions. The mere fact of having white skin still usually protects people from certain degrading, distasteful, and discriminatory experiences (Baruth & Manning 2007). Betsy Lucal (1996) points out that, generally speaking, whites do not have to expend psychological and monetary resources on recovering from other people's prejudices.

White Privilege and Counseling

According to Leroy Baruth and Lee Manning (2007), white counselors respond to white privilege in different ways. They report that white counselors experience a range of emotional responses from anger, guilt, self-protectiveness, sadness, hopelessness, and confusion. There are variations in how responsible white counselors feel about the role of advocacy in challenging racism and privilege in their communities. Danica Hays, Catherine Chang, and Jennifer Dean (2004) argue that it is good when white counselors experience strong emotions regarding white privilege, as it may increase their awareness of issues around oppression, advocacy, and counselor awareness. However, our interest is not so much in getting people to feel strong emotions as in getting them to participate in actions toward change. The link between feelings of guilt and motivation to work for change is more often assumed than demonstrated. So it remains questionable.

Differing Perspectives on Understanding and Addressing Racism

Racism and its effects can be understood from a variety of perspectives. One's worldview and one's understanding of how power and oppression work will influence how one addresses racism and whether its deleterious consequences will diminish. In earlier chapters in this book, we discussed three approaches to power relations—liberal humanist, structuralist, and poststructuralist—and how they shape counseling practice. In this chapter we would like to show how these versions of power relations can be applied to give different accounts of racist practices. We shall also explore how racism may be addressed through the lens of these contrasting conceptual tools.

Liberal Humanism and Racism

Liberal humanism, as we explained in Chapter 6, views the individual as the prime mover, responder, and initiator, while the functions of institutional conditions and social structures are downplayed or ignored. Individual free will is favored over any assumption that wider sociocultural influences and colonizing history might shape or determine human volition and action. If individuals are basically free to do as they will, then individual decisions are at the base of discriminatory behavior. Power and the abuse of power is a personal phenomenon and originates from inside the individual and is then acted out against other individuals.

Racism, from this perspective, is commonly understood as an individual attitude of mind or an expression of that mind in behavior. Liberal humanist thinking usually directs us to focus on racism at the individual level. For example, many people consider racial prejudice to be constructed through an individual's making a preconceived judgment or deriving an opinion about a whole group of people on the basis of limited and distorted information. In other words, racial stereotyping is primarily a failure to treat people as individuals. From the liberal humanist perspective, the source of racism might best be understood as located in the corrupted logic of the individual mind. It is an instance of personal failure or is a personal deficit of character. Some have even argued that racism results from the early "hurt" experiences of racist individuals (reported by Ponterotto & Pedersen, 1993). Sometimes people think of it as diseased or irrational thinking that shapes the personal attitudes of individual people. From this perspective, racism has its origins in individual faulty thinking, or personal prejudice, or irrational stereotyping, which is then manifested in discriminatory decisions, practices, laws, and so forth. Thus, racism originates in the individual's psychology, and there will be individual variation in the extent to which racist behavior is expressed.

From a liberal humanist perspective, racism is also understood as a misdirection of a person's personal power. It becomes more damaging when the racist individual has accrued more power than the victims of racism, who may have less personal power and less ability to protect themselves. Racism from this perspective is a by-product of the individual's personality and relational style. Thus, accusing somebody of being racist when he doesn't believe he is racist goes right to the heart. Accused persons experience their essence as being under siege and often go on the attack to protect themselves. The recipient of the racist behavior responds in kind and accepts the protective attack as a personally motivated action that justifies the original accusation. Usually, frustration is the main product of such interactions. Some of the frustration results from conceiving of racism as an intimate act generated and acted out by one individual against another.

From this perspective, the eradication of racism would need to involve a process of individual psychological change in which racist persons are identified, or identify themselves, and then receive corrective training to eliminate their irrational thinking and replace it with more accurate, rational thinking. The role of the counselor or psychotherapist delivering this corrective training might be to help the client "own" her racism and take personal responsibility for her abusive behavior. By helping the client connect with oppression in her own life, the counselor might help her understand and then change her oppressive behaviors.

The liberal humanist perspective on racism is limited, however. Individuals do not usually invent the racist ideas that pepper their utterances and social practices. They more often borrow them from the discourse in which they have been enculturated. They are not in this way the originators of their own thoughts. Most racist social practice comes packaged and ready made, with little individual thought necessary. It happens because people just accept and go along with how things are done. It is powerful precisely because it seems natural, familiar, and unable to be questioned.

Structuralism and Racism

Another way to understand racism and address its harmful effects is to consider a structural analysis, as discussed in Chapter 7. Racism from this perspective is understood as a systemic process that consistently advantages one group over another based on race (Wellman, 1977). It emphasizes the underlying social structure as the source of racism, rather than racism being a personal property of the individual. Because the structural analysis regards the individual as a product of his position in a social structure, individual people are viewed as having limited abilities to make choices. Since individuals have such little influence within the structure, emphasis is placed on analyzing and changing the structures that shape and influence lives. Those with a structural orientation tend to focus on mobilizing individuals who are the victims of the oppressive structures—that is, those who are victims of racism—and helping them see how the structural constraints are negatively affecting their lives.

A structural analysis is directed at how racism is institutionalized. Institutional racism and discrimination occur when people are excluded or deprived of rights and opportunities as a result of the normal operations of the institution. A structuralist analysis can show that even while individuals hold no malicious racist intentions or are unaware of how others are being harmed, there can still be racist outcomes. As Sonia Nieto (2000) notes, racist practices can be produced in schools through inequitable testing practices, rigid ability tracking, low expectations of students based on their identity, and inequitably funded schools. Claude Steele (1992), speaking to the issue of institutional racism, suggested, "Deep in the psyche of American educators is a presumption that black students need academic remediation, or extra time with elemental curricula to overcome background deficits" (p. 77). Steele spoke of stigma vulnerability, another phrase for racism, and demonstrated how such stigmata are based on the systematic devaluation faced by blacks and other people of color in schools. Of course, schools are only one location where institutionalized racism occurs. Rewards and punishments are also structurally expressed in the systematic organization of access to housing, employment, and health.

As racist behaviors are understood from a structural perspective separate from the individual, people are inevitably cast into social groups that represent their structural position in a society. They are considered less as individuals than as members of a group. And that group occupies a structurally determined position that is either oppressing or being oppressed. Individuals may protest their innocence or difference, but they are still seen as part of the group. Beverly Tatum (1999) reserves the term *racist* only for "behaviors committed by whites in the context of a white-dominated society" (p.10). While Tatum acknowledges hateful behavior and hate crimes perpetrated by people of color, her overriding concern is to define racism in relation to the structural power differentials afforded whites in the United States. These power differentials translate into white superiority and white advantage. Individual racism is the downstream effect of this structural superiority. Tatum argues that people of color cannot be racist because they do not automatically benefit from racism and because there is no institutional support for racism by blacks or other people of color. Jerry Diller (2007) has a similar perspective when he says that while all people hold prejudices, whites, because of their access to positions of power, are actually racist, while people of color can only be prejudiced. His formula is that prejudice plus power equals racism. The structuralist perspective shows that racism is a product of systematic privilege for some categories of personhood and systematic penalty for other categories. This structural definition is employed by many people working in the multicultural field. It is a very understandable definition when we consider the history of systematic oppression in the United States. It accounts for racist practice that is anonymous, pervasive, and seemingly not the fault of any individual intent. Many whites continue to benefit from the cultural privileges that accompany being white and experience considerable distress, anger, and guilt when confronted with this reality.

A therapist using a structural analysis will seek to help individuals identify more closely with their racial group membership. He or she will then teach his or her clients how they are victims of institutional practices and thus help them focus on and identify the oppressive structures rather than blame themselves for the suffering they have experienced. An additional role is to help oppressed groups to rebel and challenge the racial injustices implicit in the institutions that shape day-to-day lives. A counselor focusing on a structural orientation would seek to challenge members of groups that benefit from racist structural conditions to acknowledge their privilege and to use their positions in power structures to help to change the system. This can be very discouraging work, as many individuals question whether they can do anything about institutional racism. They may argue that they are not responsible for an institution's policies. To challenge or question exclusionary practices might seem beyond one's power to change. The typical response is, "I am hardly in a position to change policies I am not responsible for." As Diller (2007) suggests, this is similar logic to that used in the response, "I should not be held responsible for what happened two hundred years ago at the time of the slave trade." People question why they should make sacrifices now to address injustices that happened long ago. Other constraints on action include the sheer effort required to change the status quo, which is often vulnerable to change only at a time of crisis or when the system is completely malfunctioning. For many people, it is difficult to even know where to start.

Box 14.1. Racism in Prison

There is no worse place to see the ugly face of racism than among the over 2,000,000 inmates locked in prison facilities around the United States. It is widely accepted among social scientists that people of color receive harsher sentences than whites. According to Terry Kupers (1999), 50% of the current inmate population are African American and 15% Latino or Latina, numbers well in excess of population proportions. Jerry Diller (2007) suggests that by 2020, one third of all African Americans will be in the criminal justice system. Currently, 90% to 95% of the inmates of maximum security units are blacks and Latino, while minimum security units are primarily white. The prison populations are drawn sharply along racial lines, and in many prisons, when there is trouble, people quickly organize themselves into racial groups. According to Kupers (1999), prisoners of color are more likely than whites to be sent to solitary confinement rather than receive appropriate psychological treatment. Prison life reminds prisoners of color about all of the systemic injustices in the world. In many prisons the majority of the prison staff are white, including those sitting on hearing and appeals panels. Kupers suggests that prisoners of color are treated in stereotypical ways, resulting in large numbers of complaints against guards on the basis of racial discrimination. He also comments that supervisory positions and training tend to be allocated along racial lines, with higher-status positions going to white inmates.

Closely associated with institutional forms of racism are the phenomena of culturally racist practices in North America. An example is the dominant culture's acknowledging holidays and celebrations such as Christmas and Thanksgiving while ignoring many holidays associated with non-European cultures. Cultural racism can also come in the form of disdain for cultural expressions derived from communal and collective practices and the favoring of individuality and assertiveness. Standard English is expected to be spoken in most institutions in North America, while standard of dress is always measured against European criteria. For example, Afros and braids worn by African Americans can be deemed "ethnic" and not appropriate in many companies and organizations. Cultural icons such as Jesus and Mary are often portrayed as white while Christ's betrayer Judas is shown as black. Meanwhile, Band-Aids that are called "skin color" come in shades that approximate only white skin colors.

Some counseling models are constructed so as to empower oppressed groups to challenge the structural inequalities caused by oppressor groups. For example, the Just Therapy Model developed in New Zealand explicitly aims to structure counseling in a way that addresses cultural and racial oppression. One of the interventions aimed at addressing oppression and racism is the forming of caucusing groups among social service agency employees. The dominant group, which could be either white or male, takes responsibility for raising its own consciousness and addressing potential or actual abuse of power and unconscious assumptions of racism. The dominant group takes responsibility for stopping harmful behaviors or discriminatory practices and makes itself accountable to the evaluation and feedback of the nondominant group with regard to its efforts. Group members who are representative of marginalized populations (Maori or Samoan or women) are taught how to identify oppressive practices and to challenge them when they occur (Waldegrave, Tamasese, Tuhaka, & Campbell, 2003). Partnership between the caucuses and accountability of the dominant group to the marginalized is the key to success. Counseling is provided for families and individuals on the basis of establishing a match between counselor and client with regard to ethnicity and gender.

Another emergent therapeutic model that is in alignment with some of the structural elements described here is the Cultural Context Model (CCM; Hernandez, Almedia, & Dolan–Del Vecchio, 2005). The CCM postcolonial model utilizes culture circles made up of client groups in same-gender or same-race groups. They use a systemic cultural analysis process that involves identifying a variety of forms of domination, including those that relate to racism, and incorporating the analysis and the challenging of oppressive practices into therapeutic work.

TO DISCUSS

Have a discussion in small groups on the topic of racism, prejudice, and discrimination.

1. How would you define *racism*, *discrimination*, and *prejudice*?
2. Which definitions included in this chapter do you prefer? Why?
3. How do you think that people learn to behave in racist ways and to show prejudice, and to discriminate against others?
4. What experiences of the various forms of racism described in this chapter have you either experienced or witnessed?
5. What would it mean to you to be described as a racist?
6. Do you know a racist, or is everybody in the world a racist?
7. How do you deal with racism when you encounter it?
8. Can a person change racist behavior? How?
9. Can racism be eliminated? How would you suggest that it could be done?
10. What steps have you taken to help deal with racism?
11. How can counseling practice make a difference to the existence of racism?

Problems With a Purely Structural Analysis of Racism

While Beverly Tatum (1997) eloquently names the insidious, systematic processes of racist behavior and oppression, a challenging part of her analysis occurs when she locates racism as an essential characteristic of white group membership. To call people racist on the basis of their ethnic group membership falls into the same structural logic as racism itself. Like racism, it is an example of essentialist thinking. Structural analyses often create an impression of the inevitability of personal racism that precludes the possibility of personal moral choice about whether or not to resist structural positioning. When people engage with others, they are constructed as falling into alignment with their positions in an organized system of social relations, rather than considered to be speaking out of their personal experience. A structural analysis tends to produce binary groupings made up of oppressors and oppressed. From a structuralist perspective, the oppressor group sets the stage on which the subordinate group operates. The relationship of the oppressor to the oppressed is often one in which the oppressor group assigns itself high status while devaluing the oppressed group in demeaning ways.

While this analysis gets at some important aspects of how discourse operates, to fix people as part of an oppressor or oppressed class limits where you can go in the conversation to address racism and other forms of social injustice. For example, if whites are part of an oppressor class because they are white and blacks are part of an oppressed class because they are black, there isn't much room for either group to exercise agency. A range of differential responses within each group is obscured from view. It is hard to see how people can make decisions to extricate themselves from these binary positions. A structural analysis also does not easily account for contradictions, reverse racism, white activism against racism, or the subtle nuances of race relations that do not straightforwardly divide into structural binaries.

Shelby Steele (2006), a black activist of the 1960s whom some describe as a black conservative, speaks about how blacks who embrace the status of victims or the oppressed can diminish the extent to which they can act responsibly and powerfully in the world. He states, "Suddenly I could use America's fully acknowledged history of racism just as whites had always used their race—as a racial authority and privilege that excused me from certain responsibilities, moral constraints, and even the law" (p. 54). He reminisces about authentic black militancy of the kind shown by Malcolm X, which he termed "hard work militancy," that follows the principles of self-sacrifice, delayed gratification, and the hard-core work ethic. He talks about the troubled analysis of certain social processes that legitimate blacks' not taking responsibility for their lives and their future. Steele explains why the comedian Bill Cosby is criticized by black elites for suggesting that poor blacks need to take more responsibility. To accept Cosby's suggestions, he points out, would be a betrayal of the critics' oppressed identity. Maintaining an identity as an oppressed victim can undermine people's efforts to take action on their own behalf rather than waiting for the oppressor to stop oppressing them. The assumptions underlying the psychological constructs of internal and external loci of control, first discussed by Julian Rotter (1966), may be of assistance here. An internal locus of control refers to the notion that individuals believe they are in control of their own fate, whereas an external locus of control refers to the notion that individuals are at the mercy of external forces. What is at stake is here is agency, although the internal locus of control idea assumes a liberal humanist version of the ideal individual self. Many of the multicultural writers, such as Derald Wing Sue and David Sue (2003), have enunciated in depth the influence of the locus of control literature on our understanding of various ethnic groups' responses to change processes. Sue and Sue note how many people of color have developed an external locus of control because of systematic patterns of oppression and believe they are not in charge of their own fate. Charles Ridley (2005) also addresses this issue:

Shackled by self-doubt, fear, and helplessness, many minorities forgo chances to exploit their potential and opportunities because they are reenacting their past victimization. The secondary gains these individuals realize from such reenactment include avoidance of the consequences of relinquishing the victim role. (p. 115)

He goes on to explain the secondary gains, which include avoiding head-on confrontation with racism, avoiding the discovery of one's true abilities, and avoiding the scorn of other minorities who still hold on to their victim status.

There are further problematic aspects of the dominant/subordinate, oppressor/oppressed binaries. For example, a structural analysis of the abuse of power and the mechanisms of oppression place the following identities in the oppressor category: white, male, able-bodied, heterosexual, Christian, middle class, urban, educated, thin, and attractive. Identities in the oppressed category include: colored, female, disabled, bisexual, homosexual, non-Christian, poor, rural, uneducated, fat, and unattractive. It is likely that any reader of this text who is placed in some of the categories of the oppressed class will also have membership in oppressor categories. The notion of discrete structural binaries begins to break down when, in any one moment, people are simultaneously part of both oppressor and oppressed polarities. The structural analysis becomes weakened when this kind of diffusion occurs.

One of the unfortunate consequences of a structural analysis of racism is that people get seduced into what Elizabeth Martinez (2001) calls the Oppression Olympics—an endless and irresolvable competition among diverse groups seeking a prize for the most victimized and oppressed group. Krishna Guadalupe and Doman Lum (2005) regretfully report that the multicultural movement has been held back because of the conscious or unconscious prioritizing of one set of human diversity attributes over another.

To be called racist is to be labeled with one of the most blameworthy descriptions that can be given a person, especially if the accusation is made by a person of a different ethnicity. *Racist* has become such a loaded word that it often produces a nasty emotional wake, leading to people's withdrawing from one another and erecting barriers to further discussion. We have witnessed many encounters in which an individual or a group of people are told they are racist because of their ethnic membership. Whether the accusation is accurate or not, the quality of the conversation often deteriorates from there. Talking about racism can be intimidating in a roomful of people where some have a family history of active participation in racism while others have a family history of being the recipients of racist acts.

Poststructuralism and Racism

We have emphasized in this book the growing interest in a poststructuralist perspective and its value in our understanding of power and how to intervene to diminish its harm in our communities. As already outlined in Chapter 5 and Chapter 8, a poststructuralist lens challenges the notion that the world is neatly divided into categories of oppressors and the oppressed. Racism is not assumed to be inherent in the nature of either individuals or groups, or even in social structures.

Instead, we would start from the assumption that racism inheres in social practices, which are performed in discourse. We would argue that these social practices and the discourses that inform assumptions about race are where racism originates. The attitudes of persons, the characteristics of groups, and the structure of social arrangements are all derived from the constant reproduction of these practices. Personal racism is not invented by those individuals who perform racist hate crimes as much as it exists before they are born, and for a complex array of reasons they become recruited into speaking its lines. Structural and institutional racism is not essential to any system, even when it appears to stabilize that system. Neither does structural racism make personal racist assumptions inevitable for members of "oppressor" groups. Nor does it make victimhood and the psychology of abjection essential for members of "oppressed" groups.

The poststructuralist reasoning is instead that social structures are sustained only by pieces of discourse that will shift and change their shape as people remake social discourse. Discourse assigns people positions from which to think, and these are codified and reified into social structures and institutions, but people can and do refuse to act from these positions. They actively contest and modify them on a daily basis.

A poststructuralist analysis of racism needs to take such nuances into account, particularly if we as counselors are intent on helping individuals negotiate their way through life in the midst of a confusing array of positions. From this perspective, the complexity of life makes for a more indeterminate, fluid set of circumstances. People on a moment-to-moment basis make efforts to influence the quality of their own lives and those of others. A poststructuralist analysis pays attention to the microdynamics that both support and undermine racism. To do so means that we don't have to wait for a structural revolution to bring about meaningful change. Nor do we have to rely on changing racism one person at a time. A poststructuralist analysis opens to view a variety of opportunities to challenge the discourse of racism and to diminish its effects.

Discourse, deconstruction, and positioning, as discussed in Chapter 5, are useful conceptual tools that help us name and examine the effects of the cultural discourses that embody racism. The analysis of discourse helps us identify cultural histories that position blacks as less intelligent than whites, that suggest that men are superior to women, that see heterosexuals as normal and homosexuals as aberrant. Rather than assigning individuals because of one identity into a dominant group or a subordinate group and hanging an oppressor or an oppressed label over them, we can explore the effects of these discourses on relations between people. Apart from anything else, labels always run the risk of fixing people in place. A focus on the discourse of racism and its effects provides many avenues to address the problem without resorting to totalizing statements that define people as essentially racists. Such totalizing is no different from defining some people as evil and others as pure. Human beings are always more complex than simplistic descriptions can ever capture.

Addressing racism as a discourse disrupts the tendency to tie the term *racist* in an essential way to a person or to a group. While the emphasis moves on to the discourse and its effects, in no way does this discount the systematic and patterned applications of racist practice that advantage some groups of people over others. Racial privilege can still be deconstructed. Nor does it excuse individuals (of all races and ethnicities) from the challenge of taking moral responsibility for the existence of the social practices of racism. In fact, it opens up the possibility that people who are positioned in places of privilege and people who are positioned in places of marginalization can actually work together against racism. Below is a classroom story that brings out a focus on racism as a discourse that systemically affects groups of people in painful ways and enlists others to perpetuate harm in painful ways.

Box 14.2. Famous Statements About Race

"Racism . . . made me less than I might have been."

—George Jackson, 1971

"The inseparable twin of racial injustice is economic injustice."

—Martin Luther King, Jr., 1963

"Slavery is essential to democracy. For where there are great incongruities in the constitution of society, if the American were to admit the Indian, the Chinese, the Negroes, to the rights to which they are justly jealous of admitting European emigrants, the country would be thrown into disorder, and if not, would be degraded to the level of the barbarous races."

—Lord Acton, 1861

"Blood mixture and the resultant drop in the racial level is the sole cause of the dying out of old cultures."

—Adolf Hitler, 1924

"Never yet could I find that a black had uttered a thought above the level of plain narration."

—Thomas Jefferson, 1785

"The mental inferiority of the negro to the white or yellow races is a fact."

—Encyclopedia Britannica, 1911

"Now as to the Negroes! I entirely agree with you that as a race and in the main they are altogether inferior to the Whites."

—Theodore Roosevelt, 1906

> *"I believe in White supremacy until the Blacks are educated to a point of responsibility. I don't believe in giving authority and positions of leadership and judgment to irresponsible people."*
>
> —John Wayne, 1971

Racism in the Multicultural Class

In a multicultural counseling class, there was a heated exchange among students wrestling with the issues of racism. Half the group were people of color and the remainder were white. Three women who identified as persons of color expressed serious concerns about a white student who had made a series of racist remarks and told her in direct and strong terms that she was a racist. One of the students had heard the white student relay a comment to another person to the effect that "black people are homophobic." Now it was being spoken about in the multicultural counseling class.

As the conversation developed, one of the students of color spoke about how much she hated white people. She hated them for what they had done to people of color and how they continued to perpetuate harmful racist behavior as well as support racist cultural practices. The tensions and distress in the room rapidly began to rise. A number of people were feeling under attack for different reasons. The perceived level of safety, which had been very high at an earlier stage, was rapidly being eroded by fear and mistrust.

Some people, both white students and people of color, began linking the racist comment with other remarks that this same white student had made. They began to infer racist undertones in each of these other comments, which further confirmed the opinion of the three students that this white student was indeed racist. Some other group members agreed she was making racist implications, while others disagreed. The accused white student was now shut down and frozen. Many other white students were feeling under attack in the same way that the students identifying as people of color were feeling. The interactions were ready to spiral out of control, and people either wanted to leave the room immediately or began to shut down.

Many educators who have taken on the difficult job of addressing racism have witnessed similar difficult interactions. Exploring the effects of racism is a sensitive and sometimes dangerous task and often runs the risk of unraveling a group. Because many people deny that they are affected by racist attitudes, when they are brought to the surface, it is often very difficult and very painful. That is why many people choose to keep the subject of racism off the table along with discussions about religion, gender issues, and homophobia. Interactions between group members can so quickly move to attack and defend modes, and then to counterattack and self-protection. Ultimately what is produced is depression, disengagement, and bitterness, rather than significant change toward rooting out racism.

There is no doubt that racism was present during these painful interactions. The problem was that individuals were totalized as either racist or as members of a hateful group, and the possibility of challenging racism in a more productive way was shut down. Such conversations also close off opportunities to educate and ultimately address racist behaviors in school, in the workplace, and in the community. We would argue that it is more useful to start from the assumption that racism as discourse is present in all of us. This does not mean that its deleterious effects are felt by all in the same way. Its effects are clearly distributed unfairly. But it does mean that we might share in the process of examining how we are positioned by racist discourse in order to work together to challenge it.

In the next meeting, the facilitator of the class asked permission of the group to talk about the subject of racism in a different way. Instead of attacking the individuals for their various painful remarks, it was suggested that the group identify how they were affected by painful comments rather than going on the attack. Instead of using language like, "I hate white people," "You are a racist," or "You are a perpetrator of injustice," students were asked if they would be prepared to name the discourses of racism that they were personally affected by. Many students used externalizing phrases (White & Epston, 1990) that named the racist behavior without attacking the person. Some students were willing to rephrase their statement "I hate white people" as "I hate what white privilege has done to me."

The group members were able to have some success in referring to the effects of discourse on their lives and to how racism affected them personally. As they continued to practice naming the discourse and its negative effects, the group was able to learn about racism without the conversation's turning into personal attack and counterattack. Rather than describing individuals as personally racist, students discovered value in describing as racist the assumption of natural entitlement to privilege on the basis of being white and the reproduction of the ideology that entrenches these entitlements in patterns of social interaction. Focusing on discourse, we can talk about white privilege and how it can systematically favor Anglo Americans.

This approach is very different from saying that all white people are privileged. We all know of numerous examples of people identified as white who have been exposed to unimaginable suffering from life-threatening disabilities, poverty, and homelessness or from gay bashing persecution and religious bigotry. While individual people may engage in racist behavior, it is the presence of racist discourses and the social practices they produce that need to be addressed. Individuals participate in the reproduction of these discourses and so become implicated in them, sometimes unconsciously. This perspective is very different from saying that they are the sources of the racist discourse in which they are implicated. Neither does racism originate mysteriously out of the social structures that determine how individuals act. That too would be an essentialist assumption. People are not puppets of institutional or structural racism. They are not programmed to speak and act in racist ways without the possibility of doing otherwise. Asking people to identify systemic patterns of racism in their own families is helpful in addressing and undermining the ongoing effects of racism. Here are two examples of white students who traced racism and gross human injustices in their own family while seeking to play their part to ensure that these histories do not continue.

I had a great, great, great uncle who was what my grandpa referred to as a "used slave salesman." This uncle owned more than 150 slaves, whom he sold and rented out to make a profit. It is shameful for me to claim roots in a family system that has played such a blatant role in setting the racist foundation of our country. I have spent the last 10 years of my life living in communities where the dominant groups are people of color. I have had black boyfriends in the past and my present boyfriend is black. I really have an affinity with the black community in my neighborhood and work hard as a school counselor to address racism in the school and community I work in.

—Sara

My great-grandfather was a member of the Ku Klux Klan from 1920 to 1932. My great-grandfather preached about "the Klan" all the time. He told my father not to let the black man or the Mexican take what the white man had earned in America. To my great-grandfather, the KKK was the pride of our family's history. The belief in a superior white race was taught to my grandmother at a young age. Once she came to California, she only saw whites, so the feeling was not as strong, but I still see evidence of her beliefs today. She still refers to African Americans as "colors" and has even used the word "nigger" in front of me. My father believes that this part of our family's history is gone, but I can still hear negative judgments of other races come from his mouth. While they are not as apparent as "colored" or "nigger," they are still there. I don't believe that this aspect of our family has been passed on to my siblings and me, and I hope it never revisits our cultural world again. It is shameful to admit that my family is associated with a racist past. When racism became socially unacceptable during the civil rights movement of the 1960s, my grandmother hid this aspect of our family. My father hid it from his family as well. I did not learn of our shameful past until recently. At first, I thought that I should keep it hidden, but I realized that this is part of my family's history and I don't need to hide it. Now that I am aware of it, I am making sure that I give back what I believe my family took away from a future integrated society.

—Nate

Internalized Racism

Internalized racism occurs when racist discourses are taken on or adopted by individuals and groups of people targeted by negative stigmatized messages. Racist discourses are all pervasive. The concept of internalized racism is related to the explanation of hegemony that we canvassed in Chapter 7. We believe it is best explained within a poststructuralist analysis of how power operates through discourse. It would make sense that racist discourse as a way of thinking and speaking would be picked up and internalized by people of all races, rather than only by those who benefit from it. Thus, people of color are also easily implicated in the repetition of discourse that disadvantages themselves. This does not make them racist. Instead it points to the function of discourse as producing racist effects.

Here is an illustration of how internalized racism works. In 2006, a young black filmmaker (Davis, 2006) replicated the research of black psychologist Kenneth Clark, who over 67 years ago explored young black children's responses to white and black dolls. Black children around six years of age were asked which doll they preferred—the white doll or the black doll. The black children overwhelmingly chose the white doll. The children were asked which was the good doll. In large numbers, the children selected the white doll as the good doll and the black doll as the bad doll. Internalized racism starts at a very early age.

Because discourse is constructed in the exchange of conversation, there is no one who does not participate in it. The contexts where racist discourse is reproduced are the home, the community, and public institutions such as schools, hospitals, and prisons, as well as the most definitive source in the modern world—the mass media. Discourse exchange is the basis of all movies, newspapers, television programs, videos, computer games, Internet sites, and magazines. For generations, racist discourse has penetrated and been reproduced within the very families who have been victims of it. They have often unwittingly handed negative messages on to other family members. Family members who have features most different from Anglo American phenotypic characteristics can be marked as unattractive and can learn within their own family to possess all of the negative traits portrayed by racist discourse, simply because they have darker skin or because their nose is too broad or their hair too kinky. Negative perceptions held by blacks of other blacks often arise from individuals described as fitting the criteria of a preencounter racial identity, as discussed in Chapter 12. Embracing negative stereotypes of blacks and viewing whites in stereotypical positive terms is an example of internalized racism. It often takes hard work to root out the effects of such internalized discourse.

Many students of color consistently have negative models portrayed for them in the school, the community, and the media. They grow up with a very limited range of models and mentors of their same ethnicity and of whom they can feel proud. So often in schools, most of the historical and contemporary leaders, educators, famous historians, and inventors are Anglo American. The media continue to be full of images such as that of a young black woman who is a school dropout, a single parent addicted to drugs, and a victim of domestic violence. A young black male is portrayed with his hands cuffed behind his back, having been arrested for a recent crime. These images dominate even though they do not represent the majority of young black men and women. The effect of such discourse as it becomes internalized is sometimes a loss of self-belief and a devaluation of members of one's own ethnic community, including oneself. The result is that many people of color attempt to embrace "whiteness." Camara Jones (2000) describes this process as one of accepting limitations about one's humanity and the right to determine one's future and constraining or limiting one's self-expression. The use of bleaching creams to lighten the skin, the use of hair straighteners, and the use of cosmetic surgery to reshape the nose and eyes are all examples of internalized racism at work. Other examples include the rejection of one's ancestral or indigenous community, the adoption of racist nicknames, engaging in at-risk behaviors, and failing in school.

Because of the ugliness of racist discourse and the shaming effects it has on victims of this discourse, people of color can minimize or even fail to recognize the implicit and explicit characterizations of racist acts by embracing the apparent safety of being in a state of denial (Henze, Lucas, & Scott, 1998). The oppositional patterns of identity described above also illustrate internalized racism. Beverly Tatum (2003) describes how certain styles of speech, music, dress, and behavior can become characterized as "authentically black." These behavioral styles may be harmlessly embraced by many black youth. However, there are also more harmful behaviors that young black youth can get caught up in that are destructive to themselves, their families, and the community. Being authentically black to these youth might come to mean engaging in intimidating and threatening behavior, being disrespectful to any authority figure, and failing to study, leading to low grades and ultimately school failure. Some black youth are ridiculed by their black peers for doing their homework, succeeding in school, and respecting their teachers, because this behavior is perceived as "acting white." This is one of the most harmful forms of internalized racism.

When minority counselors are affected by internalized racism, they can feel self-hatred and anger toward their clients of the same ethnicity. Instead of showing empathy with their clients regarding the effects racist practices have had on them, therapists of color can make harsh judgments and be very demanding and blaming. An example might be where a therapist says, "If I can be successful in America, so can you."

Internalized racism also helps explain serious racist practices that occur between ethnic minority groups in the United States. Racist treatment of others occurs between Latinos and blacks, Asians and blacks, and within each of these ethnic groupings. Black-on-black violence is often a consequence of internalized racism, and the same thing can happen among Latino and Asian communities. When we trace these actions back through a deconstruction of the internalized effects of racism, however, we can often see that such demonstrations of racism within and between people of color are outgrowths of Western colonizing discourse that is more than 400 years old.

Racism and Stereotyping

Another concept that needs to be distinguished in relation to racism is the concept of stereotyping. Many people use the term *stereotyping* to refer to assumptions that fit easily into racist discourse, and many efforts to combat racism aim at disrupting stereotyped thinking. Dictionary definitions of the word *stereotype* commonly refer to conventional but simplistic thinking whereby distorted views of a person or a group become fixed and resistant to being challenged by countervailing information. Kwame Appiah (2005) helps us penetrate farther into the concept of stereotyping by making distinctions among three different types of stereotyping. We shall outline his distinctions here.

Appiah calls the first form of stereotyping *statistical stereotyping*. It occurs when a property is ascribed to an individual on the basis that it is characteristic of a social group to which the individual belongs. If, for example, it is generally thought that women are more "intuitive" than men, then ascribing one woman's responses to her intuitiveness on the basis of this generalization would be an example of stereotyping. Statistical stereotyping, as the name suggests, happens in much social research where statements about a group are made on the basis of probabilities that may not always apply to each individual member of the group. Such stereotyping may not be problematic at the level of generalization but may become problematic if rigidly applied to individuals.

Appiah calls the second form of stereotyping that he identifies *simply false stereotypes*. These are descriptions of a group of people founded on false generalizations or beliefs. As Appiah remarks, many ethnic stereotypes are of this type. They ascribe to a group of people a characteristic that frequently does not pertain to members of that group any more than to any other group. Examples might be that "Scots are stingy," "Americans are loud," "Women can't think rationally," "Feminists are man-haters," "Mexicans are lazy," and so forth. Such stereotypes frequently create a negative burden for members of the group, which they must work to dispel. They are rationally and empirically false as well as morally wrong in their discriminatory effects.

The third form of stereotyping that Appiah identifies is referred to as *normative stereotyping*. This form of stereotyping occurs when someone does not ascribe a characteristic of a group to an individual but rather judges an individual on whether she is conforming to what a member of a group *should* do. The example Appiah cites is when employers expect women to match gender stereotypes and, for example, wear more "feminine" clothing. Such stereotypes can be thought of as resulting from the normative effects of dominant discourses. They specify how a "proper" or "real" member of a group should behave. They cannot be disproved, as the other two forms of stereotyping can, by challenging their veracity. They cannot be shown to be irrational or incorrect as much as they can be shown to be limiting or restrictive. Indeed, as a result of the work done by dominant discourse, they may often be all too "true" in an empirical sense, because they have the effect of inducing many people to conform to their injunctions. It is Appiah's third category of normative stereotypes that must be examined for its effects on internalized aspects of identity. Such stereotypes are more insidious in getting into our heads than the other two forms. The other two forms of stereotyping can lead to discriminatory acts by others, but this last form conforms to the kinds of internalized technologies of power described by Foucault (see Chapter 8).

With regard to racism, all three forms of stereotyping may be found. They are tools for perpetuating the assumptions of racial superiority and the advantages of racially based privilege. We should be careful, however, of assuming that racism is founded on stereotyping. Racism cannot easily be contested on logical or empirical grounds, as can Appiah's first two forms of stereotyping. Unfortunately, in the history of modernist thinking, racism has not been considered illogical or irrational. It has been all too commonplace. Appiah's third form of stereotyping can be contested not on empirical grounds but on ethical and moral grounds. As a result, it will not be as susceptible to legal challenge on the grounds of discriminatory action or through a rights discourse. It is particularly important because of its insidious insertion into the identity of members of a group. Here is an area of racism that counselors may often find themselves dealing with. Aspects of identity formed by normative processes are of the kind that counselors can be very effective in helping their clients engage with as they encourage them to reconsider their own preferences.

Racism and Counseling Practice

Charles Ridley (2005) judges that the most harmful forms of racism in the mental health professions are associated with the most influential positions in the social services and mental health systems. According to the American Psychological Association, Norine Johnson (2001, cited by Ridley) reported that approximately 5% to 6% of psychologists in the United States are people of color. Because of the small number of minority therapists, many more inequities may be brought to bear on minority clients because of the lack of understanding of racism and because of racist behaviors perpetuated by white therapists. There may also be a greater presence of institutional and cultural racism when there are so few people of color to challenge the effects of racist assumptions. Minority clients are sometimes struggling to manage their day-to-day affairs and are so negatively affected by racist practices in their communities and in their schools that they often feel hopeless and disoriented. Thus, for counselors to ignore the impacts of institutional racism on their clients is for them to unknowingly collude in blaming those who are most victimized by racism. Counselors can sometimes participate in victim blaming practices by labeling people of color resistant or untreatable and by overdiagnosing minority populations. Diagnostic systems such as the *Diagnostic and Statistical Manual of Mental Disorders* do not attune counselors and psychologists to look for the effects of racist discourse in people's lives. Only when counselors understand the harmful effects of their behavior will they be in a position to address it.

Many people of color who use counseling services will be resistant to trusting "white institutions staffed by white professionals." Charles Gelso and Bruce Fretz (2001) argue that trust is the most important contribution to building a working therapeutic relationship. Minority clients often enter a therapy with a significant amount of fear and anxiety. Clients of color are often suspicious of therapy. They are alert to themes of concealment and disguise. To many clients of color, white counselors represent societal oppression. Many scholars continue to find a common theme of mistrust of white counselors among African American, Asian American, Latino, and Native American clients (Sue & Sue; 2003; Ridley, 2005; Whaley, 2001). Sometimes clients of color don't trust minority therapists because they feel these professionals have sold out to white establishments and no longer care about minority rights and social justice. Thus, overcoming a client's mistrust may lead to the greatest success in terms of therapeutic outcome.

It would be a mistake to interpret such resistance in terms of transference originating in family-of-origin dynamics. Since white professionals represent a dominant racist culture to other ethnicities, many people of color may be either guarded or somewhat reactive and ready to act out their frustrations. Charles Ridley (2005) describes this "cultural paranoia" as a healthy reaction to racism by a person of color. It might be disclosed to a black therapist but not to a white therapist. He also suggests that minority clients may show negative feelings toward white therapists during a counseling session because of what he calls cultural transference. The concept of cultural transference suggests that ethnic minority clients can transfer their sufferings caused by racist practices onto a white therapist, who symbolizes and embodies white racist attitudes. Ridley then describes how cultural countertransference can occur when white counselors inappropriately attribute psychological deficiencies to their minority clients because of their own unconscious racist attitudes.

Therefore, there can be significant obstacles to establishing a strong therapeutic alliance between white therapists and people of color. Sensitivity by white therapists to the history of institutional and cultural racist practice is critical in the creation of a strong counselor-client relationship. Ridley (2005) points out that therapists can have good intentions in working with minority clients and yet still engage in racist behavior because of their lack of awareness, knowledge, and understanding of institutional racism. This lack of awareness comes in the form of counselors' assumption that their values, worldview, and life experiences are predominantly shared by their clients. Because of colonizing discourse and its systematic privileging of white culture and demeaning of other ethnicities, black clients and white counselors, for example, have very different experiences of an American way of life. A poststructuralist analysis of racism nevertheless alerts us to the need to study the practices that might build such trust, rather than assuming that it is either possible or not possible on the grounds of the counselor's group membership.

When a white counselor says, for example, "I don't see color; we are all the same underneath," the counselor and client may be immediately talking past each other. The black client is often immediately in touch with how racism produces systematic oppression and is shocked to hear a white counselor make a comment like this. Meanwhile, the white counselor may be shocked to find that a client is upset, because the intention of the comment was to demonstrate equal treatment of people of all races.

Sarah Knox, Alan Burkard, Adanna Johnson, Lisa Suzuki, and Joseph Ponterotto (2003) found that African American therapists in their sample routinely addressed the subject of race with clients of color and with clients whose race was part of their psychological presentation but that white psychologists were uncomfortable discussing race and normally avoided mentioning racial issues with their clients. Jairo Fuertes, Lisa Mueller, Rahul Chauhan, Jessica Walker, and Nicholas Ladany (2002) suggest that counselors who are most effective in working across the majority/minority divide show interest in and express appreciation for a client's ethnicity and cultural heritage. There is compelling evidence to suggest that white counselors who directly address race issues with minority clients can establish strong therapeutic relationships with those clients. When this does not occur, minority clients may avoid speaking about race so their therapists won't feel offended or alienated, even when racism is a clear concern.

If counselor values are influenced by racist assumptions, then the potential harm in counseling interactions is all the more alarming. There are many subtle ways in which counselors can act from an unspoken belief that their values are superior to those of their clients. For example, counselors might believe that individualistic decision making is preferable to, say, a collective, more communal decision making process. A person being challenged to move from a communal or collective perspective on a decision to deciding for himself and rejecting family or community opinions might be perceived by the counselor as making therapeutic progress. The client, however, may simply be aligning with the counselor's value system and worldview. Another example is labeling a client passive when he is behaving in an appropriately deferential position according to his own cultural community.

When clients prematurely cancel their sessions or are subject to psychiatric diagnoses shaped by Eurocentric assumptions, racist discourse can be shown to produce negative outcomes for minority clients. David Smart and Julie Smart (1997) note how the mental health profession generally fails to take into account cultural considerations for diagnosis. They point out that the whole construction of psychiatric and psychological models is based on Eurocentric assumptions with little respect for other cultural practices. For example, several epidemiological studies revealed significant differences between African Americans and whites with regard to rates of diagnosis of affective disorders. Gordon Johnson, Samuel Gershon, and Leon Hekimian (1968) studied three years' worth of admissions at Bellevue Psychiatric Hospital and did not find a single case of an African American patient diagnosed with a manic depressive disorder. Carl Bell and Harshad Mehta (1980) suggest that misdiagnosis of African American patients is rooted in the notion that manic illness is clustered in higher socioeconomic brackets and is not featured among poor or black communities. Because lower class black patients are denied treatment for affective illnesses, the withholding of appropriate services can be analyzed as a covert form of racism that is institutionalized in psychiatry. When clients are misdiagnosed, they receive inappropriate psychotherapy and medication, fail to receive benefits they would have gained from appropriate treatment, and often are subjected to inappropriate psychopharmacological therapy.

When already misdiagnosed, clients are more likely to be caught in a further cycle of misdiagnosis. Gerald Russell, Diane Fujino, Stanley Sue, Mang-King Cheung, and Lonnie Snowden (1996) sampled 9,000 adults in the Los Angeles County mental health system. They examined the relationship between therapist-client ethnic matching and the therapist's evaluation of overall client functioning based on the Global Assessment Scale. Interestingly, findings indicated that ethnically matched therapists were more likely to judge their clients as having a higher mental health status than therapists and clients working together from different ethnicities. Since most therapists, psychologists, and psychiatrists are white in the United States, it is probable that their clients with nonwhite identities are more likely to be pathologized.

Other examples of institutional racism in mental health agencies include setting agency fees above the range of what ethnic minority clients can afford and thus excluding them from treatment. Standardized psychological tests that do not include data from minority cultural groupings reflect biased test construction and thus perpetuate cultural inequity.

Counselors' unrealistic expectations for therapeutic outcomes for minority clients are other examples of inequitable and possibly racist practice. Therapeutic goals set too low can become self-fulfilling prophecies, while goals set too high can be impossible for clients to achieve. Other forms of unequal treatment can occur when counselors have to spend a long time with their clients to learn about their cultural background when the clients feel that the counselor should already have a basic knowledge of their ethnic community and its cultural history.

Counseling and White Guilt

Writers in the multicultural field have begun to address the role that "white guilt" plays in setting the scene for how whites and blacks relate to one another. Essentially, white guilt is the collective and individual shame that Anglo Americans experience as they consider the effects of historical and contemporary oppression thrust upon the black community by slavery and white institutional racism. Shelby Steele (2006) has made a powerful argument for how white guilt holds back both white and black communities from making progress in building meaningful and productive relationships with one another and stalls positive social and economic initiatives. White guilt can also impact white therapists' behavior with black clients. For example, Alison Jones and Arthur Seagull (1977) argued that some white professionals are motivated to counsel minorities almost completely out of their guilt about racism. The problem with this motivation is that white counselors are then operating from their own insecurities and trying to work out their own issues rather than being fully present for their clients. In addition, this dynamic of guilt can cause white counselors to seek approval from their minority clients. Charles Ridley (2005) suggests that white therapists may be so focused on their efforts to be nonracist that they set themselves up for countermanipulation by their minority clients, who may be keenly aware of their therapists' vulnerability and emotional insecurities. Thus, much time can be wasted on alleviating counselor anxiety, directing the therapy away from meaningful client outcomes.

The Problem of Overidentification With Clients of the Same Ethnicity

According to Charles Ridley (2005), minority counselors can hurt minority clients by assuming that the experiences of clients who look like them are the same as theirs. Even if counselors and clients come from similar backgrounds and have similar upbringings, it does not follow that they share exactly the same challenges. Overidentifying with clients keeps the counselor from being curious about the client's unique circumstances. Counselor interactions become stereotypically based and inflexible. This overidentification produces what Courtland Lee (1996) terms a monolithic perspective. According to Charles Ridley (2005), some counselors gain personal satisfaction from unloading on their clients pent-up feelings from their own experiences of racism. Counseling sessions can then inappropriately become a forum for therapists' own race-related distress.

Counseling Strategies to Circumvent Racist Practices

Because of the complexity and difficulties associated with addressing racism, multiple approaches are necessary to address its causes and effects. Ongoing legal and institutional changes are required. In addition, how to deal with racism should be addressed in counselor training programs and with counseling supervisors and administrators. Racist issues are made all the more difficult when the immediate issues a client struggles with are not directly related to racism but invoke older painful memories. Shelby Steele (1990) considers the memory of racial victimization to be a particularly powerful wound:

> I think one of the heaviest weights that oppression leaves on the shoulders of its former victims is simply the memory of itself. This memory is a weight because it pulls the oppression forward, out of history and into the present, so the former victim may see his world as much through the memory of his oppression as through his experience in the present. (p. 150)

In this section we look at the important micro-level approaches that counselors might use to address racism in the counseling room. We have discussed at length the value of developing historical and sociocultural awareness of the issues that can negatively affect the work between counselors and clients. An honest examination of one's personal biases, agendas, preferences, and prejudices and how they might impact ethnically different clients is important to undertake. Charles Ridley (2005) says counselors themselves can benefit from seeing a therapist of another race to address their cultural encapsulation and build cultural empathy and understanding.

Charles Ridley (2005) and Larry Lee (2004) have outlined helpful practices in addressing the effects of racism on clients and building trust during counseling, including some of the following:

1. Believe your clients when they describe their experiences of racism.

2. If you are white or are perceived as white by a client of color, don't inadvertently invite your client to behave in a deferential manner.

3. Don't make your client feel she has to diminish her emotional response or reaction to racism. A strong and angry response to an experience of racism may be the client's first step toward rebuilding her dignity and finding her voice. Not accepting and acknowledging the pain caused by racism can lead to an early termination of counseling.

4. When you are conducting psychological assessments, ensure that documentation is made of the effects of racism in a client's profile along with environmental and social factors.

5. Provide information about the counseling time frame. Be careful about how you end the counseling session, especially when a client is preparing to introduce some new information, as he can feel disrespected when the time is up.

When Clients Are Racist

Many multicultural texts focus on helping white counselors grapple with racism and its effects on clients of color. There is currently a growing literature that supports ethnic minority counselors' working with white clients who may exhibit racist behavior. Counselors can sometimes experience troublesome interactions with their clients when clients exhibit blatantly racist behavior. Take this example mentioned by Larry Lee (2004). Lee describes a scenario in which he is counseling a white man and his family. The client has his own tech company and employs many Asians. Lee is Asian American. After the client has engaged in an angry exchange with his wife, Lee makes efforts to interrupt and redirect him. His client spins around and tells him, "Don't interrupt me when I'm speaking. I don't need your help. I can handle this very well without your interference. You know, I really don't know if you are really qualified to help us. I work with a lot of Asians and see that we're different" (p. 95).

These interactions are excruciatingly painful, and counselors can be blindsided by them. Lee gives a wonderful response: "You have a right to express your opinions although I am not comfortable with what you have expressed" (p. 96).

Here are some of the suggestions made by Azmaira Maker (2004) and Larry Lee (2004) to assist minority counselors working with clients from a majority culture:

1. Explore with the client what it is like to work with someone who looks and sounds so different.

2. Ask your client to make an honest response while reassuring her that it is safe to share her feelings and reactions.

3. Adopt an inviting response by asking questions like, "Where do you think I come from?" "Are you wondering about my values and religious beliefs and what I think about you and your family?" and "Do you worry that I might not be able to understand and relate to your experiences?"

TO DISCUSS

1. How easy is it to discuss racism in your class? What constraints do you experience? What might make those constraints interfere less?

2. What examples can you recall from your experience of internalized racism?

3. Collect examples of each of Appiah's three forms of stereotyping. Discuss whether these are examples of racism or not.

4. What do you see as the advantages and disadvantages of the poststructuralist analysis of racism?

5. How can counselors work against racism in their practice?

First Response to Chapter 14

Kobus Maree

Kobus Maree, D.Ed., Ph.D., D.Phil., is a professor in the Faculty of Education at the University of Pretoria. His research focuses on optimizing the achievement of disadvantaged learners and providing cost-effective career facilitation to all persons. As the author or coauthor of more than 40 books and chapters and 90 articles in accredited scholarly journals and the recipient of numerous awards for his research, he is frequently interviewed on radio and television. He received the Exceptional Academic Achiever Award at the University of Pretoria from 2004 to 2009. Professor Maree was elected as a member of the South African Academy for Science and Arts in 2003 and as a member of the Academy of Science of South Africa (ASSAf) in 2006. He is the editor in chief of *Perspectives in Education*, a consulting editor of *Gifted Education International*, and a member of the editorial boards of six more scholarly journals.

The experiences of Alfred, a brilliant fourth-year student from a rural background, illustrate the many one-dimensional notions of cultural groups that are rife in South Africa (SA).

I really struggled during my first 18 months at the university (particularly with chemistry, physics, and mathematics). The medium of instruction was my biggest problem. Although the lecturers were not unwilling to help, some of them were also experiencing problems lecturing in their second language. One put it this way: "I don't understand why they bothered to bring blacks who cannot speak or understand Afrikaans or English properly, to this campus; they have their own universities."

Alfred's quote highlights the fact that blacks at South African universities are often still assigned inferior status, in typical colonial fashion, and doomed to inferior and diminished opportunities. The embedded suggestion in this remark is the following: "You do not deserve state-of-the-art education." (By and large, black South African universities have historically been, and still are, greatly disadvantaged).

Alfred does not accept being marginalized.

I have as much right to be here as they do. It is my country, my university, my city too; I visit the same clubs and I belong to the same organizations. Why pick on me?

Alfred intuitively draws attention to the poststructuralist view of racism. He assumes a discursive position in which he refuses to be branded as a helpless, oppressed victim who should merely accept his fate.

Seemingly even a modern university such as this one is not sufficiently geared toward accommodating people from diverse cultures. When I lost my grandmother (the person who had raised me from birth), I indicated that I, as a member of the extended family, needed to attend her funeral. However, it proved almost impossible to convince many of my lecturers of the need to attend the funeral. One simply retorted, "It seems that all black people are related to each other. Imagine if every student would apply to attend the funeral of every relative who passed away!"

The lecturer's distorted discourse is a clear example of simply false stereotyping. She shows blatant disrespect for the power and importance of the student's cultural beliefs, and she chooses to discriminate against an already severely traumatized young person.

I was informed by a lecturer that many persons objected to the fact that blacks had been "dumped" on "their" university and were "virtually destroying the traditional culture of the place."

This lecturer accepts that her own social privileges have been earned and well deserved, at the same time assuming that the student deserves to be excluded from these privileges.

> We were constantly reminded, directly and indirectly, that blacks generally achieved poorer results at the end of Grade 12, which "proved" that we did not have the capacity to achieve at the university level.

The lecturers clearly verbalize their support for the stereotypical racist view expressed here, namely that, based on perceived ethnic differences, blacks are unintelligent (i.e., whiteness is superior and blackness inferior).

> Acceptance by fellow students was a particularly painful stumbling block. All my fellow black students consistently complained about racism, being called names, and not being greeted in turn by white students, irrespective of the prevailing circumstances. As one fellow student put it, "Many of us were victims of discrimination this year. It seems as if whites think that, just because you're black and poor, you are an animal. I tried to befriend whites, but they didn't have time to greet me or listen to me."

According to Alfred, black students continue to suffer rejection and social exclusion at the hands of whites on account of perceived ethnic (bodily) differences and outmoded colonial practices.

> Much as students complained about orientation, we, on the whole, accepted this as a necessary evil. In some instances, though, we perceived the underlying racial motives it created, as well as the lingering bitterness and animosity. In the words of one black student: "Here we had people who did not respect my culture at all. I felt like a slave, being forced to do things against my will."
>
> Some students whose achievement was not satisfactory at the end of their first, second, or third year were put on a so-called waiting list for residences (*waglys*). This almost inevitably doomed them to a life of roaming the streets of adjacent suburbs (they have no support structures in the region) until (hopefully) one day they are lucky enough to regain access to residences. Conversely, some students turn to squatting as a way of handling an untenable situation with little or no help from administration, which does not seem to understand the frame of reference of changing socioeconomic circumstances and the changing demographic profile of the campus.

Unchallenged, outmoded, and persistent colonizing discourses, which include colonizing patterns of behavior, conspire with unearned white privilege to predestine black students to untenable situations.

I do not believe that it is useful to single out any one of the rigorous arguments in Chapter 14. Instead, I believe Alfred's narrative highlights the need not only to combat racism on all fronts, but, indeed, to strive toward more inclusive perspectives on multicultural counseling, especially an epistemology that would respond satisfactorily to questions about some of the existing theoretical concepts in the field of counseling. In South Africa, in particular, racism impacts the lives of people across diverse cultures. It manifests itself in various forms and in various forums— for example, educational institutions (e.g., schools and universities) and the workplace (where racism and discrimination still abound, despite the best efforts of the powers that be to eradicate this scourge).

Whereas traditional, positivist counseling has failed the needs of the majority of the global population, social constructionism and its emphasis on multiple realities highlights the need for multiple and flexible approaches to data (objective and subjective) collection, for combining approaches, for meaning making and mattering, and offers a window of opportunity—a novel lens that potentially enables psychologists to enter the phenomenological world of clients from across the racial continuum. In South Africa in particular, where "the problem is that entrenched racism dictates that justification must be found for the persisting white fears of *die swart gevaar* [the black danger]" (Mbeki, 2007), it is fundamentally important to achieve this aim.

Second Response to Chapter 14

Nola Butler-Byrd

Nola Butler-Byrd, Ph.D., is an African American scholar and an assistant professor in the Community-Based Block program in the Department of Counseling and School Psychology at San Diego State University. Her research interests include experiential multicultural education and counseling for social justice, indigenous healing and worldview, somatic body work, multicultural identity development, multi-ethnic faculty retention, and service learning.

As a faculty member in the Community-Based Block (CBB), a highly diverse multicultural counselor preparation program with a strong social justice orientation, I am extremely fulfilled and challenged. Each year, 27 students join our program from a wide range of ethnic, cultural, sexual orientation, and socioeconomic backgrounds and bring with them a great deal of knowledge and experience to share about how they came to be who they are in the world. I never cease to be amazed by their depth, their passion for learning and giving to others, and the emotional intelligence and stamina they develop in the program. Our learning community uses a critical theoretical framework that works to collapse the hierarchy between students and faculty though our collaborative teaching, learning, and decision making processes. These processes are very challenging, because students have to learn to balance their individual needs with the needs of the community. They also learn to differentiate individualism from the appreciation of individual uniqueness and gifts that strengthen community.

Community is a critical issue that I feel is often missing in discussions about racism. Often, discussions and texts address racism as a problem focused primarily on people of color. I bristle at the way that people of color are often problematized or pathologized in many multicultural texts and discussions on racism. Most scholars have good intentions when they draw attention to racism's effect on people of color. After its overt racist denial for so long, this is an understandable reaction. Yet I feel that, by its failure to look at or minimization of focus on Euro-Americans, it is a form of covert racial microaggression, which Derald Wing Sue, Jennifer Bucceri, Annie Lin, Kevin Nadal, and Gina Torino (2007) describe as "brief, everyday exchanges that send denigrating messages to people of color because they belong to a racial minority group. These exchanges are so often dismissed and glossed over as being innocuous" (p. 72). By making people of color the problem while excluding or minimizing the problems and pathology of European Americans, people of color experience negative psychological effects. I often come away from these exchanges or texts with the feeling that only European Americans have value and that people of color are in deficit or bankrupt.

While the issues, symptoms, and sufferings of oppression are very real and serious, I feel that giving little or no focus to racism's negative effects on European Americans has deleterious consequences for everyone, including European Americans. I look forward to the day when I read a text that begins its discussion with the sadness, loneliness, and soullessness that many European Americans suffer as a result of this racist, colonizing system; the negative consequences of consumerism on relationships and families; and the hunger of malnourished European American souls for community and individuality versus individualism. I'd like to hear more about European Americans who seek and benefit from the spiritual strength and beauty of people of color, from their knowledge, science, cultures, and traditions.

This is why the work of indigenous scholars like Malidoma Somé gives me so much hope. Somé (1998) discusses the symbiotic relationship between the West and disenfranchised cultures and communities throughout the world. While disenfranchised cultures suffer physical deprivation and poverty, the dominant Euro-American culture suffers a horrific soul hunger that is threatening to consume the world.

One of my female European American students shared her despair at the beginning of our program on September 7: "Last week I had a panic attack. I've only had three in my lifetime and my panic attack last week was just as strong as my first one three years ago. I presume the cause of my panic attack was for fear of being pushed out of the group. Consciously, I know that I'm a member of the community and will be, yet I felt because [an African American Male] viewed me as being prejudiced against black people, I felt that I wasn't a welcomed group member. Since the reasons for my panic attacks in my past have been because I wasn't allowed to participate in particular groups, my solution has been to leave those groups. Thus, having a panic attack last week not only challenged me to control myself physically and emotionally, but it also challenged me to continue to be a part of the community."

As she continued to participate in the CBB learning community, she reflected on her understanding about racial differences and individuality on November 3: "CBB has impacted how I think about other people *every day*. I have never before noticed people's skin colors more than I do now. I can't go through a day, through an interaction, watch television, or be in an environment without noticing everyone's skin colors. Even though I've been at SDSU for over two years now, I saw SDSU in a new light when I was walking on campus to meet you yesterday, Nola. I now notice more than ever little nonverbal language from black people when they interact with white folks. I now wonder if they feel uncomfortable or what they may really be thinking but not saying."

On March 14, she reflected about her sense of belonging and group membership: " . . . Even though I know that it's a natural need for people to feel a sense of belonging to a group, it's even more apparent how people relate with one another when it comes to one's culture. In CBB, I notice how people of color feel the need to connect with those identifying with the same ethnicity. I've also noticed how people from the LGBT community feel the same need to share a sense of belonging with other members of the LGBT community in CBB. I've primarily lived my life cultureless and I know being white has had a huge impact on these feelings. It has been since the start of CBB that I've developed the same want and need to relate with other white folks because we're so few and far between within CBB. I can no longer feel comfortable being white all the time because I am no longer within a sea of my own kind."

Racism is a community problem, and therefore everyone's problem. When we address racism as a community issue from which everyone suffers and which therefore needs everyone's investment to heal, individuals and communities can flourish.

CHAPTER 15

Social Class, Poverty, and the American Dream

Social class and socioeconomic status are fundamental variables that shape and influence the way life is lived. Class, wealth, and poverty systematically structure our communities, organize where we live, affect our quality of life, constrain or invigorate our aspirations and dreams, impact the quality of our education, channel our access to health care, and orchestrate virtually every other aspect of our lives. Social class membership translates into privilege for some and disadvantage for others. It opens or closes the doors of opportunity in life. Since most people agree that social class position is in no way biologically natural, it has to be considered an aspect of the cultural forces that constitute people's lives. It is therefore implicated in the stories that clients tell to counselors, individuals' very access to counseling services, and the resources clients have available for addressing problems.

What Is Social Class?

Defining class is an elusive task. William Ming Liu, Geoffrey Soleck, Joshua Hopps, Kwesi Dunston, and Theodore Pickett (2004) suggest that counselors and health care providers speak about class as though everybody knows what it is. According to Liu and his colleagues, counselors too easily assume that they can identify clients' social class membership status. Counselors also often assume that people in a particular class share a homogenous worldview, have similar consumer habits, and aspire to similar lifestyle preferences. Evidence, however, is to the contrary. There is research that suggests enormous variation in these factors (see Fletcher, 2001). First, it is difficult to separate class from its multiple interactions with other salient social divisions, such as ethnicity, gender, religion, sexuality, geographic location, and mental health status. Class membership makes sense only in relation to other classes and economic privilege or disadvantage and must always be relative to features of a particular social context. The context in which we discuss class shapes our very definition of it. Jodie Kliman (1998) gives examples of how context is important in our understanding of perceptions of social class: "A professor may be seen as in a superior position in terms of class than a contractor with equal income, but not if she is a Latina and the male contractor is from an old family of British stock" (p. 51). Furthermore, a wealthy black professional man may have less effective class status than a white professional man when they attempt to hail a cab. In other words, social class status is affected by a variety of contextual dimensions. It is a not a fixed or essential category into which people are born and to which they immutably belong.

Another source of confusion is that the very terms in which social class is talked about are not agreed on. The terms *social class* and *socioeconomic status* have very different academic histories, are based on different assumptions, and are used for different purposes. *Socioeconomic status* refers primarily to social groups defined by income level. It is based on a Weberian tradition of sociological research. It informs the collection of data through the census and other databases and is used by social planners to categorize communities on the basis of things like mean income. It lends itself to a liberal humanist account of social relations (see Chapter 6 for the liberal humanist account of power relations).

The categories commonly used to define socioeconomic status (SES), such as upper, upper middle, middle, lower middle, and lower socioeconomic status, don't always convey the profound differences between wealth and privilege or between poverty and oppression. We live in an era in which the disparities in income between the wealthy and the poor have been widening for several decades. Socioeconomic status can result from both earned and unearned income. Earned income is that produced by employment and occupation. Unearned income includes assets, inheritances, credit lines, employment security, debt load, and how close one can be to homelessness. All these sources of income are also shaped by ethnicity, gender, and physical and mental well-being.

The term *social class*, on the other hand, has been most strongly influenced by a Marxian analysis of social relations. The Marxian tradition does not so much focus on income level as on positions in economic relations. People are positioned in social classes by their roles as employers or employees, owners of businesses or wage earners, those who have capital to invest and those who sell their labor for wages. Karl Marx (1932) describes classes as being organized in the shape of a pyramid, with the ruling class at the top. The hierarchy is as follows: the ruling class; the non-ruling capitalist class; the professional/managerial middle class; the working class, which includes salaried workers of lower social class status; and the lower working class, who live with low wages and no benefits or security. Some writers also discuss an underclass, which consists of poor people who live outside the legitimate economy at the margins of society (Inclan & Ferran, 1990).

Jean Anyon (1980) offers a clear definition of social class. She describes it as the sum of the effects of people's relationships with three dimensions of life: their relationship with systems of ownership of the workplace and things within it (e.g., physical or symbolic capital); their relationship with others in the work context (e.g., having authority over others or having to submit to others' authority); and their relationship with the content and process of their own productive activity (e.g., the ability to benefit materially from one's own labor or alienation from the possibility of such benefits).

The middle classes and ruling classes have the most decision making power in the social world and stand to gain the most from economic growth. The working class earns their living by their own labor, and their conditions of work are often characterized by the condition of "alienation." This means that they have no material interest in the economic outcome of their work. If they were to work harder and produce more, they would still earn the same wage. To some extent, the cultural experience of social class is also determined by how free people are in the workplace. Some people are governed as to whether they can have a bathroom break, while others can choose to give themselves bonuses or lay other people off work. In the 19th century, by far the majority of the Western population were working class and there was a relatively small group in the ruling class and a modest-sized middle class.

One of the problems with a rigid application of the Marxian analysis of class is that the configuration of society has changed since the 19th century. The middle classes have ballooned in size. There have developed a range of occupations that do not fit so easily into the working class category or the middle class category. Workers might have some middle class conditions of work but still be paid working class wages. The contrast between middle class workers' interest in and working class workers' alienation from their work has often become less starkly drawn than it was in the 19th century and has become more complex than previously thought. The range of ways in which people develop relations with economic production and the world of work have become much too diverse to be described by a simple binary opposition between middle class and working class interests. Also, the development of an underclass of unemployed and homeless persons has added to the complexity of the picture of social relations.

There are other problems with the way that social class has been talked about. Essentialist habits of thinking have not been uncommon in relation to social class. For example, many explanations of class are given as distinct and separate from the sociocultural world that people inhabit. For example, Donna Langston (1992, in Harley, Jolivette, McCormick, & Tice, 2002) reported on an account of social class as a phenomenon that has always existed, occurs "naturally," and probably exists in various forms throughout the world. Other explanations of class culture refer to individuals' personal and moral attributes, such as dishonesty, laziness, dedication, a strong work ethic, and moral virtue (Henry, 1994), as contributors to their social class position. Class is thus assumed to be an indication of one's personal worth, and one's social position is merited on the basis of personal talent. Sometimes class is simply taken to mean how much money somebody has and the power she can yield through buying power. The social science literature overwhelmingly stresses the structural, institutional, systemic, political power relations that define and shape class and how it is infused with the dynamics of gender and ethnicity (Harley et al., 2002; Langston, 1992; McGoldrick & Giordano, 1996; Williams, 1999). This is despite the fact that many Americans view events in a historical context of individual happenings rather than as a product of long-term social trends that affect every aspect of our cultural lives.

Figure 15.1   Photographs of homeless citizens from Paris, France. Courtesy of Ian Douglas.

Class Culture

Social research over many years has revealed the complexity of the cultural dimensions of social class identification. People do not just belong to a social class; they construct cultural worlds out of their class membership. These cultural worlds include value systems, habits of thought, relationship patterns, ways of speaking, behaviors, and attitudes toward others. In one important example of such research, social psychologist Melvin Kohn established over a sustained period of research some strong patterns of difference between the child rearing practices of middle class parents and those of working class parents (Kohn, 1989). On the basis of extensive data collection, Kohn argued that one clear difference in child rearing was causally correlated with the employment conditions of parents. It focused on the degree of emphasis on "self-direction." According to Kohn, middle class parents train their children to be self-directed and responsible for their own decisions in life. Such training is argued to reflect the importance of self-directed behavior in the working conditions of middle class parents. By contrast, working class parents work in contexts where they are not expected to be self-directed as much as they are to do as they are told by their bosses. Kohn shows how working class parents translate these working conditions into child rearing behavior in which they emphasize children's doing the right thing and doing what they are told, rather than being self-directed and learning to reason through responsible decision making.

Kohn's research has important implications for counseling. The values that are expressed in counseling theories of self-actualization may often be said to reflect middle class valuation of self-directed behavior. When counselors look for and reward self-directed behavior in their clients, they may be inadvertently favoring cultural values that are middle class in origin and contradicting the cultural training that working class children have received in their families.

TO DISCUSS

1. How do you locate yourself in terms of social class and socioeconomic status?

2. In what circumstances does locating yourself become complicated?

3. Compare yourself with your parents and grandparents. What have been the generational patterns and trends of social class in your family?

4. From what social class backgrounds do people come into the profession of counseling? Take a poll in your class.

5. What are the conditions of your workplace? What sort of impact do they have on your identity and on your relations with others in the workplace?

6. What does alienation from your work mean? Have you experienced it? What effect does it have on you?

7. What are some stories about how to do things that you have been exposed to in your family and neighborhood? How are these stories shaped by social class values?

Being Poor in America

Jesse Jackson gave a speech at the 2000 American Psychological Annual Convention in which he said,

> Most poor people work every day. Most poor people in the U.S. are not black, not brown. Most poor people are white, female, young, invisible, and without national leaders.
>
> Most poor people are not on welfare.
>
> They raise other people's children. . . . They put food in our children's schools. . . . They clean our offices. . . . They cut grass. . . . They pick lettuce. . . . They work in hospitals, as orderlies . . . no job is beneath them. (p. 329)

While the poor contribute so much to our society, they are subject to elevated rates of threatening and uncontrollable life events, noxious life conditions, high infant mortality, violent crime, and homicide. As Bernice Lott (2002) noted, physicians on the whole tend to avoid working in poor areas, even when tempted by generous salary packages. Jonathan Kozol (1992) found that the same is true for the best teachers, who gravitate toward the wealthier school districts, where they are paid more. Mental health workers often feel uncomfortable with low-income clients, finding it difficult to empathize with them. Low-income clients are more likely than middle-income clients to receive therapy that is brief (if they receive any at all) and drug centered. They are often treated by students and low-status professionals. Lawyers are reluctant to provide services to the poor, and less than a third of low-income people who need an attorney get one. Crime victims who are poor or homeless receive less attention in the media than those who are more affluent (Viano, 1992). According to a United States Justice Department report ("Deadly Disparities," 2000), 82% of the 682 defendants facing capital charges in federal courts since 1995 were members of a minority and poor. Seventy-four percent of the 183 recommended for the death penalty were also members of a minority and poor.

Poverty is a constant threat to children's well-being. Poor children rarely get access to high-quality child care facilities. Since poorer parents often work more than one low-paying job and often cannot afford quality child care at all, there is often very little adult supervision of children in poverty-stricken communities. These same parents usually work in circumstances where there is inadequate sick leave or vacation time. When extended family networks are unavailable, which is increasingly the case, children are frequently left alone. Without adult supervision, children are more likely to spend time engaged in potentially harmful activities, such as watching hours and hours of unmonitored television full of adult sexual and violent content (Garbarino & Bedard, 2001). Children are often free to circulate in a community that is prone to serious unemployment, violence, drugs, deteriorating housing, and declining health care services. As a result of violence and gang warfare, children are often isolated and have little access to any form of social support or even physical recreation in the neighborhood (Vera & Shin, 2006). These conditions constitute an ongoing hazardous situation to all members of the community. See Box 15.1 for some statistical summaries of the trends in income levels.

Box 15.1. Poverty and Wealth Statistics

According to Alemayehu Bishaw and Sharon Stern's (2006) report on the poverty rate estimates in 2003 from the United States Census Bureau, approximately 12.5% of all individuals are below the poverty line, with 28% of them being from sole female parent households. In the United States, over 12 million children (or one child in six) live in poverty. This rate of child poverty leaves the United States at the bottom of the heap in the industrialized world in its ability to care for the poor (Sengupta, 2001). The cavernous differences between the rich and poor around the world are growing at an extreme rate. In the United States, Conrad Phillip Kottak and Kathryn Kozaitis (2003) report that the top 5% of the population received 24% of the total income in 1989, up from 18% in 1977. In comparison, the bottom 60% of the population's share of national income decreased 5% in the same period. In 1998, the top 5% of Americans had more wealth than 95% of the population, and 10% of the richest families owned 90% of the business assets (Wolff, 2003). It has become almost a cliché to say that the rich are getting richer and the poor are getting poorer. Andrew Hacker (1995), reporting on this phenomenon, noted that a typical CEO in the mid 1970s made 40 times as much as a typical American worker. Twenty years later the ratio had swelled to 190 times as much. Roughly 1% of the population owns nearly 40% of the wealth (McNamee & Miller, 2004). In the United States, the lack of welfare reform in recent decades has also exacerbated the disparities and the stratification of class in our society, causing the effects of class inequities to intensify (Harley et al., 2002).

John Hartigan, Jr. (1997), and Annalee Newitz and Matt Wray (1997) observed that, in general, Americans love to hate the poor. They noted that, instead of being sympathetic and understanding of the poor, middle class Americans frequently have reactions of disgust and hostility toward the poor and typically stereotype them as lazy, stupid, and refusing to work. The poor are often assumed to live in a female-headed household in an inner-city ghetto and to be undeservedly on welfare (Robinson & James, 2003).

The American Dream

Many people believe that the fate of the poor and marginalized results from their own life choices. The notion that everybody in North America has a chance at the good life if he is willing to work hard and obey the rules continues to be widespread. No one really cares if the boss earns 300 times more than the average worker, as long as the average worker can hope someday to have a shot at the top job. In fact, 8 out of 10 Americans believe that those who start off poor, if they work hard, can still make pots of money ("Inequality and the American Dream," 2006). This is a central part of the American dream.

The American dream was popularized by the historian James Truslow Adams (1931), who defined the dream of a "land in which life should be better and richer and fuller for every man, with opportunity for each according to his ability or achievement" (p. 404). The dream was based on the idealistic hope that everybody had the right to individual freedom and the chance to succeed. Built into the American dream is the incentive for everyone to strive for upward social class mobility and to become wealthier than she currently is. The dream requires a Protestant work ethic, acceptance of a delay of gratification, individualism, and industriousness. Research on upward mobility suggests that people internalize an expectation to succeed to such an extent that those who are unsuccessful are regarded as deviant (Liu & Pope-Davis, 2003).

The American dream invites us to consider poverty a failure of personal initiative. It is predicated on the persuasive view that, as individuals, "we are the masters of our own destiny." With this view, the existence of poverty constitutes an irritating reminder of the dark side of the American dream. The American dream is built on individualism. It assumes a valorization of individuals' talents and abilities and a belief in the pervasiveness of personal opportunity. The self envisaged is acontextual to the extent that the constraints on such opportunity put in place by a person's position in relation to social class, race, gender, and disability are at least downplayed, if not trivialized. The spirit of the American dream is firmly rooted in the religious, economic, political, and dominant cultural notions of mainstream America. These frameworks of belief place most of the burden of accountability for poverty on the poor. They should "pull themselves up by their own boot straps." Those who do not achieve such advances are easily deemed worthless as well as poor. This denigration of the poor feeds ongoing political attacks on the United States welfare system and supports plans to dismantle it without providing any alternatives.

bell hooks (2000) claims that "many greedy upper and middle class citizens share with their wealthy counterparts a hatred and disdain for the poor that is so intense, it borders on pathological hysteria" (p. 45). She suggests that American citizens are socialized to view the poor as "parasites and predators" whose ongoing needs inhibit others' ability to enjoy a good life.

Most social scientists and economists who research patterns of wealth and poverty pretty much agree that the American dream is illusory. Bernice Lott (2002) argued that American psychologists have consistently worked under the assumption that the United States is a classless society, making it seem that socioeconomic status is not an important factor in the treatment of the poor. In America today, parental income is a better predictor of whether someone will be rich or poor than it is in most other countries, including Canada and most European countries. In America, about half of the income disparity in one generation is generally reflected in the next. By comparison, in Canada and Nordic countries, that proportion is about a fifth. In other words, the American dream is more possible in Canada than it is in the United States. From every measure, it is clear that there has been a continuous trend since 2000 toward a further concentration of income at the very top. No other country has seen such extreme shifts in recent times. The latest research suggests that only 3% of students in the top colleges come from the poorest quarter of the population ("Inequality and the American Dream," 2006). Poor children are often trapped in run-down schools, while wealthier parents are in a position to spend more cash on tutoring their children to ensure they succeed. For many ethnic minorities, new immigrants, and people in the lower socioeconomic strata suffering from institutional discrimination, it is more appropriate to speak of an American nightmare than an American dream (McNamee & Miller, 2004).

In fact, the American dream is systematically denied to numerous social groups by discrimination on the basis of sexual orientation, disability, religion, regional location, and level of physical attractiveness. While gender and ethnicity are generally deemed the most common bases for discrimination, when discrimination happens on other grounds, it is no less real for the victim. Nevertheless, the myth of the American dream holds out hope for many. It can be harmful, however, when it provides an incomplete explanation of an individual's success or failure, or when it continues to mistakenly praise the rich and demonize the poor.

There is a serious disparity between the rich and poor who wish to fulfill the American dream. The wealthy in North America are born near the finish line in terms of maintaining their existing wealth and producing more of it. The poor have a slim chance of accumulating wealth and making the American dream occur in their lives. We hear the success stories in the media of poor individuals who have accrued unimaginable wealth in their short lifetimes. Their numbers, however, are tiny. Success for this population is almost always based on a working class work ethic and good luck. Table 15.1 shows the immense distance the poor must travel to be financially successful.

Table 15.1   The journey of "financial success" for the wealthy and the poor

Source: Adapted from McNamee & Miller, 2004. International race to get ahead p. 50

My mother was a single parent raising two children on welfare. I can vividly recall many of the struggles we endured as a family. The two main constants in my childhood were worrying if we would have enough food and worrying about where we would live. As a child I was always hungry. My brother and I often went to bed without dinner, and the only meal that I could count on was my free lunch at school. The free lunches were not exactly free because of the high emotional price one had to pay by standing in the free lunch line. The school cafeteria always had two lunch lines: one for the kids who paid cash for their lunches and a much smaller line filled with children holding blue cards and dressed in less-than-popular clothes, who paid for their lunches with their pride. I can remember begging my mom to pack me a lunch so I could feel free of the daily humiliation. Unfortunately, there was never anything to pack.

Because of our poverty, chaos and instability were a part of my daily life. By the time I was in fifth grade, I had gone to 12 different schools (all of which subscribed to the segregated lunch lines). Along with the constant moving came periods of homelessness. These times of living on the streets and staying in strangers' houses were both confusing and frightening. I can recall being displaced from my home on more than several occasions. We had nowhere to go, and we spent many days sleeping at the houses of strangers who had picked us up while we were walking.

From there, things got worse; my family was separated in ways that are almost too painful to discuss. As a family we were separated for many months, but my mom fought her way back to us and we were reunited as a family again.

My mother had clever ways of coping with our poverty. Without a penny to her name, she would take us to the grocery store and fill our shopping cart with the most delicious and desirable food items. She would open up various packages of crackers and cookies and feed my brother and me. Once we were fed, my mom would abandon the shopping cart and we would quickly exit the store.

I know now that my mother did her best at the time, but for me the poverty I experienced as a child made me feel isolated, ashamed, and constantly yearning for a place to call my own. As a child I was obsessed with drawing pictures of houses, furniture, and clothing. I thought it was because I was artistic, but I believe now it was because these were the material things I longed for. I dream of poverty as a tidal wave. It is crushing; it destroys everything in its path; it can be deadly and it is very hard to escape. In my dreams I am always running from it, always trying to find shelter to protect myself. Over the years, my dreams have become less frequent, but whenever life gets particularly rough, the nightmare reappears. While I am very grateful that I do not wake up every night gasping for air, I am not ready to completely let go of these dreams yet.

—Joyce

Joyce Everett experienced many hardships as a child growing up in the United States.

We were constantly on the move. We evaded landlords and collectors by sneaking out and moving in the middle of the night. Our last names are different so that loan sharks couldn't make the connection within the family in case they came after my father. I can still remember my mother sleeping with a machete by her bed at night for protection. I remember her warning us to be careful if we were home alone. *You don't know what these kind of people are like,* she said. *Your dad borrowed a lot of money from them. They're looking for him, they want their money. But if they can't get money, they'll take your life instead. And believe me, your dad won't care.*

I grew up never knowing what stability was like. We moved at least once a year, from house to house and then from motel room to motel room. When I was in the seventh grade, we moved into our car. All eight members of my family lived in the same car for six months. We used to drive to McDonald's every morning to use the bathroom and brush our teeth before school. We would rent a motel room once a week to shower and do laundry. We ate porridge when we had it; otherwise we ate nothing. I remember my mom saying one night that she was going to steal from the grocery store so we could eat something. I told her not to do it, that she was even more useless to us if she was in jail. What kind of daughter says that to her own mother? What kind of mother would let her children go to sleep hungry? What kind of father would let this happen?

—Jamie

The Growth of Consumer Culture

Sut Jhally (1998), a communications professor from the University of Massachusetts, has eloquently described the emergence of consumer culture as one of the dominant cultural trends in our world today. He describes consumer culture and its impact on our global community as "the *ground* on which we live, the *space* in which we learn to think, the *lens* through which we come to understand the world that surrounds us" (p. 1).

We are, whether we like it or not, a part of the consumer culture. A belief in capitalism and consumerism tells us that Americans live in a land of opportunity. Government laws and regulations are designed to protect capitalism, businesses are accorded the right to maximize profit with few restrictions, and our job as consumers is to buy material objects, even if we have to amass debt to do it. Within this culture we are all under tremendous pressure to conform to the tenets of consumerism. Many of us have our worldviews molded and our identities shaped to live our lives according to goals of consumer practice, such as watching commercial television, shopping in the mall, investing in the stock market, and spending a paycheck.

Jhally (1998) identifies advertising in the media as playing a significant cultural role in the definition of our values and morals. It tells us what we should deem to be virtuous and worthwhile as well as what is bad and immoral. In fact, some of the most creative minds have dedicated enormous effort to selling consumer consciousness. Most of the television and print media have been developed primarily as a delivery system for marketers to tell us that happiness is fulfilled through the consumption of products. The more goods we own and consume, the happier and more contented we will be. The advertising machine not only promises to fulfill all of our human needs but also simultaneously creates them. To illustrate this point, retail analyst Victor Liebow made the following comment many years ago:

> Our enormously productive economy . . . demands that we make consumption our way of life, that we convert the buying and the selling of goods into rituals, that we seek our spiritual satisfaction, our ego satisfaction in commodities. . . . We need things consumed, burned up, worn out, replaced, and discarded at an ever increasing rate. (cited by Durning, 1992, p. 153)

As Jeffrey Kottler (1999) suggests, "We are enculturated to want things. We are brainwashed to assess our worth and image according to the products we acquire" (p. 48).

Consumer culture endorses notions of identity that say that we are what we can buy. Everyone, no matter what his class, is susceptible to the marketing machine of consumer culture, in which a person's value is defined by the acquisition of objects. For the poor, the acquisition of material objects is often used as an antidote to the shame of poverty.

Television pumps consumer messages to us through sitcoms, dramas, game shows, and reality television, many of which extol the virtues of acquisition and consumerism. Advertisers have sophisticated techniques to convince us to buy. Tim Kasser, Richard Ryan, Charles Couchman, and Kennon Sheldon (2004) report on the positive correlation between television watching and materialism. Products are being used by famous people or those we find attractive, and we are coached into believing that we might enjoy some of their success if we simply buy that product. Psychological techniques such as classical conditioning and social learning theory (Bandura, 1971) are used to teach us consumptive behavior.

Consumer culture creates cruel illusions as it projects images in the media of human happiness but ultimately does not deliver these things. Consumer culture has colonized so much of what we have historically valued, like interpersonal connections, that we have instead become part of what Tibor Scitovsky (1976) refers to as "the joyless economy." Jeffrey Kottler (1999) noted that despite the fact that the United States has gotten wealthier, the number of "very happy" people has declined. More tellingly, the 100 richest people in America are only a little happier than the average person (Myers & Diener, 1996). Because of the success of advertising, more and more young people are becoming materialistic and consumer focused. In 1973, one third of American young people surveyed in their 20s declared that having lots of money was an extremely important goal. In 20 years, that percentage doubled (Hornblower, 1997). Tim Kasser and Alan Kanner (2004) report on a growing body of research that demonstrates that people who are strongly oriented toward money, possessions, and image report lower subjective well-being.

Consumer culture directs us away from being members of society with an interest in collective issues and focuses us on individual greed and selfishness. It does not promote an interest in the general plight of large portions of the human population who live in poverty, receive limited health care, and have inadequate housing and few opportunities. Tim Kasser and Richard Ryan (2001, cited in Kasser & Kanner, 2004) describe a decrease in the likelihood that people oriented toward materialism and consumerism will behave in a prosocial manner. People strongly focused on materialistic values have a lower societal interest and display less prosocial behavior (Kasser & Ryan, 2001, and McHoskey, 1999, cited in Kasser & Kanner, 2004). People with a materialistic focus compete more than cooperate and have more greed and heightened consumption. In addition, people strongly affected by materialistic values care less about environmental issues and engage in fewer environmentally friendly behaviors (Sheldon & McGregor, 2000, cited in Kasser & Kanner, 2004). Thus, there is good evidence to suggest that the culture of consumption not only negatively impacts psychological well-being but heightens the dangers of serious environmental and social problems. It also undermines our ability to look for collaborative solutions to our problems.

The Third World and Consumer Culture

There is today a stark difference between people who are raised in a consumer culture and those raised in traditional communities where ancient systems of social organization are prominent. These differences have a great bearing on the meanings individuals attribute to their being poor and socially and economically deprived.

In isolated communities in the developing world, the large majority of people have very little in the way of material resources and are surrounded by many others in exactly the same circumstances. There are countless villages and towns whose citizens are struggling to sustain basic material needs and who have little conception of the tremendous wealth and resources available to others in the West. Many do not envisage any possibility that they will have access to a Western middle class lifestyle, and for the most part, they are entirely accurate in this assessment. This does not mean, however, that people in the third world do not aspire toward the acquisition of material goods that might relieve day-to-day life burdens.

There are still communities who accept low material status without contest, faultfinding, or shame about their contributions to their own plight. Citizens from countries with caste systems, such as India, Pakistan, and Sri Lanka, or from societies with highly elaborate social class systems have tended to be more accepting of social inequities. Religious systems such as Hinduism and Buddhism teach their adherents to accept their lowly status and the inevitability and finality of their life's circumstances in this present plane of existence. The poor may believe they are promised greater things after death or in another life. To some extent, their inherited status in the social order is accepted. When traveling to many parts of the globe, we continue to be struck by how many people in jarring and unspeakable poverty are among the most generous, contented, and kindly folk that you could meet anywhere. While the physical consequences of being poor are devastating in developing and third-world countries, there are also serious physical as well as psychological consequences of being poor in a consumer-dominated society.

TO DISCUSS

1. What brands or popular products were "all the rage" when you were an adolescent in school?

2. What impact did having these products have on your personal and social life?

3. What happened if you were not able to afford these brand name products?

4. How does the same thing happen now that you are an adult?

5. For those who are parents, how does consumer culture work on your children?

The Psychological Effects of Being Poor

Where the consumer culture has taken hold, the social inscriptions of what it means to be poor change. The power of marketing and advertising adds momentum to the myth of a classless society in which wealth is potentially attainable by everyone. bell hooks (2000) suggests that transnational media present consumer culture as a democratic system that is open and free and where anything is possible. The rich are represented as heroic champions of hedonistic consumerism, and the media promote the notion that people already have an equal right to buy anything. hooks makes a case that the poor are demonized in the media and are portrayed as corrupt and dysfunctional, while the rich are depicted as caring and generous. Popular reality television unabashedly celebrates beauty and wealth. The rich and famous dominate our television screens and other forms of media, and many of us vicariously live our lives with them through this medium. We can imagine rising to fame and fortune and think that we too can be part of the fantasy of working for Donald Trump, or have our home shown on the popular MTV program *Cribs*. hooks gives an example of how consumer culture has undermined the spiritual and moral integrity of young black leaders:

> While young black gangsta' rappers stand up at award ceremonies and give thanks to God for their fame and fortune, the Christian and Islamic religious beliefs they evoke do not shape their moral values or their actions in the world. They (and their non-black counter parts) mock their gods, and their wanton worship of wealth encourages the young to believe that God is useful only as a tool for taking you to the top. And this top is not Martin Luther King's mountaintop where one embraces a divine vision of social justice and democratic union. (p. 87)

The discourse through which poverty is understood inevitably becomes internalized into the psychological experience of the poor. They are susceptible to the invitation to hold themselves personally to blame for their grim and impoverished material circumstances. Many of the lower class and working poor experience feelings of desperation and hopelessness. They are surrounded by middle class culture and wealth, but none of it seems accessible. As Charles Waldegrave, Kiwi Tamasese, Flora Tuhaka, and Warihi Campbell (2003) have argued, counselors with a commitment to multicultural understandings should be prepared to inquire into and work with the effects of poverty and unemployment. They should understand, for example, the depression that can result from difficult life circumstances as contextually produced rather than just as the result of the action of chemicals in the brain.

The production of hedonistic consumerism has created a generation of youth who see little value in hard work but believe that status and power lie only in getting one's material needs met. Success is measured by demonstrating excesses of material consumption. Young African American youth from poverty-stricken communities who become stars in the music industry and in the sporting world often overexaggerate displays of the conventional status symbols of success to win the respect and approval of their peers. The platform large diamond-studded necklaces and the fashion of wearing diamond-studded teeth grills is only a different version of materialistic display from those exhibited by movie stars, entrepreneurs, and recipients of inherited wealth who show off jet planes, large yachts, and collections of cars and palaces as status symbols.

Consumer discourse promotes the envy that is exploited by modern advertising. This dynamic has produced a predatory culture in poor urban neighborhoods where young people are slaughtered for their material possessions. Many youth attempt to hide their shame about being poor by masking their background with clothing and material possessions. This is most noticeable in schools, where adolescents often make strong requests to their parents about wearing the current designer labels in order to escape being ridiculed by their peers for wearing out-of-date clothing.

When youth in poor communities are served by poor health and education services, they can look to expedient methods to be free from the shame of being poor and the feelings of worthlessness that can accompany their failure to realize the American dream. In the face of limited possibilities in the inner city, many in the underclass resort to hustling, pimping, prostitution, and drug dealing. In these poor urban communities, families get pulled into the immediate attractions that a prolific drug culture can provide them. Selling drugs buys the necessities and provides the prospect of rapid access to luxuries. The downstream psychological effects of addiction result. Sadly, the infestation of the drug culture in poor communities further undermines the attempts of its citizens to escape the exploitation and violation that accompany drug trafficking. Illicit drugs become attractive pathways to acquiring monetary rewards, allowing an otherwise poor person to drive the same cars and wear the same clothes as the middle and upper classes. Drugs also ease the pain of shame and humiliation and numb the sorrow accompanying entrapment in poverty. Paradoxically, however, it is the same drug culture that frequently destroys the familial bonds that once mitigated the hardships of poverty.

We shall now present two stories that illustrate some of the identity effects of poverty. In this first example, notice how the sense of shame produced by the general negative stereotyping of poverty develops.

My family, I have noticed, do not always seem proud of who they are. I remember the times I would ask my mother or father if friends could come over to play when I was young, and my parents would say no because they were ashamed of themselves: their low socioeconomic status, their alcoholism, their "Okie" ways. I can remember when I internalized that shame. I stopped asking friends to come over altogether. My immediate family is ashamed of the way they live, knowing that it is different from my friend's family's lifestyle. My extended family has some pride and shame issues as well, especially my Nanny (my father's mother). I remember that every time I would tell her about a new boyfriend, she would ask about his family's financial standing. She would recommend, "Marry for money, and eventually you will love him." This disturbed me when I was in my idealistic, romantic stage. However, now I see the struggles that our family went through financially and I understand her convictions. Though she would never leave my grandfather, her life would have been a lot easier had she married for money. My family's shame of being in the low SES category is also evidenced when they see or talk about people who do have money. Their jealousy is very apparent. The issues of shame with regard to money have been passed down from previous generations, all of whom had low or middle SES and all of whom were concerned with how they appeared to other people.

—Maryanne

Notice how strongly in Maryanne's story the discourse of personal worth has been constructed around having money. There is little in this statement that might represent, for example, pride in being a member of the honest working class. Indeed, the concept of social class is absent and is replaced by the concept of socioeconomic status, a measuring tool by which individuals and families are placed on a normal scale. On this scale, Heather finds herself placed at the low end and feels the shame of this intensely.

Status and social class are very important to my family. My family classifies themselves as middle class, but I believe that they are very low middle class. My family is very insecure about the way they are viewed by others in terms of appearing wealthy or poor. Growing up, I have always been aware of our low socioeconomic status. I think that a lot of the insecurity about money stems from struggling for so long. My Nanny, for example, takes great pride now in driving an older Mercedes.

—Diane

TO DISCUSS

1. What is it like to be poor? Share experiences of temporary or long-term poverty among your class.

2. Is temporary poverty different from long-term poverty?

3. What effect does poverty have on children?

4. Research the psychological effects of poverty and the educational effects. Share findings.

5. What does it mean to live below the official poverty line? Find out how many people live below that line in your country, state, city, and community.

Classism

Classism is the cultural expression of prejudice on the basis of social class membership. It involves the making of a negative judgment about the worth of a person, either oneself or another, on the basis of perceived social class membership. It is similar to racism in that people judge others on the discursive significance of particular attributes and evaluate them on a scale. The scale usually leads to an assumption of superiority or inferiority. Classist discourse is constantly at work informing the perceptions that individuals form about others' being above them, below them, or just like them. It becomes a form of rationalization for the assignment of "in" groups and "out" groups.

Classist behavior can show itself in all sections of society. Children engage in this behavior when they tease others because they dress funny or look dorky. Adults warn their children not to get big ideas in life and show them up as inferior. Classist discourse functions as an explanatory system to account for why some people deserve to accumulate resources while others do not. Liu and his colleagues (2004) identify four versions of classism: upward, downward, lateral, and internalized. Upward classism is prejudice and discrimination directed toward individuals who are perceived to be of a higher social class. They are judged to be elitist, snobbish, pretentious, and self-absorbed. Affluent people can be perceived as ruthless, selfish, and uncaring. Downward classism involves prejudicial attitudes and behaviors against people and groups that are perceived by the observer to be "lower" or "below" them. They are assumed on little or no evidence to be lazy, dirty, violent, or a drain on society. Lateral classism is best illustrated by the concept of "keeping up with the Joneses," a phrase that refers to how individuals within a certain economic structure compete with others in that social group to demonstrate that they not only belong to that class grouping but are a little superior to the others. Those who violate the cultural norms of their class are at risk of being jettisoned from that social group. Lateral classism involves a strong discourse of conformity to the social group, and an individual who moves to the margins of that group may be deemed unworthy to belong. Last, internalized classism functions as a discourse that works on the inside. It occurs when individuals transgress the boundaries of their own internalized cultural norms and expectations. On the basis of deterioration in their financial position or some social or behavioral misdeed, people can judge themselves to be inadequate and to have failed to meet the cultural standards of their class.

There are significant counseling implications for classist behavior, which can be demonstrated by both counselors and clients. For clients experiencing internalized classism, strong feelings of shame, anger, frustration, and depression can dominate their experience (D'Andrea & Daniels, 2001). Men in particular can be deeply troubled when they have not been able to meet their own expectations of wealth accumulation and fail to live up to their own social class worldview.

William Ming Liu and Donald Pope-Davis (2003) have suggested that counselors who have not confronted their own classist attitudes may be prone to displaying disrespectful and sometimes abusive behaviors toward their clients that are akin to racism. As therapy is a talking form of healing, the discourse used in the therapy room can be infected with classist language and assumptions. Thus, counselors need to be aware of biases and not judge clients on the basis of, for example, their use of nonstandard English or slang or their particular accent.

Social Mobility Through Education

Despite the powerful constraining effects of social class, there are many people who are socially mobile. They grow up in working class families and achieve entry to middle class occupations and lifestyles. Educational achievement is the main pathway to this mobility. Indeed, the opportunity for such educational achievement is sometimes held out to the poor as if it is equally open to all. The impression created is that those who do not achieve social mobility are morally weak and thus less deserving. Many people from a range of nonwhite ethnic backgrounds and from working class families nevertheless do achieve educational success. In many cases, these individuals overcome great odds to succeed in school, the university, and the workplace.

Sometimes this success happens because the institutions themselves make efforts to respond to culturally different backgrounds. Affirmative action is an example. More often, however, socially mobile individuals have not only learned the culture of middle class America, but in many cases also learned to thrive in it. Thriving in the discourse of education is much more straightforward for those groomed in white middle class culture from birth (Croninger & Lee, 2001; Holt, 1997). They are said to have accumulated "cultural capital" (Bourdieu & Passeron, 1977) that gives them profound advantages in the marketplace of education. After they accumulate educational qualifications, they translate this cultural capital back into economic capital through the extra money they can earn in the workplace.

Liu et al. (2004) adds to Pierre Bourdieu and Jean-Claude Passeron's account by distinguishing between social capital, cultural capital, and human capital. Social capital, for example, is defined by privileged access to specific relationships that enable advancement. It is explained by the well-known phrase, "It's not what you know but who you know." Human capital is based on personal charisma, interpersonal skills, physical ability, or physical beauty as these things are valued by a particular community. Cultural capital was first defined by Bourdieu to refer to the particular tastes and aesthetic sensitivities cultivated in one's social class as signals to others that one belongs.

Many middle and upper class individuals are groomed to take full advantage of the cultural, social, and human capital they acquire and to translate it into educational achievement and economic advancement. Others who have not been brought up with cultural capital have to acculturate to the dominant culture of the middle class, sometimes at great cost to themselves and to their indigenous cultural heritage. Sometimes the costs outweigh the advantages, as the stresses of acculturation itself lead to drug addiction, mental illness, family breakup, loneliness, and isolation.

There are numerous statistics to support the idea that dynamic and complex shifts in social mobility through education are taking place in North America. Box 15.2 summarizes a few key statistics.

Box 15.2. Race, Class, and Education Statistics

When statistics are collected about race and social class, clear links are detected. Blacks still lag behind whites in numbers of young people attaining a high school graduation. While only 79% of black students graduate from high school, 89% of white students do (McKinnon, 2003). At the college level, those categorized as Asian had the highest proportion of college graduates at 50% in 2004. About 30% of whites and 17% of blacks completed a bachelor's degree. In 1993, 24% of whites and 12% of blacks were college graduates. According to a U.S. Census Bureau news release (United States Department of Commerce, 2004), women have made large gains in earning college degrees. Over the past decade, women with a bachelor's or higher degree have jumped nearly 7 percentage points, from 19% to 26%. During the same time, men have had a 4-percentage-point increase from 25% to 29%. In 2004, for the second year in a row, women had a slightly higher proportion of high school graduates (85%) than men (84%). (United States Department of Commerce, 2004).

Social Class Culture in the Workplace

Achieving success in education and in the workplace in the modern world requires the ability to adhere to specific behavioral protocols. Acculturation into these protocols determines to a large extent where one falls in the division between the "haves" and the "have nots." To survive and thrive in educational and corporate institutions, people must negotiate their way through a series of nuanced political requirements and become adept at joining and maintaining a network of positive relationships, especially with those above them in the hierarchy.

Those who are most successful in meeting the cultural expectations of large economic and educational institutions know how to fulfill a complex array of both subtle and not-so-subtle daily tasks. They know the importance of following repetitive routines and managing time. They are able to understand and work within hierarchical structures and are willing to do so. In addition, they learn how to follow the cultural conventions of business and educational etiquette. They can deliver and receive information and acquire particular technological know-how. Less obvious because it is so taken for granted but most important is their ability to hold fast to particular standards of dress and hygiene, demonstrate nonverbal attentiveness by engaging in a high degree of eye contact, and demonstrate verbal agility while responding quickly to requests and demands. Successful individuals must also display a particular voice tone, accent, and dialect that mirror the pattern of communication of those who are high in the hierarchy. Those who succeed in contemporary economic systems are generally able to speak fluently in the accents and dialects of the dominant language, which in North America is middle class English.

There are always a small minority of individuals in diverse cultural communities who "make it" in a capitalist culture even when they do not meet or demonstrate the necessary cultural expectations of the white middle class in school and in business. Many youngsters from underrepresented and marginalized communities aspire to be professional sportsmen and sportswomen, such as professional football, basketball, or baseball stars or rap or hip-hop artists. In part, these young people know at an early age that their lives do not conform to the cultural expectations prized in school settings. They see physical prowess or musical and dancing talent, rather than the attainment of business acumen or professional mastery in any of the possible career paths that exist, as a way to attain monetary success and social prestige.

The dominant cultural practices in economic institutions may have their origins many hundreds of years ago in Greek, Roman, Chinese, Japanese, and Islamic civilizations. They have been honed and refined by the dominating European civilizations over the last 400 years. In a contemporary American context, the individuals who are most likely to excel in workplace culture are from middle and upper class backgrounds and have either a European American or Asian ancestry. In part, they have excelled because their ancestors played a significant role in establishing the cultural practices that accompanied the development of modern-day institutions such as schools, universities, banks, retail stores, factories, hospitals, and construction industries. People without the cultural background that teaches the cultural nuances of contemporary institutions have struggled harder to achieve success in these contexts.

The argument presented here does not deny the history of discrimination that has positively excluded people from success in the workplace on the grounds of skin color or gender. Instead, it explains how privileged access to occupational success is also founded on what happens in our minds and in our daily relational practices. This is the domain of psychology rather than, say, legal rights. It is the psychology of the internalized cultural knowledge that is passed on from generation to generation, much of which we are barely aware of. Its effects are not always immediately obvious, but they are worked out over a lifetime.

Counseling Needs of the Underclass

Members of cultural communities who struggle to participate successfully in the current education system and who drop out and fail to graduate from high school often fall into a large underclass. Included in this group are those who find themselves unemployed or underemployed or working in menial jobs in dangerous environments at or below the minimum wage. This group typically is caught in a hopeless cycle of poverty from which escape is very difficult. They are also commonly exposed to neighborhood and gang violence and police brutality. They are provided with inadequate social services, and yet they are the most in need of health and counseling services. Current counseling services in North America are mostly underprepared to work with this large and alienated group. While this underclass is made up of many people from African American, Mexican American, Native American, Caribbean, and Pacific Island communities, it also includes many whites from lower class backgrounds. People with physical and mental disabilities frequently end up in this underclass, as do seniors who find themselves without adequate financial resources.

In many ways, members of this financially poor, alienated underclass share more day-to-day experiences with each other than they do with more well off members of the same race, ethnicity, religion, or sexual orientation. A Community Development Authority report produced by the United States Department of Labor revealed, for example, that the major factors producing child poverty in the United States result from welfare dependence and single parenthood (Rector, Johnson, & Fagan, 2001). They state that race per se is not a factor in producing child poverty and does not directly increase or decrease the probability that a child will be poor. When white groups with high levels of single parenthood and welfare dependence (matching those typical in the black community) are compared to black groups, the poverty rates for both groups are nearly identical. Yet black American children are three times more likely to live in poverty than white children are, primarily because black children are far more likely to live in single-parent families and to be on welfare.

Counseling Services and Cultural Acculturation

Counseling and social services need to be tailored for the poor as well as respond to the unique needs of different ethnic groups and gay and lesbian communities. The shared cultural experiences of those who are of the same socioeconomic class are critical resources for the development of culturally respectful and effective counseling approaches for this population.

Those who are schooled in the conventions of middle class culture are more likely to utilize and benefit from mainstream counseling and psychotherapy services than those who have been rejected, failed, and marginalized by the educational and economic institutions of dominant culture. And yet the frames of reference for most counseling and psychotherapy models are congruent with the cultural assumptions embedded in these same institutions. Many approaches to therapy have been developed by therapists working with middle class clients. It would therefore not be surprising to find that such approaches do not fit with the cultural values of those who are members of the working class or in poverty. A notable exception to this generalization is Salvador Minuchin's (1974) approach to structural family therapy, which was largely developed among families living in the slums of Philadelphia.

Counseling in Poor Communities

There are some immediate practical issues that need to be taken into account by counselors working in poor communities. Derald Wing Sue and David Sue (2003) point many of these out. For example, it is easy to overlook the struggles that many clients with no reliable means of transportation have in attending counseling sessions. Many working class families also have great difficulty making long-term appointments. People doing shift work or whose working schedule is constantly changing have little control over their working hours and cannot easily schedule services way into the future. They may face greater risk of losing their jobs by taking time off to attend appointments than middle class clients. Setting 50-minute appointments a week or two in advance may work well for middle class clients but not always so well for lower class clients who are concerned with day-to-day survival (Sue & Sue, 2003). As a result, many families can benefit from mental health services only if counselors are willing to conduct home visits. And yet counselors are often reluctant to make these home visits, particularly in neighborhoods where they feel endangered.

Many people in poor communities have had frequent negative experiences in dealing with public and community agencies, some of which are poorly run and poorly resourced. They also frequently experience such agencies as serving a governing role over their lives rather than working in solidarity with them in their struggles. As a result, Sue and Sue suggest that many poor people have low regard for punctuality, as they have had numerous experiences of waiting for hours on end in mental health centers, police stations, and various government agencies, just for a few minutes of the professional's time. It is not surprising that clients who have repeatedly had these experiences lack enthusiasm for another appointment and feel indifferent toward counseling professionals. Members of poorer communities have sometimes been described by mental health professionals as more likely to be distrustful and to become frustrated with authority figures. There is perhaps an expectation that mental health professionals won't listen to them and may not value the same things. These self-protective responses may easily be wrongly assessed as poor motivation for counseling.

Living in a harsh environment in a poverty-stricken community does not invite long-range planning and sophisticated, indirect therapeutic strategies. Many people want immediate, concrete advice and tangible support. Salvador Minuchin (1974) describes family relationships in such circumstances as often characterized by a chaotic pattern. He therefore advocates therapeutic interventions that address the building of greater structure in family members' lives. Clients who live in poverty often don't have the resources to pay for mental health treatment and are almost certain not to have health insurance. Instead, they can be completely reliant on public nonprofit health services, which may vary dramatically in quality of services.

It is sometimes said that many people who live in poor communities do not necessarily respond to talk therapies. We want to be very cautious about this conclusion, which can be a quite patronizing and pathologizing assumption made by middle class counselors who interpret working class patterns of language use as a lack of intelligence or a lack of ability to communicate. Just because working class people do not talk in counseling in the ways that a counselor is familiar with or in ways that match the expectations of a particular therapeutic approach does not mean that such clients cannot benefit from talking through their struggles with a counselor. The crucial issue is whether the counselor is willing to enter the cultural values implicit in the client's language world rather than whether talking to a counselor at all is of no use. In circumstances where such a question arises, the onus is on the counselor to make the effort to join with and respect the client's cultural knowledge and linguistic frames of reference rather than to write the client off as lacking the skills necessary for participation in counseling. This issue is even more salient when the client's first language is not English. Monolingual English-speaking therapists can easily slip into pathologizing and writing off clients because they do not understand them.

Now we shall turn from the pragmatic issues to the substantive issues that working class and poor clients raise with counselors. Counselors and therapists can have great difficulty understanding and relating to circumstances and day-to-day challenges that people face in poor communities. It is easy for therapists to interpret failure to overcome powerful systemic and discursive constraints as failures in client awareness or moral courage. In other words, it is easy to individualize the effects of social forces and impute to clients a personal deficit of some kind. Given many of the knowledges that dominate psychology, we can even say that it is understandable that counselors would be pulled in such a direction by their training and professional knowledge base. But what is understandable is not always good enough. It is possible for counselors to understand the processes by which the poor come to internalize feelings of inferiority and failure and become dominated by helplessness (Sue & Sue, 2003), not because of some personal failure, but because these are the interpretations that they are invited to make of themselves by the cultural context in which they live. Jeanne Slattery (2004) comments that sometimes lower class and working poor clients feel so hopeless about the quality of their lives and their economic well-being that this hopelessness is transferred to their expectations about therapy. It is also possible for counselors to open opportunities in counseling for clients to contest the negative identity conclusions that they have internalized from the cultural and economic contexts of their lives. They can also help clients to develop qualities and skill sets that build the resilience, strength, and perseverance necessary to survive in tough and unforgiving communities.

Other times, clients are struggling with basic survival needs, such as having a reliable shelter and finding an adequate source for food. These needs take precedence over some of the agendas important to the counselors assigned to work with folks who are struggling. At the same time, there are internal experiential dimensions and identity stories about obtaining basic survival needs that counseling can help clients process.

Middle Class Culture and Graduate School

In general, there is very little emphasis on the impact of social class on counseling in counselor training programs. In many programs, counselors are prepared to work with middle class cultures rather than with the working class and the poor. This emphasis is largely due to the pervasiveness of middle class culture in many university institutions. As Tracy Robinson (2005) suggests, graduate culture is steeped in economic privilege. Counselor education programs are shaped and developed within middle class culture. Graduate students are drilled in cultural practices requiring self-reliance, standard English, and the middle class work ethic of delayed gratification. Even if members of the student body have not come from well-resourced communities, graduate students have distinguished themselves by succeeding amid the rigors of academia and have acculturated in a middle class direction, with an emphasis on competing in an individualistic way. Students who have made considerable personal and financial sacrifices to participate in advanced professional training would prefer jobs that show their middle class standing and salaries and lifestyle opportunities commensurate with their middle class grooming.

There is compelling evidence to suggest that many counselors are drawn toward working with the young, attractive, verbal, intelligent, and successful client group described by the acronym YAVIS (Schofield, 1964, cited by Robinson, 2005) rather than working with clients from lower social classes who speak nonstandard English and express themselves in slang and street talk. This tendency is cause for concern in counselor education programs, and counselors who are committed to working in a multicultural way need to address their own assumptions on these issues.

Therapists and Class

For many therapists, it is easy to overlook the constraining social factors pertaining to class and socioeconomic status that are impacting their clients. The isolation, self-loathing, and immobilization that occurs for families struggling to survive in poor urban communities can be downplayed. When therapists understand the power of class and socioeconomic factors in shaping people's identities and aspirations, they can help clients feel understood and accepted. Feelings of humiliation, remorse, guilt, and resentment can be alleviated, freeing the individual or family to draw on family and community resources that were not previously available to them. As Jodie Kliman (1998) suggests, "deconstructing class relations in therapy both counters their shaming effects and helps therapists guard against falling back on privilege themselves" (p. 58). Careful questioning can help families who are denied mortgages and loans to see that their problems may indeed be economic systemic issues rather than their own failings.

Counselors and therapists must be prepared to own their socioeconomic privilege, where it exists, and to be watchful about how their class differs from that of their clients and how this gulf may impact the therapeutic relationship. It is not wrong to be economically privileged. The important issue is not *being* privileged as much as how one *uses* one's privilege. If it is used to make a difference in the lives of others who are less privileged, then there should be no criticism. In order to start making such a difference, counselors need to develop consciousness of their own social class influences and be careful of imposing their own class-related assumptions on their clients. Such middle class markers as speaking standard English can become barriers for therapists whose clients have not learned to look, speak, and act like the middle class. Counselors can, however, work intentionally at minimizing such barriers.

Monica McGoldrick (2005) makes the point that therapists who are representative of dominant groups, such as the middle class, tend to view their own values as the norm, and therefore must be careful not to judge the meaning of client behaviors or impose their own methods and timetable for when change should occur. She suggests that sometimes even when behavior does not represent a therapist's humanitarian or equitable values, we must understand the cultural context in which a behavior has developed, even as we try to change it. Respectful collaborative conversations about therapists' class dilemmas in therapy can guard against therapists' imposition of social class judgments on individuals of a class different from their own. As we have emphasized repeatedly in this book, it is essential that counseling approaches and theories be examined and redeveloped to address the discourses (historical and current) that underpin present attitudes regarding social class and how it impacts the counseling process.

On the other hand, counselors who have themselves experienced shame and humiliation pertaining to poverty and the prejudices against those who belong to the working class can be immensely positive resources in the lives of poverty-stricken clients. Specifically, therapists can help clients locate the source of their shame and humiliation in the wider cultural practices of the community rather than inside their character or personal foibles.

But social class differences do not occur only between the middle class counselor and the working class client. It can also be challenging for working class counselors to work with wealthy clients without being intimidated. In this context, counselors may become sensitive to the inadequacies of their physical environment and may evaluate their physical space as not worthy of their client and might imagine being negatively judged by their client. Jeffrey Kottler, Marilyn Montgomery, and David Shepard (2004) describe how listening to clients talk about their successes can leave therapists feeling ashamed and inadequate about their own lives. Therapists are just as prone as everybody else to measuring their self-worth according to their financial achievements.

Implications of Poverty and Class for Counseling

Poor or economically disenfranchised clients may perceive the counselor who is middle class (even when she is of similar ethnicity) to have "bought into" Anglo American middle class values and cultural practices. Or they may have difficulty disclosing problems to counselors for fear of being judged out of the middle and upper class tendency to vilify the poor. Overtly naming clients' possibly distrustful responses is a helpful way to proceed. For example, a middle class client attempting to build trust with a client from a lower socioeconomic grouping might say,

"I notice that you look very uneasy talking to me. We have already established that we are of the same ethnic background, but I am wondering whether you distrust me because my way of talking is very different from yours. It would be really helpful to me if you can be really honest with me and identify any barriers that you think might be getting in the way of our working together."

In many communities where counseling is a foreign practice, there may be significant barriers that keep families from taking advantage of counseling services. The barriers are even greater when these communities are poor and economically disenfranchised. In these communities, people will often take advantage of help from other extended family members, from a family friend, or from somebody deemed to have healing powers, such as a minister or priest. Counselors can play an important role in supporting families' efforts to take advantage of such local resources rather than competing with them.

Linguistic differences and problems with physical accessibility are further barriers between client and counselor. The counselor's knowledge of the language and dialect of the client can be crucial in providing assistance. Counselors who are familiar with nonstandard English can build strong empathy with their clients. There are almost always dialect differences between classes. For example, in some African American communities, a counselor's fluency in ebonics can be a powerful resource for counselors. Understanding and respecting the speech patterns of different cultural communities helps build the kind of counselor-client rapport that is prerequisite to effective counseling.

Counselors who have access to middle class privilege (perhaps by means of their own social mobility) must be watchful of how they use this privilege with economically disadvantaged clients. Families from lower class communities can be jealous, cynical, and untrusting of a counselor's economic privileges. Sometimes counselors are tempted to distance themselves from the effects of poverty because of the level of struggle they witness their clients experiencing. Financial hardship may depress client motivation and engagement with the counseling process. Hopelessness caused by the daily struggle to survive does not typically motivate clients to eagerly engage in counseling interactions. Counselors who have been subjected to poverty in their own lives need to remember the experience and empathize. But to do so, they may have to struggle against an inclination to distance themselves from their own memories of the shame, humiliation, and daily grind they were subjected to in their childhood.

Middle class clients, on the other hand, may appear to be highly motivated toward the promise of upward economic and social mobility. However, in the desire to "keep up with the Joneses," they may compromise their personal convictions in an effort to "look the part" and achieve material success. Middle class clients may have suppressed feelings that contradict class-oriented goals of perfection, beauty, and what Jeanne Slattery (2004) calls "interpersonal smoothness." When emphasis is placed on what is expected rather than on what is personally valued, private aspirations for one's life can be compromised. Good counseling can explore the dilemmas that result.

By contrast, some people in lower socioeconomic groups are less concerned about people pleasing—especially when it comes to addressing authority figures. Counselors are often perceived to be authority figures and can be the target of angry and cynical responses by clients who have suffered at the hands of other authority figures. Poor clients may even anticipate adversarial interactions from middle class professionals and adopt a position of expecting neither to be heard nor to have their strong feelings (including anger) validated. Day-to-day suffering can cause people to develop a tough and invulnerable exterior in which strong, angry emotions serve a protective function.

Whereas middle class clients may be concerned with attaining beauty and perfection, many lower socioeconomic communities prize resilience, strength, perseverance, and outspokenness. Counselors can provide acknowledgment of these different value systems. Lower class directness of verbal and physical expression may not conform to middle class cultural conventions of how to deal with strong emotions. Appreciating these differences as cultural styles can help counselors to not be afraid of such intense emotions.

Response to Chapter 15

Pilar Hernández-Wolfe

Pilar Hernández-Wolfe, Ph.D., is an associate professor in the Department of Counseling and School Psychology at San Diego State University. She was born and raised in Colombia. She is heterosexual and middle class. In the United States, she is an immigrant and a woman of color. She is passionate about social justice and human rights and works in the fields of trauma, resilience, and social justice approaches to counseling.

The authors outline three general guidelines to challenge the negative impact of "totalizing" assumptions about class and poverty: (a) understanding the processes by which "the poor" come to internalize feelings of inferiority and failure and exhibit helplessness as the result of cultural interpretations that they are invited to make of themselves in the context in which they live; (b) opening up opportunities in the counseling process to contest the negative identity conclusions these individuals have internalized from the cultural and economic contexts of their lives; and (c) assisting clients in developing qualities and skill sets that build the resilience, strength, and perseverance necessary to survive in tough and unforgiving communities.

I would like to call attention to one more way to challenge the negative impact of class-based views on the poor: listening to, tracking, and elaborating on the subjective perception that clients have of their social status. In spite of the real lack of economic resources and quality education and services and the presence of multiple social ills, it is important to explore how clients perceive their social status in relation to their families and communities. Tapping into people's construction of their social status might prove pivotal in facilitating therapeutic change. The following story illustrates a therapeutic relationship in which many social location factors were salient. However, I would like to emphasize the importance of social status to illustrate my point.

I met Carmen when working at a community mental health center serving low income clients in New York. She was a client assigned to me after intake with a common description given to female clients—"depressed." Carmen showed symptoms of depression, and at a first glance she fit the profile of many other clients we served: middle aged, currently unemployed, and living alone, with a high school education, a family history of alcoholism and abuse, a personal history of abusive relationships with men, and two children in their early 20s.

Carmen was soft-spoken and verbal. During our first sessions she candidly shared her personal history and current troubles with me. Carmen was from Puerto Rico and I was from Colombia. Carmen grew up on the island, but her family had migrated to New York in search of better opportunities. However, their economic situation never changed. They struggled to make ends meet. I was an immigrant with a middle class upbringing and doctoral level education currently living a middle class life in the United States.

In spite of these class differences, I realized that we both shared an interest in spirituality. I noticed that she mentioned spirituality a few times here and there in our conversations, and I "knew" that her bracelets and collars had a spiritual meaning based on my knowledge of curanderismo and alternative forms of spirituality. When I engaged her in talking with me about her spiritual beliefs, I tapped in to a treasure full of resources. *Carmen was a spiritual priestess.* Carmen's construction of her social status in relation to her family and community and her actual standing in her social circle played a fundamental role in her perception of who she was as a Puerto Rican woman, mother, and community member. She was a healer, like me.

I believe that there were two elements that changed the nature of the therapeutic relationship at this point: (a) she felt treated with the respect that she deserved as a spiritual priestess and (b) we were able to discuss how healers might not be able to heal themselves. Together we embarked on a process of learning from each other about healing. She helped me understand the meaning of her depressive symptoms in relation to the spiritual test that she had to overcome but until then had not been successful at mastering. I helped her understand the family legacies around gender, class, sexual orientation, and ethnicity that influenced her experience of abusive relationships with men. I tapped into strengths based on her social status: her power, responsibility, and ability to assert and advocate for herself. We integrated our knowledges to help her overcome the spiritual test that the master spirits had given her. This test involved mourning the loss of a romantic relationship, identifying its abusive aspects, and making the changes necessary to prevent further emotional abuse from happening. We culminated our work with a letting-go ritual at a place near the ocean. At the end of our 18 sessions, Carmen was not taking any medication and the depressive symptoms had disappeared.

I believe that therapeutic change was facilitated by multiple factors, as is the case in any therapeutic relationship. However, discovering, acknowledging, and bringing into therapy Carmen's social status as it mattered to her in her community helped me see and work with her strengths. In the same vein, exploring the role of African

American women in their church might bring a wealth of strength to work with, as might looking into immigrants' occupation and status in their country of origin. In her work on health and social class, psychologist Karen Fraser Wyche (2001, 2006) identifies three key dimensions in assessing the subjective meaning of social class: perception of one's positioning in a social status hierarchy; comparison of self to others in the neighborhood, at work, and the community; and adaptive skills resulting from the class-based perception that one can advocate for oneself and can navigate a system. I believe that incorporating these elements in the assessment and treatment process helps counselors expand their ways of working with people in economically poor communities.

CHAPTER 16

The Production and Reproduction of Culture in School Counseling

Schools are small communities. To some degree, they mirror the larger communities in which they exist. Therefore, we might expect them to manifest the cultural relations of the world around them. Schools are also places where young people spend a large amount of time. There is no other social institution in which people are compulsorily kept for such large proportions of their daily lives. The cultural groups that make up a residential community are thrown together in close proximity in the population of a public school (although those who attend private schools often do not get the same experience of cultural heterogeneity). For this reason, counselors who work in schools have a special opportunity to work with young people in their formative years in a context where they may encounter cultural diversity as fully and as directly as at any other time of their lives. The school is, therefore, an important site for the construction of a multicultural community.

Schools as Sites for Cultural Transmission

Schools are places where children learn far more than how to read, write, and compute. Schools also have an express social role of producing and shaping young people for life in the community around them. Counselors have a part to play in this social role. Schools are sites where basic attitudes to life, social skills, and a range of values are transmitted from adults to the next generation. At school children learn things like how to manage time, how to relate to others in the world around them, how to wait their turn, how to be patriotic citizens, how to work toward a substantial goal rather than just an immediate reward, how to present their views to others, how to argue a case, how to make room for the different views of others, and so on. They also acquire values. Such values will necessarily represent the values of the community around the school. For example, children might learn in school to value knowledge, learning, orderly behavior, particular versions of rational thought, gender roles, individual competition, democratic participation, submission to authority, imagination, and respect for others.

These skills and values can never be free from cultural definition and influence. For example, the construction of time can be quite different from one cultural world to another (Levine, 1997), and the way timeliness is expected to be observed in school is likely to represent the domination of one tradition of cultural observance, usually associated with the modernist tradition that invented the modern methods of measuring time objectively. Learning to be submissive in the face of authority prepares young people to work as good employees. Learning the rituals of national identity, such as how to sing the national anthem, say the pledge of allegiance, and honor the flag, prepares them for patriotic citizenship. Even the subject matter in school curricula is not value free. History classes are built on particular versions of national identity and will usually represent the perspective of dominant social groups. Economics classes build on the assumption of particular capitalist economic values and lifestyles. Math and science classes teach what Valerie Walkerdine (1988) has called the "mastery of reason." By this she means that particular attitudes toward life and about our relationship with the world around us are conveyed in procedures that make up logical and scientific thought. She has also analyzed in depth the ways in which the texts used for mathematical study construct gendered roles and relationships with the world. English literature classes have been built on the recognition of a canon of established great works (usually written by white men) considered worthy of study. Many writers in the field of cultural studies (e.g., Edward Said, 1978/1994) have challenged the dominance of this canon on the grounds of the particular Western cultural traditions and values represented in it, while other cultural traditions are implicitly devalued by their exclusion.

The point here is that knowledge itself is not neutral. It is shot through with cultural influences. What is taught is always taught from a cultural perspective. For example, textbooks on the history of America seldom are written from the perspective of native peoples, or ordinary working class folk, or women. A critical perspective on pedagogy raises countless questions about what children are taught in school and whose lives are privileged (and whose diminished) as a result. Peter McLaren (2005) lists examples of such questions:

> What is the relationship between social class and knowledge taught in schools? Why do we value scientific knowledge over informal knowledge? Why do we have teachers using "standard English"? . . . What accounts for some knowledge having high status . . . while the practical knowledge of ordinary people or marginalized or subjugated groups is often discredited and devalued? (p. 410)

If schools are places where culture is transmitted and called knowledge, we always need to ask questions about which cultural narratives are being transmitted. And we need to pay attention to the cultural narratives that are being neglected or marginalized in the process. For counselors, paying such attention also includes monitoring the personal effects of cultural messages of value for students whose values and attitudes are being formed in the context of these narratives.

The Explicit Curriculum and the Hidden Curriculum

As counselors in schools meet with young people who are subject to this process of cultural transmission, they will necessarily encounter its effects on the identity of children and young people. However, in their understanding of their social role, counselors should take on board more than just the explicit agenda of schooling. They should also pay attention to what has been called the "hidden curriculum" of schooling. We shall examine both the explicit and the hidden agendas of schooling.

The explicit agenda of schools is known to everyone. It is to educate young people in academic skills, provide them with a secure environment in which to develop, inculcate them with the values of the community around them, and prepare them to graduate with the requirements for higher education or for other career paths. Counselors have an acknowledged role to play in relation to this explicit curriculum.

Texts on school counseling, including the American School Counseling Association's national model for school counseling (American School Counseling Association, 2003), commonly divide the functions of counselors in schools into three concentrations: academic counseling, career counseling, and personal/social counseling. Each of these concentrations of counseling practice has important cultural dimensions to it. Academic counseling involves working with young people in the context of their cultural positioning as learners. Career counseling involves helping young people develop and work toward a vision of their future lives, which can only be lived in a cultural landscape. And personal and social counseling is always about helping young people formulate responses to the current cultural developments in their families, peer groups, and communities.

School counselors who approach their counseling only as work with individuals and neglect to notice the cultural networks in which their clients are situated will fail to address many of the cultural forces at play in these areas. In academic counseling work, counselors are working with children and young people who bring their cultural experience and background to their learning in very important ways. As learners, they are not blank slates. Nor are they, as Paulo Freire (1976) has argued, to be thought of as banks into which knowledge is deposited. Many approaches to learning have tended to regard children in this vein (Reynolds, 2005). For example, the behaviorist theorizing of learning scarcely mentions the cultural context in which learning takes place and treats learning as solely a technical process by which the instructor and the school manage the contingencies that produce learning. A multicultural approach to learning, however, has to be based on a recognition of the learner as a participant in the social and cultural process of learning (Bruner, 1996). As a participant, the learner brings to the learning task a linguistic background, an incipient value system, a family-generated orientation to life, a social class living situation, and a cultural background that wraps education itself in a system of meaning. Each time a child opens his mouth or attempts to learn something, all of this cultural knowledge is applied to his engagement with what is being learned. All of this is included in the explicit curriculum of schooling.

If we now consider the "hidden curriculum," we can see that there are many other things that children are learning that are not explicitly taught. The hidden curriculum is sometimes referred to as the "unintended outcomes of the schooling process" (McLaren, 2005, p. 413). It is what children pick up by way of osmosis, by being immersed in a sociocultural environment, by experiencing the constitutive effects of discourse. The hidden curriculum offers them social positions to occupy and constructs their expectations of themselves and of their lives. It is contained in the school rules, in the way classrooms are organized rather than in what is taught, through the teaching and learning styles favored in an institution, through the physical environment of the school, through the grading procedures employed. No teacher explicitly teaches the hidden curriculum, and yet children inevitably learn it. It is an inferred curriculum of normalized knowledges and behaviors that children acquire through their participation in school. In short, the hidden curriculum is the cultural knowledge that is transmitted by the experience of being schooled.

The phrase "hidden curriculum" has been around for a while. It was reportedly coined by the sociologist Phillip Jackson (1968) and developed by Benson Snyder (1973) in his book *The Hidden Curriculum*. Snyder was interested in analyzing the social norms inculcated into children as a process of their school experiences that did not necessarily always work in favor of the educational goals of the explicit curriculum. One of his interests, for example, was how it was that some academically gifted students chose to drop out of school early. In relation to the hidden curriculum, the role of the counselor can be considered as one of consciousness raising. Through asking careful questions, counselors can invite students to think about how they are being positioned by the hidden curriculum, whether they like being positioned in this way, and whether they have well-thought-out strategies to counter the effects of the hidden curriculum.

For example, consider what happens to minority students who are caught breaking school rules. School principals always have to interpret the seriousness of the offense and then exercise discretion about whether to reprimand, punish, or expel students in this situation. It is far more likely that minority students will be punished more severely, rather than reprimanded for "acting out of character." School counselors should check the statistics for this in the schools in which they work. When I (John) did this as a school counselor, many of the school teachers and administrators were surprised to learn how disproportionate the statistics were. To their credit, they set about doing things to change the situation.

What the hidden curriculum teaches minority students through such situations are some perspectives on cultural relations with authority. Treating some groups of students consistently as troublemakers increases the likelihood that these students will adopt antisocial attitudes and eventually translate this into criminal behavior. In this way, schools play a role in the reproduction of a social world that has disproportionate numbers of members of ethnic minorities in prison. Counselors who are conscious of the effects of the hidden curriculum can be helpful to such students by calling teachers' attention to what might be happening in the school and by generating conversations with students about whether they are willing to just let these trends continue or whether they want something different for themselves.

Schooling and Social Reproduction

There is a literature in the sociology of education that examines the kinds of social relations that are reproduced in the process of schooling. School counselors who are interested in social justice and in combating processes that confer automatic privilege on the basis of gender or race or social class should pay attention to this literature. We shall introduce it here.

Social reproduction theory analyzes the ways in which schools function through the hidden curriculum to reproduce existing relations of inequality in the next generation. Children from privileged families are educated in ways that produce them as members of the ruling class, while children from poor, working class families are schooled to learn to do what they are told and not buck against authority. In a society that institutes social class divisions along racial lines, children from nonwhite families are shown to be systematically blocked from opportunity. Meanwhile, gender relations that privilege men as active leaders in business and politics are reproduced in school practices that reward boys for showing these qualities and conversely reward girls for being neat and tidy, but docile and submissive. Thus, schools are not just socially neutral places that offer equal opportunity for all. Instead, they are argued to serve a social sorting function for the society as a whole. Schools reproduce the social and cultural relations of the world around the school in the lives of the next generation of young people.

How does this process happen? Samuel Bowles and Herbert Gintis (1976, 2005) represent one perspective on the process of social reproduction in schools. For Bowles and Gintis, reproduction is built on the "correspondence principle," whereby hierarchical relations between employers and workers in the workplace are reproduced in schools by a corresponding relation between teachers and children. Just as most workers have little opportunity to control their jobs, so students have little opportunity to control their learning. Grades function like wages, and the threat of expulsion functions like the threat of being sacked. Bowles and Gintis also stress the ways in which schools "reward docility, passivity, and obedience" (2005, p. 199) in the majority of students through the application of anonymous rules and regulations handed down from higher authorities. They characterize "behavior modification" as a repressive process that coerces children into becoming passive citizens who conform and do what they are told. Meanwhile, creativity and critical consciousness are actively penalized. For Bowles and Gintis, despite the movement toward progressive education, schools do little to disrupt the inequalities of the wider social system. Although they grant that some parents, teachers, and students do manage to assert a more egalitarian consciousness, their view is a largely pessimistic one that concentrates on the role of schools in aiding the economic repression of the masses in a capitalist society that is fundamentally unjust. Schools in the long run mirror the structural hierarchies (theirs is a structuralist argument; see Chapter 7) of the social class system and reproduce the inequalities of social class in the way that they perform their task. These authors argue that educational attainment remains dependent on social class background. Schools really do little to either add to or subtract from the inequities of the economic system.

A valuable aspect of this explanation is that it balances the overly optimistic liberal view of education, which suggests that public education can be a force for equalizing injustices through providing opportunity for all. From this perspective, education is automatically regarded as a positive force that we should think of as a form of investment in a better society. Everybody has access to education, and therefore all can improve their social and economic position. Social mobility is seen as the answer to oppression and injustice. (For an outline of this argument, and also for a summary of Bowles and Gintis's work, see Swartz, 2003). The corollary of this liberal view is that those who do achieve success through educational attainment are able to congratulate themselves on their merited economic success, while those who do not are assumed to have only themselves to blame. We can all point to just enough individuals who achieve social mobility through education to support this argument. The problem is that, when we step back and view the larger picture, it doesn't bear out. The reality doesn't match the dream. Bowles and Gintis were among the first to point out that the reason education does not eradicate economic injustice is that schooling also serves functions other than its overt purpose—especially the function of selecting some people out for privileged lives and others (the majority?) for oppressive life circumstances.

During the 1980s, Jean Anyon (1980, 2005) completed a famous ethnographic study into the learning cultures of five different elementary schools from five different areas in New Jersey. Each school differed in the wealth and resources that the community could call on. Her five schools were categorized on the basis of broad features of the affluence of the neighborhoods they were in, the types of occupations the children's parents held, and the mean income levels in the community. Two schools were categorized as *working class* schools, one as *middle class,* one as an *affluent professional* school, and one as an *executive elite* school. Anyon found that the same curriculum was taught in the five schools but that the teaching methods varied considerably and that the messages conveyed to children through the hidden curriculum were very different.

In the working class schools, the emphasis was on learning through repetition of mechanical behaviors, "following the steps of a procedure" (Anyon, 1980, p. 73), or rote learning, rather than on planning or thinking for oneself. Teacher control of student behavior was heavily emphasized, and the knowledge taught was about other people's lives. Teachers in these schools rarely explained why something should be learned.

In the middle class school, the emphasis was on getting the right answer more than following procedure, and getting to the right answer involved figuring out the steps and making decisions. Rather than copying what they were told by the teacher or in books, children were encouraged more to "put it in your own words" (p. 79). Critical curiosity, though, was not encouraged in case it provoked parental complaint about dealing with controversial topics.

In the affluent professional school, the children's work was often more creative and they were expected to work independently, develop and express individual thoughts, interpret empirical realities, and make decisions about how to represent findings. There were relatively fewer rules, the teacher was constantly negotiating with children rather than telling them to do what they were told, and the children were encouraged to "think about the consequences of their actions" (p. 82).

In the executive elite school, the emphasis in learning was much more on developing analytical skills, on developing rules and then applying them. Children were encouraged to disagree with "right" answers and develop reasons for their conclusions. Topics were taught as ways to understand systems, and children were given many opportunities to do presentations in which they experienced being in charge. Rules and bell times were much more flexible than in the other schools, and children were regularly told that "it is up to you," "you must control yourself," and "you are responsible for your work" (p. 86).

Jean Anyon's argument is that in each of these different styles of schooling, children are being enculturated differently. They are being offered a differential hidden curriculum that does not necessarily have to do with better or worse standards of teaching, but it does prepare them for different relationships in the social and occupational world. The working class children are being taught the culture of compliance and resistance. The executive elite children are being prepared for roles in which they are expected to design the rules for others and exercise authority. Jean Anyon's approach to the processes of social reproduction is more cultural than strictly structural in its focus. It is an effort to explain how a sense of entitlement to privilege is constructed in the cultural world of a school. It also explains how the opposite experience of having to comply and bow to authority, accept one's meager lot in life, and not raise too many challenges is also constructed in children's minds through the hidden curriculum of schooling. School culture is not the only context where these messages are conveyed to children. Nor does schooling precisely determine children's futures, but Anyon argues that the culture of a school operates subtly and effectively in accord with other social forces to produce people's lives. It does so in ways that make individual will to differ from the culturally prescribed patterns, while not impossible, at least challenging.

Pierre Bourdieu has contributed to this analysis through his study of the process by which schooling transmits social privilege from one generation to the next. Bourdieu argues (Bourdieu & Passeron, 1977) that what is communicated in the process of teaching in schools is not just knowledge but a style of speaking and behaving. This style is culturally specific to the ruling classes within a particular social world. It is legitimated through social processes outside of the school but is translated into the ways of speaking and acting that are called forth and granted recognition in the school system. Bourdieu developed a term to describe and summarize these ways of speaking and acting. He called them *habitus*. Bourdieu contends that school performance and successful academic achievement are not just a matter of individual differences in intelligence but to a substantial degree a reflection of students' mastery of the dominant habitus. He describes habitus as an "analogue of genetic capital" (Bourdieu & Passeron, p. 32), or intelligence. Here there are clear differences among groups of students. Some are brought up in family surroundings where they are advantaged by exposure to the linguistic resources of the ruling classes just as importantly as they are advantaged materially with extra resources such as books, computers, and travel opportunities. Others are not so well resourced with these aspects of cultural background. Habitus is added to in the school system by pedagogic agents (teachers and schools), who develop and refine the habitus children bring to school with them.

Bourdieu analyzes this habitus in terms of "cultural capital." While not quite the same as financial capital, it serves an equivalent purpose in the education system. As children go through school, they invest their cultural capital in their learning and earn returns on the investment. Those who have more cultural capital at their disposal of course earn bigger returns, while those with less cultural capital to invest struggle much more to obtain educational success. Eventually, the combination of education and cultural capital produces school and university qualifications, which can then be exchanged in the occupational marketplace for economic capital.

Access to the necessary cultural capital for success in school is differentially distributed. Those who are not native speakers of the language of instruction start off with a disadvantage. Those who speak in a dialect, in an accent, or in a style that is not legitimized by the dominant classes in the social and economic world, or within the school system, are quickly judged to be less academically capable. Over time, they gradually internalize these judgments as personal expectations. On the other hand, those whose social and economic interests are closely aligned with the dominant habitus of the school system are quickly marked for academic success and channeled consistently toward such success. An abundance of the right kind of habitus is generally misrecognized as "natural talent" in the school system and rewarded so that individuals come to identify strongly with their own success. In Bourdieu's analysis, success in school is not ascribed to a combination of native intelligence and hard work so much as to the investment of cultural capital, which eventually earns returns in diplomas and credentials. In the words of Nick Crossley (2003), "School launders cultural advantages and turns them into the clean currency of qualifications" (p. 43). Conversely, educational failure is not explained so much by lack of effort or ability as by lack of the necessary cultural capital that would make academic success easy.

The School Accountability Movement

The value of reproduction theory in relation to education is that it helps us understand how educational success is built on more than intelligence and individual effort. The often-told story that anyone can succeed in life if she studies hard and applies enough effort is ingrained in many people's beliefs about education. It is part of the dominant discourse of liberal education. Reproduction theory complicates this story considerably. School counselors and school psychologists who take it seriously are less quick to form summary judgments of individuals with regard to their natural ability or their willingness to work. Similarly, school success is not just an automatic outcome of good teaching, and school failure cannot simply be blamed on poor teaching. In the United States, over the last two decades, there has been a concerted effort to make schools and teachers "accountable" for the academic success or failure of their students. The No Child Left Behind (NCLB) Act of 2001 was the culmination of this movement. The main thrust of this accountability movement has been to emphasize teacher and school responsibility for educational outcomes. If some groups of children are not succeeding in school, then it must be because they are attending poor schools and receiving poor teaching. Of course, there is plenty of evidence of poor schools and poor teaching to be found, and these explanations cannot be discounted. The accountability movement has entailed substantial efforts to make sure that all teachers are properly qualified. And it has sought to identify schools that are not producing adequate outcomes and to label these schools first of all "in need of improvement" and then later as "failing schools" (see Popham, 2004, for a full explanation of the No Child Left Behind Act). The chief method of arriving at these descriptions has been through the increased testing of children using standardized testing methods. These tests are often referred to as "high stakes tests" because of the heavy consequences for school administrators and school districts that are built into the system as a result of the tests.

Let us look at the results that are starting to emerge out of this accountability movement in education in relation to cultural capital. The picture is still far from clear. While there are those who claim that general educational achievement standards (as far as these can be measured by the tests used—very much an open question) are rising, politicians and administrators who are eager to show success stories rush to statistics that appear to prove their point. In general, it seems that test performance scores in recent years have improved by modest amounts, at the most by 5 percentage points.

Under the NCLB law, however, tests scores are disaggregated for race and socioeconomic status. A key goal has been the closing of gaps between minority groups and the majority. It should be noted that there are huge problems with identifying the minority groups, which should lead us to view all disaggregated figures with caution. Take the "Hispanic" racial group. There are those who criticize the designation of such a group. Kenneth Carlson (2004) argues that there is in fact "no sound argument for disaggregating groups by race" (p. 379) in the first place, and in the second place that the category "Hispanic" subsumes an array of nationalities, each with its own set of subcultures (p. 380). Be that as it may, the emerging disaggregated results show a clear picture. The achievement gaps between white students and minority groups are not closing. For example, in one report (Morial, 2006), the percentage of African American fourth-graders reading at or above "proficiency level" grew between 1992 and 2005 from 8 to 12 percentage points. The problem is that the percentage of white children reading at the same level grew during the same period from 35 to 41 percentage points. The gap between the two groups was increased in size by 1 point. Even though there are specific examples of grade levels, local schools, and school districts that buck this trend, that pattern is the same elsewhere (Dillon, 2006; Hsu, 2007). The achievement gap is not closing and may even be increasing.

In the meantime, it has been estimated that over 70% of schools in the United States are in the process of being designated "failing schools" (Berliner, 2005), because, despite considerable effort to improve teaching, the test scores have not been showing the hoped-for improvements. Reproduction theory helps us understand why. Standardized testing does not take into account cultural capital. In fact, it starts from the assumption that all children bring with them basically the same cultural capital, and differences in testing results are accounted for by differences in individual intelligence or differences in teaching quality. To really improve school success for currently disadvantaged groups of children would take a much more substantial intervention in the lives of those who are currently not succeeding in school. For instance, it would take a concerted, society-wide effort to address the role that poverty plays in handicapping many children (Berliner & Biddle, 1995).

All of these circumstances pose particular challenges for counselors and psychologists working in schools. Clearly, counseling cannot on its own lift children out of poverty. On the other hand, poverty is not completely determining of educational success or failure. There are many examples of individual schools and teachers who do excellent work to offer opportunity for success to students who come from a background of poverty. And yet, increasingly, counselors in schools are asked to be more accountable for the outcomes of schooling for all students. It is in the context of a general accountability movement for schools that the national model for school counseling (ASCA, 2003) has been devised. (See the American School Counseling Association's Web site at www.schoolcounselor.org for an executive summary of the national model.) Trish Hatch and Judy Bowers (2002) specify the link between the accountability movement and the national model for school counseling when they say that the national model "reflects current education reform movements, including the No Child Left Behind legislation, which mandates all federally funded programs be accountable for and directly connected to student learning and student improvement" (p. 15).

There are many aspects of the national model for school counseling that we shall not go into in detail. We shall, however, give a brief overview of the national model and then look more closely at what it says about culture, social reproduction, and social change. One of the goals of the national model is to establish a more comprehensive and systematic approach to counseling in schools. This involves a commitment to providing counseling and guidance services to all students, not just to those who are at risk or to those who are already demonstrating the necessary cultural capital to succeed in school (Gysbers, 2001; Hatch & Bowers, 2002). Another goal is for schools to establish a systematic proactive guidance program rather than random and isolated responsive services. The program will be managed by school counselors, but they will not provide all of the services themselves. The guidance program will be goal focused and will specify goals in terms of enhancing academic success rates for students. And school counselors are encouraged to collect data to demonstrate the effects of their work. An increased role for school counselors envisaged within the national model is that of change agent advocacy on behalf of students or groups of students lagging behind in academic achievement (Trusty & Brown, 2005). Such advocacy is aimed at "closing the gaps" (Hatch & Bowers, 2002, p. 17) in achievement outcomes so that all students can experience success and all schools can be designated succeeding schools. In order to identify gaps that need to be closed and groups of students who require intervention, school counselors are expected to seek out data about student progress, disaggregate the data for individuals and for groups, and design programs that will address the gaps.

The national model for school counseling can be seen to be idealistic in its goals and methods. It clearly has much to recommend it in terms of professional revitalization for the school counseling profession. The systematic approach and the development of the role of advocacy means that counselors are being encouraged to think in more systemic terms and to take cultural forces seriously rather than to aim their services only at individuals. As counselors disaggregate school achievement data from different groups of students on the basis of ethnicity, race, disability, gender, second language learning, and so on, they will no doubt discover many gaps that need closing. The heightened awareness of neglected educational needs, coupled with the optimistic assumption that schools can address such needs, has much to recommend it.

There are, however, several questions that need to be asked about the chances of closing these gaps. In the first place, the definition of success seems to be tied a little too firmly to academic performance on standardized achievement tests as specified in the NCLB act. One of the effects of the NCLB agenda has been an effective shift in the discourse that specifies what academic learning in schools is. The dangers of measuring success in such narrow ways, often fallaciously, are spelled out by, among others, James Popham (2004). The ideological assumptions of NCLB are all-too-easily imported with the emphasis on accountability—for example, the assumption that academic failure results primarily from poor teaching, lack of intelligence, or lack of personal effort. It is too easy to move toward blaming the disadvantaged for their own disadvantage if we believe these assumptions. The national school counselor model should perhaps separate itself more from the NCLB version of accountability, which seems doomed to failure.

Second, we need to ask whether aspects of cultural capital might be addressed by the national model for school counseling or whether the processes of social reproduction of privilege and disadvantage are left intact. Reproduction theory would warn us against assuming that simple interventions to close the gaps in educational outcomes can produce substantial results, particularly if the rest of the forces that contribute to social reproduction (in the economic system and in the media, for example) remain intact. In fact, there are voices of warning in the school counseling literature that suggest that, despite some preliminary supporting evidence, school counselors may not easily be able to demonstrate the effects of counseling programs on student performance on academic tests (Brown & Trusty, 2005; Sink, 2002). They warn against claiming that counseling can do too much for fear that such claims can come back to bite the counseling profession if its efforts are not successful. They also point out that current research data do not strongly support the notion that counseling by itself can close the gaps. At best, most of the data are correlational and less than conclusive.

What Can Counselors Do?

Perhaps the picture we have painted so far appears too pessimistic. So let us finish this chapter by balancing the concerns about the forces of cultural reproduction with some ideas about how counselors can make a difference. The question that needs to be asked is whether counseling can address in some modest ways the development of cultural capital. Pierre Bourdieu's theoretical perspective is helpful here. Bourdieu argued that we should remember that social reproduction is not an automatic process. His approach is less rigid than the structuralist account of Samuel Bowles and Herbert Gintis. In modern democratic systems, there clearly is greater opportunity for social mobility than there is in other social contexts. Moreover, social movements do have effects, and social change is always possible (Crossley, 2003). The outcomes of the schooling process are therefore not completely predictable for any individual student. The process of social reproduction always remains indeterminate to some degree. The intense anxiety of many middle class parents about the educational success of their children attests to this. They are often really worried that their children will not be able to attain their own degree of educational, and therefore economic and social, success.

Bourdieu points out that there is always a degree of struggle that takes place. People do not simply accept with resignation diminished chances in life for their children. They are not puppets of the processes of social reproduction. They are actors in the process. They are always to some degree aware of what is going on, even if they have not articulated it clearly. They therefore frequently take action on their own behalf or on behalf of their children. The processes of social reproduction and of social mobility that do eventuate are therefore not all structured in advance. They are worked out on the ground in the daily exchanges of power relations and negotiated in the midst of the messiness of life.

Counselors who are willing to listen can hear these negotiations going on. They can hear how children, as they progress through school, seem to sense the ways in which they are being destined for success and failure, and they can help them articulate and then examine the paths that are being drawn for them. They can hear their cries of protest and, through the good listening that counselors are trained to offer, help make these cries achieve greater clarity. Very often young people, as they sense the power of the forces of cultural reproduction, develop a sense of inarticulate rebellion. This rebellion may be expressed in a number of ways, from refusal to study to subtle undermining of school rules to gang membership and all the way through to extreme violence. Often young people's rebellion is self-destructive and succeeds mainly in bringing down on them more of what they are rebelling against. Good counseling at this point should not just modify behavior so that the rebels fit back into the model of a normal docile student and accept their lot. It can help young people articulate their protest in more constructive ways. It can "conscientize" them in relation to cultural capital, cultural dominance, and their respective effects (along the lines advocated by Paulo Freire, 1976; Allen Ivey, Michael D'Andrea, Mary Bradford Ivey, and Lynn Simek-Morgan, 2006, have also advocated the concept of conscientization in relation to counseling; see also Sue, Ivey, & Pedersen, 1996). It can invite young people into a critical consciousness and invite them to take up positions of agency in relation to their own future. We would therefore advocate that the national school counseling model's emphasis on advocacy on behalf of children be tied more to the concept of conscientization in order to increase its effectiveness.

Students can be taught some of the skills that constitute the habitus that produces success in school. Counseling may be able to assist in the development of identity stories that can serve as counterpoints to the identities of school failure that might otherwise be reproduced. There are probably many examples that can be found of such possibilities.

Counselors and students can thus join in a project of social reproduction of a different sort. This kind of reproduction might be deliberate and conscious rather than driven by the hidden aspects of curriculum. It sets about the creation of a social world through the construction of lives that might drive it. It needs to recognize that individuals cannot just produce a life on their own. Social forces that are seeking to reproduce people in certain directions are stronger than any individual can alone withstand. But schools are not just collections of individuals. They are small communities. Therefore, there are opportunities in a school context, within a school district, within a professional counseling community, to affect and, at least to some degree, to shape the contours of the forces of reproduction. In its best aspects, this is what the ASCA national model for school counseling is advocating. Kwame Appiah (2005, citing Amy Gutmann) asserts that education should stand for a particular democratic virtue: "the ability to deliberate, and hence to participate in conscious social reproduction" (p. 162). Here he ties a notion of conscious social reproduction to the central aspects of a functioning democracy. By implication, he also criticizes the unconscious processes of reproduction as undemocratic.

Ruby Payne's (2005) work on poverty addresses the process by which schools can influence the process of social reproduction. Her work offers much promise for how school counselors can engage with the social reproduction of poverty-determined lives. Payne analyzes the economic stratification of people's lives into groups defined by poverty, middle class membership, and wealth as governed by sets of hidden rules about how to talk and act. Access to monetary economic resources plays a substantial role in children's success or failure in school, but it is not the only factor. Also important is knowledge of the appropriate language registers, cognitive strategies, and discourse patterns needed for participation in the worlds of education and employment. Lack of access to and knowledge of the hidden rules about how to speak and act prevents those raised in poverty from using education to improve their life situation.

The hidden rules that Payne refers to are based in discourse patterns that derive from the social and economic worlds that people occupy. Here are some examples of these patterns: In the discourses that dominate in contexts defined by poverty, stories about life are told more commonly in a casual register than in a formal register. And yet familiarity with a more formal register is necessary for success in schools. Stories are also structured differently in different discourse worlds. Middle class cultural capital includes constant practice in structuring stories in a linear sequence. Those who are not exposed to this cultural capital but to the worlds in which immediate responses to the environment are privileged and rewarded are likely to tell stories in a more episodic way, from a point in the middle rather than from the beginning. They are less likely to construct a story with a tidy beginning, middle, and end and to emphasize linear causality. Mastering the problem solving method that is central to economic advancement in the modern world requires that people develop the cultural capital of story organization that middle class children are brought up with. The discourses within which money, possessions, clothing, education, and family are talked about are shaped differently in poverty and in middle class contexts. Even styles of humor and orientation to time differ from one discourse world to another.

Payne advocates that teachers and counselors learn about the internalized discourses of poverty and the shape that these discourses take in children's interactions with the school. Then she advocates explicitly teaching the rules of the game to those who have not implicitly developed such knowledge through their upbringing. In other words, she suggests bringing the hidden rules into the open so that those who are being excluded from opportunity on the basis of these rules can make their own choices about whether they want to play the game or not. What she is advocating, in Bourdieu's terms, amounts to deliberate augmentation of the habitus, or cultural capital, of those raised in poverty so that they can learn how to speak and perform in middle class contexts.

The aim of what Payne is advocating is not to turn children raised in poverty into good middle class children. She carefully specifies that counselors and teachers should not disparage the discourse worlds of those brought up in poverty and set about "correcting" this discourse on the grounds that it is wrong. She wants to avoid a process of cultural colonization through schooling. Instead, she is arguing for a process of helping children learn how to cross cultural boundaries when they need to, rather than urging them to identify solely within their familiar cultural worlds. She assumes that children can become at least bicultural, can occupy the borderlands, and can develop culturally hybrid identities if given the chance. Her focus on teaching an understanding of discourse is a powerful idea that deserves the attention of counselors in schools.

Conclusion

We remain positive that counselors can impact the cultural experiences that young people in schools occupy. They can do this best if they are equipped with a useful analysis of the forces at work in schooling. This analysis needs to include a focus on the functions that schooling plays in a sociocultural world, functions that stretch far beyond, and often confound, the overt academic goals of education. We think that having an understanding of the critical role that schools play in the process of cultural reproduction and in the creation of social divisions is an important aspect of this analysis. In this chapter, we have focused more on the socioeconomic aspects of this process of social reproduction than on, say, the reproduction of gender relations or racial relations, but the same principles can be extended to those other dimensions.

We have also endeavored to strike a balance between optimism and pessimism in this chapter. Some versions of reproduction theory can appear too structurally deterministic and seem to render action by counselors and teachers, not to mention by students themselves, irrelevant. We are more inclined to see the field of power relations in schooling as more fluid and contested than such rigid accounts allow. Hence, we believe there are options for transformative reproduction, or for the kind of counseling that aims at the deliberate production of students' lives in contradiction to the influence of the forces of reproduction. It is possible to close the gaps in habitus. But in order to do so effectively, counselors should understand clearly the rules of the game and not expect that everything that happens in school will be in the best interests of children. Counselors who are alert to how reproduction of inequality and injustice happens can also be alert to opportunities to interrupt those processes, to advocate on behalf of individuals and groups of students, and to actively teach students about the hidden discourse rules that govern the education system.

TO DISCUSS

1. Share examples from your own experience or stories you have witnessed of how cultural conditions of life are reproduced in the next generation.

2. How do schools function as "gatekeepers" in the way that Trish Hatch gives an example of below?

3. Share stories of how people have resisted being assigned to a certain place in life and have struggled to overcome the forces of reproduction.

4. Role-play a counseling conversation with someone who is expressing resistance to the forces of reproduction in destructive ways and discuss ways to engage this person in more conscious resistance.

Response to Chapter 16

Trish Hatch

Trish Hatch, Ph.D., is the coauthor of *The ASCA National Model: A Framework for School Counseling Programs* and the coauthor of *Evidence Based Practice in School Counseling: Making a Difference with Data Driven Practices* with two national leaders in school counseling. Trish is the director of the Center for Excellence in School Counseling and Leadership (CESCaL) and the director of the School Counseling Program at San Diego State University. She is a former school counselor and site level and central office administrator over school counseling programs. She has received the Lifetime Achievement Award and the Administrator of the Year title from the American School Counseling Association. She is nationally recognized as a passionate and engaging keynote speaker, trainer, and consultant.

Changing the "culture" of opportunities for all students in schools requires counselors and other educators to address institutionalized gatekeeping, in addition to the sorting and selecting of students into paths that may determine their future economic potential.

A few years go, on my first day in my new role as assistant principal at a high-needs high school, I was approached by an 11th-grade Latina student who pleaded, "Can you please help me get into a Spanish class? I need to take Spanish so I can go to college!"

"Of course you do. Let's get you an appointment to see your school counselor and have that class added."

"No, you don't understand! The counselor told me that she can't put me in because it's against the rules. That's why I'm asking you to help me."

"What rule?" I queried.

"The book says I have to have a B or better in English/language arts before they will let me take Spanish, and last year I got a C, so my counselor says the teacher will find out and take me out of the class! But I know I can do the work. I have good grades in my other classes and I speak Spanish and I really want to do well in it—please can you help me?"

Ridiculous! I thought. How could this be? Deny a student access to a college prep course? Further, deny access to a Latina student who has Spanish as her native language because she hasn't gotten a B or better in her second language? *Impossible.*

I set out to find the bible of course enrollment requirements, called the "curriculum guide," and proceeded to learn about the culture of my new school. Some examples included the requirement of a B or better in life sciences (non–college prep) before students were allowed to take biology (college prep), unless of course they were honors students. A B or better in a prerequisite course was required before one could take any honors or advanced placement courses. Further dissection of the curriculum guide revealed many "gatekeeping" rules. Attempts to advocate change in the rules to encourage more students to take college prep courses produced telling cultural comments. One biology teacher shared that if the rules were changed and the counselors were allowed to put the "riffraff" into his class, he would shift his curriculum and not use the microscopes, as the "hoodlums" were not going to touch his expensive science equipment. Imagine the culture of the classroom when he teaches college prep as opposed to non–college prep classes!

In every way, the cultural message was clear: some of the students (a select few) will go to college, but most will not, as we do not expect, nor will we provide opportunity for, all to go. What social reproduction message is being sent to the ninth-grade class of students when it is discovered that only 40% of the senior English classes are college preparatory? Sixty percent are not expected to go to college, whether they were planning to or not.

School counselors must shift their role from allowing gatekeeping to becoming advocates for all students (Hart & Jacobi, 1992). *The ASCA National Model: A Framework for School Counseling Programs* encourages counselors to be leaders, advocates, and systems change agents (American School Counseling Association, 2005). Rather than telling the students that the rules won't allow them to take Spanish, why not address the issue from an access and equity perspective? Perhaps (as I later came to learn) it was because the school counselor had also learned to be "submissive in the face of authority" (p. 464). The school counselor, who possessed little social capital, allowed the hidden curriculum at this high school to decide who would get to college prep and who wouldn't.

In one year I learned the "culture beneath the culture" and partnered with counselors as they became advocates for students "systematically blocked from opportunity" (American School Counseling Association, 2005, p. 468). Indeed, the practices in this school were set up to "reproduce the inequities of social class" in the way that they had designed the very nature of access to the curriculum (p. 468), but things didn't have to stay that way. Counselors began to realize that every encounter was an opportunity to add to or subtract from the student's experience (p. 468), recognizing that there was no neutral interaction regarding this idea. Either they advocated changing gatekeeping policies or they became part of the status quo—one that would impact the future economic potential of the students they served.

These advocates no longer tolerate other educators' stating that students "only have themselves to blame" (American School Counseling Association, 2005, p. 469) because they should have gotten a higher grade to get entry into the course they wanted. Rather, they now lead the conversations that remind us all that we will have only *ourselves* to blame when our students fail, as we provide the culture that supports this outcome. School counselors must possess a passion for promoting social justice and an ability to advocate for students and systems change (Hatch, 2006). They must possess an awareness of themselves in appropriate roles as student advocates and systems change agents (while refraining for being seen as aggressive or militant). Today's school counselors must be vital members of the education team, ensuring equity and access to rigorous educational opportunities for *every* student (Hatch, 2006). They must advocate open access to challenging courses and the revision of prerequisites to ensure rigorous opportunities for every student. They must have confidence in and passion for their role as vital contributors on the leadership team and an awareness of the partnership necessary among all educators.

The leaders we are waiting for are the ones who use the same advocacy voice in these circumstances that they use for students who are victims of child abuse (Hatch, Holland, & Meyers, 2004). School counselors can no longer stand by helplessly and blame the rules or the system. Instead, they must be a part of a team that raises countless questions about what children are taught in schools and about how this impacts "whose lives are privileged (and whose diminished) as a result."

CHAPTER 17

Multicultural Competence Examined

Multicultural writers have dedicated over three decades to developing multicultural counseling practices that will help make counseling practitioners more competent in working with diverse client groups. The advances they have made in promoting what is known in the field as "cultural competence" have been significant for therapists and clients alike. Today, in most major professional organizations offering mental health care, there is a call to all professionals to be culturally competent (Middleton, Stadler, & Simpson, 2005). Clinical multicultural competence has been introduced and then formalized in program accreditation standards such as those of the American Counseling Association (2005), American Psychological Association (2002), Council for Accreditation of Counseling and Related Education Programs (2001), Association of Multicultural Counseling and Development (1996), Association for Counselor Education and Supervision (1993), and National Career Development Association (1997). Efforts have been made to help counseling organizations as a whole become much more culturally aware, more knowledgeable, and ultimately more competent in catering to culturally diverse populations.

In this chapter we would like to discuss some of these developments in the cultural competence movement. We address both the key concepts underpinning cultural competence and some of the challenges to the notion of acquiring cultural competence. We also outline some additional elements that might be helpful in advancing culturally respectful therapeutic practices with diverse populations, particularly as such practices relate to working with ethnic differences, racism, and social justice.

Nonutilization of Counseling Services

A relatively small proportion of the North American population ever considers utilizing counseling and psychological services, let alone takes advantage of therapeutic help. In the popular media, however, therapeutic practices are growing in popularity. Movies and television shows frequently feature characters who consult therapists. Newspapers reporting on traumatic events customarily mention that survivors are receiving counseling. In the first decade of the 21st century, pseudopsychology talk shows have grown in popularity in addition to the television shows conducted by professional psychologists such as Dr. Phil, Dr. Keith Ablow, and Dr. Ruth. Yet, despite this popularity, seeing a counselor, therapist, or psychologist is still an alien notion to many people. In the public sphere, we continue to hear people speak about avoiding seeing therapists for fear of being labeled crazy by others who have judgments about the value and role of mental health professionals. In Chapter 9, we discussed how alien an idea seeking psychological or counseling assistance is for many men.

The most likely reason that people troubled by the notion of going to therapy will end up seeing a counselor is that they are forced to by somebody else. Their personal troubles have become so distressing that conventional health care professionals or federal or state agencies have become involved and have ended up mandating psychological treatment. Alien as the experience of seeing a counselor or therapist is to many people in the white middle classes and in dominant Western cultural groupings, it is an even greater source of alienation, estrangement, and mystery for minority and marginalized populations (Sue & Sue, 2007). There are many explanations for this, and we will identify some specific issues below.

Many individuals do not perceive counseling and psychotherapy as an activity with which they have a positive relationship. It is foreign to many people to sit down with a perfect stranger and, within a brief time, disclose deeply personal material in a supposedly private forum, and thus become immensely vulnerable to this stranger's efforts to be helpful. How much greater might the risk appear when the client and counselor inhabit very different cultural worlds and where the counselor is straining to make meaning of the client's experience, which only remotely matches the counselor's. For example, Derald Wing Sue and David Sue (2007) suggest that for Asian Americans, discussing family problems with a stranger is a source of embarrassment and an indication of failure. In fact, for many cultural groups, seeing a counselor is deeply embarrassing and perhaps even humiliating.

Harm Caused by Eurocentric Counseling Practices

Sadly, harm has been caused to members of specific racial, ethnic, and other cultural groups, who out of desperation or mandated external pressure have had to attend counseling and therapy sessions and have had very negative experiences. Clients who already felt ashamed, guilty, and embarrassed have experienced a range of serious negative consequences within the counseling that have left them feeling even less equipped to deal with difficult personal and family problems. It is this series of multiple negative consequences experienced by underrepresented populations that has galvanized the development of the multicultural counseling competency movement. These consequences have been well documented in the multicultural counseling literature. According to the President's Commission on Mental Health (*Report to the President*, 1978), counseling clients reported that they often felt harassed, intimidated, and abused by nonminority personnel. Derald Wing Sue and David Sue (2007) reported that many people of color complained that mental health professionals could not relate to their life circumstances and were insensitive to their needs. Many described how they did not feel respected and were treated with arrogance and contempt when they received services.

At the heart of the move toward cultural competence is the recognition that counseling practices have often been enormously harmful to specific racial and ethnic populations. Nonwhite ethnic populations in particular have had their cultural belief systems and cultural practices labeled at worst deviant and pathological and at best unhelpful and outdated. Such invalidation of peoples' life experiences and treasured cultural beliefs has denied many communities access to culturally appropriate resources that could have assisted them with serious mental health concerns and threats to their physical, psychological, and socioemotional well-being. Dominant cultural practices that have been found to be unhelpful and irrelevant to marginalized populations have often been imposed on communities in such a manner as to alienate those most in need of assistance.

As a consequence, the multicultural counseling literature has documented that people of color are almost twice as likely as whites to terminate counseling services early (Sue & Sue, 2007). The aim of the cultural competence movement is to address these serious negative consequences for minority populations. In this context, it is ironic that the "minority" populations are steadily heading toward becoming the "majority" in the United States (see Box 17.1).

Box 17.1. Demographic Shifts

In 1992, the U.S. population was 75% European American. By the year 2050, it is anticipated that the population will be 52.8% European American. The Latino population will more than double from 9% in 1992 to 24.5% in 2050. During this same period, it is expected that the Asian American/Pacific Islander population will more than double, while the African American population will stay at about the same level (Kocarek, Talbot, Batka, & Anderson, 2001). Interestingly, by 2020, in California, Hawaii, New Mexico, and Texas, populations that have been traditionally described as minorities (nonwhite) will be in the majority (Diller, 2007). According to a survey conducted by the California Association of Marriage and Family Therapy, 94% out of 12,900 family therapists surveyed were European American, whereas 66% of their clients were from other racial groups (Green, 1998). It is clear that there is a serious absence of minority therapists in heath care. It is also understandable that multiculturalists are anxious to ensure that therapists develop more skills in working with ethnically diverse clients.

Defining Cultural Competence

There are many perspectives that might define multicultural competence, and yet the multicultural counseling literature has been dominated in the last two decades by the three-pronged developmental model composed of awareness, knowledge, and skills (Fowers & Davidov, 2006). These three dimensions have become widely accepted, and addressing multicultural awareness, multicultural knowledge, and multicultural skills has been elaborated into a prolific literature base (e.g., Arredondo, Toporek, & Brown, 1996; Lum, 2007; Sue, Arredondo, & McDavis, 1992; Sue et al., 1982). In their book on cultural competence, Derald Wing Sue and his colleagues (1998) named a much broader summary that includes the understanding of multiculturalism as a national resource and treasure. They emphasized the importance of understanding and valuing cultural diversity, pluralism, equity, social justice, and cultural democracy and advocated the study of multiple cultures and multiple perspectives.

Despite the large body of literature exploring multicultural competence, there is still no clear definition of it (Ridley, Baker, & Hill, 2001; Ridley, Mendoza, & Kanitz, 1994; Sue, 2001). Doman Lum (2007) refers to multiple definitions drawn from multiple authors. While there are some common themes in the definition of cultural competence, there is often a failure to name the epistemological foundations of this construct. Donald Atkinson, George Morten, and Derald Wing Sue (1998) commented that there is still no conceptual framework underlying the multifaceted dimensions of cultural competence. Sue (2001) even suggested that it is not possible to have a unified definition of cultural competence, as it is still evolving. However, that does not constrain him from articulating a working definition of cultural competence:

> [Cultural competence is] the ability to engage in actions or create conditions that maximize the optimal development of clients and client systems. Multicultural counseling competence is defined as the counselor's acquisition of awareness, knowledge, and skills needed to function effectively in a pluralistic democratic society (ability to communicate, interact, negotiate, and intervene on behalf of clients from diverse backgrounds), and on an organizational/societal level, advocating effectively to develop new theories, practices, policies, and organizational structures that are more responsive to all groups. (p. 802)

If we take this statement as a working definition, there are many specific questions still to address. Of all the possible range of awarenesses, or cultural knowledges, or practice skills, which ones are important to acquire? Once we have decided that, how much of this learning represents competence? Indeed, from what cultural basis might we decide that competence has been achieved? One challenge for those seeking to define cultural competence is the determination of which groups therapists will learn to be competent working with. The challenge centers around how inclusive or exclusive the development of multicultural competence should be. A group of researchers (Dumas, Rollock, Prinz, Hops, & Blechman, 1999) studied cultural competence and what it might mean from the vantage points of different racial and ethnic groups. They posed the question of whether it should focus on micro or macro levels of analysis. Their results were inconclusive as far as exactly what broad-based practices should be established to address the multiple needs of diverse groups. They argued for the development of an adequate conceptual framework to guide further explorations of cultural competence and to form a clearer picture of the needs of diverse clients.

Derald Wing Sue (2001) expressed concern about having too wide and inclusive a definition of cultural competence. He sees a danger of its becoming so broad that developing competency to work across racial and ethnic differences gets watered down by the need to address other competing cultural differences. A wide umbrella definition of cultural competence might risk avoidance of any thorough effort to address racial discrimination and racial oppression in the context of myriad unique cultural identity claims. Sue (2001) points out that, for example, counselors and psychologists may focus more on gender, socioeconomic status, and religious orientation than on race and ethnicity issues, because, he argues, race and ethnicity are the most uncomfortable for counselors and psychologists to address. This is, of course, an Americentric perspective. In Northern Ireland or in the Middle East, for example, issues of religious orientation might indeed be more uncomfortable to address. Sue has been challenged by some of his colleagues (Ridley et al., 2001) for focusing too much on the specific needs of discrete categories of persons based on their race and ethnicity. However, Sue's (2001) retort is that if ethnic groups are not identified as having unique needs, the next step could become a focus on "individual differences," and concerns over racist and unjust therapeutic practices could be lost. Doman Lum (2007) contends that cultural competence should go beyond racial and ethnic groups to include gender, social class, and sexual orientation groups. He suggests that where there are advocates for women, gays, lesbians, immigrants and refugees, and "spiritual" persons, there will be a broad application of cultural competence with diverse populations. These debates are not conclusive and will no doubt continue, but they seem to militate against the establishment of any consensus on what kind of cultural competence should be aimed at.

Being Culturally Competent

While the competence movement emphasizes the development of awareness, knowledge, and skills, there is an assumption that the attainment of competence involves a profound personal journey of self-exploration. Derald Wing Sue and David Sue (2003) point out that competence is gained by facing the painful realities about oneself, about one's cultural group, and about society as prejudiced and racist. Such an assertion targets cultural competence especially in those who identify with dominant cultural groups. Thus, cultural competence really involves addressing one's personal cultural constraints and blindnesses and doing so through extensive personal transformation. Blaine Fowers and Barbara Davidov (2006) make a case for going beyond the mere application of knowledge and skills and engaging in something much more profound in realizing cultural competence.

At the heart of the journey of transformation is the demonstration of the ability to deeply care for and build a relationship with clients who are in psychological pain. Fowers and Davidov suggest that therapists must be interested in the various dimensions of diversity, demonstrate the character strength of compassion, be open minded, and become "better human beings" in order to move toward being culturally competent.

Developing multicultural competence is, for most authors, a lifelong process that involves a change of lifestyle in all aspects of one's dealings with others. It permeates all of one's life and is characterized by a concern for justice and equity, expressed through a demonstration of respect toward others.

Nancy Arthur (1998) suggests that, while on the journey to becoming more culturally competent, therapists need to challenge the "cultural encapsulation" caused by ethnocentrism in the majority culture. Cultural encapsulation is "a psychological phenomenon characterized by the belief in the superiority of a set of values and a world view that evolves from one's own cultural, ethnic, or racial group" (Daniels & D'Andrea, 1996, p.157). As these authors point out, the group or groups one identifies with will significantly influence the way one makes sense of life experiences and will lay out the norms against which appropriate and inappropriate behaviors are judged.

Patricia Arredondo and Miguel Arciniega (2001) suggest that being culturally competent requires therapists to question, challenge, and change the operating norms and assumptions of their culturally formed worldviews. They suggest that therapists need to continually revise their self-perceptions and expectations to maintain awareness of the cultural values and biases expressed in the counseling room, as well as to be aware of the client's worldview in order to devise culturally appropriate interventions. Arredondo and Arciniega suggest that psychotherapists and counseling professionals should engage in cultural learning on an ongoing basis in order to be responsive to the cultural differences in the worldviews and expectations of their clients. Doman Lum (2007) proposes that multicultural clients and communities should be included in the discussion on the development of cultural competence. He proposes multicultural advisory consumer boards to monitor services delivered to diverse communities.

Problematizing Cultural Competence

It is wonderful for mental health professionals to learn to be more responsive, respectful, compassionate, and effective with all culturally diverse clients. We applaud the efforts of those who have gone before us in introducing the cultural competence movement into the counseling and helping professions and who have helped us grapple with the important changes required of a multicultural practitioner. Like our colleagues, we are mindful of the enormous complexity involved in demonstrating effective and respectful engagement with those who inhabit very different cultural worlds from our own. In fact, many authors recognize the profound nature of the transformation that must take place if we are to become effective with diverse cultural communities. Some observe that we never arrive at the point where we can say we are now fully competent to engage with the culturally different Other. We would like to discuss this point a little further, because we think it requires considerably more attention.

Competence is generally defined as being well qualified to perform a particular role. As mental health professionals, we have engaged in long periods of graduate study, completed rigorous licensing requirements, and are required to continually engage in lifelong education to remain up to date with the changing needs of the discipline. We wish to convey to our clients, to our employers, and to those who supply resources for our activities that we are competent to perform the multiple and complex tasks of a mental health professional. Demonstrating competence is an important indicator of professional attainment. Cultural competence implies that a counselor or therapist will be *successful* at developing the necessary awareness, knowledge, and skills to work with a culturally different Other.

The construct *cultural competence* has a strong association with the epistemology of modernism—the very same modernism that gave rise to racism and justified it "scientifically." As we have already established in previous chapters, the agendas of modernism are an outgrowth of the colonizing movement of 19th and 20th century Europe. There is a surprising irony in that multiculturalists committed to advancing the cause of social justice, equity, and respect in counseling practices toward all ethnic and other cultural groups are using the tools of modernist epistemology to facilitate change. There is literature on cultural competence that suggests using the modernist practices of rationality, analysis, and measurement to investigate whether somebody has the awareness, knowledge, and skills to work with culturally different Others. Reductionist and deductive quasi-scientific tools, bolstered by procedures that lay claim to validity and reliability, are being used to determine whether somebody is culturally equipped to perform specific counseling functions across culturally diverse groups. Perhaps this trend in the multicultural movement mirrors other similar assessment practices in psychology that sharply delineate the correctness or inadequacies of particular behavioral characteristics. The likelihood that people will be judged according to questionable truth-based practices as having deficits or strengths is reminiscent of modernist practices that have, often inadvertently, turned out to be harmful to minorities. Pseudoscientific practices have in the past frequently turned into judgments that are interpreted as real but in actuality are cultural constructs produced out of 19th century Euro-American colonizing practices.

Another problem with the construct of cultural competence is that it easily becomes a punitive cultural product by which people are scrutinized and analyzed in tests and exams. The right answers on these tests may or may not be close to what people actually do in confidential counseling and psychotherapy interactions. The cultural competence movement risks becoming, and sometimes seems to be seeking establishment as, a source of institutional scrutiny that subjects individuals to particular forms of evaluation based on the latest iteration of Western psychological theory.

An unexamined use of the phrase "cultural competence" suggests that competence is actually attainable (despite the fact that many leading authors call it an unattainable lifelong pursuit). There is of course substantial difficulty in determining whether somebody can be evaluated as culturally competent. Doman Lum (2007) indicates a concern about the evaluation of the competence of students through measurement instruments. He utilizes outcome measures through the attainment of teaching and learning objectives to determine his students' cultural competence. Numerous studies have been conducted to explore the attainment of cultural competence (e.g., Constantine & Sue, 2005; Green, 2005; Teasley, 2005). Many of the instruments are self-report surveys in which people tend to overinflate their evaluation of their cultural competence because it has become socially desirable to be culturally competent. Moreover, we have noted that counseling students often naively rate themselves highly on measures of competence in the early part of multicultural course work and then rate themselves lower on these same measures at the end of their training. They have learned to realize how complex and difficult it is to truly engage, understand, and assist others who come from different cultural backgrounds and different worldviews. It is problematic for more sophisticated understandings of cultural complexity to be reflected in outcome measures of competence that produce decreased rates of self-assessed competence. As practitioners and writers working in the multicultural field, we would like to exercise substantial caution about defining ourselves as competent and thus well qualified to work effectively across diverse cultural contexts. There are many elements of effective communication, negotiation, and intervention with the multiple and contradictory identities that human beings perform in diverse communities. Claims to have achieved competence in these elements have to be treated as suspect.

There are so many contextual elements playing out in our field that much of what we do remains very foggy. Consider how difficult it is for many of us to be culturally competent within our own families. Family members are often acculturated in a different way from ourselves, because they are members of a different generation. The influence of a peer group impacted by diverse cultural assumptions presented in the popular media can lead to very different cultural understandings between family members across generations. Many of us have firsthand awareness of the painful conflicts, misunderstandings, and experiences of disrespect that can occur within one's own household. If we had attained cultural competence, we should at least be able to apply it to the cultural differences present under our own roof. Let's elaborate further on what it might mean to attain cultural competence within therapy—a cultural practice within itself.

Therapy as a Cultural Practice

All therapeutic practice is, of course, a cultural system in itself. The culture of therapy refers to sets of belief systems, assumptions, and theories about the nature of the self, the family, and the community; the origins and causes of psychological problems; and the preferred cultural pathways toward solutions. Multiculturalists acknowledge that therapy is inherently a cultural product and shaped by sociocultural, historical, and sociopolitical forces. Patricia Arredondo and Miguel Arciniega (2001) suggest that counseling practices and ethics are infused with values informed by cultural elements. Clearly, the cultural, economic, and institutional context of mental health practice shapes the definition of clients' problems and influences what might be deemed appropriate therapeutic responses.

Just as specific cultural identities can influence and shape worldviews, so too are the theoretical orientations of mental health professionals influenced by cultural values. Unfortunately, in our view, the selection of the three main areas of cultural competence (awareness, knowledge, and skills) frequently leaves out a questioning of counseling and psychological knowledge itself. The knowledge usually focused on is knowledge of the cultural worldviews of clients rather than the knowledge that informs counseling itself. Lisa Tsoi Hoshmand (2005) makes the comment that counseling systems not only mirror their cultures of origin, but continue to replicate what is portrayed in popular culture. She adds that dominant cultural viewpoints lie at the cornerstone of the psychology professions and are seldom considered problematic, because they are products of our age and support the basic assumptions and beliefs of the dominant Western culture. Philip Cushman (1990, 1995) suggested somewhat cynically that psychotherapy is "syntonic" with American culture, as it offers lifestyle solutions to clients. Psychotherapy seeks to sooth consumers the same way that the consumption of material goods satisfies people's existential emptiness.

Derald Wing Sue (2001) argues that much of what counts as professional knowledge, supposedly constructed on a sound empirical base, actually emerges from folk wisdom and from the cultural assumptions and traditions of the dominant cultures in the West. So much of therapeutic practice taught in graduate school has evolved from therapeutic outcomes with the white middle class. He quite rightly identifies that many of the cultural conventions of therapy contravene the cultural practices of some indigenous communities that don't embrace the therapeutic taboos. If these biases are part and parcel of the discourse practices of counseling itself, then it is not surprising that counselors struggle not to impose their personal cultural biases and assumptions on their clients. Derald Wing Sue and David Sue (1999) suggest that most Euro-American psychotherapies share common therapeutic characteristics that make it difficult to attend to the unique cultural requirements of some client groups. For example, therapy most often occurs in a one-to-one relationship, and the responsibility for change in client behavior belongs with the client. The therapeutic medium is usually verbal, and clients are expected to self-disclose their most intimate thoughts and feelings. These are all cultural assumptions that no amount of empirical testing can validate.

In addition, many counseling practices suggest that clients should not receive advice, because it can encourage dependency, and that the giving of advice defies the therapeutic imperatives of helping clients connect with their own resources and strengths. Some clients expect that they will be given advice when they see a therapist, and there is thus a significant cultural disconnection that can occur. Most counselors and psychologists are trained not to disclose their thoughts and feelings, because to do so is perceived as unprofessional. Yet many clients resent the fact that they are expected to be trusting, highly disclosing, and vulnerable, while the therapist wears a professional mask and hides a compassionate and caring human response. We are taught that bartering with clients is inappropriate because it negatively affects the therapeutic relationship, yet gift giving in some communities is essential to developing respect and a bond of mutuality. These ethical practices may contravene the dominant modes of respectful human interaction among some client groups, and yet the counselor or therapist is somehow still required to exhibit cultural competence in what is for the client a foreign medium.

Sue (2001) links Western psychology with the philosophical traditions of the Greek scholars, such as Socrates, Hippocrates, Plato, and Aristotle. He finds the link between contemporary psychology and these ancient philosophers' writings in the idea that individualistic, autonomous, independent behavior is illustrative of good mental health. He contrasts these theories with those of the ancient Chinese scholars, such as Lao Tzu, Confucius, and Mo Tzu, whose theories about healthy living stressed collectivism and interpersonal connectedness, values very much marginalized by a Western worldview. Unearthing the genealogy of Western psychological ideas in this manner shows how embedded cultural assumptions are in contemporary psychological theory. It is not surprising, then, that therapists and psychologists, rather than considering an epistemological foundation that could support a more collective or communal approach to working with families, are pulled into an individualistic mindset when they approach their clients. The emphasis on individualism, psychological mindedness, and so-called rational approaches to problem solving is so pervasive in therapeutic practice that many practitioners would be challenged to exhibit cultural competence in a strong collectivist environment. In such a context, interdependence, instead of being perceived as healthy, might be pathologized as codependency and enmeshment.

Given that our counseling theories and research are dominated by Eurocentric belief systems and assumptions about culturally respectful practice, practitioners must pay special attention to how underlying worldviews direct and influence therapeutic moves in the counseling room. Being culturally skilled and respectful will require therapists to continually deconstruct the cultural assumptions embedded in our theory and practice and guard against imposing these cultural practices on communities that do not share Eurocentric belief systems. This is easy to say and hard to do. Becoming skilled and practiced at the process of deconstruction might be the best that most counselors can do. The notion that one can attain cultural competence and can be qualified to work with all of the complex identities that people perform in our communities might produce a dangerous form of assuredness that can be harmful to the next culturally different client.

Morality, Power, and Privilege

Let's consider the influence of moral decision making and the effects power and privilege have on the counseling relationship and how they might impact cultural competence. If we were to thoroughly deconstruct all of the main notions that underpin Western psychology, we would most likely find it embedded within a complex social and political nexus. Its influence goes well beyond the reach of simple descriptive techniques that are supposed to work with people from different cultural communities. As Lisa Tsoi Hoshmand (2005) suggests, value issues are seldom part of the therapy discourse. Inherently, the scientific method that has so dominated the field of psychology hides the very epistemological foundations it is built on. It is the scientific assumption of neutrality or objectivity in psychology that leaves psychotherapists and counseling practitioners unconscious of the extent to which they are actually facilitators of moral reflection. This assumption explains why counselors and therapists avoid facing the very real moral and political challenges in working across diverse communities.

As Hoshmand (2005) contends,

> the old approach of attempting to maintain neutrality has to be replaced by a conscious attempt to acknowledge the moral spaces in which psychotherapists and clients are located as well as the role we play in enabling, questioning, or diminishing the clients' moral responsibilities. (p. 16)

If counseling is a place for moral reflection on clients' intentions and purposes in their lives, then surely it is important for therapists to be more consciously aware of how they are engaging clients in inevitable moral consequences and dilemmas on the basis of their interventions. This requires much more than knowing some general outline of how to counsel a particular group of people. When counselors consider the basis of their moral, social, and political acts in their exchanges with clients, they are going beyond the mere application of "how-to" techniques with different cultural and ethnic groups.

Increasingly, multiculturalists do not speak about addressing multicultural competence without acknowledging the power differentials that exist within a counseling relationship. As Hervé Varenne (2003) notes, the authority granted to therapists by the wider community places them within political structures of social control. Because of the differential access to power, influence, and privilege that therapists have, it is not enough to claim to be culturally competent with specific racial and cultural groups (Suzuki, Ponterotto, & Meller, 2001), especially when such competence is granted within the same relations of power that govern clients' lives. It is more important for therapists from different cultural positions to understand and address how power and privilege work in the lives of counselors and clients as well as in the lives of diverse cultural groups.

There is clear evidence (Sue & Sue, 2007) that sociopolitical forces that influence the mental health delivery systems produce differing levels of service for different groups. In North America, it is the lower socioeconomic groups and especially poor people of color who are consistently shortchanged. Culturally competent behavior involves working at systemic levels to promote social justice in order to provide equal access and opportunity. Competence involves helping remove barriers so that everyone gets access to fair mental health services. These are some of the overarching principles that must guide the practice of cultural respect. From this perspective, therapists should abandon a passive role of working competently with diverse client groups and must act as change agents in rectifying injustice, racism, and discrimination at the wider system level. The systemic operation of power needs to be analyzed far more for the role it plays in producing the psychological distress that the poor and people of color present to counselors. Such an analysis would lead to counseling theories different from those that are usually taught, relying as they do on explanations that focus on family-of-origin dramas and the frequent blaming of mothers.

David Nylund (2006) speaks of different versions of multiculturalism and comments on the extent to which they grapple with issues such as racism, classism, social justice, and equity. He describes a conservative version of multiculturalism as ultimately an assimilationist model where the lens through which cultural differences are understood is primarily white or Eurocentric. Peter McLaren (1994) describes conservative multiculturalism as having an ahistorical analysis and as devoid of any economic or class analysis. He criticizes it for failing to link racism with economic injustice. Similar to conservative multiculturalism is liberal humanism, which Pamela Perry (2002) describes as purveying a form of cultural tourism wherein ethnicities are described by chapter and strategies are outlined for working with particular ethnic minority groups. What is missing from these versions of multiculturalism is discussion of the dominant cultural lens. Nylund (2006) terms whiteness the "unmarked norm against which other ethnic groups are compared" (p. 29). Perry (2002) suggests that this form of multiculturalism constructs people of color as "tightly bound fictive identities that reproduce notions of inherent, durable and unbridgeable differences between people" (p. 197).

Advancing the field in multiculturalism and extending the discussion on cultural competence requires a move away from believing there are specific tightly bound identities that share the same worldviews. Such a fiction originates in European fantasies about people of color that can be traced back to the era of colonization. Rather, it is time to bring forth a contextual analysis that acknowledges the contradictions and complexities involved in being culturally respectful. Counselors need to learn about the cultural location, unique history, life experience, language, family, and peer culture of those they are working with before they can begin to recognize their counseling needs. This is not the same as treating clients as unique individuals who share the same underlying human needs. Rather, it is considering how the dominant cultural ideas or dominant discourses are working on people's lives, producing their identities and shaping their possible modes of expression. These dominant ideas work on both those who identify with the cultures that are dominant and on those who do not. But the effects are quite different. We need to understand racist and sexist discourse, and the discursive affects of classism, homophobia, ableism, and fundamentalism, in order to be culturally respectful. On the other hand, it is also necessary to consider how people shield themselves from these influences, assert other cultural narratives and traditions, make choices of accommodation and resistance, and invent new cultural modes of expression all the time. This all happens so fast that it would be impossible for any individual to keep up with all of the possible cultural nuances and thus to be called competent in working with them.

Whiteness

David Nylund (2006) distinguishes "being white" from the effects of the "discourse of whiteness" and reflects on the discourse of whiteness as a useful tool with which to name the systemic patterns of racism and injustice. He suggests that cultural competence is better understood by making visible the sociohistorical construction of whiteness. Deconstructing whiteness exposes the everyday practices that are often subtle and covert but nevertheless continue to secure the power and privilege of people who benefit from this discourse. Much of it happens outside the consciousness of white people through the work done by discourse to structure consciousness. The discourse of whiteness produces racist and inequitable systems and normalizes injustice. Raka Shome (1996) suggests that it maintains its power largely because it "remains unmarked, unnamed and unmapped in contemporary society" (p. 503). The whiteness discourse does not embrace a tightly knit cultural group. Its effects are felt in the consciousness of people of color as well as those with white skin. It is not a monolithic, fixed category. In this respect, it is just like any other identified cultural grouping. Whiteness might mean many different things, depending on the context. John Hartigan, Jr. (1997), points out that there is a different meaning of whiteness for poor whites, for example. Whites of a lower socioeconomic status are not associated with economic privilege.

Reconstructing Whiteness

There is an interesting notion being proposed in the transformational multicultural literature that proposes the possibility of a white identity not characterized as a salient negative identity. It amounts to an attempt to step out of essentialist assumptions of what it means to be white. Instead, it traces a white identity that is oppositional to racism and oppressive practices. Henry Giroux (2002) remarks that, historically,

> whiteness is a marker of identity confined to the notion of domination and racism that leaves white youth no social imaginary through which they can see themselves as actors in creating an oppositional space to fight for equality and social justice. (p. 144)

An alternative discourse of whiteness can create space for people characterized or identifying as white to become advocates for social justice while diminishing the effects of guilt and shame that the dominant discourse of whiteness casts on people striving to make the difference in race relations and social and economic equity. Giroux (2002) sums up his notion of oppositional whiteness:

> By re-articulating whiteness as more than a form of domination, white students can construct narratives of "whiteness" that both challenge, and, hopefully provide a basis for transforming the dominant relationship between racial identity and citizenship, one informed by oppositional politics. (p. 164)

Politicizing whiteness in this manner opens up new possibilities for whites to construct new subject positions that strengthen their resolve to support a politics of difference and be partners with people of color in addressing unequal power differentials and unequal distribution of material resources. Alternative discourses of whiteness will be grounded in a political, historical, cultural, and social reality rather than the previously unmarked and benignly perceived category. Nylund

(2006) has experienced this reconstruction of whiteness as an approach that can help whites support African American students who wish to express their distress and strong feelings about slavery without their feeling the need to shut down this expression because of the presence of white guilt. Nylund suggests the reformulation of whiteness as a discourse of social justice that offers white students an ability to act and not become immobilized by feelings of guilt and shame. Deconstructing whiteness and positioning it in a discourse of advocacy for justice, equity, and the eradication of racism can be understood as a form of cultural positioning. It provides an opportunity for white students to develop greater cultural respect and is a step toward being culturally responsive to difference.

TO DISCUSS

1. When in the United States did *white* become a term used to describe a group of people?

2. How did families identifying as German, Finnish, Irish, or Italian come to identify as white or simply American?

3. Are there any white cultural practices? Is there a white culture? Why do we find it difficult to answer those questions if we are white?

4. How have white people been shaped by the wider culture?

5. How has racism affected their daily lives?

6. How has whiteness been used politically?

7. What current issues center around whiteness?

8. What does whiteness mean to you?

9. How could whites become antiracist allies?

Source: Adapted from Helfland & Lippin, 2001, p. 12.

Social Constructionism and Cultural Competence

In an extensive exploration of culturally competent practice, Doman Lum (2007) identifies social constructionism as a robust theoretical underpinning to the rather elusive construct of cultural competence. We have used this theoretical lens to view the whole multicultural movement in general. Let's consider now the value of social constructionism as a way of grappling more fully with the cultural competence construct and the challenges of attaining meaningful and effective therapeutic outcomes across cultures.

Social constructionism does not embrace the notion of the therapist as the content expert. Rather than aspiring to cultural competence, the constructionist aspires to what we call a persistent curiosity (Monk, Winslade, Crocket, & Epston, 1997). Clients are considered experts on their own lives and assumed to possess detailed local knowledge (Geertz, 1983) of cultural significance that can serve as the wellspring of resourcefulness for change. Therapists cannot hope to learn enough about the details of clients' cultural contexts to know what will make a difference. Rather, they can use their expertise to help clients deconstruct the complexity of the cultural issues that are in different ways both constraining and strengthening their responses to the challenges they face (De Jong & Berg (2002). Gerald Corey (2008) suggests that constructionism in fact disavows the role of the therapist as expert and places greater emphasis on client consultation and collaboration.

In the first chapter, we referred to sample quotations from the work of Sigmund Freud, Carl Jung, B. F. Skinner, Carl Rogers, and Fritz Perls, all of whom who played leading roles in shaping psychological practice. In different ways they drove the modernist agenda in its search for understanding the essence of what it meant to be a human being. Today, that quest is being displaced by a desire to understand the wider sociocultural world and how it constructs persons as cultural beings. Gerald Corey (2008) describes the changes in epistemology like this: "The modernist search for human essence and truth, is being replaced with the concept of socially storied lives" (p. 386). Corey suggests that constructionists are distrustful of "knowing" because the dominant culture becomes the lens by which families and society are understood. A constructionist approach emphasizes a curious posture where there is a mutual search for understanding and exploring of ways to solve problems. Harlene Anderson and Harold Goolishian (1992) describe this quality as a "talking with" rather than a "talking to" one another. They articulated a "not knowing" position in therapy as a useful stance from which to come to understand the culturally different Other. This stance requires an active curiosity unbound by a strong therapist agenda about what should be explored. Taking a not knowing position is about entering the world of another with a fierce curiosity and a persistent interest in codiscovery between therapist and client. The expectation here is not that one can become a cultural expert in the way that some literature on cultural competence appears to suggest. Instead, therapy from this position involves an open and inquiring stance of wanting to come to understand what the client is conveying and actively eschewing any certainty that one has fully understood.

Solution-focused therapy (Corey, 2008), for example, is in alignment with this philosophy and emphasizes clients' capacity to engage effectively with challenging circumstances but assumes that they are temporarily blocked from accessing their cultural and linguistic resources. Clients are perceived from this perspective as having the capacity to change and adapt and as doing the best they can while confronted with difficult problems. John Walter and Jane Peller (2000) suggest that therapists should work alongside their clients and trust clients' intentions to solve their problems.

Social constructionist approaches emphasize the value of seeking to understand the dominant narratives or life stories in the counseling process. From this perspective, problem situations are communicated indirectly through narratives. These narratives speak not only to the past but to what is currently taking place and what is possible in the future. Even when they amount to reports of what has already happened, they are also constructions that have effects on the decisions that shape this future. Some traditional psychotherapy models define health and illness through a dominant cultural lens. A constructionist orientation operates on the central premise that problems and solutions lie in the social, political, and historical discourse rather than within the nature of individuals. Narrative therapists, for example, concentrate on the cultural narratives that are dominating and subjugating at both the personal level and at the wider sociocultural level. At the heart of this work are sociopolitical assumptions about how problems are constructed. A social constructionist embarks upon therapeutic work in a deconstructive spirit to more clearly expose the cultural assumptions that are part of the client's difficulties. When people become aware of how social practices can oppress them, they can then notice opportunities for new perspectives to emerge. Out of the plot elements of problem stories can emerge the coproduction of preferred, uplifting, and resourceful narratives.

Discursive Empathy

Even when counselors employ a not knowing stance and a fierce and yet respectful curiosity, there are often domains of human experience that may not be understood. Clients' stories of experience cannot always be translated into forms that are understandable to therapists (Cushman, 1990; Lutz, 1988; Monk, 1998). In contradiction to liberal humanist claims of universality, there are discourses that position clients in places that may not be shared in the experience of counselors. For example, it would be a challenge for a therapist who has spent much of her life positioned in discourses that are predominantly racist to be empathetic with clients who have been directly targeted by those very discourses.

A constructionist approach invites therapists to develop discursive empathy whereby they constantly review the dominant cultural discourses that shape their relationships with clients. Therapists do not presume to understand their clients' experiences with any assurance of accuracy; rather, they spend time unpacking simultaneously the cultural knapsacks that they and their clients' carry. Discursive empathy acknowledges both the client's immediate feelings and concerns and also the wider cultural backdrop. One of the difficulties of therapy is that, by oneself, it is hard to identify discourses without the perspective of difference. The practice of discursive empathy enables the therapist to be much more open to cultural assumptions that are initially difficult to grasp. In other words, discursive empathy points to developing an awareness of dominating discourses and of how these discourses position us and our clients.

Overall, the questions that the therapist can most profitably ask identify assumptions that guide clients' behavior. The therapist can also help clients to identify and draw out their own expertise as a resource to assist in the resolution of difficulties. Counselors can identify such "local knowledge" (Geertz, 1983) more profitably than they can employ generalized social science knowledge because of its likely superior contextual relevance. In practicing discursive empathy, the therapist invites a willingness and openness from clients to locate their problems not as naturally occurring, independent objects, devoid of cultural significance, but rather as outcomes of various positions taken up among a sea of discourses.

Conclusion

Despite deconstructive knowledge and expertise, therapists are going to have varying degrees of success. Confronting one's cultural encapsulation and cultural limitations can be deeply distressing and can engender a genuine sense of dislocation. Seeking cultural competence requires an extraordinary degree of openness and sensitivity, serious introspection, and painful self-discovery. It involves confronting the emotional impact of one's attitudes, beliefs, and feelings on members of communities who have been poorly understood and have suffered greatly from majority culture and its goals and aspirations. The journey is unsettling and can be deeply anxiety provoking. We are often fearful because we realize the changes required are significant and, to some extent, life changing. Profound change comes only from immersion in the lives and communities of those who are the most culturally different from oneself.

Developing a deep sense of cultural awareness and understanding requires continual effort to overcome those deeply entrenched life experiences that produce knee jerk reactions to events that are culturally new and different. Success comes after an arduous process of thoroughly questioning one's lifelong loyalty to the presumed rightness and universality of a cultural worldview.

As Blaine Fowers and Barbara Davidov (2006) suggest, developing cultural competence does not have an end point. They speak of prolonged and courageous effort that requires a character strength involving generosity, honesty, and openness. To be truly competent in understanding the culturally different Other is a desirable goal. In many ways, however, attaining cultural competence is like being drawn to a mirage in the desert that looks identifiable and attainable but as we get closer breaks up. We are confronted with the harsh reality of a journey that is not really over. The goal, however, is still worth striving for.

TO DISCUSS

1. Find some books that have chapters on how to counsel particular ethnic groups. Locate yourself in relation to one of these groups. Consider the advice given. How would this advice be helpful to you as a client? How would it not be helpful?

2. Discuss another chapter with someone else of a different ethnicity from yours. Interview this person about what he or she would find helpful or not helpful.

3. Discuss what aspects of who we are escape descriptive accounts of ethnic groups.

4. Research the list of multicultural competencies promoted by one professional organization. What are the strengths and weaknesses of these lists?

Response to Chapter 17

Charles R. Ridley

Charles R. Ridley, Ph.D., received his doctorate from the University of Minnesota. He is a professor and codirector of training of the doctoral program in counseling psychology at Indiana University in Bloomington. He also is a former associate dean of research and of the university graduate school at that institution. He is a fellow in Divisions 17 and 45 of the American Psychological Association. His various scholarly interests include multicultural counseling, training, and assessment; organizational consultation; the use of religious resources in psychotherapy; and therapeutic change. His book, *Overcoming Unintentional Racism in Counseling and Therapy: A Practitioner's Guide to Intervention* (2005), was the recipient of the Gustavus Myers Center award for Human Rights.

The topic of multicultural competence, as the authors point out, has gained significance in the mental health field. Few constructs have garnered as much attention, and some scholars regard it as a defining feature of applied psychology (Sue, Bingham, Porche-Burke, & Vasquez, 1999). There are several advantages of this attention. The multicultural agenda remains in the forefront of conversations in the field. There has been a staggering proliferation of research and scholarly activity on the topic, and old perspectives about race and culture are giving way to new sentiments. Despite the flurry of research and scholarship on the topic, the concept continues to lack a coherent definition. In the absence of a sound definition, professionals cannot state definitively whether their behaviors and interventions in counseling reflect multicultural competence or multicultural incompetence.

Furthermore, the current state of affairs poses an interesting challenge to professionals whose only option is to treat diverse populations of clients. They somehow must bridge the chasm between theory and practice in an attempt to provide quality service delivery. Armed with all their training and considerable information but paradoxically an inadequate conceptualization of what it means to be multiculturally competent, these professionals nevertheless are expected to uphold the ideals of the profession, behave ethically, overcome the noted disparities in the field, and facilitate positive therapeutic change. Indeed, this is a monumental problem.

Unfortunately, the problem is exacerbated by the confusion over the use of the words *competence* and *competencies*. Much of the thinking about multicultural competencies is predicated on the tripartite model proposed by Derald Wing Sue and his colleagues (Sue, Arredondo, & McDavis, 1992; Sue et al., 1992). The model organizes the competencies into the domains of attitudes/beliefs, knowledge, and skills. Patricia Arredondo and her colleagues (1996) subsequently elaborated on the tripartite model, yielding 31 Competency Statements and 119 Explanatory

Statements. While the competencies are aspirational, they also are descriptive but not prescriptive. They inform practitioners what they should do in counseling, but they provide no guidance in how to behave competently.

Consider the Explanatory Statement "Use assessment instruments appropriately with clients having limited English skills." What does the statement really mean? Consider the range of possibilities. How should practitioners use so-called culture-fair or culture-free tests? Should practitioners use so-called standardized norms in making interpretations? How should practitioners use so-called standardized norms in making interpretations? Should practitioners develop and use culturally specific norms? How should practitioners develop and use culturally specific norms? Should practitioners use assessment instruments to formulate clinical hypotheses? How should practitioners use assessment instruments to formulate clinical hypotheses? Should practitioners use assessment instruments to confirm or disconfirm clinical hypotheses? How should practitioners use assessment instruments to confirm or disconfirm clinical hypotheses? Should practitioners use interpreters? How should practitioners use interpreters?

Without a prescription, practitioners really do not know how to *use* assessment instruments *appropriately* with clients having limited English skills. For the field to move forward, a conceptually sound, internally consistent definition of multicultural competence is essential.

CHAPTER 18

On the Horizon

Next Steps in Multicultural Counseling

I n this final chapter, we consider a vision for the future of multicultural counseling that we would like to see happen. We shall outline what kind of social world we might create and how counseling can contribute to it. In this chapter, we may become a little more provocative than we have been in previous chapters. You need not always agree with us. We are, after all, attempting to scan the horizon, and we can easily misread what is there. Others may see different possibilities from whatever vision their particular vantage point affords.

We start from the assumption that clinical practices for the counseling and psychology fields have been dominated by individualistic psychology models over the last 30 years. Multiculturalism in the end brings us into some form of head-on challenge with such practices. Or perhaps the challenge will be more side on. Seeing a person predominantly as an individual does not produce a sharp focus on the cultural networks that shape individual experience. For multiculturalism to advance, it needs to take note of the efforts to rethink this focus on a narrowly individual psychology. Derald Wing Sue, Allen Ivey, and Paul Pedersen (1996) state it bluntly: "Current theories of counseling are inadequate to describe, explain, predict, and deal with cultural elements of counseling across multiple cultures" (p. 250).

Our only concern with this statement is the possible qualification (some might read it as a let-out clause) implied in the expression "cultural elements of counseling." We want to ask, are there any elements of counseling that are not cultural elements? Certainly all counseling involves the use of language, discourse, and concepts, each element of which is a product of a cultural world.

Improving Democracy

In the end, the goal of the multicultural movement, in counseling as in other aspects of social life, must be a democratic one. We are not referring here just to the process of electing governments through majority voting. There are many instances of what are called "democratic" elections where democratic conditions of life are not upheld. The democratic vision is much more than electoral politics. It must be about ensuring a more just and respectful world that recognizes cultural differences and embraces them, rather than using them to establish lines of division along which privilege is granted or withheld. It must be about promoting equality and an equal right to participate in the social world. Multiculturalism is in the end about giving everyone a fair chance in life, about providing all individuals an opportunity to have a real say in designing the conditions of their own lives. It is also about ensuring that these possibilities are not withheld from some groups of people on account of their cultural, ethnic, racial, gender, or religious backgrounds or on the basis of their sexuality or disability. In the end, the goal of multiculturalism must be to improve democracy and to make it more just for more people. Multicultural counseling is about working to ensure that counseling practices participate in and promote such improvement. As we see it, the multicultural agenda is first and foremost about creating social change.

The philosopher Jacques Derrida speaks about "democracy to come." In French, there is an added strand of meaning to this phrase. *Democratie á l'avenir* has a double meaning because the word *avenir* refers to what is arriving or coming and also to the future. So Derrida is speaking about the democracy of the future, and he is at the same time speaking about democracy as always in the process of arriving, as always promising a future, better world. Derrida was serious about the hope that his own work was aimed at this process of improving democracy, of excavating the hidden possibilities in the idea of democracy and exposing them to light. He saw his idea of "deconstruction" as endeavoring to give birth to new meanings and new possibilities. We like this idea, and we see it as critically relevant to multicultural counseling. There is much in the social world and in the practice of counseling that can benefit from the kind of deconstruction that opens up new possibilities. At its best, we think counseling is not about adjusting people to accept the "reality" of the imperfect world in which they live but about generating and unleashing forces of change that would create new realities, albeit primarily in the limited and local domains of personal living.

There are two corollaries that go with this assertion. One is that multicultural counseling must embrace the idea that there is much in current reality that needs changing. We do not live in a world that readily embraces cultural difference. Rather, we live in a world that values and rewards practices of unification, domination, and exclusion on racial, cultural and other grounds. This is in some instances as true in the so-called developed countries that trumpet democracy around the world as it is in those that would not presume to call themselves democracies. However, the old practices and institutions of the modern world and the discourses that have supported them have given birth to some noble and useful democratic traditions in our political systems that need not so much to be jettisoned as further developed.

The other corollary is that multicultural counseling must embrace an analysis of power in order to understand the personal effects of cultural relations in people's lives and to be effective in offering movement toward change. We are not alone in saying this. Here is a statement made by Derald Wing Sue, Allen Ivey, and Paul Pedersen in 1996: "Issues of dominance and power have been insufficiently considered in helping theories" (p. 25).

There are different accounts of power, as we have outlined in Chapters 6, 7, and 8. We have also argued that the poststructuralist analysis of power has much to recommend it. It is responsive to developments in the technologies of power that are current and specifically modern in their application. It is not so much a centralized vision of how power works but a distributed one that allows us to see the work done by power, sometimes behind our backs, in the minute experiences of daily life. We believe that it is potentially very useful for counselors who are working with people's detailed stories of daily life. We therefore believe that a poststructuralist analysis of power promises a more finely tuned understanding of how power becomes manifest in the lives of those who consult counselors. It also does not require social revolution before change can take place. In fact, it points to the fact that every conversation can potentially be a site for social change. It thus offers special promise for counseling conversations to recognize and then shift the cultural and discursive formations of power at work in the production of counseling relationships and of people's lives.

The American Constitution begins with the resounding phrase, "We the people . . ." It has served as a catch cry for democracy, at least as a cultural product of the 18th century. Multiculturalism, as Kwame Appiah (2005) points out, asks us to consider a symbolic rewording that enhances democracy: "We the peoples . . ." (p. 203). But counselors are usually working with individuals at the level of what affects "me the person." Appiah suggests that all three perspectives have to be considered and their enmeshment acknowledged. The study and appreciation of the detail of such enmeshment is what multicultural counseling might aim to achieve in order to play its part in the development of democracy.

Our concern is that multiculturalism needs to be taken much more seriously in the counseling field. We are also aware that to do so might be an uncomfortable and challenging task. There is much talk about multiculturalism's representing a "fourth force" in counseling (e.g., Pedersen, 1991; Sue, Ivey, & Pedersen, 1996; Sue et al., 1998). We support this effort to legitimate the status of multicultural counseling and like our colleagues believe that there is more to be done to realize it. To justify such a claim, we need to do more than just assert it. We need to keep working with the concept of culture in ways that render it central to what counseling is about. All counseling might thus become "culture-centered" (Sue, Ivey, & Pedersen, 1996, p. 30).

Multiculturalism has sometimes been treated as an add-on to the usual practices of counseling. Derald Wing Sue and his colleagues (1998) refer to multiculturalism as "complementary" (p. 3) to psychodynamic, behavioral, and humanistic frameworks for counseling. There are many textbooks that have responded to the multicultural agenda by adding new sections or new chapters about multicultural issues. While this effort should be appreciated, we do not believe it goes far enough. If the field of counseling were to take multiculturalism more seriously, it would require more substantial revisions of all of the other chapters or sections in such textbooks. It would grapple more with the places where multiculturalism does not so much complement as conflict with or even undermine conventional frameworks. Counseling theories and practices would have to go through some significant changes.

Like many of our multicultural colleagues, we believe that multicultural counseling should not focus just on understanding *clients* in multicultural terms. We want *counseling itself* to be more rigorously examined through a multicultural lens. As we look at the horizon, we see the need for much painful revision of many psychological concepts, models, and theories. The easy assumptions of Eurocentrism that are built into counseling and psychological knowledge and that masquerade as solid and universal scientific truth need to be opened up to make room for a more cultural analysis. For example, Derald Wing Sue, Allen Ivey, and Paul Pedersen (1996) suggest that concepts like "self-actualization" and "autonomy," the valuation of "I-statements," "assertiveness" training, and the avoidance of advice giving or counselor self-disclosure might all be considered culturally encapsulated. The truths of psychology and counseling often need to be understood as more local than universal, which does not have to rob them of all their value. This shift is indeed happening in some quarters, but there is much more room for this trend to develop.

Looking Beyond Ourselves

It is also fair to say that a reliance on the discipline of psychology as a source of ideas for multicultural development will not suffice. Psychology has, in general, been slow to include a cultural perspective. Derald Wing Sue (in Sue et al.,1998) suggests that the mental health professions in general have been at best "reluctant" (p. xi) to embrace cultural issues. We would argue, therefore, that multicultural counseling needs to look for inspiration beyond the discipline of psychology.

Fortunately, there are some fruitful places to look. The new discipline of cultural studies has developed much material that is worth paying attention to. We would like to see it referenced a lot more in multicultural counseling texts. Postcolonial studies are producing a range of useful insights that deserve the attention of counselors and psychologists. They point to the need for the voices of the colonized around the world to be given a much greater hearing, and they have developed theories of cultural relations that offer promise for cross-cultural counseling. At the moment, the voices of the colonized are often patronized as curiosities rather than treated as of central importance in the counseling field. There are voices in the counseling literature advocating indigenous helping methods (e.g., Lee, 1996), but these methods are sometimes seen in the profession as appropriate for particular cultural groups rather than as having something to teach the mainstream counseling profession.

The more established discipline of anthropology also has many innovative ideas that move beyond the cookie-cutter versions of culture that were in vogue in anthropology some decades ago. The political philosophy of multiculturalism has thrown up a series of searching and innovative conceptual challenges in recent years. Postmodern and poststructuralist social theory offers some important lines of inquiry that might lead the counseling field out of the narrow positivist scientism that has been largely inhospitable to differences in cultural meaning.

There are many new developments in counseling itself that take these ideas seriously. Yet they often remain on the margins of the profession as a whole. Derald Wing Sue, Allen Ivey, and Paul Pedersen (1996) suggest that a multicultural perspective in counseling is more at home with constructivist orientations to subjective experience, to dialogic views of the self, and to narrative understandings of life. Sue and his colleagues (1998) argue that multiculturalism needs to embrace a postmodern orientation. They suggest that multiculturalism and postmodernism intersect with regard to the following assumptions (p. 4):

1. The acceptance of multiple worldviews, each of which is neither right nor wrong.

2. The assumption that people construct their worlds through social processes (social constructionism).

3. The rejection of universal psychology in favor of a contextual approach.

4. The understanding of language as relational rather than representational.

We agree with these conclusions, although we prefer to speak of social constructionism and poststructuralism rather than constructivism. We are dubious about whether some traditional approaches to counseling can be modified to include such assumptions. There are now a number of fresh approaches to counseling practice that explicitly take on board these basic theoretical orientations. They are variously known as constructivist therapy, narrative therapy, solution-focused brief therapy, social constructionist therapy, just therapy, collaborative language systems therapy, possibility therapy, and various others. We would like to see these approaches embraced more strongly in the multicultural counseling field. To do so might offer more promise than revising traditional models.

Another issue that arises pertains particularly to counseling within the United States. Multiculturalism in the United States is arguably struggling more than in some other places. The particularly painful historical legacies of slavery and westward colonization lie probably at the source of the emotionally loaded conversations about these issues in the United States, as do the often unspoken American ambitions for empire in the world. The political urge for the United States to act as a "superpower" in the world does not work in favor of creating a multicultural social vision within the United States or elsewhere. And yet Americans seem often unaware of what is happening elsewhere, from which they could learn much. For example, a glance across the border to Canada would be highly profitable. We suggest that Canada has done far more as a nation to incorporate multiculturalism into the fabric of its political and social life than has the United States. There are other examples around the world as well. We are acutely conscious of the particular bicultural initiatives that have happened in New Zealand. South Africa, since the end of apartheid, has undertaken some courageous initiatives that should be studied by multiculturalists everywhere. At the time of writing, British society is currently engaged in some significant debates about the limits of multiculturalism in the wake of the discovery of homegrown terrorists amid their cultural minorities. There are similar debates happening in European countries like France and the Netherlands. These debates deserve to be given attention in the United States as well. We are not suggesting that straight copying from other contexts is advisable. But a study of counseling in cultural context for the purpose of learning about more culturally responsive counseling practices might be more profitable than is often envisaged.

The Shifting Conception of Culture

One way in which multiculturalism needs to be taken seriously is by according it the honor of thoroughly interrogating and theorizing concepts like culture itself, as well as related concepts such as race and ethnicity. We have attempted to do this in this book, and we also invite readers to continue in this work. Concepts are cultural products, constructed in conversation between people. They often shift and change and can seldom be fixed by definition. Multiculturalism needs therefore to stay alert to ways in which taken-for-granted assumptions about what constitutes a race, an ethnic group, a culture, a gay person, a disability, and so forth are moving targets.

The meaning of culture appears to be going through a shift at present, as we traced in Chapter 1. The conventional idea that everyone belongs to a singular culture and that cultures are definable, discrete wholes that can be studied and learned about is giving way to some new understandings of culture that stress a multiplicity of cultural influences. All of us are subject to a range of these influences and can best be thought of as hybrid creatures rather than as being squeezed into an integrated singularity. The metaphor that is increasingly being used is that of cultural narratives rather than cultural wholes. There are implications for multicultural counseling in these conceptual shifts, and we believe that they will be taken on board in the counseling literature more and more in the future. What will have to give way are some textbook chapters that teach students the best way to counsel African Americans, Asians, Latinos, and Native Americans. Such chapters assume much greater homogeneity and stability of culture than can stand up in the complexity of people's lives. They implicitly buy into census definitions of race and culture that are at best dubious. Test questions in standardized tests that are used for counselor credentialing will also need to be revised if they require counselors to make forced choices on the basis of the assumption of one-to-one correspondence between the individual and a singular culture.

The concept of race is also under challenge, even though its existence will probably prove to be persistent and stubborn for the historical reasons we have traced in earlier chapters. It continues to serve as an organizing idea in people's heads and in the government of lives that far outweighs its intellectual substance. We do think that the multicultural field needs to take careful cognizance of the new writing emerging out of critical race theory. What we believe will emerge out of the shifts taking place in thinking about race will be a greater emphasis on the concept of racism than on the distinctions of race itself. Some people assume that the existence of race is a given and that racism is a distortion of it. We suspect that it is the other way around. Racism has been the given of the modern world and the available concepts of race are derived from it. But an emphasis on the interrogation of power relations and of dominant discourse implied within the analysis of racism still has much to offer the counseling profession.

Racism also has to be thought about carefully. Under the aegis of an individual emphasis, it is often, we believe wrongly, cast in psychological literature as a feature of individual personality, or as an emotional state. We believe that it is neither of these things. It is more productive to think of it as a feature of social discourse that is owned by no one and yet affects everyone. If we are correct about this, it makes less sense to identify racism in individuals as if they were the source of it and makes more sense to identify racism as it exists in discourse and trace its effects on individuals' thinking and practice. This is a deliberately less blaming approach and runs fewer risks of ending up in the frustrating cycles of accusation and denial that often produce silence and inaction more than change. We are much more interested in what produces change with regard to the practices of racism than we are in producing a sense of righteous blame, even when that blame appears justified.

Social theory also introduces new concepts from time to time. We have argued for the value of the concept of discourse and discursive positioning in this book. In various contexts, we think these concepts are more precise ways of talking about things that the concept of culture gets at more clumsily. We envisage, therefore, the growth of an understanding in multicultural counseling of people being shaped and influenced by a raft of cultural discourses, rather than by a singular monolithic culture. Some of these discourses are likely to dominate others, reflecting the power relations in the world. Some discourses will be in competition with others, while others will be largely compatible. The effects of these discourses will be heard in the words that clients say to counselors on a daily basis, since utterances are constructed out of elements of discourse.

One of the chief advantages we see for using the concept of discourse is that it enables us to extract ourselves from the strongly entrenched habits of thought that we referred to in Chapter 2 as essentialism. Essentialism predisposes us to search for essences at the core of a word, a person, or a culture. Cultural essentialism, in particular, is a necessary subject of study for the multicultural counseling movement. It is expressed in the various assumptions of a stable and authentic cultural norm for a particular culture. The assumption of such a norm is needed before the common practice of judging someone's authenticity is possible. Whenever you hear someone talk about another person as not a true Native American, not a real feminist, not an authentic black, you can hear essentialist assumptions operating in the background. Such assumptions are present too when a person is pitied for having to "struggle" with an identity or lifestyle or social context that is bicultural, biracial, bilingual, bisexual, binational, or in any other way bifurcated. Such pity underscores an assumption that to be singular and stable is normal and ideal, despite the fact that such assumptions stereotype and exclude probably the majority of people. It seems far more normal for the majority of people to be pulled in different directions by multiple cultural influences than to be singular and stable. In fact, we believe that the understanding of individuals in singular terms greatly advantages the cause of racism, the cause of sexism, and the agenda of homophobia. We believe that on the horizon of multiculturalism, there will be less and less emphasis on essentialist thinking, and we believe that there are many new possibilities that can open up as a result.

One way in which counselors and psychologists can step out of essentialist thinking is through thinking more in terms of culture as historical narrative. We can more fully appreciate the concepts and customs of cultural groups if we understand them as produced within particular historical conditions than if we treat them as suspended only in the present. A historical perspective allows us to see culture as in a process of development. Even the concepts of culture and race themselves, as we have seen, are historical products and subject to development. Kwame Appiah (2005) makes the point eloquently: "To create a life . . . is to interpret the materials that history has given you" (p. 163).

Culture and history provide the substances out of which identity can be constructed. Multicultural counselors should have a sense of history, particularly cultural history, as they help people deliberate on how to fashion a life. Not to be aware of the effects of history always risks one's being culturally encapsulated. Counselors are dealing on a day-to-day basis with manifestations of their clients' personal histories, and these are better understood if we conceive of them as connected with cultural and historical trends.

Counseling is about working with people as individuals or in small groups. It requires a conceptualization of the relationship between individuals and cultural groups. A common approach to this task is to think of people as individuals first and then of culture as the surrounding context in which they live. This approach itself fits nicely into European cultural worldviews but does not jibe so easily with perspectives drawn from other cultures. There are alternative approaches that multiculturalism should continue to explore. For example, cultural studies writer Nick Couldry (2000) suggests starting from the reverse assumption: that we are all members of a cultural world first and become individuals. He suggests that we study individuation as the process of "how we all become individuals" (p. 7). From a cultural perspective, we become individuals from the background of our cultural influences. Psychologist Jerome Bruner, who has been influential in the development of a "cultural psychology," has said a similar kind of thing. He argues for a reversal of "the traditional relation between culture and biology with respect to human nature" (Bruner, 1990, p. 34). In this relation, biology is assumed to be the prime original force in the construction of human nature and culture gets the second bite of the cherry. Bruner wants us to see things in reverse.

It is the character of man's biological inheritance . . . that it does not direct or shape human action and experience, does not serve as the universal cause. Rather it imposes constraints on action, constraints whose effects are modifiable.

Cultures characteristically devise "prosthetic devices" that permit us to transcend "raw" biological limits—for example the limits of memory capacity or the limits of our auditory range. The reverse view I am proposing is that it is culture, not biology, that shapes human life and the human mind, that gives meaning to action by situating its underlying intentional states in an interpretive system. (p. 34)

Such an idea gives multiculturalism in general, and psychological practice in particular, a strong mandate for what it does. It is about the shaping of human nature rather than, say, the discovery of human nature. Biological influences such as genetic inheritance, or the workings of the brain, impose constraints on what kinds of persons we might be, but human beings are *by nature* cultural beings, constantly finding ways to exceed the limits of biology.

Becoming an individual does not have to mean something like freeing ourselves from the influence of the cultural environment around us, as some theorists in the counseling field have postulated. Rather it can mean fashioning and shaping a life that brings together pieces of cultural narrative, values them, works with them, investigates how they interact with other cultural formations as well as with biological forces, and, if necessary, refashions them.

Developing New Social Imaginaries

In order for multiculturalism to develop, it needs to keep working at developing a vision of a social world that is inclusive of difference. In this section, we shall use Charles Taylor's (2004) term "social imaginaries" for this purpose (see Chapter 13 for more explanation). One message that we can take (among others) from Martin Luther King's famous "I have a dream" speech is the power of such dreams as social imaginaries. Dr. King's speech is remembered probably because it articulated an imagined social world that people could act on. The civil rights movement out of which this speech came had a vision of a series of legal changes that would grant black people in the United States greater equality as full citizens. The feminist movement has produced a new set of social imaginaries for family life, personal relations between genders, and women's careers. The gay or lesbian lifestyle has been constructed as a social imaginary too.

In relations between cultural groups, the "melting pot" has served as a powerful social imaginary in the United States for many decades. But we should be clear about what it imagines. It is about a modernist idea of integration into a singular culture rather than the pluralistic inclusion of difference. And it never has stretched itself across the color line or included Native Americans. It is, therefore, a tired metaphor that should be rejected as too limited. As we reject it, however, we should be prepared to engage in the search for new imaginaries around which people can be galvanized, in the way that they were behind Dr. King's speech.

So-called mosaic multiculturalism is one possible option. It has been given a degree of official sanction in Canada. However, as we have seen in Chapter 2, there are problems with this idea because it is based on an essentialist account of culture.

As Seyla Benhabib (2002) has pointed out, we need to create not just an appreciation of diversity but a context for negotiated relations of value between cultural worlds. In other words, we need something like a meta-cultural vision. We need places where cultural dimensions can be weighed and assessed and some working agreements negotiated about how differences will be handled. There are many questions that need to be answered along these lines. For example, will we work to eliminate female genital cutting, even though it is valued in some cultures? Can Muslim women be forced to abandon the wearing of the hajib in contexts where they are obliged to meet uniform dress codes (the army, the police, private schools)? Although, as conservatives assert, it has long been the case that marriage has been assumed to be the preserve of heterosexual couples, can we make room for new cultural developments in the meaning of marriage that are inclusive of gay and lesbian couples? These are questions that mosaic multiculturalism finds hard to address.

At issue here are the relations between culture and government. There are many cultural groups clamoring for official government recognition. It is easy to argue for government to be culturally neutral and to provide equal recognition of various groups. In practice, this is virtually impossible. As Kwame Appiah (2005) points out, the standardized use of language in a governmental jurisdiction, for a start, assumes a choice in favor of a set of cultural values embedded in the chosen lingua franca.

We do not think it is clear yet what alternative social imaginaries there are to the melting pot. However, we do see on the horizon some aspects of what such a social imaginary might aspire to. It would need to avoid slotting people into simple boxes. It would need to be flexible enough to affirm the complexity and multiplicity of modern lifestyles. It would need to offer recognition of different cultural traditions and also subcultural aesthetic styles. It would need to be sharply vigilant about processes of exclusion from social privilege. It would need to avoid the destructive mistakes of assimilation or integration but at the same time maintain a vision of a larger society. It would need to be, as Nick Couldry (2000) suggests, a "community without closure" (p. 135), a place where people can go on articulating difference without essentializing the differences encountered.

It would need to be more than an expression of the principle of tolerance, too. The concept of tolerance is historically tied to the centuries-long struggle in Western Europe for the disestablishment of Catholic or Protestant religious beliefs in national politics. The idea of toleration of some groups with different beliefs was a compromise solution that emerged out of several centuries of warfare and bloodshed. Many of the cultural groups that migrated to America in its first century of colonization were seeking the freedom to practice their faiths in places where they did not have to worry about whether or not they would be tolerated. Toleration as a concept was initially tied to a notion of religious freedom. It was later extended to refer to racial or cultural tolerance. The limits of the concept of tolerance are explained by Jacques Derrida (Borradori, 2003). He argues that toleration is always granted by (and therefore controlled by) the established majority. It is an expression of "charity" that "says to the other from its elevated position, I am letting you be, you are not insufferable, I am leaving you a place in my home, but do not forget that this is my home." (p. 127). It is, therefore, in some sense always an expression of the power of dominant groups and represents the "reason of the strongest" (p. 27). It has little to say to those in the position of minority other than perhaps that they should be grateful to the majority for their magnanimity. Derrida argues that we can do better than toleration. He explored, by contrast, the notion of hospitality. A concept like hospitality carries with it a stronger sense of welcoming and valuing of those who are different from us. It conveys a sense of obligation to form positive relations between cultural groups.

Respect for the Other is required by a thoroughgoing version of multiculturalism. And this means respect for the other as Other, not just on the basis that, despite his otherness, the person who is other is underneath the same as us. It is this higher standard of respect that is needed for multicultural counseling. It is not enough just to tolerate difference but to find ways to appreciate it or even learn from it. In the counseling room, the person who is receiving the particular form of professional attention that counseling offers will be sensitive to the difference between being tolerated and being fully accepted and respected. She will know the difference between being allowed just to maintain her differences in worldview and being encouraged to celebrate her cultural background as a reservoir of resources from which to draw in the process of living.

Some have advocated ethnic matching between counselor and client as much as possible. We think that this to some extent increases the likelihood that clients will be granted the kind of respect that we are talking about, although it does not guarantee it. On the other hand, it is clearly not always practicable. Besides, it often relies on the acceptance of the kind of essentialist versions of culture that we have been at pains to problematize throughout this book. If we think in terms of multiple cultural influences being represented in each and every client, rather than thinking of each client in simplistic essential terms as a member of a cultural group, it is even harder to meet the requirements for cultural matching. The same drawback applies to the idea of developing culture-specific counseling theories and practices. Such resolutions of the challenges of multiculturalism have more potential for enrichment of the counseling field in general than they ever have of meeting the counseling needs of every specific counseling client. Imagine the task of developing separate counseling approaches for every ethnicity, for male and female genders and transgendered persons, for each religious persuasion, for gay, lesbian, and straight cultures, for the deaf and for the physically disabled, and then for every combination of the above. The profession of counseling could itself be splintered asunder into many fragments. Culture-specific models of counseling are not unimportant, however. They have much to recommend them where they can be applied. But they need to be thought of more as temporary compromises than as essential answers.

Multicultural counseling also needs to develop approaches that can support cross-cultural conversation, that is, conversation across differences. It needs to develop further at the level of a meta-theory of culture that allows practitioners to make sense of and work with a range of cultural narratives that are presented to them. As we look over the horizon, we can speculate about what such a meta-theory might look like. It might first of all avoid some pitfalls. Conversations across difference need to resist the modernist temptation to reduce the sense of difference by searching out the commonalities of culture, an approach that has all too often led back to a Eurocentric emphasis that can paper over differences and patronize minority cultural positions. It might emphasize instead a welcoming of the indeterminacy and contradictions of competing cultural allegiances and see these as deeply implicated in the struggles people experience in their daily lives. In other words, it might theorize psychological problems from a cultural perspective in a way never contemplated in many of the major theories of personality, human development, and counseling that populate counseling textbooks and classrooms. It might make us less eager to pursue the unification of voices and more curious about the multiplication of them.

There are a variety of writers and thinkers who are exploring the possibilities that can be glimpsed on this horizon. Lisa Tsoi Hoshmand (2005) suggests it might be much more profitable to focus on the relationship between the personal and the political than to continue "teaching and learning about descriptive differences between ethnic groups" (p. 8). She argues for a vision of culture as the symbolic nexus of the personal and the social and invites counselors to consider how culture "offers [people] both possibilities and constraints" (p. 11). She also cautions that we need to see counseling and therapy as cultural systems in themselves. Counseling has appeared at a certain point in history, in particular cultural contexts, and it always rests on and conveys to clients certain cultural values that will not fit with every other cultural influence. Nevertheless, there are varieties of helping relations and often designated helping roles that are similar to those of the counselor in every cultural context (Lee, 1996).

Within contexts that are meeting points for people shaped by various cultural narratives, such as professional organizations, there need to be continued efforts to create opportunities for dialogue and negotiation about issues of value. Issues of value must always be approached from cultural perspectives, and a democratic meta-theory needs to foster a sense of obligation to talk across difference. Donna Harraway (cited by Couldry, 2000, p. 34) looks toward the formation of alliances across difference where this obligation is held paramount. Such alliances will need to be forged between those who have been disadvantaged and those who have been privileged by particular cultural dividing practices.

What is needed more than ever is a vision of dialogue that does not require differences to be collapsed into universal truths about human nature or integrated into singular, all-inclusive perspectives. The American Counseling Association's multicultural competencies that stress awareness, skills, and knowledge can certainly be helpful in promoting such a dialogic perspective. But we would like to see this agenda expanded. Calling them competencies is in itself problematic, because it sounds like acquiring known truths, rather than exploring new territories. The field of knowledge most needs expansion into more dialogic and relational forms. We have sought to do that in this book by treating concepts such as culture, race, social class, and gender not so much as givens but as worthy of discussion. No doubt some will claim that such discussions are overly academic and not relevant to the practical realities of counseling practice on the ground. We would disagree. As we indicated in Chapter 1, we have witnessed many conversations that have become mired in frustration because of inadequate thinking about these issues.

Counselors need to think about issues of culture, and to do so they need to investigate the tools they have to think with, especially when such tools are not serving them well. This is of enormous practical import, since it will shape what professionals do in their practice.

A critical piece in the necessary dialogues about and across difference is a sharpened awareness of how power operates in sometimes subtle ways in interactions between people. Hence, we have emphasized the understanding of power relations in this book. We believe that counselors who can contribute to a more just society need to develop an alertness to such processes of power. We also believe that this alertness needs to go, on the one hand, beyond thinking of power in personal terms, and on the other hand, beyond rigid, structural analyses that do not give enough credence to personal agency. It needs to investigate just how the cultural conditions of people's lives are being produced and organized systematically and yet having very personal effects. The word *awareness* is not robust enough to describe the kind of alertness we are speaking of. It implies that something is obvious if we would only open our eyes to its reality. What we are advocating is more a critical consciousness of all material that counselors are exposed in the counseling process. This consciousness does not apply just to what clients tell counselors. It must be brought to bear on the processes of counseling itself, on the power that inheres in the role of counselor, and on our understandings of what constitutes ethical practice.

A multicultural vision of what counseling might offer to the world is therefore an effort to promote social justice. It must be a dialogic vision rather than a one-size-fits-all vision. It must be more than tolerant of difference. It must welcome people and offer them hospitality on the very basis of their difference. But it must not get trapped in what Jacques Derrida (Derrida & Roudinesco, 2004) refers to as the "cult of the identitarian" or the "narcissism of minorities" (p. 21). That is, it must not constitute differences in such as way as to create essentialized totalities.

Let us conclude by one more time emphasizing the emergent understandings of culture that we referred to at the end of Chapter 2. For us, they represent the new horizons in multicultural counseling. We state them as a series of propositions:

- That it is more useful to think in terms of people's being shaped and influenced by cultural narratives than it is to simply identify them as belonging to a culture
- That the concept of discourse enables us to think in a more discriminating way about how certain cultural influences become dominant and others remain subjugated
- That cultural identifications always exist in the context of cultural power relations, which are constantly shifting and changing
- That counseling knowledge itself needs constant reexamination with regard to its cultural assumptions and its colonizing potential
- That personal identity is not an essential given on the basis of naturalized versions of either personality or culture but something that is best considered an achievement of living through the process of engagement with cultural narratives

- That there are always competing axes of cultural membership and that we cannot reduce these to singular dimensions without creating distortions and expecting that people will fit neatly into cultural boxes

On the horizon, we see many new forms of counseling emerging that will take up these propositions. They will be more wisely informed by an appreciation of cultural difference than by psychological models of a singular self. And they will stand a better chance of meeting the needs of those who do not fit into the mainstream boxes that modern social worlds too narrowly prescribe.

References

Abrams, L., & Trusty, J. (2004). African Americans' racial identity and socially desirable responding: An empirical model. *Journal of Counseling & Development, 82*(3), 365–374.

Adams, J. T. (1931). *The epic of America.* Boston: Little, Brown.

Adler, J. (2005, August 29). In search of the spiritual. *Newsweek* (U.S. ed.), p. 46.

Adorno, T., Aron, B., Levinson, M., & Morrow, W. (1950). *The authoritarian personality: Studies in prejudice.* New York: Norton.

Agronick, G., O'Donnell, L., Stueve, A., Doval, A., Duran, R., & Vargo, S. (2004). Sexual behaviors and risks among bisexually and gay–identified young Latino men. *AIDS and Behavior, 8*(2), 185–197.

Ahmad, S., Waller, G., & Verduyn, C. (1997). Eating attitudes and body satisfaction among Asian and Caucasian adolescents. *Journal of Adolescence, 17*(5), 461–470.

Akan, G. E., & Grilo, C. M. (1995). Sociocultural influences on eating attitudes and behaviors, body image, and psychological functioning: A comparison of African-American, Asian-American, and Caucasian college women. *International Journal of Eating Disorders, 18*(2), 181–187.

Alexander, M. G., & Fisher, T. D. (2003). Truth and consequences: Using the bogus pipeline to examine sex differences in self-reported sexuality. *Journal of Sex Research, 40*(1), 27–35.

Alinsky, S. D. (1969). *Reveille for radicals.* New York: Vintage Books.

Allen, L. (2003). Girls want sex, boys want love: Resisting dominant discourses of (hetero)sexuality. *Sexualities, 6*(2), 215–236.

Almeida, R., Woods, R., Messineo, T., & Font, R. (1998). The cultural context model: An overview. In M. McGoldrick (Ed.), *Revisioning family therapy.* New York: Guilford Press.

Altabe, M. (1998). Ethnicity and body image: Quantitative and qualitative analysis. *International Journal of Eating Disorders, 23*(2), 153–159.

American Psychiatric Association. (1987). *Diagnostic and statistical manual of mental disorders* (3rd ed., revised). Washington, DC: Author.

American Psychiatric Association. (2000). *Diagnostic and statistical manual of mental disorders* (4th ed., text revision). Washington, DC: Author.

American Psychological Association. (2002). *American psychological association guidelines on multicultural education training, research, practice, and organizational change for psychology.* Retrieved from www.apa.org

American Psychological Association. (2007). *Affirmative action: Who benefits?* Retrieved August 13, 2007, from http://www.apa.org/pubinfo/affirmaction.html

American School Counseling Association. (2003). *American School Counselor Association national model: A framework for school counseling programs.* Alexandria, VA: Author.

American School Counseling Association. (2005). *The ASCA national model: A framework for school counseling programs* (2nd ed.). Retrieved January 1, 2007, from http://www.school counselor.org/files/Natl%20Model%20Exec%20Summary_final.pdf

Anderson, B. (2000). *America's salad bowl: An agricultural history of the Salinas Valley.* Monterey, CA: Monterey County Historical Society.

Anderson, H., & Goolishian, H. (1992). The client is the expert: A not-knowing approach to therapy. In S. McNamee & K. J. Gergen (Eds.), *Therapy as social construction* (pp. 25–39). Thousand Oaks, CA: SAGE.

Anderson, S. K., & Middleton, V. A. (2005). *Explorations in privilege, oppression and diversity.* Belmont, CA: Thomson Brooks/Cole.

Anderson, W. (2001). *All connected now: Life in the first global civilization.* Boulder, CO: Westview Press.

Anyon, J. (1980). Social class and the hidden curriculum of work. *Journal of Education, 162*(1), 67–92.

Anyon, J. (2005). Social class and school knowledge. In E. R. Brown & K. J. Saltman (Eds.), *The critical middle school reader* (pp. 409–418). New York: Routledge.

Appiah, K. A. (2005). *The ethics of identity.* Princeton, NJ: Princeton University Press.

Archer, J. (1996). Sex differences in social behavior: Are the social role and evolutionary explanations compatible? *American Psychologist, 51,* 909–917.

Archer, J., & Lloyd, B. (2002). *Sex and gender* (2nd ed.). Cambridge, UK: Cambridge University Press.

Arnold, M. (1865). *Essays in criticism.* New York: Macmillan.

Arnold, M. (1869). *Culture and anarchy: An essay in political criticism.* New York: Macmillan.

Arthur, N. (1998). Counsellor education for diversity: Where do we go from here? *Canadian Journal of Counselling, 32*(1), 88–103.

Arredondo, P., & Arciniega, G. M. (2001). Strategies and techniques for counselor training based on the multicultural counseling competencies. *Journal of Multicultural Counseling and Development, 29*(4), 263–273.

Arredondo, P., Toporek, R., & Brown, S. K. (1996). Operationalization of the multicultural counseling competencies. *Journal of Multicultural Counseling and Development, 24*(1), 42–78.

Arts, L., & Kamalipour, Y. R. (2003). *The globalization of corporate media hegemony.* Albany: State University of New York Press.

Ashcroft, B., & Ahluwalia, P. (2001). *Edward Said.* London: Routledge.

Association for Counselor Education and Supervision. (1993). *Ethical guidelines for counseling supervisors.* Retrieved from http://www.acesonline.net/ethical_guidelines.asp

Association of Multicultural Counseling and Development. (1996). *Standards for multicultural assessment.* Association for Assessment in Counseling. Retrieved from http:// www.aac.ncat.edu/Resources/documents/

Atkinson, D. R., & Hackett, G. (Eds.). (2004). *Counseling diverse populations* (3rd ed.). New York: McGraw-Hill.

Atkinson, D. R., Morten, G., & Sue, D. W. (Eds.). (1989). *Counseling American minorities: A cross-cultural perspective* (3rd ed.). Dubuque, IA: Brown.

Atkinson, D. R., Morten, G., & Sue, D. W. (Eds.). (1993). *Counseling American minorities* (4th ed.). Dubuque, IA: Brown.

Atkinson, D. R., Morten, G., & Sue, D. W. (Eds.). (1998). *Counseling American minorities* (5th ed.). New York: McGraw-Hill.

Austin, J. L. (1962). *How to do things with words* (J. O. Urmson, Ed.). Cambridge, MA: Harvard University Press.

Avis, J. M. (1987). Deepening awareness: A private study guide to feminism and family therapy. *Journal of Psychotherapy and the Family, 3,* 15–46.

Avis, J. M. (1996). Deconstructing gender in family therapy. In F. Piercy, D. Sprenkle, J. Wetchler, & Associates, *Family therapy sourcebook* (2nd ed., pp. 220–255). New York: Guilford Press.

Axelson, J. A. (1994). *Counseling and development in a multicultural society.* Monterey, CA: Thomson Brooks/Cole.

Bakhtin, M. (1986). *Speech genres and other late essays* (C. Emerson & M. Holquist, Eds.; V. W. McGee, Trans.). Austin: University of Texas Press.

Bakhtin, M. M. (1981). *The dialogic imagination* (C. Emerson & M. Holquist, Trans.). Austin: University of Texas Press.

Baldwin, E., Longhurst, B., McCracken, S., Ogborn, M., & Smith, G. (2000). *Introducing cultural studies.* Athens: University of Georgia Press.

Ballou, M., & Gabalac, N. W. (1985). *A feminist position on mental health.* Springfield, IL: Charles C Thomas.

Bancroft, J. (2002). Biological factors in human sexuality. *Journal of Sex Research, 39*(1), 15–21.

Bandura, A. (1971). *Psychological modeling: Conflicting theories.* Chicago: Aldine-Atherton.

Bandura, A. (1977). *Social learning theory.* Englewood Cliffs, NJ: Prentice Hall.

Barnes, P., & Lightsey, O. (2005). Perceived racist discrimination, coping stress, and life satisfaction. *Journal of Multicultural Counseling and Development, 33,* 48–61.

Barrett, M., & Phillips, A. (Eds.). (1992). *Destabilizing theory: Contemporary feminist debates.* London: Polity Press.

Bartky, S. L. (1988). Foucault, femininity, and the modernization of patriarchal power. In I. Diamond & L. Quinby (Eds.), *Feminism and Foucault: Reflections on resistance* (pp. 61–86). Boston: Northeastern University Press.

Baruth, L. G., & Manning, M. L. (2007). *Multicultural counseling and psychotherapy: A lifespan perspective* (4th ed.). Upper Saddle River, NJ: Pearson Merrill Prentice Hall.

Battiste, M. (Ed.). (2000). *Reclaiming indigenous voice and vision.* Vancouver, British Columbia, Canada: UBC Press.

Beals, K., & Peplau, L. (2005). Identity support, identity devaluation, and well-being among lesbians. *Psychology of Women Quarterly, 29,* 140–148.

Bell, C. C., & Mehta, H. (1980). The misdiagnosis of black patients with manic depressive illness. *Journal of the National Medical Association, 72,* 141–145.

Bell, D. A. (2000). After we're gone: Prudent speculations on America in a post-racial epoch. In R. Delgado & J. Stefancic (Eds.), *Critical race theory: The cutting edge* (2nd ed., pp. 2–8), Philadelphia: Temple University Press.

Benedict, R. (1945). *Race and racism.* London: Routledge and Kegan Paul.

Benedict, R. (1959). *Race: Science and politics.* New York: Viking Press.

Benhabib, S. (2002). *The claims of culture: Equality and diversity in the global era.* Princeton, NJ: Princeton University Press.

Benshoff, H. M., & Griffin, S. (2004). *America on film: Representing race, class, gender, and sexuality at the movies.* Malden, MA: Blackwell.

Beren, S. E., Hayden, H. A., Wilfley, D. E., & Striegel-Moore, R. H. (1997). Body dissatisfaction among lesbian college students: The conflict of straddling mainstream and lesbian cultures. *Psychology of Women Quarterly, 21*(3), 431–445.

Berger, J. (1972). *Ways of seeing.* London: Penguin Books.

Bergeron, S. M., & Senn, C. Y. (1998). Body image and sociocultural norms: A comparison of heterosexual and lesbian women. *Psychology of Women Quarterly, 22*(3), 385–401.

Berliner, D. C. (2005). The near impossibility of testing for teacher quality. *Journal of Teacher Education, 56*(3), 205–213.

Berliner, D. C., & Biddle, B. J. (1995). *The manufactured crisis: Myths, fraud, and the attack on America's public schools.* Reading, MA: Addison-Wesley.

Bernard, J. (1969). Functions and limitations in counseling and psychotherapy. In D. Hansen (Ed.), *Explorations in sociology and counseling* (pp. 369–378). Boston: Houghton Mifflin.

Berne, E. (1973). *Games people play.* New York: Ballantine Books.

Bernstein, R. (1983). *Beyond objectivism and relativism: Science, hermeneutics, and praxis.* Philadelphia: University of Pennsylvania Press.

Berry, J. W. (1980). Acculturation as varieties of adaptation. In A. Padilla (Ed.), *Acculturation: Theory, models and some new findings* (pp. 9–25). Boulder, CO: Westview Press.

Berry, J. W. (2001). A psychology of immigration. *Journal of Social Issues, 57*(3), 615–631.

Betancourt, H., & López, S. R. (1995). The study of culture ethnicity and race in American psychology. In N. Goldberger & J. Veroff (Eds.), *Culture and psychology* (pp. 87–107). New York: New York University Press.

Betcher, R. W., & Pollack, W. S. (1993). *In a time of fallen heroes: The re-creation of masculinity.* New York: Atheneum.

Bigby, J. (Ed.). (2003). *Cross-cultural medicine.* Philadelphia: American College of Physicians.

Billinger, M. S. (2007). Another look at ethnicity as a biological concept: Moving anthropology beyond the race concept. *Critique of Anthropology, 27*(5), 5–35.

Birman, D. (1994). Acculturation and human diversity in a multicultural society. In E. Trickett, R. Watts, & D. Birman (Eds.), *Human diversity: Perspectives on people in context* (pp. 261–284). San Francisco: Jossey-Bass.

Bishaw, A., & Stern, S. (2006). *Evaluation of poverty estimates: A comparison of the American Community Survey and the Current Population Survey.* Retrieved July 11, 2007, from https://ask.census.gov

Blanchett, W., Brantlinger, E., & Shealey, M. (2005). *Brown* 50 years later—exclusion, segregation, and inclusion. *Remedial and Special Education, 26*(2), 66–69.

Blazina, C., & Watkins, C. E., Jr. (1996). Masculine gender role conflict: Effects on college men's psychological well-being, chemical substance usage, and attitudes toward help-seeking. *Journal of Counseling Psychology, 43,* 461–465.

Bly, R. (1990). *Iron John: A book about men.* Reading, MA: Addison-Wesley.

Bodenhorn, N. (2005). American School Counselor Association Ethical Code changes relevant to family work. *Family Journal: Counseling and Therapy for Couples and Families, 13*(3), 316–320.

Bordo, S. (1993). *Unbearable weight: Feminism, Western culture, and the body.* Berkeley: University of California Press.

Borradori, G. (2003). *Philosophy in a time of terror: Dialogues with Jürgen Habermas and Jacques Derrida.* Chicago: University of Chicago Press.

Bourdieu, P., & Passeron, J.-C. (1977). *Reproduction in education, society and culture.* London: SAGE.

Bowles, S., & Gintis, H. (1976). *Schooling in capitalist America: Educational reform and the contradiction of economic life.* New York: Basic Books.

Bowles, S., & Gintis, H. (2005). Schooling in capitalist America. In E. R. Brown & K. J. Saltman (Eds.), *The critical middle school reader* (pp. 197–202). New York: Routledge.

Bowling, D., & Hoffman, D. A. (2003). *Bringing peace into the room: How the personal qualities of the mediator impact the process of conflict resolution.* San Francisco: Jossey-Bass.

Brammer, R. (2004). *Diversity in counseling.* Belmont, CA: Thomson Brooks/Cole.

Braun, V., Gavey, N., & McPhillips, K. (2003). The "fair deal"? Unpacking accounts of reciprocity in heterosex. *Sexualities, 6*(2), 237–261.

Brooks, G. R., & Good, G. E. (2001). Introduction. In G. R. Brooks & G. E. Good (Eds.), *The new handbook of psychotherapy and counseling with men* (Vol. 1, pp. 3–21). San Francisco: Jossey-Bass.

Brouwers, M. (1990). Treatment of body image dissatisfaction among women with bulimia nervosa. *Journal of Counseling & Development, 69*(2), 144–147.

Brown, D., & Trusty, J. (2005). School counselors, comprehensive school counseling programs, and academic achievement: Are school counselors promising more than they can deliver? *Professional School Counseling, 9*(1), 1–8.

Brown, L. S. (1995). Lesbian identities: Concepts and issues. In A. D'Augelli & C. Patterson (Eds.), *Lesbian, gay, and bisexual identities over the lifespan* (pp. 3–23). New York: Oxford University Press.

Browning, C., Reynolds, A. L., & Dworkin, S. H. (1998). Affirmative psychotherapy for lesbian women. In D. R. Atkinson & G. Hackett (Eds.), *Counseling diverse populations* (2nd ed., pp. 317–334). Boston: McGraw-Hill.

Bruner, J. (1990). *Acts of meaning.* Cambridge, MA: Harvard University Press.

Bruner, J. (1996). *The culture of education.* Cambridge, MA: Harvard University Press.

Brunner, J. J. (1998). *Globalización cultural y postmodernidad* [Cultural and postmodern globalization]. Santiago, Chile: Fondo de Cultural Economica.

Buber, M. (1978). *Between man and man.* New York: Macmillan.

Burman, E. (1994). *Deconstructing developmental psychology.* London: Routledge.

Burr, V. (1995). *An introduction to social constructionism.* New York: Routledge.

Burr, V. (2003). *Social constructionism* (2nd ed.). London: Psychology Press.

Buss, A. R. (1979). *A dialectical psychology.* New York: Irvington.

Buss, D. M. (1995). Psychological sex differences: Origins through sexual selection. *American Psychologist, 50,* 164–168.

Buss, D. M. (2000). The evolution of happiness. *American Psychologist, 55,* 15–23.

Butler, B., & Petrulis, J. (1999). Some further observations concerning Sir Cyril Burt. *British Journal of Psychology, 90*(1), 155–160.

Butler, J. (1990). *Gender trouble: Feminism and the subversion of identity.* New York: Routledge.

Butler, J. (1992). Contingent foundations: Feminism and the question of postmodernism. In J. Butler & J. W. Scott (Eds.), *Feminists theorise the political* (pp. 3–21). London: Routledge.

Calvert, S. (1994, March). Psychology and a feminist practice: Opponents or complements? *Bulletin of the New Zealand Psychological Society, 80,* 21–23.

Campo-Flores, A., & Fineman, H. (2005, May 30). A Latin power surge. *Newsweek* (U.S. ed.), p. 24.

Camus, A. (1937). *L'envers et l'endroit* [Betwixt and between]. Paris: Gallimard.

Caramel, L., & Laronche, M. (2000). We must fight for cultural diversity. *Le Monde.*

Carlson, K. (2004, January). Test scores by race and ethnicity. *Phi Delta Kappan,* pp. 379–380.

Carter, R. T. (1990). Does race or racial identity attitudes influence the counseling process in black and white dyads? In J. Helms (Ed.), *Black and white racial identity: Theory, research, and practice* (pp. 145–164). Westport, CT: Greenwood Press.

Carter, R. T. (1990b). The relationship between racism and racial identity among white Americans: An exploratory investigation. *Journal of Counseling & Development, 69,* 46–50.

Carter, R. T. (1995). *The influence of race and racial identity in psychotherapy: Toward a racially inclusive model.* New York: Wiley.

Carter, R. T. (Ed.). (2004). *Handbook of racial-cultural psychology and counseling: Training and practice* (Vol. 2). New York: Wiley.

Carter, R. T., Helms, J. E., & Juby, H. L. (2004). The relationship between racism and racial identity for white Americans: A profile analysis. *Journal of Multicultural Counseling and Development, 32*(1), 2–17.

Cash, T. F., & Henry, P. E. (1995). Women's body images: The results of a national survey in the U.S.A. *Sex Roles, 33*(1–2), 19–28.

Cass, V. C. (1979). Homosexual identity formation: A theoretical model. *Journal of Homosexuality, 4*(3), 219–235.

Castellano, M. B. (2002). *Aboriginal family trends: Extended families, nuclear families, families of the heart.* Retrieved July 10, 2007, from http://www.vifamily.ca/library/cft/aboriginal.html

Cavanaugh, C. J., & Lemberg, R. (1999). What we know about eating disorders: Facts and statistics. In R. Lemberg (with L. Cohn; Ed.), *Eating disorders: A reference sourcebook* (pp. 7–12). Phoenix, AZ: Oryx.

Cejka, M. A., & Eagly, A. H. (1999). Gender-stereotypic images of occupations correspond to sex segregation of employment. *Personality and Social Psychology Bulletin, 25,* 413–423.

Challenging disabling practices: Talking about issues of disability. (1997). *Dulwich Centre Newsletter, 4.*

Chan, J. M., & Ma, E. (2002). Transculturating modernity: A reinterpretation of cultural globalization. In J. M. Chan & B. T. McIntyre (Eds.), *In search of boundaries: Communication, nation-states and cultural identities* (pp. 3–18). Westport, CT: Ablex.

Chan, J. M., & McIntyre, B. T. (Eds.). (2002). *In search of boundaries: Communication, nation-states, and cultural identities.* Westport, CT: Ablex.

Chaplin, J. (1988). *Feminist counselling in action.* London: SAGE.

Chasin, R., Herzig, M., Roth, S., Chasin, L., Becker, C., & Stains, R. (1996). From diatribe to dialogue on divisive public issues: Approaches drawn from family therapy. *Mediation Quarterly, 13*(4), 323–344.

Chernin, K. (1981). *The obsession: Reflections on the tyranny of slenderness.* New York: Harper & Row.

Chesler, P. (1972). *Women and madness.* New York: Doubleday.

Chomsky, N. (1966). *Topics in the theory of generative grammar.* The Hague, Netherlands: Mouton.

Chomsky, N. (2003). *Hegemony or survival: America's quest for global dominance.* New York: Henry Holt.

Chouliaraki, L., & Fairclough, N. (1999). Language and power in Bourdieu: On Hasan's "The disempowerment game." *Linguistics and Education, 10*(4), 399–409.

Chubbuck, S. (2004). Whiteness enacted, whiteness disrupted. The complexity of personal congruence. *American Educational Research Journal, 41*(2), 301–333.

Chung, R. (2005). Women, human rights, and counseling: Crossing international boundaries. *Journal of Counseling & Development, 83,* 262–268.

Chung, R., Bemak, F., & Wong, S. (2000). Vietnamese refugees' level of distress, social support, and acculturation: Implications for mental health counseling. *Journal of Mental Health Counseling, 22,* 150–161.

Cleary, L. M., & Peacock, T. D. (1998). *Collected wisdom: American Indian education.* Boston: Allyn & Bacon.

Clifford, J. (1986). Introduction: Partial truths. In J. Clifford & G. E. Marcus (Eds.), *Writing cultures: The poetics and politics of writing ethnography.* Berkeley: University of California Press.

Coe, M. D. (1996). *Mexico: From the Olmecs to the Aztecs.* New York: Thames & Hudson.

Coleman, E. (1982). Developmental stages of the coming out process. *Journal of Homosexuality, 7,* 31–43.

Collins, P. H. (1990). *Black feminist thought: Knowledge, consciousness, and the politics of empowerment.* Boston: Unwin Hyman.

Comas-Diaz, L., & Greene, B. (Eds.). (1994). *Women of color: Integrating ethnic and gender identities in psychotherapy.* New York: Guilford Press.

Comstock, D. (Ed.). (2005). *Diversity and development: Critical contexts that shape our lives and relationships.* Belmont, CA: Thomson Brooks/Cole.

Connell, R. W. (1995). *Masculinities.* Berkeley: University of California Press.

Constantine, M. G., & Sue, D. W. (Eds.). (2005). *Strategies for building multicultural competence in mental health and educational settings.* Hoboken, NJ: Wiley.

Cook, N. D. (1981). *Demographic collapse, Indian Peru, 1520–1620.* New York: Cambridge University Press.

Coontz, S. (2005). *Marriage, a history: From obedience to intimacy, or How love conquered marriage.* New York: Viking Press.

Corey, G. (2008). *Theory and practice of counseling and psychotherapy* (8th ed.). Belmont, CA: Thomson Learning.

Corey, G., Corey, M. S., Callanan, P., & Russell, J. M. (2003). *Group techniques* (3rd ed.). Belmont, CA: Wadsworth.

Cornell, S., & Hartmann, D. (1998). *Ethnicity and race: Making identities in a changing world.* Thousand Oaks, CA: Pine Forge Press.

Cortina, L., & Wasti, A. (2005). Profiles in coping: Response to sexual harassment across persons, organizations, and cultures. *Journal of Applied Psychology, 90*(1), 182–192.

Couldry, N. (2000). *Inside culture: Re-imagining the method of cultural studies.* London: SAGE.

Council for Accreditation of Counseling and Related Education Programs. (2001). Council for Accreditation of Counseling Standards. Alexandria, VA: CACREP. Retrieved from http://www.cacrep.org/2001Standards.html

Cournoyer, R. J., & Mahalik, J. R. (1995). Cross-sectional study of gender role conflict examining college-aged and middle-aged men. *Journal of Counseling Psychology, 42*(1), 11–19.

Courtenay, W. H. (2000). Constructions of masculinity and their influence on men's well-being: A theory of gender and health. *Social Science & Medicine, 50,* 1385–1401.

Crabtree, R. D., & Malhotra, S. (2003). Media hegemony and the commercialization of television in India: Implications to social class and development communication. In L. Artz & Y. R. Kamalipour (Eds.), *The globalization of corporate media hegemony* (pp. 213–228) New York: State University of New York Press.

Crawford, J., Kippax, S., & Waldby, C. (1994). Women's sex talk and men's sex talk: Different worlds. *Feminism & Psychology, 4,* 571–587.

Croninger, R. G., & Lee, V. E. (2001). Social capital and dropping out of high school: Benefits to at-risk students of teachers' support and guidance. *Teachers College Record, 103*(4), 548–581.

Crosby, F., Iyer, A., Clayton, S., & Downing, R. (2003). Affirmative action: Psychological data and the policy debates. *American Psychologist, 58*(2), 93–115.

Crose, R., Nicholas, D. R., Gobble, D. C., & Frank, B. (1992). Gender and wellness: A multidimensional systems model for counselling. *Journal of Counseling & Development, 71,* 149–156.

Cross, W. E. (1971). The Negro to Black conversion experience: Toward a psychology of Black liberation. *Black World, 20*(9), 13–27.

Cross, W. E. (1978). The Thomas and Cross models of psychological nigrescence. *Journal of Black Psychology, 5*(1), 3–19.

Cross, W. E. (1991). *Shades of black: Diversity in African American identity.* Philadelphia: Temple University Press.

Crossley, N. (2003). From reproduction to transformation: Social movement fields and the radical habitus. *Theory, Culture & Society, 20*(6), 43–68.

Croteau, J., Lark, J., Lidderdale, M., & Chung, B. (Eds.). (2005). *Deconstructing heterosexism in the counseling professions: A narrative approach.* Thousand Oaks, CA: SAGE.

Curthoys, A. (1988). What is the socialism in socialist feminism? *Australian Feminist Studies, 6,* 17–24.

Curtin, P. D. (Ed.). (1971). *Imperialism.* New York: Walker.

Cushman, P. (1990). Why the self is empty: Toward a historically situated psychology. *American Psychologist, 45*(5), 599–611.

Cushman, P. (1995). On tapestries and entanglements: A response to commentary on constructing the self, constructing America. *Psychohistory Review, 24*(1), 77–98.

Cushner, K., & Brislin, R. (Eds.). (1994). *Improving intercultural interactions: Modules for cross-cultural training programs (Vol. 2)*. Thousand Oaks, CA: SAGE.

Dana, R. H. (1998). *Understanding cultural identity in intervention and assessment*. Thousand Oaks, CA: SAGE.

D'Andrea, M. (2000). Postmodernism, constructivism, and multiculturalism: Three forces reshaping and expanding our thoughts about counseling. *Journal of Mental Health Counseling, 22*, 1–17.

D'Andrea, M., & Daniels, J. (2001). RESPECTFUL counseling. In D. Pope-Davis & H. Coleman (Eds.), *The intersection of race, class, and gender in multicultural counseling* (pp. 417–466). Thousand Oaks, CA: SAGE.

Daniels, J. (2007). Feminist counseling and therapy. In A. E. Ivey, M. D'Andrea, M. B. Ivey, & L. Simek-Morgan (Eds.), *Theories of counseling and psychotherapy: A multicultural perspective* (6th ed., pp. 321–358). Boston: Allyn & Bacon.

Daniels, J., & D'Andrea, M. (1996). Implications for ameliorating ethnocentrism in counseling. In D. W. Sue, A. E., Ivey, & P. D. Pedersen (Eds.), *A theory of multicultural counseling and therapy* (pp. 157–173). Pacific Grove, CA: Thomson Brooks/Cole.

Daniluk, J. C., Stein, M., & Bockus, D. (1995). The ethics of inclusion: Gender as a critical component of counselor training. *Counselor Education and Supervision, 34*(4), 294–307.

Das, A. K. (1995). Rethinking multicultural counseling: Implications for counselor education. *Journal of Counseling & Development, 74*(1), 45–52.

D'Augelli, A. (1994). Identity development and sexual orientation: Toward a model of lesbian, gay, and bisexual development. In E. Trickett, R. Watts, & D. Birman (Eds.), *Human diversity: Perspectives on people in context* (pp. 312–333). San Francisco: Jossey-Bass.

Davies, B. (1990). The problem of desire. *Social Problems, 37*(4), 501–516.

Davies, B. (1993). *Shards of glass: Children reading and writing beyond gendered identities*. St. Leonards, New South Wales, Australia: Allen & Unwin.

Davies, B., & Harré, R. (1990). Positioning: The discursive production of selves. *Journal for the Theory of Social Behavior, 20*(1), 43–63.

Davies, N. (1995). *The Incas*. Niwot: University Press of Colorado.

Davis, F. J. (1991). *Who is black? One nation's definition*. University Park: Pennsylvania State University Press.

Davis, K. (2006). *A girl like me* [Motion picture]. (Available at http://www.uthtv.com/umedia/show/2052/)

Deadly disparities. (2000, September 17). *New York Times*, p. 18.

Dean, M. (1999). *Governmentality: Power and rule in modern society*. London: SAGE.

De Jong, P., & Berg, I. K. (2002). *Interviewing for solutions* (2nd ed.). Pacific Grove, CA: Thomson Brooks/Cole.

de Lauretis, T. (Ed.). (1986). *Feminist studies, critical studies*. Bloomington: Indiana Universitiy Press.

Deleuze, G., & Guattari, F. (1983). *On the line*. New York: Semiotext(e).

Delgado, R., & Stefancic, J. (Eds.). (2000). *Critical race theory: The cutting edge* (2nd ed.). Philadelphia: Temple University Press.

Delucia-Waack, J. L., & Donigian, J. (2004). *The practice of multicultural group work*. Belmont, CA: Thomson Brooks/Cole.

Denborough, D. (Ed.). (2002). *Queer counseling and narrative practice*. Adelaide, South Australia: Dulwich Centre.

Deng, F. M. (1997). Ethnicity: An African predicament. *Brookings Review, 15*(3), 28–31.

DePoy, E., & Gilson, S. F. (2004). *Rethinking disability: Principles for professional and social change*. Belmont, CA: Thomson Brooks/Cole.

Dericco, J., & Sciarra, D. (2005). The immersion experience in multicultural counselor training: Confronting covert racism. *Journal of Multicultural Counseling and Development, 33,* 2–8.

Derrida, J. (1976). *Of grammatology* (G. C. Spivak, Trans.). Baltimore: Johns Hopkins University Press.

Derrida, J. (1978). *Writing and difference.* Chicago: University of Chicago Press.

Derrida, J. (1994, Autumn). The deconstruction of actuality: An interview with Jacques Derrida. *Radical Philosophy, 68,* pp. 28–41.

Derrida, J., & Roudinesco, E. (2004). *For what tomorrow: A dialogue* (J. Fort, Trans.). Stanford, CA: Stanford University Press.

Dial M for Mujahideen. (2006, May 18). *Economist,* p. 45.

Diamond, I., & Quinby, L. (Eds.). (1988). *Feminism and Foucault: Reflections on resistance.* Boston: Northeastern University Press.

Diamond, J. (1999). *Guns, germs and steel: The fates of human societies.* New York: Norton.

Dienhart, A. (2001). Engaging men in family therapy: Does the gender of the therapist make a difference? *Journal of Family Therapy, 23,* 21–45.

Diller, J. V. (2004). *Cultural diversity: A primer for the human services* (2nd ed.). Belmont, CA: Thomson Brooks/Cole.

Diller, J. V. (2007). *Cultural diversity: A primer for the human services* (3rd ed.). Belmont, CA: Thomson Brooks/Cole.

Dillon, S. (2006, November 20). Schools slow in closing the gaps between races. *New York Times* (late ed., East Coast), p. A1.

Dominguez, V. R. (1986). *White by definition: Social classification in Creole Louisiana.* New Brunswick, NJ: Rutgers University Press.

Dovidio, J., & Esses, V. (2001). Immigrants and immigration: Advancing the psychological perspective. *Journal of Social Issues, 57*(3), 375–387.

Downing, N. E., & Roush, K. L. (1985). From passive acceptance to active commitment: A model of feminist identity development for women. *Counseling Psychologist, 13*(4), 695–709.

Drewery, W. (1986). The challenge of feminism and the practice of counselling. *New Zealand Counselling and Guidance Association Journal, 8*(1), 18–28.

Drewery, W. (2005). Why we should watch what we say: Position calls, everyday speech and the production of relational subjectivity. *Theory & Psychology, 15*(3), 305–324.

Drewery, W., & Monk, G. (1994). Some reflections on the therapeutic power of post-structuralism. *International Journal for the Advancement of Counselling, 17*(4), 303–313.

Drewery, W., Winslade, J., & Monk, G. (2000). Resisting the dominating story: Toward a deeper understanding of narrative therapy. In R. Neimeyer & J. Raskin (Eds.), *Constructions of disorder: Meaning-making frameworks for psychotherapy* (pp. 243–264). Washington, DC: American Psychological Association.

Dumas, J. E., Rollock, D., Prinz, R. J., Hops, H., & Blechman, E. A. (1999). Cultural sensitivity: Problems and solutions in applied and preventive intervention. *Applied & Preventive Psychology, 8*(3), 175–196.

Duran, E. (2006). *Healing the soul wound: Counseling with American Indians and other native peoples.* New York: Teachers College Press.

Duran, E., & Duran, B. (1995). *Native American post colonial psychology.* Albany: State University of New York.

Durie, M. H. (1989). A move that's well overdue: Shaping counselling to meet the needs of Maori people. *New Zealand Counselling and Guidance Association Journal, 11*(1), 13–23.

Durning, A. T. (1992). *How much is enough? The consumer society and the future of the earth.* New York: Norton.

Dworkin, S. (1984). Traditionally defined client, meet feminist therapist: Feminist therapy as attitude change. *Personnel and Guidance Journal, 62,* 301–305.

Eagly, A. H., & Wood, W. (1999). The origins of sex differences in human behavior: Evolved dispositions versus social roles. *American Psychologist, 54,* 408–423.

Ehrenreich, B., & English, D. (1979). *For her own good: 50 years of the experts' advice to women.* New York: Doubleday.

Eko, L. (2003). Globalization and the mass media in Africa. In L. Artz & Y. R. Kamalipour (Eds.), *The globalization of corporate media hegemony.* Albany: State University of New York Press.

Eliot, T. S. (1949). *Notes towards the definition of culture.* New York: Harcourt, Brace.

Ellis, A. (1961). *A guide to rational living.* Englewood Cliffs, NJ: Prentice Hall.

Ellis, A. (1985). *The case against religion: A psychotherapist's view and the case against religiosity.* Austin, TX: American Atheist Press.

Emmons, L. (1992). Dieting and purging behavior in black and white high school students. *Journal of the American Dietetic Association, 92*(3), 306–312.

Enns, C. Z. (1993). Twenty years of feminist counseling and therapy: From naming biases to implementing multifaceted practice. *Counseling Psychologist, 21*(1), 3–87.

Erikson, E. H. (1950). *Childhood and society.* New York: Norton.

Erikson, E. H. (1968). *Identity: Youth and crisis.* New York: Norton.

Entwhistle, H. (2000). Educating multicultural citizens: Melting pot or mosaic. *International Journal of Social Education, 14*(2), 1–15.

Escoffier, J. (1991). The limits of multiculturalism. *Socialist Review, 21*(3–4), 61–73.

Evans, K., Kincade, E., Marbley, A., & Seem, S. (2005). Feminism and feminist therapy: Lessons from the past and for the future. *Journal of Counseling & Development, 83,* 269–277.

Fadiman, A. (1998). *The spirit catches you and you fall down: A Hmong child, her American doctors, and the collision of two cultures.* New York: Noonday Press.

Fairclough, N. (1992). *Discourse and social change.* Cambridge, UK: Polity Press.

Falco, K. L. (1991). *Psychotherapy with lesbian clients: Theory into practice.* New York: Brunner/Mazel.

Falicov, C. J. (1998). *Latino families in therapy.* New York: Guilford Press.

Fall, K., Levitov, J., Anderson, L., & Clay, H. (2005). African-Americans' perceptions of mental health professions. *International Journal of the Advancement of Counseling, 27*(1), 47–56.

Faludi, S. (1999). *Stiffed: The betrayal of American men.* New York: Morrow.

Fanon, F. (1963). *The wretched of the earth.* New York: Grove Press.

Fassinger, R. (1998). Lesbian, gay and bisexual identity and student development theory. In R. Sanlo (Ed.), *Working with lesbian, gay and transgender college students: A handbook for faculty and administrators* (pp. 13–22). Westport, CT: Greenwood Press.

Fay, B. (1987). *Critical social science: Liberation and its limits.* Cambridge, UK: Polity Press.

Feingold, A., & Mazzella, R. (1998). Gender differences in body image are increasing. *Psychological Science, 9*(3), 190–195.

Ferdman, B. M., & Gallegos, P. I. (2001). Latinos and racial identity development. In C. L. Wijeyesinghe & B. W. Jackson III (Eds.), *New perspectives on racial identity development: A theoretical and practical anthology* (pp. 32–66). New York: New York University Press.

Ferree, M. M., Lorber, J., & Hess, B. B. (Eds.). (1999). *Revisioning gender.* Thousand Oaks: SAGE.

Fier, E., & Ramsey, M. (2005). Ethical challenges in the teaching of multicultural course work. *Journal of Multicultural Counseling and Development, 33,* 94–107.

Fingerhut, A., Peplau, L., & Ghavami, N. (2005). A dual framework for understanding lesbian experience. *Psychology of Women Quarterly, 29,* 129–139.

Fischer, A. R., & Good, G. E. (1997). Masculine gender roles, recognition of emotions, and interpersonal intimacy. *Psychotherapy, 34,* 160–170.

Fisher, P., & Maloney, T. (1994). Beliefs, assumptions and practices of two feminist therapists. *Bulletin of the New Zealand Psychological Society, 80,* 17–20.

Flax, J. (1990). Postmodernism and gender relations in feminist theory. In L. J. Nicholson (Ed.), *Feminism/postmodernism* (pp. 39–62). New York: Routledge.

Flax, J. (1992). The end of innocence. In J. Butler & J. W. Scott (Eds.), *Feminists theorise the political* (pp. 445–463). London: Routledge.

Fletcher, J. (2001, March). When a million isn't enough. *Wall Street Journal,* pp. W1, W14.

Flores, R., Tschann, J., Marin, B., & Pantoja, P. (2004). Marital conflict and acculturation among Mexican American husbands and wives. *Cultural Diversity and Ethnic Minority Psychology, 10*(1), 39–52.

Fordham, S., & Ogbu, J. U. (1986). Black students' school success: Coping with the "burden of acting white." *Urban Review, 13*(3), 17–206.

Foster, G. A. (2005). *Social mobility in film and popular culture.* Carbondale: Southern Illinois University Press.

Foucault, M. (1969). *The archaeology of knowledge* (A. M. S. Smith, Trans.) London: Tavistock.

Foucault, M. (1972). *The order of things: An archaeology of the human sciences* (A. M. S. Smith, Trans.). New York: Pantheon. (Original work published 1966)

Foucault, M. (1978). *The history of sexuality: An introduction* (Vol. 1; R. Hurley, Trans.). New York: Vintage Books.

Foucault, M. (1980). *Power/knowledge: Selected interviews and other writings.* New York: Pantheon Books.

Foucault, M. (1983). *This is not a pipe* (J. Harkness, Trans.). Berkeley: University of California Press. (Original work published 1973)

Foucault, M. (2000). *Power: Essential works of Foucault, 1954–1984* (Vol. 3; J. Faubion, Ed.; R. Hurley, Trans.). New York: New Press.

Foucault, M. (2005). *The hermeneutics of the subject: Lectures at the College de France* (F. Gros, F. Ewald, & A. Fontana, Eds.; G. Burchell, Trans.). New York: Palgrave Macmillan.

Fowers, B. J., & Davidov, B. J. (2006). The virtue of multiculturalism: Personal transformation, character, and openness to the other. *American Psychologist, 61*(6), 581–594.

Fox, R. C. (1995). Bisexual identities. In A. R. D'Augelli & C. J. Patterson, *Lesbian, gay, and bisexual identities over the lifespan: Psychological perspectives* (pp. 48–86). New York: Oxford University Press.

Fraga, D., Atkinson, D., & Wampold, B. (2004). Ethnic group preferences for multicultural counseling competencies. *Cultural Diversity and Ethnic Minority Psychology, 10*(1), 53–65.

Frankenberg, R. (1993). *White women, race matters: The social construction of whiteness.* Minneapolis: University of Minnesota Press.

Freiberg, P., & Sleek, S. (1999). New techniques help men uncover their hidden emotions. *Monitor on Psychology, 30,* 28.

Freire, P. (1976). *Pedagogy of the oppressed.* Harmondsworth, UK: Penguin Books.

Freud, S. (1938). *The basic writings of Sigmund Freud* (A. Brill, Ed. & Trans.) New York: Modern Library.

Friedman, T. L. (2005). *The world is flat: A brief history of the twenty-first century.* New York: Farrar, Straus and Giroux.

Fuertas, J. (2004). Supervision in bilingual counseling: Service delivery, training, and research considerations. *Journal of Multicultural Counseling and Development, 32*(2), 84–94.

Fuertes, J. N., Mueller, L. N., Chauhan, R. V., Walker, J. A., & Ladany, N. (2002). An investigation of European American therapists' approach to counseling African American clients. *Counseling Psychologist, 30,* 763–788.

Fukuyama, M. A., & Sevig, T. D. (1999). *Integrating spirituality into multicultural counseling.* Thousand Oaks, CA: SAGE.

Fuss, D. (1989). *Essentially speaking: Feminism, nature and difference.* London: Routledge.

Garbarino, J., & Bedard, C. (2001). *Parents under siege.* New York: Free Press.

Garner, D. M., Garfinkel, P. E., & Schwartz, D. (1980). Cultural expectations of thinness in women. *Psychological Reports, 47*(2), 483–491.

Garrett, M., & Barrett, B. (2003). Two spirit: Counseling Native American gay, lesbian, and bisexual people. *Journal of Multicultural Counseling and Development, 31,* 131–142.

Gavey, N. (1996). Women's desire and sexual violence discourse. In S. Wilkinson (Ed.), *Feminist social psychologies: International perspectives* (pp. 51–65). Philadelphia: Open University Press.

Gavey, N., & McPhillips, K. (1999). Subject to romance: Heterosexual passivity as an obstacle to women initiating condom use. *Psychology of Women Quarterly, 23,* 349–367.

Geertz, C. (1983). *Local knowledge: Further essays in interpretive anthropology.* New York: Basic Books.

Geertz, C. (1995). *After the fact.* Cambridge, MA: Harvard University Press.

Geertz, C. (2000). *The interpretation of cultures.* New York: Basic Books.

Gelso, C., & Fretz, B. (2001). *Counseling psychology* (2nd ed.). Fort Worth, TX: Harcourt.

Gergen, K. (1991). *The saturated self: Dilemmas of identity in contemporary life.* New York: Basic Books.

Gergen, K. J. (1994). *Reality and relationships: Soundings in social construction.* Cambridge, MA: Harvard University Press.

Gergen, K. J. (1999). *An invitation to social construction.* London: SAGE.

Gergen, K. J., & Davis, K. (Eds.). (1985). *The social construction of the person.* New York: Springer.

Gibson, M., Ladd, A., Davey, B., & McEveety, S. (Producers), Gibson, M. (Director), & Wallace, R. (Writer). (1995). *Braveheart* [Motion picture]. United States: Paramount Pictures.

Gilbert, L. A. (1980). Feminist therapy. In N. A. Brodsky & R. T. Hare-Mustin (Eds.), *Women in psychotherapy* (pp. 245–265). New York: Guilford Press.

Gilden, J. (2005). As the number of fliers soars, expansion efforts are underway. Retrieved July 10, 2007, from http://www.latimes.com/news/local/valley/la-tr-airports23jan23,1, 29058.story

Giroux, H. A. (2002). *Breaking into the movies: Film and the culture of politics.* Malden: MA: Blackwell.

Glazer, N., & Moynihan, D. P. (1970). *Beyond the melting pot* (2nd ed.). Cambridge: MIT Press.

Goh, M. (2005). Cultural competence and master therapists: An inextricable relationship. *Journal of Mental Health Counseling, 27,* 71–82.

Goldberg, D. T. (1993). *Racist culture: Philosophy and the politics of meaning.* Cambridge, MA: Blackwell.

Goldner, V. (1985). Feminism and family therapy. *Family Process, 24,* 31–47.

Goldstein, J. R. (1999). Kinship networks that cross racial lines: The exception or the rule? *Demography, 36*(3), 399–407.

Gonsiorek, J. C., & Rudolph, J. R. (1991). Homosexual identity: Coming out and other developmental events. In J. C. Gonsiorek & J. D. Weinrich (Eds.), *Homosexuality: Research implications for public policy* (pp. 161–176). Newbury Park, CA: SAGE.

Gonzalez, G. M. (1997). The emergence of Chicanos in the twenty-first century: Implications for counseling, research, and policy. *Journal of Multicultural Counseling and Development, 25,* 94–106.

Good, G. E., Dell, D. M., & Mintz, L. B. (1989). Male role and gender role conflict: Relations to help seeking in men. *Journal of Counseling Psychology, 36,* 295–300.

Good, G. E., Gilbert, L. A., & Scher, M. (1990). Gender aware therapy: A synthesis of feminist therapy and knowledge about gender. *Journal of Counseling & Development, 68,* 376–380.

Good, G. E., & Sherrod, N. B. (2001). Men's problems and effective treatments: Theory and empirical support. In G. R. Brooks & G. E. Good (Eds.), *The new handbook of psychotherapy and counseling with men* (Vol. 1, pp. 22–40). San Francisco: Jossey-Bass.

Good, G. E., & Wood, P. K. (1995). Male gender role conflict, depression, and help seeking: Do college men face double jeopardy? *Journal of Counseling & Development, 74,* 70–75.

Goodman, N. (1978). *Ways of worldmaking.* Indianapolis, IN: Hackett.

Goodwin, G. C. (1977). *Cherokees in transition: A study of changing culture and environment prior to 1775.* Chicago: University of Chicago, Department of Geography.

Gore, J. (1992). What we can do for you! What can "we" do for "you"? Struggling over empowerment in critical and feminist pedagogy. In C. Luke & J. Gore (Eds.), *Feminisms and critical pedagogy* (pp. 54–73). New York: Routledge.

Gorospe, J. (2007, March). *Deadly silent: Filipino American adolescents and emotional disturbance.* Paper presented at the annual conference of the National Association of School Psychologists, New York.

Gossett, T. F. (1963). *The history of an idea in America.* Dallas, TX: Southern Methodist University Press.

Gramsci, A. (1971). *Selections from the prison notebooks.* New York: International.

Granello, D. H., & Beamish, P. M. (1998). Reconceptualizing codependency in women: A sense of connectedness, not pathology. *Journal of Mental Health Counseling, 20*(4), 344–358.

Grant, M. (1921). *The passing of the great race.* New York: Scribner.

Gray, J. (1992). *Men are from Mars, women are from Venus.* New York: HarperCollins.

Green, R. (1998). Race and the field of family therapy. In M. McGoldrick (Ed.), *Re-visioning family therapy: Race, culture, and gender in clinical practice* (pp. 93–110). New York: Guilford Press.

Green, R. G., Kiernan-Stern, M., Bailey, K., Chambers, K., Claridge, R., Jones, G., et al. (2005). The multicultural counseling inventory: A measure for evaluating social work student and practitioner self-perceptions of their multicultural competencies. *Journal of Social Work Education, 41,* 191–208.

Green, T. (2005). *Multicultural counseling lecture series.* Unpublished PowerPoint presentation, Department of Counseling and School Psychology, San Diego State University, San Diego, CA.

Greenspan, M. (1983). *A new approach to women and therapy.* New York: McGraw-Hill.

Gremillion, H. (2003). *Feeding anorexia.* Durham, NC: Duke University Press.

Grimshaw, J. (1986). *Philosophy and feminist thinking.* Minneapolis: University of Minnesota Press.

Grossberg, L., Nelson, C., & Treichler, P. (1992). *Cultural studies.* New York: Routledge.

Guadalupe, K. L., & Lum, D. (2005). *Multidimensional contextual practice: Diversity and transcendence.* Belmont, CA: Thomson Brooks/Cole.

Guay, A. T. (2001). Advances in the management of androgen deficiency in women. *Medical Aspects of Human Sexuality, 1,* 32–38.

Guilfoyle, M. (2005). From therapeutic power to resistance? Therapy and cultural hegemony. *Theory & Psychology, 15*(1), 101–124.

Gunew, S. (1993). Feminism and the politics of irreducible differences: Multiculturalism/ ethnicity/race. In S. Gunew & A. Yeatman (Eds.), *Feminism and the politics of difference* (pp. 1–19). St. Leonards, New South Wales, Australia: Allen & Unwin.

Gurian, M. (1999). *A fine young man: What parents and educators can do to shape adolescent boys into exceptional men.* New York: Tarcher.

Gysbers, N. C. (2001). Guidance and counseling in the 21st century: Remember the past into the future. *Professional School Counseling, 5*(2), 96–105.

Hacker, A. (1995, November 19). The rich: Who they are. *New York Times Magazine,* pp. 70–71.

Hacking, I. (1999). *The social construction of what?* Cambridge, MA: Harvard University Press.

Hagan, W. T. (1993). *American Indians* (3rd ed.). Chicago: University of Chicago Press.

Haley, A. (1976). *Roots: The saga of an American family.* New York: Doubleday.

Hall, S. (2000). Foreword. In D. A. Yon, *Elusive culture: Schooling, race & identity in global times* (pp. ix–xii). Albany: State University of New York Press.

Hall, S. (2005). From representation: Cultural representations and signifying practices. In E. R. Brown & K. J. Saltman (Eds.), *The critical middle school reader* (pp. 409–418). New York: Routledge.

Ham, M. D. (1993). Empathy. In J. L. Ching, J. H. Liem, M. D. Ham, & G. K. Hong (Eds.), *Transference and empathy in Asian-American psychotherapy: Cultural values and treatment needs* (pp. 35–62). Westport, CT: Praeger.

Hammond, A. (2005). *Pop culture Arab world! Media, arts, and lifestyle.* Santa Barbara, CA: ABC-CLIO.

Hammoud-Beckett, S. (2007). Azima ila Hayati—an invitation in to my life: Narrative conversations about sexual identity. *International Journal of Narrative Therapy and Community Work, 2007*(1), 29–39.

Haraway, D. (1990). A manifesto in cyborgs: Science, technology and socialist feminism in the 1980s. In L. Nicholson (Ed.), *Feminism/postmodernism* (pp. 190–233). London: Routledge.

Hare-Mustin, R. T. (1987). The problem of gender in family therapy theory. *Family Process, 26,* 15–27.

Hare-Mustin, R. T. (1994). Discourses in the mirrored room: A postmodern analysis of therapy. *Family Process, 33,* 19–34.

Hare-Mustin, R. T., & Marecek, J. (1994a). Asking the right questions: Feminist psychology and sex differences. *Feminism & Psychology, 4,* 531–537.

Hare-Mustin, R. T., & Marecek, J. (1994). Feminism & postmodernism: Dilemmas and points of resistance. *Dulwich Centre Newsletter, 4,* 13–19.

Harkless, L., & Fowers, B. (2005). Similarities and differences in relational boundaries among heterosexuals, gay men, and lesbians. *Psychology of Women Quarterly, 29,* 167–176.

Harley, D. A., Jolivette, K., McCormick, K., & Tice, K. (2002). Race, class and gender: A constellation of positionalities with implications for counseling. *Journal of Multicultural Counseling and Development, 30*(4), 216–238.

Harper, F. D., & McFadden, J. (2003). *Culture and counseling: New approaches.* Boston: Pearson Education.

Harper, G., Jernewall, N., & Zea, M. (2004). Giving voice to emerging science and theory for lesbian, gay, and bisexual people of color. *Cultural Diversity and Ethnic Minority Psychology, 10*(3), 187–199.

Hart, P. J., & Jacobi, M. (1992). *From gatekeeper to advocate: Transforming the role of the school counselor.* New York: College Entrance Examination Board.

Hartigan, J., Jr. (1997). Name calling: Objectifying "poor whites" and "white trash" in Detroit. In M. Wray & A. Newitz (Eds.), *White trash: Race and class in America* (pp. 41–56). New York: Routledge.

Harvey, D. (1989). *The condition of postmodernity.* Oxford, UK: Blackwell.

Hatch, T. (2006). Today's school counselor. *School Counselor, 44*(2), 28–34.

Hatch, T., & Bowers, J. (2002). A block to build on. *ASCA School Counselor, 39*(5), 12–17.

Hatch, T., Holland, L., & Meyers, P. (2004). When it's time to change. *School Counselor, 41*(3), 18–23.

Hawton, K. (2005). Introduction and overview. In K. Hawton (Ed.), *Prevention and treatment of suicidal behavior: From science to practice* (pp. 1–10). Oxford, UK: Oxford University Press.

Hays, D. G., & Chang, C. Y. (2003). White privilege, oppression, and racial identity development: Implications for supervision. *Counselor Education and Supervision, 43*(2), 134–145.

Hays, D. G., Chang, C. Y., & Dean, J. K. (2004). White counselors' conceptualization of privilege and oppression: Implications for counselor training. *Counselor Education and Supervision, 43,* 242–257.

Hechter, M. (1975). *Internal colonialism: The Celtic fringe in British national development, 1536–1966.* London: Routledge and Kegan Paul.

Heder, D. (Ed.). (2004). *Class and news.* Lanham, MD: Rowman & Littlefield.

Heesacker, M., & Prichard, S. (1992). In a different voice, revisited: Men, women, and emotion. *Journal of Mental Health Counseling, 14,* 274–290.

Heesacker, M., Wester, S. R., Vogel, D. L., Wentzel, J. T., Mejia-Millan, C. M., & Goodholm, C. R., Jr. (1999). Gender-based emotional stereotyping. *Journal of Counseling Psychology, 46*(4), 483–495.

Heffernan, K. (1996). Eating disorders and weight concern among lesbians. *International Journal of Eating Disorders, 19*(2), 127–138.

Heinberg, L. J. (1996). Theories of body image disturbance: Perceptual, developmental, and sociocultural factors. In J. K. Thompson (Ed.), *Body image, eating disorders, and obesity: An integrative guide for assessment and treatment* (pp. 27–47). Washington, DC: American Psychological Association..

Helfland, J., & Lippin, L. (2001). *Understanding whiteness/unraveling racism: Tools for the journey.* Cincinnati, OH: Thomson Learning Custom Publishing.

Helms, J. E. (1990a). *Black and white racial identity: Theory, research and practice.* Westport, CT: Greenwood Press.

Helms, J. E. (1990b, August). Black and white racial theory and professional inter-racial collaboration. In J. G. Ponterotto (Chair), *The white-American researcher in multi-cultural counseling: Significance and challenges.* Symposium conducted at the 98th annual convention of the American Psychological Association, Boston.

Helms, J. E. (1994). The conceptualization of racial identity and other "racial" constructs. In E. Trickett, R. Watts, & D. Birman (Eds.), *Human diversity: Perspectives on people in context* (pp. 261–284). San Francisco: Jossey-Bass.

Helms, J. E., & Cook, D. A. (1999). *Using race and culture in counseling and psychotherapy: Theory and process.* Boston: Allyn & Bacon.

Hemming, J. (1970). *The conquest of the Incas* (1st American ed.). New York: Harcourt, Brace, Jovanovich.

Henriques, J., Hollway, W., Urwin, C., Venn, C., & Walkerdine, V. (1984). *Changing the subject: Psychology, social regulation, and subjectivity.* London: Methuen.

Henry, W. A., III. (1994). *In defense of elitism.* New York: Doubleday.

Henze, R., Lucas, T., & Scott, B. (1998). Dancing with the monster: Teachers discuss racism, power, and white privilege. *Urban Review, 30*(3), 187–210.

Hernandez, P., Almedia, R., & Dolan–Del Vecchio, K. (2005). Critical consciousness, accountability, and empowerment: Key processes for helping families heal. *Family Process, 44*(1), 105–119.

Herzog, D. B., Newman, K. L., Yeh, C. J., & Warshaw, M. (1992). Body image satisfaction in homosexual and heterosexual women. *International Journal of Eating Disorders, 11*(4), 391–396.

Hesse-Biber, S., Clayton-Matthews, A., & Downey, J. A. (1987). The differential importance of weight and body image among college men and women. *Genetic, Social, and General Psychology Monographs, 113*(4), 509–528.

Hickson, J., & Kriegler, S. (1996). *Multicultural counseling in a divided and traumatized society: The meaning of childhood and adolescence in South Africa.* Westport: Greenwood Press.

Hindmarsh, J. H. (1987). Letting gender secrets out of the bag. *Australia and New Zealand Journal of Family Therapy, 8*(4), 205–211.

Hindmarsh, J. H. (1993). Alternative family therapy discourses: It is time to reflect (critically). *Journal of Feminist Family Therapy, 5*(2), 5–28.

Hitler, A. (1923). *Mein kampf* [My struggle]. Munchen, Germany: Zentralverlag der NSDAP.

Hochschild, A. R. (1997). *The time bind: When work becomes home and home becomes work.* New York: Metropolitan Books.

Hoffman, R. (2004). Conceptualizing heterosexual identity development: Issues and challenges. *Journal of Counseling & Development, 82*(3), 375–380.

Hogan, M. (2007). *The four skills of cultural diversity competence: A process for understanding and practice* (3rd ed.). Belmont, CA: Thomson Brooks/Cole.

Hollinger, D. (1995). *Postethnic America: Beyond multiculturalism.* New York: Basic Books.

Holt, D. B. (1997). Poststructuralist lifestyle analysis: Conceptualizing the social patterning of consumption in postmodernity. *Journal of Consumer Research, 23*(4), 326–350.

Hong, G. K., & Ham, M. D. C. (2001). *Psychotherapy and counseling with Asian American clients.* Thousand Oaks, CA: SAGE.

hooks, b. (1991). *Yearning: Race, gender and cultural politics.* London: Turnaround.

hooks, b. (1995). *Killing race: Ending racism.* New York: Henry Holt.

hooks, b. (2000). *Where we stand: Class matters.* New York: Routledge.

Hornblower, M. (1997, June 9). Great expectations. *Time International,* pp. 54–62.

Horsman, R. (1981). *Race and manifest destiny: The origins of American racial Anglo-Saxonism.* Cambridge, MA: Harvard University Press.

Hoshmand, L. T. (Ed.). (2005). *Culture, psychotherapy, and counseling: Critical and integrative perspectives.* Thousand Oaks: SAGE.

Hoshmand, L. T., & Polkinghorne, D. E. (1992). Redefining the science-practice relationship in professional training. *American Psychologist, 47*(1), 55–66.

Howard, J. A., & Hollander, J. (1997). *Gendered situations, gendered selves: A gender lens on social psychology.* Thousand Oaks: SAGE.

Hsu, C. (2007, January 4). Many still left behind: Student scores rise yet test gaps persist. *San Bernardino,* p. 1.

Huntington, S. P. (2004). *Who are we? The challenges to America's national identity.* New York: Simon & Schuster.

Hwang, W., Chun, C., Takeuchi, D., Myers, H., & Siddarth, P. (2005). Age of the first onset of major depression in Chinese Americans. *Cultural Diversity and Ethnic Minority Psychology, 11*(1), 16–27.

Ibrahim, F. A. (1991). Contribution of cultural world view to generic counseling and development. *Journal of Counseling & Development, 70*(1), 13–19.

Iceland, J. (2004). Beyond black and white metropolitan residential segregation in multi-ethnic America. *Social Science Research, 33,* 248–271.

Inclan, J., & Ferran, E. (1990). Poverty, politics, and family therapy: A role for systems theory. In M. Mirkin (Ed.), *The social and political contexts of family therapy.* Boston: Allyn & Bacon.

Inequality and the American dream. (2006, June 15). *Economist,* p. 28.

Israel, T., & Selvidge, M. (2003). Contributions of multicultural counseling to counselor competence with lesbian, gay, and bisexual clients. *Journal of Multicultural Counseling and Development, 31,* 84–98.

Ivey, A. E. (1986). *Developmental therapy: Theory into practice.* San Francisco: Jossey-Bass.

Ivey, A. E. (1993). On the need for reconstruction of our present practice of counseling and psychotherapy. *Counseling Psychologist, 21*(2), 225–228.

Ivey, A. E., D'Andrea, M., Ivey, M. B., & Simek-Morgan, L. (2006). *Theories of counseling and psychotherapy: A multicultural perspective* (6th ed.). Boston: Allyn & Bacon.

Ivey, A. E., Ivey, M. B., & Simek-Morgan, L. (1993). *Counseling and psychotherapy: A multicultural perspective* (3rd ed.). Boston: Allyn & Bacon.

Iyer, A., Leach, C., & Crosby, F. (2003). White guilt and racial compensation: The benefits and limits of self-focus. *Personality and Social Psychology Bulletin, 29*(1), 117–129.

Jackson, P. W. (1968). *Life in classrooms.* New York: Holt, Rinehart & Winston.

Jackson, R. L. (1999). White space, white privilege: Mapping discursive inquiry onto the self. *Quarterly Journal of Speech, 85*(1), 38–54.

James, W. (1981). *The principles of psychology,* Cambridge, MA: Harvard University Press. (Originally published 1890)

Jeffries, J. P. (1869). *The natural history of the human races.* New York: Edward O. Jenkins.

Jencks, C. (1992). *The postmodern reader.* London: Academy Editors.

Jenkins, A. (1990). *Invitations to responsibility.* Adelaide, South Australia: Dulwich Centre.

Jenkins, A. H. (2001). Humanistic psychology and multiculturalism: A review and reflection. In K. J. Schneider, J. F. T. Bugental, & J. F. Pierson (Eds.), *The handbook of humanistic psychology: Leading edges in theory, research, and practice* (pp. 37–45). Thousand Oaks, CA: SAGE.

Jenkins, R. (2003). Rethinking ethnicity: Identity categorization and power. In J. Stone & R. Dennis (Eds.), *Race and ethnicity: Comparative and theoretical approaches* (pp. 59–71). Oxford, UK: Blackwell.

Jensen, R. (2004). Homecoming: The relevance of radical feminism for gay men. *Journal of Homosexuality, 47*(3–4), 75–81.

Jhally, S. (1998). *Advertising and the end of the world* [Video documentary]. Northampton, MA: Media Education Foundation.

Johnson, A. G. (2005). *The gender knot: Unraveling our patriarchal legacy* (Rev. ed.). Philadelphia: Temple University Press.

Johnson, G., Gershon, S., & Hekimian, L. J. (1968). Controlled evaluation of lithium and chlorpromazine in the treatment of manic states: An interim report. *Comprehensive Psychiatry, 9*(6), 563–573.

Johnson, N. G. (2001). Women helping men: Strengths of and barriers to women working with men clients. In G. R. Brooks & G. E. Good (Eds.), *The new handbook of psychotherapy and counseling with men* (Vol. 1, pp. 696–718). San Francisco: Jossey-Bass.

Jolliff, D. L., & Horne, A. M. (1996). Group counseling for middle-class men. In M. P. Andronico (Ed.), *Men in groups* (pp. 51–68). Washington, DC: American Psychological Association.

Jones, A., & Guy, C. (1992). Radical feminism in New Zealand: From Piha to Newtown. In R. Duplessis, P. Bunkle, K. Irwin, A. Laurie, & S. Middleton (Eds.), *Feminist voices: Women's studies texts for Aotearoa/New Zealand* (pp. 300–316). Auckland, New Zealand: Oxford University Press.

Jones, A., & Seagull, A. A. (1977). Dimensions of the relationship between the black client and the white therapist. *American Psychologist, 32*(10), 850–855.

Jones, C. P. (2000). Levels of racism: The theoretical framework and a gardener's tale. *American Journal of Public health, 90*(8), 1212–1215.

Jones, E. E. (1985). Psychotherapy and counseling with black clients. In P. Pedersen (Ed.), *Handbook for cross-cultural counseling and therapy* (pp. 173–179). Westport, CT: Greenwood Press.

Jones, S. R., & McEwen, M. K. (2000). A conceptual model of multiple dimensions of identity. *Journal of College Student Development, 41*(4), 405–414.

Julia, M. (Ed.). (2000). *Constructing gender: Multicultural perspectives in working with women.* Belmont, CA: Thomson Brooks/Cole.

Jung, C. (1983). *Jung: Selected writings* (A. Storr, Ed.). London: Fontana.

Kahn, A. S., & Yoder, J. D. (1989). The psychology of women and conservatism. *Psychology of Women Quarterly, 13*, 417–432.

Khan, J. A., & Khan, P. (2003). *Advancement of women: A Bahá'í perspective.* Wilmette, IL: Bahá'í Publishing Trust

Kamalipour, Y. R., & Rampal, K. R. (Eds.). (2001). *Media, sex, violence, and drugs in the global village.* Lanham, MD: Rowman & Littlefield.

Karpman, S. (1968). Script drama analysis. *Transactional Analysis Bulletin, 7*(26), 39–43.

Kasser, T., & Kanner, A. D. (Eds.). (2004). *Psychology and consumer culture: The struggle for a good life in a materialistic world.* Washington, DC: American Psychological Association.

Kasser, T., & Ryan, R. M. (2001). Be careful what you wish for: Optimal functioning and the relative attainment of intrinsic and extrinsic goals. In P. Schmuck & K. Sheldon (Eds.), *Life goals and well-being.* Gottingen: Hogrefe.

Kasser, T., Ryan, R. M., Couchman, C. E., & Sheldon, K. M. (2004). Materialistic values: Their causes and consequences. In T. Kasser & A. D. Kanner (Eds.), *Psychology and consumer culture: The struggle for a good life in a materialistic world* (pp. 11–28). Washington, DC: American Psychological Association.

Katz, J. H. (1985). The socio-political nature of counseling. *Counseling Psychologist, 13*(4), 615–624.

Kendall, P. (2006). *Worldwide cellular user forecasts, 2005–2010.* Retrieved August 15, 2007, from http://www.strategyanalytics.net/default.aspx?mod=ReportAbstractViewer&a0=3483

Kim, B., Ng, G., & Ahn, A. (2005). Effects of client expectation for counseling success, client-counselor worldview match, and client adherence to Asian and European American cultural values on counseling process with Asian Americans. *Journal of Counseling Psychology, 52*(1), 67–76.

Kim, B., & Omizo, M. (2005). Asian and European American cultural values, collective self-esteem, acculturative stress, cognitive flexibility, and general self-efficacy among Asian American college students. *Journal of Counseling Psychology, 52*(3), 412–419.

Kim, C. (2004). Imagining race and nation in multiculturalist America. *Ethnic and Racial Studies, 27*(6), 987–1005.

Kim, E. Y.-K., Bean, R. A., & Harper, J. M. (2004). Do general treatment guidelines for Asian American families have applications to specific ethnic groups? The case of culturally-competent therapy with Korean Americans. *Journal of Marital and Family Therapy, 30*(3), 359–374.

Kimmel, D., & Yi, H. (2004). Characteristics of gay, lesbian, and bisexual Asians, Asian Americans, and immigrants from Asia to the USA. *Journal of Homosexuality, 47*(2), 143–171.

Kimmel, M., & Levine, M. (1989). Men and AIDS. In M. Kimmel & M. Messner (Eds.), *Men's lives* (pp. 344–354). New York: Macmillan.

King, J. C. (1981). *The biology of race.* Berkeley: University of California Press.

King, J. E. (1991). Dysconscious racism: Ideology, identity, and the miseducation of teachers. *Journal of Negro Education, 60*(2), 133–146.

King, M. (2003). *The Penguin history of New Zealand.* Auckland, New Zealand: Penguin Books.

Kitaoka, S. (2005). Multicultural counseling competencies: Lessons from assessment. *Journal of Multicultural Counseling and Development, 33*(1), 37–47.

Klein, M. A. (1998). *Slavery and colonial rule in French West Africa.* New York: Cambridge University Press.

Kliman, J. (1998). Social class as a relationship. In M. McGoldrick (Ed.), *Re-visioning family therapy: Race, culture, and gender in clinical practice* (pp. 50–61). New York: Guilford Press.

Knox, S., Burkard, A. W., Johnson, A. J., Suzuki, L. A., & Ponterotto, J. G. (2003). African American and European American therapists' experiences of addressing race in cross-racial psychotherapy dyads. *Journal of Counseling Psychology, 50*(4), 466–481.

Kocarek, C. E., Talbot, D., Batka, M., & Anderson, M. Z. (2001). Reliability and validity of three measures of multicultural competency. *Journal of Counseling & Development, 79*(4), 486–496.

Kohn, M. (1989). *Class and conformity: A study in values.* Chicago: University of Chicago Press.

Kottak, C. P., & Kozaitis, K. A. (2003). *On being different: Diversity and multiculturalism in the North American mainstream* (2nd ed.). New York: McGraw-Hill.

Kottler, J. A. (1999). *Exploring and treating acquisitive desire.* Thousand Oaks, CA: SAGE.

Kottler, J., Montgomery, M., & Shepard, D. (2004), Acquisitive desire: Assessment and treatment. In T. Kasser & A. D. Kanner (Eds.), *Psychology and consumer culture: The struggle for a good life in a materialistic world* (pp. 149–168). Washington, DC: American Psychological Association.

Kozol, J. (1992). *Savage inequalities: Children in America's schools.* New York: Harper.

Kroeber, A. L., & Kluckhohn, C. (1952). *Culture: A critical review of concepts and definitions.* Cambridge, MA: Peabody Museum of Harvard University.

Kupers, T. A. (1999). *Prison madness: The mental health crisis behind bars and what we must do about it.* San Francisco: Jossey-Bass.

Lacan, J. (1977). *Ecrits: A selection* (A. Sheridan, Trans.). New York: Norton. (Original work published 1966)

Langston, D. (1992). Tired of playing Monopoly? In M. L. Andersen & P. H. Collins (Eds.), *Race, class, and gender: An anthology* (pp. 110–120). Belmont, CA: Wadsworth.

Larner, W. (1993). Changing contexts: Globalisation, migration and feminism in New Zealand. In S. Gunew & A. Yeatman (Eds.), *Feminism and the politics of difference* (pp. 85–102). St. Leonards, New South Wales, Australia: Allen & Unwin.

Larner, W. (1995). Theorising "difference" in Aotearoa/New Zealand. *Gender, Place and Culture, 2*(2), 77–191

Larsson, C. B. (1997). Masculinities: A social constructionist perspective (Doctoral dissertation, Massachusetts School of Professional Psychology, Boston). *Dissertation Abstracts International, 58,* 5B.

Lather, P. (1992). Post-critical pedagogues: A feminist reading. In J. Gore & C. Luke (Eds.), *Feminisms and critical pedagogy* (pp. 120–137). New York: Routledge.

Lawrence, V. J. (1997). Multiculturalism, diversity, cultural pluralism . . . "Tell the truth, the whole truth and nothing but the truth." *Journal of Black Studies, 27*(3), 318–333.

Lawson–Te Aho, K. (1993). The socially constructed nature of psychology and the abnormalisation of Maori. *New Zealand Psychological Society Bulletin, 76,* 25–26.

Lax, W. D. (1989). Postmodern thinking in a clinical practice. In J. Shotter & K. J. Gergen (Eds.), *Texts of identity* (pp. 69–85). London: SAGE.

Leahy, T. (1994). Taking up a position: Discourses of femininity and adolescence in the context of man/girl relationships. *Gender & Society, 8,* 48–72.

Lears, T. J. (1985). The concept of cultural hegemony: Problems and possibilities. *American Historical Review, 90*(3), 567–593.

Lee, C. C. (1996). MCT theory and implications for indigenous healing. In D. W. Sue, A. Ivey, & P. Pedersen, *A theory of multicultural counseling and therapy* (pp. 86–98). Pacific Grove, CA: Thomson Brooks/Cole.

Lee, C.C. (Ed.). (1997). *Multicultural issues in counseling: New approaches to diversity* (2nd ed.). Alexandria, VA: American Counseling Association.

Lee, L. J. (2004). Taking off the mask: Breaking the silence—the art of naming racism in the therapy room. In M. Rastogi & E. Wieling (Eds.), *Voices of color: First-person accounts of ethnic minority therapists* (pp. 91–115). Thousand Oaks, CA: SAGE.

Lee, R. (2005). Resilience against discrimination: Ethnic identity and other-group orientation as protective factors for Korean Americans. *Journal of Counseling Psychology, 52*(1), 36–44.

Lee, R., & Su, J. Y. (2005). Coping with intergenerational family conflict among Asian American college students. *Journal of Counseling Psychology, 52*(3), 389–399.

Leiblum, S. R. (2002). Reconsidering gender differences in sexual desire: An update. *Sexual and Relationship Therapy, 17,* 57–68.

Lemelle, A., & Battle, J. (2004). Black masculinity matters in attitudes toward gay males. *Journal of Homosexuality, 47*(1), 39–51.

Lepore, J. (1998). *The name of war: King Philip's war and the origins of American identity.* New York: Knopf.

Lerner, H. G. (1987). Is family systems theory really systemic? A feminist communication. *Journal of Psychotherapy and the Family, 3,* 47–63.

Levine, R. (1997). *A geography of time: The temporal misadventures of a social psychologist.* New York: Basic Books.

Lévi-Strauss, C. (1967). *Structural anthropology.* Garden City, NY: Anchor Books.

Lévi-Strauss, C. (1969). *The elementary structures of kinship.* Boston: Beacon Press.

Lévi-Strauss, C. (2001). Race, history and culture. *UNESCO Courier, 54*(12), 6–9.

Lewis, J. A., Lewis, M. D., Daniels, J. A., & D'Andrea, M. J. (2003). *Community counseling: Empowerment strategies for a diverse society* (3rd ed.). Pacific Grove, CA: Thomson Brooks/Cole.

Lews, G. (2004). Were American Indians the victims of genocide? *Commentary, 118*(2), 55–64.

Linehan, C., & McCarthy, J. (2001). Reviewing the "community of practice" metaphor: An analysis of control relations in a primary school classroom. *Mind, Culture, and Activity, 8*(2), 129–147.

Liu, W. M., Ali, S. R., Soleck, G., Hopps, J., Dunston, K., & Pickett, T. (2004). Using social class in counseling psychology. *Journal of Counseling Psychology, 51*(1), pp. 3–18.

Liu, W. M., & Pope-Davis, D. B. (2003). Moving from diversity to multiculturalism: Exploring power and its implications for multicultural competence. In D. B. Pope-Davis, H. L. K. Coleman, W. M. Liu, & R. L. Toporek (Eds.), *Handbook of multicultural competencies in counseling and psychology* (pp. 90–102). Thousand Oaks, CA: SAGE.

Liu, W. M., Soleck, G., Hopps, J., Dunston, K., & Pickett, T., Jr. (2004). A new framework to understand social class in counseling: The social class worldview model and modern classism theory. *Journal of Multicultural Counseling, 32*(2), 95–122.

Locke, D. C. (1990). A not so provincial view of multi-cultural counseling. *Counselor Education and Supervision, 30*(1), 18–25.

Locke, J. (1960). *Two treatises on government.* Cambridge, UK: Cambridge University Press.

Lokken, J., & Twohey, D. (2004). American Indian perspectives of Euro-American counseling behavior. *Journal of Multicultural Counseling and Development, 32,* 320–331.

Lopez, I. F. H. (2000). Institutional racism: Judicial conduct and a new theory of racial discrimination. *Yale Law Journal, 109*(8), 1717–1884.

Lorber, J., & Farrell, S. A. (1991). *The social construction of gender.* Newbury Park, CA: SAGE.

Lott, B. (2002). Cognitive and behavioral distancing from the poor. *American Psychologist, 57*(2), 100–110.

Lucal, B. (1996). Oppression and privilege: Toward a relational conceptualization of race. *Teaching Sociology, 24,* 245–255.

Luke, A. (1999). The jig is up: An alternative history of psychology or why current concepts of identity and development are part of the problem rather than part of the solution. In J. Winslade (Ed.), *Proceedings of the New Zealand Association of Counsellors Conference 1999* (pp. 26–34). Hamilton, New Zealand: New Zealand Association of Counsellors.

Lum, D. (2000). *Social work practice and people of color: A process-stage approach.* Belmont, CA: Wadsworth.

Lum, D. (Ed.). (2007). *Culturally competent practice: A framework for understanding diverse groups and justice issues* (3rd ed.). Belmont, CA: Thomson Brooks/Cole.

Lutz, C. A. (1982). The domain of emotion words on Ifaluk. *American Ethnologist, 9*(1), 113–128.

Lutz, C. A. (1988). *Unnatural emotions: Everyday sentiments on a micronesian atoll and their challenge to western theory.* Chicago: University of Chicago Press.

Lutz, C. A. (1990). Morality, domination and understandings of "justifiable anger" among the Ifaluk. In G. R. Semin & K. J. Gergen (Eds.), *Everyday understanding: Social and scientific implications* (pp. 204–226). Thousand Oaks, CA: SAGE.

Lyness, K. S., & Thompson, D. E. (2000). Climbing the corporate ladder: Do female and male executives follow the same route? *Journal of Applied Psychology, 85*(1), 86–101.

Lyotard, J. F. (1984). *The postmodern condition: A report on knowledge* (G. Bennington & B. Massumi, Trans.). Minneapolis: University of Minnesota Press. (Original work published in 1979)

Lyotard, J. F. (1993). *The postmodern explained: Correspondence, 1982-1985* (J. Pefanis & M. Thomas, Eds.). Minneapolis: University of Minnesota Press.

Maalouf, A. (2000). *On identity.* London: Routledge.

Magdoff, H. (1978). *Imperialism: From the colonial age to the present.* New York: Monthly Review Press.

Mahalik, J. R., Good, G. E., & Englar-Carlson, M. (2003). Masculinity scripts, presenting concerns, and help seeking: Implications for practice and training. *Professional Psychology: Research and Practice, 34,* 123–131.

Maisel, R., Epston, D., & Borden, A. (2004). *Biting the hand that starves you: Inspiring resistance to anorexia/bulimia.* New York: Norton.

Maker, A. H. (2004). Post 9/11: Combating racism in the sanctity of healing. In M. Rastogi & E. Wieling (Eds.), *Voices of color: First-person accounts of ethnic minority therapists* (pp. 155–168). Thousand Oaks, CA: SAGE.

Marcia, J. E. (1966). Development and validation of ego identity status. *Journal of Personality and Social Psychology, 5,* 551–558.

Marcia, J. E. (1980). Ego identity status, formal operations, and moral development. *Journal of Youth and Adolescence, 9,* 87–99.

Marecek, J. (1995). Gender, politics and psychologies of ways of knowing. *American Psychologist, 50*(3), 162–163.

Marshall, B. L. (1994). *Engendering modernity: Feminism, social theory and social change.* Boston: Northeastern University Press.

Marshall, J. D. (2007). Michel Foucault: Educational research as problematisation. In M. A. Peters & A. C. Besley (Eds.), *Why Foucault? New directions in educational research* (pp. 15–28). New York: Peter Lang.

Martinez, E. (2001). *Latino politics: Seeing more than black & white.* Retrieved from http://www.zmag.org.zmag/articles/may94martinez.htm

Martinez, E. (2007). Seeing more than Black and White: Latinos, racism, and the cultural divides. In M. L. Andersen & P. H. Collins (Eds.), *Race, class, and gender: An anthology* (6th ed., pp. 105–111). Belmont, CA: Wadsworth/Thomson Learning.

Marx, K. (1932). *Capital, the communist manifesto and other writings by Karl Marx* (M. Eastman, Ed.). New York: Modern Library.

Maslow, A. H. (1956). Self-actualizing people: A study of psychological health. In C. E. Moustakas (Ed.), *The self* (pp. 160–194). New York: Harper Colophon.

Masson, J. M. (1984). *The assault on truth: Freud's suppression of the seduction theory.* New York: Farrar, Straus and Giroux.

Mathews, G. (2000). *Global culture/individual identity: Searching for home in the cultural supermarket.* New York: Routledge.

Mbeki, T. (2007). Freedom from racism—a fundamental human right. *ANC Today, 7*(10), 1–10. Retrieved March 23, 2007, from http://www.anc.org.za/ancdocs/anctoday/2007/at10.htm

McAuliffe, G. (2007). *Culturally alert counseling.* Thousand Oaks, CA: SAGE.

McCarn, S. R., & Fassinger, R. E. (1996). Revisioning sexual minority identity formation: A new model of lesbian identity and its implications for counseling and research. *Counseling Psychologist, 24,* 508–534.

McCarthy, J., & Holliday, E. L. (2004). Help-seeking and counseling within a traditional male gender role: An examination from a multicultural perspective. *Journal of Counseling & Development, 82,* 25–30.

McGoldrick, M. (1998). *Re-visioning family therapy: Race, culture, and gender in clinical practice.* New York: Guilford Press.

McGoldrick, M., & Giordano, J. (1996). Overview: Ethnicity and family therapy. In M. McGoldrick, J. K. Pearce, & J. Giordano (Eds.), *Ethnicity and family therapy* (pp. 1–27). New York: Guilford Press.

McGoldrick, M., Giordano, J., & Garcia-Preto, N. (2005). *Ethnicity and family therapy* (3rd ed.). New York: Guilford Press.

McHoskey, J. W. (1999). Machiavellianism, intrinsic versus extrinsic goals, and social interest: A self-determination theory analysis. *Motivation and Emotion, 23,* 267–283.

McIntosh, P. (1989, July/August). White privilege: Unpacking the invisible knapsack. *Peace and Freedom,* pp. 10–12.

McKinley, N. M. (1998). Gender differences in undergraduates' body esteem: The mediating effect of objectified consciousness and actual/ideal weight discrepancy. *Sex Roles, 39*(1–2), 113–123.

McKinley, N. M. (1999). Women and objectified body consciousness: Mothers' and daughters' body experience in cultural, developmental, and familial context. *Developmental Psychology, 35*(3), 760–769.

McKinley, N. M. (2000). Constructing and deconstructing the body: A review of recent body images videos. *Feminist Collections: A Quarterly of Women's Studies Resources, 21,* 5–7.

McKinley, N. M., & Hyde, J. S. (1996). The Objectified Body Consciousness Scale: Development and Validation. *Psychology of Women Quarterly, 20*(2), 181–215.

McKinnon, J. (2003). *The black population in the United States: March 2002.* Retrieved July 10, 2007, from http://www.census.gov/prod/2003pubs/p20-541.pdf

McKinnon, L., & Miller, D. (1987). The epistemology and the Milan approach: Feminist and socio-political considerations. *Journal of Marital and Family Therapy, 13*(2), 139–155.

McLaren, P. (1994). *Critical pedagogy and predatory culture: Oppositional politics in a postmodern era.* New York: Routledge.

McLaren, P. (2005). Critical pedagogy and the social construction of knowledge. In E. R. Brown & K. J. Saltman (Eds.), *The critical middle school reader* (pp. 409–418). New York: Routledge.

McNamee, S., & Gergen, K. J. (1992). *Therapy as social construction.* London: SAGE.

McNamee, S., & Gergen, K. J. (1999). *Resources for sustainable dialogue.* Thousand Oaks, CA: SAGE.

McNamee, S. J., & Miller, R. K., Jr. (2004). *The meritocracy myth.* Lanham, MD: Rowman & Littlefield.

McNay, L. (1992). *Foucault and feminism: Power, gender, and the self.* Boston: Northeastern University Press.

Meichenbaum, D., & Gilmore, J. B. (1984). The nature of unconscious processes: A cognitive-behavioral perspective. In D. Meichenbaum & K. Bowers (Eds.), *The unconscious reconsidered* (pp. 273–298). New York: Wiley.

Mellin, L. M., Irwin, C. E., & Scully, S. (1992). Prevalence of disordered eating in girls: A survey of middle class children. *Journal of the American Dietetic Association, 92,* 851–853.

Memmi, A. (1967). *The coloniser and the colonised.* Boston: Beacon Press.

Messner, M. A. (1998). The limits of "the male sex role": An analysis of the men's liberation and men's rights movements' discourse. *Gender & Society, 12*(3), 255–276.

Meth, R. L. (1990). The road to masculinity. In R. L. Meth & R. S. Pasick (Eds.), *Men and therapy: The challenge of change* (pp. 3–34). New York: Guilford Press.

Meth, R. L., & Pasick, R. S. (Eds.). (1990). *Men in therapy: The challenge of change.* New York: Guilford Press.

Middleton, R. A., Flowers, C., & Zawaiza, T. (1996). Multiculturalism, affirmative action, and Section 21 of the 1992 Rehabilitation Act Amendments: Fact or fiction? *Rehabilitation Counseling Bulletin, 40*(1), 11–31.

Middleton, R. A., Stadler, H. A., & Simpson, C. (2005). Mental health practitioners: The relationship between white racial identity attitudes and self-reported multicultural counseling competencies. *Journal of Counseling & Development, 83*(4), 444–456.

Midgett, T. E., & Meggert, S. S. (1991). Multicultural counseling instruction: A challenge for faculties in the 21st century. *Journal of Counseling & Development, 70,* 136–141.

Mintz, L. B., & Betz, N. E. (1986). Sex differences in the nature, realism, and correlates of body image. *Sex Roles, 15*(3–4), 185–195.

Minuchin, S. (1974). *Families and family therapy.* Cambridge, MA: Harvard University Press.

Mio, J. S., & Awakuni, G. 1. (2000). *Resistance to multiculturalism: Issues and interventions.* Philadelphia: Brunner/Mazel.

Mock, K. (1997). 25 years of multiculturalism—past, present, and future, part 1. *Canadian Social Studies, 31,* 123–127.

Monk, G. (1998). *Developing a social justice agenda for counsellor education in New Zealand: A social constructionist perspective.* Unpublished doctoral dissertation, University of Waikato, Hamilton, New Zealand.

Monk, G., Winslade, J., Crocket, K., & Epston, D. (Eds.). (1997). *Narrative therapy in practice: The archaeology of hope.* San Francisco: Jossey-Bass.

Montagu, A. (1962). The concept of race. *American Anthropologist, 65*(5), 919–928.

Moore, D., & Leafgren, F. (Eds.). (1990). *Problem-solving strategies and interventions for men in conflict.* Alexandria, VA: American Association for Counseling and Development.

Moradi, B. (2005). Advancing womanist identity development: Where we are and where we must go. *Counseling Psychologist, 33*(2), 225–253.

Morales, E. S. (1989). Ethnic minority families and minority gays and lesbians. *Marriage & Family Review, 14*(3–4), 217–239.

Morial, M. H. (2006). Achievement gap between white and black students seems to be widening even as scores rise. *Washington Informer, 43*(7), 18.

Morson, G. S., & Emerson, C. (1990). *Mikhail Bakhtin: Creation of a prosaics.* Stanford, CA: Stanford University Press.

Mosher, D. L. (1991). Macho men, machismo, and sexuality. *Annual Review of Sex Research, 2,* 199–247.

Mouffe, C. (1992). Feminism, citizenship and radical democratic politics. In. J. Butler & J. W. Scott (Eds.), *Feminists theorise the political* (pp. 369–384). London: Routledge.

Moy, S. (1992). A culturally sensitive, psychoeducational model for understanding and treating Asian-American clients. *Journal of Psychology and Christianity, 11*(4), 358–367.

Munley, P., Lidderdale, M., Thiagarajan, M., & Null, U. (2004). Identity development and multicultural competency. *Journal of Multicultural Counseling and Development, 32,* 283–295.

Murphy-Shigematsu, S. (2002). *Multicultural encounters: Case narratives from a counseling practice.* New York: Teachers College Press.

Myers, D. G., & Diener, E. (1996, May). The pursuit of happiness. *Scientific American,* pp. 10–19.

Nadal, K. (2004). Filipino American identity development model. *Journal of Multicultural Counseling, 32*(1), 45–62.

Narayan, U. (2000). Essence of culture and a sense of history: A feminist critique of cultural essentialism. In U. Narayan & S. Harding (Eds.), *Decentering the center: Philosophy for a multicultural, postcolonial & feminist world* (pp. 80–100). Bloomington: Indiana University Press.

National Career Development Association. (1997). *Career counseling competencies* (Rev. ed.). Columbus, OH: Author.

Neimeyer, R. A. (1998). Social constructionism in the counseling context. *Psychology Quarterly, 11*(2), 135–149.

Nelson, M. L., & Holloway, E. L. (1990). Relation of gender to power and involvement in supervision. *Journal of Counseling Psychology, 37,* 473–481.

Newitz, A., & Wray, M. (1997). What is "white trash"? Stereotypes and economic conditions of poor whites in the U.S. In M. Hill (Ed.), *Whiteness: A critical reader* (pp. 168–186). New York: New York University Press.

Nghe, L., Mahalik, J. R., & Lowe, S. (2003). Influences on Vietnamese men: Traditional gender roles, the refugee experience, acculturation, and racism in the United States. *Journal of Multicultural Counseling and Development, 31*(4), 245–261.

Nichols, M. P., & Schwartz, R. C. (1998). *Family therapy: Concepts and methods* (4th ed.). Boston: Allyn & Bacon.

Nieto, S. (2000). *Affirming diversity: The sociopolitical context of multicultural education* (3rd ed.). New York: Longman.

Nolen-Hoeksema, S. (1998). *Abnormal psychology.* Boston: McGraw-Hill.

Noll, S. M. (1966). Correlational and experimental tests of body shame as a mediator. (Doctoral dissertation, Duke University, Durham, NC). *Dissertation Abstracts International, 57,* 09B. (UMI No. 9704732)

Nutt, R. (1991). Ethical principles for gender-fair family therapy. *Family Psychologist, 7*(3), 32–33.

Nylund, D. (2006). Critical multiculturalism, whiteness, and social work: Towards a more radical view of cultural competence. *Journal of Progressive Human Services, 17*(2), 27–42.

Obama, B. (2006). *The audacity of hope: Thoughts on reclaiming the American dream.* New York: Crown.

Offen, K. (1988). Defining feminism: A comparative historical approach. *Journal of Women in Culture and Society, 14,* 119–157.

Ohlson, T. H. (1993). The Treaty of Waitangi and bicultural issues for psychologists. *New Zealand Psychological Society Bulletin, 76,* 8–9.

Okin, S. M. (1999). *Is multiculturalism bad for women?* In J. Cohen, M. Howard, & M. Nussbaum (Eds.), *Is multiculturalism bad for women?* (pp. 9–24). Princeton, NJ: Princeton University Press.

Olssen, M. (1991). Producing the truth about people. In J. Morss & T. Linzey (Eds.), *Growing up: The politics of human learning* (pp. 188–209). Auckland, New Zealand: Longman Paul.

O'Neill, J. M. (1990). Assessing men's gender role conflict. In D. Moore & F. Leafgren (Eds.), *Problem-solving strategies and interventions for men in conflict* (pp. 23–38). Alexandria, VA: American Counseling Association.

Orange, C. (1987). *The Treaty of Waitangi.* Wellington, New Zealand: Allen & Unwin.

Orlinsky, D. E., & Howard, K. L. (1980). Gender and psychotherapeutic outcome. In A. M. Brodsky & R. T. Hare-Mustin (Eds.), *Women and psychotherapy* (pp. 3–34). New York: Guilford Press.

Paltoo, D., & Chu, K. (2004). Patterns in cancer incidence among American Indians/Alaska natives, United States, 1992–1999. *Public Health Reports, 119*(4), 443–449.

Parham, T. A. (Ed.). (2002). *Counseling persons of African descent: Raising the bar of practitioner competence.* Thousand Oaks, CA: SAGE.

Parham, T. A., & Helms, J. E. (1981). The influence of black students' racial identity attitudes on preferences for counselor's race. *Journal of Counseling Psychology, 32,* 431–440.

Parker, I. (1992). *Discourse dynamics: Critical analyses for social and individual psychology.* London: Routledge.

Parker, R. G., & Gagnon, J. H. (1995). *Conceiving sexuality: Approaches to sex research in a postmodern world.* Rio de Janeiro, Brazil: State University of Rio de Janeiro.

Parker, W. M. (1998). *Consciousness-raising: A primer for multicultural counseling* (2nd ed.). Springfield, IL: Charles C Thomas.

Parks, C., Hughes, T., & Matthews, A. (2004). Race/ethnicity and sexual orientation: Intersecting identities. *Cultural Diversity and Ethnic Minority Psychology, 10*(3), 241–254.

Patterson, C. H. (1996). Multicultural counseling: From diversity to universality. *Journal of Counseling & Development, 74,* 227–231.

Payne, R. K. (2005). *A framework for understanding poverty* (4th ed.). Highlands, TX: Aha! Process.

Pedersen, P. (1993). The multicultural dilemma of white cross-cultural researchers. *Counseling Psychologist, 21*(2), 229–232.

Pedersen, P. (1995). *The five stages of culture shock: Critical incidents around the world.* Westport, CT: Greenwood Press.

Pedersen, P. B. (1976). The field of intercultural counseling. In P. B. Pedersen, W. J. Lonner, & J. G. Draguns (Eds.), *Counseling across cultures* (pp. 17–41). Honolulu: University of Hawaii Press.

Pedersen, P. B. (1991). Multiculturalism as a generic approach to counseling. *Journal of Counseling & Development, 70*(1), 6–12.

Pedersen, P. (Ed.). (1999). *Multiculturism as a fourth force.* Philadephia: Brunner/Mazel.

Pedersen, P. B., & Carey, J. C. (Eds.). (2003). *Multicultural counseling in schools: A practical handbook* (2nd ed.). Boston: Allyn & Bacon.

Pedersen, P. B., Draguns, J. G., Lonner, W. J., & Trimble, J. E. (Eds.). (1989). *Counseling across cultures* (3rd ed.). Honolulu: University of Hawaii Press.

Pence, E. (1993). *Education groups for men who batter: The Duluth model.* New York: Springer.

Pennachio, D. (2004). Caring for your Filipino, Southeastern Asian, and Indian patients: More than half of Asian Americans say their doctors don't understand their cultures: Sensitivity to diversity is essential for good patient care. *Medical Economics, 81*(2), 36–42.

Perkins, J. (2004). *Confessions of an economic hit man.* San Francisco: Berrett-Koehler.

Perls, F. (1972). Four lectures. In J. Fagan & I. Shepherd (Eds.), *Gestalt therapy now.* London: Penguin Books.

Perls, F. (1973). *The Gestalt approach & eye witness to therapy.* Palo Alto, CA: Science & Behavior Books.

Perry, P. (2002). *Shades of white: White kids and racial identities in high school.* Durham, NC: Duke University Press.

Peters, M. A., & Besley, A. C. T. (2006). *Building knowledge cultures.* Lanham, MD: Rowman & Littlefield.

Petras, J. (1993). Cultural imperialism in the late 20th century. *Journal of Contemporary Asia, 23,* 139–148.

Phan, L., Rivera, E., & Roberts-Wilbur, J. (2005). Understanding Vietnamese refugee womens' identity development from a sociopolitical and historical perspective. *Journal of Counseling & Development, 83,* 305–312.

Phillips, U. B. (1968). The slave economy of the old south. In E. D. Genovese (Ed.), *Selected essays in economic and social history* (p. 269). Baton Rouge: Louisiana State University Press.

Philpot, C. L. (2001). Family therapy for men. In G. R. Brooks & G. E. Good (Eds.), *The new handbook of psychotherapy and counseling with men* (Vol. 1, pp. 622–638). San Francisco: Jossey-Bass.

Phinney, J. (1989). Stages of ethnic identity development in minority group adolescents. *Journal of Early Adolescence, 9*(1–2), 34–49.

Phinney, J. (1990). Ethnic identity in adolescents and adults: Review of research. *Psychological Bulletin, 108,* 499–514.

Plath, S. (1963). *The bell jar.* London: Heinmann.

Pleck, J. H. (1981). *The myth of masculinity.* Cambridge: MIT Press.

Pleck, J. H. (1987). *The myth of masculinity* (3rd ed.). Cambridge, MA: MIT Press.

Pleck, J. H. (1995). The gender role strain paradigm: An update. In R. F. Levant & W. S. Pollack (Eds.), *A new psychology of men* (pp. 11–32). New York: Basic Books.

Poindexter-Cameron, J. M., & Robinson, T. L. (1997). Relationships among racial identity attitudes, womanist identity attitudes, and self esteem in African American college women. *Journal of College Student Development, 38,* 288–296.

Pole, N., Best, S., Metzler, T., & Marmar, C. (2005). Why are Hispanics at greater risk of PTSD? *Cultural Diversity and Ethnic Minority Psychology, 11*(2), 144–161.

Polkinghorne, D. E. (2004). *Practice and the human sciences: The case for a judgment-based practice of care.* Albany: State University of New York Press.

Pollack, W. S. (1998). *Real boys: Rescuing our sons from the myths of boyhood.* New York: Basic Books.

Ponterotto, J. G. (1988). Racial consciousness development among white counselor trainees: A stage model. *Journal of Multicultural Counseling and Development, 16,* 146–156.

Ponterotto, J. G., Casas, J. M., Suzuki, L. A., & Alexander, C. M. (Eds.). (1995). *Handbook of multicultural counseling.* Thousand Oaks, CA: SAGE.

Ponterotto, J. G., & Pedersen, P. B. (1993). *Preventing prejudice: A guide for counselors and educators.* Newbury Park, CA: SAGE.

Pope, N. (1995). The "salad bowl" is big enough for us all: An argument for the inclusion of lesbians and gay men in any definition of multiculturalism. *Journal of Counseling & Development, 73*(3), 301–304.

Pope-Davis, D. B., & Coleman, H. L. (Eds.). (2001). *The intersection of race, class, and gender in multicultural counseling.* Thousand Oaks, CA: SAGE.

Popham, J. (2004). *America's "failing" schools: How parents & teachers can cope with No Child Left Behind.* New York: Routledge/Falmer.

Poster, M. (1989). *Critical theory and poststructuralism: In search of a context.* Ithaca, NY: Cornell University Press.

Poston, W. C. (1990). The biracial identity development model: A needed addition. *Journal of Counseling & Development, 69*(2), 152–155.

Potter, J., & Wetherell, M. (1987). *Discourse and social psychology: Beyond attitudes and behaviour.* London: SAGE.

Potts, A. (1998). The science/fiction of sex: John Gray's Mars and Venus in the bedroom. *Sexualities, 1(2)*, 153–173.

Prey, L., & Roysircar, G. (2005). Effects of acculturaltion and worldview for white American, South American, South Asian, and Southeast Asian students. *International Journal for the Advancement of Counseling, 26(3)*, 229–248.

Price, C., Raymond, J., & Zissu, A. (2005, September 27). Viva Botox! *Health*, p. 27.

Pride, R. A., & Woodard, J. D. (1985). *The burden of busing: The politics of desegregation in Nashville, Tennessee*. Knoxville: University of Tennessee Press.

Rabin, C. L. (2005). *Understanding gender and culture in the helping process: Practitioners' narratives from global perspectives*. Belmont, CA: Thomson Wadsworth.

Rabinowitz, F. E., & Cochran, S. V. (2002). *Deepening psychotherapy with men*. Washington, DC: American Psychological Association.

Radina, M., & Barber, C. (2004). Utilization of formal support among Hispanic Americans caring for aging parents. *Journal of Gerontological Social Work, 43(2–3)*, 5–23.

Rahman, O., & Rollock, D. (2004). Acculturation, competence, and mental health among South Asian students in the United States. *Journal of Multicultural Counseling and Development, 32*, 130–142.

Rawlings, E. I., & Carter, D. K. (1977). Feminist and non-sexist psychotherapy. In E. I. Rawlings & D. K. Carter (Eds.), *Psychotherapy for women* (pp. 49–76). Springfield, IL: Charles C Thomas.

Real, T. (1995). Fathering our sons; refathering ourselves: Some thoughts on transforming masculine identities. *Journal of Feminist Family Therapy, 7(1–2)*, 27–44.

Rector, R., Johnson, K. A., & Fagan, P. F. (2001). *Understanding differences in black and white child poverty rates* (Heritage Center for Data Analysis Report No. CDA01–04). Washington, DC: Heritage Foundation.

Reed, I. (1989). America's "black only" ethnicity. In W. Sollors (Ed.), *The invention of ethnicity* (pp. 226–229). New York: Oxford University Press.

Report to the president from the President's Commission on Mental Health (Vol. 1; Stock No. 040–000–00390–8). (1978). Washington, DC: U.S. Government Printing Office.

Reynolds, A. L., & Constantine, M. G. (2004). Feminism and multiculturalism: Parallels and intersections. *Journal of Multicultural Counseling and Development, 32*, 346–357.

Reynolds, S. (2005) *Learning is a verb: Psychology for teaching and learning* (2nd ed.). Scottsdale, AZ: Holcomb Hathaway.

Ricciuti, H. (2004). Single parenthood, achievement, and problem behavior in white, black, and Hispanic children. *Journal of Educational Research, 97(4)*, 196–206.

Richardson, F. C., & Zeddies, T. J. (2001). Individualism and modern psychotherapy. In B. D. Slife, R. N. Williams, & S. H. Barlow (Eds.), *Critical issues in psychotherapy: Translating new ideas into practice* (pp. 147–164). Thousand Oaks, CA: SAGE.

Ridley, C. R. (2005). *Overcoming unintentional racism in counseling and therapy: A practitioner's guide to intentional intervention* (2nd ed.). Thousand Oaks, CA: SAGE.

Ridley, C. R., Baker, D. M., & Hill, C. L. (2001). Critical issues concerning cultural competence. *Counseling Psychologist, 29(6)*, 822–832.

Ridley, C. R., Mendoza, D. W., & Kanitz, B. E. (1994). Multicultural training: Reexamination, operationalization, and integration. *Counseling Psychologist, 22(2)*, 227–289.

Rigazio-DiGilio, S. A., Anderson, S. A., & Kunkler, K. P. (1995). Gender-aware supervision in marriage and family counseling and therapy: How far have we actually come? *Counselor Education and Supervision, 34(4)*, 344–355.

Rigazio-DiGilio, S. A., Ivey, A. E., Kunkler-Peck, K. P., & Grady, L. T. (2005). *Community genograms: Using individual, family, and cultural narratives with clients*. New York: Teachers College Press.

Rigazio-DiGilio, S. A., Ivey, A. E., & Locke, D. C. (1997). Continuing the postmodern dialogue: Enhancing and contextualizing multiple voices. *Journal of Mental Health Counseling, 19,* 233–255.

Ringel, S. (2005). Therapeutic dilemmas in cross-cultural practice with Asian American adolescents. *Child & Adolescent Social Work Journal, 22*(1), 57–69.

Robertson, J. M. (2001). Counseling men in college settings. In G. R. Brooks & G. E. Good (Eds.), *The new handbook of psychotherapy and counseling with men* (Vol. 1, pp. 146–169). San Francisco: Jossey-Bass.

Robertson, J. M., & Fitzgerald, L. F. (1990). The (mis)treatment of men: Effects of client gender role and life-style on diagnosis and attribution of pathology. *Journal of Counseling Psychology, 37,* 3–9.

Robertson, J. M., & Fitzgerald, L. F. (1992). Overcoming the masculine mystique: Preferences for alternative forms of therapy among men who avoid counseling. *Journal of Counseling Psychology, 39,* 240–246.

Robinson, J. D., & James, L. C. (Eds.). (2003). *Diversity in human interactions: The tapestry of America.* New York: Oxford University Press.

Robinson, T. L. (1999). The intersections of dominant discourses across race, gender, and other identities. *Journal of Counseling & Development, 77*(1), 73–79.

Robinson, T. L. (2005). *The convergence of race, ethnicity, and gender: Multiple identities in counseling* (2nd ed.). Upper Saddle River, NJ: Prentice Hall.

Robinson, T. L., & Howard-Hamilton, M. F. (2000). *The convergence of race, ethnicity, and gender: Multiple identities in counseling.* Upper Saddle River, NJ: Prentice Hall.

Rodgers, M. E. (2005). *Mencken: The American iconoclast: The life and times of the bad boy of Baltimore.* New York: Oxford University Press.

Rodin, J., Silberstein, L., & Striegel-Moore, R. (1985). Women and weight: A normative discontent. In T. B. Sonderegger (Ed.), *Psychology and gender: Nebraska Symposium on Motivation* (pp. 267–307). Lincoln: University of Nebraska Press.

Rogers, C. (1967). Toward a modern approach to values: The valuing process in the mature person. In C. Rogers & B. Stevens (Eds.), *Person to person: The problem of being human: A new trend in psychology* (pp. 13–28). Lafayette, CA: Real People Press.

Rogers, C. (1970). *On encounter groups.* New York: Harper & Row.

Rogers, C. R. (1973). *Carl Rogers on encounter groups.* New York: Harper & Row.

Rogers, M. F. (1999). *Barbie culture.* Thousand Oaks, CA: SAGE.

Root, M. P. P. (2003). Bill of rights for racially mixed people. In Root, M. P. P., & Kelly, M. (Eds.), *The multiracial child resource book: Living complex identities.* Seattle, WA: Mavin Foundation.

Rosaldo, R. (1993). *Culture and truth: The remaking of social analysis.* Boston: Beacon Press.

Rosaldo, R. (1994). Cultural citizenship and educational democracy. *Cultural Anthropology, 9*(3), 402–411.

Rose, N. (1985). *The psychological complex: Psychology, politics and society in England, 1869–1939.* London: Routledge and Kegan Paul.

Rose, N. (1990). *Governing the soul: The shaping of the private self.* London: Routledge

Rose, N. (1999). *Powers of freedom: Reframing political thought.* New York: Cambridge University Press.

Rosenthal, D. (2004). Effects of client race on clinical judgment of practicing European American vocational rehabilitation counselors. *Rehabilitation Counseling Bulletin, 47*(3), 131–141.

Rotter, J. B. (1966). Generalized expectancies for internal versus external control of reinforcement. *Psychological Monographs, 80*(1), 1–28.

Rowan, J. (1997). *Healing the male psyche: Therapy as initiation.* New York: Routledge.

Roy, A. (2004). *An ordinary person's guide to empire.* Cambridge, MA: South End Press.

Rumbaut, R. (2003). Assimilation and its discontents. In J. Stone & R. Dennis (Eds.), *Race and ethnicity: Comparative and theoretical approaches* (pp. 237–259). Oxford, UK: Blackwell.

Russell, G. L., Fujino, D. C., Sue, S., Cheung, M.-K., & Snowden, L. R. (1996). The effects of therapist-client ethnic match in the assessment of mental health functioning. *Journal of Cross-Cultural Psychology, 27*(5), 598–615.

Russell, M. N. (1984). *Skills in counseling women.* Springfield, IL: Charles C Thomas.

Sabnani, H. B., Ponterotto, J. G., & Borodovsky, L. G. (1991). White racial identity development and cross-cultural counselor training. *Counseling Psychologist, 19*(1), 76–102.

Sadeghi, M., Fischer, J., & House, S. (2003). Ethical dilemmas in multicultural counseling. *Journal of Multicultural Counseling and Development, 31*(3), 179–191.

Said, E. W. (1976). Interview. *Diacritics, 6*(3), 30–47.

Said, E. W. (1993). *Culture and imperialism.* New York: Vintage Books.

Said, E. W. (1994). *Orientalism.* New York: Vintage Books. (Originally published 1978)

Said, E. W. (1994). *The pen and the sword: Conversations with David Baramian.* Monroe, ME: Common Courage Press.

Samantrai, K. (2004). *Culturally competent public child welfare practice.* Pacific Grove, CA: Thomson Brooks/Cole.

Sampson, E. (1989). The deconstruction of the self. In J. Shotter & K. J. Gergen (Eds.), *Texts of identity* (pp. 1–19). London: SAGE.

Sanchez, D., & Crocker, J. (2005). How investment in gender ideals affects well-being: The role of external contingencies of self-worth. *Psychology of Women Quarterly, 29,* 63–77.

Santiago-Rivera, A. L., Arredondo, P., & Gallardo-Cooper, M. (Eds.). (2002). *Counseling Latinos and la familia: A practical guide.* Thousand Oaks, CA: SAGE.

Sarason, I. G., & Sarason, B. R. (2002). From mental health research data. In J. Archer & B. Lloyd (Eds.), *Sex and gender.* Cambridge, MA: Cambridge University Press.

Saussure, F. de. (1986). *Course in general linguistics* (R. Harris, Ed. & Trans.). Peru, IL: Open Court. (Original work published 1972)

Savage, T., Harley, D., & Nowak, T. (2005). Applying social empowerment strategies as tools for self-advocacy in counseling lesbian and gay male clients. *Journal of Counseling & Development, 83,* 131–137.

Savickas, M. (1992, August). Innovations in counseling for career development. In L. J. Richmond (Chair), *New perspectives on counseling for the 21st century.* Symposium conducted at the annual convention of the American Psychological Association, Washington, DC.

Schlesinger, A. M. (1991). *The disuniting of America: Reflections on a multicultural society.* New York: Norton.

Schofield, W. (1964). *Psychotherapy: The purchase of friendship.* Englewood Cliffs, NJ: Prentice Hall.

Schutz, A. (1976). *Collected papers II: Studies in social theory.* The Hague, Netherlands: Martinus Nijhoff.

Schwarzbaum, S. (2004). Low-income Latinos and dropout: Strategies to prevent dropout. *Journal of Multicultural Counseling and Development, 32,* 296–306.

Scitovsky, T. (1976). *The joyless economy: An inquiry into human satisfaction and consumer dissatisfaction.* New York: Oxford University Press.

Scollon, C., Deiner, E., Oishi, S., & Biswas-Diener, R. (2004). Emotions across cultures and methods. *Journal of Cross-Cultural Psychology, 35*(3), 304–326.

Scott, A. (Ed.). (1997). *The limits of globalization.* London: Routledge.

Scott-Clark, C., & Levy, A. (2003, June 14). Fast forward into trouble. *Guardian Weekend,* pp. 14–20.

Scott, S., & Morgan, D. (Eds.). (1993). *Body matters: Essays on the sociology of the body.* Washington, DC: Falmer Press.

Seidman, S. (1994). *The postmodern turn: New perspectives on social theory.* Cambridge, UK: Cambridge University Press.

Selden, S. (1999). *Inheriting shame: The story of eugenics and racism in America.* New York: Teachers College Press.

Sengupta, S. (1996). Understanding consumption related values from advertising: A content analysis of television commercials from India and the United States. *Gazette: The International Journal of Communication Studies, 57,* 81–96.

Sengupta, S. (2001, July 8). How many poor children is too many? *New York Times,* pp. 4–3.

Shay, J. J. (1996). "Okay, I'm here, but I'm not talking!" Psychotherapy with the reluctant male. *Psychotherapy, 33,* 503–513.

Sheldon, K. M., & McGregor, H. (2000). Extrinsic value orientation and the "tragedy of the commons". *Journal of Personality, 68,* 383–411.

Shome, R. (1996). Race and popular cinema: The rhetorical strategies of whiteness in "City of Joy." *Communication Quarterly, 44*(4), 502–518.

Shotter, J. (1990). Getting in touch: The metamethodology of a postmodern science of mental life. *Humanistic Psychologist, 18,* 7–22.

Shotter, J., & Gergen, K. J. (1989). *Texts of identity.* London: SAGE.

Shultz, E. B., & Tougias, M. J. (1999). *King Philip's war: The history and legacy of America's forgotten war.* Woodstock, VT: Countryman Press.

Silberstein, L. R., Striegel-Moore, R. H., Timko, C., & Rodin, J. (1988). Behavioral and psychological implications of body dissatisfaction: Do men and women differ? *Sex Roles, 19*(3–4), 219–232.

Silverstein, B., Perdue, L., Peterson, B., & Kelly, E. (1986). The role of the mass media in promoting a thin standard of bodily attractiveness for women. *Sex Roles, 14,* 519–532.

Silverstein, S. (2005, January 31). Racial issues lose urgency, study finds. *Los Angeles Times,* p. B.

Sinclair, S. L. (2007). Back in the mirrored room: The enduring relevance of discursive practice. *Journal of Family Therapy, 29*(2), 147–168.

Sinclair, S. L., & Monk, G. (2004). Moving beyond the blame game: Toward a discursive approach to negotiating conflict within couple relationships. *Journal of Marital and Family Therapy, 30*(3), 335–347.

Sink, C. A. (2002). In search of the profession's finest hour: A critique of four views of 21st century school counseling. *Professional School Counseling, 5*(3), 156–163.

Skinner, B. F. (1968). *The technology of teaching.* Englewood Cliffs, NJ: Prentice Hall.

Slattery, J. M. (2004). *Counseling diverse clients: Bringing context into therapy.* Belmont, CA: Thomson Brooks/Cole.

Smart, D. W., & Smart, J. F. (1997). DSM-IV and culturally sensitive diagnosis: Some observations for counselors. *Journal of Counseling & Development, 75*(5), 392–398.

Smith, G. H. (1992, November). *Tane-nui-a-Rangi's legacy, propping up the sky: Kaupapa Maori as resistance and intervention.* Paper presented at the joint conference of the New Zealand Association of Research in Education and the Australian Association of Research in Education, Geelong, Australia.

Smith, L. T. (2001). *Decolonizing methodologies: Research and indigenous peoples.* New York: Zed Books.

Smith-Adcock, S., Rogers-Huilman, B., & Choate, L. H. (2004). Feminist teaching in counselor education: Promoting multicultural understanding. *Journal of Multicultural Counseling and Development, 32,* 402–413.

Snyder, B. (1973) *The hidden curriculum.* Cambridge: MIT Press.

Somé, M. (1998). *The healing wisdom of Africa: Finding life purpose through nature, ritual and community.* New York: Jeremy P. Tarcher/Putnam.

Sophie, J. (1985–1986). A critical examination of stage theories of lesbian identity development. *Journal of Homosexuality, 12*(1), 39–51.

Sowell, T. (1994). *Race and culture: A world view.* New York: Basic Books.

Sowell, T. (1998). *Conquests and cultures: An international history.* New York: Basic Books.

Spence, J. T. (1995). Achievement American style: The rewards and costs of individualism. *American Psychologist, 40,* 1285–1295.

Spickard, P. R. (1992). The illogic of American racial categories. In M. P. P. Root (Ed.), *Racially mixed people in America* (pp. 12–23). Thousand Oaks, CA: SAGE.

Spickard, P. R., & Fong, R. (1995). Pacific Islander Americans and multiethnicity: A vision of America's future? *Social Forces, 73*(4), 1365–1383.

Spitzack, C. (1990). *Confessing excess: Women and the politics of body reduction.* New York: State University of New York Press.

Stam, H. J. (Ed.). (1998). *The body and psychology.* Thousand Oaks, CA: SAGE.

Steele, C. M. (1992, April). Race and the schooling of black Americans. *Atlantic Monthly,* pp. 68–78.

Steele, I. K. (1994). *Warpaths: Invasions of North America.* New York: Oxford University Press.

Steele, S. (1990). *The content of our character: A new vision of race in America.* New York: St. Martin's Press.

Steele, S. (2006). *White guilt: How blacks and whites together destroyed the promise of the civil rights era.* New York: HarperCollins.

Steinem, G. (1992). *Revolution from within: A book of self-esteem.* Boston: Little, Brown.

Stewart, A. J., & Lykes, M. B. (Eds.). (1985). *Gender and personality: Current perspectives on theory and research.* Durham, NC: Duke University Press.

Stiglitz, J. (2003). *Globalization and its discontents.* New York: Norton.

Stone, J. (2003). Max Weber on race, ethnicity and nationalism. In J. Stone & R. Dennis (Eds.), *Race and ethnicity: Comparative and theoretical approaches* (pp. 28–42). Oxford, UK: Blackwell.

Stone, S., & Han, M. (2005). Perceived school environments, perceived discrimination, and school performance among children of Mexican immigrants. *Children and Youth Services Review, 27*(1), 51–66.

Story, M., French, S. A., Resnick, M. D., & Blum, R. W. (1995). Ethnic/racial and socioeconomic differences in dieting behaviors and body image perceptions in adolescents. *International Journal of Eating Disorders, 18*(2), 173–179.

Straubhaar, J., & La Pastina, A. (2003). Television and hegemony in Brazil. In L. Artz & Y. R. Kamalipour (Eds.), *The globalization of corporate media hegemony* (pp. 151–160). New York: State University of New York Press.

Striegel-Moore, R. H., Silberstein, L. R., & Rodin, J. (1986). Toward an understanding of risk factors for bulimia. *American Psychologist, 41*(3), 246–263.

Strong, S. M., Williamson, D. A., Netemeyer, R. G., & Geer, J. H. (2000). Eating disorder symptoms and concerns about body differ as a function of gender and sexual orientation. *Journal of Social and Clinical Psychology, 19*(2), 240–255.

Strong, T., & Paré, D. A. (2004). Striving for perspicuity. In T. Strong & D. A. Paré (Eds.), *Furthering talk: Innovations in the discursive therapies* (pp. 1–14). New York: Kluwer Academic/Plenum.

Stuart, B. (1997). Sentencing circles: Making "real differences." In J. Macfarlane (Ed.), *Rethinking disputes: The mediation alternative* (pp. 201–232). London: Cavendish.

Sue, D. W. (1993). Confronting ourselves: The white and racial/ethnic-minority research. *Counseling Psychologist, 21*(2), 244–249.

Sue, D. W. (2001). Multidimensional facets of cultural competence. *Counseling Psychologist, 29,* 790–821.

Sue, D. W. (2003). *Overcoming our racism: The journey to liberation.* San Francisco: Jossey-Bass.

Sue, D. W., Arredondo, P., & McDavis, R. J. (1992). Multicultural counseling competencies and standards: A call to the profession. *Journal of Counseling & Development, 70,* 477–486.

Sue, D. W., Bernier, J. E., Durran, A., Feinberg, L., Pedersen, P., Smith, E. J., et al. (1982). Position paper: Cross-cultural counseling competencies. *Counseling Psychologist, 10*(2), 45–52.

Sue, D. W., Bingham, R. P., Porche-Burke, L., & Vasquez, M. (1999). The diversification of psychology. A multicultural revolution. *American Psychologist, 54*(12), 1061–1069.

Sue, D. W., Bucceri, J., Lin, A. I., Nadal, K., & Torino, G. (2007). Racial microaggressions and the Asian American experience. *Cultural Diversity and Ethnic Minority Psychology, 1*(13), 72–81.

Sue, D. W., Carter, R., Casas, J. M., Fouad, N., Ivey, A., Jensen, M., et al. (1998). *Multicultural counseling competencies: Individual and organizational development.* Thousand Oaks, CA: SAGE.

Sue, D. W., Ivey, A., & Pedersen, P. (1996). *A theory of multicultural counseling and therapy.* Pacific Grove, CA: Thomson Brooks/Cole.

Sue, D. W., & Sue, D. (1981). *Counseling the culturally different: Theory and practice.* New York: Wiley.

Sue, D. W., & Sue, D. (1990). *Counseling the culturally different: Theory and practice* (2nd ed.). New York: Wiley.

Sue, D. W., & Sue, D. (1999). *Counseling the culturally different: Theory and practice* (3rd ed.). New York: Wiley.

Sue, D. W., & Sue, D. (2003). *Counseling the culturally diverse: Theory and practice* (4th ed.). New York: Wiley.

Sue, D. W., & Sue, D. (2007). *Counseling the culturally diverse: Theory and practice* (5th ed.). New York: Wiley.

Suzuki, L. A., Ponterotto, J. G., & Meller, P. J. (2001). Multicultural assessment: Trends and directions revisited. In L. A. Suzuki, J. G. Ponterotto, & P. J. Meller (Eds.), *Handbook of multicultural assessment: Clinical, psychological, and educational applications* (2nd ed., pp. 569–574). San Francisco: Jossey-Bass.

Swartz, D. L. (2003). From correspondence to contradiction and change: Schooling in capitalist America revisited. *Sociological Forum, 18*(1), 167–186.

Szasz, T. (1974). *The myth of mental illness.* New York: Harper & Row.

Szymanski, D. (2005). Heterosexism and sexism as correlates of psychological distress in lesbians. *Journal of Counseling & Development, 83,* 355–360.

Tamesese, K., & Waldegrave, C. (1993). Cultural and gender accountability in the "just therapy" approach. *Journal of Feminist Family Therapy, 5*(2), 29–45.

Tannen, D. (1991). *You just don't understand: Women and men in conversation.* New York: Ballantine.

Tatum, B. V. (1997). *"Why are all the black kids sitting together in the cafeteria?" And other conversations about race.* New York: Basic Books.

Tatum, B. V. (1999). Color blind or color conscious? *School Administrator, 56*(6), 28–30.

Tatum, B. V. (2003). *"Why are all the black kids sitting together in the cafeteria?" And other conversations about race* (Rev. ed.). New York: Basic Books.

Taylor, C. (2004). *Modern social imaginaries.* Durham, NC: Duke University Press.

Taylor, J., Gilligan, C., & Sullivan, A. (1995). *Between voice and silence: Women and girls, race and relationship.* Cambridge, MA: Harvard University Press.

Taylor, M. (1991). How psychoanalytic thinking lost its way in the hands of men: The case for feminist psychotherapy. *British Journal of Guidance & Counselling, 19*(1), 93–103.

Taylor, M. (1994). Gender and power in counselling and supervision. *British Journal of Guidance & Counselling, 22*(3), 319–326.

Teasley, M. L. (2005). Perceived levels of cultural competence through social work education and professional development for urban school social workers. *Journal of Social Work Education, 41*, 85–98.

Thernstrom, S., & Thernstrom, A. (1997). *America in black and white. One nation, indivisible.* New York: Touchstone.

Thomason, T. C. (1991). Counseling Native Americans: An introduction for non–Native American counselors. *Journal of Counseling & Development, 69*(4), 321–327.

Thompson, J. K., Heinberg, L. J., Altabe, M., & Tantleff-Dunn, S. (1999). *Exacting beauty: Theory, assessment, and treatment of body image disturbance.* Washington, DC: American Psychological Association.

Tocqueville, A. (1945). *Democracy in America* (Vol. 1). New York: Vintage Books.

Todosijevic, J., Rothblum, E., & Solomon, S. (2005). Relationship satisfaction, affectivity, and gay-specific stressors in same-sex couples joined in civil union. *Psychology of Women Quarterly, 29*, 158–166.

Toperak, R., Ortaga-Villalobos, L., & Pope- Davis, D. B. (2004). Critical incidents in multicultural supervision: Exploring supervisees' and supervisors' experience. *Journal of Multicultural Counseling and Development, 32*(2), 66–83.

Torres, L., & Rollock, D. (2004). Acculturation stress among Hispanics: The role of acculturation, coping, and intercultural competence. *Journal of Multicultural Counseling and Development, 32*(3), 155–167.

Townsend, K., & McWhirter, B. (2005). Connectedness: A review of the literature with implication for counseling, assessment, and research. *Journal of Counseling & Development, 83*, 191–201.

Toynbee, A. J. (1987). *A study of history: Abridgement of Volumes I–VI* (Abridged by I. Dolutsky). London: Oxford University Press.

Treadgold, R. (1983). Two issues in the counselling of women. *New Zealand Counselling and Guidance Association Journal, 5*, 23–29.

Troiden, R. R. (1988). *Gay and lesbian identity: A sociological analysis.* Lanham, MD: Rowman & Littlefield.

Troiden, R. R. (1989). The formation of homosexual identities. *Journal of Homosexuality, 17*(1–2), 43–73.

Troiden, R.R. (1993). The formation of homosexual identities. In L. Garnets & D. Kimmel (Eds.), *Psychological perspectives on lesbian and gay male experiences* (pp. 191–217). New York: Columbia University Press.

Trusty, J., & Brown, D. (2005). Advocacy competencies for professional school counselors. *Professional School Counseling, 8*(3), 259–265.

Trusty, J., Looby, E. J., & Sandhu, D. S. (Eds.). (2002). *Multicultural counseling: Context, theory and practice, and competence.* New York: Nova Science.

Tse-Tung, M. (1967). The united front in cultural work. In *Selected works of Mao Tse-Tung* (Vol. 3, p. 235). Peking, China: Foreign Languages Press. (Original work published 1944)

Tucker, R. C. (1978). *The Marx-Engels readers* (2nd ed.). New York: Norton.

Tuckwell, G. (2002). *Racial identity, white counsellors and therapists.* Buckingham, UK, Open University Press.

Turner, T. (1993). Anthropology and multiculturalism: What is anthropology that multiculturalists should be mindful of it? *Cultural Anthropology, 8*(4), 411–429.

Twenge, J. (2001). Changes in women's assertiveness in response to status and roles: A cross-temporal meta-analysis, 1931–1993. *Journal of Personality and Social Psychology, 81*(1), 133–145.

Twohey, D., & Volker, J. (1993). Listening to the voices of care and justice in counselor supervision. *Counselor Education and Supervision, 32,* 189–197.

Tylor, E. (1871). *Primitive culture.* New York: Harper.

Udelson, J. H. (1990). *Dreamer of the ghetto: The life and works of Israel Zangwill.* Tuscaloosa: University of Alabama Press.

United Nations, Population Division. (1999). *World urbanization prospects: The 1999 revision.* Retreived July 11, 2007, from http://www.un.org/esa/population/pubsarchive/urbanization/urbanization.pdf

United Nations, Population Division. (2004). *World population prospects: The 2004 revision.* Retrieved July 11, 2007, from http://www.un.org/esa/population/publications/WPP2004/wpp2004.htm

United States Department of Commerce. (2004). *U.S. Census Bureau News.* Retrieved from http://www.census.gov/

Vacc, N., DeVaney S., & Wittmer, J. (1995). *Experiencing and counseling multicultural and diverse populations.* Philadelphia: Accelerated Development.

Valery, P. (1919). The crisis of the mind. In D. Folliot & J. Mathews (Eds.), *The collected works of Paul Valery* (Vol. 10, pp. 23–36). New York: Bollingen.

Valsiner, J. (2000). *Culture and human development: An introduction.* London: SAGE.

Van Wormer, K. S., Wells, J., & Boes, M. (2000). *Social work with lesbians, gays, and bisexuals: A strengths perspective.* Boston: Allyn & Bacon.

Varenne, H. (2003). On internationalizing counseling psychology: A view from cultural anthropology. *Counseling Psychologist, 31*(4), 404–411.

Vera, E. M., & Shin, R. Q. (2006). Promoting strengths in a socially toxic world: Supporting resiliency with systemic interventions. *Counseling Psychologist, 34*(1), 80–89.

Vessey, J. T., & Howard, K. I. (1993). Who seeks psychotherapy? *Psychotherapy: Theory, Research, Practice, Training, 30,* 546–553.

Viano, E. C. (1992). The news media and crime victims: The right to know versus the right to privacy. In E. C. Viano (Ed.), *Critical issues in victimology: International perspectives* (pp. 24–34). New York: Springer.

Vicario, B., Liddle, B., & Luzzo, D. (2005). The role of values in understanding attitudes toward lesbians and gay men. *Journal of Homosexuality, 49*(1), 145–159.

Vontress, C. E. (1988). An existential approach to cross-cultural counseling. *Journal of Multicultural Counseling and Development, 16,* 73–83.

Wagner, R. (1981). *The invention of culture.* Chicago: University of Chicago Press.

Wahoo, E., & Olson, L. (2004). Intimate partner violence and sexual assault in Native American communities. *Trauma, Violence, & Abuse, 5*(4), 353–366.

Waldegrave, C. T. (1985). Mono-cultural, mono-class, and so called non-political family therapy. *Australia and New Zealand Journal of Family Therapy, 6*(4), 197–200.

Waldegrave, C. T. (1990). Just therapy. *Dulwich Centre Newsletter, 1,* 6–47.

Waldegrave, C. T. (1992). Psychology, politics and the loss of the welfare state. *New Zealand Psychological Society Bulletin, 74,* 14–21.

Waldegrave, C. T. (1994). A conversation with Kiwi Tamasese and Charles Waldegrave. *Dulwich Centre Newsletter, 1,* 20–27.

Waldegrave, C., Tamasese, K., Tuhaka, F., & Campbell, W. (2003). *Just therapy: A journey.* Adelaide, South Australia: Dulwich Centre.

Walkerdine, V. (1988). *The mastery of reason: Cognitive development and the production of rationality.* London: Routledge.

Walter, J. L., & Peller, J. E. (2000). *Recreating brief therapy: Preferences and possibilities.* New York: Norton.

Want, V., Parham, T., & Baker, R. (2004). African American students' ratings of Caucasian and African American counselors varying in racial consciousness. *Cultural Diversity and Ethnic Minority Psychology, 10*(2), 123–136.

Waterhouse, R. (1993). The inverted gaze. In S. Scott & D. Morgan (Eds.), *Body matters* (pp. 105–121). Washington, DC: Falmer Press.

Weedon, C. (1987). *Feminist practice and poststructuralist theory.* Oxford, UK: Blackwell.

Weinrach, S. G., & Thomas, K. R. (1998). Diversity-sensitive counseling today: A postmodern clash of values. *Journal of Counseling & Development, 76*(2), 115–122.

Wellman, D. (1977). *Portraits of white racism.* Cambridge, UK: Cambridge University Press.

Wester, S. R., Vogel, D. L., & Archer, J., Jr. (2004). Male restricted emotionality and counseling supervision. *Journal of Counseling & Development, 82,* 91–98.

Wetherell, M., & Potter, J. (1992). *Mapping the language of racism: Discourse and the legitimation of exploitation.* New York: Harvester Wheatsheaf.

Whaley, A. L. (2001). Cultural mistrust of white mental health clinicians among African Americans with severe mental illness. *American Journal of Orthopsychiatry, 71*(2), 252–256.

Whelehan, I. (1995). *Modern feminist thought: From the second wave to "post-feminism."* New York: New York University Press.

White, M. (1989). The externalisation of the problem and the re-authoring of relationships. In M. White, *Selected papers.* Adelaide, South Australia: Dulwich Centre.

White, M. (1992). Deconstruction and therapy. In D. Epston & M. White (Eds.), *Experience, contradiction, narrative, and imagination* (pp. 109–152). Adelaide, South Australia: Dulwich Centre.

White, M. (2002). Addressing personal failure. *International Journal of Narrative Therapy and Community Work, 2002*(3), 33–76.

White, M., & Epston, D. (1990). *Narrative means to therapeutic ends.* New York: Norton.

Wijeyesinghe, C., Griffin, P., & Love, B. (1997). Racism curriculum design. In M. Adams, L. A. Bell, & P. Griffin (Eds.), *Teaching for diversity and social justice: A sourcebook* (pp. 82–109). New York: Routledge.

Wilcox, D. W., & Forrest, L. (1992). The problems of men and counseling: Gender bias or gender truth? *Journal of Mental Health Counseling, 14,* 291–304.

Williams, D. M. (1999). Hardiness, John Henryism and the stress-illness link among low socioeconomic status women (African-Americans). *Dissertation Abstracts International, 60,* 6B.

Williams, R. (1958). *Culture and society, 1780–1950.* New York: Columbia University Press.

Willig, C. (2001). *Introducing qualitative research in psychology: Adventures in theory and method.* Buckingham, UK: Open University Press.

Winslade, J. (2005). Utilising discursive positioning in counseling. *British Journal of Guidance & Counselling, 33*(3), 351–364.

Winslade, J., & Monk, G. (1999). *Narrative counseling in schools: Powerful & brief.* Thousand Oaks, CA: Corwin Press.

Winslade, J., & Monk, G. (2007). *Narrative counseling in schools: Powerful and brief* (2nd ed.). Thousand Oaks, CA: SAGE.

Winslade, J., Monk, G., & Drewery, W. (1997). Sharpening the critical edge: A social constructionist approach in counselor education. In T. L. Sexton & B. L. Griffin (Eds.), *Constructivist thinking in counseling practice, research, and training* (pp. 228–248). New York: Teachers College Press.

Wise, T. (2005). *White like me: Reflections on race from a privileged son.* New York: Soft Skull Press.

Wiseman, C. V., Gray, J. J., Mosimann, J. E., & Ahrens, A. H. (1992). Cultural expectations of thinness in women: An update. *International Journal of Eating Disorders, 11*(1), 85–89.

Wolf, E. R. (1989). *Europe and the people without history.* Berkeley: University of California Press.

Wolff, E. (2003). The wealth divide: The growing gap in the United States between the rich and the rest. *Multinational Monitor, 24*(5), 11–15.

Woodhouse, S. (2002). The historical development of affirmative action: An aggregated analysis. *Western Journal of Black Studies, 26*(3), 155–158.

Wooley, S. C., & Wooley, O. W. (1984, February). Feeling fat in a thin society. *Glamour,* pp. 198–252.

Wrenn, C. G. (1962). The culturally encapsulated counselor. *Havard Educational Review, 32,* 444–449.

Wyche, K. F. (2001). Sociocultural issues in counseling for women of color. In R. K. Unger (Ed.), *Handbook of the psychology of women and gender* (pp. 330–340). Hoboken, NJ: Wiley.

Wyche, K. F. (2006). Healthy environments for youth and families. In J. Worell & C. D. Goodheart (Eds.), *Handbook of girls' and women's psychological health: Gender and well-being across the lifespan* (pp. 218–228). New York: Oxford University Press.

Yakushko, O., & Chronister, K. (2005). Immigrant women and counseling: The invisible others. *Journal of Counseling & Development, (83),* 292–298.

Yang, D. (1991). Generational conflict among the Hmong in the United States. *Hmong Forum, 2,* 35–38.

Yeatman, A. (1993). Voice and representation and the politics of difference. In S. Gunew & A. Yeatman (Eds.), *Feminism and the politics of difference* (pp. 85–102). Sydney, Australia: Allen & Unwin.

Yeh, C. (2003). Age, acculturation, cultural adjustment, and mental health symptoms of Chinese, Korean, and Japanese immigrant youth. *Cultural Diversity and Ethnic Minority Psychology, 9*(1), 34–48.

Yon, D. A. (2000). *Elusive culture: Schooling, race, and identity in global times.* Albany: State University of New York Press.

Yoon, S. (2005). The characteristics and needs of Asian American grandparent caregivers: A study of Chinese American and Korean American grandparents in New York City. *Journal of Gerontological Social Work, 44*(3–4), 75–94.

Zinn, H. (2003). *A people's history of the United States: 1492–present.* New York: HarperCollins.

Zuckerman, M. (1990). Some dubious premises in research and theory on racial differences: Scientific, social, and ethical issues. *American Psychologist, 45,* 1927–1303.

Index